INDEX TO THE 1810 CENSUS OF KENTUCKY

INDEX TO THE 1810 CENSUS OF KENTUCKY

Compiled by

ANN T. WAGSTAFF

CLEARFIELD

Reprinted for
Clearfield Company, Inc. by
Genealogical Publishing Co., Inc.
Baltimore, Maryland
1994, 1996, 2002

Library of Congress Catalogue Card Number 80-66547
International Standard Book Number 0-8063-0896-6
Made in the United States of America

FOREWORD

The 1810 Federal Census lists only heads of households. All other household members are indicated numerically, the totals divided into age groups by sex, with separate columns for free persons of color and slaves.

All entries in this index have been copied verbatim. No attempt has been made to standardize or change spellings, and uncommon spellings, where possible, are keyed to common spellings. The reader should be aware that the order of the entries varies in the original census enumerations, i.e. the surname may appear either first or last. In some few cases it was impossible to tell whether the surname was inverted with the given name or not, so these are entered both ways in the index. Note also that superscripts such as *Ab^m* appear as *Abm.* in this index.

Employees at the National Archives cooperated in making the original bound volumes of the census returns available to me to make comparisons and corrections, and indeed I was able to make a complete page to page comparison of the microfilm copy with the original returns. One page in the original does not appear in the official microfilm copy—page 136 of Lincoln County. Data on that page can be found here in Table II. Table I, following, contains a multitude of information pertaining to this publication which may be helpful to the reader.

I wish to express thanks to my family for their encouragement, their assistance, and their patience when work on this index was given priority.

Ann T. Wagstaff

TABLE I

Name of County	Abbreviation	Microfilm #252-	Page Numbers	Population	Partially Alphabetical
Adair	Adr	5	3-19	6,011	x
Barren	Bar	5	19-54	11,286	
Boone	Boo	5	53-61	3,608	x
Bourbon	Bou	5	68-133	12,945	x
Bracken	Bra	5	141-153	3,706	
Breckenridge	Bre	5	156-169	3,430	
Bullitt	Bul	5	173-187	4,311	x
Butler	But	5	192-198	2,181	x
Caldwell	Cal	9	3-20	4,268	
Campbell	Cam	9	24-33	3,473	
Casey	Cas	9	37-48	3,285	
Christian	Chr	9	53-117	11,020	
Clark	Clr	9	121-147	11,519	x
Clay	Cly	9	147-160	2,398	
Cumberland	Cum	9	165-186	6,191	x
Estill	Est	6	1-9	2,082	
Fayette	Fay	6	11-60	21,370	x
Fleming	Fle	6	61-92	8,947	
Floyd	Flo	6	95-105	3,485	x
Franklin	Fra	6	107-180	8,013	x
Gallatin	Gal	6	183-197	3,307	x
Garrard	Gar	6	199-236	9,186	x
Grayson	Gra	6	237-244	2,301	
Green	Grn	6	245-266	6,730	
Greenup	Grp	6	269-278	2,309	
Hardin	Hrd	6	281-304	7,531	

Harrison[1]	Hrs	6	305-324	7,752	
Henderson	Hnd	6	325-348	4,703	
Henry	Hnr	6	351-369	6,777	
Hopkins	Hop	6	371-381	2,964	
Jefferson	Jef	7	3-34	13,399	x
Jessamine	Jes	7	35-62	8,377	x
Knox	Knx	7	63-92	5,875	
Lewis	Lew	7	95-104	2,357	
Lincoln[2]	Lin	7	107-143	8,676	x
Livingston	Liv	7	145-160	3,674	
Logan	Log	7	161-196	12,123	
Madison[3]	Mad	7	197-250	15,540	x
Mason[4]	Mas	7	251-310	12,459	x
Mercer	Mer	7	313-343	12,630	x
Montgomery	Mon	7	345-384	12,975	
Muhlenberg	Mul	7	385-408	4,181	
Nelson[5]	Nel	8	1-48	14,078	x
Nicholas	Nic	8	51-65	11,808	x
Ohio	Ohi	8	68-104	14,070	
Pendleton	Pen	8	105-117	6,897	
Pulaski	Pul	8	121-157	3,792	x
Rockcastle	Rck	8	159-166	1,731	
Scott	Sco	8	167-193	12,419	
Shelby	She	8	197-242	14,877	
Warren	War	8	243-282	11,937	
Washington	Wsh	8	286-350	13,248	x
Wayne	Way	8	351-374	5,430	
Woodford[6]	Woo	8	376-402	9,659	
				419,301 Total	

[1] Page 305, last name torn off
[2] Page 136 missing, see Table II
[3] Helpful marginal notes
[4] Occupations given
[5] No page 2
[6] Page 399 follows page 400

TABLE II*

Lincoln County, Lincoln City—Page 136 missed on microfilm

Name	Census
Robert Tucker	2 0 0 1 0 - 3 2 0 1 0 0 2
Zacarias Tucker	1 0 0 1 0 - 2 0 1 0 0 0 2
Elijah Trotter	0 1 1 0 0 - 1 0 1 0 0 0 0
Willm. Tisdall	3 2 0 0 1 - 1 0 0 1 0 0 1
John Thurmond	0 2 2 0 1 - 0 0 2 0 1 0 1
Littlebury Tucker	0 0 0 1 0 - 0 0 0 0 0 0 1
H. James Tompson	0 0 2 1 0 - 2 0 1 0 0 0 4
C. John Thurman	1 0 0 1 0 - 0 2 0 1 0 0 3
Pleasant Tucker	1 0 0 1 0 - 2 0 1 0 0 0 0
Frederick Trump	1 2 1 0 1 - 2 2 1 1 0 0 1
George Thornton	1 0 1 1 0 - 0 0 1 0 0 0 2
Peter Thornton	1 0 0 1 0 - 3 0 0 1 0 0 0
John Tindal	2 0 0 1 1 - 0 0 1 1 1 0 0
David Thurmond	2 1 0 0 1 - 1 1 0 1 0 0 2
John Tayler	3 0 2 0 1 - 1 1 1 0 1 0 0
Walter Tayler	1 0 0 0 1 - 1 0 0 2 1 0 15
John Thomas	3 0 1 1 0 - 3 2 1 1 0 0 3
A. Nelson Thompson	1 0 0 1 0 - 2 0 1 0 0 0 7
Sarah Thompson	0 0 0 0 0 - 0 2 3 1 1 0 11
William Tate	1 1 0 0 1 - 3 2 0 1 0 0 5
Willm. Thompson	2 0 0 1 0 - 2 1 0 1 0 0 0
Mathias Talisman	0 0 2 0 1 - 0 1 0 0 1 0 0
Alexr. Thompson	1 0 0 0 1 - 1 2 2 0 1 0 1
George Thompson	1 1 0 1 0 - 2 0 0 1 0 0 1

* From left to right the columns signify white males under 10 years of age, white males from 10 to 16, from 16 to 26, from 26 to 44, and from 45 and upwards; then the same age categories for white females, followed by a column for all other free persons and a column for slaves.

INDEX TO THE 1810 CENSUS OF KENTUCKY

INDEX TO THE 1810 CENSUS OF KENTUCKY

Name	County	Page
..., Susa	Adr	5
...an.s, ...	Bar	46
...g.., ...y	Bar	53
...s, R...	Hrs	311
...s, A...	Mon	379
...son, Jer...	Mon	380
-- A --		
Aarnold, Josiah	Mul	392
Aaron, Miller	Fay	50
see Miller, Aaron		
Aayres, Samuel	Fay	11
Abannion, Joseph	Bar	36
Abbay, Jonathan	Mon	371
Abbet, James	Cly	149
John	Log	192
Abbett, Geo	Hnr	360
Abbitt, Jonathan	Fra	109
Robt	Woo	390
Abbot, Joseph	Mon	371
William	Jes	35
Abbott, Bivin	Clr	121
Harry	Sco	174
James	Hnr	364
James	Jef	3
John	Jef	3
Joseph	Sco	174
William	Fra	109
William	Sco	174
William, Jr.	Sco	184
Abdil, George	Hrs	320
Abel, Ben	Hrd	291
Jos.	Jef	24
Abell, Elizabeth	Nel	1
Enoch	Wsh	350
Enock	Nel	1
Francis	Nel	1
James	Wsh	349
Jesse	Wsh	350
John Barton	Wsh	350
Joseph Abner	Wsh	349
Joshua	Wsh	350
Margaret	Wsh	350
Pollard	Nel	1
Saml.	Nel	1
Saml. T.	Nel	1
Samuel	Wsh	350
Abernathy, Blaxton	Fay	19
Abinather, Robert	Chr	54
Able, Caleb	Jef	3
William	Nel	1
Abner, Burry	Est	6
Abner, Elisha	Cly	160
Elisha, Jr.	Cly	160
John	Est	5
Joshua	But	192
Abney, John K.	Grn	255
William	Est	9
Abrams, Elias	Mad	215
Joseph	Mad	215
Tho.	Mad	215
Tho., Jr.	Mad	215
Abrel, James	Adr	3
John	Cas	44
Abrell, Jacob	Adr	4
James	Adr	4
Abrims, Gabril	Cly	149
Absalom, Atkinson	Adr	3
Absher, James	Ohi	91
Thomas	Adr	3
William	Adr	3
Abshire, Abram	War	263
John War 263		
Accan?, Daniel	Cas	39
Accles, John J.	Bra	147
Achels, Nancy	Fay	39
Acherson, James	Jes	35
Killus	Mon	374
Nathan	Mon	381
Wm.	Mon	374
Wm. Sr.	Mon	374
Aclin, Joseph	Cam	24
Acman, Wm.	Cam	30
Acock, Robert	Chr	75
Acre, Wm.	Boo	57
Acres, Henry	Bou	117
Solomon	Flo	100
Valentine	Flo	100
Acrey, John	Way	354
Wm.	Way	355
Acton, Aron	Gar	201
Jas.	Gar	201
John	Way	360
Smallwood	Clr	121
Acuff, Christopher	Sco	172
Adair, Benjamin	Fra	109
James	Hrs	312
John	Chr	96
John	Mer	340
John	Way	364
Joseph	Bou	117
Wile I.	Grn	265
William	Bou	72
William	Mer	340
William P.	Bou	73
Adall, Jacob	Cas	37
Adam, Jacob M.	Grp	273
Shoemaker	Bre	163
Adams, Aandrew	Bra	144
Aaron	Bou	73
Abraham	Gar	202
Abraham	Mad	197
Abraham	She	235
Abriham	Chr	89
Absalam	Fay	48
Absalom	Gar	200
Alexander	Mer	340
Alexander	Pul	122
Andrew	Hnr	363
Ann	Fay	11
Archibald	Mer	339
Archibald	She	217
Benj.	Nel	1
Benja.	Flo	95
Benjamin(freeman)	Fay	11
Conrad	Wsh	350
Daniel	Gar	200
Daniel	Knx	81
Daniel	Lin	107
Daniel	Lin	107
Danl.	Way	351
David	Hnr	367
David	Mer	339
David	Mer	339
Drury	Chr	93
Eleaner	Log	180
Eli	Ohi	93
Elijah	Grn	256
Elijah	Pul	122
Elisha	Clr	121
Elisha	Nel	4
Elisha	Wsh	286
Elizbh.	Boo	57
Elkanah	Log	191
Ellender	Jef	3
Francis	Bou	72
Francis	Jef	24
Francis	Mer	341
Geo.	Gar	201
George	Fay	11
George	Fay	11
George	Fay	11
Adams, George	Fra	110
George	Mul	385
Girau	Hnr	354
Hugh	Pul	122
Isaac	Cum	171
Isaac	Sco	172
Jacob	Liv	157
Jacob	Mad	197
Jacob	Sco	188
James	Cal	5
James	Chr	108
James	Fay	34
James	Fay	49
James	Fra	110
James	Hop	375
James	Mer	339
James	Ohi	84
James	Pul	123
Jeremiah	Pul	123
Jerh.	Sco	176
Jesse	Est	5
Jesse	Hop	375
Joel	Mad	216
Jno.	Hnr	351
Jno.	Mad	197
Jno.	Mad	216
John	But	192
John	Cas	42
John	Chr	76
John	Chr	95
John	Clr	121
John	Clr	121
John	Flo	95
John	Flo	95
John	Flo	100
John	Fra	107
John	Gar	200
John	Knx	77
John	Knx	81
John	Mer	340
John	Mon	367
John	Nel	4
John	Sco	189
John, Dr.	Flo	95
Joseph	Fra	107
Joseph	Mas	304
Joseph	Mon	364
Joseph	Nel	1
Joseph	War	263
Joseph	Wsh	286
Joshua	Way	372
Leaven	Mad	216
Levan	Sco	188
Luke	Gar	201
Lydea	Mer	340
Mathew	Mon	359
Martin	Mer	339
Martin	Mer	339
Mary	Clr	121
Matthew	Jew	24
Matthew	Ohi	87
Matthias	Ohi	81
Mattw.	Hop	372
McNemar	Mad	216
Moses	Flo	95
Moses	Sco	167
Nathan	Clr	121
Nathan	Mad	216
Nathan	Sco	188
Nathaniel	Mas	303
Peter	Cam	30
Peter	Wsh	286
Pleasent	Cas	44
Polly	Mer	339
Randolph	Knx	84
Reuben	Gal	195
Richard	Cas	44

Adams, Robert Pul 122
Robt. Gar 202
Robt. Hop 375
Sally Mad 197
Saml. Hnr 351
Samuel Log 176
Samuel Mer 339
Samuel Mer 341
Sinchs Knx 69
Spencer Clr 121
Spencer Flo 95
Stephen Flo 95
Stephen Flo 100
Sylvester Pul 123
Tho. Hop 373
Thomas Chr 108
Thomas Fay 20
Thomas Fra 109
Thomas Lin 107
Thomas Mon 355
Thomas Pul 123
Thos. Boo 57
Thos. Pul 123
Thos. R.G. War 268
Walter Gar 201
Walter Mad 197
William Fay 23
William Flo 100
William Grn 249
William Grp 274
William Log 180
William Mer 340
William She 208
William She 212
William She 218
William Woo 379
Williams Chr 90
Williams Hnr 359
B
Wilson Gar 200
Wm. Gar 200
Wm. Jef 3
Wm. Mad 216
Wm. Way 351
Wm. jur Mad 216
Zachariah Pul 122
Adamson, James Mas 303
Joseph Mas 303
Ruth Mas 302
Stephen Mas 303
Adan, John War 277
Adans, Wm. Bra 149
Adcock, Edmund She 218
Addams, Absolem Hrs 318
George Hrs 319
Henry Hrs 318
John Cal 7B
John Hrs 310
John Hrs 316
John Hrs 318
John Pen 112
John Pen 115
Robt. Cal 8
William Hrs 310
Wm. Hrs 318
Wm. Hrs 319
Wm. Hrs 319
Addcock, Edmund She 239
Addison, Thos. Sco 186
Ader, Cathrine Grn 262
Adkason, Seth Mul 389
Adkaxn, Elisha Mul 398
Adkerson, Elias Mad 215
Thomas Mon 352
Adkin, Thomas Jef 25
Adkins, Abner Ohi 92
Bartlett Flo 95
Adkins, Cornelius Log 178
Cornelius Log 194
Isham Flo 95
Jacob Way 374
James Pul 122
Jesse Flo 95
Joel Flo 95
John Adr 3
John Log 196
John Mer 339
Joseph Flo 95
Joshua Knx 66
Martha Mer 341
Moses Flo 100
Noton Flo 95
Owen Way 361
Spencer Flo 100
Thomas Flo 95
Thomas Knx 64
William Bul 183
William Clr 121
Adkinson, Wm. War 280
Adkison, Thomas Mer 341
Adley, Dorhety Adr 3
Admire, George Hnr 355
Henry Hnr 365
Henry, Jr. Hnr 355
James Hnr 358
Adya?, Nicholas Grn 262
Aerexon, Benjn. Jef 15
James Jef 15
James Jef 24
Aexander, Abel Chr 95
Agen, Wm. Jef 24
Aggy, (Negro free) Fay 111
Agnell, James Hrs 321
Agnew, Robert Hnd 343
Agors, Geo. Cam 25
Ahull, Mr. Fay 59
Aiken, James Cum 166
Aikens, Garland Cum 185
Aikins, Joseph Cum 166
Peggy Gar 200
Wm. Gar 200
Aikman, James Bou 73
John Bou 73
Aikmon, John Knx 89
Ailer, Abraham Mer 341
Ailes, Fanny Jef 28
Aills, William Lew 101
Ailor, Benjn. Boo 57
Aines, Reuben Cas 41
Airbuckle, Samuel Chr 82
Thomas Chr 82
Airs, John She 238
Samuel She 238
Akeheart, Christopher Mas 302
Aken, John She 227
Akers, Abner Bar 29
Benjamin She 204
Drury She 203
Geo. Bar 28
Isaac Bar 28
John Bar 34
John Jes 35
Joseph Mad 197
Joseph She 203
Michael Chr 91
Michael Chr 95
Simon She 202
Stephen Jes 35
Tho. Bar 24
Thomas Jes 35
Akes, Federick Rck 162
Peter Rck 159
Akin, Alexander She 222
Akin, James Grn 265
James Woo 379
John Lin 107
John Woo 379
Jos. Grn 262
William Woo 388
Akins, James Liv 148
Akree, Wm. Way 351
Akrey, Ephm. Way 373
Alander, George Bou 73
Albaugh, John Gar 200
Alben, Greenwell Nel 30
see Greenwell, Alben
Albert, Davis Hnr 368
Sinion But 192
Albin, Delina Nel 3
James Hnd 328
William Bul 173
Albion, Absolem Ohi 103
Albrook, Starlisy Liv 148
Alcorn, George Pul 123
James Mas 304
John Mas 305
Robert Clr 121
Thos. Gar 201
Alderman, James Clr 121
Alderson, Aron Bar 34
Benja. Gar 201
Benjamin Mer 340
Henry Fay 41
Aldman, Saml. Hop 378
Aldredge, Nathl. Nel 1
Aldridge, Elijah Cly 154
Jas. Gar 200
John Gar 199
Joshua Jes 35
Nathaniel Fay 20
Nicholas Clr 121
Saml. Nel 4
Thomas Fay 27
Thomas Hnr 362
William Clr 121
Wm. Jr. Boo 57
Wm. Senr Boo 57
Aldrige, Saml. Cum 179
Alen, Adnen Hnr 363
James D. She 222
Whiley But 192
Alender, Andrew Est 6
Thomas Bul 173
Alexander, Aaron Fay 33
Abey Grp 274
Amos Ohi 98
Andrew Hrd 294
Annes Fle 72
Archd. Mas 302
Benjamin Cal 7
Benjamin Fra 109
Bin Est 4
Charles Hnd 332
David Mon 376
Ebenezer Hop 373
Edvin Mer 339
Elizabeth Fay 20
Hugh Fra 107
Hugh Mon 381
Hugh Sco 168
Isaac Mer 341
James Bul 173
James Est 4
James Fay 19
James Fle 84
James Mer 341
James Mon 357
James Mon 360
James She 197
Jas. Bou 117

Alexander, Jas. Gar 202
Jas., jr Mad 216
Jas. R. War 265
Jesse Nic 65
Jno. Gal 195
Jno. M. Cum 168
John Clr 121
John Cum 168
John Log 168
John Mon 362
John Mon 331
John She 224
Jonathan Sco 170
Joseph Fle 77
Joseph Jef 25
Josua Cal 18
Mary Fay 19
Mathew Log 187
Nicholas Way 369
Peter Woo 395
Polly War 270
Randal Pul 122
Randel Bou 73
Reubin War 253
Robert Fay 19
Robert Woo 390
Robert V. Hrd 290
Robt. Cum 167
Roling Fle 78
Samuel Chr 92
Sarah Bou 72
Thomas Chr 69
Thomas Est 7
Thomas Knx 74
Thomas Mon 381
Thos. Cum 168
Thos. Nic 65
Tnos. Pul 123
Travis Sco 174
Washington Gal 195
William Bou 117
William Fay 11
William Fay 24
William Fle 84
William Mer 339
William Mer 341
Wilson Bou 72
Wm. Boo 57
Wm. Mad 216
Wm. Pul 122
Wm. Sco 172
Zacheus Bou 73
Zackariah Fle 84
Alexandr, Zenus Chr 95
Alexandra, John Cas 44
Alexandre, John Grp 274
John Grp 275
Alexnder, Robert Fle 89
Alford, Charles Gar 200
Chrals Lin 107
James Lin 107
John Lin 107
Kellices Cas 46
Nancy Gar 200
Nancy Mad 215
William Jes 35
Alfred, Thos. Sco 173
William Jes 35
Alfreys, Abraham Mon 354
Algar, Jerimiah Way 374
Algee, John Cal 5
Alimon, Solomon Nel 4
Alington, Jacob Mon 353
Alison, Ezekiel Cum 165
Hugh She 208
John Chr 106
Joseph Bra 148
Alison, Joseph Chr 65
Joseph Chr 67
Lewis Cum 165
Robert Chr 67
Robert Chr 110
Robert She 221
Samuel Mul 401
Alkier, William Bou 117
All, Aquilla Nel 11
Benjamin Nel 3
James Nel 11
Thomas Nel 3
Alla, Petre Pul 122
Allbright, Adam Hnd 336
Allbriton, James Fay 43
Allcock, Council Mul 387
Darin Mul 387
Sarah Mul 388
Allcom, George Mad 215
Allcorn, Geo. Cly 151
Jessee Way 373
Jno. Mad 216
John Way 374
Robt. Cly 151
Allcoun, Robert Fay 56
Allegree, Giles Mad 216
Allen, Archabald Jef 27
Archibald Hrd 304
Adoniram Cly 155
Ananias Adr 3
Anderson Fra 109
Andrew Log 168
Andrew She 237
Anna Mon 359
Azeriah Fay 44
Barnabas Mas 303
Bejamin Cas 42
Ben Hrd 295
Benjamin Clr 121
Benjamin Fay 11
Benjamin She 217
Beverly Jes 35
Beverly A. Log 194
Charles Fra 109
Charles She 241
Charles War 260
Charles H. Fay 23
Davice Grn 265
David Bou 72
David Bre 164
David Grn 250
David Nel 4
David Sco 185
David Wsh 349
Davis Fay 11
Elijah Log 188
Elisha Bar 35
Elisha Nel 1
Ely Mer 340
Erasmus Gar 201
Francis Fay 23
Francis Woo 399
George Clr 121
George Flo 95
George Mer 340
George Mon 359
George Nel 41
Granvil Bou 72
Hugh Woo 383
Isaac Bou 117
Isham Clr 121
James Adr 3
James Cas 46
James Chr 95
James Grn 265
James Hrd 302
James Log 194
Allen, James Mas 304
James Mas 305
James Mer 341
James Nel 1
James Nel 3
James Nel 4
James She 205
James She 220
James She 223
James Way 356
James Wsh 350
Jane Cum 165
Jeremiah Clr 121
Jessee Bou 117
Jno. Hrd 295
Jno. Pul 122
John Adr 3
John Adr 4
John Bou 72
John Cas 44
John Clr 121
John Cly 155
John Cly 158
John Cum 165
John Cum 170
John Jes 41
John Knx 86
John Knx 89
John Mon 359
John Mon 371
John Mon 383
John Nel 4
John Nic 65
John She 201
John She 223
John She 238
John Woo 378
John Woo 381
John Woo 383
Jos. Cly 156
Joseph Bre 169
Joseph Clr 121
Joseph Fay 36
Joseph Mas 305
Joseph Mer 340
Joseph Mon 383
Joseph She 241
Josiah Clr 121
Memucan Senr Fra 107
Mountgomery Hnd 348
Nisbat Knx 71
Patcy Adr 8
Peggy Grn 253
Polley Bou 117
Reuben Log 194
Richd. Gar 201
Robert Bou 73
Robert Bre 158
Robert Cas 44
Robert Cum 174
Robert Mas 304
Robert Ohi 90
Robert Sco 181
Robert P. She 210
Saml. Way 364
Sampson Cum 165
Samuel Bou 73
Samuel Bre 156
Samuel Fle 86
Samuel Pul 122
Sarah Flo 95
Solomon Mer 341
Stephen She 240
Stephen She 242
Stephen Way 356
Theophelus Ohi 70
Thomas Bul 173

Allen, cont.
Thomas Clr 121
Thomas Flo 95
Thomas Mas 303
Thomas Mas 304
Thomas Mer 339
Thomas She 221
Thos. Cas 44
Tobias Gar 202
Washington She 215
William Adr 3
William Bou 72
William Bou 72
William Bou 73
William Clr 121
William Clr 121
William Cum 165
William Fay 43
William Fay 59
William Flo 95
William Hnd 347
William Hrd 301
William Jef 24
William Mas 304
William Nic 64
William Nic 65
William She 213
William Wsh 286
William Wsh 350
William Wsh 350
William, Senr Hrd 282
Will She 225
Wm. Bar 48
Wm. Cly 151
Wm. Gar 202
Wm. Hrd 294
Allender, George Fle 81
Allentharp, Betsey Bou 73
Alleson, Benjamin Mer 339
Samuel Mer 339
Allexander, Zachakriar -
- Fle 81
Alley, Jas. Way 359
Allifant, Obedeah Bar 37
Allfray, James Nic 65
Allfree, John Fle 62
Allin, Benjamin Fay 30
Daniel War 249
Elisha Fay 11
Isaac War 249
Isaac War 268
James Boo 57
James Chr 112
James Hop 381
John Bar 35
John Fay 23
John M. Bou 72
Joseph Bar 48
[illegible] 268
[illegible] 31
[illegible] 215
Rebecca Lin 107
Richard Fay 20
Richardson Fay 11
Thos. Boo 57
Thos. O. Bou 73
Wm. Bar 35
Wm. War 264
Allison, Achilas Mul 395
Alexr. Nic 65
David Bul 173
Elijah Clr 121
Enoch Bul 173
Henry Jef 25
Hugh Knx 73
James Log 179
Jno. Mad 197

Allison, cont.
John Nic 65
John B. Bou 73
Joseph Mas 305
Nancy Jef 15
Patrick Fle 64
Tho. Mad 197
Thos. Hnr 359
B
William Mul 399
Allnutt, William Fay 19
Allowaye, William She 199
Allred, John Log 186
Soloman War 249
Allspaugh, Isaac Mer 341
Allumbaugh, Pet. Mad 197
Ally, Buford Bar 47
David Bar 47
John Bar 49
Merral Bar 50
Wm. Bar 47
Wm., Junr Bar 49
Alnet, James Log 168
Alnut, James Log 196
Aloway, Archelus Boo 57
John Boo 57
Alphin, Reubin Ohi 97
Shelton Ohi 88
Alplin, Zebulun Cam 26
Alred, James Ohi 95
Alsep, Spencer Fay 11
Alsman, Andrew Jes 35
Alsop, Bartlett She 235
James Knx 90
John Knx 65
John Mon 373
Joseph She 228
Thos. Woo 380
Wm. Sco 180
Alstot, Marey Cas 44
Alte, Emanuel Fay 11
Alton, John Cal 3
Altorn, Wm. Cal 11
Altsman, Robert Liv 152
Alverson, Benja. Gar 201
Jas. Mad 216
Pleasant Gar 202
S. John Gar 200
Wm. Mad 197
Alves, John Fay 23
Alvey, Ann Wsh 349
Bennett Wsh 350
Betsy Wsh 349
George Wsh 350
James Hnd 330
John Hnd 330
John Wsh 350
John F. Hnd 332
Robert Hnd 329
Thomas, Junior Bre 168
Alvis, Jesse She 224
Alwell, Hugh Mas 304
Alxander, John Cly 155
Ambros, Joseph Adr 4
Ambrose, Isaac Bra 151
Jacob War 281
James Bra 144
Mats Nel 4
Wm. Bra 145
Ament, Anthony Hrd 289
Gabl. Bar 54
Jno. Hrd 298
Jno. V. Hrd 300
Philip Bou 117
Amerman, John Pen 116
Amis, Cathrine Cly 154
Lincoln Cly 160

Amiss, Benjn. War 269
Gabriel Pen 106
Ammermon, Isaac Bou 72
John Bou 72
Philip Bou 72
Will Bou 72
Will Bou 73
Ammons, John Bar 37
Thomas Bou 73
Amos, Charles Bar 32
Ditto Bou 73
Elijah Bou 73
Francis Bar 33
James Bar 33
Margaret Bou 73
Mordica Bar 33
Nicholas Bou 73
Nicholas D. Bou 73
Ranson Bar 33
Thomas Bou 73
Wm. Bar 33
Amslom, Goodman Adr 8
Amus, Reuben Adr 3
Anders, Robert Fle 91
Andersen, Isaac Nel 1
Jerey Nel 3
John Nel 4
Anderson, Abihue Mon 350
Abihue Mon 370
Abraham War 246
Alexr. Cal 5
Alexr. War 248
Ambrose Cal 12
Amos She 223
Andrew Fle 82
Andrew Liv 148
Andrew War 279
Andrew Woo 379
Anna Boo 57
Arc[illegible]s Gar 200
Ar[illegible] Nel 3
Ar[illegible]d Hnd 331
Athel Ohi 79
B. Thos. Lin 107
B. Wm. Bar 46
Benjn. War 276
Betsy Mer 341
Carter Hrs 323
Charles Bra 153
Charles Mad 197
Charles Mas 302
Charles Mas 305
Charles Mon 365
Claibourne Mas 303
Cornelius Gar 200
Daniel Knx 82
Danil Nic 65
Davd. O. Bar 42
David Grn 261
David Mon 368
David Nel 41
Dixey Bou 73
Edward Nic 65
Eli Mas 305
Elija Cam 30
Elijah Fre 109
Elijh. Lew 102
Enock Boo 57
Francis Hrs 317
Geo. Cam 29
George Bre 162
George But 192
George Fay 11
George Fle 83
George Mas 305
George Nic 65
George War 263

Anderson, cont.
Henry Boo 57
Henry Bou 117
Henry Cam 29
Hugh Jes 35
Isaac But 192
Isaac Mad 216
Isaac War 275
Isiah Hrd 299
Izrael War 265
Jacob Lew 95
James Bar 25
James Bra 150
James Cal 9
James Cal 16
James Chr 77
James Clr 121
James Fay 54
James Hnr 361
James Liv 147
James Mer 339
James Mer 340
James Mer 340
James Mon 347
James Mon 359
James Mul 408
James Ohi 100
James Pul 123
James She 211
James She 242
Jas. Gal 195
Jas. Gar 202
Jas. Mad 216
Jas. Nel 3
Jeremiah Hnr 362
Jesse Mul 396
Jno. Hrd 289
Jno. jur Mad 197
John Adr 19
John Bar 19
John Boo 57
John Bou 72
John Cal 17
John Cam 29
John Cas 43
John Cas 44
John Chr 92
John Cly 160
John Cum 174
John Fay 11
John Fay 60
John Gar 202
John Grp 276
John Hnd 331
John Hrs 323
John Hrs 323
John Hrs 324
John Log 169
John Mad 216
John Mon 348
John Mon 358
John Nel 1
John Nel 3
John Nel 3
John Nic 65
John Ohi 104
John, Jr Log 168
John, Sen Mad 197
John, Ser Mon 348
John B. Mul 396
John D. Hnd 343
John H. Bar 19
Jonathan Gra 243
Jos. Boo 57
Joseph Bar 52
Joseph Fre 109
Joseph Grn 265

Anderson, cont.
Joseph Ohi 70
Josiah Cal 13
Josiah Nel 3
Lydea Cal 18
Mary Mad 216
Mathew Clr 121
Miason Nel 3
Moses Way 364
Nancy Nel 4
Nathan Bar 49
Nathan D. Hnd 344
Nelson Hnd 325
Nimrod Mon 350
Nimrod Mon 350
Polley Jef 24
Polly Log 183
Pouncey Grn 259
Presley Mon 373
Reuben Fra 109
Reuben Grn 259
Rhubin Hrs 309
Richard C. Jef 24
Robert Fay 23
Robert Hnr 353
Robert Mas 304
Robert Mul 401
Robert Nel 1
Robert Nel 3
Robt. Cum 175
Robt. Gar 202
Robt. Mad 216
Sally Mer 340
Saml. Bar 37
Saml. Bar 39
Saml. Cum 177
Saml. Mad 215
Saml. Nel 1
Saml. Nel 1
Saml. Y. Log 184
Sarah Chr 77
Sarah Nic 65
Stephen Grn 256
Stokes Mas 303
Theophilus Gar 202
Tho. Hop 375
Thomas Cal 13
Thomas Hnr 359
A
Thomas Jef 31
Thomas Mas 302
Thos. Boo 57
Thos. Gar 201
Turner Hnd 343
Vardamon Pul 123
Vincent Cal 9
Walter Lin 107
Will Bou 69
William Cal 5
William Fay 49
William Gra 242
William Hnd 340
William Hrs 324
William Jes 35
William Knx 67
William Liv 147
William Log 162
William Log 168
William Log 196
William Mad 243
William Mer 341
William She 218
Willm. Nel 4
Wm. Bar 41
Wm. Boo 57
Wm. Cam 25
Wm. Cum 177

Anderson, cont.
Wm. Gar 202
Wm. Gar 202
Wm. Hop 373
Wm. Mad 215
Wm. Mon 370
Wm. Nel 3
Wm. War 247
Wm. War 270
Wm. Way 364
Wm., jr Mad 216
Andres, Henry Mad 197
Peter Mad 197
Wm. Mad 197
Andrew, Goodman Adr 8
James Ohi 94
Mark War 262
Negro Log 186
Andrews, Alexander Ohi 100
Alexr. Woo 394
Danl. Way 368
Elexander Adr 3
George Fay 23
Jas. Way 364
John Bou 73
John Grn 265
John Log 181
John Woo 377
Wm. Cum 178
Androse, Lewis Ohi 76
Aneswerth, Levin Chr 84
Aneswirth, William Chr 104
Angel, George Log 168
George Log 194
John Gar 202
Martin Pul 122
Robert Sco 174
Thos. Hrd 297
Angle, Ann Hrs 319
George Pen 111
Permelia Pen 115
William Pen 109
Angleton, Wm. Boo 57
Anglin, James Cly 150
Anglton, John Sco 169
Anno, William Mas 309
Ansley, William Fle 70
Anson, Frances Log 168
Henry Log 186
Anthoney, Daniel Jes 35
Anthony, Adam Nel 11
Jacob Mul 386
John Chr 80
Philip Mul 394
Philip Nel 11
Philip Nel 13
Joseph War 271
William Chr 80
William Hnd 344
Antle, Henry Adr 3
Jacob Cum 172
John Cum 172
Mary Cum 172
Michael Adr 3
Antles, Peter Sco 189
Antrobus, Amos Mad 216
John Bou 71
Wm. Mad 216
Anyan, James But 192
Apelgate, Benja. Fle 62
Richrd. Fle 68
Apelton, William Fay 42
Appelgate, Benja. Fle 80
Apperson, Fras. Cum 177
John Cum 177
Richard Fra 109
Apple, John Cas 44

Appleby, John Cum 170
  Philip Gar 202
Applegate, Benjamin- She 223
  Danl. Hnr 351
  Elijah Jef 24
  George Mas 302
  Jacob Mas 304
  Jos. Jef 25
  Joseph Jef 24
  Richard Mas 303
  Saml. Jef 24
  Tunis Jef 24
  Wm. Hnr 368
Arbough, Henry Jes 35
Arbuckle, James Clr 121
  James Fra 107
  John Fra 109
  Saml. Gar 202
  Samuel Clr 121
  Samuel Fra 107
Archer, Cavell Cas 44
  Edmond Jef 3
  Edward Hrs 314
  James Nic 65
  James She 232
  John Jef 3
  John Nic 65
  Joseph She 206
  John She 206
  Josiah liv 153
  Meredith Adr 4
  Sampson Nic 64
  William Adr 4
Archerd, John Mas 304
Archibal, Jno. Hrd 291
Ard, Jacob Way 372
  John Way 371
  Rueben Way 370
Ardary, Alexander Hrs 315
  Wm. Hrs 322
Ardry, James Nic 64
  Robt. Nic 65
Arduy, John Bou 73
Argo, Purnal Fle 69
Arher, John Jef 3
Arick, Frederick Chr 94
Arington, Aaron Ohi 83
  Charles Ohi 82
  Henry Ohi 81
  James Lin 107
  John Ohi 82
  Margaret Ohi 82
  Moses Ohi 82
  Samuel Ohi 82
Arion, Francis Jef 24
Arissmith, Wm. Bou 117
Arledge, Jona Hop 373
Armer, William Gra 238
Armestrong, Robt. War 254
Armstong, John Mul 397
Armstrong, Alex Mer 340
  Alexander Liv 159
  Alexander Mer 339
  Alexr. Fle 73
  Ambrose Fay 20
  Andrew Fay 44
  Archabald Cas 46
  Benjamin Chr 57
  Benjamin Chr 111
  Benjamin Mer 340
  Benom She 240
  Edward Fra 109
  Elizebeth Mas 303
  Geo. Hnr 353
  George Jes 35
  George Mul 397

Armstrong, cont.
  George She 222
  Henry Adr 3
  Henry Lew 101
  Irvin Nic 65
  Jacob Clr 121
  James Bra 141
  James Chr 56
  James Fra 110
  James Mon 371
  James War 253
  James Woo 381
  Jas. Cam 31
  Jno. Mad 216
  John Cal 16
  John Chr 107
  John Fle 65
  John Fra 107
  John Log 186
  John Mas 300
  John Mas 302
  John Mer 339
  John Woo 380
  John Woo 382
  Julius Mad 215
  logan Cal 16
  Mattw. How 371
  Plunket Bou 117
  Polley She 207
  Richard Mer 340
  Robert Chr 100
  Robert Fay 34
  Robert Fra 107
  Robert Mer 341
  Robert Mon 372
  Robert Sco 189
  Robert, Junr Fle 66
  Robert, Senr Fle 66
  Samuel Clr 121
  Samuel Jes 35
  Santy Mer 339
  Santy Mer 340
  Susanna War 279
  Thomas Fay 23
  Thomas Mas 303
  Thos. Mas 304
  William Chr 82
  William Fay 42
  William Fay 44
  William Fle 66
  William Hrs 310
  William Log 195
  William Mer 339
  Wm. Cal 16
  Wm. Hrs 323
  Wm. Mon 378
Arnald, Chs. Nel 3
Arnel, Anthony Hrs 323
Arnet, James Fay 23
  John Mon 381
  Lea[illegible]en Mad 216
Arnett, David Knx 78
  David Lin 107
  Elizabeth Knx 78
  Marrian Nel 4
  Reuben Knx 78
  Samuel Clr 121
  Sarah Clr 121
  Stephen Knx 78
  Thomas Mon 382
Arniss, William Jes 35
Arnold, Adam Jef 24
  Benet Rck 159
  Benjamin Cal 7B
  Cader But 192
  Charles Fle 67
  David Jes 35

Arnold, cont.
  David Lew 97
  Edward Log 180
  Edward Log 187
  Grace Wsh 350
  H. Lewis Nic 64
  Isaac Bra 145
  Jacob Log 186
  James Cum 174
  James Fra 109
  James Mul 390
  James Woo 402
  Jeremiah Mul 395
  John Bou 73
  John But 192
  John Cam 28
  John Clr 121
  John Fra 107
  John Fra 107
  John Gal 195
  John Gar 202
  John Hrd 301
  John Woo 385
  John H. Log 168
  Joseph Mul 395
  Josiah Mul 395
  Lewis Woo 393
  Lott But 192
  Moses Cal 13
  Nancy Fra 107
  Nancy Woo 391
  Nicholas Bou 73
  Patsey Fra 109
  Peggy Gar 200
  Peter Lew 97
  Philip Log 168
  Price Mer 341
  Rice W. Clr 121
  Saml. Boo 57
  Silas Fra 107
  Thomas Bou 69
  Thomas Gal 195
  Thomas Log 179
  Thompson Fle 67
  Weden Log 185
  William Bou 73
  William Bou 73
  William Pen 111
  Willis H. Bou 70
  Wm. Hrd 283
  Yos. Jef 24
  Younger Log 167
  Ziba Fra 107
Arntt, Samuel Nic 64
ArraSmith, James Sco 169
  see Smith, James Arra
Arrasmith, Richd. Bou 72
  Thos. Bou 72
  Westley Bou 72
Arrington, Jordan Mad 197
Arry, George War 262
Art, Robert Fay 51
  William Nic 65
  William, Junr Nic 65
Arteburn, Elijah Jef 3
  John Jef 24
  Presley Jef 24
  Saml. Jaf 24
  Wm. Jr Jef 24
  Wm. Sr Jef 24
Artelany, John Wsh 286
Arter, David Cas 45
  Jenkenias Cas 45
  Wm. Cas 45
Arters, Thomas Chr 66
Arthur, Dolly Fay 11
  Elias Knx 71

Name	County	Page
Arthur, cont.		
John	Kns	74
John	Log	171
John, Jr	Knx	89
Joseph	Knx	70
Margaret	Mas	305
Mathew	Mas	304
Samuel	Knx	71
Stephen	Mon	352
Thomas	Knx	75
Thomas	Knx	80
Artis, Mathew	Mas	304
Artman, Adam	Gra	242
Jacob	Gra	241
John	Gra	237
John, Senr	Gra	242
Michael	Gra	240
Artonhouse, Conrod	Jes	35
Artree, John	Bar	53
Arvin, John	Lin	107
William	Lin	107
Asa, James	Hnd	344
Asakey, Richard	Wsh	286
Asbel, Willm.	Mad	215
Asbell, John	Est	7
William	Est	7
Asberry, Joseph	Adr	3
Wm.	Cum	181
Wm.	Fle	76
Asbons, Elijah	Cas	40
Asbrey, Linsey	Hrs	309
Asbury, George	Mas	305
Henry	Nic	65
Landman	Mas	304
Squire	Mas	305
William	Nic	65
William	Nic	65
Asby, Coleman	Pen	110
Ash, Andw.	Bar	26
Chas.	Hrd	298
Dolly	Nel	3
Henry	Hrd	299
Henry	Nel	3
John	Bul	173
Mul 388		
John	Nel	1
Peter	Nel	1
Reubin	Gra	240
Wm.	Hrd	291
Ashbaugh, Andr.	Nel	1
Ashbeau, Polly	Bul	173
Ashbey, Holt	Grp	269
Nathaniel	Fay	31
Ashbough, Jacob	Bra	148
Joseph	Bra	148
Ashbourne, James	Log	194
Ashbrok, John	Pen	111
Ashbrook, Levy	Clr	121
Thos.	Hrs	315
Ashburne, Henry	Log	161
Ashby, Alexr.	Bou	68
Benjn.	She	239
Blady	She	236
David	Chr	89
David	Ohi	80
Fielding	She	221
George	Ohi	96
Hankins	She	239
Horatio	Ohi	96
Jane	She	227
Jessee	Ohi	74
John M.	She	241
Landen	She	227
Peter	Hop	376
Robert	She	229
Sarah	She	239
Stevin	Chr	89
Ashby, cont.		
Thomas	Ohi	80
Thomas	She	220
Thomas	She	235
Thompson	She	219
Tinson	She	227
Warner	Ohi	96
Washnigton	She	213
William	Ohi	96
Ashcraft, Abisha	Hrd	304
Abner	Hrd	304
Amos	Pen	112
Ann	Hrd	304
Daniel	Gra	242
Elijah	Hrd	300
Ephraim	Nic	65
Jacob	Nic	65
James	Est	6
James	Pen	112
Jas.	Mad	197
Jediah	Pen	105
Jno.	Hrd	291
Ashen, Thomas	Mas	303
William	Mas	304
Asher, Bartlett	Jef	24
Dillian	Cly	151
Dillion	Cly	149
William	Hnr	355
William	Mul	408
Wm.	Cal	4
Ashford, John	Jes	35
John, Senr	Woo	388
Thomas	Jes	35
Thomas	Woo	389
Ashley, Absalom	Hop	372
Charles	Pul	122
Daniel	Hop	375
Elenor	Hop	371
George	Fra	110
George	Hop	376
Henry	Hop	381
James	Woo	375
Jemima	Hop	372
Jesse	Hop	371
Jno.	Hop	372
Jno.	Pul	122
Joel	Woo	387
Josiah	Clr	121
Stephen	Hop	372
Thomas	Mon	368
Thomas	War	263
William	Log	169
Ashlock, John	Lin	107
Richard	Lin	107
Thos.	Cum	179
Ashly, Bounds	Hop	378
Ashmore, James	Log	195
Ashton, Richard	Fay	11
Ashurst, Henry	Pul	123
Robert	Fay	20
Ashworth, Mitter	Bar	53
Starting	Bar	53
Askey, Zachariah	Liv	148
Askins, Courtney	Bre	164
Edward	Wsh	286
Edward	Wsh	349
Philamon	Gra	239
Askren, John	Wsh	286
William	Wsh	286
Askridge, George	Fle	89
Alky, Jonathan	Gar	202
Aslen, John	Log	170
Asque, Wm.	Bar	42
Aston, David	Mer	341
Geo.	Mad	215
Jinkins	Grn	265
Atchison, Alexander	Fay	23
Atchison, cont.		
Hamilton	Fay	23
Jeremiah	Mas	303
Jerry	Fle	76
Jesse	Fle	76
John	Fay	23
Silas	Mas	305
William	Fay	23
Wm.	Cal	5
Ategg, Henry	Mas	300
Ateway, John	Chr	74
Atha, William	Bou	117
Athel, Benjamin	Clr	121
Atherton, Henry	She	241
Joha.	Gra	240
William	She	236
Atkerson, David	Liv	159
Atkins, Absalom	Sco	172
Alexr.	Sco	177
Allen S.	Clr	121
Amos	Nel	3
Benj.	Way	361
Charles	Cum	185
Gawen	Sco	172
Hinch	Wsh	286
James	Clr	121
James	Clr	121
James	Sco	181
James	Sco	181
Jesse	Grn	253
John	Gal	195
John	Woo	385
Philip	Mas	305
Roling	Adr	3
William	Rck	163
William	Sco	184
Atkinson, Benjamin	Fay	11
Henry	Woo	394
Isaiah	Adr	3
John	Fle	64
Joshua	Grn	263
Spencer	Grn	259
Thomas	Adr	3
Aton, Hery	Adr	3
Atterberry, Charles	Gra	242
David	Gra	239
Edwd.	Hrd	284
Elijah	Hrd	284
Elijah	Hrd	286
Isaiah	Gra	242
Israel	Gra	241
James	Gra	242
Melchezedick	Gra	241
Michael	Gra	241
Michl.	Hrd	285
Nathan	Gra	242
Thos.	Hrd	283
Thos.	Hrd	285
Thos.	Hrd	300
Wm.	Hrd	284
Atterbury, Richard	Ohi	101
Attison, Michael	Log	181
Saml.	Log	178
Attkins, Henry	Gar	200
Atwell, Joseph	Bul	173
Solomon	Way	362
Atwood, James	Adr	3
James	Woo	378
Jos.	War	263
William	Woo	379
Wm.	Adr	3
Auberiry, Henry	Fay	19
Auberry, John	Nel	4
Aud, Armstead	Nel	4
James	Nel	3
Joseph	Bul	173
Philip	Nel	1

Aud, cont.
Thomas Nel 3
Thomas Nel 3
Zackerl Nel 3
Audley, Charlen Cum 172
Audubon, John Hnd 345
Augden, William Fay 38
Augustus, David Jef 25
Jacob Jef 25
Aulday, Seth Pul 123
Auldham, Newport Cly 158
Auldridge, Francis Pul 122
Aulich, Charles Pen 114
Ausbin, Squire Cly 156
Ausbrooks, Mary War 272
Austen, Nathl. Mad 215
Austin, David War 279
George She 214
James Wsh 286
Janas Cas 37
John Gar 200
John Jef 3
Nath. Cly 156
Obediah Bou 73
Saml. Mad 197
Thomas Gar 202
Auston, Chas. Bar 39
John Hnd 333
Mary Hnd 336
Autrey, Alexr. Cum 176
Auxi, Nathaniel Flo 95
Auxier, John Flo 95
Michael Flo 95
Simon Flo 95
Thomas Flo 95
Ave, Jacob Jes 35
Avery, Craven Nel 4
George Fay 20
John Wsh 286
Payton Fay 20
Samuel Wsh 349
Avit, Richard Bre 168
Avry, Zachariah Bre 165
Awbrey, Rowland Bre 159
Awkward, Wm. Cam 31
Awler, Edwd. Hrd 285
Leonard Hrd 283
Awley, Peter Grn 254
Awlsberry, Thomas Chr 53
Axley, James Liv 152
Pleasant Liv 152
Robert Liv 155
Axton, Isham Mer 341
William Mer 341
Axun, Micajah Hop 378
Ayers, Coleman Gal 195
James Gal 195
Nahanel Way 363
Thomas Gal 195
Wm. Gal 195
Aynes, James Woo 397
Ayres, David War 269
Gentry Way 351
Henry Log 161
Jane Log 178
Saml. Way 371
Thomas Wsh 349
Walter Woo 388
Ayris, Daniel Bou 72
Thomas Bou 72
William Bou 72

-- B --

Babb, Martain Cas 45
Babb, cont.
Stephen Bar 37
Babell, Jno. Nel 5
Thos. Nel 5
Baber, George Mer 338
Isham Clr 123
Obediah Clr 123
Standley Clr 123
Bable, William Cal 9
Back, Harmon Fay 22
John Flo 99
Jos. Gar 203
Backster, Bethuel Est 7
Bacon, Edmond Fra 117
Elizabeth Fay 43
John Fra 114
Langston Fra 117
Lyddall Fra 113
Bacy, Edmond Jef 28
Badder, Moses Cam 28
Badders, Moses Bou 75
Phinnis Bou 75
Badger, David Mon 375
Badget, Jno. Mad 214
Badin, Stephen T. Wsh 340
Bagbey, Will Bou 75
Bagby, Charles Mas 301
David Mas 292
Nathan Mon 372
Robert Lew 98
Robert, Junr Mas 300
Robert, Senr Mas 292
Wm. Lew 98
Baggess, William Bou 118
Baggs, Archibal Mul 398
John Jef 21
Robert Mul 390
Bagley, Henry Cly 149
John Cly 152
Will Cly 152
Bagwell, John She 198
Thos. Sco 179
Baid, Arcd. Lew 102
Bailes, Joseph Bar 49
Bailey, Abm. Sco 173
Alectious She 241
Alexander Log 180
Archebald Fra 115
Banja. Flo 99
Bennet D. Mul 393
David She 234
Elijah Lin 109
Elisha Adr 4
Ezekiel Knx 71
Gabriel Log 194
Hezekiah Grn 258
Hezh. Adr 4
James Flo 98
James Gal 197
James Hop 381
James Knx 64
James Lin 109
James Mas 301
Jane Log 192
Jane Mas 294
Jno. Nel 12
John Fay 19
John Lin 109
John Nel 11
John Nic 62
John Sco 167
John War 255
John, Jur Rck 161
John, Senr Sco 167
Joseph Flo 99
Joseph Gal 193
Joseph She 218
Bailey, cont.
Lewis Knx 89
Mary Knx 86
Peter Rck 163
Reuben Grn 258
Reuben Grn 260
Reuben Rck 163
Robert Grn 263
Robert Log 192
Robert She 234
Saml. Bra 145
Sarah Bou 119
Simon Fra 112
Stephen Gal 194
Syntha Log 177
Thomas Log 183
Thomas Nel 12
Thomas Wsh 342
Thos. Lin 109
Thos. Sco 167
Wifley Grn 252
William Bou 118
William She 233
Wm. Cum 177
Wm. H. Nel 8
Bailis, John Bar 41
Baily, Andrew Pen 110
Benj. Bar 42
Callum Bar 46
Callum H. Jun Bar 29
Chas. J. Bar 27
Clodeus Bar 27
Edwd. Gar 202
George Log 186
James Cal 16
Jessee Bar 27
John Bar 42
John Bar 48
John Hop 377
John Log 175
John Log 186
Lewis Gar 201
Richd. Bar 40
Richd. Hop 376
Saml. Log 170
William Gar 202
Zacariah Cal 16
Bain, George Woo 390
Johnson Hnr 356
Lewis Hnr 355
Patterson Fay 12
Richd. Lew 102
Robert Knx 87
Bainbridge, Absalom - Fay 33
Absalom Fay 44
Petr. Gar 199
Baine, Leroy Hnr 357
Thomas Log 177
Baines, John Log 177
Baird, Bedant Bre 162
Charles She 208
James She 203
James, Junr Ohi 69
James, Senr Ohi 77
Jno. Hrd 294
Jos. Hrd 292
Samuel Bre 165
Robert Bre 161
Saml. Lew 101
Stanly Log 172
Taylor Hrd 294
Thos. Hrd 292
Baire, William Chr 64
Baisden, S. John Flo 99
Baiseaw, Patrick Bar 51
Baker, Abner Cly 155

Baker, cont.
Abraham Bou 76
Abraham Bra 142
Abraham Gar 203
Absalom Wsh 343
Andrew Hnd 331
Andrew Log 189
Andw. Hnr 365
Aron Bra 146
Baily Chr 87
Bazel Mad 210
Bazel, Jr Mad 210
Benja. Pul 125
Benjamin Bou 76
Blake Cal 3
Boling Cly 151
Brice Knx 79
Charles GAr 203
Charles Mad 209
Charles Way 352
Conrod Cas 39
Coonrod Log 174
David Fay 20
David mad 210
David Pul 124
E. Holland Mas 300
Edmund Mon 358
Edward War 260
Edward Way 360
Eleaner Fay 13
Elijah War 269
Federick Grn 258
Francis Fle 69
Geo. Cly 151
George Clr 122
George Jef 21
George Mad 213
Henry Cam 32
Henry Mas 296
Hugh Hnr 368
Isaac Bou 76
Isaac Jes 62
Isaac Mad 214
Isaac. Way 359
Isaac Way 373
Jacob Nic 64
James Cum 166
James Hop 377
James Jes 62
James Log 183
James Mad 208
James Nic 63
Jas. Gar 205
Jesse Gal 193
Jincy Mon 383
John Bar 41
John Cam 31
John Chr 87
John Chr 88
John Clr 124
John Cum 166
John Cum 183
John Fra 115
John Gar 204
John Hnr 359
B
John Log 170
John Mad 206
John Mas 297
john Nel 11
John Nic 63
John Nic 64
John Pen 105
John War 248
John Way 359
John Way 360
John, Jun Cly 155

Baker, cont.
John, Sr Cly 154
John, Senr Cum 166
Jonathan Gal 193
Jonathon War 243
Jos. Gar 203
Joseph Cas 38
Joseph Knx 77
Joseph Mon 347
Joseph M. Way 352
Joshua Cam 28
Joshua Gal 193
Judimian Pul 125
Julianna Hrs 317
Lathy Gar 204
Lewis Jes 61
Martin Bou 76
Martin Gar 205
Martin Nic 63
Michael Mad 212
Miles Cal 18
Moses Gal 193
Moses Mon 350
Nathan Gal 192
Nathaniel Jes 59
Nathaniel Jes 62
Obediah Cum 166
Patsy Lin 111
Peleg Pul 129
Peter Hrs 318
R. Simon Mas 294
Reason Mad 212
Reubin Fra 111
Richd. Hop 377
Robert Chr 99
Robert Log 170
Robt. Cly 151
Saml. Cam 26
Samuel Adr 19
Samuel Chr 87
Samuel Log 171
Samuel Log 174
Sarah Cum 166
Seth Cal 7
Thomas Bou 77
Thomas Chr 58
Thomas Cum 166
Thomas Jef 29
Umphrey Cam 32
Umprey Grp 273
Vachel Mad 212
Wandley Mad 210
Wandley, jur Mad 210
Warner Cas 46
William Bou 77
William Knx 79
William Log 172
William Log 182
William Mas 296
William Mas 298
William Wsh 349
William, Senr Mas 301
Wm. Cum 166
Wm. Hnr 367
Wm. Nic 63
Bakerer, Jacob Pul 125
Bal, Hugh Bou 76
Balance, Willis Mer 343
Balard, Hyram Fay 19
Balddin, James Fra 114
Balden, Mary Pul 121
Balding, Moses Fay 41
Baldock, Ann Lin109
James Sco 188
Levi Lin 111
Reuben Cas 39
Willim. Lin 111

Baldridge, Saml. Adr 5
Thos. Adr 4
Baldwin, Danl. Sco 169
Henry Mas 291
James Mas 304
Jno. Grn 260
John Sco 186
Joseph Rck 165
Samuel Mas 304
Thos. Nel 11
William Hop 374
Balenger, Frances Fay 52
Jeramiah Bra 149
John Bra 149
Baler, David Lin 111
Bales, Alex Cly 152
Jacob Grn 261
James Cal 12
James Cly 151
James S. Liv 155
Balew, Absalom Cum 171
Massa log 195
Baley, Andrew Pul 124
Basil Nic 63
David Fay 30
David Fay 55
Elijah Pul 126
John Fay 55
Joshudy Lew 99
Samuel Hrs 317
Simon Hrs 321
Syrus Jef 22
Balintine, Thomas Fle 73
Ball, Benjamen Adr 4
Benjamin Mas 298
Daniel Lin 111
David Hrs 320
Drucilla Fay 47
Edmond Woo 377
Edward Mas 304
Henry Fay 12
James Fay 19
James Gal 194
James Gar 201
James Nel 5
Jno. Hrd 299
Jno. Mad 212
John Bou 77
Polly Gar 204
Richard Lew 100
Robert Grn 252
Robt. Adr 5
Samuel Hop 372
Thomas Lin 109
William Fay 20
William Jes 62
Willm. Lin 109
Wm. Cum 178
Wm. Gar 203
Wm. P. Lew 97
Ballad, Harris Grp 270
Ballaher, Susanah Fle 83
Ballance, Mary Clr 124
Ballard, Appleton E Fle 84
Bentley War 262
Blan W. She 197
Charles Cum 175
Geor. Mon 358
George Sco 176
James Clr 123
James She 209
James B. Mad 243
Jesse She 237
John Jef 30
John Mad 243
Johnson Woo 389
Larkin Mad 212

Ballard, cont.
  Laving Gra 237
  Margery Gar 203
  Mary Nel 11
  Philip Clr 123
  Proctor Nel 10
  Reubin War 262
  William Clr 123
  Wm. War 262
BAllding, Edward Mad 209
Ballenger, Achelles Gar 205
  Benjm. Adr 5
  Edward Knx 85
  Henry Gar 205
  John Adr 5
  Richard Knx 83
  William Mas 293
  Wm. Nic 63
Baller, Walker Cas 45
Ballew, Thomas Mad 209
Ballingal, David Nic 64
Ballinger, Jane Fra 116
  John Sco 182
  William Mas 295
Ballow, John Cum 173
  Mary Knx 65
  Richard Knx 77
  Robert Knx 78
Ballwin, Reubin Boo 57
Balsel, John Nel 8
Balshie, Robt. Way 352
Balt, John Adr 4
Baltzill, George Fra 117
Balwin, Wm. Mon 348
Bandurant, Joseph She 221
Bandy, Hugh Grn 253
Bane, Clotilda Nel 6
  John Nel 11
  Peter Chr 95
  Richard Clr 123
Banefiled, Robert Mon 375
  Samuel Mon 375
Banerster, Joseph Cas 44
Banes, John Log 161
Banester, John Bou 74
Banfield, Thomas Grp 275
Banister, Boliam War 275
  Wm. Cal 15
Bankinship, Wm. Flo 100
Banks, Adam Pul 124
  Cuthbert Fay 11
  Cuthbert Mon 362
  Hugh Log 187
  Jarret Gar 205
  Jas. Gar 201
  Jerrard Fra 117
  John Gar 203
  John Jef 22
  John Snr Gar 205
  Joseph Log 187
  Reuben Gar 203
  Rivors Log 185
  Samuel Adr 4
  Somerton Adr 4
  Thomas Adr 4
  Thomas Pul 129
  Vandr. Adr 4
  Wm. Gar 201
Bann, Leroy Hnr 367
Bannan, William Fle 61
Banning, Clark Cum 182
Banta, David Jes 61
  Henry Mad 209
Banton, Henry Gar 199
  Jno., Jnr Gar 199
  John Log 174
  Josua War 254

Banton, cont.
  Willm. Lin 109
Baragar, Peter Mad 215
Barar, Henry Fay 20
Barbary, David War 262
  Peter War 253
Barbee, Danl. Gal 194
  Elias Grn 245
  John She 210
Barber, Edward Bar 42
  Edward Mas 299
  James Mer 341
  Jas. Jef 3
  John Knx 83
  Moses Mad 243
  Nathl. Way 369
  Sally Mon 352
Barbey, Ezekiel Mer 331
  Jessee Bou 118
  Joseph Bou 118
  Joseph Fay 12
  Joshua Mer 331
Barbour, Ambrose Hnd 344
  Ambrose Wsh 348
  Philip Hnd 327
  Philip Wsh 342
  Richard Jef 3
  Thomas Jef 3
Barclay, Geo. Gar 204
  Hugh War 252
  James Lew 95
  John Mad 206
  Saml. War 269
Bare, Adam Bre 164
  Johns Bre 164
Barefield, Thomas Mul 399
Barfield, James Bou 118
Barger, Abraham Cly 155
  Adam Bre 165
  George Bre 165
  Jacob Bre 157
  John Cly 154
  John, Jr Bre 167
  John, Sr Bre 167
Bargo, John She 213
  Peter Nel 9
  William She 219
Barhan, E. Nel 7
Barier, Abreham Pul 128
  Martin Pul 128
Barinner, Jonathan Cal 19
Barkaloe, Wm. V. Hop 381
Barkeloo, Edward Grp 270
  Ruth Grp 270
Barker, Amas Chr 94
  Ananias Log 190
  Ann Fay 12
  Aron Nel 13
  Elias Est 3
  Elizabeth Ohi 94
  George Fay 37
  James Est 3
  Jacob Hop 374
  John Mas 292
  John Pul 127
  John H. Pen 109
  Joseph Est 3
  Joseph Fay 35
  Joseph Mon 361
  Joseph Chr 109
  Mary Mas 292
  Richd. Gar 205
  Saml. Nel 6
  Stephen Est 3
  Thomas Bou 77
  Thomas Fay 33
  Thomas Mon 351

Barker, cont.
  Thomas Nel 6
  William Est 3
  William Fay 19
  William Fay 57
  William She 214
Barkerlow, William Fay 12
Barkewell, Joel Jes 60
Barkley, George Jes 62
  James Sco 182
  John, Jr Jes 62
  John, Sr Jes 62
  Mathw. Jur Sco 168
  Mathw. Senr Sco 168
  Robert Sco 171
  Samuel Jes 62
  Thos. S. Sco 186
  William Clr 123
  William Sco 191
Barksher, Dickey Boo 57
  Jeremh. Boo 57
Barkshire, Joshua Hrs 318
Barkshre, Green-berry Hrs 316
Barlar, Christopher Wsh 348
  Cornelius Wsh 348
  Jacob Wsh 340
  John Wsh 348
Barlaw, Joshua Bar 41
  Thos. Cal 15
Barlee, Andrew Fay 54
Barley, Urial Log 195
Barlor, Jenny Wsh 340
Barlow, Aaron Boo 57
  Ambros Bar 31
  Danl. Boo 57
  David Bou 75
  Enoch Sco 177
  Ephrm. Boo 57
  Heny. Adr 4
  Jesse Nic 62
  Jesse Pul 128
  John Nic 62
  Lewis Adr 4
  Lewis Liv 151
  Michl. Boo 58
  Michl. Hrd 289
  Nancy Gar 203
  Simon Way 368
  Theophilus Gra 237
  Thomas Pul 128
  Thomas Pul 131
  Thompkins Bou 76
  Thos. Hrs 318
  Thos. Sco 167
  Wm. Nic 62
Barn, Beal Clr 122
Barnaby, George Fle 73
Barnard, Heny. Adr 5
  Jesse B. Log 188
  William Ohi 70
Barner, Francis War 254
  Wiley J. Log 161
Barnerd, Elizabeth Clr 122
Barnes, Aaron Fay 20
  Aquilla Est 3
  Bazel Fle 63
  Bingman Gal 194
  Brinsley Est 6
  Brinsley, Junr Fay 19
  Brinsley, Senr Fay 19
  Cado Chr 89
  Charles Clr 124
  Charles Way 360
  Charles Woo 393
  Daniel Bre 161
  Ephram Fle 65

Barnes, cont.
Federick War 257
Francis, Jr Gal 195
Francis, Sr Gal 194
George Chr 79
Harry Ohi 86
Hugh Mas 296
Isaac Chr 113
James Chr 106
James Est 5
James Mon 369
John Est 6
John Ohi 80
Joseph Ohi 69
Joshua Hop 371
Joshua Wsh 348
Josshua Fle 63
Lemmon Mas 297
Martha Wsh 342
Moses Fay 19
Nancyq Fay 37
Neriah Fle 65
Robert Clr 124
Ruthy Chr 98
Samuel Log 169
Shedrick Gal 192
Thomas Chr 84
Thomas Est 6
Thomas Mon 364
Weaver Ohi 70
William Pen 113
Wm. Way 359
Zackariah Est 2
Barnet, Abner Mon 378
Absolom Bar 26
Absolom Bar 44
Benjn. Boo 57
James Hrs 318
Jas. Way 353
Jereimiah War 257
John Mon 377
John Way 374
Jonathan Mon 376
Joshua Mon 377
Martin Wsh 349
Paul Hrs 317
Robert Bou 75
Solomon Wsh 348
William Wsh 349
Wm. Bar 44
Wm. Mon 377
Wm. Way 373
Barnett, Alex Mad 209
Alexander Bou 74
Alexander Ohi 76
Ambrose Nic 62
Andrew Grn 264
Andrew Log 168
Andrew Log 184
Andrew Ohi 103
Ann Jef 34
Ann Lin 109
Betsey Mon 364
Daniel Hnr 361
David Log 172
David Log 195
David Mer 334
Eddy Gar 205
Edwd. Gar 202
Eleazer Gar 202
Elijah Log 168
George Bou 76
George Mon 356
Guilbert Flo 100
Henry Est 6
Henry Mon 382
Isabella Hnd 342

Barnett, cont.
Jacob Ohi 73
James Bou 76
James Lin 109
James Log 188
James War 247
James War 252
James War 274
Jams. Collo Mad 209
Jeremiah Est 3
Jesse Flo 99
John Bou 76
John Bou 76
John Bou 77
John Lin 111
John Log 170
John Liv 155
John Log 176
John Log 187
John Mad 209
John She 224
John She 228
John War 243
John War 274
John Woo 388
John M.K. Log 188
Joseph Hnr 359A
Joseph Mad 207
Joseph Ohi 72
Kitty Bou 76
Mary Cly 152
Robert Lin 109
Robert Log 184
Saml. Cal 5
Samuel O. Mer 333
Samuel Hnd 337
Sarah Hnd 337
Schuyler Mad 213
Spencer Bou 77
Thos. War 247
Umphrey Hnd 336
William Bou 77
William Liv 155
William Mad 207
Willm. Adr 4
Wm. Hrd 284
Wm. Jef 21
Wm. (Jockey) Mad 209
Zachariah Mer 333
Barnhart, John War 276
Barnhill, Daniel Sco 181
James Hnr 359A
Robert Hnr 359A
Saml. Sco 167
Saml. Jur Sco 167
William Hnr 359A
Wm. Jef 23
Barnit, Abner Chr 65
James Chr 65
James Chr 66
William Chr 67
Wm. Bar 40
Barns, Abraham Mad 210
Abraham Pul 128
Amus Pul 130
Archibald Nel 11
Benjamin Pul 125
Betsy Mer 334
Charles Nel 11
Elias Mad 212
Elijah Pul 124
Elijah Pul 125
Elijak Nel 10
Elisha Mad 243
Elizabeth Pul 124
George Pul 125
George Pul 127

Barns, cont.
Henry Mer 337
James Hrs 318
James Mer 335
Jane Hrs 313
John Hrs 319
Nicodemus Way 353
Noble Mon 364
Oliver Hrs 319
Phil Mad 212
Philemon Mon 368
Rebecka Mad 212
Reuben Fra 113
Richd. Pul 125
Robt. Jur Fle 65
Saml. Mad 213
Saml. Nel 11
Shadrach Mad 215
Thomas Gra 237
Tice Mon 368
William Adr 12
see William, Barns
William Mer 335
William Mer 335
William Pul 128
Zachariah Mer 335
Barntt, John Nic 62
Baron, Augustin Wsh 344
Charles Bra 153
Barnod, Pheby Fay 48
Barr, Agnas Fay 22
Amelia Bou 76
George Jes 62
Hugh Bou 75
James Jef 31
Jnr. Hnr 365
John Hnr 359
John Jes 62
R.V. Thomas Fay 13
Robert Bou 76
Robert Fay 45
Robert Mon 354
Thomas Fay 35
Thomas Fay 54
Thomas, Senr Fay 30
William Chr 60
William Nel 11
Zachariah Jes 62
Barraw, Jacob Wsh 348
Barrell, Christian Jef 28
Barren, Aron Pul 129
Jno. Pul 130
Barret, David Cly 150
George Mul 403
John Grn 265
Robt. Grn 265
BArrett, Fras. Cum 170
Isaac Mad 215
John Jes 60
Peter Hrs 323
Thomas Ohi 69
William Nel 5
William Ohi 72
Barrickman, Jacob Cam 33
Barritt, Wm. Grn 262
Barron, Jno. Hrd 296
Martha Liv 149
Barrot, Elijah Fay 19
George Mul 398
Barrott, Elijah Jes 59
Barrough, Peter Mas 300
Barrow, Daniel Way 359
Elizabe Pul 129
David Mon 350
David Pul 129
Hinchea Mon 350
Jno. Pul 129

Barrow, Nathan Mon 349
William Pul 129
Barry, Archibald Chr 85
Daniel Chr 58
James Chr 111
James War 252
John Jes 61
John K. War 252
Thomas Chr 94
Bart, George Mer 341
Bartee, Rececka Chr 91
Barter, John Mer 330
Bartett, Wm. Bra 151
Bartle, John Cam 31
Bartleson, Jno. Way 366
Bartlet, Edmd. Cum 171
Elijah Hrd 283
Geo. Hrd 284
Solomon Bar 43
Tho. Bar 48
Bartlett, (free negro) Fay 32
Ant Hnr368
Charles Clr 123
Dahiel Clr 122
Daniel Clr 122
Ebnezar Nic 64
Edmund Hnr 358
Foster Hnr 359
Frederick Jef 22
Harry Fra 113
Harry Hnr 369
James Bre 160
James Hnr 359B
James Jef 34
John Clr 122
John Fra 113
John Jef 22
John Sco 181
Joseph Nic 64
Joshua Clr 122
Mycage Bra 151
Nathan Liv 159
Nathan Mon 349
Nimrod Gra 243
Owen Log 187
Saml. Nic 64
Samuel Clr 122
Stephen Log 187
Thomas Fra 115
Thos. Hnr 363
Will Hnr 366
William Clr 122
Wm. Nel 9
Wm. Nic 64
Bartley, George Pul 130
James Bra 149
Joshua Grp 278
Bartlow, James Bra 152
Bartly, Joseph Cal 17
Bartoe, Thomas Chr 102
Barton, Abner Bar 52
Andrew Bou 75
Cessia Fay 12
Clark Gra 243
David Fay 55
David Hop 377
Elijah Bou 69
Jacob Bar 52
James Bar 25
James Pen 109
John Cly 150
John War 268
Josiph Chr 89
Joshua Bou 77
Mary Hnd 338
Mary Log 193

Barton, cont.
Ravister War 268
Samuel Chr 67
Susana Knx 72
Thos. Cum 168
William Chr 65
William Chr 67
William Knx 79
Bartson, Wm. Way 367
Bartwell, Stevin Chr 102
Barum, Amy Lin 111
Basarrd, Philip Hrd 300
Basey, Richard She 203
William Hrs 307
William Mer 329
Bash, Henry Vou 118
Basham, Bartlet A. Bre 164
Obediah Bre 165
Obediah Bre 167
Bashiers, Edin Hrd 296
Edwd. Hrd 294
Marsham Hrd 288
Baskell, Thomas She 208
Baskett, Jesse Nic 63
Job She 221
John She 233
Lucy She 235
Martin She 231
Thomas She 231
Wm. War 255
Baskum, William She 199
Bass, Henry Grn 251
Jos. Grn 252
Josiah Gra 238
Jourden Log 162
Mathew Bul 173
Narril Grn 255
Nathaniel Bar 54
Norril Grn 252
Olden Log 192
Peter Grn 252
Philimon Bar 29
Thos. Grn 261
Tiry Grn 261
Winney War 261
Basset, Abner Mer 333
Amas Bra 148
Amous Grp 271
Benjamin Mas 297
Elijah Bra 148
Bassett, John Gar 201
William Fra 113
Bast, David Lin 111
Peter Lin 111
Bastin, Richd. Woo 383
Baswell, Walter Chr 106
Basye, Alfred Bou 118
Basys, Elezamon Bou 118
Bate..., Elias Mad 208
Bate, Jas. S. Jef 3
John Jef 3
Bateman, John Fle 71
Nancy Fle 80
Shadruk Fle 83
Thomas Fle 80
William Fle 79
Bates, Daniel Rck 165
Danl. Mad 207
George Mul 396
Humphry Gar 204
James Bar 34
James Cum 182
James Jes 59
James Ohi 93
John Cly 156
John Gar 204
John Jef 32

Bates, cont.
Joseph Cal 19
Joseph, Jur Sco 174
Marmaduke Fra 114
Matthew Wsh 342
Moses Jef 22
Richard Hnr 366
Samuel H. Bre 169
Thomas Mad 208
Thos. Way 367
Thos. Sr Hnr 367
Warren Bou 76
William Rck 166
Batey, Robert Fay 12
Bathe, John Bou 75
Bathuram,Benjn. Jr Rck 161
Benjn. Ser Rck 163
David Rck 163
Isaac Rck 161
Wm. Rck 163
Batman, Isaac Jef 21
John Fle 64
Margaret Jef 21
Thomas Jef 21
Batson, Jonathan Bcu 76
Mordica Bcu 76
Robert Bou 77
Battershell, Fran-cis Clr 123
John Clr 123
Batterton, Benjn. Bou 77
Henry Mad 243
Jeremiah Mad 206
Moses Mad 208
Saml. Bou 119
Battleton, Amos Adr 4
Battoe, Peter Chr 94
William Chr 94
Battoss, John Lin 111
Batty, Adrew. Lew 96
Baty, Charles Chr 59
John Bou 119
Baucher, Peter War 263
Baugh, Abraham Gar 204
Alexander Mad 208
Henry Pul 125
Joseph Mad 207
Philip Bar 29
William Mod 207
Wm. Bar 42
Baughman, John Knx 76
Bauldin, Elisha Liv 152
William Liv 152
Baunty, Henry Mer 330
Henry Mer 337
Jacob Mer 337
Baurne, Benjamin She 203
Bausley, James Cas 47
Baw, Elizabeth Fra 110
Bawers, Jacob Mul 403
Bawman, Joseph Cal 7B
Baws, Thomas Way 360
Bawsly, John Mer 331
Baxdale, John Mer 331
Baxley, Jesse Mad 211
Baxter, Jenjamin Mad 206
Edm. Mad 214
Edmond Bou 76
Francis Hnr 364
Geo. Mad 214
Jacob Sco 192
James Adr 5
James Fay 19
James Hnr 364
James Jes 61
Jesse Clr 122
Jessy Hnr 368

Name	County	Page
Baxter, cont.		
Rebecka	Fay	19
Saml.	Gal	193
Saml.	Jef	24
Samuel	Fay	20
Samuel	Fay	51
Silr.	Mad	214
Thomas	Fay	19
William	Clr	123
William	Hrs	313
William	Wsh	343
Wm.	Cas	47
Wm.	Jef	22
Bayles, Benj.	Mas	304
Jesse	Mas	292
Stephen	Mas	300
Bayley, James	Lin	111
John	Lin	111
John	Mon	377
John	Mon	381
Ralph	Lin	109
Robert	Mon	364
Warren	Mon	364
Willm.	Adr	4
Wm.	Mon	361
Wm.	Mon	379
Baylor, Catharine	Hrs	309
George W.	Bou	75
John G.W.	Log	196
John W.	Bou	77
Robert	Log	177
Robert T.	Log	176
Walker	Bou	77
William	Mas	291
Baylow, Elijah C.	Fra	113
Bayls, Eden	Mad	208
Bayne, Walter	Nel	12
Bays, Edward	Hnr	356
John	Hnr	369
John	Ohi	82
Richard	Mas	299
Bayty, Daniel	Mon	367
Thomas	Mon	367
Bazey, Elizth.	Nel	41
Bazle, John	Bou	77
Beach, Baley	Fay	37
Joseph	Fay	19
Beacham, Jessy	Fay	39
Beachem, James	Jef	33
Beackam, Samuel A.	Fay	32
Beacum, Hugh	Bou	74
Beadle, Daniel	Bre	165
Elizabeth	Mon	375
Nathan	Bre	164
Samuel	Mon	360
Beadles, Edmond	War	252
Beagle, Edmond	Jef	3
James	Jef	3
Joseph	Hrs	320
Wm.	Jef	3
Beal, Samuel	Fay	19
Bealer, Henry	Fay	52
John	Jef	22
Beall, Eliza	Cam	32
Jannet H.	Cam	27
John	Bou	74
Norborne B.	Jef	21
Richard	Wsh	344
Robt.	Grn	260
Walter, Sr	Nel	12
William	Wsh	342
Bealor, John	Ohi	101
William	Ohi	99
Beam, Fielding	Grn	256
George	Nel	6
Jacob	Bar	40
Jacob	Wsh	344

Name	County	Page
Beam, cont.		
Michl.	Hnr	359B
Saml.	Nel	11
Beames, James	Knx	67
Beams, Conrad P.	Wsh	348
Bean, Abner	Fay	12
Baldwin	Lew	100
Bennet	Wsh	347
Daniel	Chr	104
Isaac	Jef	32
John	Clr	123
John	Clr	146
Russell W.	But	192
Thos.	Hrd	286
Wm.	Hrd	287
Beane, Charles	Bou	118
William	Clr	124
Beantly, John	Bou	74
Bear, Christopher	Clr	122
John	Fra	116
Beard, Abraham	Pul	131
Abram	Woo	377
Alexr.	Nel	9
Andrew	Hrs	319
Andw.	Bar	39
David	Log	187
David	Mas	294
Elizabeth	Gal	196
George	Mon	381
Hugh	Adr	4
Hugh	Adr	4
Hugh	Sco	184
James	Adr	4
James	Nel	12
Jno.	Pul	130
John	Adr	5
John	Adr	19
John	Cum	186
John	Mul	402
John	War	279
John P.	Ohi	99
Joseph	Fay	23
Joseph	Wsh	341
Leanna	Gal	197
Mary	Mon	356
Rebecca	Mul	398
Saml.	Adr	4
Saml.	Lin	109
Samuel D.	Mon	356
Stephen	Nel	7
Thomas	Pen	115
Thomas	She	224
William	Fay	23
William	Knx	76
William	Nel	9
Wm.	Jef	24
Wm.	Mon	382
Zebulon	Mas	291
Beardin, John	Cal	7B
Silas	Cal	17
Thourney?	Cal	7B
Bearding, Richd.	War	265
Bearns, Saml.	Fle	84
Bearry, Jennet	Mon	367
Beas, Nace (Free-man)	Fay	26
Beasley, Jas.	Gar	203
John	Fay	22
John	War	250
William	Fay	19
Willm.	War	276
Wm.	War	250
Beasly, Catharine	Woo	385
Charles	Woo	397
Edmond	Woo	397
Beason, Richard	Pul	127
Roger	Way	355

Name	County	Page
Beatee, John	Way	369
Beatem, Adam	Fay	53
Beates, John	Boo	57
Wiley	Boo	57
Beatle, John	Mon	362
Beatley, Daniel	Flo	100
Beatly, Sally	Sco	169
Beaton, John	Nic	63
Beats, Wm.	Boo	57
Beatton, James	Grn	258
Beatty, Adam	Gra	241
Edward	Fay	31
George	Sco	171
Henry	Est	4
James	Sco	175
James	Sco	180
Joseph	Gra	241
Nancy	Sco	185
William	Gra	242
Willm.	Sco	172
Beaty, Adam	Mas	304
Alexr.	Cum	184
David	Mas	295
Edward	Fay	60
James	Cum	184
James	Fay	40
Thomas	Way	364
Wm.	Cum	184
Beauchamp, Causton	Wsh	348
Cot.	Nel	8
Isaac	Sco	171
Jereboam	Wsh	348
Josh	Nel	8
Newel	Nel	13
Samuel	Fay	40
Stephn.	Bar	52
Tho.	Bar	52
Beaughcamp, Wm.	Hrs	320
Beaumont, Wm.	Gar	203
Beaven, Austin	Nel	11
Chas.	Nel	7
Edward	Wsh	342
Henry	Nel	7
John	Wsh	341
Joseph	Wsh	341
Nicholas	Wsh	348
Richard	Wsh	344
Thompson	Nel	7
Beaver, B. Mathias	Hrs	310
John	Cam	27
Michael	Hrs	309
Michael	Hrs	310
Beavers, Abraham	Flo	100
John	Mon	374
William	Hrd	302
Beavis, Juliana	Woo	389
Beazly, Hiram	Hnr	363
Philip	Wsh	347
Beck, Athony	Fle	80
Danl.	Bar	28
Edwd.	Cum	173
Jacob	Bar	28
Jacob	Way	354
James	Fay	50
Jeremiah	Mas	298
Jesse	Jef	33
John	Bou	76
John	Fay	12
John	Hnd	339
Joseph	Way	371
Moses	Cum	173
Polly	Mad	212
Preston	Cum	186
Stephen	Hnd	331
Thomas	Cal	6
Thomas	She	201
Beckam, Elizabeth	Jes	59

Beckam, cont.
John Hnd 327
Becket, John Bou 75
John Hrs 319
John Hrs 319
John Hrs 319
Joseph Bou 118
Joseph Hrs 319
Joseph Hrs 319
Josiah Cum 185
Robert Mer 333
Samuel Mas 299
Beckett, Benjamin Est 1
Humphy Fle 66
Nelson W. Pen 109
Becklehamer, David Cam 32
Beckley, Henry She 237
Levi She 209
Beckly, John W. She 234
Becknell, Tho. Mad 210
Beckner, Fredrick Fle 73
Henry Fle 70
Peter Fle 73
Becktel, Henry Jef 22
Beckum, John Woo 383
Beckweth, Wadding Clr 124
Beckwith, John Bul 173
John Bul 174
John W. Bul 174
Becraft, Benjn. Mon 362
Binjn. Mon 369
Jonathan Bou 75
Bedford, Archd. Bou 118
Benjn. Bou 118
Jno. Nel 13
John Cum 178
Little Berry Bou 119
Stephen Cum 176
Thos. Cum 176
Bedster, Jno. Mad 211
Bedwell, Bailey Nel 12
Robert she 211
Thomas Jef 33
Beechly, William Mas 301
Beechum, Barberry Chr 102
Beeding, Milly Mas 297
Tabitha Mas 298
Beedles, John Mer 333
Rice Lin 109
Beegle, Soloman Clr 122
Beeler, Chrits. Nel 8
George Fle 76
Beeles, George Fle 70
Beemen, Daniel Boo 57
John Boo 57
Been, Benjamin Mas 299
James Hrs 312
Leonard Mas 298
Phantleroy Mas 301
William Mas 294
Beesly, Ezekiel Mas 291
Beeson, Henry Way 369
Beetle, John War 278
Beetly, James Mer 332
Beggerly, Isaac Jef 23
Beggs, Alexander But 192
Begle, Thos. Cam 27
Begles, Citon Pul 126
Begley, Thomas Knx 79
Behany, James Bar 39
Belber, Robert Pul 127
Belche, Jeremiah Jef 23
Belcher, Isom Cal 16
James Knx 71
John Liv 155
Beleart, David Fay 12
Belee, Joel She 198

Belee, cont.
Peter She 197
Belen, John War 264
Samuel Log 175
Belew, David Adr 5
John Gar 203
Joseph Gar 203
Peter Log 167
Belill, Zedock Log 192
Belinger, Saml. Bar 49
Bell, A. Thomas Mas 297
Andrew But 192
Andrew Hop 373
Archd. Bou 118
Asa Bou 75
Benjamin Mas 297
Charles, Junr Mas 298
Charles, Senr Mas 300
Clement Fra 115
Daniel Mas 297
David Fay 30
David Fay 55
David Hnr 359A
David Mer 341
Edward Clr 124
Eli Ohi 92
Elijah Rck 162
Frances Cas 44
Frances Fay 19
Francis Way 354
George Ohi 78
Hennery Cas 37
Henry Bar 34
Henry S. Nel 5
Hugh Hrs 323
Humphrey Lew 104
Isaac Grn 248
Israel Mas 294
Jabish Ohi 79
James Bou 75
James Fay 19
James Fay 19
James Hnd 348
James Jef 34
James Woo 382
Jane Nic 61
Jane Nic 63
Jas. Way 362
Jesse Nel 13
Jno. Hrd 285
John Bul 173
John Cas 37
John Cum 170
John Fay 11
John Fay 60
John Fle 89
John Fra 114
John Gar 204
John Hrs 323
John Hnr 357
John Hrs 320
John Jef 27
John Lew 99
John Lin 109
John Nel 8
John She 234
John Wsh 341
John D. Fle 79
John M. Hop 373
Jophanna Grn 248
Jos. War 262
Joseph Hrs 323
Joseph Sco 172
Joseph She 236
Josiah Mul 388
Lewiana Fay 11
Louisa Mon 376

Bell, cont.
Nathaniel Ohi 93
Patrick Jef 34
Patterson Jef 34
Peggy Clr 122
Peter Nel 11
Rezin Clr 122
Richard Mas 294
Robert Hnr 354
Robert Mul 390
Robert Nel 9
Robert Ohi 103
Robt. F Hnr 369
Salley Mad 207
Saml. Bar 46
Samuel Hrs 323
Samuel Nel 8
Samuel she 208
Sarah Sco 177
Sary Bar 31
T. John Fay 12
Thomas Bou 76
Thomas Grp 272
Thomas Hnd 325
Thomas Mon 376
Thomas Mul 401
Thomas Nel 7
Thomas she 215
Thomas Woo 390
Thos. Nel 9
Will She 226
William Est 1
William Fay 12
william Fle 84
William Gal 193
William Hnr 354
William Log 179
William Mad 206
William Mul 397
Wm. Bar 34
Wm. Bar 51
Wm. Cas 44
Wm. Mon 357
Wm. Way 365
Wm. Way 368
Zachariah Clr 124
Zedick Fay 44
Zepheniah Bar 37
Bellamy, John Mad 243
R. Reuben Mad 206
Bellert, Matthias Jef 30
Bellinger, G. M. Nic 61
Bellows, John Sco 169
Mary Sco 178
Peter Mer 331
Peter, Jur Mer 331
Bells, John Pul 124
Belmare, Saml. Nel 8
Belmere, Jeremiah Jef 23
Beloo, Charles she 228
Elward she 211
Below, Saml. Rck 162
Belsford, Nathan Chr 103
Belsha, Jas. Mad 214
Saml. Mad 215
Thomas Mad 208
Belsher, Berry Grn 247
George Flo 99
John Flo 99
Belshire, Moses Mon 347
Belt, Higason Bou 119
Higgerson Ohi 74
Joseph C. Fle 65
Josiah Jef 31
William Jes 60
Belus, Hirom Adr 5
Bembridge, Absolem Jef 22

Bembridge, cont.
  Eliza Jef 29
Bemus, John Nel 13
Ben, a free man of
  colour Clr 123
Ben Hrd 292
  Free Jef 28
Benaugh, George Grp 273
Bence, Daniel Flo 99
  Lawrence Flo 99
Bencher, George Mer 330
Bender, John Mas 304
Benedeck, Benja. Bar 37
Benedick, John Lin 109
Benedict, Nicholas Wsh 341
Benet, Bartlett Hrs 309
  John Bra 150
Benett, Bazl. Nel 12
Benge, David Cly 150
  Joel Mad 213
Bengi, David Knx 89
Benham, Benjamin Chr 115
  Daniel Chr 115
  David Chr 115
  Robert Wsh 340
Bening, Isaac War 261
Benington, Nihm. Nic 61
Benjaman, Henry Lin 111
Benjamin, Robert-
  son Fay 49
  see Robertson, Benjamin
Benley, Jarves Lin 109
Benn, Benjamin Clr 124
  Samuel Bou 118
Bennedick, Jacob Lin 109
Bennefield, Stroud Bou 75
  Wm. Bou 74
Bennerfield, John Grn 260
Bennet, Evens Hnd 347
  Fisher B. Bar 40
  George Woo 387
  Jesse Mas 299
  John Adr 4
  John Cum 176
  John Mas 300
  John Nel 13
  John Wsh 344
  Richd. Sco 179
  Stephen Bar 30
  Thomas Fay 19
  Tunnis Mas 294
  William Bul 173
  William Hrs 307
  William Mas 292
  William Mas 298
  William Mas 299
  Wm. Bar 30
Bennets, Samuel Mul 396
Bennett, Aaron Log 173
  Ab She 241
  Anna Mon 373
  Asa She 217
  Benjamin Fra 112
  Benjamin Wsh 342
  Brooke Hnr 357
  Charles Mer 338
  Coleman Liv 156
  Cornilious Log 173
  Daniel she 202
  Elijah Mad 210
  Elisha But 192
  James Jes 60
  James War 253
  Jeffries Nic 69
  Jerh. Nel 6
  Jesse Bou 75
  Jno. Mad 214
Bennett, cont.
  Jno. Nel 6
  John Est 4
  John Fra 110
  John Gar 203
  John Knx 73
  John Ohi 73
  John, Junr Ohi 74
  Joseph Mad 210
  Josha. Nel 8
  Moses Mad 210
  Nathan Liv 155
  Philip Nel 6
  Richard Fra 112
  Robert Fay 20
  Samuel Ohi 81
  Sarah Mad 214
  Solomon Knx 82
  Stephen Liv 156
  Tho. Mad 206
  Thomas Liv 156
  Thomas Ohi 70
  William Liv 156
  Willm. Adr 4
Bennick, Jarimiah Cas 38
Bennifield, George Clr 124
Benning, Anthony Jef 34
  James Fay 19
Bennington, Jno. Bou 76
  Thomas Fle 79
  William (B) Fle 91
  Wm. Fle 92
Bennit, Benjamin chr 77
  Benjamin Mas 299
  Elijah Cal 7B
  Fisher Grn 249
  James Chr 75
  James Log 180
  Joseph Chr 77
  Larkin Cal 5
  Legro Chr 71
  Steven, Jur Cal 7B
  Walter Chr 54
  Walter Chr 101
Bennom, James Fra 112
Benson, Chichester She 199
  David War 273
  James Mon 362
  James, Senr Mon 362
  Jane Jef 30
  Martin But 192
  William Fay 58
Bent, Amasa Jef 23
  Asa Jef 23
Benthall, Thomas Hnd 327
Bentley, James Fay 19
  John Lin 109
  John E. Hnd 347
  Levey Cas 43
  Reuben Log 178
  Thos. Cum 174
  William Nel 11
Bently, Danl. Mad 213
  James Lin 111
  John Lin 111
  John Mad 213
  Lawrence Mad 213
  Micheel Nic 64
  Wm. (Cuusin) Mad 214
  Wm. Nel 11
  Wm. Sen Mad 213
Bentol, John Chr 105
Benton, Benjamin Ohi 72
  Betsey Mad 209
  David War 253
  Erasmus Sco 192
  Hezekiah Mon 377
Benton, cont.
  John, Snr Gar 203
  Joshua Mul 399
  Richd. Mad 215
  Robert Mad 209
  William Mul 399
  William Mul 399
Benvele, Saml. Cam 27
Berbenridge, Rob-
  ert Grp 276
Berch, John Pen 114
Berchfield, Elias Mon 368
Bereman, John N. Fra 111
  Thomas Mer 334
Berey, Robt. Nic 63
Berge, John Jef 23
Bergen, Isaac Mas 298
Berger, Peter Cum 169
  Philip Hrd 301
Bergin,William She 235
Bergman, Francis Bul 174
Berican, Wm. Cal 17
Berk, James Mon 367
  Peter Mon 372
  Robert Mon 368
Berkley, Elijah Hrs 308
  Elizabeth Jef 22
  Robert Mon 362
  Samuel Bou 75
Bernard, Chas. Adr 5
  John Adr 5
  John B. Gal 194
Bernaugh,Taliafass Lin 111
  Thos. Lin 111
  Willm. Lin 111
Berns, John Bou 77
  John, Jr Bou 77
Berrimon, Samuel Fay 19
Berry, Abraham Way 356
  Allen Woo 402
  Austin Bar 25
  Bazel Bou 77
  Bazil Bou 77
  Ben Hrd 295
  Benja. Hop 376
  Benja. Hop 376
  Benjamin Fay 19
  Benjan. Bou 75
  Benjn. Sco 183
  Benjn. War 267
  Benjn. Woo 387
  C. Elijah Mas 301
  C. William Mas 291
  Edward Wsh 347
  Edwin Clr 122
  Elijah, Senr Mas 201
  Elisha E. Fle 65
  Enoch Mas 294
  Enock Hnd 339
  Ephraim Gar 204
  Francis Hnd 330
  Francis Wsh 347
  Garrett Mad 206
  Geo. Bar 31
  George But 192
  George But 192
  George Fay 22
  George Mas 301
  George Sco 190
  George Way 370
  George, Senr Mas 295
  George H. Boo 57
  Henry Fra 111
  Henry Mas 299
  Isaac Bou 77
  Isaac Flo 99
  James Mas 300

Berry, cont.
James Mon 354
James Nel 12
Jamis Mad 206
Jams. Mad 212
Jesse Lin 109
Joel Hnd 339
Joel Pen 105
John Cum 174
John Fay 32
John Hop 376
John Hrs 308
John Hrs 317
John Hrs 322
John Knx 70
John War 277
John W. She 242
Joseph Bar 28
Joseph Grn 256
Joseph Mas 301
Lewis Clr 122
Michael Jef 21
Morris Wsh 344
Peggy Hrd 299
Rachel She 232
Reuben Hop 372
Reuben Mas 299
Richard Wsh 347
Richd. Gar 201
Saml. jr Woo 375
Saml. Senr Woo 387
Thomas Clr 122
Thomas Mas 292
Thomas, Jr Clr 122
Thomas, Sr Clr 122
Thomas H. Clr 123
Thos. Grn 260
Washington Cam 27
William Fay 23
William Hnd 330
William Hop 375
William Mas 292
William Mas 294
William Mas 295
William Pen 107
William Wsh 347
Willm. Lin 109
Willm. War 271
Withers Mas 301
Wm. Grn 263
Wm. Hop 376
Wm. Mad 212
Berryer, John Wsh 347
Berryman, Jesse War 258
John Mon 363
Josiah Bou 118
Sarah Sco 189
Bersian, Isaac Lin 109
Bertchett, Benja. Flo 99
Berthoud, James Jef 30
Berton, Allen Pul 129
Eady Clr 123
Elijah Pul 129
George Pul 131
James Pul 126
James Pul 126
James Pul 128
James Pul 131
Jesse Pul 127
Jno. Pul 128
Jno. Pul 128
Jno. J. Pul 126
John Mon 381
Thomas Pul 126
Will S. Pul 126
William Bou 77
William Pul 129

Berton, cont.
William Pul 129
Beryman, G. B. Nel 8
Beson, Mosis Chr 73
Best, Cornelius Bul 173
David Clr 124
Ebenezer Gar 204
Edward She 212
Humphrey Mad 208
Humphry Gar 204
James Clr 124
James Mas 299
Joseph Pen 113
Josiah Hrd 296
Samuel She 212
Stephen Mad 209
Beswick, George Wsh 347
Philip Wsh 347
Bethel, James Hnd 341
Joshua Mad 211
Margat. Nel 11
Saml. Mad 214
Wm. Nel 11
Bett, Carlton Log 196
Bettersworth,
Richd. Mad 214
Wm. Mad 215
Bettis, John Gar 205
Betts, Cromstock Log 178
James Sco 191
Joseph Sco 187
Thos. Sco 173
Betty (free woman) Fay 12
Betty (free woman) Fay 13
Beuford, Leroy Liv 150
Miles Liv 150
Beven, Clenit Nel 12
Bevens, Alex Mad 207
Trueman Mad 208
Beverly, John Jef 22
Bevines, Richard Fay 37
Bevins, John Lin 111
Bewley, Nathan Lin 111
Bias, John Mer 336
Susanna Woo 379
Bibb, Ann Fay 19
George M. Log 188
James Bar 25
Richard, Junr Log 194
Richard, Senr Log 195
Thomas Lin 111
Thomas Sco 172
Thos. Gal 192
Bibee, David Clr 123
James Clr 123
Neal Clr 123
Biby, Biram Bar 50
Can Bar 46
John Bar 46
Joseph Bar 51
Lee Bar 46
Pleasant Bar 47
Sherod Bar 41
Sherod Bar 51
Bice, Coonrod She 213
Dennis Mer 338
Evert Mer 337
Jacob Mer 332
John She 219
Nicholas Mer 330
Bick, John Adr 4
Bickelshimer, Danl Mad 206
Bickers, Wm. Sco 175
Bicket, William Wsh 347
Bickett, Henry Gar 205
Bickham, Solomon Fra 113
Biddle, Richard Bou 119

Biddle, cont.
Stephen Mas 297
Bidwell, Daniel Mul 395
Levie Mul 393
Bigers, Wm. Mon 376
Bigger, William Wsh 346
Biggers, Joel Mer 329
William Clr 124
Biggerstaff, Aaron Cum 175
Hiram Mad 211
Saml. Cum 175
Saml. Senr Cum 175
Samuel Mul 405
Thomas Mul 398
Biggim, Saml. Cal 18
Biggins, David Jes 61
(freeman of colour)
Joshua Cal 17
Biggleman, Lewis Log 169
Biggs, Andrew Fay 13
Andrew Mon 384
Andrew Sco 179
Davis Hrs 313
Dearington Log 170
Elisha Log 174
Francis Cum 184
James Bou 76
John Gar 204
John Grn 261
Margarett Bou 74
Simeon War 261
William Bou 77
Bigham, David Sco 189
James Mad 207
John Mer 338
John Mer 338
Bigler, John Mer 332
Bigs, Duglis Grp 274
Stephen Bar 53
Bilbo, Archibald Mer 333
John Mer 333
William Mer 333
Bilderback, Jacob She 238
Biles, James Fay 23
Joseph Fra 111
Bill, John War 243
Billinger, Wm. Bar 48
Billings, Abraham Mul 402
Abraham Mul 403
Ardin Mul 405
William Mul 403
Billingsly, Tho. Bar 48
Bills, Samuel Fay 12
Billy, negro Fle 86
Bilt, Thos. Fle 64
Bingaman, Christian Gar 204
Henry Lin 109
John Gar 204
Petr. Gar 204
Bingerman, Lewis Log 193
Bingham, Reuben Rck 161
Thomas Mer 331
Wm. Rck 161
Bingherman, Lewis Log 172
Bingman, Jacob Fay 52
Binkly, Benja. Bar 45
Binns, Danl. Cum 169
Birch, George Clr 124
George Clr 124
Joseph Sco 188
Davd. Hrd 294
Birchum, Joseph Mer 330
Bird, Abraham Bar 38
Edward Wsh 341
Francis Cam 29
Henry Est 6
Henry Mad 206

Bird, cont.
James Bar 35
James Cal 6
James Log 172
James Log 186
John Bar 19
John Bou 76
John Cam 32
John Log 172
John Log 196
John Mas 294
Jonathan Bar 38
Joshua Nel 9
Lee Sco 173
Markes Fay 49
Mathew Bar 33
Miles Log 169
Reuben Grn 253
Richard Est 1
Robt. Bar 31
Samuel Bul 174
Shadrick Chr 105
Thomas Adr 4
William Log 172
Wm. Bar 31
Wm. Bar 33
Birdal, James Bar 49
Birds, Abraham Fay 49
Birdsong, Henry War 268
Birdwell, Jas. Bar 48
Birdwhistle, James Sco 181
Thos. Cam 31
Birgin, John Cly 158
Birk, Arnal Bar 39
Henry Pul 130
Thomas Pul 125
Thomas Pul 130
Birkhead, Abraham Wsh 340
Birks, George Mer 334
John Mer 330
John Mer 335
John, Junr Bar 30
John, Senr Bar 54
Birney, James Mer 331
Birt, Benjn. Sco 187
James Sco 187
Milly Sco 178
Birton, Betsy Mer 337
Biscoe, James Fra 115
Bishars, Robert Pul 126
Bishaw, William Bou 75
Bishey, Joseph Pul 131
Bishop, Abner Adr 5
Benjamin Clr 123
Benjn. Bou 74
Daniel Bul 173
Daniel, Jr Bul 173
David Adr 4
Edmund Bar 52
Eli Hop 374
Elisha Hnr 352
Elisha Hnr 366
George Clr 123
George Fle 85
Jane Woo 388
John Nel 9
Joshua Clr 123
Joshua War 243
Laurence Bul 173
Lowry Bar 39
Maler Knx 63
Richard Bou 76
Richard Hrs 319
Robert Fay 22
Saml. Cly 151
Solomon Nel 9
Tho. Nel 9

Bishop, cont.
Thomas Clr 123
Wachel Mer 329
William Knx 70
Wm. Hop 371
see Wm, Bishop
Wm. Senr Bar 46
Bisset, Rachl. Nel 11
Bisshey, Thomas Pul 130
Biswell, Jeremiah Wsh 347
Biter, John Cum 185
Bith, Joseph Fle 64
Bitner, Nichs. Sco 168
Bivan, John Jef 27
Bivans, Thomas Flo 99
Bivens, Covester Glo 99
Valentine Cum 179
Bivin, Bennet Woo 380
Samuel Bre 166
Bivins, Zacariah Cal 18
Bixler, John She 235
Blacard, Chas. Bar 48
Eli Bar 48
Black, Alexander Fay 37
Andrew Cas 40
Andrew Mad 213
Anny Bou 74
Benjam. Pul 128
Benjn. Boo 57
Charles Mas 295
Christo. Jef 24
David Knx 91
Ezekeel Mon 383
Geor. Mon 382
George Boo 57
Henry Mul 386
James Bar 54
James Boo 57
James Bou 74
James Bra 145
James She 225
James She 240
James Woo 389
Jeremiah Grn 255
Jno. Mad 210
Jno. Pul 125
Jno. J. Pul 126
Jno. S. Pul 126
John Bar 34
John Bou 74
John Bou 74
John Bou 74
John Bra 145
John Bra 145
John Bra 151
John Chr 55
John Grn 264
John Hnd 325
John Hnr 369
John Knx 65
John Mer 329
John Sco 168
Joseph Cam 24
Joseph Chr 76
Moses Grn 263
Moses Mer 330
Nathan Pul 126
Patrick Grn 263
Robert Bar 53
Robert Hnd 340
Robert Ohi 88
Robert Woo 399
Robert, Junr Hnd 336
Rudolph Bra 153
Saml. Bou 74
Saml. Bou 74
Saml. Bou 77

Black, cont.
Saml. Bou 77
Saml. Cal 15
Saml. Gar 204
Samuel Cal 4
Samuel Chr 53
Samuel She 212
Sarah Bou 74
Thomas Chr 54
William Bre 162
William Clr 123
William Clr 123
William Hnd 331
Willm. Bou 77
Wm. Bra 142
Wm. Mad 212
Blackborn, H. Julius Nic 64
Blackbourn, Edward Fay 23
Ephram War 259
Robt. War 277
Saml. Fra 111
Saml. War 277
Thos. Flo 100
Wm. Flo 100
Wm. B. Woo 397
Blackburn, Alexander Pen 114
Benjamin Mas 294
David Hrs 319
George Woo 389
James Lin 109
James Mad 208
John Hnr 361
John Hrs 313
Jonathan Woo 388
Joseph Hnr 359
Julius Sco 184
Robt. Hrs 319
Samuel Mon 380
Thomas Mas 292
William Grp 275
Wm. Cas 46
Blackeby, Thadius Gar 201
Thomas Gar 201
Blackenburgh, Jacob Fay 12
Blackenship, Levi War 249
Blackerby, Jeduthan Mas 295
Blackford, Abigail Woo 387
Benjamine Jes 59
Wm. Nel 6
Blackiter, Norman Mer 332
Rachel Mer 332
William Mer 332
Blackgrave, An Cam 29
Banister Mer 333
Blacklege, Jno. Pul 129
Blackling, Acabud Pul 131
Blacklock, Joseph Bul 174
Thos. Nel 10
Blackmon, William Mul 392
Blackmore, James Hnr 356
John Woo 378
Moses Grn 253
Blackwell, Ann War 276
Benjamin Clr 124
Francis Hnd 331
James Est 3
James Fay 50
James Hnr 359B
Jeramiah War 263
John Clr 122
Randolph Mad 214
Robert Fra 111
Robt. Hrd 286
Robt. Sr Hnr 365

Blackwell, cont.
Thornton Hnr 359B
Thos. Nel 8
Thos. War 276
William Hnd 341
William Mad 209
Blackwood, James Chr 113
Joseph Mer 334
Josn. Lin 109
Richd. Cum 174
Saml. Grn 258
William Chr 113
Blacky, Reutser Lin 111
Blades, Francis She 236
George she 236
John She 233
Saml. Bra 145
William Fay 51
William She 236
Zadoc Mas 292
Blain, Alexr. Lin 109
Alexr. Snr Lin 109
Ann Lin 109
Geo. Bar 41
James Bre 157
James Grn 262
John Lin 111
Michael Bre 159
Robert Wsh 341
William Pul 128
Blair, Alexr. Adr 4
Alexr. Bar 28
Alexr. Nic 61
Charles Knx 85
Col. Adr 5
Henry Hrd 283
James Flo 99
James Fra 113
James Jef 21
James She 235
Jas. Hrd 283
John Cly 155
John Fle 82
John Jef 21
John Lin 109
John Liv 149
Joseph Lin 111
Molly Fay 19
Peter Wsh 344
Saml. Hrs 307
Samuel Fay 22
Sarah Nic 61
Thomas Nel 6
Blake, Archabald Knx 69
Bartholomew Bre 163
James Jef 23
James She 241
Jno. Hrd 288
Joshua Cum 184
Kenath Grp 270
Peter Way 358
Rebeca Knx 68
Robert Bou 74
Wm. Cum 180
Blakeley, Charles Knx 83
Blakely, Curtis Knx 82
James Chr 85
John Chr 85
Robert Knx 75
Samuel Chr 85
Thomas Mas 297
Blakeman, Aaron Jes 59
Adam Jes 59
Blakeney, John Bou 76
Martha Bou 76
Blakey, George Log 175
James Sco 172
Blakey, cont.
Thos. Cum 175
Blakley, John Liv 151
Blaky, Field Bar 52
Fulas Adr 5
Wm. Bar 52
Blalock, Jer. Gar 204
Blanchard, David Mas 291
Jacob Bre 165
John Bra 141
William Log 180
Willis Log 168
Blanchart, H.T.B.-
Asa Fay 11
Blanchet, Jas. Way 368
Bland, Charles Gar 201
Charles Wsh 341
Danl. Nel 9
Elijah Nel 9
Grissy Mad 206
Isaac Nel 13
James Liv 156
Jesse Cum 175
John Cum 175
John Nel 5
John Wsh 347
Margaret Mas 299
Micajah Mas 291
Moses Jef 33
Osburn, Junr Cum 175
Osburn, Senr Cum 175
Rolly Wsh 343
Saml. Nel 12
Samuel Wsh 347
Thomas Wsh 346
Willm. Nel 12
Blandford, Aquila Wsh 347
Charles T. Wsh 340
Jno. B. Nel 12
Nathaniel Wsh 340
Blane, Joseph Mas 293
Blanford, Edward She 237
Henry L. Sco 172
Richard Bul 174
Walter Bul 174
Blanfort, John B. Hnd 330
Blanken, Shep Adr 5
Blankenbaker,
Felix Jef 20
Hannah Jef 20
Henry Jef 20
Jacob Jef 20
Nicholas She 212
Samuel She 212
Thomas Jef 20
Blankenship, Abel Cum 172
Daniel Grp 273
Elijah Mad 207
Elisha Cum 185
Hudson Cum 171
Jesse Cum 171
John Grp 278
Noel Cum 172
Noel Lin 109
Wm. Cum 180
Blanketship, Jos. Grn 257
Blankinbaker, Saml. Jef 20
Blankinship, Asa Cly 157
Condy Flo 100
Obedh. Flo 100
Blanks, Lidia Lin 109
Blanten, Abner Gra 237
Blanton, Carter Fra 116
Elijah Gar 201
James Gal 193
James Woo 401
Jesse Jef 21
Blanton, cont.
Joshua Jes 61
Nancy Woo 390
Sally Fay 47
Shackleford Jef 26
Thomas Woo 385
Thompson Fra 116
William Knx 84
William Mer 330
Wm. Gal 193
Blasengan, James Bra 144
Blasingam, Polly War 277
Blastengem, Wm. Nic 64
Blayer, Nancy Mon 355
Blazer, Moses Hnd 336
Bleak, Jas. Way 373
Bleakley, Robert Hrd 281
Bledsau, Elijah Mon 376
Lucy Mon 376
Bledsoe, Abnr. Gal 194
Ben Cum 169
Benjamin Mas 294
Elizabeth Knx 81
Ezekiel Mad 207
Isaac Gal 193
Isbel Clr 123
Jacob Gal 194
Jesse Fay 37
John Fay 20
Jos. Gal 195
Jos. Gar 204
Joseph Cum 169
M. Wm. Gar 204
Moses O. Fra 117
O. Moses Gar 204
Rice Gal 197
Richard Fay 19
Thomas Clr 124
Wm. Gal 192
Wm. Sco 180
Blembaugh, Benjn. Mad 207
Blemmer, Joseph Mas 300
Bless, Anthony Fay 11
Blevens, John She 235
Blevin, John Lin 111
Saml. Lin 111
Blevine, Daniel Knx 91
Blevings, James But 192
William But 192
Blevins, Berry Pul 129
Daniel Lin 109
Elisha Way 366
Green Way 370
John Way 360
John Way 361
Jonathan Way 361
Jonathan Way 362
Lemual Gar 205
Richd. Way 359
Richd. Way 366
Sally Mer 337
Samuel Lin 109
Talton Way 360
Blew, John Chr 107
John Fay 19
Richard Clr 122
Blewford, William Fay 19
(free negro)
Blewitt, Eli War 262
Blincoe, Benjamin Bre 162
Jas. Hrd 288
Joseph Nel 11
Thomas Bre 162
Blinger, John Cam 31
Blisset, Geo. Hrd 298
Rezin Hrd 303
Blithe, Daniel Cly 154

Blizard, Joshua Log 183
  William Log 183
Blocksome, William Mas 300
Bloid, Elijah Bar 34
  John Bar 34
Blois, Jane Wsh 340
Bloomer, Henry Boo 57
Bloomhuff, Abraham Mas 292
Blount, John Grn 252
  Levy Grn 252
Bloyd, Hezekiah Grn 247
  John Grn 257
  Purnel Pul 127
  Stephen Grn 247
  Tubby Grn 264
  William Grn 264
Blue, David Fle 61
  David Hnd 330
  Jacob Bou 74
  James Hnd 337
  Jno. Lew 103
  John Hnd 337
  Paul Lew 104
  William Fle 65
Blunk, And. Jef 21
  Jno. Hnr 359B
Blunt, Andrew Bou 76
  Bartholemew Fay 12
  Henry Gal 192
  Miles Cas 38
  Moses Mer 335
  Riding Fle 76
  Sally Sco 172
Bly, David Lin 111
  David Rck 165
  John Rck 165
  William Rck 161
Blyth, James Fay 11
Blythe, Hugh Liv 158
  John Clr 123
  John Cly 158
  Robert Clr 124
  Samuel Chr 55
  William Fay 20
Boale, Robert Hnr 356
Boals, James Chr 101
Boar, James Bou 74
Board, Absolam Bre 167
  Elijah Bre 157
  George Bou 75
  James Bre 158
  Micajah Bre 161
  Stephen Bre 160
  William Bre 157
Boardman, James Fay 11
Boardmon, Benjn. Bou 76
  Joseph Bou 76
Boas, Henry Sco 183
  John Sco 183
Boateman, Robert Jes 60
  Robert Jes 60
Boatman, Henry Jes 59
  Henry Nic 62
  James Mad 210
  John Lin 109
  Richd. Cum 178
  Simon War 255
Bobbet, James Pul 128
Bobbit, Clabourn War 260
  Isham Chr 55
  John Chr 55
  John War 260
  Nancy Chr 79
  Randolph Cam 30
  Stevin Chr 103
  William Chr 55
Bobbs, John Fay 12
Bobbs, cont.
  William Fay 12
Bobo, Absolum Chr 91
  Jerramiah Chr 95
Boddy, Thomas Mer 341
Bodine, Chas. Nel 5
  Isaac Nel 9
  Jacob P. Mul 394
  Jno. Nel 5
  John Log 183
  John Nel 13
  Peter Hrd 281
Bodkin, Richd. Knx 67
  William Hrs 313
Bodle, James Rck 163
Bodley, John Fay 12
  Thomas Fay 12
Bogan, James Log 171
  James Log 192
  James, Jr Log 171
  Lewis Log 170
  Samuel Log 171
  William Log 171
Bogard, Cornelius Bul 173
Bogert, Isaac Mer 335
Bogey, Andrew Mad 211
  James Mad 211
Boggas, Thos. Nic 64
Boggass, Vincent Boo 57
Boggess, Henry Fra 112
  John Fra 112
  Joseph Fra 112
  Martin Fra 112
  Vincent Fra 112
Boggs, Asa She 211
  Bazel She 211
  Charles Clr 124
  George C. Clr 124
  James Mad 213
  James She 212
  Jno. Mad 215
  John Fay 12
  Joseph Est 5
  Robert Fay 19
  Robert Mad 210
  William Clr 122
  William Liv 154
  Wm. Boo 57
Boggus, Robert Mul 387
  Warren Mul 403
Bogguss, Joel Mul 404
  Peter Mul 404
  Lemuel Mul 391
  Richard Mul 404
  William Mul 387
Bohan, John Mer 335
Bohannon, Abraham She 209
  Austin Fre 111
  Elliott Woo 378
  Ezekiel Mer 331
  George Jef 33
  John Woo 394
  Julius Jef 34
  Larkin Jef 33
  Richard Jef 34
  Robert Jef 3
  Simeon Jes 62
  William She 232
  William Woo 400
Bohanon, German Woo 378
  Richd. B. Woo 399
Bohn, William Mer 337
Bohon, Benjamin Mer 334
  John Mer 329
  Thomas She 214
  Walter Mer 329
Boice, Willm. Sco 188
Boid, Jno. Lew 96
  Robert Pul 128
  Samuel Pul 128
Boide, Robert Hnd 340
Boiles, Charles Mer 333
Boils, John Log 177
Boilston, John Bar 32
Boiner, Robert Bre 160
Boise, William Fay 45
Boken, John Cam 32
Boland, David Way 373
Boldin, Thomas Bou 71
Bolding, Joseph War 277
  Willm. War 278
Bolen, Joel Fay 19
  John Hrs 319
  Nicholas Nel 13
  Wm. Hrs 316
  Wm. Hrs 320
Boler, John Fay 37
  Nutty Fay 11
  William Fay 37
Boles, John Nic 63
  John B. Sco 174
  Robert Hrs 319
  William Nic 64
Bolew, Stewart Gar 202
Boley, Isaac Lin 111
  Jno. Nel 13
  John Bre 161
Bolin, Jona. Hrd 287
  Thos. Hrd 285
  Thos. Nel 11
  William Chr 106
Boling, Christopher Cly 152
  Daniel War 245
  Ely Cly 151
  Isham Cly 150
  James Cas 48
  James Cly 151
  Jessee Cly 155
  John Cas 48
  John Cly 151
  Joseph Cly 150
  Justus Cly 155
  Sims She 237
  Wm. Cly 151
Bollen, Mary Mas 296
Bolling, James Cal 12
  Thomas Cal 15
  Wm. Cal 11
Bolt, Benjamin Gra 242
Bolton, James Bul 173
  James Lin 109
  Sally Lin 109
Boman, Abraham Bou 77
  Andrew Chr 101
  Andrew Pen 115
  Eligah Cly 158
  Elisha Cly 158
  George Bou 75
  Jacob Cly 158
  Jno. Pul 126
  John Jes 56
  John She 209
  Sarah Cly 158
  Thos. Cly 158
  Will Cly 157
  Wm. Way 373
Bond, Anthony Fra 112
  George Cum 135
  George Nel 11
  George Ohi 76
  Hopkins Cum 183
  Isaac Way 366
  James Grn 247

Bond, cont.	
Joel	Way 371
John	Wsh 346
Joseph	Way 360
Masten	Wsh 346
Robert	Sco 183
Solo	Hnr 359A
Thomas	Cal 15
Walker	Sco 172
Winfry	Cal 15
William	Cal 9
William	Fra 112
William	Hnd 336
William	Sco 176
Wm.	Cal 15
Wm.	Way 369
Bonderant, Benjn.	Woo 378
Bonds, John	Gal 192
Thomas	Chr 64
Bondurant, Caleb	Clr 123
Bond, Cornelius	Hop 374
Jno.	Mad 213
John	Hop 374
Boner, Barnet	Pen 107
Charles	Pen 107
Edward	Nel 7
Mary	Pen 105
Bones, John	Wsh 343
Bonham, Amariah	Fle 76
Bonner, Wm.	War 259
Bonnie, Mosis	War 265
Bonnifield,	
Dorothy	Cly 124
Mircen	Clr 123
Bonta, Cons.	Hnr 351
Danl.	Hnr 365
Henry	Hnr 351
Henry	She 231
Henry, Jr	Bou 76
Henry, Sr	Bou 76
Peter	Hnr 367
Bonwell, Arthur	Bra 149
Jas.	Bra 141
Thos.	Bra 146
Booe, Benjn.	Boo 57
James	Boo 57
Booer, Jno.	Mad 214
Book, Henry	Hnd 340
Michael	Hnd 340
Booker, Abraham	Knx 87
" (Conrod)	Fay 50
David	Jef 34
Edward	Jef 22
Edward	She 211
Elizabeth	She 230
George	Jef 23
Isaac	Jef 23
Jacob	Jef 23
John	Flo 98
John	Mer 335
John P.	Jef 23
Richard	She 198
William M.	Clr 123
Boon, Abner	Hrs 320
Benjn.	Jef 21
Enoch	Hrd 299
George	Clr 123
George	She 212
George G.	Fay 34
Isaiah	Hrd 299
Jeremiah	Pul 128
Jesse	War 258
Joab	Hrs 318
John	War 251
Jonathan	Bou 118
Joseph	Bar 36
Josiah	She 215
Boon, cont	
Ovid	Bou 119
Ratliff	War 258
Samuel	Bul 174
Samuel	Fay 35
Squire	Fay 35
Thomas	Clr 124
William	Fay 22
Boone, Edward	She 215
Francis	Wsh 340
George	Gal 192
Henry	Wsh 340
Hezekiah	Woo 382
Jacob	Mas 301
Jessa B.	Grp 269
Jno. L.	Gal 194
Joseph	Mad 206
Josiah	Woo 383
Levi	Mas 300
Philip	Wsh 340
Saml.	Hnr 366
Solomon	Woo 381
Squire	Mad 214
Walter	Nel 11
William	Mad 215
Booth, Charles	Wsh 339
James	Mad 212
John	She 221
Samuel	Bou 76
William	Bou 75
William	Jes 60
William	Wsh 345
Boothe, Harrison	Bou 77
James	Bou 77
John	Boo57
John	Clr 123
Joseph	Mas 293
Stephen	Bou 74
Waid	Grn 259
Wm. A.	Jef 23
Wm. H.	Jef 3
Booton, Thos.	War 254
Travis	Mad 207
Boots, Bartes	Fra 114
Bartes	Fra 114
Jacob	Fra 114
Joseph	Fra 114
Boottes, Roland	Boo 57
Borah, George	But 192
Jacob	But 192
Boran, Jas.	War 263
Mathew	War 271
Nancy	Cas 42
Willm.	War 272
Bord, John	Fay 37
Philip	Mer 338
Borden,	
Christopher	Knx 87
Borders, Henry	Wsh 343
John	Flo 99
Matthias	Wsh 339
Michael	Flo 99
Michael	Mer 336
Boren, Thos.	Bra 145
Bornes, Thomas	But 192
Borwell, Joseph	Fay 12
Boshart, Jacob	Fay 12
Boshere, Isaac	Chr 60
Ithry	Chr 74
Jerramiah	Chr 60
Thomas	Chr 60
Bosley, Abraham	Lin 111
B. Thos.	Lin 111
Benad.	Nic 62
Isaac	She 221
Bosly, Gidian	Lin 109
Bostan, John	Cas 46
Bostec, Truman	Jef 28
Bostice, John	Clr 122
Bostick, Ezra	War 250
Boston, George	Fay 22
Jas.	Jef 23
Jenny	Wsh 339
John	Fay 19
Reubin	Mer 335
Taylor	Cam 26
William	Bou 74
Boswell, George	Fay 52
George	She 205
Henson	Sco 183
John	Boo 57
John	Clr 146
John	Sco 183
John	She 205
Priscilla	She 205
Thomas	Fay 34
William	Hrs 312
Bosworth, Benajah.	Fay 13
Bottam, Robert	Grn 245
Bottom, William	Wsh 346
Botts, Charles	Mon 370
George W.	Fle 61
John	Mas 295
Joseph	Mas 295
Joseph	Mon 370
Joshua	Mon 370
Laurence	Mon 370
Moses	Mon 362
Richard	Mas 295
Robert	Mon 370
Seth	Clr 124
Thos.	Nel 7
Wm.	Mon 361
Bottum, Turner	Mer 336
Bottums, Edmund	Mer 336
Jacob	Mer 337
John	Mer 336
Martin	Mer 337
Micajar	Mer 338
William	Mer 336
William	Mer 337
Boua, John	Hrs 321
Bouar, Arthur	Fay 36
Boucher, Amos	War 244
Richard	Mas 293
Bouetan, Margaret	Knx 71
Bougher, Jacob`	Bou 77
Boughner, Peter	Bra 142
Boughton, John	War 254
Boul, Ignatius	Nel 12
Bouls, John	Mer 336
Boulton, John	Mad 211
Joseph	Bou 119
Boulware, Esther	Fra 116
John	Fra 113
Mordica	Fra 115
Ramsey	Fra 115
Richard	Fra 115
Theoderick	Fra 115
Thomas	Clr 123
Bound, Cornelious	Fay 51
Bounds, Joseph	Chr 94
Bounty, Henry	Mer 338
Peter	Mer 338
Bourer, Volentine	Pen 107
Bourien, John	Fay 19
Bourland, Benja.	Hop 380
Ebenezer	Hop 377
John	Hop 377
Patsy	Hop 374
Bourn, Abner	Bar 41
Ambrose	Fay 20
Daniel	Jes 42

Bourn, cont.
Elleanor Fra 114
Francis Gar 201
Peggy Gar 201
William Fra 112
Bourne, Andrew Jes 60
Hannah Jes 60
John Jes 60
John Sco 169
Moses Jes 61
Moton Jes 61
Thomas Jes 61
William Jes 61
Bout, George Mon 379
Bow, Henry Cum 183
Jesse Cum 183
Nathl. Cum 183
Bowden, Uriah Chr 92
Bowdery, Latitia Woo 396
Lewis Woo 396
Bowels, Thos. War 247
Bowen, Adam Flo 99
Duzella Bul 173
Elener Bou 77
Elijah Jes 61
Fredrick Mon 352
George Jes 62
Polly War 251
Robert Bou 75
William Mer 330
Wm. Jef 24
Wm. Nic 62
Bowers, Jacob Mul 388
John Mul 388
Willm. Lin 109
Bowin, David Grn 258
James Lin 109
James Mon 366
Joseph Chr 74
Robert Grn 258
Samuel A. Chr 53
Bowing, William Fle 79
Bowland, William Woo 379
Bowler, Anderson Mad 208
Archer Jef 23
John Jef 34
John Log 175
John Mad 208
Lucey Cas 41
Wm. Jef 23
Bowles, David Bou 75
Hughes Bou 75
Ignatius Nel 11
James Fle 91
James Nel 13
Jno. Nel 6
Jno. Nel 13
John Wsh 339
Joseph Wsh 342
Mary Mad 206
Nelson Bou 75
Thomas Bou 76
William Wsh 339
Bowley, Vincent Gar 201
Bowlin, John Mad 209
Wesley Mad 212
Bowling, Benjamin Hnd 329
Garrard Hrd 291
George Gal 195
James Wsh 342
John Liv 156
John Wsh 340
John Wsh 340
William Mer 334
William Wsh 343
Wm. Hnr 364
Wm. Hrd 299
Bowls, Cliburn Bar 47
Elija Bar 43
Jessee Bar 51
Jessee, Jr. Bou 75
Jessee, Senr Bou 75
John Bar 51
Robert Mon 357
Stephen Bou 75
Wm. Bar 51
Bowman, Abraham Fay 23
Abraham Mas 293
Ben Cum 175
Casper Bra 152
Casper, Jr Bra 142
Charles She 204
Cornelius Mad 206
Corns. Jr Mad 206
David Jes 42
Elisha Rck 160
Geo. Gar 203
Granville Cum 180
Herman Woo 393
Hesekiah Est 9
Jacob Bul 174
Jacob Sco 176
Jno. Hrd 286
John Bra 143
John Bul 174
John Mer 329
John Mer 330
John Sco 183
John Wsh 346
Joseph, Jr Jes 61
Joseph, Sr Jes 61
Judah Wsh 342
Nathl. Cum 175
Richard She 204
Sarah Clr 124
Thomas Bul 174
William Clr 123
William Hnr 366
Wilson Hrd 286
Wm. Cas 37
Wm. Cum 175
Bowmar, Benjm. Adr 4
Robert, Senr Woo 401
Bownser, William Jes 62
Bowruff, John Ohi 97
Bowyers, John Jef 21
Box, Robert Liv 156
Samuel Knx 90
Boyce, Richard Log 161
Robert Gar 203
Willis War 246
Boyd, Abriham Chr 96
Andrew Cal 6
Andrew Cal 19
Andw. Bar 54
Ann Wsh 346
Arthur Hrs 321
Benjamin She 232
Charles Mon 364
Elizabeth Mas 297
George She 227
Hugh Lin 109
Hugh Sco 179
Hugh Sco 186
James Bra 150
James Lew 102
Jno. Pul 125
John Bra 150
John Cas 42
Boyd, John Fay 54
John Hrs 314
John Log 172
John Log 194
John Mas 300
Boyd, cont.
John Mon 375
John Nic 62
John Nic 62
John Pen 106
John She 202
Jorden Way 363
Lettice Cum 171
Mary Fle 73
Matthw. Log 172
Richard Mon 361
Robert Knx 70
Robert Liv 149
Ruthy Log 192
Samuel Adr 5
Samuel Bou 118
Susanna Bar 27
Thomas Mon 383
Thos. Cam 29
Thos. Hrs 314
William Fra 111
William Lew 100
William Pul 125
William She 206
William She 231
William She 214
William G. She 209
Wm. Mon 357
Wm. Mon 377
Boydine, Thomas Log 181
Boydston, Benjn. War 256
Boye, Jesse War 246
Boyer, G. John Fay 11
Boyers, Jacob Bra 144
John Bra 152
Boyken, James Log 171
Boykin, James Log 181
Solomon Log 182
Solomon Log 183
Boyl, Elenor Log 184
Boyle, Alexr. Gar 204
James Clr 122
James, Sr Clr 124
John Clr 122
John, Jnr Gar 201
John, Snr Gar 204
Stephen Clr 122
William Nel 12
Boyles, Andrew Nel 9
Henry Cam 24
Boyls, Henry Bul 183
Boys, John Bra 152
Boyse, Abraham Bra 152
James Bra 144
Wm. Bra 144
Boysaw, John Log 161
Boze, John Woo 391
John, Senr Woo 384
Will Cly 157
Bozier, Abner Chr 83
Josiph Chr 90
Bozman, Jacob War 250
Rob War 282
Bozorth, Jerry Gra 237
John Gra 237
John Gra 239
Jonathan Gra 240
Bozwell, Harrison Knx 86
Bra...n, William Mer 342
Braaddus, Beverly Cly 156
Bracher, Thomas Gra 242
William Gra 239
William Gra 239
Brack, John Mer 336
Bracken, James Mon 374
Mathew Mon 381
Theophilous Mon 360

Name	Co.	Page
Brackenridge, Jas.	Bou	75
Mary	Fay	56
Preston	Fay	42
William	Fay	55
Bracker, John	Gra	240
Bracket, John	Knx	76
Thomas	Mul	391
Brackett, Hawkins	She	202
John	She	217
Wm.	War	253
Brackinridge, Preston	Fay	31
Brackonridg, Robert	Mon	358
Bradberry, Joel	She	208
Wm.	She	207
Bradbourn, Joseph	Fay	19
Bradburn, John	Boo	57
Jonn	Chr	53
William C.	Chr	103
Braden, Bartleson	Fay	19
John	Cum	176
Joseph	Cum	171
W..	Sco	188
Bradford, Adam	Wsh	342
Alexr.	Sco	173
Austin	Sco	170
Daniel	Fay	11
Benjn.	Sco	175
Enoch	Sco	181
Fielding	Sco	181
Jno.	Mul	385
John	Fay	12
William	Mul	385
Wm.	Bra	144
Bradin, George	Adr	5
Bradley, Andrew	Cly	157
Benjamin	Chr	100
Charles	Chr	111
Charles	Woo	384
Chs.	Hop	377
Daniel	Nic	63
David	War	246
Dennis	Fay	19
Elijah	Hrd	291
Elisha	Bou	75
Ewd. R.	Clr	124
George	Flo	100
George	Nic	63
Hannah	Sco	185
Isaiah	Mad	209
James	Chr	62
James	Hrs	322
Jno.	Mad	213
John	Bou	75
John	Chr	62
John	Chr	92
John	Lin	109
John, Senr	Sco	169
John W.	Sco	168
Layton	Bou	119
Lion	Adr	4
Nancy	Hrd	291
Philip	Sco	185
Richard	Pul	130
Samuel	Chr	62
Senka	Fay	34
Terah	Cum	172
Terra	Fay	19
Tho.	Mad	213
Thomas	Fra	115
Thos. P.	Sco	168
William	Chr	62
William	Fay	35
William	Rck	163
Wm.	Hop	381
Wm.	Mon	371
Bradly, Beverly	Bar	54

Name	Co.	Page
Bradly, cont.		
John	Cal	7B
John, Snr	Lin	109
Robt.	Nic	63
Bradock, Genl.	Hrd	298
Bradshaw, Amos	But	192
Benja.	Mer	329
Benjamine	Jes	59
Charles	Chr	113
Charles	Mad	208
Claybourn	Mer	329
David	Mon	354
David	Nic	61
Edward	Chr	110
George	Grp	271
James	Bou	74
James	Mon	350
James	She	239
John	Bou	118
John	She	241
Jonathan	Log	175
Marah	Bou	74
Moses	Rck	159
Robt.	Bou	74
Shaderick	Mer	329
Thomas	Mon	354
Thomas	She	207
William	Grn	264
William	Grp	269
William	Jes	59
William	Mer	329
William	She	199
Bradwell, David	War	252
Brady, A. Thos.	Lin	109
Charles	Cam	31
Emila	Fay	12
John	Gra	241
John	War	272
Jonathan P.	She	215
Joseph	Mon	364
Josiah	Gar	199
Michael	Cam	31
Saml.	Cal	12
Susana	Hrd	303
Wm.	Boo	57
Brag, Calep	Log	170
Gabriel	Adr	4
Bragg, Ezel.	Adr	5
Norman	She	231
Thomas	Lew	100
Braggs, Joseph	Mer	337
Brags, Moor	Hrs	312
Braiden, John	Adr	4
Braidin, James	Adr	4
Brain, John	Bou	77
Brakefield, George	Log	174
Bramble, Thos.	Fle	65
Wm.	Gar	204
Bramblet, Henry	Bou	75
Hugh	Bou	74
Jas.	Way	353
Lewis	Bou	74
Martin	Hrs	315
Peggy	Bou	75
Ruben	Chr	88
William	Bou	75
Bramblett, Polly	Gar	205
Bramson, Roland	Way	359
Thos.	Way	359
Branaman, Christian	Mad	207
Branard, Benja.	Fle	63
Brand, John	Fay	12
Pleasant	Bou	76
Richard	Bou	74
Thos.	Bou	74
William	Hnd	347
Branden, Richd.	Bou	74

Name	Co.	Page
Branden, cont.		
Walter	Bou	74
Brandenburg, Heny.	Hrd	299
Jona.	Hrd	304
Joseph	Est	3
Saml.	Est	3
Solm.	Hrd	289
Brandinburg, David	Clr	124
Esther	Clr	122
Brandis, James	Jes	60
John, Sr	Jes	59
Brandon, Ebenizar	Bou	118
James	Bar	45
John	Log	193
Jonathan	Bou	74
Joseph	Bou	74
Joseph	Bou	118
Peter	Log	196
Brands, Thos. Sr	Fle	71
Tobiah	Fle	71
Branham, Benjn.	Sco	172
David	Flo	99
David	Flo	100
Edmond	Flo	100
Gaten	Sco	184
Harlin	Bou	74
James	Sco	187
John	Flo	100
John	Sco	174
John	Sco	184
John	Sco	189
Lynn	Sco	174
Margaret	Bou	74
Matsy	Pul	127
Richd.	Sco	169
Robert	Sco	180
Tanner	Sco	189
Tavener	Sco	174
Tavener	Sco	185
Thomas	Fra	114
Thos.	Sco	171
Turner	Flo	100
Will	Bou	74
Wm.	Flo	100
Branin, Richd.	Sco	170
Brank, Robt.	Gar	204
Brann, Francis	Pen	107
Joseph	Boo	57
Joseph	Pen	107
Thomas	Pen	110
Brannam, John	Grp	270
Brannon, Carns	Hrs	313
David	Bra	146
David	Bra	146
Thomas	Hnr	353
Branock, Robt.	Bou	76
Branon, Samuel	Hrs	307
Branson, Hannah	Hop	376
Lenor	Hop	372
Branstetter, Michl.	Bar	50
Brant, Christopher	She	197
Edward	Ohi	100
John	She	197
Brants, John	She	220
Brashea, Jos.	Nel	4
Brashear, Ignatious	Bul	174
Loy	Nel	11
Lucy	Bul	173
Richard	Bul	174
Robert	Nel	11
Talbot	Jes	61
Thomas C.	Bul	174
Walter	Nel	10
William	Bul	173
Brashears, Delila	Bra	149

Brashears, cont.
James Nel 9
Joseph Bre 163
Judson Sco 185
Lilbron Log 184
Reason Jes 59
Samuel Ohi 85
Brasher, Aquila Liv 156
Charles Boo 57
Brashere, Dennis Mer 332
Brasier, Isaac Jef 34
Brass, Peter Mer 334
Brassfield,
James E. Clr 124
Jas. Gar 201
Wiley R. Clr 122
Bratchee, John Way 372
Bratcher, Clemon Bra 150
Elizabeth War 278
John War 246
Bratton, Andrew Hop 374
Benjamin Mas 296
David Mas 294
David Mon 354
Hugh Hop 379
James Hop 379
James Mas 296
Jno. Mad 214
John Grn 260
Wm. Hop 379
Brawdy, Richard Chr 90
Brawford, John Fra 110
Brawn, Daniel Cal 17
David Cal 6
Isaac Cal 16
Isaac Cal 20
John Cal 7B
Joseph Cal 7
Peggy Cal 9
Saml. Cal 4
William She 210
Wm. Cal 11
Brawning, Elias Bra 148
Bray, Abrahm. Nel 11
Edward Bar 48
John Mad 208
John Mas 297
John Way 374
Peter Knx 88
Reuben War 268
Samuel Jef 22
William Nel 6
Braydey, Joseph Mad 210
Brayfield, John Mas 298
Brayles, Elisabeth Lin 109
Brazier, Elijah Chr 56
Equilla Chr 55
John Chr 54
John Chr 56
Larrance Chr 54
Thomas Chr 56
Brazilton, John Mer 331
Breadlove, John Knx 73
Breadus, John Jr Jes 62
Breakin, Edward Wsh 342
Breathitt, Card-
well Log 182
Breckenige, James Mad 207
Breckenridge,
Alexr. Jr Bou 119
Alexr. Sr Bou 118
Geo. Bou 76
James Jef 26
Jane Jef 22
Jas. Bou 119
Jno. Bou 76
Johny Bou 118

Breckenridge, cont.
Robert Jef 22
Breden, Aaron Wsh 342
James Rck 161
Bredon, David Chr 83
James She 201
Bredwell, Cuthbt. Nel 42
Danl. Nel 12
George Nel 42
Henry Nel 7
Isaac Nel 10
J. Fielding Fay 11
Presley Nel 12
Simon Nel 8
Breed, Nathan Bar 44
Breeden, Abraham Cas 44
Elijah Boo 57
Elijah Gal 192
Elijah Gal 194
Richd. Gal 192
Wm. Gal 192
Breeding, Caleb Hrs 323
Jacob Bar 35
Breedlove, James Mad 207
Major Sco 185
Nathan Sco 185
William Mad 207
Breedon, Fanny She 201
Breedwell, William Fra 114
Breeze, John Mas 299
John, Senr Mas 299
Bremer, Jacob Bre 160
Brendon, (see Burdon)
John But 192
Brenham, Charles Jef 22
Nancy Jef 34
Robert Fra 117
Robert Jef 34
Brent, Catherine Hnd 344
Dick Bou 69
Hugh Bou 68
James Hnr 363
James Way 374
John Hnr 364
Thos. Sco 190
William Sco 173
Wm. Lew 102
Brenthinger, Andrew Jef 22
Brenton, Eliza Nic 62
James Nic 62
Joseph War 267
Brents, Jos. Grn 257
Saml. Grn 263
Brest, John Bou 74
Brethit, William Chr 76
Brett, Thomas Log 192
Brewen, Winford Bra 148
Brewer, Abraham Mer 337
Arthur Fay 30
Benjn. Mad 209
Charles Nel 9
Daniel Mer 328
Daniel Mer 331
Daniel She 239
Edwd. Lew 102
Garret Mer 337
George She 203
James Nel 13
James Wsh 343
John Knx 86
John Mer 329
John Mer 329
John Mer 338
John She 203
Joseph Nel 6
Lewis She 229
Mark Hrd 293

Brewer, cont.
Peter Hrd 292
Peter Log 168
Pious She 203
Saml. Hrd 293
Thomas Nel 6
Thos. Hnr 361
Vincent Mer 336
William Hnr 361
William, Jr Hnr 361
William M. Liv 158
Wm. Grn 262
Brewnen, Henry Cal 7
Brewner, John Nel 7
Brians, Josiah Mon 352
Briant, Abnen Pul 124
Alexander Gra 240
Allen Log 169
Bailey Lew 97
Benjamin Jes 62
Edmond Jes 62
Edward Log 170
Elijah Log 170
Elijah Log 195
Enoch Fay 54
Enock Log 167
Ezechal Chr 61
George Fay 54
George Jes 62
James Jes 62
James Knx 83
James Log 167
Jessy Fay 51
John Chr 53
John Grp 272
John Jes 62
John Knx 91
John Way 363
Joseph Fay 54
Nicholas Mon 348
Nicholas Mon 355
Peter Knx 69
Richard Chr 102
Thomas Chr 91
Thomas Chr 99
William Knx 81
William Log 171
Zachariah Wsh 343
Zephaniah Grp 270
Briarly, Margaret Mas 292
Briary, George Mas 300
Brice, James Cal 7B
Samuel Bou 75
Thomas Clr 122
Brichan, William wsh 343
Brichen, William Wsh 345
Bricken, John Cas 47
Bricket, Henry Wsh 342
Bridge, Olley Nel 10
Bridgeford, Richd. Woo 397
Thomas Jef 23
Bridges, Absalom Lin 111
Agatha Clr 124
Aron Nel 12
Benja. Bar 38
Benja. Jef 29
Catharine Fle 82
David Boo 57
Elizabeth War 277
Ephram War 249
George Jef 34
Hirem Mon 351
Isham Jef 34
James Nel 10
Jeremiah Bar 30
John Bou 118
John Fay 11

Bridges, cont.
John Fay 11
John Liv 160
John Mas 295
John Mer 336
John Nel 10
Jonathan Bar 37
Joseph Chr 88
Joseph Mas 293
Lewis Fle 82
Martha Bar 41
Nancy Bar 35
Peggy War 249
Peter War 259
Polly Liv 151
Thos. War 259
Thos. War 266
William Chr 88
Wm. Cum 178
Wm. Grn 252
Wm. Mon 383
Wm. War 259
Bridgewater, Jonn. Adr 4
Saml. Nel 9
William She 217
Bridgewaters,
Elisha Log 181
Levi She 204
Sal. Jr Nel 9
Bridgfarmer,
Martin Cum 173
Bridgis, Drury Chr 98
Briers, Kitty Jes 59
Briges, Benjamin Chr 61
William Bul 174
Brigg, Robert War 252
Briggs, Benn. Lin 109
David War 252
Ebenezer Hnd 328
George Log 182
Thomas Fle 85
Thompson War 246
Bright, Albert Fay 58
Daniel Chr 64
David Lin 111
Henry Fay 58
Henry Lin 111
Henson Mon 355
Hopkins She 200
Jacob Mer 336
Jas. Gar 202
John Handsom Wsh 342
Jos. War 266
Tobias War 280
Thomas Fay 58
Thoms. Log 174
Wm. Mon 355
Brightman, Walter Jef 23
Brigs, Benj. Nel 11
William Hrs 314
Briles, Adam Wsh 346
Michael Mer 332
Brill, Solomon Liv 151
Brim, Chruchwell Mer 329
Brimbarger, Fred-
erick Fay 40
Brimberry, Isaac War 261
Brimigham, Patrick Fay 24
Brimigin, Isac Fay 56
Brimm, Loddy Mer 334
Brinagar, Linvill Fay 54
Brindle, Wm. Mon 375
Brindger, Jacob Fle 71
Briner, Danl. Bou 68
Briney, Peter Nel 41
Bringle, George Wsh 346
John Log 166

Brinigar, Samuel Clr 123
Brink, Hybert Fay 19
Phillip Fay 19
Robt. Est 2
Brinker, Jos. Hnr 368
Brinkley, Timothy Log 171
Brinkman, George Jef 20
John Jef 30
Martin Jef 23
Brinnigar, Adam Clr 124
John Clr 124
Brinnger, Thos. Cly 158
Brinson, Emilly Pul 130
John Nic 64
Thos. Nic 64
zebulon Mon 353
Brinton, Briant Cas 48
James Cas 46
John Gal 193
John Hnr 355
Mary Gal 193
Robt. Gal 193
Brisbey, James Jes 61
Brisburn, William Chr 54
Brisby, Nancy Fra 116
Brischo, John Knx 70
William Knx 70
Brisco, Harrison Bul 174
Phillip Bul 174
Robert Bul 174
Samuel Bul 174
Willm. Lin 111
Briscoe, Andrew Mad 212
Edward Wsh 346
Henry Jef 22
James M. Sco 175
Jeremiah Mer 333
John Nel 10
John Sco 175
John She 234
Parms. Nel 10
Phil Mad 212
Samuel Ohi 103
Thomas Ohi 103
Walter Hrd 297
William Mad 206
William Ohi 104
Brisler, James Log 171
Bristo, Archibald Clr 124
James Cum 181
John Log 171
Bristoe, Catharine She 234
Isaac Cum 181
Jasper She 209
James She 209
John Mon 369
John Mon 376
Sarah She 234
Wm. Cum 173
Wm. Cum 173
Briston, Gideon She 233
Bristow, James Bou 118
John Clr 122
William Ohi 85
Brit, Robert Chr 116
Britain, Nathan Gal 192
Brite, Albert She 229
Catharine She 229
Jane Hnr 361
William Gra 237
Britinham, German Woo 400
Jarman Fay 37
Briton, Jessy Chr 71
William Chr 70
William Chr 71
Brittain, Andrew Mas 292
Benjamin Mas 297

Brittain, cont.
George Knx 90
Levy Knx 79
Britten, William Nel 9
Britton, Joseph Bar 30
Parke Bar 54
Saml. Mer 335
Brizendine, Lewis Fra 110
Broaddus, Edward Mad 206
Eligah Cly 160
Richard Mad 207
Schs. Cly 154
Broadice, Edwin Fay 37
Broadnax, H.P. Nel 11
Broadus, Milley Mad 210
Broadwell, Ashlerry
Samuel Hrs 314
Brock, Aaron Knx 64
Aaron Aco 175
Even Lin 109
George Knx 90
Brock, Henry Fra 115
Henry Jef 20
James Knx 73
Jesse Knx 84
John Hop 376
John Mer 338
John Sco 191
Joshua Rck 164
Major Bar 24
Marthew Pul 127
Marthew Pul 130
Mashack Clr 122
Micajah War 256
Perry Hop 375
Russel Bar 41
Russel Hop 376
Saml. Jef 20
Sharrard Gar 204
William Pul 127
William Pul 130
Brockman, Andrw. Boo 57
Elijah Sco 169
Joseph Fay 44
Moses Boone 57
Saml. Gal 192
Stevin Chr 103
Thomas Mad 211
Wm. Boo 57
Wm. Sr Boo 57
Brockner, Saml. Grn 256
Brodrick, James Mas 293
Brofferd, Robt. Adr 4
Brohard, James Clr 124
Broils, Wm. Jef 3
Brokaw, Abram mer 332
Peter Mer 332
Brokmon, John Adr 5
Broks, Hanah Nic 63
Bromagim, Thomas Mon 377
Bromajim, Jarves Mon 361
Bromfield, James Jes 61
Joel Jes 59
John Jes 61
William Hrd 281
William Jes 35
Bronagh, George Bou 75
Bronaugh, William Mas 296
William Mas 299
Broner, George Jes 62
Brook, Elizabeth War 262
George Mas 301
James Bar 41
John War 252
John B. War 262
Joshua She 204
Brookbank, Abraham Mas 293

Name	County	Page
Brooke, Ezekle B.	War	278
Brooken, John	Sco	182
Brookes, Geo.	Cas	48
Wm.	Hrd	287
Brookhart, Caty	Jef	22
Jacob	Jef	22
Philip	Jef	21
Brookie, John	She	242
Brooking, John W.	Woo	398
Robert	Clr	122
Samuel	Woo	375
Brookman, John	Mer	331
Brooks, Abijah	Clr	122
Archi	Mon	348
Benjamin	Mad	207
Boaz	Mas	301
Christr.	Cum	165
Dabny	Bar	33
David	Bul	173
Dorcas	Wsh	346
Elijah	Cal	10
Elisha	She	204
Elizabeth	Gra	241
Geo.	Bar	33
Grizzy	Sco	167
Hen. jur	Mad	214
Hen, Sen	Mad	214
Henry	Fra	114
James	Bar	33
James	Nel	6
Jesse	Mer	333
Jessy	Chr	115
Jno.	Mad	214
Jno. jun	Mad	205
John	Bar	33
John	Bar	33
Jonathan	Mad	214
Joseph	Bul	173
Joshua	Cum	166
Lynch	Mad	214
Lynch, jur	Mad	214
Miles	Bar	33
Nancy	Mas	293
Paul	She	239
Squire	Bul	174
Squire	Jef	22
Thomas	Cal	10
Thos.	Way	352
Thos. Jun	Cal	10
William	Chr	115
William	Mas	291
William	Sco	177
Wm.	Cum	165
Wm.	Gar	202
Zackh.	Nic	62
Zadoc	Mas	293
Brooksher, Hughes	Clr	123
Jesse	Clr	122
Brooky, William	Hnr	359
Broshears, Thos.	Bou	141
Brothers, Absalom	Mon	380
James	Wsh	339
Jeremiah	Wsh	339
John	Bar	26
John	Mon	378
John	Wsh	339
Robert	Mon	379
Wm.	Bar	25
Broughton, John W.	Clr	123
Jos.	Cly	155
William	Clr	123
William	Cly	155
Broun, James	Fle	61
Brow, John	Chr	114
Browden, Uriah	Chr	95
Browder, Isham	Hop	376
Tho.	Hop	373
Browlee, Alex	Grn	264
Brown,......	Jes	41
Absalom	Gar	203
Absalom, Jnr	Gar	202
Absolum	Chr	67
Adam	Ohi	77
Alexander	Bou	74
Alexander	Bul	173
Alexander	Mon	376
Alexander	Wsh	343
Alexr.	Bar	25
Alexr.	Bar	26
Alexr.	Way	374
Allin	Pul	127
Andrew	Mon	359
Androw	War	248
Anthony	Wsh	339
Aphia	Mad	212
Arabia	Gar	202
Archibald	Bou	74
Archibald	Wsh	345
Armsted	Rck	166
Arnston	Mer	331
Austin	But	192
Barlow	She	207
Barna	Hnr	364
Bartlett	Gar	201
Barzilla	Gra	113
Bazilla	Hnr	368
Benja.	Gar	201
Benjamin	Fra	111
Benjamin	Log	182
Benjamin	Wsh	343
Bennet	Log	175
Beverly	Gar	202
Beviley	War	250
Bolen	But	192
Boswell	Chr	54
Brazell	Gar	202
C. Thos.	Flo	98
Caleb	Fay	12
Caleb	Mad	213
Charles	Gar	204
Charles	Mad	209
Charles	Mer	334
Charles	Nel	11
Charles L.	Cum	169
Charlotte	Ohi	85
Chas.	Bar	28
Christian	Mer	332
Christn.	Adr	5
Claiburn	Way	374
Coldamin	Chr	61
Coleman	Hrs	310
Coleman	Wsh	342
Dad.	Way	374
Daniel	Fle	81
Daniel	Flo	100
Daniel	Fra	110
Daniel	Hop	378
Daniel	Mul	407
Daniel E.	Fra	116
Danl.	Grn	261
Danl.	Grn	265
David	Bul	173
David	Liv	147
David	War	243
Dawson	Woo	397
Dixon	War	243
Drury	War	270
Eak	Cas	43
Edward	Liv	149
Edward	mad	212
Eli	Bul	174
Elias	Adr	5
Elijah	Lin	111
Elijah	Log	170
Brown, cont.		
Elisha	Mon	364
Elliott	Woo	388
Ezekiah	Log	195
Ezekial	Lin	111
Ezekiel	Lin	109
Francis	Fle	71
Francis	Hrs	305
Franky	Mas	294
Frederick	Gar	201
Frederick	Hrd	286
Geo.	Hop	373
Geo.	Way	374
George	Fay	40
George	Fay	57
George	Flo	99
George	Fra	110
George	Fra	115
George	Jef	22
George	Jef	29
George	Knx	85
George	Log	182
George	Log	183
George	Mer	335
George	Ohi	85
George	Wsh	346
George J.	Woo	385
Hannah	Sco	177
Hannah	Woo	400
Harry	Fra	113
Harvy	Gar	202
Henry	Gra	240
Henry	Way	374
Henry	Woo	393
Henry, Jnr	Gar	203
Henry, Snr	Gar	202
Heny.	Adr	4
Hezekiah	Fra	111
Hezekiah	Log	177
Hezekiah	Way	374
Hobson	Hop	373
Hugh	Bar	26
Hugh	Bul	174
Hugh	War	248
Ignatious	Grn	260
Isaac	Bul	174
Isaam	Pul	125
J. Arabia	Gar	202
Jacob	Bul	173
Jacob	Ohi	95
James	Bou	74
James	Bou	76
James	Bou	118
James	chr	104
James	Cum	168
James	Cum	180
James	Fay	44
James	Fle	77
James	Flo	99
James	Flo	100
James	Hnr	366
James	Hop	371
James	Hrd	302
James	Hrs	307
James	Jef	21
James	Jef	24
James	Lew	95
James	Liv	148
James	Mas	292
James	Mer	331
James	Nel	5
James	Nel	8
James	Nic	62
James	Nic	63
James	She	237
James	War	258
James	War	265

Brown, cont.
James, Senr Bou 76
James B. Woo 386
James J. Est 5
Jas. Gar 203
Jas. Hrd 290
Jas. Hrd 293
Jas. War 245
Jeremiah Mer 330
Jeremiah Nel 11
Jery Nel 5
Jesse Fra 116
Jno. Mad 213
Jno. Pul 124
Jno. Pul 126
Jno. Pul 129
Jno. L. Gal 194
Joel Pen 111
John Adr 5
John Bar 32
John Bar 32
John Boo 57
John Bou 74
John Bou 118
John Chr 59
John Chr 93
John Chr 93
John Clr 123
John Clr 123
John Fay 53
John Flo 100
John Fra 113
John Fra 116
John (B2) Gal 191
John (B1) Gal 193
John Grp 272
John Grp 273
John Hnr 361
John Hrs 305
John Hrs 305
John Jef 21
John Jef 21
John Knx 86
John Liv 147
John Log 170
John Mad 207
John Mas 299
John Mer 330
John Mer 332
John Mon 383
John Nel 5
John Nel 7
John Nel 8
John Nel 10
John Nic 63
John Nic 63
John Nic 64
John Ohi 85
John Rck 164
John Sco 171
John Sco 189
John War 267
John Way 363
John Woo 395
John Wsh 342
John, Jr Flo 100
John, Junr Ohi 95
John, Senr Fle 62
John, Sur Fle 81
John G. Chr 90
John P. She 197
Johnson Nel 7
Jona. Hrd 298
Jonas Bar 28
Jos. Gar 203
Joseph Bou 75
Joseph Bou 118

Brown, cont.
Joseph Bul 174
Joseph Jef 30
Joseph Liv 147
Joseph Mas 304
Joseph Nel 6
Joseph Nel 7
Joseph Ohi 96
Josha. Nel 7
Joshua Cum 167
Joshua Fay 22
Joshua Knx 86
Joshua Mad 213
Josiah Cum 181
Josshua Fle 80
Juda Gar 202
Larkin Adr 12
Lazarus Hop 374
Lensey Hop 373
Leroy Gar 202
Lewis Hrd 285
Lewis Knx 83
Lydia Sco 177
Manley Fle 78
Margat Nel 13
Mary Chr 61
Mary Mas 293
Mary Mas 300
Mary Way 356
Maryan Mon 384
Mathew Mon 357
Mathew Rck 160
Maxamilian Clr 122
Melyar Hop 373
Morgan Jes 62
Morriss Lin 109
Nancy Mad 211
Nathaniel Mer 332
Nathaniel She 232
Nathl. Nel 5
Nelson Grp 272
Nicholas Mad 208
Nicholas Nel 10
Oliver Fra 116
Parker Nic 61
Paten But 192
Patrick Hrd 290
Patsy Wsh 339
Peter Log 171
Peter Nel 8
Peter Nel 11
Peyton Cas 42
Peyton Log 172
Presely Jef 3
Prestly Mer 331
Preston W. Woo 400
Raphael Wsh 341
Reuben Gra 239
Reubin Ohi 96
Richard Mon 351
Richard Nel 8
Robert Flo 99
Robert Fra 113
Robert Hop 381
Robert Jef 31
Robert Liv 149
Robert Mon 367
Robert Mon 371
Robert Nel 42
Robert She 204
Robt. Gar 203
Saml. Flo 99
Saml. Gar 203
Saml. Hrs 308
Saml. Nel 6
Saml. Nel 6
Saml. War 265

Brown, cont.
Samuel Bul 173
Samuel Log 181
Samuel Nel 5
Samuel Nel 8
Samuel Ohi 104
Scott Fra 111
Shadrack Hrd 300
Spill C. Hop 373
Stephen Lin 111
Swanson Clr 124
Swebston Bul 174
Thomas Fle 83
Thomas Flo 100
Thomas Gar 203
Thomas Lin 111
Thomas Nel 7
Thomas Sco 186
Thomas Wsh 346
Thos. Cam 25
Thos. Cum 168
Thos. (B) Gal 194
Thos. War 265
Timothy Chr 59
Timothy Chr 59
Wiley Bar 25
William Bul 174
William Clr 123
William Fle 61
William Gra 240
William Hrd 301
William Hrs 324
William Mad 206
William Mer 330
William Nel 5
William Nel 10
William Wsh 346
William, Junr Liv 147
William, Senr Fra 110
William, Senr Liv 147
Willm. Sco 189
Wilson Woo 398
Wily Bar 39
Wm. Bar 38
Wm. Bar 49
Wm. Bar 51
Wm. Boo 57
Wm. Cum 181
Wm. Cum 181
Wm. (Sailor) Fra 112
Wm. Gar 204
Wm. Hop 373
Wm. Hrd 285
Wm. Jef 21
Wm. Mon 380
Wm. Nic 62
Wm. She 237
Wm. War 270
Wm. Way 355
Wm. Jnr Gar 203
Wm. Snr Gar 202
Wm. F. Gal 193
Wm. G. Fra 115
Zekel Fay 42
Brownen, Micajah Hrs 319
Browner, Frank Adr 5
Frank Adr 5
Brownfield, Geo. Hrd 290
James Chr 90
James Pen 107
John Cam 32
Richard Chr 90
William Chr 91
Wm. Hrd 289
Browning, Abner Log 185
Bazel Fle 78
Benjm. Bra 144

Browning, cont.
Caleb Pen 108
Charles Nel 5
Danl. Bar 44
Edmon Bra 151
Eliah Clr 123
Frank Pul 124
Haney Log 182
Henry Clr 122
Jacob Bou 77
James Clr 122
James Fay 56
Jesse Sco 167
Joseph War 274
Joshua Bou 76
Reuben Log 185
Thomas Mas 295
Toliver Clr 122
William Fle 80
Willm. Bou 118
Brownlea, Charles Grn 255
Brownlee, George Fay 12
Jno. Grn 261
Brownlow, James log 172
Bruce, Alexr. War 253
Ambrose Clr 123
Austin Clr 123
Geo. W. Bou 118
Barnet Clr 123
Charles Gal 192
Henry Chr 65
Henry Fle 63
James Nel 8
John, Jnr Gar 204
John, Snr Gar 204
Maddill G. Fay 55
Milly Clr 123
O.Stanton Gar 204
William Hnd 329
William Hnr 364
William Lin 111
Bruel, Alex Bra 151
Bruff, James Liv 158
Bruice, Temperance Fay 55
Bruington, George Bre 158
Bruise, Peter Mul 395
Bruks, Betsey Fay 12
(free woman)
Brumback, Charles Mad 211
Jno. Mad 208
Jno. Mad 211
Paul Mad 215
Petr. Gar 203
Brumell, Ben Cum 166
Brumfeild, Heny Fle 86
Brumfield, Elizabeth Wsh 345
Jno. Lew 103
John Bar 40
John Bar 47
John Hrs 318
Obadiah Grn 250
Obediah Ohi 100
Richd. Hrd 294
Robert Mer 333
Robert She 202
Samuel H. Wsh 345
Skiner Grp 277
William Mer 333
Wm. Hrd 295
Brumit, Shine? Pul 127
Brumley, Barnabas Way 351
Daniel Jes 59
Daniel She 216
John Gal 194
Thos. Gal 192
William Grp 272
Brummet, Geoe. Adr 5
James Knx 83
Reece Knx 88
Brummit, James Knx 65
Brummt, William Knx 83
Brundredge, Peggy Clr 123
Soloman Clr 123
Bruner, Adam Bre 156
Christian Jes 60
Edward Lew 104
George Bre 162
George Bre 164
George, Senr Bre 162
Henry Bre 165
Henry Jes 60
Jacob Boo 57
Jacob She 201
John Bre 165
John Clr 146
John Jef 21
Leonard Bre 167
Peter Bre 164
Peter Bre 164
Samuel Jes 59
Thomas Jes 62
Bruning, William Fle 89
Brunk, Christopher Gra 238
David Grn 248
Jacob Chr 83
Jacob Hrd 283
Jesse Grn 248
Jno. Hrd 296
John Gra 238
Brunson, Stout War 263
Brunt, John Grn 255
Peter Cum 173
Peter War 259
Brunts, Durham Wsh 345
James Cum 182
John Wsh 345
Brunty, Thomas War 258
Bruse, William Grp 275
Brush, Isaac Mas 299
James She 223
Jas. Way 361
John Hnd 338
John She 220
Richd. Rck 164
Wm. Way 361
Bruster, Alexander Liv 147
James Knx 81
Zadock Knx 82
Bruton, David Mad 213
David Way 351
George Way 351
Isaac Mad 215
Samuel liv 152
Wm. Way 372
Bruzau, Chas. Bou 118
Bryan, Barrock Hnr 352
Edward Jef 23
George Bou 119
Jas. Gar 203
John Mer 336
Morgan Hnr 368
Morgan, Jr Hnr 363
Richard Bou 119
Thomas Fra 116
Thomas Ohi 69
Thomas Pen 113
William Pen 114
Williamson Mer 333
Wm. Adr 12
Bryant, Alexdr. Bou 75
Allen Knx 66
Andrew Bou 75
Aron Nel 7
Bryant, cont.
Banits Nel 10
Charles Gal 191
Chas. Hrd 293
Daniel Fay 23
David Fay 19
David Lin 111
David Mas 299
Elizabeth Log 181
Frans. Nel 6
G. Jas. Gar 201
Hardy Liv 152
Henry Nel 13
James Bou 75
James Jef 34
Jesse Jef 3
Jessee Rck 164
Jno. Nel 13
John Adr 5
John Fay 11
John Gar 201
John Gar 201
John Jef 34
Jonathan Clr 124
Joseph Jef 33
Joseph Mad 208
Josiah Grn 258
Mary Hrd 293
Morgan H. Jef 3
Nancy War 280
Patsey Jef 33
Peter Nel 7
Peter She 199
Philip Nel 5
Richd. Woo 396
Robert Lin 111
Robert War 246
S. Geo. Gar 201
Sally Nel 7
Sam Pul 127
Samuel Jef 34
Samuel She 237
Tho. Hop 377
Tho. Hop 381
Thomas Fay 22
Thomas She 209
William Cly 159
William Est 1
William Hnd 338
William Knx 66
William Lin 111
William Ohi 97
William, Jr Cly 159
Wm. Hrd 292
Bryars, Richd. Way 365
Brydon, Robert Fra 115
Bryent, John Adr 4
Bryers, John Jef 20
Brymant, Thom. Pul 127
Bryney, Henry Nel 6
Bryson, Abner Cum 180
James W. Cam 33
Bucey, Jacob She 219
Matthew She 231
Samuel She 231
Buchanan, Joseph Woo 398
Levi Woo 381
Patsy Gar 201
Petr. Adr 4
Simeon Woo 382
Buchannan, David Boo 57
George Way 360
Nathaniel Way 361
Spence Bou 118
Thos. Bou 119
Wm. Bou 118
Buck, Charles Woo 399

Buck, cont.
  James Pul 124
  James Pul 131
  Jno. Pul 124
  John Way 365
  John, Senr Woo 386
Buckalew, Moses Mad 209
Buckham, John War 256
Buckhanan, Margt. Lew 95
  Phebe Nic 64
  William Grp 275
  Wm. Hrs 309
Buckhannan, Alexr. Grn 258
  David Grn 259
  John Clr 146
  Mary Grn 258
  Victor Gal 195
Buckhannen, James Jef 23
  James Jef 23
Buckhannon, Benjn. War 268
  David Clr 124
  George Mer 334
  James Mer 335
  John Grn 258
  John Log 187
  Jon. War 280
  Joshua War 269
  Nancy Mer 333
  Wm. Grn 258
Buckhanon, A. Nel 11
  Andrew Sco 176
  John Fay 45
  Sally Hnr 363
  Will Bou 76
Buckingham, Wm. Cal 18
Buckler, Cornelious Liv 157
  Henry Wsh 345
  Richard Wsh 345
  Robert Wsh 345
  Stephen Nic 64
  William Mul 401
Buckles, Jno. Hrd 299
Buckley, Jeremiah Woo 391
Buckly, Warfiels - farm Samuel Fay 41
  William She 235
Buckman, Charles Wsh 341
  Clement Wsh 341
  Francis Wsh 341
  John Wsh 341
  Joseph Wsh 343
  Joseph Wsh 344
Buckner, Benjamin Hnd 335
  Elizabeth Hnd 335
  George Sco 187
  Haley Jef 21
  Henry Fay 50
  Henry Nic 62
  James Grn 259
  John Grn 247
  Nicholas Jef 22
  Peter B. Clr 122
  Philip Bar 34
  Philip Bra 141
  Richd. A. Grn 247
  Robert Nel 5
  Saml. Nic 62
  Thomas Jef 21
  Thomas Jef 34
  Thornton Grn 247
  Walker Hnd 335
  Wm. Bra 141
  Wm. Grn 247
Buckridge, James Cum 184
Bucks, Wills Way 363
Bucner, Jno. Grn 263

Bud, John Bul 173
Buff, Reecy Mas 298
Buford, Abm. Sco 175
  Abrahans Bou 118
  Ambse. Bou 118
  Henry P. Rck 163
  James Jr Bou 118
  James Sr Bou 118
  John Gar 202
  John Woo 379
  Simeon Bar 41
  Simeon Bou 118
  Simeon Woo 387
  Thomas Gar 199
  William Bre 158
  William Woo 388
  William, Ser Rck 163
Bugg, Samuel Hnd 332
Buitt, Thos. Bou 57
  Thos. Senr Boo 57
Bukey, Rodolphus bul 173
Bulcher, William Mad 208
Bulger, John Log 168
Bulinger, Josiph Chr 108
Bulington, Benjn. War 256
  Robt. War 256
Bull, Bennett Mer 338
  Edward She 197
  Isaac She 238
  Isaiah Knx 88
  James Knx 64
  John Knx 64
  John, Sr Knx 64
  Robert Mas 304
Bullard, Catharine She 232
  Isaac Liv 154
  Reuben She 214
  Thomas Mad 209
  Will She 228
Bullentine, Lemmuel Mas 296
Bullerston, Jonah Adr 5
Bullett, Alexr. S. Jef 22
  Cuthbert Jef 24
  Thomas Jef 24
  Wm. Jef 23
Bulling, Edwd. Bou 118
Bullington, John Mer 328
  Josh. Adr 5
  Wm. Bar 35
Bullock, Bolden Pul 129
  David Clr 123
  David Cly 149
  Edmond Fay 19
  Edwd. Grn 265
  Garland Gal 194
  James Jay 19
  James Pul 130
  Jessee Pul 130
  Jno. Nel 7
  John Wsh 344
  John H. She 210
  Lewis Mas 301
  Nathaniel Fay 20
  Reuben Pul 129
  Robert Mas 295
  Thomas Woo 392
  Thomas Wsh 345
  Waller Fay 19
  William Clr 123
  William Pul 130
  Wingfield She 240
Bulloo, Solomon Pen 106
  Thomas Pen 105
Bumgarner, Dl. Adr 4
Bumpass, Augustin Cal 15
Bun, John Bul 174

Bunch, Archd. Cum 174
  Calloway Mer 328
  George Knx 75
  George War 262
  Israel Cum 174
  James Boo 57
  James Knx 89
  Jos. Hrd 285
  Mary Liv 155
  Micajah Chr 61
  Nancy Mon 350
  Nancy War 261
  Rawdon Cum 174
  Richard Mer 328
  Simmeon War 258
  Solomon Knx 71
  William Pul 124
  Zacariah Hrd 285
Bunderant, Joseph Mon 383
Bunds, Rachel Mad 210
Bundurant, Edw. Mad 213
Bundy, George Pul 125
  Reuben Pul 125
Bungar, Philip Mer 332
Bungas, Henry Mer 332
Bunnel, Jeremiah Bar 53
  Samuel Mer 334
Bunnell, William Hrd 301
Bunt, Jeremiah Way 363
Buntain, John Wsh [illegible]
  Thomas Wsh [illegible]
Buntan, John Cly [illegible]
Buntlinger, Mary Jef 32
Bunton, Andrew Fra 111
  Andrew Nic 61
  George Mer 338
  Isaac Cly 149
  James Cly 149
  James Nic 61
  John Mer 334
  John Nic 62
  Rachel Mer 336
  Samuel Mer 338
  William Jes 59
  William Nic 61
Buoy, Robert Pen 110
Burbage, George Sco 183
Burbridge, Aaron Adr 4
  Elijah Woo 401
  Jeremh. Adr 5
  Linchfield Clr 124
  Rowland Mon 375
  Willm. Adr 4
  Wm. Mon 370
Burch, Benjn. Lin 111
  Cheadle War 247
  Darius Cam 32
  Henry Jes 42
  Jesse Bul 174
  John Jes 42
  Leonard Hrd 281
  Lydia Bul 173
  Moza Gar 204
  Samuel Bul 174
  Samuel Jes 59
  Samuel Jes 61
  Walter Nel 5
Burcham, Samuel Mon 356
Burchet, John Cum 173
Burchfield, Jon. War 251
  Meshack War 264
  Robert Fra 112
Burden, Chas. Nic 63
  Elijah Pul 124
  John But 192
  John Nel 11
  Sam Pul 125

Burdet, John Bul 173
William Bul 173
William, Jr Bul 173
Burdett, Enoch Gar 203
John Rck 162
Jos. Gar 203
Joshua Gar 203
Spencer Gar 202
Burdine, Amos Wsh 340
Betty Wsh 340
Elizabeth Fra 114
Burdit, Lewis Bre 163
Richard Bre 163
Tompkins, Jr Bre 163
Tompkins, Jr Bre 165
Wm. Way 374
Burditt, John Wsh 343
Burdon, Benjamin But 192
John But 192
Burdsong, William Cal 6
Bureham, Elizabeth Bar 48
Burford, Daniel Mer 334
John Mer 329
John Mer 330
Burg, Robison Pul 124
Burgan, Charles Mad 212
Christo. Hnr 362
Dennis Mad 212
Geo. Hnr 362
Jacob Mad 214
Robt. S. Bar 42
Thomas Mad 214
Burge, Jos. War 252
Woody She 214
Burges, Hardin War 261
Henry Fle 86
Mason Jef 3
Thomas Clr 123
Burgess, Bazil Mas 300
Edward Flo 99
Edward Flo 99
Edwd. Sco 184
Garland Flo 99
Henry Flo 99
John Flo 99
John Hrs 322
Joshua Mas 300
Osgood Mas 295
Thos. Jur Sco 167
Walter Mas 292
William Flo 99
Willm. Lin 109
Burgher, John Bou 77
Joseph War 250
Michael Bou 77
Nicholas Est 2
Burgin, Thomas Clr 122
Burgis, Henry Chr 104
Jesse Clr 124
John Chr 82
Burich, Charles She 234
Burise, Henry Fle 82
Burk, Benj. Way 365
Elihu Knx 66
James Woo 386
John Fle 71
John Jes 61
John Knx 77
John, Senr Fle 71
Joshua Mad 205
Michael Mad 209
Patrick Woo 380
Randolph Cal 19
Richard She 211
Samuel Fay 23
Samuel Fle 71
William Fle 76

Burk, cont.
William She 236
Burke, Andrew Hnd 328
Enock Boo 57
George Boo 57
James Boo 57
Martin Sco 184
Robert Bou 77
Robt. Gal 192
Wm. War 265
Burkes, Allen Cas 42
Levey Cas 43
Roland Cas 37
Willies Cas 38
Wm. Cas 43
Burkett, Bazel Nel 8
Lar Nel 13
Thos. Nel 7
William Nel 9
William Nel 12
Burkham, Charles Cly 149
Zilpha Mas 291
Burkhart, Andrew Hrd 287
Geo. Hrd 287
Geo. Hrd 294
George Hrd 290
Burkhead, Ab. B. Nel 12
Abr. Nel 13
C. Nel 7
Eleazor Nel 13
Philip Nel 12
Burkheart, George Knx 63
George Nel 10
Burks, Charles Cum 166
Charles Wsh 344
George Mad 211
Isham Cum 166
James Bul 174
John Bul 173
Leonard Liv 155
Mattew Lin 111
Nicholas Bul 174
Silas Grn 257
Thompson Gar 203
Burlaw, Peter Grn 249
Burlison, Jonathan War 267
Burn, Philip Wsh 344
Burnam, Frederick Mul 387
Henry Est 7
Jno. Mad 212
Joel Mad 209
John (H's son) Mad 206
Burner, Abrm. Hrd 288
Danl. Hrd 288
Burnes, Benjamin Cas 46
Burnet, Isum Way 356
Jas. Bar 30
John Gra 240
Margaret Woo 382
Mathew Gra 243
Richd. Grn 250
Robert Wsh 345
Roland Way 361
Rueben Way 362
Burnett, Car Nel 5
John War 266
Joseph C. She 229
Micajah Mad 208
Nicholas Knx 70
Robert Jef 23
Thomas Jef 34
Thos. Hnr 359
William Hnd 329
William Hnr 358
William Hnr 359
William Mad 207
William She 232

Burnham, James Pul 127
Burns, Andrew Mon 352
Brice Cly 159
Caleb Fay 11
Dennis Mon 358
Edward War 258
Enoch Mon 353
Equilla Chr 80
Garrad Hrs 324
Hannah Hrs 319
Horran Grn 263
Ignatius Nel 10
Isaac Knx 84
Isaac Wsh 399
James Cam 30
James Knx 75
Jno. Nel 5
John Nel 11
John Nic 62
John Nic 63
John Sco 174
John War 281
Nicholas Mon 356
Pricilla Nel 10
Thos. Cam 30
William Bou 75
William Flo 99
William Pul 127
Wm. Bra 148
Wm. Jef 23
Wm. Sco 182
Wm. Jur Sco 185
Burnside, Jas. Gar 203
Jno. Mad 209
John Gar 201
Robt. Gar 201
Robt. mad 208
Burten, John Fay 50
Burtin, Abraham Mad 211
Jesse Gar 203
Sharrard Gar 203
Burtle, Andrew Gra 237
Benjamin Gra 240
James Gra 242
William Gra 242
Burton, Abednigo Grp 271
Absalom Mer 335
Allen Ohi 80
Ambers Mer 334
Archibald Lin 109
Bassett Ohi 78
Charles Fle 86
Charles War 269
Cuthbert War 244
Drury War 266
E. Nel 5
Elijah Rck 161
Elisha Pul 126
George Cal 5
Henry Mad 211
Huchin Adr 4
Isaac Mad 211
James Woo 392
Jane She 229
Jas. Grn 263
Jeremiah Jef 34
Jerrard Mas 293
Jesse Mad 211
Jno. Pul 126
John Jef 34
John Jef 34
John Wsh 348
John Wsh 348
Josiah Nic 61
Josiah W. She 200
Julius Mad 211
Major Adr 5

Burton, cont.
May Mer 334
Moses Mas 291
Rewlen Jef 33
Richard Mad 211
Richd. Adr 4
Robert Mer 337
Saml. Mad 206
Samuel Cal 7
Thos. Grn 263
Walthl. Nel 10
Willm. Adr 5
Wilson [illegible] 10
Wm. Mad 213
Wm. Sco 171
Zery Mad 211
Burus, Samuel Fra 111
Buryman, Anna Mon 355
Burres, John But 192
Burress, Arnet Fay 23
John Nic 62
Nathaniel Fay 12
Burrhus, Wm. Sco 177
Burris, Charles Mad 210
Edmund Mer 336
Isaiah Cly 158
Isaiah Mad 211
Jacob Mad 213
Job Hrd 297
John Gar 205
Joseph Hrd 301
Nancy Mad 210
Nathaniel Mer 335
Peter Chr 87
Thos. Hrd 288
William Hrd 281
Zadock Fle 83
Burrise, Bazel Fle 77
Benja. Fle 76
Charles Fle 81
Henry Fle 70
Henry Fle 82
Joseph Fle 69
F Nathan Fle 76
William Fle 76
William Fle 83
Burriss, Thos. Cly 158
Burrks, Christian Flo 97
Burroughs, Benjamin Mas 299
Benjamin Mas 300
Peter Mas 297
Robert Mad 297
Thomas Mad 297
Burroughes, Benjamin Wsh 345
Burrows, Archibald Wsh 339
Franky Wsh 345
Hezekiah Bou 76
Jonathan Bou 74
Nancy Boo 57
Thomas Fay 48
Thos. Boo 58
Burrus, Isaiah Est 2
Isaiah Est 3
John Jef 34
Michael Clr 124
Thomas Est 5
Thomas, Jr Clr 122
Thomas, Sr Clr 122
Thos. War 275
Busarrd, Wm. Hrd 289
Busbey, John Bou 118
Busby, James Fay 50
Matthew Nic 63
William Nic 63
Busey, Isaac She 229

Busey, cont.
John Fra 111
Bush, Ambrose Clr 121
Ambrose Fay 53
Ambrose, Sr Clr 123
Charles Fay 53
Chris. Hrd 304
Elijah Hrd 292
Elizabeth Fra 116
Elkinon Bou 74
Fanny She 226
Francis Clr 122
Geo. Bar 50
Geo. Hrd 290
Henry Hrd 287
James Clr 122
John Bar 26
John Boo 57
John Clr 122
John Est 2
John G. Clr 121
John V. Clr 121
Jonathan Clr 122
Joseph Clr 122
Joshua Est 5
Mary Clr 122
Matthias Fra 113
Patsy Clr 122
Philip Clr 124
Philip War 277
Robert V. Clr 122
Samuel Hrd 281
Thos. Hrd 287
Wiatt Clr 121
William Clr 121
William Est 3
William Pen 111
William W. Clr 122
Wm. Bar 21
Wm. Hrd 290
Wm. T. Bar 19
Bush MD, John H. Cal 15
Bushenberry, (see also Cushenberry)
Zacheus Bar 41
Busher, Isabella Way 369
Bushin, Robert Chr 102
Bushman, Henry Cam 27
Bushong, George Bar 49
Henry Bar 49
Jacob Bar 49
Buskirk, Abraham She 218
John Mas 293
John She 219
Lewis Pen 113
Michael She 203
Thomas Pen 113
Busley, Jno. Pul 127
Busnell, Isaac Clr 123
Bussel, Sarah Mas 296
Bussell, Moses Boo 57
Bustard, David Pul 126
John Jef 26
Robert Mon 370
William Pul 130
Buster, Benjn. Bar 31
Benjn. Grn 262
Robt. Mad 208
Wm. Gar 204
Butcher, Gasper War 247
George Mas 293
Isaac Mad 211
Isaac Mon 380
James Mon 379
John Cas 47
Samuel Mon 380
Wm. Gar 204

Butlar, James Hnr 369
Butler, A. Log 188
Caner Adr 5
Charles Hop 379
Charles Mas 300
Cornelius Sco 167
Daniel She 230
Delisa? Mon 378
Ebenezer Log 188
Edmund Clr 124
Edward Log 172
Edward Mas 304
Elijah Hnd 330
Elizabeth War 253
Enoch Hrd 295
George Mon 379
Isaac Adr 4
Isaac Adr 12
Jacob Mon 358
James Adr 5
James Adr 5
James Gra 241
James Knx 85
James Mer 334
James Nel 4
James Sco 179
James Sco 190
James C. Woo 392
Jessa Mon 379
Joel Hrd 295
Joel War 277
John Adr 4
John Bar 34
John Chr 86
John Mas 291
John Mon 367
John, Jun Bar 35
Joseph Bar 36
Joseph Hnd 337
Joseph Hnr 364
Joseph Mon 370
Letty Mas 304
Mary Mas 296
Mary Sco 187
Mildred War 271
Nathan Mon 378
Peggy Grn 246
Seman Hrd 297
Sidner Adr 5
Tho. Mad 213
Thomas Fle 82
Thomas Jes 59
Thos. Sco 177
Tobias Jef 21
Tompson Fay 19
William Bou 119
William Bou 119
William She 218
Willm. Adr 4
Wm. Hnr 369
Wm. Way 365
Butner, Adam Mad 212
Edwd. Hop 378
William Mad 207
Butram, Cornelus Way 360
Jacob Way 363
John Bar 27
John Way 363
Nichs. Way 360
Wm. Way 363
Butt, Atison Pul 125
Vance Hnd 337
William Mas 300
Butten, James Grn 249
Basdale Mon 354
Butter, Betsy Hrd 283
George Fra 110

Name	County	Page
Butter, cont.		
John	Fra	110
Nancy	She	222
Percival	Gal	194
William	Grn	253
Butterfield, John	Grn	246
Butterton, Abra.	Mad	213
Button, Jacob	Bar	47
John	Bar	36
John	Bar	47
John	Hnr	357
Thomas	Clr	123
William	Hnr	354
William	Hnr	359A
William, Jr	Hnr	356
Buxton, John	But	192
Wm.	Cam	25
Buyer, Philip	Jef	23
Buyors, Jacob	Hrs	308
Buzzard, Jacob	Hrs	317
John	Hrs	317
Soleman	Fay	11
Byars, Anthony	Grn	252
Edmund	Gar	203
Byas, Jessee	Bar	34
John	Chr	89
Robert	Hop	371
Thomas	Jef	28
Bycoats, Edward	Jef	3
Felix	Jef	34
Sylas	Jef	3
Bye, John	Ohi	94
Jonas	Bre	159
Byers, Daniel	Gra	240
David	Nic	61
James	Gra	240
John	Nic	61
John	Ohi	94
Thomas	Gra	240
Byland, Saml.	Bra	145
Byram, Augustin	Nic	62
Henry	Mad	210
James	Mad	210
Lewis	Bar	26
Lucy	Mas	291
Valentine	Mad	291
William	Mas	301
Wm.	Mad	211
Wm. Jr	Mad	210
Byrch, Henry	Nel	4
Byres, James	Fle	88
Byrn, Michael	Wsh	341
Byrne, James	Wsh	342
Byrns, Arthur	Wsh	341
Catherine	Fra	116
John	Wsh	344
Patrick	Fra	114
Thomas	Clr	123
Byrum, Ridley	Mer	333
Bysher, Cristly	Cam	29

-- C --

Name	County	Page
Cabaniss, Charles, Jr	Grn	261
John, Sr	Grn	261
Cable, Frederick	Woo	387
Joseph	Grn	260
Saml.	Grn	259
Caddell, James	Knx	80
Cade, William	Liv	150
Cadle, Ranson	Log	184
Caffman, Chrisley	Jes	60
Cagle, Leonard	War	280
Cagle, cont.		
Sampson	War	280
Cahill, James	Mas	290
John	Mas	281
John	Mas	284
Laurence	Mas	290
Roger	Mas	284
Thomas	Mas	289
Caho, John	She	225
Roger	Wsh	333
Cain, Ben	Cum	182
Daniel	Knx	79
Dennis	Mas	290
Elizabeth	Jef	32
Jacob	Grp	273
Job	Grp	274
John	Est	4
John	Grp	269
John	Mul	401
Mathew	Nel	16
Moses	She	231
Michael	Nel	18
Peter	Knx	65
Peter, Jr	Knx	79
Thomas	Grp	272
William	Liv	153
William	Pul	137
Wm.	Cum	182
Caine, Patrick	Gra	240
Cains, Richard	Flo	-8
Cairer, Jonathan	Cas	43
Cake, George	Grn	266
Calab, John	Cas	43
Calaham, James	Fay	55
Calahan, Chas.	Bou	78
Calaway, Abraham	Bou	78
Calderwood, Adam	Mas	289
Caldiron, Conrod	Knx	90
Caldwell, Adam	Fra	122
Alexr.	Nic	60
Allen	Woo	399
Andrew	Fay	58
Andrew	Fle	84
Andrew	Log	187
Andrw.	Fle	87
Beverly	Grn	251
Beverly	Grn	255
Charles	Chr	117
Davd.	Adr	5
David	Mer	325
David	Nic	60
David	Nic	60
Davis	Mer	326
Elizebeth	Mas	289
Francis	Cal	14
Francis	Cal	4
George	But	192
George	Fay	37
George	Mer	325
George	Mer	326
Hardy	War	275
Henry	War	276
Henry	Woo	386
Isaac	Bou	81
James	Bou	120
James	Bou	78
James	Bou	79
James	Bul	176
James	Mer	326
James	Mon	366
James	Wsh	335
James	Woo	387
Jane	Mon	365
John	Fay	13
John	Grn	251
John	Grn	258
John	Hrd	303
Caldwell, cont.		
John	Nel	10
John	Cam	24
Jos.	War	280
Joseph	Mas	287
Josiah	Lin	113
Jno.	Hrd	298
Mary	Hrs	317
Mary	Mer	326
Mathew	War	268
Nancy	Bou	81
Polly	Gar	236
Robert	Mad	244
Robert	Mon	365
Robert	Nic	60
Robt.	Adr	6
Robt.	Bou	79
Robt.	Cam	27
Robt.	Nic	59
Robt.	Nic	60
Samuel	Fay	57
Samuel	Log	183
Thomas	Jes	59
Thos.	Grn	259
Thos.	Nic	59
Thos.	Nic	60
Walter	Nic	59
William	Adr	19
William	Bou	81
William	Jes	59
William	Pen	105
William T.	Wsh	337
Wm.	Bou	119
Wm.	Cam	32
Wm.	Mon	355
Wm.	Nic	58
Wm.	Nic	60
Calends, Philip	Sco	185
Caleway, Jessee	Fay	13
Calfa, Marget	Wsh	332
Calfee, John	Adr	5
Calfrey, Nelly	Mad	201
Calh, Wm.	Mon	347
Calhoon, David	Way	352
Eliza	Fra	121
Geo.	Hnr	366
Hugh	War	253
John	Cas	42
John	Wsh	342
Patrick	Liv	156
Thos.	Way	352
Wm.	Way	355
Wm.	Way	362
Calhoun, James	Cum	173
James	Grn	263
Call, Hannah	Bou	79
Jacob	Log	193
Samuel	Bou	78
Samuel	Bou	78
William	Bou	78
Callahan, Anderson	Fle	85
Cathrin	Fle	85
Edward	Fle	85
Callahen, John	Fle	69
Callam, Richd.	Lew	104
Callan, David	Jef	25
Callander, Isaac	Jes	60
Callaway, Abrhm.	Bou	80
James	Bou	119
William	Est	7
Calleham, Edward	Cly	156
Callender, Abraham	She	236
Callerman, John	Fle	64
Callicoat, Ebern.	Adr	7
Calimes, Marquis	Clr	126
William	Clr	126

Callimus, Henry Clr 124
Callins, Joseph She 226
Callis, Francis Bou 80
Sally Bou 80
Callisman, Bennett Jes 60
Callison, Absalom Gar 206
Joseph Lin 112
Callitt, Isaac She 222
Calliway, Edward Clr 124
Calloway, Chisley Ohi 81
Chisley, Junr Ohi 82
Jno. Hnr 356
Saml. Jef 20
Callums, Daniel Knx 78
John Knx 63
Callyer, Wm. Hrs 318
Callyhan, Dennis Mer 324
Calman, Saml. Cas 41
Calmes, Marcus Woo 378
Caloway, George Log 171
Calphant, Abner Bul 174
Calquhoun, Jas. Boo 58
Calvert, Elijah Fra 119
George Fay 60
Jerrard Mas 299
Jesse Mas 289
John Bou 120
John Wsh 334
Levi Fay 60
Peyton Fra 120
Thomas Fra 119
William Wsh 333
Zeal Mas 287
Calvin, Luther Mas 283
Rawleigh Mas 281
Calwell, John She 236
Thomas She 197
Will Pul 135
Cambell, James Bou 120
Joshua Fle 78
William Hrs 313
Cambers, William Est 4
Camblin, Sarah Lin 112
Cambridge, Wm. Bra 150
Cambrige, Benjamin Chr 60
Cambron, Bazin Wsh 334
Henry Wsh 334
Ignatious Wsh 332
Ignatius Wsh 333
James Wsh 331
John Wsh 332
John B. Wsh 332
Joseph Wsh 332
Leonard Wsh 332
Samuel Wsh 331
Thomas Wsh 333
William Wsh 332
Camden, Geo. Cam 33
Wm. Gar 236
Camel, Wm. Cam 30
Camerer, Peter Fle 64
Cameron, Archebal She 239
Robert Sco 170
Thomas Wsh 337
Cammac, Thomas Pul 135
Cammack, [illegible]erly Gal 190
Henry B[illegible] [illegible]1
Cammel, [illegible] Bou 120
John Fay 48
John Mon 381
Cammock, Christr. Fra 122
Camnel, Robert Fay 53
Camp, Benjamin But 192
Edward Hrs 319
James Bra 147
Jane Bou 80

Camp, cont.
John Rck 163
Joseph Pul 132
Campbel, Joseph Cas 41
Rebecca Mas 288
Campbell, Aaron Log 196
Abraham Bar 24
Alex Cas 39
Alex C. Sco 168
Alexander Log 173
Alexander Pul 135
Alexr. Sco 173
Allen Log 188
Allen Sco 184
Andrew Grn 258
Andrew Ohi 101
Andrew Pul 135
Archibald Fay 14
Archibald Log 170
Arther Fay 14
Arthur Fay 37
Arthur Knx 76
Audley Mad 201
Ben Cum 186
Benjamin Mer 327
Benjamin P. Chr 58
Caty Chr 109
Charlse Fay 22
Charles Gar 206
Charles Liv 147
Charles Mul 385
Charls Cal 13
Chs. Nel 15
Daniel Chr 56
Daniel Chr 66
Daniel Est 4
Daniel Fra 1[illegible]
Daniel Nic 59
Danl. Hop 375
David Cal 19
David Chr 69
David Knx 64
David Mer 326
David Mul 401
David Sco 174
David Woo 400
Duncan Gal 190
Elizabeth Mul 398
George Chr 115
George Log 186
George She 215
Gilbert Boo 58
Henry Hnd 333
Isaac Cum 170
Jac Hnr 352
James Bar 24
James Chr 66
James Chr 108
James Cum 172
James Fle 90
James Grn 258
James Hnr 352
James Knx 72
James Knx 80
James Mad 199
James Mas 284
James Mas 288
Ja[illegible]s Mas 289
James Mer 328
James Nic 58
James Pul 132
James Sco 168
James She 224
Jane Bou 78
Jane Mad 200
Janson Grp 271
Jas. Bou 78

Campbell, cont.
Jessa Grp 271
Joannah Woo 386
John Bou 78
John Bou 78
John Cas 38
John Clr 125
John Cly 153
John Cly 155
John Cum 179
John Fay 13
John Fle 70
John Fra 118
John Gra 242
John Hnr 355
John Jes 61
John Knx 86
John Lew 102
John Log 170
John Mas 284
John Mer 326
John Nic 60
John Sco 175
John, Senr Log 170
John B. Chr 53
John G. Bou 78
Jose Mad 205
Joseph Gra 242
Joseph Mer 326
Josius Nic 59
Laurence Grn 257
Linsey Sco 189
Malhew Bar 48
Mathew Hnr 355
Michael Cal 19
Migret Pul 136
Moses Bar 27
Moses Gar 206
Nathaniel Hrs 324
Nely Chr 66
Owen Log 169
Patrick Cal 4
Robert Clr 125
Robert Clr 126
Robert Fay 14
Robert Jes 60
Robert Mas 288
Robert Mer 326
Robt. Bou 78
Robt. Bou 78
Saml. Lin 112
Saml. War 281
Saml. Woo 384
Samuel Chr 67
Samuel Chr 90
Samuel Fra 120
Samuel Mad 201
Samuel Mas 285
Samuel R. Chr 53
Sarah Chr 80
Solomon Gar 206
Theopilus War 260
Thomas Cal 18
Thomas Chr 108
Thomas Est 5
Thomas Mad 203
Thon Pul 136
Will Bou 78
Will Cly 152
William Cal 13
William Clr 126
William Est 1
William Jes 61
William Knx 70
William Log 170
William Mad 204
William Mas 284

Campbell, cont.
William Mul 385
William Ohi 102
William Sco 180
William Woo 386
William Woo 391
William, Jr Knx 85
William M. She 197
Wm. Cam 32
Wm. Cum 172
Wm. Sr Knx 66
Wm. H. Fle 63
Campbells, Duncan Fle 66
Campden, Zephiniah Bou 79
Campel, Ed. Bra 141
Camper, Henry Fay 46
Letis Fay 46
Reubin Mon 369
Thornton Lin 112
Thos. Hrs 321
Tilman Fay 46
Wm. Mon 377
Camren, Thomas Hnd 339
Camron, James Flo 97
Jas. M. Nel 15
John Bul 176
John Grp 273
Milbourn Nel 19
Newbel Mon 358
Samuel Nic 61
William Chr 87
Camso, Christopher Hnr 356
Camuck, Henry Sco 174
Camwell, Joseph Lin 112
Canadey, Joseph Cas 41
Canady, John Mon 381
Canald, Loudan Cam 26
Canard, James Mon 381
Canary, Christian Wsh 336
Canatyer, Abm. Way 356
Andw. Way 356
Canby, Samuel Mas 301
Cancer, Michael Mer 324
Cane, Asle Cam 25
Charles Adr 6
Mathias Mad 199
Jacob Cly 150
James Hnd 338
John Mad 200
Seley Mad 200
Canerway, Thomas War 254
Canetso, Christopher Mad 202
Jacob Mad 202
Canidey, John Cas 38
Canine, Cornelius She 241
Peter She 241
Ralph She 241
Richard She 241
Cann, James Mon 358
Joseph Mon 358
Wm. Bar 32
Cannadey, James Cas 40
John Cas 43
Cannefax, Wm. Rck 161
Cannel, George She 212
Cannelly, Will She 229
Canner, Philip She 234
Cannon, Agnes Mon 359
Archibald Wsh 335
Bird Grn 256
Geor. Mon 358
James Chr 109
John Hrd 304
John Wsh 334
Jno. Grn 264
Newton Sco 182
Cannon, cont.
Rachael Cal 18
Robert Wsh 334
Robert Wsh 336
Robt. Hrd 297
Samuel Chr 110
William Mer 323
Zachariah Jes 62
Canny, William Mas 282
Canover, Joseph Pen 114
Canote, Jacob Mad 202
John Mad 204
John, Sen Mad 202
Cansley, James Chr 59
Canterbury, Asa Mon 374
Benjamin Grp 272
Nimrod Grp 272
Reubin Grp 272
Canterbuary, John Grp 271
Cantral, Christopher Mon 353
Joshua Mon 360
Levy Mon 360
Wm. Mon 354
Zebulon Mon 374
Zebulon G. Mon 360
Cantrel, Joseph Bou 78
Joseph Knx 66
Cantrell, Charles Knx 67
Edward Cal 16
Edwd. Cal 12
James Knx 82
John Knx 67
Cantril, Mary Grn 248
Cantrill, William Knx 82
Canute, John Flo 98
Caoch, Dedrick Cas 47
Cape, Elizaberth Fay 13
John, Junr Cum 171
John, Senr Cum 171
Capehart, Frederick Jes 59
Thamas War 267
Capel, David Fay 36
John Fay 37
Caper, Edward Pul 135
Caperten, William Mad 202
Caperton, James Mad 204
Caple, Andrew Jef 29
Caplinger, Adam She 223
Adam She 241
George Woo 377
Henry She 213
Henry She 228
Henry She 241
Jacob Woo 380
Cappel, William Bul 175
Cappes, Fransis Mul 388
Joshua Mul 388
Capps, Calep Clr 125
Capshaw, Essex Liv 154
Caraco, Thomas Gal 191
Carander, Dad. Way 372
Carathers, Elias Liv 153
Hugh Liv 153
Thos. Nic 60
Caraway, James Cal 4
Carbin, John Hnr 354
Carbone, Daniel Cal 7B
Carby, Jesse Hrd 296
Card, Dan Bar 55
Carden, James Grn 260
Robt. Bar 37
Cardery, Charles Chr 114
John Chr 114
Cardin, Robert Ohi 89
Cardwell, George She 229
Cardwell, cont.
George She 240
Jesse She 227
John Chr 86
John Mer 324
John Mer 324
John Mer 324
Peren Adr 6
Sally Mer 324
Thos. Adr 6
Wilcher Mer 324
William Sco 189
William She 217
Wm. Hnr 369
Care, John Chr 95
John Chr 99
John Chr 106
Thomas Chr 83
Thomas Chr 99
Thomas Chr 106
William Chr 97
William Chr 106
Caree, Benjn. Boo 58
Carehart, Adam Flo 97
Adam Flo 97
John Flo 98
Carell, Levy Hrs 324
Caresey, James Nic 59
John Nic 59
Carey, Archybald Hrs 324
Edmond Clr 125
Edward She 226
Hugh Sco 190
Robert Fay 34
Robert Fay 52
William Clr 126
Cargel, Thomas Chr 79
Cargil, John Chr 80
Carico, James Bul 175
Levi She 208
Carington, Samuel Mon 371
Thomas Mon 372
Caris, Simon She 234
Carithers, Adam She 210
James She 210
Shephen She 210
Carland, John She 206
Matthias She 205
Carlile, James Grn 246
John Fay 22
John Grn 259
John War 254
Nancy Fay 20
Richard Wsh 332
Thos. Grn 250
Wm. Grn 250
Carlin, thomas She 211
Carlisle, Basil Woo 378
Danl. Sco 178
George Woo 377
Henry Log 196
James Grn 260
John Cam 30
Carlock, David War 276
Carlow, Phillip Rck 166
Ransom Rck 166
Carlton, Edmond Woo 392
Isaac Boo 5
John F. Fra 119
Kimbal Bre 158
Carmac, Jonathan Cam 27
Carman, Wm. Cas 39
Carmeens, John Cum 169
Josiah Cum 169
Carmible, Isbal Pul 133
Carmic, Eliza Nel 14
Carmichael, James Jef 17

Name	County	Page
Carmickle, Andrew	Hrd	296
Peter	Hrd	295
Wm.	Hrd	297
Carmin, Caleb	Mas	299
Carmon, Edward	Bre	166
Elijah	Cas	41
Elizabeth	She	240
Isaac	She	212
John	Cas	40
Carn, Edward	She	235
John	She	235
Carnady, John	Hrs	312
Carnage, John	Mon	368
Carnagy, John	Sco	168
Carnague, James	Cly	149
Carnahan, James	Hnr	368
James	Mas	280
James	Nic	58
James	Nic	58
Robert	Nic	59
Carnard, George	Adr	6
Carneal, Thomas	Fra	120
Carneel, Elizabeth	Hrs	314
Carnes, James	Fay	13
Job	Adr	6
Thos.	Adr	6
Carney, John	Sco	182
Pleasant	Sco	182
Wm.	Jef	20
Wm.	Jef	33
Carnihan, John	Chr	116
Carns, Adam	Nic	59
Bathsheba	Wsh	332
David	Gar	205
Carnson, James	She	240
Carpender, John	Mul	395
Carpenter, Andrew	Bar	28
Boston	Cal	7B
Catharin	Cas	41
Christophe	Chr	113
Christopher	Chr	69
Coonrad	Lin	113
George	Lin	112
Henry	Chr	116
Henry	Lin	113
Heny	Fle	85
Hirum	Chr	63
Jacob	Cas	39
James	Mon	348
Jane	Mad	205
Jesse	She	212
Jno.	Mad	205
Joel	Bul	175
John	Clr	126
John	Cum	181
John	Fle	82
John (B.Smith)	Mad	205
John	Pen	112
John	Woo	398
Jonathan	Woo	384
Michael	Mon	369
Michl.	Nel	18
Moses	Mad	200
Richard	Fle	81
Robt.	Gar	206
Rufus	Gar	206
Saml.	Bar	26
Saml.	Nel	10
Simon	Fle	61
Timothy	Cum	173
William	Fle	82
Wm.	Cas	41
Zacheus	She	212
Zenith	Gar	206
Carr, Absolam	Bre	156
Charles	Fay	22
David	Hrd	296
Carr, cont.		
Edward	Woo	395
Elijah	She	220
Eliza.	Fle	67
Ezekiel	Sco	182
Gilbert	Fay	20
Hannah	Lin	112
Henry	Hrs	312
James	Bou	120
James	Hnr	352
James	Lew	101
James	Mon	372
James, Jr	Hnr	353
Jas.	Hrd	286
John	Cly	152
John	Fay	20
John	Hnr	365
John	Nel	17
John	She	203
John	War	259
Jonathan	Ohi	99
Joseph	Bou	78
Letitia	Bou	81
Nathan	Fay	39
Patrick	Fay	45
Peter	Fra	117
Peter	Log	171
Reuben	Wo[illegible]	[illegible]
Richard	M[illegible]	[illegible]
Robt.	L[illegible]	[illegible]
Rosanna	Me[illegible]	[illegible]
Samuel W.	H[illegible]	[illegible]
Susanna	Pul	1[illegible]
Thomas	Fay	20
Thomas	Lin	112
Wiltia	Fay	20
Wm.	Jef	19
Wm.	Jef	19
Wm.	Lew	101
Ws.	Way	367
Carrabough, Jacob	Hrs	317
Carrel, Andrew	Mon	381
George	Mad	204
Joseph	Clr	126
Peter	Bul	176
Samuel	Bul	176
Carrell, George	War	246
Jacob	Woo	399
Carren, James	Fay	33
Carrick, James	Cal	16
John	Cal	16
John	Liv	159
Carrico, Bazel	She	237
Corns.	Nel	15
Dennis	Mas	280
James	Nel	15
James	Wsh	333
John	Nel	18
Joseph	Nel	19
Joseph	Wsh	333
Lovine	Wsh	333
Nathan	Wsh	333
Thos. J.	Nel	17
Vincent	Nel	16
Walter	Wsh	333
Wilford	Nel	16
Carrier, Henry	Gar	205
John	War	279
Carrigan, Joseph	Cum	168
Carril, Thomas	Woo	381
Carrington, [illegible]	Lew	98
Carrns, Thomas	Fay	20
Carrobough, Peter	Nic	60
Carrol, Daniel	Bou	80
Daniel	Mas	289
Danl.	Hrd	288
Elizebeth	Mas	281
Carrol, cont.		
Enoch	Sco	170
Nancy	Hrd	296
Sandford	Mas	301
Carroll, Dempsy	Sco	181
John	Jes	59
Thomas	Jes	59
Wm.	Sco	189
Carron, Wm.	Pul	133
Carry, Willm.	Sco	187
Carsidy, George	Jef	30
Carson, Alex	Grn	264
Andrew	Chr	77
Ann	Fay	14
David	Rck	162
Elizabeth	Cas	43
Isaac	Sco	183
James	Cas	39
James	Fay	22
James	Knx	81
Jno.	Hrd	297
John	But	192
John	Chr	113
John	Hrs	321
John	Way	365
Joseph	Cam	32
Joseph	Rck	159
Lindsey	Mad	204
Robert	She	218
Saml.	Cas	39
[illegible]ml.	Way	357
[illegible]homas	But	192
[illegible]homas	But	192
Wade	Bar	31
William	But	192
William	She	218
Wm.	Bar	46
Wm.	Hrs	322
Wm. (Judge)	Rck	162
Wm.	Sco	174
Carstarphan, Robert	Fay	57
Cart, John	Bre	156
Leonard	Bre	164
Carter, Abednigo	Nel	19
Abert	Lew	104
Abraham	Fra	121
Allin	Mad	205
Barb.	Nel	19
Barberry	Chr	94
Barnabus	Hrd	290
Charles	Lin	112
Charles	Pul	133
Charles	Pul	135
Coleman	Mad	201
Collin	Lin	113
Dale	Mas	289
Daniel	Clr	126
Daniel	Nic	61
Danl.	Bar	33
Edward	Lin	112
Edward	Nel	16
Edward	Nel	18
Eldrige	Chr	112
Friend	Nel	19
Gabriel	Liv	156
Geo.	Bar	36
George	Chr	96
Goodloe	Woo	377
Harry	Fle	85
Harry	Hnr	359B
Hebe	Grp	276
Henry	Bar	36
Henry	Mad	200
Hugh	Mul	397
Isaac	Knx	79
Jacob	Hrd	295
James	Bar	52

Carter, cont.
James Liv 156
James Bou 80
James Cum 165
James Mas 284
James Mer 325
Jas. Hrd 296
Jesse Jef 19
Jesse Lin 112
Jesse Way 352
Jno. Pul 133
Jobe Fay 20
Joel Pul 133
John Adr 6
John Boo 58
John Bou 78
John Bra 141
John Cum 181
John Hop 371
John Lin 112
John Log 177
John Mon 382
John Nel 19
John Ohi 83
John Rck 162
John Woo 397
John F. Ohi 102
John F. Woo 395
Jonathan Nic 59
Joseph Bra 145
Joseph Cum 173
Joseph Mon 369
Joseph Nel 14
Joseph Wsh 333
Joshua Jes 62
Kinyan Mon 378
Landen Cum 181
Martin Mer 328
Masha Jef 13
Nicholas Nel 14
Nicholas Nel 18
Obediah Fay 54
Peter Lin 112
Rex Log 193
Saml. Cum 165
Soloman Lin 112
Solomon Mon 363
Stephen Lin 112
Suky Hrd 298
Tandy Sco 173
Thomas Adr 6
Thomas Bou 78
Thomas Nel 19
Thos. Adr 6
Thos. Boo 58
Travace Bar 35
Turner Cal 17
William Mul 393
William Mul 400
William Ohi 83
William She 236
Wm. Bar 36
Wm. Bra 143
(see also McCarter)
Wm. Hrd 292
Wm. Mon 378
Wm. Way 361
Cartere, Benjamin Wsh 338
Carter's Family,
John (Wm. Son) Fle 75
Cartmale, Elijah Bul 175
Cartmell, Elijah Fay 37
John Mon 353
Thomas Mon 377
Cartmil, Andrew Mon 360
Samuel Mon 360
Cartmill, John Hrs 315

Cartmill, cont.
Susanah Hrs 315
Thomas Mon 370
Wm. Mon 351
Cartor, Charles Jes 62
Henry Jes 60
John Jes 60
Joshua Jes 60
Cartright, Bennett Hop 373
Cartwell, Jacob Nel 20
Cartwright, John Adr 6
Carty, Charles Mas 282
James Cum 169
John Cum 170
John Fay 14
Morris Cum 170
William Hnr 367
Caruthers, Wm. Sr Nel 18
Carvat, Nelipy Bar 45
Carvenah, Charles Chr 64
William Chr 64
Carven, Andrew Sco 181
Andrew Sco 191
Carver, Cornelius Bar 45
James Fay 47
James Mad 202
John Gra 240
Kneel Gra 244
Pleasand Gra 239
Reuben Bou 78
Thomas Gra 240
William Gra 240
William Mad 202
Henry Jes 62
Carvin, John Bar 26
Cary, Ebenezer Mer 323
John Fay 59
John Mer 323
Joseph Hop 372
Lemuel Log 184
Ludwell Fay 36
Casaday, Daniel Nic 58
Jerry Nic 58
Casady, James Nic 59
John Bre 168
Casan, George War 250
Casat, David Mer 323
Jacob Mer 323
Casbear, David Mul 391
Frederick Mul 406
Jacob Mul 394
Casberry, James Cal 17
Case, Benjamin Wsh 335
Delilah Bou 120
Edward Bra 143
George Bou 119
Goldsmith Bra 150
James Bra 143
James Bra 149
James Mas 285
John Wsh 335
Joseph Bou 120
Lydia Wsh 335
Nathl. Nel 19
Shederick Bra 146
Thiophelous Mon 366
Thomas W. Woo 382
Thos. Bra 142
Wayne Jef 19
William Bul 176
William She 218
Zeph. Bra 149
Casebolt, John Flo 97
Caseman, William Jes 59
Casey, Abner War 270
Charles She 199
David Wsh 335

Casey, cont.
James Grn 261
John War 273
John Wsh 331
John Wsh 332
John Wsh 332
Joseph Cam 28
Josiah Fra 121
Lewis Lin 113
Moses Hrd 294
Peter Hnd 330
Riley She 197
Robert Wsh 334
Saml. War 270
Willm. Adr 5
Cash, Calep Mon 362
Claiborne Hrd 284
Elizabeth Wsh 332
Howard Cal 7B
James Flo 98
Jeremiah Hrd 297
John Mas 288
John Nel 21
Josiah Woo 393
Nancy Mas 287
Warren Hrd 285
William Nel 14
Cashaw, Benoni Mon 381
John Mon 356
Cashler, Henry She 232
Cashman, Conrod Liv 145
Martin Bre 168
Peter Bre 168
Cashner, David Chr 99
Jonas Cum 174
Leonard Cum 174
Cashwiler, Betsy Mer 324
Christine Mer 324
Casick, Christopher Lin 112
Casil, Jacob Fay 13
Casine, Cornelius Mer 324
Garrett Mer 327
John Mer 325
Caskey, Robt. Adr 5
Robt. Adr 6
Casky, Josiph Chr 110
Thomas Flo 97
Casley, John Wsh 338
Cason, Edmond War 273
John Hrs 309
Reuben Log 175
Seth But 192
Cassell, Abraham Jes 59
Abraham Jes 60
David Fay 56
Henry Woo 379
Cassety, John Senr Mon 354
Cassidy, Micheal Fle 83
Peter Fle 64
Thomas Fle 61
Will Bou 79
Cassity, David Mon 369
Isaac Mon 371
Jacob Mon 351
John, Junr Mon 354
Peter Mon 368
Peter Mon 375
Wm. Mon 368
Cassledine, John Mon 364
Cast, Robert Clr 126
Casteel, John Cly 150
Joseph Cum 177
Caster, Conrod Hrd 287
Casterson, George Chr 87
Castile, I. Joseph Flo 98
Castilow, John War 275
Castlebery, Fleming Cal 18

Castleberry,
  Martin Hop 374
  Wm. Cal 17
Castleman, Jacob She 223
  Jas. Hrd 295
  John Fra 121
  Lewis Woo 390
Casto, Abijah Mas 301
Caswell, Basil Flo 98
  Hannah Bul 175
  James Fay 14
  Jno., Junr Hrd 286
  Jno., Senr Hrd 286
  Potter Mon 381
  Wm. Hrd 286
Casy, Stephen Lin 112
Catchem, Tempy Mer 327
Catcher, Benjamin Knx 87
  John Knx 66
Caterim, Peter Way 353
Catermous, Elisha Jef 18
  Elizabeth Jef 18
  James Jef 18
Cates, Richard Est 8
Cathers, Edward Knx 89
Catherwood, Chas. Nic 61
  Saml. Nic 60
Cathy, Samuel Flo 98
Catlet, Alexander Grp 278
  Alexandre Grp 270
  Fraces Fay 45
  Horatio Grp 270
Catlett, John Jes 62
Catlin, Seth Wsh 337
  Theodorus Wsh 337
  William Wsh 337
Cato, Henry Chr 62
  Henry Chr 62
  Nathan Chr 62
Catoe, Sterling Chr 62
Caton, George Mer 326
Catril, Thos. Nic 60
Catt, Michael Lew 103
  Thos. Lew 97
Catterson, Robt. Gal 190
Cattrell, Abel She 209
  Richard She 209
Catty, Elijah She 219
Caudle, Ransom Log 173
Caughey, David Nic 59
  John Fay 33
  John Fay 53
  John Nic 59
Caughman, Christ Nel 17
  Isaac Mer 326
  Jacob Nel 16
Caughril, John Fay 20
Caulk, Benjamin Wsh 332
Cavanah, David Hop 376
Cave, Henry Sco 192
  Jeremiah Jes 59
  John Boo 58
  Reuben Woo 392
  Richard Bou 81
  Richard Woo 390
  William Bou 81
  Wm. Boo 58
Cavell, Saml. I. Cas 45
  Wm. Cas 44
  Wm. Sin Cas 44
Cavender, Fielding Fay 36
  James Hnd 342
  John Hnd 342
  Margaret Sco 184
  Thomas Sco 181
Caves, Benjamin Mon 368
  Wm. Mon 369
Cavin, James Chr 80
Cavinder, Thomas Fra 122
Cavins, Edward Fay 60
  John War 247
Cawa, John Jes 60
  Martin Jes 60
Cawan, Wm. Cal 11
Cawley, Jas. Gar 206
  Jonathan C. Bre 167
Cawood, Aquilla Bou 79
  Stephen Bou 79
Cawson, Abel Boo 58
  Juleanna Boo 58
Cawthon, Charles Mad 200
  Leforce Woo 390
Caysey, Merideth Gar 206
Cayton, Margarett Gal 191
  Noah Lin 113
  Philip Gal 191
  Wm. Gal 191
Caywood, Asa Mon 376
  Thomas Mon 372
Cazee, Benjamin Pul 136
  Edward Rck 164
Ceally, Peggy Gar 206
Cecil, Bresley Way 359
  Elender Nel 16
  Ignatius Nel 20
  Jno. Nel 14
  Jno. Nel 17
  Joseph Nel 20
Cemp, Ambrose Jef 33
  Michael Jef 33
Ceneay, Vincent Mas 304
Cenebaugh, Jas. Bar 44
Ceoghan, Wm. Jef 20
Cerbey, John Fay 23
Cerrick, Walter Fay 53
  William Fay 42
Cesar (freeman) Fay 22
Chace, William HNR #%¢
Chadd, David Bou 81
  James Bou 79
  Saml. Bou 79
  Samuel, Sr Bou 81
Chafen, Stanley Jef 32
Chaffen, Mordica Bra 147
Chaffin, David Flo 98
  Ellis Chr 70
  James Flo 98
Chaifin, Jordan Grp 274
Chain, David Lew 95
  Thomas Lew 95
  William Lew 95
Chalfant, Thos. Gal 189
Chalfin, Aaron Hrd 302
  John Hrd 301
  Joseph Hrd 281
Chalk, James Sco 190
Chalkley, Ben Cum 166
Challen, William Fay 13
Chamber, Wm. Cam 26
Chamberlain, Cha. Cum 167
  David Adr 6
  Fielding Wsh 333
  John Wsh 331
  Liles Wsh 335
  Silas Wsh 331
  Thomas Wsh 331
  Thomas Wsh 334
  Thomas Wsh 335
  Thos. Cum 167
  Wm. Est 5
Chamberland, Wm. Bar 50
Chamberlane, John Mas 282
  John, Jun Mas 282
Chamberlin, Fed Mer 323
Chamberling, John Fay 13
Chambers, Abraham Sco 187
  Ahs. Nel 16
  Alexander Hnr 358
  Asa Hrd 300
  Benjn. Bra 145
  Emilia Bul 176
  Enock Jes 62
  Hugh Pul 134
  James Hrs 324
  James Mas 301
  James Sco 172
  Jiles Bre 167
  John Est 4
  John Mad 203
  John Mas 304
  Joseph Fay 12
  Mordichai Pul 137
  Nathanl. Mad 203
  Phillip Hrs 310
  Phillip Hrs 321
  Richard Log 170
  Richard Log 178
  Robert Fay 41
  Robert Fay 53
  Rowland Woo 387
  Silas Bou 120
  Thomas Hnd 338
  William Fay 40
  William Jes 60
Chamblin, Geo. Bou 120
Chamlers, Ricd. D. Log 170
Chamman, James Hnd 335
Champ, Jane Bou 80
  Robt. Bou 79
  Thos. Bou 79
  William Mad 204
Champin, Edmund Mer 328
Champion, Drury Liv 155
  John Wsh 334
  Mary Liv 148
  Thomas Liv 155
  Thomas Wsh 337
  William Liv 152
  Willis Liv 155
Chance, Ezekiel Rck 161
  James Rck 160
  John Gar 206
  Wm. Bar 42
  Zebulon War 258
Chanceller, David Gra 237
Chancellor, John Mas 289
Chancey, Wiley Cum 180
Chandlain, John Grn 261
Chandler, Abednigo Chr 63
  Charity Mas 285
  Clabourn Hrs 307
  Danl. War 270
  Edward Wsh 330
  Haratia Grn 245
  John Chr 59
  John Cum 168
  John Grn 246
  John Wsh 336
  Joseph Cal 6
  King Cal 4
  Rankin Lin 112
  Reuben Cum 179
  Richard Log 169
  Richard Wsh 338
  Richard, Jr Log 169
  Richd. Jnr Log 178
  Robert Mad 201
  Shadrick Knx 91
  Susanna Wsh 330
  Thos. Cum 168
  William Cas 4

Chandler, cont.
William Hnr 358
William Hrs 316
Wm. Bar 38
Zacariah Cal 3
Chandoin, David Grn 262
Chaney, Charles She 204
Edward Lew 100
Heritage Bou 79
James Nic 60
Jas. Lew 97
John Clr 125
John Nic 60
John J. Way 365
Leanord Fay 44
Leonard Fay 32
Richard Clr 126
Thomas Bou 79
Wm. Nic 60
Thomas Log 172
Channonhouse, Abel Jef 30
Chantor, William She 235
Chany, Ambrose Bou 79
Chapel, John Hop 376
Solomon Mad 200
Stephen Hop 374
Chapland, Abraham Jes 60
Chaplin, Abraham Mer 322
James Mad 204
Jeremiah Bul 175
Willm. War 281
Chapman, Abner War 258
Alexandr. But 192
Amos She 236
Asa Cum 170
Benj. Fra 118
Daniel Lin 112
Edmond Clr 126
Geo. Bar 22
James Hnr 355
Jas. Lin 112
Geo. Cum 169
Jeremiah War 276
Jesse War 252
Job Lin 112
John Hnd 336
John War 257
John A. Fra 120
Joseph War 274
Joshua Ohi 72
Joshua Ohi 81
Josshua Fle 77
Mary Fle 77
Naaman Fle 82
Neel Bar 35
Payton Adr 5
Richd. Lin 112
Sarah Hnd 336
Thos. War 252
Thos. War 258
Thos. War 258
William Fle 70
William Fle 70
Willis Ohi 69
Wm. Bar 30
Wm. Flo 98
James Hnr 354
Chapmon, William Cal 9
Chappel, Abraham Bul 176
James Bul 176
Jesse Cas 37
Robert Bul 176
Chappell, Archd. Sco 182
Ballard Cas 43
Henry Sco 182
James Fle 63
Jesse Nel 21

Chappell, cont.
John Sco 182
Wm. Cas 42
Chappezi, Henry Nel 10
Chapple, James Pul 136
Chaptan, Wm. Nel 15
Chapton, Andr. Nel 15
Charles (freeman) Fay 21
Charles Way 356
Charles, Absalom Bul 175
James Mon 373
Philip Mon 373
Charley, George Jef 17
Charms, Sarah D. Sco 191
Charndler, James Fay 20
Charter, Jno. Pul 134
Chary, Jno. Pul 135
Miles Mul 389
Chase, William Flo 97
Chaslain, James Mad 204
Chastain, John War 259
William Mad 243
Chatham, Benjamin Mer 325
Thos. Hnr 354
Chatman, James Bar 44
James Grp 270
Reubin Grp 270
Chattain, Joseph War 277
Chattsen, Robert Hnr 356
Chaunch, Jacob Mer 326
Cheak, Hardin Chr 83
James Chr 75
Lewis Chr 74
Winney Chr 75
Cheaney, John Nic 59
Cheatham, Daniel Wsh 336
David Mon 368
Edward Hnd 341
James Mon 368
John Mon 348
Joseph Mad 201
Leonard Mon 384
Major Woo 384
Obadiah Wsh 336
Reuben Wsh 336
Check, Nicholas Jef 33
Cheek, Henry Adr 6
John Cal 9
Nicholas She 206
Shadrick Chr 71
Cheeks, George Way 374
Cheers, Jencey War 247
Cheeseman, William Mas 281
Cheetham, Christr. Cum 166
Edmd. Cum 165
Edmund Hnd 340
Hezekiah Cum 166
Richardson Cum 166
Wm. Cum 165
Chelton, Thos. Adr 6
Chenault, Chris Nel 14
David Mad 203
John Nel 20
William, Jr Mas 204
Wm. Mad 203
Chenowith, Abslam. Cam 29
Chenoworth, Wm. Nel 18
Chepley, Robert Fay 13
Stephen Fay 14
Cherry, Mary Boo 58
Nicholas Cam 27
Wm. War 250
Wm. War 282
Chesery, Robert Hop 376
Tho. Hop 376
Cheser, William Knx 80
Cheshire, William Mad 204

Chesholm, John War 282
Chesure, Jonathan Bul 175
Thomas Bul 175
Chesnut, Abraham Knx 89
Benjamin Knx 63
Jacob Rck 161
John Knx 63
Saml. Cly 157
Samuel Knx 89
Sarah Chr 113
Chesshire, Benjamin Wsh 336
John B. Wsh 336
Chester, Jacob Chr 107
Chestham, Leond. Lin 112
Cheston, Thos. Way 369
Chew, Richard Jef 31
Saml. jef 20
Samuel Mon 357
Thomas Jef 20
Chewning, Hardin Grn 255
Chick, James Knx 75
Wm. Bra 149
Childers, Abraham Flo 97
Goldsberry Gar 206
Henry Pen 107
Henry, Jr Pen 112
James But 192
John Pen 112
Joshua Mer 327
Joshua Pen 111
Major Pen 111
Robert Pen 107
Lolomon Pen 110
Thomas Pen 110
Susannah Hrs 321
William Pen 110
William, Jr Pen 111
Childis, Jackson Knx 67
Childras, Thos. War 265
Childres, Saml. War 264
Chiles, Alexander Mul 398
David Mas 283
Elizabeth Mer 325
Henry Clr 125
John Jes 60
Phebe She 236
Thomas Mer 325
Urias Hrs 309
Wm. Mon 384
Chimley, John Bou 79
Chin, Ely Hrs 313
George Hrs 313
John Hrs 313
Thos. Hrs 316
China (free woman) Fay 13
China, Obid. Grn 263
Chindler, George She 214
Chineth, Jonothan Mul 391
Chiney, Ezekiel Mas 280
Isaiah Mas 280
John Fle 64
Chinn, Achilles Nel 10
Benjanim Grp 269
Elijah Mas 299
Joseph Bou 81
Rawleigh Mas 283
Sythe Bou 81
Will B. Bou 81
Chinneth, Samuel Log 169
Samuel Log 193
William Mas 282
Chinnith, James She 221
Chinoeth,
Arther, Jr. Jef 18
Arther, Sr. Jef 17
Ellender Jef 18
John Jef 18

Name	County	Page
Chinoeth, cont.		
Margaret	Jef	19
Thomas	Jef	19
Chinoweth, Nichs.R	Gal	190
Chinworth, Jacob	But	192
Chipley, John	Bou	80
Chipman, Draper	Mon	381
Parris	Mon	381
Chipmon, Perry	Pen	109
Chisnam, Thomas	Jes	59
Chishm, George	Bar	21
Chisnolm, Benjn.	Grn	256
Joseph	War	250
Wm.	Grn	256
Chism, Chicheter	Hrs	320
Gabriel	Clr	125
George	Sco	174
George	Sco	180
Jacob	Bar	43
James	Bar	43
James	Sco	185
Jesse	Hrd	288
John	Boo	58
John, Sen	Bar	26
Michl.	Bar	44
Thomas	Clr	125
William	Fay	59
Wm.	Bar	44
Chissenhall, Samuel	Hnd	343
William	Hnd	343
Chitwood, James	Pul	135
John	Cum	171
Pleasant	Pul	135
Zalerous	Pul	135
Chity, Joseph	Mad	201
Chivaly, Jacob	Grn	260
Chowning, Charles	Fay	46
Laurence	Mas	288
Robert	Fay	47
Chrise, Christian	Mul	400
Chrisham, Benjamin	Jes	59
Chrisler, Allin	Boo	58
David	Boo	58
David, Sr	Boo	58
Elisha	Boo	58
Leonard	Boo	58
Lewis	Boo	58
Silus	Boo	58
Chrisman, Abraham	Fay	20
George	Chr	59
Hugh	Jes	59
Isaac	Way	373
Jacob	Fle	72
Jacob	Fle	90
Joseph	Cum	165
Joseph	Jes	59
Joseph	Jes	62
Methew, Sen	Fle	72
Chrismass, William	Log	193
Christ, Frederick	But	192
Christerson, John	Grn	259
Christeson, John	Cas	48
Christian, Gilbert	Hop	373
John	Cum	180
John	Hnd	332
Matthew	Hnd	332
Paul	Sco	175
Robert	Adr	6
Titus	Nel	10
William	Fay	20
Christison, Molly	Mer	326
Thos.	Cas	46
Christman, Jonas	Woo	378
Christopher, David	Mad	203
Jno.	Mad	205
Lewis	Jef	19
Wm.	Woo	397
Christopher, cont.		
Wm. jr	Woo	402
Christwell, Elijah	War	263
Christy, Ambrose	Clr	124
David	Boo	58
James	Fle	61
John	Clr	124
Joseph	Fle	85
Samuel	Fle	85
Samuel	Way	354
Chriswell, David	Sco	187
Chruchfield,		
Richard	Mer	342
William	Mer	326
Chumley, John	Knx	81
Church, Henderson	Fra	119
Joshua	Cal	8
Robert	Hnd	325
Robert, Jr	Fra	120
Robert, Senr	Fra	121
Thomas	Fay	30
Thomas	Fay	33
Thomas	Fay	55
Thomas	Fra	120
William	Fra	121
Churchill, George	She	231
Henry	Jef	19
Jno.	Hrd	290
Mary	She	236
Samuel	Jef	17
Cills, Bigh	Way	356
Elias	Way	356
Cimbley, Isaac	Jef	30
Cinclear, Geor.	Mon	378
Thomas	Mon	376
Wm.	Mon	376
Cisna, Wm.	Hrd	293
Cisney, Robert	Mul	392
Cissell, Augustin	Wsh	331
Francis	Wsh	329
Henry B.	Wsh	338
James	Wsh	331
James	Wsh	331
James R.	Wsh	331
Jeremiah	Wsh	338
Matthew	Wsh	331
Nancy	Wsh	331
Sylvester	Wsh	338
Wilfred	Wsh	331
William	Wsh	334
Zachariah	Wsh	331
Clack, John	Bar	36
Clagete, Euphon	Fay	20
Clair, Allen	Pul	132
Clampet, Henry	Clr	146
Clampett, Moses	Lin	113
Clancey, William	Fle	76
Clank, William	Pul	133
Clanton, Samuel	Log	171
Sterling	Log	171
Clardy, Norman	War	276
Clare, Francis	Pul	121
James	Bou	80
Claren, Andrew	Fle	64
Claringen, Jessee	Cal	6
Clark, Aaron	Hop	371
Abner	Bra	143
Abner	Jes	59
Abner	Log	171
Abraham	Bar	53
Alexander	Liv	152
Alexander	Mul	395
Amos	Fra	120
Andrew	Liv	152
Ann	Mas	282
Ansley	Liv	152
Bazel	Jef	24
Clark, cont.		
Ben	Hrd	298
Benj.	Nel	19
Benj.	Nel	20
Benja. Jun	Bar	39
Benja. W.	Bar	39
Benjamin	Mad	204
Benjamin	Mas	280
Benjamin	Mul	388
Benjamin	Nic	61
Benjamin	She	235
Benjm.	Nic	60
Bennett	Est	6
Bolen	War	257
Boling	Clr	124
Catharine	Fay	22
Charles	Bre	160
Charles	Fay	50
Charles	Hnr	361
Charles	Hnr	363
Charles, Jr	Hnr	363
Christopher	Chr	62
Christopher	Mad	202
Clemt.	Nel	17
David	Adr	6
David	Cly	150
David	Mad	203
David	Nic	60
David	Wsh	335
Davis	Nel	20
Drury	Pul	134
Edmond	Jef	26
Elias	Bre	159
Elizebeth	Mas	286
Ephram	Hrs	305
Everet	Bar	53
Geo.	Bar	33
George	Fay	22
George	Hop	374
George	Lew	104
George	Mas	280
Godfrey	She	200
Harry	Bra	151
Henry	Adr	5
Henry	Chr	107
Henry	Cly	157
Henry	Cum	182
Henry	Lin	112
Henry, Sen	Chr	107
Henry A.	Nel	16
Igs.	Nel	19
Isaac	Chr	107
Jacob	Bar	53
James	Chr	84
James	Hop	377
James	Jes	60
James	Log	196
James	Mad	199
James	Nel	17
James	Pen	112
James	Pen	114
Jas.	Hnr	351
Jas.	Way	359
Jesse	Bul	176
Jessy	Chr	107
Jno.	Pul	132
Jno.	Pul	134
John	Bar	33
John	Bou	119
John	Bre	163
John	Bul	175
John	Chr	84
John	Fay	41
John	Grp	276
John	Hnr	361
John	Hop	373
John	Hrs	313

Clark, cont.
John Log 193
John Mon 362
John Nel 20
John Nic 59
John She 200
John She 224
John, Snr Lin 113
Jonathan Bar 50
Jonathan Jef 31
Joseph Chr 59
Joseph Mas 290
Joseph Mon 371
Judah Mad 200
Lary Hnr 363
Ledloe Jef 19
Lewis Pen 105
Matthew, Junr Fra 119
Matthew, Senr Fra 118
Micajah Jes 60
Moses Fle 61
Moses Hrd 283
Nathaniel Bul 176
Nathaniel, Sr Bul 175
Obadiah She 229
Patience Cal 5
Patrick Jes 61
Philip Bra 143
Phineas Fay 13
Portions Fay 37
Randolph Cly 149
Reuben Flo 97
Reubin Lin 113
Richard Bre 159
Richard Chr 107
Richard Fay 44
Richard Nel 17
Robert Bou 120
Robert Nel 19
Robt. Bra 148
Ruben Bar 53
Saml. Hop 374
Samuel Fle 86
Samuel Hop 379
Samuel Mas 287
Samuel Mon 379
Samuel Nel 17
Sarah Fle 85
Sarah Nel 19
Sarah Nel 42
Sarah Pen 105
Septimus Mas 284
Solomon Adr 6
Solomon Adr 6
Solomon Liv 153
Steward Pul 134
Susanah Fay 46
Thomas Bou 80
Thomas Fay 20
Thomas Liv 147
Thomas Log 169
Thomas Mad 201
Thomas Mon 371
Thomas M. Bre 156
Thos. Cly 149
Thos. Hrd 293
Thos. Hrs 314
Thos. Hrs 315
Warner Bar 42
Wilford Bre 159
Will She 226
William Bou 120
William Cly 158
William Fay 13
William Hnd 337
William Liv 151
William Log 161

Clark, cont.
William Log 169
William Mad 200
William(B.Smith) Mad 201
William Mad 203
William Nel 17
William Nel 20
William Nic 61
William Pen 117
William Pul 134
William She 209
William She 235
Willm. War 278
Wm. Bar 31
Wm. Bar 48
Wm. Jef 19
Wm. Mon 382
Wm. Pul 132
Zachariah She 216
Clarke, Agnes Woo 377
Alice Clr 126
Benjamin Woo 378
Benjamin Wsh 331
Cary L. Sco 191
Catharine Grn 253
Charles Clr 124
Cobb V. Cal 7
Ether Sco 168
Francis Mer 325
James Bou 79
James Clr 146
James Mer 325
James Mer 325
James She 216
James She 237
Jesse She 219
John Gar 205
John Gar 206
John Gar 206
John Mer 326
John War 269
John Woo 381
John Wsh 338
Jos. Gar 205
Jos. Hrd 295
Joseph Clr 124
Joseph She 206
Joseph Wsh 331
Micajah Clr 124
Richd. E. Woo 385
Robert Clr 124
Robert Grn 257
Samuel Clr 124
Samuel Clr 124
Samuel Ohi 87
Shadrach Wsh 338
Susanna Wsh 336
Thomas Gar 199
Thomas Gar 205
Thomas Mer 326
William Hrd 301
William Woo 379
Willm. War 247
Willm. War 269
Wm. Gar 205
Wm. Jr Gar 205
Clarkeston, Franky Mer 325
Clarkson, Agness Bou 81
Anselm Bou 81
Anselm, Jr Bou 119
Charles Bre 166
David Bou 80
David, Jr Bou 120
Edward Wsh 337
Henry Wsh 343
Julius Bou 119
Julius, W. Bou 119

Clarkson, cont.
Peter Bou 120
Reubin Bou 119
Clarkston, Drury Mer 324
Joseph Mer 326
Thomas Mer 328
William Mer 325
Clary, David Lew 100
Nachil Hrs 322
Clasby, John Bar 36
Wm. Bar 36
Clatterbuck,Reuben She 231
Claunch, Barnett Ohi 88
Clauser, Leonard Mon 368
Michael Mon 368
Clawson, Jas. Way 354
Peter Bul 175
Richard Clr 125
Clay, Abraham Fay 23
Brittin Pen 111
Charles Clr 125
Green Mad 203
Henry Bou 119
Henry Fay 22
Henry, Senr Bou 120
John Bou 120
Sally Hnd 345
Thos. Mad 203
William Nic 60
Claybrook, James Jes 61
Claycomb, Balser Bre 168
Coonrod Bre 167
Frederick Bre 169
George Bre 168
Peter Bre 168
Claypole, Jesse Bou 81
Clayton, Ambrose Sco 168
David She 236
Francis Cal 17
George Mad 201
George Mon 364
Henry Cum 170
James Bar 21
James Hop 373
James Mon 364
James She 222
John Cal 6
John D. Cal 7
Joseph Nel 14
Mosses Cal 6
Samuel Bou 80
Thomas L. Hnr 359
Warren Mon 377
William Hop 378
William Mad 201
Wm. Jef 33
Claywell, Shadh. Cum 182
Shadrach, Junr. Cum 171
Claxon, Capius Fra 119
Cellestiness Fra 119
William Hnr 364
Claxton, John She 225
Joshua Woo 392
William She 213
William She 225
Clear, Andrew Fle 89
Cleary, John Fle 88
Cleaver, David Wsh 338
Stephen Gra 239
Cleavland, Ely Hrs 312
John Bou 80
Zedock Mon 382
Cleek, John Boo 58
Cleeveland, Ele Fay 20
Cleft, Benjamin Mas 290
Hansley Mas 289
Henry Mas 284

Cleft, cont.
Moses Mas 290
Nelson Mas 288
Cleland, Thomas Wsh 336
Clem, George Mon 352
Jac Hnr 352
James Bar 48
John Hnr 352
John Mon 351
Joseph Mon 351
Pheba Hnr 352
Sally Mon 347
Clemand, John Mon 380
Roger Mon 380
Clemands, John Lin 112
Clemants, Gustavus A. Fle 79
Clemen, Henry Adr 6
Clemens, Henry Bou 120
Jeremiah Mer 342
Clements, Barnett Fra 121
Bazil Wsh 332
Charles Wsh 331
Charles Wsh 334
Joseph Wsh 332
Thomas Hrd 303
William Wsh 337
Wm. Hrd 289
Clemmens, Allen Fra 119
Clemment, Isham She 204
James She 222
Clemments, Edward H. Hnd 329
Leonard Hnd 329
Clemmins, Wm. Gar 236
Clemmons, Benjamin Pen 106
Benjn. Hrs 318
Bent Nel 16
Isaac Pen 106
James Hrs 318
John Clr 125
John Hrs 318
Joseph Chr 80
Osblell.? Nel 41
Oswell Nel 20
Will Cly 153
Clemons, David Lin 112
Thomas Bre 167
Wm. Cas 48
Clemont, Benjamin Mad 202
William Bre 159
Clemonts, John Bou 80
Clendenen, Geo. W. Bou 78
James Rck 166
Josiah Rck 166
Clendennon, Isaas Bar 30
Cleneay, Betty Mas 305
Joseph Mas 305
Cleridence, Frederic Bul 175
Cleveland, Addin Jef 33
Ezer Jef 33
George Jes 59
John She 199
Lerey Cam 28
Marsena Jes 60
Micaqah Hrs 315
Wm. Clr 126
Zachue Jes 60
Clevenger, Uriah Mad 201
Clever, Benj. Nel 15
Clevinger, Jas. Sco 176
Cleyton, Austen Bar 37
Wm. Bar 37
Clice, Wm. Mon 365
Click, John Flo 97
Clifden, James Log 189
Clifford, Edward Hrs 308
John Fle 81
Michael Woo 392
Nancy Fay 20
Clift, George Mad 200
Clifton, Baldwin Mas 286
Edmond Pen 108
Elias Fay 43
George she 215
Hardin Mad 203
Job Cas 40
John Mas 304
Noah Pen 108
Susan Grn 260
William Bul 176
William Wsh 332
Clindennon, Thos. Bou 119
Cline, Daniel Bou 81
David liv 160
Jacob She 235
John Fle 90
John She 235
Nicholas Hnr 361
Peter She 234
William Fle 73
William Hrs 323
Clingensmith, George Bre 161
Clingman, Geo. Fle 80
Clinkenbaird, Wm. Bou 120
Clinkenbeard, Isaac Bou 78
Clinkinbird, Wm . Clr 126
Clinkingbeard, John Fle 75
Joseph Mon 358
Clinton, Archibald Gar 206
Moses Fra 120
Saml. Sco 172
Sion Chr 57
William Fra 121
Cliser, Joseph Bou 120
Cloa, free woman of colour Clr 125
Cloey (free woman) Fay 23
Cloise, James Chr 61
Cloke, Benjn. Woo 385
John Woo 385
Clonch, Christophe Pul 133
Jeremiah Pul 132
Clook, John Mon 374
Clopton, Jno. Hrd 289
Close, Geo. Hrd 284
Geo. Senr Hrd 284
Jno. Hrd 287
Mary Jes 60
Closier, Jacob Chr 67
Closson, Wm. Woo 393
Cloud, Bayles Boo 58
Daniel Fay 22
Jane Boo 58
Jonathan Woo 384
Wm. Boo 58
W. Caleb Fay 14
Clower, Henry Jef 19
Clows, George Gar 235
Cloyd, David Gar 206
Faithful Lin 112
James Cum 174
Jesse Pul 135
John Lin 112
John Mad 204
Samuel Wsh 329
Solomon Grn 247
Solomon Grn 259
Thos. Cum 174
Club, Peter Chr 55
Rezen Log 188
Samuel Log 188
Clubb, Elijah Mad 202
McKinsey Mad 199
William Mad 205
Cluff, Fanney Hrs 321
Reuben Fra 122
Thos. Hrs 321
Clure, Benjn. Jef 19
Elijah Jef 19
Lawrence Jef 19
Clutter, Henry Mas 290
Paul Sco 179
Simon She 233
Clygett, Thos. Woo 388
Coach, John Cas 46
Coal, Elizabeth Mer 326
Francis Mer 327
Robert Cas 48
Coalson, Sanders Chr 104
Coapland, William Wsh 330
Coatney, James Chr 90
Jno. Nel 15
John Gar 206
William She 210
Coatnig, William Chr 66
Coats, Allin Mad 203
Amos Mad 203
Celia Gar 205
Geo. Bar 32
Hezakiah Jef 17
John Bar 29
John War 254
Kinsey Adr 6
Roberts H. Bul 176
Sarah Hnr 360
Thomas Bar 32
Walter Bar 27
Wm. Bar 47
Coalter, Alice Mad 200
Andrew Chr 112
Archibald Chr 112
James Mad 200
John Chr 112
Cob, John Grp 272
Cobb, Jesse Est 6
Jessy Chr 81
John Pen 108
Josiah Cal 4
Judah Sco 178
Phillip Fle 61
Saml. Gal 190
Samuel Fle 61
Shanul. W. Liv 149
Thos. Sco 170
Wm. Sco 170
Cobbs, Ambrose Knx 67
David Fay 13
Cober, Jothn. Nel 16
Cobler, Any Bra 148
Cobourn, Saml. Flo 97
Coburn, John Mas 280
Cocherwills, Simon Mon 352
Cochram, Preston Cas 46
Cochran, Andrew Bou 79
James Bul 175
James Mad 201
Jane Mad 200
John Mad 201
Margaret Nic 60
Nathaniel Bul 175
Robert Mas 305
Robt. Mad 201
Saml. Bou 119
Samuel Mad 201
William Mad 200
Cochron, James But 192
John But 192
Cochrum, John Chr 77

Cock, Henry D. Mad 244
James Mon 372
Cocke, Jesse Way 358
John Nel 21
Richard Wsh 329
Thomas I. Wsh 338
Cockerham, Danl. War 278
William Knx 73
Cockern, Catharine Mul 390
John Fle 80
John, Sur Fle 80
Cockes, Beaveley Cas 45
Cajor Cas 45
Wm. Cas 45
Cockrall, Lewis Jr Lin 112
Cockram, Rubin Bar 39
Cockran, Andrew Bar 46
Isaac Bra 143
James Fle 77
James Jef 32
Philip Bar 25
Wm. Bar 47
Cockrell, Daniel Cly 160
John Cly 159
Simon Cly 160
Cockren, John Fle 80
Cockril, Anderson Bar 37
Wm. Bar 37
Cockrill, Elizabeth Fay 20
John Fay 35
John, Senr Fay 20
Joseph Fay 33
Susanah Fay 20
Wm. War 269
Cockrum, James Lin 112
Cocks, David Way 354
George Way 366
Jas. Way 359
Rebeckah Way 354
Wm. Way 366
Coddle, Mary War 243
Codey, John Cly 153
Coe, Jane Nel 15
Pearson Cum 170
Timothy Hrd 293
Cofer, George Mon 354
Henry Mon 384
Reuben Mon 354
William Bul 175
Coffee, Absm. Adr 6
Ambroce Pul 136
Chesley Adr 6
Cleveland Adr 6
Eli Adr 6
Fieldg. Adr 6
James Adr 6
James Adr 6
Joel Adr 6
John Knx 90
John D. Ohi 73
Jonathen Way 358
Joseph Cum 170
Nathan Adr 6
Nathen Adr 5
Newton Adr 6
Phillip Ohi 81
Richd. Adr 5
Sale Adr 6
Coffer, Ambrose Mon 363
Elijah Mad 199
Thos. Hrd 287
Coffett, Jacob Knx 79
Coffey, Asbon Cas 37
Jesse Cas 46
Lewis Way 370
Coffield, Benjamin Liv 148
Charles S. Liv 147
Coffield, cont.
Demsey Liv 148
Grisham Liv 147
Robert Liv 147
Coffman, Abraham Bou 79
Adam Log 162
David Jes 62
Henry Hop 374
Isaac Hop 375
Jacob Bou 79
Jacob Fra 118
Jacob Wsh 336
John Fra 119
Leonard Log 162
Nelly Fra 118
Coffmon, Benjamin Mul 394
Margaret Mul 394
Cogall, John Lin 112
Coger, James Jes 60
Coghill, Catharine Jes 61
James Gal 191
John Wsh 335
Matthew Wsh 335
Cogir, John Way 361
Coglin, Jos. Hrd 288
Cogswell, James Bou 120
Jediah Fle 62
Cogwell, Frederick Fra 118
John Sco 169
Zacheriah Fra 118
Cogzel, John Grp 269
Cohain, George Mer 323
Cohanour, Jacob Wsh 329
Jacob Wsh 329
Cohern, Andrew Cal 13
Hugh Cal 7
James Cal 7B
James Cal 11
James, Senr Cal 15
John Cal 8
Thomas Cal 14
Cohoon, David Chr 98
Joel Chr 98
Cohorn, John Mer 342
Cohron, Robert She 205
Coil, Jas. Way 372
Jesse Est 7
John Way 372
Patk. Way 372
Thomas Est 7
Coile, Peter Fra 121
Colaver, Elijah Mon 378
Richard Mon 378
Thomas Mon 379
Wm. Mon 378
Colbern, Wm. Mon 372
Colbert, Ann W. Lew 101
Cecelius Bou 80
Cristopher Fay 55
Elexander Fay 59
Isaac Sco 187
Jeremiah Sco 187
Jerh. Sco 187
Jessy Fay 39
John Bar 25
John Sco 174
Marget Wsh 343
Presly Sco 187
Reubin Mul 396
Richard Wsh 343
Robert Wsh 342
Saml. Bar 25
Samuel Fay 13
Thomas Gal 190
William Mas 289
Colchasier, Abraham Mon 379
Colclasier, Jacob Fay 11
John Mon 380
Mary Mon 379
Coldwell, David Liv 151
David Liv 156
John Liv 151
Robert S. Liv 149
Cole, Ann Clr 126
Aquilla Bul 175
Banett Lin 112
Charles (free negro) Jef 18
David Cum 183
David Mon 367
Edwd. Hop 376
Elijah Fra 118
James Bou 80
James H. War 254
Jesse Clr 146
Jesse Fra 121
Jesse Hrd 294
John Bou 80
John Knx 64
John Lin 113
John Liv 157
John War 247
John War 255
Joshua Hnr 354
Joshua Hnr 357
Leroy Clr 125
Mary Mon 364
Micajah Fra 117
Richd. Bar 30
Richd. Jr Woo 381
Richd. Senr Woo 381
Robert Mon 367
Saml. Cum 181
Stephen Bar 50
Will She 227
William Bou 80
William Log 196
William Mas 290
Willis Nel 19
Wm. Cum 165
Wm. J. (free Negro) Jef 18
Zachius War 270
Colehouse, Henry Fay 14
Coleman, Archibald Fay 20
Benjamin Hnr 357
Charles P. Liv 151
Daniel Clr 125
Daniel Hnr 358
Danl. Nel 20
Edward S. Fra 123
Farish Bra 148
Field Bar 46
Francis Hrs 318
Francis Pen 109
George Fay 56
George Ohi 102
Greess Bar 28
Henry Jef 20
Henry Ohi 87
James Chr 104
James Fay 14
James Hrs 323
James Nel 16
James Woo 397
John Bar 35
John Bul 174
John Cam 25
John Fay 56
John Hnr 362
John Jes 61
John Liv 147
John Log 188

Coleman, cont.
John Log 188
John Log 190
Jonathan Jes 61
Joseph Bar 28
Martin Ohi 102
Mosis Chr 98
Nathl. Nel 15
Robert Chr 110
Robert Jef 20
Robert Mer 328
Robt. Bra 145
Robt. Gal 190
Tho. Bar 36
Thomas Fay 36
Thomas Pen 113
Thomas Woo 387
Rhos. Adr 6
Thos. War 273
William Log 187
Colenge, Josiah Mon 377
Coles, Ebinezer War 245
Hugh War 265
Coleson, William Woo 382
Colgan, Henry Grn 248
Colgin, William Grp 278
Colhoon, John Woo 386
Colhoun, John Ohi 94
Coliar, Buford Pul 136
Jno. Pul 136
Colier, Jonathan Mer 323
Moses, Sr Lin 112
Solomon Lin 112
Colins, William Pul 137
Collans, Wm. Pul 133
Collard, Elijah Gra 244
John Chr 103
Richard Gra 242
Collazier, Abm. Hnr 358
Colleer, Moses Gar 236
Collens, Benjamin Bul 176
David, Sr Knx 66
George Bul 176
Isaiah Knx 77
John Bul 176
Spencer Bul 176
Spencer, Jr Bul 176
Thomas Bul 175
William Bul 175
Collet, Wm. Gar 205
Collett, Benj. Nel 14
John She 205
Joseph Jef 18
Peter Fle 61
Saml. Way 362
Colley, Jno. Lew 96
John Liv 151
Seth But 192
William Liv 151
Wm. Lew 96
Wm. Lew 99
Colliah, Charles Pul 134
Richard Pul 134
Collien, Isaac She 206
Collier, Alexr. Lin 113
Aron Gar 236
Claborne Nic 59
Coleman Nic 60
Hamlet Nic 60
Jas. Gar 236
Jno. Sen Mad 205
John Gar 236
John Nic 60
Michael She 200
Moses, Jr Lin 112
Nathaniel She 214
Nelly Pen 113

Collier, cont.
Richard Flo 97
Robt. Gar 236
Sarah Mad 200
Thos. Nel 16
Wm. Jef 20
Collins, Aaron Knx 76
Acquilla Mas 286
Adam Hrd 289
Adam War 244
Ambrose Bra 143
Benjamin Log 177
Daniel Chr 103
David Knx 90
Dennise Fle 86
Dillard Clr 125
Edmund Mas 285
Edmund Nic 59
Edward Log 171
Edward Log 194
Edward Mas 286
Eli She 225
Elijah Mas 283
Elisha Clr 125
Elisha Log 192
Foster Bou 78
Garland Mad 202
Gasper Woo 375
Henry Log 192
Henry War 269
isaac Mas 285
Isaac Nel 15
Jacob Chr 55
Jacob lin 113
Jacob She 225
James Clr 126
James Fay 22
James Fay 43
James Fle 70
James Mad 202
James Pen 111
James She 200
James She 202
Jas. M. Way 358
Jeremiah She 200
Jeremiah Woo 398
Jno. Hrd 283
John Bou 79
John But 192
John Cum 174
John Fle 77
John Jef 26
John Mas 285
John Nel 10
John Woo 386
John Woo 391
John, Snr Fle 70
Jonathan Way 355
Joseph Mad 199
Joseph Woo 392
Josiah Bou 79
Josiah Mad 199
Joshua Fra 120
Kerns She 202
Lewis Bar 29
Lewis Fay 44
Lewis Jes 59
Lewis Sco 176
Marthy Chr 103
Meredith Flo 98
Nancy Hnd 333
Ralph Pen 109
Richard Mad 203
Richd. Sco 167
Richd. War 252
Robert Fay 34
Robert Fra 118

Collins, cont.
Robert, Junr Fay 47
Robert, Junr Fra 117
Robert, Senr Fay 47
Sarah Chr 55
Stephen Est 7
Stephen Nic 61
Thomas Chr 103
Thomas Mad 199
Thomas Mas 285
Thos. Sco 168
Thos. Way 354
Uriah Jes 62
Whitfield Sco 185
William Mad 204
William She 207
Willm. War 258
Wm. Gar 205
Zacy. Adr 5
Collister, Sandy Chr 99
Colly, Andrew Chr 61
Charles Mad 204
Jacob Chr 86
William Chr 61
William Ohi 89
Colman, Philip Bar 28
Colquit, Ransom E. Fra 119
Colrim, John Cam 24
Colston, John Hrs 321
Colter, John Mer 326
John Mer 326
Joseph Mer 323
Matthias Cas 48
Thomas Mer 326
Colton, Henry Nel 14
Colvegrove, Jeri-
miah Grp 271
Colver, Jothn. Nel 19
Colvert, Christ-
opher Fay 32
James Mas 284
Walter Mas 284
William Mas 284
William, Senr Mas 284
Colvet, Mary E. Nel 18
Richd. K. Nel 14
Colvil, Joseph Bou 80
Samuel Bou 80
Colvill, Rosanna Liv 148
Colvin, Charles Bra 144
Charles B. Pen 116
George Pen 113
Henry, Sr Pen 105
James Chr 70
Jobe Chr 69
John Chr 78
John Grp 269
John Lin 113
Joseph Lin 113
Joseph Lin 113
Luke Hrd 298
Mosis Chr 77
Susannah Chr 68
William Lin 112
William Mas 286
Colwell, Joseph Pul 134
Wm. Bra 144
Colyar, John Rck 164
John, Jur Rck 162
John, Ser Rck 160
Micajah Rck 164
Stephen Rck 164
Wm. Rck 159
Comb, Jesse Cum 175
Combes, Edward Nel 18
Combess, Jacob Mas 287
Combs, Andrew She 211

Combs, cont.
Andrew Woo 397
Benjamin, Jr Clr 125
Benjamin, Sr Clr 125
Cuthbert, Jr Clr 125
Cuthbert, Sr Clr 125
Dolly War 257
Elijah Cly 152
Enock Nel 21
Francis Nel 17
Geo. Cly 152
Henry Cly 152
James Sco 172
Jeremiah Flo 97
Jeromiah Cly 152
Jeromiah Cly 155
Jno. Hop 372
Jno. Nel 16
John Clr 125
John Cly 153
John Flo 97
John Lin 113
John Lin 113
John Nel 20
Jonah Hnr 366
Joseph Clr 125
Leonard Nel 20
Mason Cly 153
Nelson Nel 16
Nicolas Cly 153
Rebecca Nel 16
Saml. Grn 263
Saml. Nel 21
Samuel R. Clr 125
Shode Cly 153
Stephen Lin 113
Thomas Bar 27
Thomas Bou 79
Thomas Nel 18
Walter Nel 18
Will Cly 153
William Nel 17
William Nel 20
Willm. Lin 112
Wm. Cas 39
Wm. Grn 253
Comely, Absalom Gar 205
Jas. Jnr Gar 205
Jas. Snr Gar 205
Mary Gar 205
Sabiett Gar 205
Comer, Mary Knx 77
Richard Lin 112
Comes, John Mon 377
Comfort, Daniel Fay 34
Comins, James Bou 80
Commins, John Bou 81
John Fra 118
Matthew, Jr Fra 119
Matthew, Senr Fra 118
Robt. B. Bou 81
Thomas Bou 78
William Fra 119
Committ, Jas. Adr 6
Compliments, Clemr. Nel 18
Compton, Abner Ful 136
Benj. Nel 19
Edmund H. Wsh 338
James Grn 247
John Grn 251
John War 260
Joseph Wsh 330
Mearideth Grn 249
Richd. Grn 252
Saml. Grn 2/9
Thomas Mas 287
Comstock, William Bre 169
Con, James Adr 5
Martin War 249
Conatzer, Nichs. Way 362
Conaway, Lewis Flo 98
Samuel Pen 111
Conckright, Abm. Clr 125
Condela, John Bou 78
Conder, George Mer 327
George Wsh 334
Jacob Bul 176
John Cas 47
John Mer 327
Martin Bul 175
Condit, Byram Ohi 69
Timothy Ohi 72
Uzal Ohi 69
Condra, Jas. Bar 45
John Bar 45
Wm. Bar 45
Condrin, William Chr 99
Condry, Stephen Pul 134
Conelius, Elihu Cly 150
Cones, Jacob Cam 28
Conger, Isaac Log 171
Congers, Wm. Bar 54
Congleton, James Bou 80
William Bou 79
William Hnd 337
Wm. Bou 78
Congo, Isaac Log 191
Joseah Bar 50
Conkerwright, Isaac Cas 45
Conkins, Isaac Hnr 354
Conkright, John Clr 126
Conley, Alexander Fay 56
Andrew N. Chr 113
David Flo 98
Henry Flo 97
James She 215
Jesse She 207
John Fay 37
John Flo 97
Sarah Jes 41
Standford She 236
Thomas Flo 97
Thompson Cam 29
Conley, Wm. Bar 42
Conly, David Bar 39
Conman, Abraham Fay 56
Conn, Andrew She 235
Benjamin Knx 76
Edward Jef 17
James Hnr 365
Jas. Jr Way 360
Jas. Sr Way 361
John Bou 80
Joseph Cum 168
John Gar 206
John Jef 32
Saml. Jef 17
Thomas, Senr Bou 78
Thomas Bul 176
Thomas, Jr Bou 79
William Bou 119
William Hnr 362
Connaway, Christ. Clr 126
Tho. Bar 37
Connel, James Bul 174
John Cal 16
Martha Mad 199
Connell, Jesse, Jr Gal 190
Jesse, Sr Gal 191
Patrick Liv 150
Samuel Gal 190
William, Jr Bul 176
Wm. Boo 58
Connelley, Arthur Mon 353
Connelly, Alexr. Boo 58
Arthr. Boo 58
Francis Mad 199
Isaac Bar 42
Jas. Adr 6
Jno. Nel 15
John Adr 5
John Adr 6
John Mad 199
Levy Lew 99
Robt. Boo 58
Thos. Boo 58
Conely, James Sco 183
Conner, Byram Way 371
Clemon Mon 365
Daniel Pul 132
Francis Log 182
Isham Hop 374
Isham Hop377
Jacob Hop 371
James Jes 41
John Boo 58
John Hrs 307
John Wsh 334
John C. Jef 18
Laurence Cum 173
Lewis Boo 58
Livingston Grn 250
Mary Nel 19
Phillin. Boo 58
Reuben Boo 58
Rice Jes 41
Richard Nel 16
Robt. Way 355
Thomas Nel 18
Thomas Pul 135
Thos. Cas 42
William Bou 120
Wm. Mon 366
Conneway, Will Bou 80
Connier, Jos. War 259
Mordica War 256
Connoh, John Mer 323
Connor, John Clr 125
William Clr 126
William Jes 62
Connote, Conrod Jef 18
Connoway, Peter Sco 188
Connyers, Benjamin She 199
Conover, Gart. Adr 6
James Fay 13
Jno. V. Gal 197
Livy Adr 6
Peter Adr 6
Wm. Bra 141
Conoway, Joseph Nel 18
Conquest, James Fay 39
Conrod, Adam Jef 17
Daniel Jef 33
Samson Liv 155
Val Jef 32
Constable, Samuel Clr 125
Constant, Elijah Grn 266
Isaac Fle 79
Jacob Clr 125
Jacob Fle 71
John Clr 126
John, Jur Fle 72
John, Senr Fle 72
Thomas Clr 125
Wm. Hrd 289
Constantine, William Fra 119
Conway, Hugh Gal 190
Jessy Chr 74
John Gal 191
John Mas 284

Conway, cont.
John Nic 60
Miles Mas 289
Richd. Lew 96
Richd. Lew 97
Thomas But 192
Volentine Cal 10
Wm. War 256
Conyers, David Bar 30
Isaac Mon 374
Conyres, Dennis Pen 110
John Pen 116
Coock, Anthony Lin 113
Charles Clr 126
George Lin 112
Henry Lin 113
John Lin 112
John Lin 113
Lewis Lin 113
Coodle, Richmond Mad 203
Cook, Abraham She 234
Aron Rck 159
Aron Rck 164
Benja. Hop 371
Catherine Grn 259
Clayton Flo 98
Coleman Sco 177
Cullen Liv 153
D.K. John Sco 191
Daniel Bre 162
Daniel Mas 283
David Bar 30
David Chr 102
David Est 6
David Lin 112
Dawson Jes 59
Edward Mul 391
Gibbs Way 361
Grove Gar 206
Henry Bar 51
Hugh Log 170
Isaac Sco 186
Isain Nel 18
James But 192
James Cal 17
James Chr 61
James Wsh 333
Jane Gar 205
John Adr 6
John Log 180
John Nic 58
John Sco 169
John War 247
Jos. Jr Log 180
Joseph Log 172
Joshua Grn 248
Jsaac Bou 81
Loftus Rck 163
Mary Bra 150
Mathew Fay 22
Moses Cum 175
Nichl. Nel 15
Nichls. Nel 42
Peter Nic 60
Philip Nel 15
Randolph Pul 133
Robert Nel 15
Robert Sco 189
Ruben Chr 88
Rubin Chr 55
Seth She 207
Stephen Mad 201
Thos. Cum 171
Vallantine Jes 61
Wiles Mon 360
William Bou 81
William Hrs 309

Cook, cont.
William Knx 77
William Mer 324
William Nel 20
William Rck 163
William She 234
William Wsh 335
William, Jr Hnr 361
Zion Bar 39
Coo[illegible] Alice War ?72
[illegible]ge Adr 6
Giles War 272
Henry Adr 6
John Adr 6
John Woo 383
John W. War 272
Mathias Cal 13
S. Payton Gar 205
Stephen Wsh 342
Thos. Grn 263
Will Hnr 369
Wm. W. She 239
Cookendaffer, Michael Hrs 308
Cookendorfer, Bd. Nel 10
Cookley, Benjamin Log 178
Cooksey, Joseph Cum 181
Wilson Log 188
Cooksy, Lidston Log 173
Cool, Benjamin Bre 162
Jacob Clr 125
Jacob Clr 126
Philip Bre 162
Cooley, Danl. Adr 6
James Fay 14
James Mad 202
James Mer 327
Jesse Jef 18
John Adr 6
John Cas 47
John, Sin Cas 48
Joseph War 260
Matthew Mer 325
Perrin Wsh 330
Reuben Cas 46
Coolly, Daniel Knx 82
Coolson, James Knx 77
Coombes, Adin Hrd 284
Coombs, Saml. Hrd 297
Coomer, Daniel Pul 133
Richard Pul 133
Wm. Pul 133
Cooms, James Log 174
Saml. Log 174
Coon, George Hrs. 313
Jacob Hrs 309
Solloman Hrs 309
Cooney, Ann Jef 28
Daniel Mer 324
Mary Mer 324
Coonfield, Isaac Hnr 358
Coonrod, Abraham Mon 379
Catharine Hrs 307
George Bou 79
Henry Fle 67
Isaac Hrs 319
Jacob Gra 242
Jacob Hrs 311
John Hrs 307
Coones, Frederick Fay 45
Coons, Adam Jef 18
Benjamin Hnr 364
Charles She 212
George Fay 13
Henry, Senr Fay 47
John Fay 46
John Hnr 364

Coons, cont.
John Mon 368
Joseph Hnr 355
Joshua Fay 46
Letty Mon 369
Martin Fay 33
Martin Fay 51
Martin Fay 55
Samuel Fay 46
Thomas Fay 46
William Hnr 355
Coonse, James Bou 79
Coontz, Philip Hnd 328
Cooper, Adam Mon 380
Archibald Cl[illegible] 126
Archibald, Sr Cl[illegible] 126
Bazil Wsh 329
Becky Hrd 293
Benjn. Nel 17
Calep Lin 113
Charles Fle 65
Charles Grp 275
Charles She 198
Christian Cam 25
Danl. Sco 175
David But 192
Devalt Mas 288
Elizabeth Mas 283
Fielding Mas 286
Francis Nel 14
Frederick Way 355
George Mon 358
Henry Mon 365
Henry Ohi 80
Isaac Mas 288
Isaac Way 364
Jacob Fle 84
James Lin 112
James Lin 113
James Mer 324
James Pul 133
James Pul 135
James She 226
Jani Mas 283
Jechonias Mas 283
Jemima She 203
Jesse Mad 203
Jesse Mas 280
Jesse Mas 286
John But 192
John Cam 27
John Clr 125
John Fle 76
John Flo 97
John Hnd 338
John Lin 113
John Log 187
John Mad 202
John Mad 202
John Mad 204
John Mas 282
John Mas 290
John Nel 20
John Nic 58
John Nic 59
Jonathan Hnr 360
Josep Pul 132
Joseph Clr 126
Joseph Fay 41
Joseph Mas 281
Layton Est 3
Levin Jef 18
Malichia Pul 136
Mary Cal 13
Micagen Pul 135
Murdock Lew 100
Mycage Bra 151

Cooper, cont.
Nancy Bra 148
Nancy Fay 14
Nathan Gar 206
Nathl. Nel 20
Nathl. Way 369
Osborn Wsh 330
Robert But 192
Robert But 192
Robert Mer 325
Saml. Gal 191
Saml. Sco 169
Samuel Mas 286
Samuel Mas 288
Sarah Fay 13
Sherid Knx 85
Spencer Lew 100
Spencer Woo 384
Tassy Cal 8
Tho. Hop 375
Thomas Woo 400
Vincent Mas 282
William Fay 41
William Ohi 75
William Pul 134
William She 201
Wm. Gar 236
Wm. Hrd 289
Wm. Mon 365
Wm. She 241
Coopper, David Pen 114
John Pen 106
Coos, Margaret Lin 112
Cootes, Shepherd She 209
Cope, Andrew Cly 156
Andrew Knx 85
David Fay 51
David Sco 171
David Sco 177
James Flo 98
Jesse Sco 177
Jonathan Sco 177
Jonathan, Senr Sco 177
Joseph Fay 51
Martin Mul 403
Wileigh Cly 159
William Flo 97
James Cal 16
Jno. Hrd 285
Copeland, John Log 180
John Mer 327
Samuel Fra 121
Copelin, Jacob Gar 206
Samuel Chr 60
Thomas Gar 206
Copenhafer, Jno. Pul 134
Copenhaver, Samuel Way 354
Copher, Ezekiel Clr 125
Jacob Clr 125
Jesse Clr 125
Thomas Clr 126
Copland, Lot Cum 169
Coplin, Abel Chr 71
Jms. Chr 83
Coppage, Alexander Wsh 330
Alexander Wsh 330
Fielding Pen 105
James Wsh 330
Travis Wsh 338
Wm. Nel 15
Coppedge, Charles Sco 185
John Sco 177
Rhoden Sco 182
Corathers, James Jes 59
William Jes 61
Corban, James Sco 183

Corban, cont.
John Sco 183
Corben, Lewis Bou 120
Corbet, Jacob Wsh 330
Corbin, Abraham Nic 59
Elijah Bra 145
James Bou 78
James Hop 377
John Jes 62
Martin Mon 378
Thomas Clr 125
William Bou 78
Cord, Asbury Nic 61
Jacob Fle 81
James Fay 42
Joseph Cam 31
Milka Fle 85
Zakeus Fle 85
Cordeley, Wm. Lew 95
Corder, Wm. War 280
Cordill, James Flo 97
Matthew Flo 97
Sampson Flo 97
William Flo 97
Cordry, Hozea Mas 284
James Mas 283
John Mas 283
William Mas 283
Core, John Jef 20
Corey, John Fle 64
Corhon, Andrew Log 190
Cork, Henry Adr 11
Jacob Grn 261
Cormack, Archabald Cal 7
Corn, Andrew Wsh 334
Aron Liv 152
David Gra 240
Ebenezer Clr 126
Geo. Hnr 351
George Boo 58
George Mer 323
Jesse Mer 328
Joseph Mer 323
Joseph Woo 394
Solomon Mer 328
Timothy Mer 323
William Gra 240
Cornelias, Jessy Chr 58
Levy Chr 58
Cornelison, Conrad Mad 205
Jesse Mad 205
John Mad 205
John, Jr Mad 205
Moses Mad 205
Cornelius, Abner Mad 203
Austin Mul 394
Jno. Mad 203
John Boo 58
John Chr 62
Wm. Boo 58
Cornell, Solomon Bul 175
Solomon, Jr Bul 176
William Bul 176
Cornett, Lidia Cly 153
Nathaniel Cly 153
Park Lin 112
Robt. Cly 155
Roger Cly 155
Saml. Cly 153
Will Cly 153
Cornick, Richard Bou 78
Cornish, George D. Woo 384
Cornog, David Fle 82
Corns, Absalam Mon 350
Cornwall, Geo. Hop 378
Jno. Hnr 351
Thomas Fle 87

Cornwell, Charles Jef 20
Daniel War 266
Dempsey Chr 74
Edd. War 255
Elisha War 270
Jeremiah Jef 20
Peter Jef 19
Simon Jef 20
Wm. Jef 20
Corr, James Pul 132
Cortney, Thomas Clr 126
Corum, John Mad 204
Coruthers, Thos. Nel 16
Corvin, Wm. Grn 247
Corwine, Amos Mas 290
George Mas 281
Richard Mas 290
Coryell, Cornelius Mas 289
Joseph Mas 281
Cosbey, Charles Mad 202
James Liv 160
Cosby, Fortunatus Jef 25
John Bar 36
Overton Nic 61
William H. Woo 400
Cosgrove, Hugh Jef 19
Cosley, Overton Nel 14
Cossa, Robt. Bar 28
Tho. Bar 28
Tho. Sinr Bar 28
Cossey, Curtes Fay 58
Costilow, Edd. War 270
Coston, Aham Jef 19
Coteny, James Hrs 309
Cotes, John Grn 259
Cotner, Frederick Wsh 338
Cotnor, John Wsh 334
Cottell, Will Cly 152
Cotten, John Bou 120
Cotterel, Henry Hrd 284
Jno. Hrd 284
Joshua Hrd 284
Cottingham, Charles Hnd 343
Cottingin, Wm. Lew 102
Cottle, Joseph Mon 348
Cotton, Berry Cal 12
Edward Nel 17
George T. Woo 393
Henry Fay 20
James Bre 161
Jas. Gar 206
John Fay 38
John Woo 379
Jothn. Nel 20
Nathl. Nel 17
Robert Nel 14
Temple Nel 17
William Clr 125
William Fay 20
William Nel 15
Young Log 196
Cottonham, George Jef 18
Cottrell, John Knx 89
Samuel Mas 286
Couch, John War 268
Moses Chr 115
Couchman, Frederick Clr 126
Melekiah Bou 78
Peggy Bou 120
Couchmon, Benedk. Bou 78
George Bou 78
Coudery, John Fay 60
Coulson, John Knx 82
Coulter, Isaiah Wsh 335
Mark Wsh 330
William Mas 285

Name	County	Page
Countryman, Jno.	Nel	19
Counts, Elisha	Liv	149
Jacob	Bou	79
Joseph	Bou	79
Courey, Polly	Log	181
Robert	Log	183
Courney, Archibald	Way	354
Courter, Abram.	Boo	58
Jos.	Boo	58
Courtney, Ann	Hrs	309
Barba.	Hrs	316
Chas. (S)	Hrs	308
Daniel	Hrs	308
Elias	Hrs	308
John	Hrs	307
John	Hrs	308
Robert	Mas	281
Samuel	Hrs	308
Steven	Hrs	315
Thomas	Mas	289
Courtny, Archibald	Way	354
Michael	Way	354
Cousens, William	Nel	10
Cousins, Jessee	Nel	17
Coutz, Henry	Hrd	290
Coventree, George	Log	194
William	Mer	323
Coverdill, Richard	Fay	39
Covert, Cornelius	Mer	323
Daniel	Mer	325
David	Wsh	329
Isaac	Mer	323
John	Mer	323
John	Mer	325
Masten	Bra	145
Covington, Abel	Jef	19
Asa	War	262
Benjn.	War	258
Benjn.	War	261
Benjn.	War	264
Edmond	War	245
Eijh.	War	261
Jos.	War	247
Joseph	War	262
Melchazadeck	Chr	111
Nathal.	War	261
Peter	War	262
Phillip	Chr	112
Richard	Log	173
Robert	Mad	199
Thomas	Fay	22
William	Mad	202
Cowan, Andrew	Cum	186
David	Cum	186
David G.	Nel	10
Henry	Hnr	359B
Hugh	Bou	120
Hugh	Sco	167
James	Cum	186
James	Jef	18
John	Jef	33
Wm.	Cum	186
Coward, Willis	Grn	263
Cowbird, James	Grn	246
Simeon	Grn	255
Cowden, Anthony	Fay	31
Elizabeth	Sco	183
James	Sco	168
John	Wsh	330
Cowel, Abraham	Bra	147
Cowen, Andrew	Pul	132
Gilmore	Pul	133
Isaac	Nic	59
James	Pul	133
Jas.	Way	353
Jno.	Pul	132
Lurauy	War	267
Cowen, cont.		
Peter	War	278
Cowenhown, Joseph	Wsh	329
Cowgil, Danl.	Cam	30
Joseph	Cam	30
Martin	Cam	30
Cowgill, Elisha	Mas	287
Ralph	Woo	390
Cowherd, Jonathan	Grn	247
Willis	Grn	247
Cowhorn, Jno.	Pul	135
Wm.	Mon	366
Cowin, Hannah	Mer	324
John	Mer	325
Thomas	Pul	136
Cowles, Henry	War	248
Cowls, Edmand	War	248
Cowly, John	Bul	175
Cowne, Augustus	Lew	97
Cownover, Domineus	Woo	380
Peter	Woo	379
Rachel	Woo	380
Cowser, Thomas	Liv	147
Cowsert, John	Liv	160
Cox, Abel	Cum	182
Allen	Pul	137
Amos	Knx	65
Amos	Knx	73
Any.	Way	372
Aris	Hnr	363
Asa	Fra	120
Benjamin	Bre	160
Benjamin	Mad	202
Benjamin	Ohi	75
Benjamin	She	228
Benjamin L.	Fra	120
Benjamin S. Jr	Fra	121
Beverly	Hrd	284
Cajor	Cas	45
Christopher	Knx	71
Coleman	War	248
Daniel	Gra	237
Daniel	Sco	189
Danl.	Sco	177
Danl.	Sco	178
David	Knx	72
David	Nel	14
David	Nel	17
Edward	Lin	113
Enoch	Mas	284
Ezechal	Chr	97
Ezechal	Chr	1[illegible]
Federick	War	25[illegible]
Flory	Flo	98
Frederick	Knx	83
Gambrel	Hrd	284
George	Cal	13
Geseph	Mul	403
Isaac	Clr	126
Isaac	Fle	76
Isaac	Nel	16
James	Adr	6
James	Clr	125
James	Est	8
James	Nel	17
James	Ohi	75
James	Pul	134
James	Woo	379
Jesse	Knx	85
Jesse	Mad	205
Jesse	Way	367
Jessy	Chr	99
Jessy	Chr	106
Jno.	Grn	260
Jno.	Nel	16
John	Adr	6
John	Bou	79
Cox, cont.		
John	Cam	25
John	Fay	13
John	Fay	57
John	Fra	118
John	Fra	120
John	Gra	237
John	Knx	81
John	Knx	83
John	Mon	353
John	Mul	391
John	War	249
John	War	248
John	Wsh	333
John	Wsh	343
John, Sr	Gra	242
John, Sr	Knx	81
Jonathan	Mad	200
Jonathan	She	217
Jos.	Cly	151
Jos.	Sco	167
Joseph	Knx	82
Joseph	Mad	205
Joseph	Mas	280
Joseph	Ohi	77
Joseph	Sco	182
Lazares	Gal	191
Matthew	War	267
Meridith	Ohi	84
Moses B.	Bar	46
Moses L.	Bar	46
Nathan	Knx	65
Nathan	Knx	80
Nathan, Jr	Knx	83
Phenias	War	248
Phenis	Gra	237
Philip	Bou	78
Phineas	War	247
Pleasant	Hop	376
Richard	Jef	18
Richard	Lin	112
Richard	Wsh	334
Russell, Junr	Fra	118
Russell, Senr	Fra	118
Saml.	Boo	58
Saml.	Lew	99
Samuel	Knx	69
Samuel	Lew	99
Solomon	Knx	74
Stephen	Clr	126
[illegible]ephen	Knx	72
[illegible]ton	[illegible]	[illegible]83
[illegible]no.	Mad	202
Thomas	Fra	121
Thomas	Knx	69
Thomas	Mer	327
Thomas	Mer	328
Thomas	Ohi	102
Tunstall	Fra	122
William	Knx	76
William	Knx	82
William	Lew	98
William	Nel	18
William	Ohi	75
William L.	Fra	122
Wm.	Lew	104
Wm.	Sco	178
Wyatt	Ohi	103
Zekiel	Fle	71
Coy, Benjn.	Nel	19
Christopher	Mad	201
Danl.	Hrd	291
Jno.	Nel	19
John	Hrd	301
Moses	Hrd	292
Samuel	Gar	205
Thomas	Gar	205

Coy, cont.
William Gar 205
Wm. Hrd 292
Coye, Saml. Mad 203
Coyle, Cornelius Fay 13
Coyne, Cornels. Hnr 362
Cozart, Josiph Chr 95
William Hrd 301
Cozens, Richard Mas 286
Crabb, Charles She 227
Jere Hnr 360
John Gar 206
Crable, Christo Jef 17
Crabtree, Abraham Cum 182
Benjamin Chr 82
Hiram Cum 182
Isaac Way 351
Isaiah Hop 376
James Chr 63
James Chr 63
Jas. Way 355
Jemima Ohi 99
Jessee Ohi 101
John Chr 101
Moses Ohi 101
Richard Way 351
Saml. Way 351
Thos. Grn 251
Wm. Cum 182
Cracraft, Joseph Mas 287
Reuben Mas 287
Samuel Mas 287
Thomas Mas 287
Craddock, Archer Bar 53
John Log 172
Richd. C. Bar 53
Thomas Ohi 78
Cradie, John Bou 80
Cradlebow, William Mad 203
Cradock, Robert War 247
Crafford, David Hrs 309
Samuel Wsh 334
Craft, Archelaus Flo 97
Fanny B. Mon 368
Frederick Chr 101
Jacob Liv 149
Michal Cum 180
Craften, Henry Fle 73
Crafton, James She 238
Crag, Whitfield Bra 143
Crage, John Chr 97
John Chr 105
Craig, Andrew Knx 63
Benj. Jr Gal 191
Benj. Sr Gal 191
David Knx 70
David She 216
Elijah Gal 197
Elijah (C) Gal 198
Elijah Sco 171
Elisabith Lin 112
George W. Knx 70
James Cam 28
James Cum 186
James Fay 37
James Fle 74
James Grn 259
James Hrs 311
James Lin 112
James Mon 353
James Mon 357
James Mul 408
James She 205
James She 241
Jeremiah Gal 190
John Boo 58
John Cal 8

Craig, cont.
John Gra 242
John Hrs 312
John Hrs 322
John Mas 304
John Mon 360
John Ohi 88
John Sco 190
John Way 358
John B. Liv 155
John D. Sco 167
John H. Boo 58
Joseph Fay 37
Joseph Fay 37
Joseph mother Fle 70
Joseph Fra 122
Lewis Fra 122
Lewis Gal 190
Lewis, Senr Mas 290
Margret Fay 22
Nathl. Sco 169
Phillip Boo 58
Reuben Sco 185
Robert Hrs 311
Robert Hrs 314
Robert Mon 354
Robert Mon 359
Robert, Jr Knx 70
Robert, Sr Knx 73
Robin L. Mon 371
Robt. Cam 29
Robt. Hrd 299
Samuel Jes 59
Samuel Mon 363
Stuman Gal 190
Thomas Gal 191
Thomas Nel 16
Toliver Sco 181
Toliver, Jur Sco 169
William Flo 98
William Grp 272
William Hrs 314
William Jes 62
William Knx 64
Willm. Lin 112
Wm. Mon 348
Craigg, Charles Gar 236
John Gar 236
Craighead, Robert Mas 282
Craigmile, James Hrs 322
Craigmiles, John Sco 192
Craigmyle, Matt Gal 190
Crail, Abslam. Cam 27
John Cam 33
Crain, James Fle 63
John Chr 85
Samuel, Senr Fle 64
Craine, Aaron Fay 22
Lewis Fle 77
Lewis Fle 90
Samuel, Senr Fle 77
Crale, James Pen 105
Wilson Pen 105
Crall, Christian Jes 62
Cramer, Peter Lin 113
Cramns, Nancy Adr 7
Crams, William Fle 90
Crane, Abrahma Jes 59
Daneil Est 5
Job Est 5
John Mer 327
John Pul 133
Joseph Pul 133
Nimrod Pen 112
Simeon Mon 354
William Pen 112
Crank, James Knx 77

Crank, cont.
Joseph Grp 273
William Flo 98
Cranmer, George Sco 188
Crapper, Laban Bou 80
Crass, George Flo 97
Craten, Caleb Est 8
Craught, Susanah Lin 113
Craul, Jacob Fay 22
Crave, Ely Chr 65
Craven, James Nel 19
John Nel 20
John Wsh 330
Levi Nel 17
Cravens, David Jes 62
Elijah Jes 60
James Jes 62
Jeremiah Boo 58
Jessee, Junr Ohi 78
Joseph Chr 84
Craver, George Bou 80
Jacob Bou 80
Craverson, Rebeca She 203
Craviens, Armon Jes 60
Cravin, David Jes 60
Hirom Adr 6
Cravins, Ester Chr 110
Jerramiah Chr 82
Jesse Ohi 69
Jessy Chr 82
Nehemiah Cal 7B
Polly Chr 101
William Chr 69
Craw, Peter Jes 61
Wm. Cal 17
Crawford, Abel Log 182
Alexander Fra 122
Alexander Pul 136
Archibald Est 4
Daved Bar 52
Hezekiah Sco 179
Hugh Fay 13
Hugh Mer 324
Hugh Mer 341
Hugh Nel 15
Isaac Gar 205
James Fle 75
James Hnr 353
James Hnr 366
James B. Sco 189
Jas. Bar 45
John Cum 171
John Hrd 281
John Mon 364
John She 202
John War 244
Joseph Est 3
Joseph Fle 81
Joshua Mas 305
Josiah Nel 14
Mason Ohi 89
Michael War 244
Nathan She 205
Orson Est 4
Phebee Bar 53
Rebecka Fay 20
Richard Lew 99
Saml. Nic 59
Saml. She 201
Saml. Junr Bre 158
Samuel Ohi 90
Thomas Mer 327
Thos. Grn 247
Thos. War 259
Valuntine Est 4
William Bre 156
William Hnr 359A

Crawford, cont.
William Mas 281
William Nic 61
William She 207
Wm. Hrd 299
Wm. Lew 97
Wm. Nel 15
Wm. Nel 18
Crawler, Wm. She 231
Crawley, Saml. Adr 6
Crawlley, Samuel Fay 22
Craycraft, Mary Mon 358
Wm. Mon 354
Crays, William Mer 324
Creacraft, Charles Grp 269
Creacroft, John Grp 271
Cready, David Hrd 292
Creager, Daniel Wsh 337
John Wsh 337
John Adam Wsh 337
Thomas Wsh 337
Creal, Elijah Hrd 288
Richd. Hrd 296
Creamo, Henry Bul 175
Creason, John Mon 377
Creath, Robert Mad 201
William Mad 201
Cree, William Flo 98
Creed, Augustin She 237
Elijah, jr Woo 400
Elijah, Senr Woo 396
Isaac War 246
Creek, Jacob War 246
John Bar 40
Killian War 246
Creekman, Eliza-beth War 272
Creekpon, Michal Grp 272
Creel, Charles Adr 6
Durram Adr 6
Hedger Adr 5
John Adr 6
Simeon Adr 5
Creeson, John Mad 200
Creighton, Henry Sco 190
Robert Sco 179
Cremer, Moses Jef 33
Crenshaw, Benja. Bar 34
Bluford Bul 175
Cosby Bul 174
James Bul 175
Jno. Bar 51
Joel Sco 168
Lewis She 214
Nelsen Bul 175
Overton Bul 175
Thompson Bar 46
William Fay 44
Creson, James Adr 6
Cress, Valentine Bou 79
Creth, Jacob Woo 386
Crewdson, James Log 171
Crews, Anderson Mad 204
David Mad 204
David, jr Mad 204
David, jur (Tho's Son) Mad 200
Elijah Mon 373
Jeremiah Hnr 359A
Joseph Mad 244
Lucy Hnr 360
Richard Jes 62
Robert Jes 60
Sarah Mad 204
Thomas Mad 243
Thomas, jr Mad 205
William Mad 200
Crews, cont.
William Pul 134
Criag, John Fle 70
Crickmore, Ballen-tine Knx 71
Crider, Daniel Liv 152
Jacob Liv 152
Samuel Liv 152
Crier, Thomas Log 169
William Log 169
William Log 179
Crigler, Abraham Bul 175
Jno. Mad 205
Crim, Ambrose Clr 126
Elias Fay 35
Elias Fay 51
Enoch Clr 125
Fielding Fay 51
Jacob Hnr 354
Joseph Fay 51
Martin She 235
Moses She 231
Nimrod War 243
Willis Hnr 359A
Crisley, Elias Jef 18
Crisswell, James Hrs 314
Saml. Mas 280
Crist, Abraham Jef 17
George She 202
Henry Bul 175
Jacob Nel 15
Nicholas, Jr Bul 175
Nicholas, Sr Nel 18
Cristean, Martin S She 218
Cristian, Judy Fay 43
Cristman, Luke Gar 206
Crostopher, Elisa-beth Lin 112
Cristy, James She 234
William She 234
Criswell, Robert Hnr 360
Critchfield, Will-iam Mas 283
Critendon, Charles W. Fay 46
Crittenden, Judith Woo 397
Crittendon, Rich.H Hnr 363
Crocker, John Mon 352
Crocket, Newbold Fay 43
Paterson Chr 102
Robert Cum 185
Robert Mon 360
Crockett, Anthony Fra 119
Ephm. Way 357
Hambleton Fra 117
James Clr 125
John Gar 236
John Way 357
Joseph Jes 60
Robert Clr 125
Robert Jes 60
William Fra 117
Wm. Junr Fra 117
Crofford, Wm. Cam 29
Crofton, Anthony She 225
Crogzort, Jesse Cum 174
Croly, Benjamin Chr 85
Cromer, Jno. Pul 136
Cromstalk, Oliver Hrd 298
Cromwell, Fielding Jef 19
Joshua Jes 61
Oliver Wsh 338
Richard Jes 61
William Jes 61
Croock, Hezekiah Cly 156
Crook, Hezekiah She 227
Jeremiah Pen 110
Crook, cont.
John Pen 116
Michael Jef 17
Zachariah She 237
Crooke, John Mad 205
Ozias Mad 202
Crooks, James Mon 375
John Mon 354
Usual Mon 353
Cropper, Bela Hnr 367
James Hnr 366
Jona. Hnr 366
Noble Hnr 353
Crosby, George Woo 378
John Sco 176
Simeon Gal 197
Crosdel, Abraham Hrs 323
Crose, Hnery Cly 125
Jonathan Bou 79
Levie Bou 119
Michael Bou 79
Cross, Benja. Gar 206
Drurey War 263
Drury War 280
Humphrey Wsh 336
Israel Adr 7
James Mul 389
James Mul 408
Jeremiah Bul 175
Joel Mad 203
John Cal 12
John Fay 13
John Log 192
John Sco 193
Joseph Cam 33
Joseph Woo 378
Joshua Mad 203
Robert Cum 183
Solomon Adr 7
William Mad 200
William Mul 408
Wm. Cum 183
Wm. Hnr 365
Zachariah Mad 200
Zachriah Log 186
Crossby, Joseph Mas 281
Katharine Mas 281
Robert Mas 285
Crossgrave, Daniel Wsh 329
Crossley, Moses Mas 286
Moses, Jun Mas 281
Crosslin, Joab Hop 378
Crossly, William Mas 285
Crosswhite, Absalom Mon 356
John Liv 155
Crosthwart, Isaac Clr 125
Mary Clr 125
Saml. Clr 125
Wm. Clr 125
Croswhite, Perry Hrs 323
Thomas Bou 78
Wm. Hrs 322
Crothers, Susannah Fay 39
Crouch, Aron Cas 40
Brihd. War 260
Charles Mul 406
David Bou 79
David Bou 79
David War 274
Francis Est 5
George Est 8
James Cum 183
John Bou 79
John Grn 248
John Hrs 318
Jonathan Bou 79
Jonathan Mon 362

Crouch, cont.
Joseph Bou 79
Robert Wsh 337
William Chr 100
Wm. Cum 184
Croucher, Robt. Gar 206
William Mad 204
Croumbaugh, Jacob Fra 122
Crouse, John Bou 80
Peter Fay 13
Crow, Andrew Lin 113
Basil Bul 175
David Grp 277
George Fle 87
Henry Bul 175
Jacob Mer 327
James Lin 112
James Mer 324
Joel Cum 170
John Clr 126
John Mon 358
John Nel 19
John She 235
Joshua Ohi 68
Leonard Bou 120
Richard Clr 126
Samuel Bul 175
Samuel Pul 132
Thomas Jef 19
Thomas Pul 132
Walter Lin 112
Warner Ohi 86
William Nel 19
Willian, Snr Lin 112
Crowder, Burrell War 269
James Hnd 342
Philip Grn 246
Polly Sco 167
Reuben Wsh 329
Starling Jes 62
Wm. Gal 190
Crowdus, William Wsh 333
Crowe, Robert Chr 108
Crowel, Calvin Mas 301
Crowford, Jno. Nel 14
Crowley, Nancy She 232
William Ohi 87
Crowly, Charles Hop 372
Prior Hop 375
Crownover, Benja. Hop 372
Gilbert Fle 79
James Fle 77
John Hop 372
Croxton, Cornelius Jef 18
Crozier, John Nel 10
Cruce, Isaac Liv 158
Crucher, Matthew Lew 102
Cruise, James Bar 32
Redmond Bar 50
Crum, Adam Flo 98
Elizabeth Jef 19
Henry Flo 98
Rebecka Lin 113
Crumbaugh, Solomon Sco 183
Crumbough, Conrod Log 183
John Fay 23
Crume, Charles Bre 161
Jesse Nel 21
Jessee Nel 17
Jno. Nel 41
John Nel 20
Philip Nel 14
Richard Nel 14
William Bre 160
Crumel, Vincen Fay 42
Crumes, Ralph Sr Bre 160
Crumfort, John Jef 20
Crummel, Benjamin Fay 60
Joseph Fay 48
Crummey, Geo. Cam 32
Crump, Havillah War 281
James Clr 126
John Bou 80
John Jes 62
Joseph Bou 79
Joshua Bar 32
Shewood Bou 80
Crums, Ralph, Jr Bre 160
Cruse, James War 250
Cruson, King Mas 282
Crutcheloe, James Bre 161
Crutcher Cebert She 204
Henry Bar 19
Henry Fra 122
Hugh Jes 61
Isaac Woo 394
Jabez Mas 280
James Hrd 281
James Jes 61
John Jes 59
John Mas 281
Patsy Fra 122
Reuben Fra 121
William Nel 17
Crutchfield, Citon Pul 136
John Fra 117
John Sco 171
Nicholas Clr 125
Thomas Jef 31
Wm. Jef 17
Wm. Jef 33
Crutchloe, John Bul 176
Crutchlow, James Hrs 318
Moses Hrs 320
Wm. Jef 19
Crutsinger, George Jef 28
Cruzan, Benjamin Mas 285
Crylick, Francis Mas 305
Crystal, William Fle 66
Cud, Jonithan Chr 98
Cugle, John Fay 20
Culberson, David Clr 125
David Clr 126
Margarett Sco 171
Sarah Clr 125
Culbertson,
Alexdr. Bou 71
David Lin 112
David Lin 113
Francis Bou 78
James Mas 281
Jos. Bou 80
Robert Mas 286
Robt. Bou 78
Samuel Mas 301
Thos. Bou 78
Culbison, John Mul 397
Cull, James Wsh 330
John Hnr 353
John Wsh 337
O. James Mas 288
Samuel Mer 341
Thomas Wsh 337
Culleham, Isaac Cly 156
Cullem, Edwd. N. Way 370
Wm. Way 369
Cullen, Charles Fay 22
William Mas 285
Culley, William Woo 387
Cullin, Benjn. War 246
Charles Sco 185
Cullum, Susanna Clr 125
Thomas Clr 125
Cullumber, Henry Mad 202
Culp, Cornilius Grp 273
Danl. Bar 22
Easter Bou 81
Thos. Nic 60
Tilman Grp 273
Culton, John Knx 75
John Mer 325
Joseph Knx 75
Culver, Benja. Est 8
Benjamin Bul 174
John Est 2
Jothn. Nel 19
Culverson, Alexr. War 269
Cumbers, James Mas 283
Cumbes, Saml. Cas 40
Cuming, James Flo 98
Cumings, Asa War 276
Asa War 276
Christo. Bra 153
Daniel Rck 162
Jas. War 272
Moses Rck 162
Stephen Rck 164
Willm. War 276
Cumins, Jacob Bou 120
James Mad 201
Jesse Log 172
John Bou 120
Joseph Hrs 311
Melkier Grp 272
William Hrs 311
Cummings, Abram Mer 323
Anthony Lew 100
Cornelius Jef 18
Henry Mer 323
Henry Mer 325
John Jef 18
John Mer 323
John Mer 325
Mary Jef 18
Michl. Nel 15
Moses Bre 160
Saml. Lew 99
Thos. Lew 99
William Bre 166
Wm. Jef 18
Cummins, Andrew Cum 167
Andrew Sco 180
Benjamin Clr 125
Daniel Clr 125
Elizabeth Gar 206
James Mer 328
Hugh Knx 82
Jas. Gar 236
John Clr 125
John Knx 64
John Log 172
John Nel 20
Joseph Pen 115
Joshua Mer 328
Moses Ohi 68
Ro. G. Nel 20
Robert Mas 286
Saml. Bar 46
Sary Gra 239
Thos. Sco 189
William Clr 125
William Clr 125
William Knx 76
Zacheriah Hnr 358
Cumpstock, Linden Fay 13
Cumpton, Aron Chr 94
Bent Nel 14
Burris Gar 206
Jacob Jef 18
Joel Bre 164
Joel Mer 327

Name	County	Page
Cumpton, cont.		
Kenith	Cam	30
Matthew	Bre	162
Richard	Jef	19
Robert	Mer	327
William	Bre	162
Cumstalk, Elizabeth	Knx	83
Isaac	Knx	74
Joseph	Knx	74
Wm.	Knx	64
Cumuns, James	Flo	105
Cundiff, Benjamin	Pul	137
James	Pul	134
Jno.	Pul	132
John	Cas	40
John	Cly	154
John	Ohi	86
John, Senr	Ohi	86
Lewis	Cas	38
Mashack	Pul	132
Richd.	Adr	6
Shadrick	Pul	133
Wm.	Cas	41
Cuning, Daniel	Mon	359
Cuningham, Jas.	Cly	149
John	Cal	12
Jonath	Flo	97
Robt.	Nel	16
Cunningham, Andrew	Wsh	336
Ephrem	Cas	41
Frances	She	202
Francis	Mer	328
Hugh	Est	6
Hugh	Woo	398
Isaac	Clr	125
James	Bul	175
James	Bul	175
James	Hrs	309
James	Liv	155
James	Sco	186
James	She	224
James	Woo	398
Jamis	Fle	79
Jas. (see also Wm)	Bou	120
John	Fra	122
John	Jes	62
John	Woo	382
Jos.	Bou	79
Joseph	Mer	328
Joseph	She	213
Joseph	She	224
Michal	Liv	145
Robert	Clr	125
Robert	Fay	13
Robert	Mer	327
Robert	She	224
Robert	Wsh	329
Robert	Bou	80
Thomas	Woo	398
Thos.	Fle	69
Will	She	224
William	She	213
William	Woo	387
Wm. (see Jas.)	Bou	120
Wm.	Bre	161
Wm.	Cas	45
Wm.	Mad	201
Wright	Bre	158
Cunnius, Jacob	Mad	203
Cunstable, Stephen	Wsh	329
Zachariah	Wsh	329
Cup, Michl.	Bar	27
Cupper, Cornelius	Way	353
Cuppy, Aron	Nel	18
Curby, Francis	Gar	206
John	Gar	206
Wm.	Gar	206
Curcheville, William	Log	161
Curchwell, Armst.	Nel	17
Curd, Benjamin	Mer	327
Daniel	Jes	61
Edmund	Log	162
Edward	Log	162
James	Jes	61
John	Log	171
Joseph	Mer	328
Lucy	Jes	61
Meryman	Jes	61
Newton	Mer	327
Price	Fay	23
Samuel H.	Log	182
Woodford	Jef	33
Curington, Thomas	Chr	94
Curksohn, John	Mer	342
Curl, Bennet	Jef	33
Dudley	Est	5
John	Bou	120
Saml.	Jef	32
Curle, Archibald	Mad	202
Currance, Mathew	Log	193
Currants, Wm.	Bra	151
Curray, William	Fra	120
Current, John	Bou	80
Thos.	Bou	80
Thos.	Hnr	361
Currethers, Hugh	Mas	301
Currie, Daniel	Jef	32
Daniel	Jef	33
Edward	Jef	33
Currins, James	Mer	324
Curry, Alexr.	Sco	169
Andrew	Hrs	308
Barthomew	Grn	262
Benjamin	Hnd	340
Charles	Grn	249
David	Fay	20
Henry S.	Grp	272
Israel	Mer	328
James	Hrs	312
James	Mer	323
James	Mer	327
Jno.	Grn	260
John	Bou	69
John	Fay	60
John	Hrs	321
John	Mer	323
John	Mer	324
John	She	212
Nicholis	Pen	111
Robert	Hnd	330
Robert	Hnd	341
Robert	Hrs	321
Robert	Mon	365
Samuel	Mer	323
William	Bou	120
William	Fay	20
William	Hrs	309
William	Mer	323
William	Mer	324
Curt, Conrod	Nel	14
Jacob	Nel	17
Curtis, Chichester	War	250
George	Mas	290
Hilry	Chr	93
James	Hop	377
James	Mas	290
Jas. W.	Bar	40
John	Mas	286
Nathl.	Knx	74
Peter	Gar	206
Russel	Chr	95
Samuel	Knx	65
Seth	Mas	287
Curtis, cont.		
William	Est	1
William	Mas	282
William, Junr	Mas	282
William, Jun	Mas	299
Curtley, Francis	Fay	34
Curtner, Elizabeth	Fay	13
Jacob	Mer	324
Curtright, Corns.	Bou	119
Danl.	Bou	119
John	Bou	119
Richd.	Bou	119
Saml.	Bou	119
Curts, Ann	Nel	18
Conrod, Sr	Nel	18
George	Nel	14
Curtus, Arnal	Bar	35
Cury, Joseph	Hrs	313
Cusenberry, Stephen	Jef	33
Cushenberry, (see also Bushenberry)		
Zacheus	Bar	41
Cushinberry,		
James H.	Clr	126
Wm.	Bou	120
Cushman, David	Mas	283
Thomas	Mas	283
Cushonberry, Aron	War	243
Danl.	War	266
Elijah	War	280
John	War	243
Nicholas	War	246
Vincent	War	280
Cussenberry, Aaron	Jef	33
Custard, Coonrod	Bou	80
Coonrod, Jr	Bou	80
Coorrod	Cam	26
Elizabeth	Hrs	310
Jacob	Bou	80
Cutbearth, Benjamin	Knx	82
Cutlin, James	Wsh	337
Cutlip, David	War	254
Cutright, John	Cly	149
Cutsinger, Alice	Wsh	336
Conrad	Wsh	335
George	Wsh	336
John	Wsh	338
Michael	Wsh	335
Cutson, George	Adr	5
Cyphers, Jos.	She	229
Matthias	She	229

-- D --

Name	County	Page
D...san, Elijah	Lin	115
Dabb, David	War	270
James	War	255
Dabny, Nathan	Way	355
Dacon, Nathan	Bul	176
Daffern, Rhoda	Way	368
Dagby, Tho.	Bar	31
Daicase?, Peter	Cly	153
Daid, Charles	Grp	274
Dailey, Bennett	Wsh	327
Elijah	Nel	24
John	Nic	58
Ralph	Bra	149
Wm.	Sco	175
Daily, Jno.	Grn	262
John	Mas	275
John N.	Log	191
Mary	Nic	58
Michael	Hnd	333
Dalany, Edward	Jes	35

Name	County	Page
Dale, Abraham	Gra	241
Abram	Woo	393
Alexr.	Woo	384
George	Woo	384
Isaac	Bar	54
James	Fle	88
James	Mad	201
John	Bar	54
John	Woo	383
Matty	Mon	359
Natur	Woo	384
Philip	Gra	242
Reuben	She	210
Robert	Woo	394
Rolly	Woo	396
Ruben	Bar	39
Thomas	Mon	360
Uriah	Fle	61
William	Woo	393
Wm.	Bar	54
Wm. Senr	Woo	384
Daley, Francis	She	226
Hezekiah	War	272
Owen	Lew	99
Wm. (mulatto)	Woo	379
Dalham, Josia M.	But	193
Richd. B.	But	193
Dallam, William S.	Woo	390
Dalland, Francis	Jes	35
Dallum, Nathaniel S	Chr	90
Dalrimple, Joseph	Log	184
Dalton, Lewis	Log	183
Moses	Mas	272
Daly, Charles	Fle	87
Laurence	Jes	35
Dalzell, Thos.	Bou	82
Dameron, Thos.	Bou	121
Damewood, Boston	Chr	102
Damfiur, Henry	Bou	82
Damon, Rachel	Liv	153
Damorel, George	Grn	252
Damron, Joseph	Flo	97
Lazarus	Flo	97
Richard	Flo	97
Robt.	Adr	7
Danaca, James	Mon	359
Danalds, Eastridge	Mon	360
Jessa	Mon	350
Danally, Epham	Lin	114
Dance, Thomas	Pen	107
William	Pen	107
Dancy, John	Knx	66
Danell, Thomas	She	225
Danelly, Saml.	Fle	62
Daniel, Aggey	Mad	201
Benjamin	Mer	320
Beverly	Clr	127
Beverly	Clr	127
Caleman	She	210
Henry	Mon	384
Isham	Flo	97
James	Grn	250
James	Knx	75
James Jr	Clr	127
James, Sr	Clr	127
James B.	Boo	58
James M.	Clr	127
John	Fay	21
John	Gal	189
John	Jef	32
John	Knx	80
John	Mad	200
John	She	215
John O.	Hrd	300
Leonard	She	238
Martin	She	215
Mary	Clr	127
Daniel, cont.		
Nancy	Cly	154
Nathaniel	She	234
Paul	Cum	179
Peter	Bre	166
Reuben	Jef	17
Robert	Knx	73
Robert	Ohi	83
Spencer	Knx	79
Thomas	Jef	31
William	Mer	320
William	She	234
Wm.	Boo	58
Wm. G.	Fra	124
Wyatt	Cum	181
Daniels, Charles	Cam	24
Peter	Cam	25
Vivion	Cam	24
Wm.	Cam	24
Danil, William	Chr	116
Danily, John	Clr	127
Dankins, John	Hnr	367
Danks, John	Log	183
Dannel, John	Liv	154
Dannell, John	Liv	154
Danread, Elijah	Chr	90
Dant, Elizabeth	Wsh	328
James	Nel	22
Joseph	Wsh	327
William	Nel	25
Danun, Aron	Grn	245
Dolin, Ebenezer	Log	172
Dapper, Richd.	Nel	22
Darby, John	Sco	168
Philip	War	246
Richd.	War	246
Daring, Daniel	Fle	90
James	Fle	61
Darington, James	Log	173
William	Log	173
Darity, Joseph	She	212
Dark, Joseph	Clr	127
Darland, Isaac	Bou	82
Darling, Abraham	Niv	57
Darnaby, Edward	Fay	52
John	Fay	46
Darnal, Jonathan	Pul	138
Nicholas	War	268
Darnald, Achd.	Est	4
Daniel	Mon	372
Elizabeth	Mon	372
Henry	Mon	376
Joseph	Lin	114
Mary	Mon	372
Nancy	Mon	373
Thomas	Est	4
Darnall, Hannah	Bou	82
Thomas	Bou	82
Darneal, Lewis	She	201
Darnel, Aaron	Woo	399
Darnell, Adam	Wsh	325
Barton	Cly	160
Charles	Fle	61
David	Bou	82
Henry	Cal	5
Isaac	Bou	82
Isaac	Bou	82
James	Mad	199
Joseph	Woo	378
Joshua	Bou	82
Levi	Bou	82
Susana	Fle	83
Thomas	Bou	82
William	Fle	70
Darniby, Nealy	Mer	320
Ned	Mer	320
Daron, Wm.	Fle	63
Darr, William	Woo	396
Darrow, James	Hrs	322
Dart, John	Way	368
Dasan, William	Nic	58
Dasey, Elijah	Bou	83
Jaspier	Bou	83
Jonathan	Bou	83
Lemuel	Bou	83
Daton, Jos.	Cly	153
Daugherty, A. David	Mas	277
Alexander	Mas	279
Charles	Bul	176
Edward	Bul	176
George	Pul	140
Hugh	Bou	82
James D.	Bra	148
John	Mas	274
John	Wsh	327
Joseph	Knx	63
Michael	Mas	277
Owen	Mas	275
Robt.	Bar	47
Robt.	War	252
Saml.	Bou	82
Thomas	Bul	176
William	Bul	176
William	Fra	124
Wm.	Bar	46
Davage, Reason	Chr	116
Davenport, Abm.	Clr	127
Fortunatus	Woo	390
George	Cal	12
Martn.	Adr	12
Priestly	Grn	247
Richard	Woo	397
William	Fay	21
Zachariah	Knx	67
Davers, James	Fay	34
Daves, Bartlet	Boo	58
Davice, Ben	Cum	184
Charles	Cum	177
David	Cum	178
James	Cum	172
Jesse	Fle	75
John	Cum	172
John	Cum	179
John	Fle	66
Joseph	Fle	66
Joshua	Cum	176
Joshua	Cum	179
Morris	Cum	178
Moses	Cum	178
Nathl.	Cum	175
Peter	Cum	181
Robert	Cum	172
Wm.	Cum	179
David, Henry	Bou	83
Henry	Hrs	314
Jacob	Bou	83
Jacob	Mas	305
John	Wsh	326
Michael	Mas	305
Richd.	Hrd	299
William	Bou	83
William	Wsh	326
Davidge, Henry	Ohi	75
Davidson,		
Alexander	Knx	66
Alexr.	Bar	46
Alexr.	Bar	55
Daniel	Cly	155
Daniel	Jef	32
Daniel	Mon	355
David	Cal	14
Elijah	Bar	31
George	Jes	36
George	Lin	114

Davidson, cont.
George War 264
Hezekiah Bar 35
James Cly 155
James Sco 169
James H. Log 184
John Bar 35
John Bar 46
John But 193
John Cal 14
John Chr 94
John Chr 96
John Cly 155
John Gar 199
John Mad 199
John Nic 57
John, Jun Nic 57
Mary Bou 121
Mary, Jr Bou 121
Mosias J. Chr 75
Reuben Sco 169
Saml. Cly 155
Saml. Lin 114
Samuel Clr 127
Thomas Bar 40
Thos. Cly 155
Wm. Bar 35
Wm. Bre 169
Davies, Elizabeth Jes 36
James Jes 35
Philip Wsh 327
Polly Jes 35
Solomon Jes 35
(freeman of colour)
William Jes 36
Daviess, James Snr Lin 115
Jane Lin 114
Saml. Lin 115
Wm. Lin 114
Davis, Abam. Adr 7
Abner But 193
Abner Grn 264
Abner Knx 82
Allen Mer 319
Alex. Mad 199
Amos Mer 319
Amos Nel 23
Aquilla Hnd 335
Aron Fle 73
Aron Mon 349
Aron Mon 366
Arthur Cal 11
Asariah Chr 82
Asel Gar 235
Asell War 249
Augustus Est 2
Azariah Hrd 283
Bacster Way 357
Barnett Fra 123
Baxter Hnd 333
Baxter Ohi 83
Benj. Way 366
Benjamin Bra 144
Benjamin But 193
Benjamin Hop 380
Benjamin Liv 154
Benjamin Sco 185
Benjamin Way 363
Benjamin Wsh 327
Benjm. Adr 7
Benjmin Mon 368
Benjn. Sco 167
Caroline Jef 16
Charles Est 1
Charles Hnd 336
Charles Hrs 318
Charles Nel 21

Davis, cont.
Chas. Lew 97
Clemont Chr 65
Danl. Sco 175
Danl. Sco 191
David Lew 100
David Liv 152
David Mas 309
Dorcas Bre 163
Edmund Mer 322
Edward Chr 108
Edward Mad 199
Edwd. Jnr Gar 235
Edwd. Snr Gar 235
Eli She 234
Elihu Hrd 289
Elijah Sco 189
Elisas Liv 157
Eliz. Hrd 289
Elizabeth Mad 199
Elizabeth Mer 321
Enoch Mon 372
Evan Jef 32
Ezekiel She 207
Ferculow Mer 318
Forest Ohi 88
Francis Lew 97
Francis Mad 201
Francis Nel 22
Fredrick Cal 9
Gabriel But 193
Gabriel Log 173
George Grn 257
George Liv 158
George Mul 394
George Mul 399
George Wsh 325
George N. Lew 100
Giddeon Ohi 77
Goldsby Grn 261
Grace Mon 380
Griffeth Gar 234
Hanah Fay 36
Harden Bar 28
Harrison Hop 377
Harrison Log 195
Harry Mul 399
Heads Way 357
Henry Bar 32
Henry Cal 13
Henry Mad 200
Henry Mon 352
Henry War 257
Henry Woo 397
Henry, Jr Nel 24
Henry, Sr Nel 24
Henry W. War 270
Hezekh. Nel 21
Hezekiah Liv 157
Hugh But 193
Isaac Chr 107
Isaac Mad 201
Isaac Mul 390
Isaac Nel 23
Isham War 253
Ishmael Lew 102
Jacob Bar 33
Jacob She 204
Jacob Wsh 325
Jacob Wsh 327
James Bou 82
James Chr 91
James Chr 108
James Clr 127
James Fay 53
James Flo 97
James Fra 124

Davis, cont.
James Hnd 332
James Hrs 323
James Jes 35
James Knx 70
James Mer 320
James Nel 23
James Nel 23
James She 201
James She 227
James Wsh 327
James, Sr Knx 85
James D. She 222
James, U.P. But 193
Jarard Fay 22
Jas. Hrd
Jas. Way 357
Jeremiah Flo 97
Jeremiah Mad 201
Jeremiah Mon 384
Jessa Mon 364
Jesse But 193
.Jesse Knx 64
Jesse Mer 320
Jesse Nel 24
Jessee Bar 50
Jno. Nel 22
Jnothn. Nel 21
John Bar 32
John But 193
John Chr 83
John Chr 106
John Chr 110
John Est 3
John Fay 14
John Gal 189
John Gar 234
John Gra 237
John Hnd 330
John Hnd 331
John Hrd 289
John Hop 376
John Jef 32
John Knx 81
John Knx 81
John Lew 99
John Mad 201
John Mas 277
John Mer 322
John Mon 374
John Mon 384
John Nel 22
John Nel 24
John Nel 24
John Ohi 98
John Ohi 103
John Pul 138
John Pul 139
John Sco 170
John Sco 179
John She 199
John She 199
John She 215
John She 219
John War 265
John Way 351
John Woo 380
John Wsh 325
John E. Hop 380
Jonathan Adr 19
Jonathan Bar 41
Jonathan Clr 127
Jonathan Knx 88
Jos. T. Nel 22
Joseph Flo 97
Joseph Hop 371
Joseph Mad 200

Davis, cont.
Joseph Mas 273
Joseph Mas 274
Joseph Mon 378
Joseph Nel 24
Joshua But 193
Joshua Mad 199
Joshua(Alex'son) Mad 199
Joshua Mer 322
Josiph Chr 108
Lamack Grp 273
Lemuel Fra 123
Leonard Way 371
Levi Bul 176
Levi Mas 277
Levi Nel 24
Levy Hrs 320
Lodawick Wsh 328
Lodowick Ohi 83
Lucy Sco 185
Luke Mon 359
Macklin Chr 104
Maeling Gra 237
Margaret Mon 365
Mark Bou 69
Mathas Liv 157
Mathew Clr 127
Mathew Nel 21
Matthias Mon 357
Maxfield Mon 365
Morgan Mer 320
Nancy Mas 272
Nancy Mon 368
Nancy Sco 171
Nathan Lin 115
Nathan Wsh 325
Peggy Way 372
Peter Mon 371
Peter Sco 169
Philemon Sco 168
Philip Mas 274
Philip Nel 22
Philip Nel 25
Phillip Ohi 98
Phineas Way 352
Polecap Nel 25
Polly Mer 318
Redzin Grp 278
Richard Gra 241
Richard Knx 76
Richard Woo 377
Richd. Cal 16
Richd. Hop 378
Robert But 193
Robert Chr 55
Robert Flo 97
Robert Hnd 327
Robert Hop 377
Robert Mer 320
Robert Mer 321
Robert Mer 321
Robert Nel 22
Robert Nic 58
Robt. Bra 141
Robt. Way 358
Robt. Jr Way 351
Ruth Wsh 327
Samuel Gar 234
Samuel Mas 272
Samuel Mas 276
Samuel Mer 319
Samuel Mer 321
Samuel Mer 341
Samuel Pul 140
Saml. Nel 23
Saml. Way 368
Septimus Clr 127

Davis, cont.
Shadrach Wsh 326
Simon Nel 23
Sneed Gra 237
Soloman Ohi 79
Solomon Gar 235
Solomon Sco 183
Solomon Woo 402
Stephen Fay 43
Stephen Mer 320
Stephen She 236
Susanna Mer 322
Temple But 193
Theophilus Gra 243
Thomas Chr 100
Thomas Clr 127
Thomas Fay 14
Thomas Hrd 281
Thomas Hrs 312
Thomas Log 186
Thomas Nic 57
Thomas Nic 57
Thomas She 222
Thomas She 226
Thomas Woo 381
Thomas Woo 388
Thomas C. Fra 124
Thomas G. Liv 160
Thomas M. Bou 121
Thos. Nel 24
Thos. Nel 24
Thos. Way 352
Tison Lew 96
Travis Nel 21
Van liv 157
Vincent Nel 22
Walter Lew 100
Widow Way 370
William Bou 121
William But 193
William Fay 14
William Fay 49
William Fle 64
William Hnd 339
William Hop 381
William Knx 81
William Log 195
William Mad 199
William Nel 21
William Nel 21
William Nic 58
William Pul 139
William She 211
William She 226
William Woo 380
Willm. Adr 7
Willm. Nel 24
Willm. Sco 169
Wily Cal 15
Wm. Bar 32
Wm. Gar 235
Wm. Gar 235
Zachariah Flo 97
Zachariah Knx 81
Davise, Arthur Cum 172
Eli Fle 85
John D. Fle 89
Joseph Fle 83
Nathanil Fle 80
Samuel Fle 84
Davison, Andrew Pul 140
David Bre 159
David Fra 123
Edward Gra 239
Elias Wsh 343
Foster Mer 319
George Mas 272

Davison, cont.
James Mer 321
John Mas 275
John Wsh 327
Joseph Mas 275
Josiah Grp 269
Philip Gra 239
Richard Pul 140
Robert Mas 272
William Log 175
William Mer 319
William Pul 140
Daviss, Abner Log 186
Briscoe War 244
Edward Cas 43
Euriah War 273
Gabriel Log 186
H. Joseph Fay 14
Israel War 270
James War 279
John Lin 114
John War 273
Joseph Lin 115
Landon Cas 43
Mary War 248
Robert Cas 38
Robert Cas 39
Thomas Lin 115
Thomas Lin 115
Wm. Cas 48
Wm. War 279
Wm. War 279
Davisson, Hugh Mas 279
Dawdle, Fautleroy She 200
Dawiton, David Fay 36
Dawkins, George Hnr 364
Thomas Fle 78
Dawling, James Wsh 326
Dawns, Zachariah Bar 35
Dawnton, Richard Fay 22
Dawpon, William Fay 36
Dawson, Abraham Mas 278
Bejamin Cas 44
Benjamin Fay 50
Christopher Clr 127
Enock Adr 7
George Adr 7
Hannah Adr 7
Isaac Mas 278
Jacob Clr 127
James Fay 50
Jeremiah Hrd 286
John Bar 24
John Bou 121
John Clr 127
John Woo 401
John, Jr Bou 121
John, Jr Woo 397
Jonathan War 272
Joseph Adr 7
Joseph Mon 365
Malin Bou 121
Peter Hnr 359B
Richard Fra 123
Robert D. Fle 81
Saml. I. Bou 82
Spencer Clr 127
Thomas Bou 121
Thomas Fay 51
William Grn 245
William Pen 110
William Woo 392
William Woo 396
Willm. Adr 7
Wm. Clr 126
Day, Archer Jef 17
Archibald Jef 17

Day, cont.
Archibald Mon 353
Asa Bra 142
Benjamin Fay 52
Christopher Bra 145
Edmund Mer 322
Elizabeth Woo 400
Francis Lin 114
Henry Log 192
Isaac Bra 144
Isaac Bra 152
James Cam 28
James Flo 97
James Nel 21
John Bou 83
John Bul 177
John Cal 3
John Fle 88
John Knx 68
John Mer 322
John Way 365
Joseph Bra 144
Joseph Gra 241
Joseph Fay 14
Joseph Nel 22
Labourn War 263
Mark Bra 142
Mary Fle 84
Reuben Flo 97
Truman Fle 65
Valentine Lin 114
William and son-in-law Fle 65
Willis Mas 274
Winny Mas 278
Dayhoof, Frederick She 202
Dayle, Richard Wsh 343
Dayley, James Fay 22
Days, Anthony Mon 352
Dayton, Garrett Nic 57
Deacon, James Nel 25
John Nel 21
Deacons, Stephen Mon 381
Deadmon, Elijah She 227
Deakins, John Cly 156
Deal, Daniel Jef 17
David Flo 97
John Nel 23
Peter War 271
Dealy, William Mad 200
Dean, Alsa Bar 38
Daniel Bra 152
Daniel Gal 189
Daniel Mon 354
Edward Clr 127
Elias Bul 176
George Clr 127
George Wsh 329
Henry Bre 161
Isaac Knx 77
James Adr 7
James Jes 36
James Mon 382
Jeremiah Clr 127
John Bar 50
John Flo 97
John Hnr 359
John Knx 77
John Wsh 328
Jonathan War 247
Joshua Way 362
Mary Lin 115
Michael Lew 95
Robt. Hnr 360
Thomas Woo 382
Thomas Wsh 326
Wm. Gal 189
Dear, Goodall Sco 189
Reubin Lin 114
Dearing, Ane Way 359
Elijsha Fle 65
John Wsh 327
Willm. War 269
Deatherage, Anne Mad 200
George Mad 200
Deatley, John Bou 121
Deatly, William Mas 275
Deavenport, Saml. Mad 200
Deaver, Thos. Hrd 296
Deavers, John Fle 67
Debaird, E½hraim Clr 127
Debell, Wm. Fle 82
Debode, William Pul 138
Debon, Abram Mer 318
George Mer 318
Joseph Mer 318
Joseph Mer 318
Samuel Mer 318
Debow, Benjamin Jes 36
Debril, John Way 370
Debrile, Charles Way 371
Debrular, Jacob Hrs 316
Jacob Hrs 318
Debruler, James Bou 83
John Bou 121
Decker, Barnet Gra 240
Calep Gra 237
Ezekiel Gra 237
George Way 359
Henry Gra 237
Jacob Nel 24
John Gra 237
John Gra 240
John Mer 322
John Way 369
Joseph Way 363
Samuel Mer 320
William Mer 322
William Pul 139
Deckinson, John Bar 48
Solomon Bar 48
Decoursey, John Cam 32
Wm. Cam 31
Dedman, Elijw. Fle 64
John Jes 35
Nathan Woo 400
Richmond Fay 23
William Fle 76
Dedvore, John Wsh 325
Deen, Ann Mer 320
Betsy Mer 318
Eleven Mer 320
Jane Bar 32
Jesse Mul 391
Job Mer 320
John Mer 319
Kizzy Mer 320
Sofiah Mer 318
Thomas Mer 320
William Mer 318
Deer, Bernard Mas 275
Lewis Mer 321
Deerin, Richard Grp 272
Deering, Antonia Grp 274
Robert Fra 123
Walker Fra 125
Dees, Sampson Chr 94
William Chr 96
Defevers, John Bar 34
Defoe, Stephen Lin 115
Deford, James Chr 108
Deforges, Huse Fay 53
Degallon, Henry Jef 27
Degraffenreed, Fras Cum 167
Degraffenreed, cont.
Jno. Cum 167
Wm. Cum 167
Dehart, Acklin Gar 234
Dehaven, Edward Bre 165
Isaac Sco 186
Jacob Sco 183
Saml. Sco 167
Deheart, William Pen 116
Dehoney, Rodes Sco 174
Dehony, James Sco 174
Deimy, William Gra 242
Dejarnet, Abijah Hrs 319
Dejarnett, James Mad 200
John Bre 158
Dejernett, John Mon 358
Dejirnett, Thos. Hnr 354
Delainy, Fieldin Hnd 329
Delane, Patrick Fay 40
Delaney, Ann Jef 28
Anthony She 197
Henry I. Liv 151
James But 193
Joseph Mad 199
William Liv 153
William Mad 201
Delany, Abner Bou 121
Danl. Bou 121
Danl. Sr Bou 121
John Boo 58
Judith Mas 273
Thomas Cal 9
Delay, Edmond Mon 373
Henry Bou 82
James Bou 82
John Bou 82
John Mon 358
Dell, John Fay 14
Dellan, Jane Jef 16
Dellon, Isaiah Fle 65
Delman, Andrew Bra 143
Andrew Bra 147
George Bra 147
Deloach, Thomas Log 182
William Log 182
Demalee, Danl. Hnr 362
Demar, Winny (mulattoe) Woo 396
Demarce, David She 225
Demarco, Samuel She 212
Demard, Peter She 239
Demarel, David She 221
Demarse, Cornelius Mer 321
Samuel Mer 321
Demaru, John Mer e19
Demcey, Coleman Fra 123
Demerea, Jas. Gar 235
Demines, John Chr 58
Deming, Jessy Chr 83
Demint, Elias Bou 121
John Fra 123
William Fra 123
Demit, Jaret Gal 189
Wm. S. Jef 16
Demitt, James Mas 276
Moses Mas 276
Richard Bou 83
Demoss, James Fle 87
John Bra 149
John Sco 186
Lewis Fle 73
Peter Pen 106
William Fle 72
Dempsy, Patrick Cam 32
Demutt, John Mer 321
Lawrence Mer 321
Peter Mer 321

Demutt, cont.
Peter Mer 321
Denbo, Solomn. Nel 24
Dency, Saml. Bar 22
Denham, David Jes 36
Hardan Jes 35
Michl. Bar 42
Obediah Pul 139
Denis, Samuel Mon 362
Denison, James Bou 121
John Flo 97
Jonathan Flo 97
Thomas Flo 97
Denler, James Adr 7
Denna, Elijah Rck 164
Dennes, Robert Fay 22
Dennesson, Daniel Fay 21
William Fay 21
Denney, Charles Way 363
Erijah Way 364
Jas. Way 356
Thos. Hrs 318
Dennica, James Clr 146
Dennie, William Ohi 102
Denning, Ant. Hnr 367
John Hnr 359B
Rachl. Hnr 361
Dennis, Abraham Mul 386
Abraham Mul 392
Absalom Cal 6
Adam Wsh 328
Betsy Wsh 328
David Jes 36
Elisha Gar 234
Hudson Gar 234
Jesse Woo 383
John Cal 10
John Mas 273
John Mul 398
Josiah Gra 238
Mary Mul 401
Samuel Fra 123
Samuel Rck 166
William Gra 238
Dennison, Benjn. Bar 31
John Mas 274
John Mas 278
Robt. Bar 47
Saml. Bar 31
Zachariah Bar 31
Danny, Alexander Gar 234
Benj. Way 364
Christopher Sco 184
David Mer 320
Fielding Sco 182
Geo. Gar 235
jaems Sco 167
James Sco 178
John Mer 320
John Way 354
Lewis Sco 171
Nancy Jef 16
Robert Mer 320
Saml. Mad 199
Samuel Mer 320
Simon She 202
Wm. Way 364
Zacharia Pul 138
Dent, Samuel Mad 200
Denton, Abraham Mon 381
Benjamin Hnd 348
David War 259
Henry Gar 233
Isaac Cum 184
James Gal 189
John Hnd 328
John Lin 114
Denton, cont.
John, Jnr Gar 236
John, Snr Gar 236
Jonathan Bar 36
Joseph Pul 141
Denton, Josiah Pul 139
Joseph Fle 77
Patton Gar 233
Robert Cas 42
Saml. Hop 371
Wm. Mon 380
Densford, James Jef 16
John Jef 32
Denum, John Chr 80
Deofendall, Phioip Nel 25
Depauer, Charles Lin 114
Depaw, John Cas 39
Depew, Abram. Boo 58
Depoyster, Thos. War 276
Depp, Wm. Bar 34
Deprest, Robert Knx 78
Depu, George Wsh 325
Depue, Willm. Adr 7
Dereer, John Cas 45
Deremiah, John Gra 240
Deringer, Jacob Woo 388
Joseph Woo 384
Martin Woo 384
Mary C. Woo 387
Michael Woo 391
Derling, Lambut Mer 319
Derly, Arter Chr 68
Jehu Cal 9
Dermon, Catharine Rck 161
Jonathan Rck 164
Wm. Rck 161
Dernam, Isaac Mon 383
Derr, Sebastin Bou 69
Derraugh, Amos Mas 278
Derret, Richard Mas 277
Derrum, William Chr 100
Derumple, Samuel Chr 73
deryberry, John War 275
Desen, William Chr 94
Desern, Edmund Grn 253
Desha, John Bou 82
Deshai, Joseph Mas 277
Deshazer, John Mad 202
Jonathan Mad 202
Deson, Argulas Chr 94
Argules Chr 96
Edward Chr 97
Desponet, David Mer 319
Devarr, Michia Mas 278
Devary, Joseph Clr 127
Devenport, Ballard hrs 311
Christop Mer 319
David Cal 3
Duke Hnd 337
Geor. Cas 40
John Cas 40
John Mer 321
John Way 363
Marmaduke Fay 55
Richard Mer 342
Thomas Mer 322
Thos. Cas 40
William Mer 319
Wm. Cas 40
Wm. Cas 43
Devers, James Fay 44
Jno. Jur Mad 201
John Mad 201
Devin, James Lin 114
Devine, Roger Fra 124
Devinn, William Mas 278
Devore, Abner Mas 273
Devore, cont.
Benjamin Mas 278
John Fay 48
Mosses Fay 48
Nicholas Mas 273
Samuel Fay 58
Devour, Christopher Bra 144
Jeramiah Bra 148
Wm. Bra 148
Dew, Peter Grp 275
Dewberry, John Cum 168
William Bul 176
Deweast, Matthew Mer 320
Dewees, Benjamin Gra 243
D Daniel Gra 243
Jesse Cum 183
Joseph Gra 242
Lewis Boo 58
Deweese, John But 193
Dewese, David Knx 74
Henry Cal 4
Dewit, Achelis Grn 262
Barnard But 193
Henry Hrd 291
Dewitt, Henry Nic 57
Martin Clr 127
Mary Clr 127
Peter Clr 127
Tarlton Hnr 359A
Dexter, Benjamin Mul 395
James Ohi 86
Silas, Junr Ohi 86
Silas, Senr Ohi 86
Dial, John Cam 31
John Log 181
Mary Log 181
Nathenial Liv 148
Thomas War 250
Diamond, James Ohi 100
Dianurt, Edward Hnr 362
Dick (free man) Fay 14
Dick (freeman) Fay 23
Dick, Abraham Bar 50
Coonrod Mul 403
Jacob Jef 32
James Pul 139
John Way 373
John Woo 389
John J. Pul 139
John S. Pul 138
Peter Mul 389
Samuel Pul 139
Dicken, Christopher Ohi 84
Ephraim Cum 177
Henry Sco 185
Thomas Knx 74
Thomas Wsh 325
William Wsh 324
Dicker, Nicholas Bra 151
Dickerman, William Woo 400
Dickerson, Archd. Cly 156
Beverly Wsh 326
David Jes 36
Fagge Jef 16
Francis C. Grn 262
George Jes 36
Griffin Chr 113
Hirum Chr 97
Isham War 255
James Jes 36
Jeremiah Jes 36
Joel War 255
John Bou 121
John Jes 41
Lewis Chr 72

Name	County	Page
Dickerson, cont.		
Lewis	Jes	36
Martin	Jes	36
Mrs.	Jef	16
Nathl.	War	261
Oba	Bou	121
Robt.	Cam	26
Robt.	War	258
Thomas	Liv	154
Valentine	War	255
Wm.	Cam	26
Wm.	Nel	21
Wm.	Nel	25
Dickeson, Mathew	Cal	11
Dickey, Adam	Mon	370
Alexander	Liv	159
Alexander	Nic	58
David	Bou	82
David	Liv	159
David	Log	173
Ebenezer	Mad	200
James	Fle	79
James	Woo	377
John	Log	173
John	Log	193
John	Sco	176
John, Senr	Log	173
Joseph	Log	184
Michael	Woo	395
Robert	Liv	159
Robert	Mon	360
William, Junr	Liv	160
William, Sr	Liv	159
Willm.	Sco	177
Dickin, John	Lin	114
Dickins, James	Boo	58
Joseph	Cam	29
Dickinson, Benj. T.	Bar	30
Henry	Bar	48
Tho.	Bar	22
Thomas	Fay	59
Dickison, Chas.	Hrd	283
Dickon, Simeon	Mer	342
Dicks, George	Mas	273
John	Mas	305
John, Senr	Mas	274
Dickson, David	Hrs	314
George	Fle	81
Greenberry	Way	364
Henry	Cly	153
Isaah	Mer	319
James	Hnd	346
John	Flo	97
John	Hnd	340
Thomas	Log	172
Dicksson, James	Lin	115
Dicktum, Richard	Boo	58
Dicky, Hase	Mer	318
John	Hnr	352
John	Mer	319
Robert	Mer	319
William	Fay	41
Dicus, Elijah	Bar	27
John	Bar	33
John	Chr	114
Joshua	Bar	26
Wm.	Bar	26
Dida (free woman)	Fay	14
Diddle, William	Adr	19
Didlake, Robert	Clr	127
Die, Avery	Mer	318
Diel, Martin	Hnd	342
Matthew	Nic	58
Digby, William	Per	112
Diggins, Alexr.	Lin	115
Diggs, David	Bou	82
Digman, Peter	Mas	276

Name	County	Page
Dike, Henry	Clr	127
John	Clr	127
Dikes, Daniel	Liv	150
George P.	Liv	152
Stephen	Liv	151
Dilany, Harris	Sco	178
Dilinder, Henry W.	Mer	31[illegible]
Jacob	Mer	[illegible]
John	Mer	[illegible]
Dilingham, James	Cal	5
Joshua	Cal	17
Josua	Cal	5
William	Cal	5
Wm.	Cal	17
Dill, Abner	Nic	58
Benjamin	Mas	272
Susanna	Mas	273
Dillar, Jeremiah	Jef	25
Dillard, Jas.	Way	352
John	Jes	36
Joseph	Rck	163
Minty	Liv	148
Dillen, Henry	Log	185
William	Mas	279
Dillenham, Cham	Adr	7
Dilliard, James	Chr	102
Joseph	Chr	58
Luke	Chr	112
Dillin?, ...	Jes	36
Dillin, John	She	222
Dilling, Edmond	Mul	405
Dillingjam, Joshua	Mad	200
Lott,	Cas	44
Michal	Cas	38
Peter	Adr	7
Vachel	Gar	234
Dillion, Peter	Cal	7B
Dillon, Abner	Fle	87
Abriah	Fle	81
Amos	Fle	87
David	Fle	87
Eli	Fle	87
Michl.	Nel	25
Saml.	Bou	82
Dills, Henry	Hrd	288
John	Hnd	341
Wm.	Way	361
Dilly, Stephen	Cam	29
Dilman, John	Bra	142
Saml.	Sco	177
Dilse, David	Hrs	324
Isaac	Hrs	312
Rachel	Hrs	312
Dilyard, Ishmael	Cum	170
Dimwiddie, Alex.	Hnr	361
Dimwiddy, Wm.	War	269
Dinaway, Willm.	Lin	114
Dine, Andrew	Mer	319
Dingle, Edward	Sco	179
William	Nic	57
Dinkin, Stephen	Wsh	328
Dinney, James	Wsh	325
Dinsmore, Henry	Nic	57
John	Fle	72
John	Nic	57
Thomas	Mon	360
Dinton, Reuben	Hnd	346
Dinwiddie, James	Mad	199
Jas., Jur	Mad	201
Thos.	Sco	191
Dinwiddie, Willm.	Lin	114
Wm.	Bou	121
Wm.	Mad	200
Dinwiddy, Alexr.	War	269
Thos.	War	270
Dinwidie, John	Lin	115
Dinwoody, Jas.	Gar	199

Name	County	Page
Dirkam, William	Cly	149
Dishay, Patrick	Grn	256
Disher, Christo.	Bra	149
Thos.	Bra	149
Dishman, James	Put	138
Jeremiah	Pul	138
Peter	Mer	321
Dismore, Heny	Nel	25
Hery S.	Nel	25
Dismuke, Joseph	Cas	38
Dismukes, Jinny	Gar	235
Wm.	Gar	235
Dison, George	Hrs	305
Roswell	Hrs	305
Sarah	Bul	177
Ditch, Henry	Mon	362
Ditterline, John	Liv	157
Ditto, Abraham	She	220
Henry	She	225
Henry, Junr	Hrd	294
Henry, Senr	Hrd	295
William	She	212
Divens, Easter	Bra	153
John	Woo	382
Dives, Ursula	Bul	176
Divinah, Samuel	Chr	81
Divine, Andrew	Mer	318
George	Mer	318
John	War	279
Samuel	Mer	319
Divinna, John	Mon	351
Divinney, Daniel	Mon	352
Diweese, William	Pul	141
Dixon, Abraham	Mon	347
Henry	Cam	25
Henry	Hnd	327
Henry	Mon	347
John	Fra	124
John	Mas	276
John	War	249
John	War	249
Peter	Mad	202
Thos.	Cam	30
Rimothy	Hrd	302
Wynn	Hnd	344
Dixson, John	Knx	85
Nathan	Knx	67
Dizerne, Nathaniel	Hnd	343
Doak, Abram	Way	361
Dobbins, Hugh	Liv	154
James	Cal	12
James	Fle	78
John	Liv	154
Matthew	Mad	199
Robert	Cal	9
Wm.	Cal	5
Dobbs, Jessee	Way	365
John	Mad	199
Wm.	Grn	246
Wm.	Way	362
Dobell, John	Fle	79
Dobenspike, Philip	Hrs	312
Dobins, Lucy	Hop	378
Dobson, Davy	Adr	7
Ellinor	Knx	72
James	Grn	260
Jos. Sr	Grn	252
Dobyes, Edwd.	Hop	373
Dobyn, John	Mul	406
Lew	Mul	406
Dobyns, Charles	Mas	279
Daniel	Mas	277
Edward	Mas	279
Enoch	Mas	276
Fanny	Mul	402
Lawson	Mas	275
Thomas	Mas	275

Docerty, John Mon 372
Cocherty, John Mon 379
Dockery, Geo. Gar 234
Robt. Gar 235
Dodd, Danl. She 232
Dolly Fay 45
Edward Jef 16
George Jef 17
George Mer 321
James Bar 36
John Fay 33
John Fay 53
John Liv 154
John, Junr Fra 124
Louisa Fra 124
Richd. Nel 22
Wm. War 280
Dodds, Francis Cal 6
James Hnr 361
James Liv 154
Jane Liv 154
John Lin 114
John Lin 114
John Mad 200
Doddy, Jos. War 260
Dodge, David Clr 146
Gimaliel Jef 30
John Hnd 340
Joseph Hrs 321
Richd. Hop 378
Sophia Hrd 290
Dodsen, Absolom Way 371
Thomas Way 355
Dodson, Abner Pul 138
Amestead War 268
Asa Pul 140
Charles Pul 138
Charles War 271
Delingham War 277
Eli She 212
George Mer 320
Jesse Hrd 302
John Hrd 301
John Jef 16
John Way 374
Mager Clr 127
Martha Way 369
William Nel 23
Doennon?, John Cal 5
Dogan, George Nel 23
Dogett, Thomas Mon 361
Thomas Mon 378
Dogget, Richard Mas 274
Doggett, Presley She 231
Dogherty, John Way 372
Tas. Way 372
Wm. Way 372
Doghne, Paul Mer 342
Dogin, Lovin Pul 140
Lucy Fay 53
Doherty, James Mer 322
Michael Chr 109
Samuel Mer 322
William Mer 322
Dohone, Hugh Mer 322
Dohoney, Rhodes Adr 7
Dohorty, Henry Hrs 320
Doing, Bennet Mas 273
thomas Mas 273
Doit, James Nel 24
Peter Nel 24
Doke, David Adr 7
James Jes 35
Jas. Hrd 283
Thomas Mer 321
William Mer 321
Dolahide, Thomas Pul 140
Dolerhite, Francis Mer 322
Dolihide, Cornel-
ius Pul 138
Dolin, Patsy Lin 115
Dollands, John Gar 234
Dollar, Will Bou 69
Dollard, Jno. Mad 202
Dollason, Jacob Log 182
Dollins, James Lin 114
William Lin 114
William Lin 115
Dollus, Henry Fle 82
William Fle 82
Dolman, Thos. Sco 190
Dolson, Moses C. Liv 153
Dolton, George War 275
Isham Mad 202
James Cal 8
Michael Jef 16
Robt. Cal 18
Domigin, Patrick Fay 50
Domorel, George Grn 258
Donaga, Thomas Mon 359
Donahow, Major Fay 36
Donald, Jas. Bou 82
Saml. Bou 82
Thomas Bou 82
Donaldson, John Jef 16
Robert Jef 16
Wm. Mon 353
Donalson, Charles War 281
James Hnr 365
Robert Mad 201
William Mad 201
Donaphin, Anderson Mas 299
Joseph Mas 277
Donathan, Hawkens Mon 347
Hawkins Mon 364
Thomas Mon 347
Thomas Mon 364
Donavain, Alex-
ander Mas 277
Aquilla Mas 272
Gilbert Mas 275
Jacob Mas 278
M. Thomas Mas 274
Philip Mas 274
William Mas 274
William Mas 277
Donaven, Danill Bra 145
Done, Benjaimen Hrs 317
Sary Hrs 317
Robert Hrs 317
Donehey, John Liv 151
Donelson, Andrew Liv 154
James Liv 154
Robt. Clr 126
Donely, James She 208
Donevin, Jas. Bou 141
Donilson, John Clr 126
Donjasly, William Lin 114
Donley, James Bul 176
Donnell, James Bou 82
Donnelly, Cornel-
ius Bou 83
Donniley, Thomas Clr 126
Donnington, Benj. Log 175
Charles Log 175
Donnohue, Daniel Clr 127
Donnor, George, Jr Jes 36
George, Sr Jes 36
Donoho, Chs. Nel 24
Danl. Nel 24
John Nel 25
Major Fay 39
Rice Mas 201
Robert Mad 199
Donovan, Ephram Fle 70
Dood, John C. Cal 14
Joseph Cal 14
Thos. Cal 14
Dooley, Aron Fra 123
Ephraim Clr 127
Henry Clr 127
Jacob Mad 199
John Clr 127
John Mer 320
Obediah Clr 127
Stephen Clr 127
Doolin, Cornelius Pul 140
Daniel But 193
David Log 190
Jacob Gar 235
James J. Pul 140
James S. Pul 140
John But 193
William But 193
William Lin 115
Dooly, Geo. Bar 50
George Bul 177
George Lin 114
Henry Bul 177
Henry Log 173
Hiram Mad 199
Jacob, Jur Mas 199
Job Mad 199
John Bra 151
John Log 173
Doom, Henry Cal 12
John Cal 4
Doome, Joseph Grn 255
Dooms, Jacob Cal 9
Dooning, Geo. T. Bar 52
Doran, Daniel Grn 259
Francis Wsh 324
John Gra 237
Dorathy, James Pen 106
John Pen 109
Dorin, John Nel 24
Dorkins, Wm. Jef 32
Dorothy, Archibald Wsh 325
Dorrel, Geor. Mon 360
Dorrell, John Rck 165
William Jes 36
Dorris, Joseph Chr 87
Dorrow, James Nic 57
Dorsey, Azel Hrd 294
Beal Hrd 294
Charles Gal 189
Delilah Log 162
Edward Fle 65
Edward Wsh 326
Greenberry Hrd 300
John Woo 397
Johnzy Wsh 326
Nimrod Jef 17
Noah Jef 16
Reason Sco 175
Richard Nel 22
Richard Wsh 326
Robt. Hrd 285
Susanna Jef 17
Thomas Wsh 326
William Fay 14
Dorsoh, John Liv 155
Dorson, George Nel 22
John Nel 25
William She 206
Dorton, Edward Flo 97
Lewis She 217
Moses Knx 78
Dorsy, Perry Log 172
Dory, Fardanan Bra 143
Doss, Ambrose Cum 174

Name	County	Page
Doss, cont.		
Aron	Pul	138
James	War	271
Joel	Pul	138
Stephen	Liv	151
William	Liv	150
dosson, Benjamin	Mad	200
Dotey, Ephraim	Mad	201
Dotson, Elijah	Bou	82
Isaac	Nel	25
James	Nic	57
Leonard	Way	356
William	Fra	123
Doty, Francis	Mer	319
Jesse	Gar	234
John	Gar	236
Douden, james	Mad	201
Doudle, Wm.	Hrd	294
Doughater, John	Est	6
Dougherty, Chas.	Cum	171
Christopher	Hrd	296
Danl.	Woo	377
George	Jef	17
Henry	Wsh	328
James	Bra	146
James	Gal	189
James	Sco	172
James	Sco	184
Jas.	Hrd	289
Jas.	Hrd	297
Jas.	Woo	377
Jesse	Jef	16
Jiss	Nic	57
John	Hrd	301
John	Jef	17
John	Jef	17
John	Jes	35
John	Nic	57
Joseph	Cum	168
Matthew	Wsh	328
Michl.	Hnr	352
Mosses	Fay	53
Noble	Wsh	328
Philip	Woo	380
Robert	Jes	36
Roger	Fle	73
Roger	Fle	86
Rubin	But	193
Samuel	Jes	35
Sarah	Hrd	294
Tho.	Fle	64
Wm.	Jef	17
Wm.	Jef	29
Doughety, Daniel	But	193
John	But	193
Doughketer, Moses	Est	5
Doughtery, William	Wsh	328
Doughty, Daniel	Way	256
Jas.	War	256
Jeremiah	War	256
John	Nic	58
John	Pen	113
Preston	War	256
Saml.	Bar	30
Sarah	Pen	113
Thos.	Nic	57
William	Nic	57
Douglas, Geo.	Bar	52
Hezekiah	Woo	382
Jas. S.	Mad	199
Jeremiah	Mad	200
Jesse	Mad	201
John	Ohi	79
S[illegible].	Bar	52
S[illegible]el	Mad	202
William	Mad	202
Wm.	Bar	52
Douglass, Alexander	Hrs	323
Andw.	Adr	7
Charles	Grn	258
David	Mon	366
Elizabeth	Hrs	324
John	Adr	7
John	But	193
John	Hrs	324
Jos.	Bou	82
Richd.	Sco	185
Robert	Hrs	312
Robt.	Grn	257
Thomas	Hrs	312
William	Hrs	311
Willm	Hrs	307
Douitte, John	She	204
Douls, William	Fra	124
Doupe, George	Jef	32
Douthart, John	Hnr	362
Thomas	Hnr	362
Douthit, Silas	Fra	124
Thomas J.	Jef	32
Douthitt, David	Hnd	336
Dovard, Sasi?	Bre	169
Dove, Francis	Gar	235
Henry	Pul	140
James	Pul	140
Doves, John J.	Pul	139
John S.	Pul	139
Dowdall, John	Wsh	326
Nathaniel	She	213
Stacy	Wsh	326
Dowdd, Elizabeth	Fay	55
Dowden, John	Mas	277
William	Fay	22
Dowdle, Anna	Liv	159
thos.	Hrd	287
Dowel, Elijah	Bre	160
Elijah	Bre	161
James	War	271
Micajah	Bre	165
Thomas	Bre	167
Dowell, John	Cum	170
Richard	Clr	126
Richd.	Clr	127
Dowes, Jesse	Knx	76
Dowing, William	Gra	243
Dowis, Isaac	Knx	84
William, Jr	Knx	66
William	Knx	75
Dowland, John	Jef	16
Wm.	Jef	16
Down, John	Nel	21
Downard, David	Cam	33
Jacob	Pen	111
Thos.	Bra	142
Downen, Josiah	Mul	399
Thomas	She	228
Downer, Benjamin	Chr	78
David	Chr	66
Downey, Abram	War	262
James	Mer	319
James	Mer	319
James	Mer	319
Joel	Mer	319
John	Hnr	362
John	Mer	319
Thomas	Fle	71
Wm.	Clr	127
Downing, Archd.	Nic	57
Ezekiel	Gra	241
Frances	Sco	170
Francis	Fay	14
Francis	Fay	21
Jailey	Clr	127
James	Bra	144
Downing, cont.		
James	Chr	68
James	Fay	36
Jane	Mas	273
Jobe	Mul	402
John	Cam	27
John	Fay	14
John	Gar	234
John	Jes	41
John	Lin	115
John	Mas	273
Joseph	Fay	14
Joseph	Mas	278
Richard	Fay	14
Robert	Mon	349
Samuel	Mon	365
Sary	Bar	39
Thomas	Mas	273
Timothy	Mas	277
Timothy	Mul	402
William	Chr	116
William	Fay	33
William	Fay	54
William	Fra	124
Downs, Barnett	Wsh	328
Benj.	Nel	23
Ezekiel	Bar	35
Francis	Nel	25
George W.	Jes	42
Jacob	Mon	360
John	Fle	64
John	Grp	276
John	Nel	25
Jonthn.	Nel	23
Richard	Gra	237
Robert	Mon	363
Tho.	Bar	35
Thomas	Mul	394
Thomas	Mul	401
William	Ohi	75
Downton, Richard	Fay	35
Downy, Andrew	Cam	27
James	Lin	114
Willm	Lin	114
Doxon, George	Clr	146
Doyall, Wm.	Boo	58
Doyel, Gregory	War	249
John	Woo	384
Doyl, Michael	Chr	96
Owen	She	238
Patrick	Sco	172
Saml.	War	249
Doyle, Allen	War	278
Charles	Nel	22
Conrod	Nel	25
Dennis	Fay	43
Farmer	She	200
Jas.	War	255
Jno.	Nel	21
John	War	268
John	War	278
Peggy	Jef	16
Dozer, James	Lew	99
John	Mon	372
Zacheriah	Mon	372
Dozier, Adam	War	262
John	Ohi	73
Josiah	Mad	199
Leonard	Mad	199
Thomas	Mad	199
Drace, Daniel	Knx	65
Dragoo, Ephraim	Bul	176
John	Ohi	84
Drain, Anthony	Bar	35
James	Mon	380
Drake, Abraham	Fay	14
Albritain	Mul	400

Drake, cont.
Allen Bar 27
Benjamin Mas 276
Braxton Cas 39
Carter Bar 27
Charles Bul 176
Cornelias Chr 57
Cornelius Mas 299
Daniel Chr 57
Edward War 274
Enoch Fay 42
Isaac Mas 279
Jacob Mas 276
James Liv 155
Jesse Bul 176
Joel Adr 7
John Mas 272
John Mas 274
John Mas 275
John Mas 279
John Nel 22
Nathaniel Jes 35
Ralph Mas 275
Runi Mas 299
Samuel Mas 279
Samuel Mul 403
Sary Bar 28
Sir Francis Log 191
Thos. Adr 7
Thos. Sco 170
Tolton War 251
William Jes 35
Drane, Joseph Wsh 328
Stephen She 225
Thomas Wsh 326
Walter Wsh 326
Drannon, Joseph Cal 14
Draper, John Bar 33
John Hrs 312
Wm. Boo 58
Dream, George Log 186
Dredden, Margaret Woo 386
Dreddin, Jane Hrs 308
Dredriger, Philip Log 173
Drenen, John Sco 168
Drew, John Mer 322
Washington Log 185
Drinkhard, Wm. Gar 234
Drinner?, Hugh Fle 63
Driscal, John Log 182
William log 182
Driscle, John Log 186
Drisedel, John Mon 379
Driskel, Jesse Cas 40
Driskill, David Hnr 366
Dennis Mer 318
Elijah mer 318
Joseph Mer 319
Peter Mas 273
Priscilla Mer 319
Driver, Dempsy Bar 39
Francis Sco 185
Jessee Bar 39
Thomas Bar 39
Drum, George Fay 49
Drummon, James Cas 39
Drummond, James Nic 57
Samuel Mas 275
Drury, Elias Hrd 290
John Wsh 327
Libby War 265
Mary Nel 23
Michael Wsh 328
Zachariah Wsh 328
Dry, George Cas 37
Jacob War 266
Dryden, John Mas 272
Dryden, cont.
Mary Mad 201
Drysdale, James Mon 371
DsPain, Soloman Grn 257
DsSpain, Peter Grn 247
Soloman Grn 251
Dubenyear, Peter Mas 277
Duck, Josiah Pul 139
Ducker, james She 225
Jas. Way 370
John Cam 28
Nathaniel Pen 112
William Fra 124
Ducket, John R. Bou 83
Thomas Bou 82
Duckett, Isaac Fle 67
John War 273
Wm. Bou 82
Duckworth, Ezekiel Mon 380
Isaac Grn 248
John Grn 248
John Mon 355
John Mon 383
Simon Mon 380
Wm. Jr Grn 248
Wm. Sr Grn 248
Dudgeon, James Boo 58
Dudggins, Willm. Lin 115
Dudgins, Willm. Lin 115
Dudley, Ambris Chr 110
Ambrose Fay 33
Ambrose Fay 46
Anne Bou 82
James Fay 45
James Knx 78
Jas. Hrd 303
Jephthah Fra 124
John Clr 127
Robert Fay 34
Robert Fay 45
Robert Mul 388
Thomas Grn 247
William E. Fay 46
Willm. Adr 7
Dudly, James Hop 374
William Fay 45
Dueart, Cornelius Bar 46
Duease, David Bar 28
Elisha Bar 29
Duerson, John Mad 200
Dueson, Thomas Jes 35
Duff, Abraham War 257
Daniel Mon 384
John Bar 30
John Gar 234
John War 278
Joseph War 267
Mary Liv 156
Robert Liv 160
Saml. War 278
Walter Cal 19
William Mas 276
Duffe, William Mad 201
Duffey, James Way 351
John Way 351
John Mas 272
Lewis Hrd 294
Dufield, Thomas Gal 189
Dufner, Jacob Hrd 293
Dugan, Hugh Gal 189
James Cam 31
James Nel 23
Jeramiah Hrs 312
Sarah She 207
Thos. Nel 23
William Nel 22
Dugger, David Bar 27
Dugger, cont.
James Knx 70
William Knx 72
Duggin, Mary Lin 125
Richard Wsh 325
Stephen Wsh 324
Duggins, Alexander Jef 32
David Mer 319
Elizabeth Gar 233
Dugglass, Nathan Gar 233
Duglas, Daniel Pul 141
John Pul 140
Thomas Chr 66
Thomas Pul 141
Wm. Lew 97
Duglass, George Mas 276
Dugless, Geo. Cas 41
Duglis, Wm. Mon 364
Duit, William Chr 95
Duke, Bazel mas 309
David Hrd 288
Geo. Bar 34
Henry Gar 234
Hezakiah Chr 67
James Wsh 328
John Ohi 102
Mathew Clr 127
Morry Bar 38
Dukes, Benjamin Mul 406
Jacob Mul 391
Samuel Mul 391
Duley, James Sco 186
James, Jur Sco 193
Thos. Sco 190
Zadoc Mas 276
Dulin, Edwd. Bou 121
Jacob Cly 157
Lod Chr 66
Thadius Fay 37
Duly, Abm. Way 365
James Hrd 302
Thomas Hrd 302
Wm. Hrd 291
Duma, Anthony C. Fay 55
Dumas, Silas Boo 58
Dumass, Lewis Fay 22
Dumet, P. William Grp 277
Robert Grp 277
Dumn, Edward Hrs 321
Dun, Abraham Nic 57
Andrew Bra 147
Benedger Hrs 318
Benjamin Hrs 321
Elijah Hrs 322
John Hrs 321
John Hrs 322
Joseph Hrs 320
Joseph Liv 151
Lewis Log 191
Nehemiah Hrs 321
Pressilla Jef 16
Robert, Junr Hrd 301
Robert, Senr Hrd 303
Samuel Hrs 307
Thos. Hrs 321
William Hrd 282
William Liv 159
Dunaga, Thomas Mon 356
Dunagan, Solomon Woo 385
Dunagem, Isaac Way 367
Dunagunn, David Jes 35
Dunahoo, Mathew Mon 367
Dunavin, John Chr 103
William Chr 69
Dunaway, Charles Pen 107
Thomas Est 1
Willm. Lin 115

Dunawho, Michael Knx 69
Dunbar, Alexr. Fle 80
James Fle 61
James, Sr Hnr 352
Jas. R. Gal 189
John Adr 7
John Nel 23
Nancy Cum 170
Nathaniel Cal 16
Robert Jef 31
Sidney Jef 30
Tho. Mad 202
William Nel 24
Willm. Adr 7
Young War 277
Duncan, Anderson Mad 199
Andrew Mon 378
Archd. Nic 57
Benjamin Fra 123
Benjamin Ohi 84
Benjn. Lin 114
Charels, C. Fle 66
Charles Jef 16
Charles Mad 199
Charles Ohi 93
Cilia Sco 178
Claboune Cas 38
Colem. Nel 22
Coleman Jef 16
Colin Sco 171
Danl. Bou 68
David, Sen Mas 279
Edw. Jur Mad 200
Edward Mad 200
Elias Pen 116
Elisha Hrd 296
Eliza Bar 54
Elizabeth Log 182
Ennis Mas 301
Enoch Pen 116
Gabriel Mad 199
George Lin 114
George Ohi 93
Hamton Lin 115
Henry Jef 24
Henry Liv 147
Henry Mad 199
Henry Nel 23
Isauc Mad 199
James Clr 127
James Hnr 356
James Hrs 308
James Hrs 310
James Log 185
James Nic 58
James Sco 171
James, Jr Bou 121
James, Junior Bre 157
James, Sr Bou 121
James, Senr Bre 161
Jas. Jef 25
Jesse Hrs 308
Jesse She 220
Jno. Nel 25
John Adr 7
John Adr 7
John Fay 55
John Knx 65
John Knx 87
John Mad 199
John Mad 201
John Ohi 92
John, W. Clr 127
Joseph Clr 127
Joseph Clr 127
Joseph Grp 277
Joseph Lin 115

Duncan, cont.
Joseph Nel 22
Joseph Nic 58
Joseph War 282
Josha. Adr 7
Joshua Clr 126
Laurance Knx 66
Marble War 267
Marshal She 204
Mathew Bou 121
Matthew Log 183
Nancy Bar 53
Nancy Woo 394
Nimrod Log 176
Nimrod She 235
Peter Rck 164
Prior War 282
Reuben Hnr 357
Rice Cum 172
Rice War 271
Robt. D. Rck 161
Roger Bou 82
Roser Hrs 322
Saml. Gar 234
Saml. Lin 115
Saml. Nel 21
Sanford Log 196
Seth Bou 121
Shadrack Hrd 293
Thos. Nel 21
Walter Mas 276
Washington Bou 82
William Fle 89
William Hnr 357
William Log 171
William Log 182
William Nic 58
William She 219
Willis Hnr 356
Willis Pen 113
Wm. Gar 234
Wm. Nel 22
Wm. Nel 23
Zachariah Liv 147
Duncann, Thos. Bou 83
Duncum, William Pul 140
Dungan, John Mer 321
Thos. Hrs 307
Dungans, George Pul 141
Dungins, Henrietta Pul 141
Jeremiah Pul 141
Dunham, Amos Mon 377
Dennis War 246
John Mad 200
John War 267
Samuel Mas 275
Dunhan, Timothy War 257
Dunhart, Christian Jef 31
Duning, Ezechal Chr 88
Hardiman Chr 89
James Chr 88
Jessy Chr 61
John R. Hop 372
Shadrick Chr 89
Dunken, George Way 355
Dunkerson, Thomas Chr 103
Dunkill, David Hnr 366
Dunkin, Charlse J[illegible] 35
Dad. [illegible] 361
Deniel P[illegible]l 139
Jesse Mer 322
Dunkin, John Cal 19
John Mer 321
John Pul 139
John Pul 140
Margaret Mon 379
Martin Mer 320

Dunkin, cont.
Melehar Chr 76
William Pul 138
Willm. Hrs 308
Wm. War 271
Dunkins, Alexander Pul 141
Dunkle, Jacob Woo 378
Dunklin, John Mer 321
Dunlap, Alexr. Woo 378
Benjamin Chr 75
Elizabeth Liv 149
George Fay 22
Henry Fle 64
James Fle 73
James Mon 348
John Mer 321
Morning Knx 87
Moses Chr 75
Robert Mon 361
William Chr 72
William Fay 22
William Fay 23
William Fay 36
Wm. Mon 348
Dunlavy, Daniel Mon 369
Dunn, Alex Hnr 367
Alex, Sr Hnr 351
Alexander Jes 35
Alexr. Cal 10
Andrew Bou 121
Andrew Cal 14
Augustine Gar 235
Benja. Gar 235
Benjamin Mer 318
Edmond War 254
Elender Mer 321
George Fay 54
Henry Fle 83
Isham Clr 126
James Fay 14
James Jes 35
James Mer 321
James War 264
James Wsh 325
Jesse Hnr 351
Jesse Mer 318
Jesse War 264
Jessy Chr 109
Jno. Hnr 353
John Bul 176
John Gar 235
John Hnr 351
John Jef 24
John Liv 156
John, Jr Clr 126
John, Sr Clr 126
Joseph Bou 82
Joseph Cal 10
Joseph Cal 14
Julias War 248
Levy Hrs 321
Mackey Wsh 325
Nathaniel Jes 62
Pharo Chr 110
Polly Cal 10
Richard Mad 199
Rier Adr 7
Robert Hnr 351
Samuel Mer 319
Thomas Bou 83
Vincent Gra 242
William Chr 110
William C. Fay 21
Wm. Gar 236
Dunnagan, John Woo 385
Dunnagin, Tho. Bar 30
Dunnam, Samuel Fay 33

Dunning, John R. Hnd 341
Micajah War 271
Dunnington, Benns Log 161
William Log 161
Dunniway, Ben Clr 127
Dunnuway, Isaac Fle 67
Dunsmore, John Way 371
Dunton, Kely Bra 143
Thos. Hrd 296
Dunwiddie, James Jes 35
Dunwiddy, James Chr 53
Dunwoody, Wm. Bar 37
Wm. Bou 121
Dunwooddy, John Bou 83
Dupen, Barby Nel 25
James Nel 25
Dupin, Freeborn Nel 23
John Nel 23
Dupu, Joseph Chr 63
William Chr 62
Dupuy, Benja. She 239
James She 207
James Woo 391
Jel Woo 385
John Hnr 354
Joseph Hnr 351
Samuel She 239
Starke She 232
William Grp 271
Durban, Austin Hrd 286
Daniel Bou 83
Durben, Christopher Knx 78
Durbin, Amous Grp 271
Christopher, Jun Mad 200
Edward Mad 202
Hosier Bou 82
John Bar 33
John, Jur Mad 200
John, Sen Mad 201
Joseph Mad 200
Melvan Grp 271
Nicholas Mad 244
Philip Mad 199
Saml. Mad 201
Tho. Bar 33
Durbon, Danl. Gal 189
Durbrow, Robt. Gal 189
Duree, Saml. Hnr 363
Saml. Hrd 296
Durham, Benj. Mer 322
Betsy Mer 321
James Grn 245
James Mer 321
James Mer 322
Jesse Mer 322
John Mer 322
John Mer 322
John Woo 381
Melton Cas 37
Samuel Grn 245
Thomas Mer 322
William Mad 201
Wm. Grn 245
Durling, Garrett Mer 321
Durly, Rhatio Cal 12
Durmon, Edward Gal 197
Durnal, James War 278
Wm. War 278
Duroset, Mary Mon 376
Durral?, Levi Grp 272
Durram, Wm. War 272
Durrell, Francis Hnr 362
Francis, Sr Hnr 353
Durret, Joel Grn 258
John Grn 257
Durrett, Paul Mon 384
Durrett, cont.
Woodson Fay 34
Woodson Fay 46
Durrum, John Knx 78
Durum, Nathaniel Pul 138
Durye, John Jun Mas 275
Dusan, Jacob Nic 58
Peter Lew 97
Duson, Thomas Jef 32
Wm. Jef 32
Dutero, Jocob Fle 88
Dutton, David Pul 138
Jessee Cam 33
Samuel Wsh 327
Duttry, Saml. Lin 114
Duty, Daniel Mas 278
William Bou 83
Duval, Claiborne Hrd 288
Daniel Ohi 77
Jacob Nel 23
Thos. Hrd 298
William P. Nel 10
Zachariah Fay 14
Duvall, Charles She 232
Claudius Log 194
Cornelius Sco 186
David Mul 386
Dennis Bul 176
Elisha Cal 4
Elizabeth Mul 392
George Woo 379
John Clr 126
John Sco 187
John Woo 395
John L. Bul 176
Lewis Mul 392
Marina Sco 186
Martha Mul 398
Mary Fay 50
Notly Mas 279
Samuel Liv 149
Silas Mas 279
Thomas Woo 384
William Clr 127
Duvaul, James Mon 351
Duwit, Elisha Gra 241
Duzan, Abraham Mas 274
Hezekiah Mas 274
John Mas 273
John Mas 278
Dwathen, Horace G. Hnd 347
Dwere, Ellis Mas 275
Dwiggins, James Cly 154
Dwolin, Edward Mon 375
Dyar, Abraham Lin 114
Dye, Fantleroy Mer 322
Isaac Cam 26
Isaac Cas 41
James War 267
Job Hrd 291
John Fay 22
John Mas 274
John Mas 277
Kenith Mas 278
Martin Grn 245
Mountur Mas 279
Peter Fle 77
Phebe Mas 273
Richard Hnd 342
Shadrick Pul 139
William Mas 276
William Pul 139
William, Senr Mas 278
Dyehouse, Edwd. Gar 235
Dyer, Abner War 261
Benjamin Chr 75
Charles Wsh 326
Dyer, cont.
Elisha War 261
Enuck Chr 58
Hezekiah Liv 156
John Chr 93
John Mas 276
John Mas 278
John Wsh 324
John Wsh 325
Milly Mer 342
Minoah War 261
Rachl. War 275
Sarah War 275
William Hnd 329
Wm. Cum 174
Dyert, Hugh Wsh 327
Dykes, John Bou 82
William Bou 121
William, Jr Bou 121
Dyllon, D. John Fay 14
Dyre, Abraham Lin 115
Dysart, Colo. J. Rck 159
John B. Rck 159
Saml. Rck 159
Dyson, Bennet Hnd 340
Hezk. Sco 177

-- E --

E..., ... Lin 116
Eadan John Lin 116
Eaden, Eliah Cas 40
Hennery Cas 39
Wliam Cas 39
Eadens, John Bul 177
Phillip Bul 177
Wm. Sin Cas 43
Eades, Carrel Mad 204
George Grn 258
Joseph Gal 188
Joseph Hnd 333
Lewis Mad 202
Eadin, James Mul 392
Eadon, Jonathan Clr 128
Zachariah Clr 128
Eads, Drury Clr 128
Howell, Clr 128
James Fay 14
John Fay 15
Robert Bul 177
Sam Log 178
Thomas Bou 84
Thomas Lin 115
Walter Clr 128
Eager, Henry Hrs 314
Eagland, Clemont Bre 159
Eaglin, Cornelius Gal 189
J. Jef 15
Zackariah Jef 29
Eakin, Olly She 232
Eakins, Henry Hnr 352
Eales, Daniel Bou 122
James Bou 122
John Bou 122
Ealley, Henry Sco 170
Ealliwine, Danil Nic 56
Ealum, Benjn. Woo 385
Ealy, Thomas Hnr 365
Eammel, John R. Fay 43
Eandy, Arazamew Mul 395
Earingten, Lovedy Hnr 366
Earle, Ann Hop 375
Edwd. H. Hop 379
John Mul 388

Earles, Frederick Cum 169
Joshua Cas 45
Samuel Cas 45
Wyatt Cum 169
Earley, James Fay 21
Joseph Knx 90
Saml. War 248
William Knx 64
Earliwine, George Nic 56
Jacob Nic 56
Earls, Rodham Mas 270
Samuel Chr 91
Early, David Fle 77
Joseph Mas 271
Mathew Chr 61
Thomas Knx 86
Thomas Mas 271
Whitefield Boo 59
William Chr 83
William Mas 299
Earnest, Aron War 261
John Log 174
Thos. War 248
William, Jr Log 174
William, Senr Log 174
Earom, Charles Jef 15
Earp, Joel Bou 84
Earrly, John Fle 81
Easaley, John Hrs 317
Easby, John War 264
Easley, Daniel Jes 37
Wm. War 274
Easom, Edward Grp 273
East, Benjamin Chr 56
James Gar 232
John Cal 15
Joseph Lin 116
Mary Cal 15
Neal Lin 116
Neal Lin 116
North Way 355
Robert (freeman) Jes 41
Safey Cas 44
Eastep, Cornelius Flo 98
Shadrack Flo 97
Shadrack Flo 98
Easter, George Mer 317
James Mad 204
John Bar 53
Patsy Bar 53
Will Gar 232
Easterday, Lewis Gal 188
Eastes, Fielding Bou 122
Litelton Fay 46
Wiet Fle 65
Wm. Hrs 321
Eastham, Joanney Fay 23
Jno. Nel 26
Marry Hnr 359B
Richard Fay 21
Wm. Sco 189
Eastige, Clemon Fay 49
Midelton Fay 49
Eastin, Augustine Bou 84
Charles She 208
John Mad 204
Nicholas Mad 204
Philip Jef 15
Robert Mad 204
Stephen Mad 203
Zacheriah Bou 84
Eastis, Nathan Jef 31
Thomas Lin 116
Eastland, Thomas Mer 318
Easly, Jesse Cum 172
Joseph Nic 57
Sally Cum 172

Easton, Danl. Adr 9
George Hrs 317
Griffin Pen 116
Isaac Hrs 317
James Jes 37
John Hrs 317
John Wsh 322
Johnson Jes 37
Eastus, Thos. Nic 56
Eastwood, Abner Hnd 332
Abraham Hnd 333
Hannah Hnd 333
John Hnd 332
Eatburington,
Richd. Bre 164
Eathel, John War 254
Eaten, Benjan. Bou 84
Daniel Bou 84
James Pul 142
Eaton, Benja. Fle 77
Benjn. Mon 382
Charles Fle 65
George She 231
Henry Jef 32
Henry War 249
Isaac War 261
Jacob Nic 56
John Knx 73
John Woo 397
Joseph Mon 379
Joseph Woo 385
Nannah Mon 375
Saml. Est 8
Saml. Way 360
Solomon Mon 379
William Gal 188
Wm. Lew 104
Eatwell, Alexander Cam 26
Eavens, John Nic 56
Eaves, William Fay 29
Eavins, John Jes 37
(Free man of colour)
Nathaniel Jes 37
Rachel Nic 56
William Jes 37
Eavy, Abraham Mul 404
Ebert, Philip Mas 305
Ecard, Leonard Cam 28
Eccles, see Accles
Henry Mer 317
Jane Mer 317
John Gal 188
Jno. Hrd 304
Eckler, Jacob Hrs 317
Oly Hrs 317
Ecton, Drusilla Clr 128
Smallwood Cly 128
Eddis, Charles Way 368
Gabl. Way 369
Eddlemon, Danl. Bou 84
John Bou 84
Peter Fay 35
Ede, William She 242
Edelen, Edward Wsh 324
Robert Wsh 323
Samuel Wsh 323
Sarah Wsh 324
Ederington, James Grn 262
Moses Grn 266
Thomas Grn 262
Will Grn 266
Wm. Grn 262
Edes, John Mas 270
Edgar, James Bar 34
James Log 173
John Bar 34
William Log 191

Edgar, cont.
Zacheriah Log 162
Edge, Benjamin Fay 29
Henry Mad 203
Jonathan Est 3
Edger, Alesancer Hrs 312
Edward Hrs 309
Henry Hrs 308
Edgerton, Benja. Gar 233
John Gar 233
Wm. Gar 232
Edgman, Thos. R. Way 367
Edins, Elias Sco 189
Edlin, Joseph Nel 26
Edminson, Tho. Mad 204
Edmison, John Fay 46
Edmiston, James Cum 178
James Hop 381
John Fay 32
Mary Woo 386
Edmond, James Mul 404
Edmonds, James Adr 7
James War 270
John War 270
Edmondson, John Jef 32
Jno. Gar 233
Edmonson, Richard Clr 128
Edmonston, Wm. Hrs 319
Edmosen, Archibald Chr 113
Edmund, Peter Cam 26
Edmunds, John Cam 26
Edmundson, Francis Wsh 324
William Wsh 323
Edmunson, James Fle 82
Edon, Jeremiah Fle 65
Edrington, Austn. Nel 26
Benj. Fra 126
Joseph Woo 394
Edson, George Log 196
John Fra 126
Edward, Emmeriah Cas 39
Ishem Cas 44
John Cas 44
Joseph Cum 179
Lewis Cas 47
Meridith Flo 97
Payne Fay 39
Travis Nel 26
William Fay 15
Edwards, Abdon Cum 179
Abner Gra 239
Alexr. Bar 54
Ambros Gar 233
Amos Log 183
Aron Cas 38
Benj. Nel 27
Benjamin Fra 125
Benjn. Bou 122
Benjn. Woo 393
Cader Bar 54
Clayburn Lin 116
Cornelius Woo 400
David Bre 157
David Gra 239
Edward Chr 70
Edward She 210
Wlisha Hrd 298
Elisha Nel 26
Elish Nel 27
Esaac Bar 27
Everus Elish Nel 27
Francis Hrs 308
Francis Mad 202
Frederick Jef 15
George Bou 84
George Lin 116
Hannah Nic 56

Edwards, cont.
Henry Acr 7
Henry Chr 55
Henry Lin 116
Henry Log 183
Hogdn. Nel 26
Isaac She 227
Isaac She 233
James Bar 52
James Fra 125
James Mas 271
James Pul 142
James War 246
James Woo 391
James Woo 395
James M. Jef 32
Jesse Gar 232
John Bou 84
John Bou 84
John Bra 150
John Chr 111
John Fay 29
John Fra 125
John Grn 255
John Grp 270
John Hop 381
John Jef 16
John Lin 116
John Liv 147
John Log 175
John Pul 142
John Way 372
John Wsh 322
John, Jr Woo 393
John, Senr Woo 393
Jonathan Hrs 319
Joseph Woo 384
Josiah Wsh 323
Langhorn Cas 39
Lewis Gar 233
Merida Log 175
Moses Woo 394
Philip Bre 159
Richard Jef 15
Richard Mul 386
Robert Log 176
Robert Mas 271
Robt. Bar 54
Simeon Woo 386
Stoutin Jef 15
Susannah Bou 84
Thomas Bre 161
Thomas Chr 73
Thomas Jes 37
Thos. Grn 263
Thos. Nel 26
Rhos. Junr Lin 116
Thos. Snr Lin 116
Uriah Cam 29
Uriah Fra 125
Uriah Woo 393
William Knx 72
William Log 175
William Mas 271
Wm. Cas 37
Wm. Clr 128
Wm. Gar 233
Wm. Jef 32
Wm. Nel 26
Wm. Nel 26
Zach. Gar 233
Eevins, John Pen 109
Efferson, Jas. Gar 232
Effett, William Nel 26
Egbert, David Fra 125
Delency Woo 401
James Mer 317

Egbert, cont.
John Nel 10
Egell, Harris Cal 4
Eggans, Thomas Mer 317
Eggleston, Benjamin Fra 126
Eglan, James Hrd 294
John Hrd 301
Thos. Hrd 292
William Hrd 303
Egnew, Isaac Hrs 317
Ehrich, David Woo 378
Eidson, James Bre 158
John Bre 169
John War 276
Ejistile, Mathias Way 354
Elage, James Mon 353
Elam, Elizabeth She 241
Godfrey Cum 166
Elambough, John Jes 37
Elberson, John Fle 74
Elbert, Henry Hrs 323
Jno. D. Fle 82
Elbird, James Bar 33
Elder, Alexander Mad 204
Andrew Mad 204
Arnold Bre 158
Arnold Bre 168
David Liv 160
David Mad 203
George Liv 158
Ignats. Nel 27
James Lin 116
James Wsh 323
John Fay 15
Matthew Fay 14
Matthew Lin 115
Peggy Liv 156
Peter Cum 177
Ro... Lin 115
Robert Liv 158
Robert Mul 385
Samuel Chr 61
Samuel Liv 157
Sylvester Wsh 323
Thomas Fay 14
Thomas Gra 242
Thos. Nel 27
William Liv 156
William Wsh 324
Wm. Cas 40
Eldridge, James Cly 152
Jas. Hnr 352
John Cly 152
Rachel Cly 153
Eleraig, T. Mul 385
Elett, William Fle 91
Elexander, Aaron Fay 52
Robert Fay 53
Elexandra, Andrew Cas 40
Elgan, Kizzy Mer 317
Elgin, Agnes Bou 122
Frederick Woo 381
Jesse She 202
Joseph Sco 182
William Bou 122
Elgins, Gusta Mon 378
Eli, Eli Log 187
Eliot, Danil Lin 116
Elijah Grn 260
George Cal 8
John Chr 60
Samuel Fay 53
William Hrs 313
Wm. Bra 142
Eliott, Elijah Bra 151
Elison, Andrew Mon 381
Frederick Bra 142

Elison, cont.
Isaac Bra 142
James Mon 374
John Mon 378
Jonathan Bra 142
Josua Mon 376
Wm. Mon 374
Eliston, Amos Lin 116
John Gal 188
Elkin, Abel Grn 266
Aylett Wsh 323
David Grn 254
Ezekiel Clr 128
James Clr 128
Robert Clr 128
William Grn 266
Zachariah Clr 128
Elkins, Pul 142
Abel Mad 203
Drury Pul 142
Frederick Mul 403
Isaiah Woo 381
James Flo 97
James Flo 97
Jesse Pul 142
Joshua Cly 155
Joshua Mul 390
Josiah Chr 72
Nathaniel War 279
Reubin Clr 146
Richard Pul 142
Elledge, Benjamin Clr 128
Boon Clr 128
Frances Clr 128
Ellen, David Sco 192
Ellender, George Fle 87
William Fle 88
Ellensworth, Bartholemew Jef 15
Elleott, Edward Fle 73
Ellerbick, Jos. Nic 56
Ellerson, Joseph Bar 38
Elles, Hezekiah Fay 35
Elless, Isaac Cas 45
Richard Cas 46
Ellet, Jonathan Mer 317
Jonathan Mer 318
Jno. Nel 27
Richd. Nel 27
Samuel Mul 390
Ellett, Joseph Pul 142
Thos. Cly 149
Elley, Henry Sco 184
Ellice, Peter Pul 142
Ellidge, Elijah Flo 98
Ellington, David Flo 98
David Grp 273
Jonathan Flo 98
Jacob Flo 98
Jacob Fra 125
Pleasant Grp 273
Elliot, Benjn. Nel 26
George Fay 43
Hanbleton Mon 363
Tho. Bar 42
William But 193
Wm. Hrd 290
Zachariah But 193
Elliott, Abel She 207
Asehel Knx 86
David Mad 204
Dosson Mad 204
Elex. Adr 7
Elizabeth Knx 84
Elizabeth Mon 375
Galen Nel 26
Geo. Gar 233

Elliott, cont.
Geo. Gar 233
James Bou 84
James Fle 64
James Flo 98
James Sco 184
James Wsh 323
John Bou 84
John Bou 122
John Fle 66
John Mad 204
John Nel 27
John She 205
John She 206
John Woo 385
Joseph Mad 203
Joseph Wsh 324
Marget Wsh 323
Mary Clr 128
Rachel She 207
Reuben Mas 270
Revd. John Sco 170
Richard Wsh 322
Robert Bou 84
Robert She 206
Sally Knx 84
Saml. Cum 169
Samuel Fay 43
Simon Wsh 323
Stephen Wsh 322
Thomas Fle 75
Thomas Mas 270
Thomas Sco 189
Thomas Wsh 323
Thos. Cum 184
William Bou 122
William Nel 26
William She 199
William She 206
William She 206
William Woo 383
William, Senr Fra 125
Ellis, Asa Bar 29
Auguston Mer 317
Benjamin Bou 84
Benjamin Bou 84
Benjamin Flo 98
Charles Flo 98
Charles Mon 372
Charles She 218
Christr. Cum 179
David Bou 122
Dudley Bou 122
Eleazer Fra 125
Elizebeth Mas 270
Elizebeth Mas 270
Henry Bou 84
Henry Gal 188
Heskiah Fay 52
Isaac Bar 37
Isaac She 198
Israel Fra 126
Jacob Fra 125
James Mas 305
James Nic 56
James Nic 56
James Pen 113
James Wsh 324
Jas. Gar 233
Jesriel Pen 110
Jesse Cum 171
Jesse Fra 126
Jesse She 227
Jesse, Jr Woo 391
Jessee, Senr Woo 390
Joel Gal 188
John Bar 21

Ellis, cont.
John Boo 58
John Bou 84
John Bou 84
John Bou 122
John Cum 173
John Mas 271
John Nic 56
John Pen 110
John She 208
Jos. Hnr 359
Joseph Bou 84
Joseph Bou 84
Joseph She 210
Joseph She 211
Joseph She 238
Joseph, Senr Bou 84
Leonard Woo 394
Letelberry Fay 54
Luke Mer 317
Obadiah Sco 180
Rhody Pen 108
Richard She 220
Richd. Boo 59
Roger She 209
Samuel Liv 148
Samuel She 240
Stephen She 238
Thomas Fay 50
Thomas Fay 52
Thomas Rck 163
William Bou 84
William Bou 84
William Fay 52
William Fay 59
William Mer 317
William Pen 108
William She 211
William She 217
Wm. Bar 25
Wm. Boo 59
Wm. M. Bou 84
Ellise, Elijah Fle 78
Ellison, Archd. Cly 154
Asa Knx 72
Baily Adr 7
Givan Hnr 364
Henry Mer 317
Isabell Bou 122
James Mad 202
John Grp 278
John War 257
Joseph Mad 204
Margaret mer 317
Moses Sco 180
Robert Hrs 309
Robt. War 257
Wm. War 261
Elliss, Charles War 253
Johnson War 269
Jona. Hnr 363
Thomas War 271
William Hnr 366
Elliston, Danl. T. Woo 392
Jacob Fra 125
Thomas Wsh 323
Ellitt, Johnson Lin 116
Ellot, Johnston Cas 41
Elmes, Samuel Liv 156
Elmore, Elisha Way 358
George Adr 7
James [illegible] 21
John [illegible] 28
Mathew Lin 116
John Lin 116
Martin War 254
Thos. Grn 259

Elmore, cont.
Travis Hrd 288
William Grn 265
Elmos, Patty Fay 44
Elms, James But 193
Margaret But 193
Thomas But 193
William But 193
Elmsbaugh, Peter Est 3
Elmsby, Geo. Hnr 357
Elridge, Abr. Nel 25
Elrod, Jeramiah Way 359
Michael Way 360
Robert Mas 270
T. John Mas 270
Elsberry, Benjamin Clr 128
Isaac Gar 232
Liddy Clr 128
Elsbury, Jacob She 225
Elsey, John Sco 182
Elsome, William Cly 160
Elson, Cornelius Lew 100
Ricd. T. Lew 100
Richard Lew 97
Elston, Benja. Hnr 366
David Hnr 368
David Hnr 369
Joseph Hnr 363
Josiah Mad 203
William Hnr 362
Elstone, Jonathan Jef 15
Elswick Bradley Flo 98
Edmond Flo 98
John Flo 98
Elum, Burrel Way 362
Elvin, James Log 167
Ely, Anthony Knx 63
Benjm. Mon 354
Isaac Mon 359
Laurance Log 191
Wm. Jr Knx 63
Wm. Sr Knx 63
Emanuel, Thomas Mon 348
Emberson, Armstead Sco 168
Francis Pul 142
John Lin 116
John Pul 143
Joseph H. Bul 177
Reuben Fay 21
Reubin Mer 317
Pleasant Bar 28
Samuel Lin 116
Thomas Pul 143
Walter Way 366
Wm. Bar 28
John Bar 48
Emberton, Susanna Bar 48
Tho. Bar 44
Embree, Caleb Clr 128
Elijah Lin 116
Elisha Cum 170
John Clr 128
John Lin 116
Joseph Clr 128
Moses Cum 170
Thomas Clr 128
Embrei, Joshua Cum 178
Embrey, Cadoc Gar 232
Isaac Gar 232
Will,Jnr Gar 232
Wm. Snr Gar 232
Embry, Burrel Gar 232
Henry Grn 260
Joel Mad 203
Joseph Mad 203
Talton Mad 202
Willis Adr 7

Embry, cont.
Wm. Grn 260
Emerson, Filley Clr 128
Henson Bul 177
James Cum 165
John Grn 265
Simpson Clr 128
Emery, Adam Hrd 301
Isaac Hrd 295
Joseph Hrd 302
Emett, Silus Boo 59
Wm. Boo 59
Emison, Ash Sco 181
Hugh Sco 172
James Sco 172
Emitt, Elexander Mon 353
Emmerson, Fras. Cum 171
Emmie?, Nicholas Bre 164
Emmins, Elisha Mas 271
Emmit, Lewis Hrd 302
Emmons, Charles Fle 86
Elijah Fle 75
James Nel 26
William Fay 15
William, Jur Fle 86
Willm. Nel 26
Empson, John Clr 128
Richard Clr 128
Ems, John Clr 128
Emston, Hannah Jes 37
Endecott, Joseph Woo 392
William Woo 391
Engard, Rachel Mad 203
Silas Mad 203
Engart, David Mad 203
England, Augustine Gar 233
Jacob Log 180
Jessa Mon 377
Jonn Cum 179
Joseph Flo 98
Mary Gar 233
Nathan Adr 7
Stephen Mon 364
Thomas Knx 88
Wm. Bar 25
Engle, George Knx 67
John Knx 84
Peter Knx 71
William Hnr 359A
English, Andrew Mon 355
Anna Gar 232
Charles Mad 204
Elisha Hnr 355
Elisha Hnr 367
James Gra 242
John Fay 56
John Hrs 310
John Mon 355
Patrick Gra 242
Robert Mas 271
Stephen Mad 204
Thomas Hnr 359
Thomas, Jr Hnr 359
William Gra 240
Wm. Hrs 310
Engram, Abraham Mon 353
Abraham Mon 373
Colenge Mon 373
John Mon 353
John Mon 372
Thomas Jef 32
Thomas, Junr Mon 372
Uriah Mon 353
Engrim, Jas. Jef 15
Enix, David Jef 31
Garret Jef 32
Isaac Jef 31
Enix, cont.
Thomas Jef 31
Enlove, Abriham Chr 90
Enlow, Abraham Hrd 302
Jacob Hrd 302
James Fle 90
Enlowe, Isom Hrd 290
Ennis, Barton Cal 7B
Charles Mas 271
George War 258
James Fay 50
John Bar 53
John Mas 271
James Fay 57
Enniss, John War 257
John War 257
Enocks, Abraham Fle 62
Entrican, John Chr 109
Enyart, Rebekah Cum 176
Eoff, Isaac Pul 142
Epason, Barnet Bou 122
Eperson, James Mon 361
James Mon 361
James Mon 371
Peter Mon 361
Robert Mon 361
Robert Mon 364
Robert, Jurr Mon 361
Wm. Adr 7
Epison, John Sr Clr 128
Epperson, Ann Fay 15
Benjn. Boo 59
Charles War 257
David Lin 116
David Mer 317
Francis Fay 21
John Lin 116
John She 209
John She 219
Peter Mon 362
Richard Jes 37
Robert Mad 202
Thomas Fay 21
Eppison, Richd. Hrd 287
Epting, Christopher Fay 15
Erby, John Log 173
Ericson see Aerexon
Erit, John Way 353
Erl, James She 240
Erles, James Pen 116
John Pen 107
Ernest, Nathaniel Ohi 82
Ervan, James Mon 380
Janes Mon 348
Thomas Mon 379
Timothy Mon 351
Wm. Mon 380
Ervene, Joseph Nel 26
Ervin, Elias Pen 105
John Fle 71
Ervine, Jameson Cly 158
Erwin, Benjamin Pul 142
Joseph Hnr 368
Joseph Pul 142
Robert Hnr 361
Robert Liv 145
William Chr 76
Erwing, Edward Ohi 89
Esely, Washam Cal 8
Esenflow, Joseph Hrs 317
Eslep, Saml. Adr 7
Esler, John H. Mad 204
Eslick, Samuel But 198
Esom, Ann Fay 41
Essary, Jona. D. Hrd 300
Essery, Thomas Liv 159
Essex, Joseph Nel 26
Essex, cont.
Thomas Hrd 281
William Fay 15
Essrey, Thomas But 193
Estam, James Nel 26
Esten, Robert Gra 239
Esters, John Chr 91
Estes, Elisha Mad 203
Elisha Mad 246
Joel Mad 203
John Cly 156
Little B. Mad 203
Littleton Fay 35
Peter Mad 203
Smith Mad 246
Spencer Mad 203
Wiatt Fle 87
William Mad 246
Estham, James Fay 41
James Pul 143
James, Sen Pul 143
John Pul 142
Esther, John Hrd 301
Estice, Abram. Adr 7
Peter Adr 7
Saml. Adr 7
Estil, William Fle 71
Estill, Benjamin Mad 202
Boud Mad 202
James Mad 203
John Mad 203
Jonathan Mad 244
Saml. Mad 202
Thos. Sco 178
Walliss Mad 202
William Fle 75
Estis, Asy Chr 96
Estiss, Thos. War 253
Estters, David Pul 142
Estwage, Abraham Lin 116
Etherington, James Fle 87
Micajah Fay 29
Peter Hrd 294
Etherton, Aron Nel 26
Benj. Nel 25
John Ohi 98
Joshua Mad 202
Ethington, William Sco 184
Ethrington, John Sco 172
Reuben Fra 125
Eubank, Achilles Clr 128
Ambrose Clr 128
James Clr 128
Joseph Mas 271
Robert She 223
Eubanks, James Knx 66
James Wsh 323
John Lin 116
John War 277
Jonathan War 263
Mortan War 271
Thos. War 274
Euebanks, Joseph Bar 45
Eulis, Jacob Sco 178
Evans, Abner War 258
Alen But 193
Andrew Knx 73
Archabald Knx 70
Archer Clr 128
Belain P. Fay 35
Bonnett H. Fle 64
Charles Mas 271
Christopher But 193
David Est 3
David Est 8
David Mad 202
David Mer 317

Name	County	Page
Fvans, cont.		
Edward	Cly	158
Edward	Rck	161
Evans	Flo	97
Fanny	Jef	15
Gabriel	Fle	84
George	But	193
Griffith	Mas	270
Harris	But	193
Henry	Ohi	90
Henry	Woo	394
Henry	Mad	203
Hugh	Mer	317
Jacob	Bul	177
James I.	Clr	128
James, Jr	Clr	128
James, Sr	Clr	128
Jas.	Way	370
Jeane	Fle	90
John	Adr	7
John	Boo	59
John	Est	5
John	Est	8
John	Fle	68
John	Flo	97
John	Hnr	363
John	Jef	27
John	Jef	32
John	Knx	76
John	Wsh	323
John, Sr	Jef	32
Joseph	Fle	84
Joseph	She	226
Josiah	Bul	177
Jno.	Hnr	360
Mabra	Clr	128
Mary	Mer	317
Moses	Hrd	283
Peter	Clr	128
Peter	Est	7
Rebecca	Fra	126
Robert	Cum	178
Saml.	Cum	171
Saml.	Nel	26
Saml.	War	258
Samuel	Woo	377
Scito	Fle	77
Soverance	Mad	203
Squire	Fle	69
Taylor	Fra	125
Theophilus	But	198
Tho.	Bar	46
Thomas	Bul	177
Thomas	Flo	105
Thomas	Rck	165
Thos.	Adr	7
W. Richd.	Flo	97
William	Bul	177
William	Knx	73
William	Mas	271
Wm. Sr	Knx	66
Eve, George	Sco	188
Evely, George	Way	367
Evens, Adam	Fay	19
Alexr.	Bar	51
Tho. Senr	Bar	46
Thomas	Fay	21
William	Grp	275
Everet, Aaron	Mul	393
Jeremiah	Bar	30
Jessee	Bar	31
Jno. D.	Lew	97
Everhart, David	Rck	161
Martin	Wsh	324
Everit, Richmond O.	Mad	244
Everitt, Isham	Woo	377
Everly, Henry	Mer	317
Everly, cont.		
Jacob	Mer	318
John	Mer	317
Jesse	Mul	390
William	Mul	390
Everman, Jacob	Grp	272
John	Grp	276
Evermon, Jacob	Mon	379
John	Bou	84
Michael	Mon	379
Michael, Senr	Mon	379
Samuel	Mon	379
Wm.	Mon	379
Everitt, Richmond	Mon	384
Eversoul, Jacob	Cly	152
John	Cly	155
Peter	Cly	155
Everton, Thomas	Mul	400
Eves William	Fay	20
Evett, John	Est	8
Evines, Alexander	Fay	21
Richard	Fay	21
Evinger, George	Jef	15
George	Jef	15
Evington, James	Fle	69
Evins, Andrew	Pul	143
Charles	Chr	63
David	Mon	355
David	Pul	143
Elijah	Gar	232
Enoch	Gar	232
Francis	Mon	359
George	Pul	143
Isaac	Mon	364
James	Mon	376
Jessy	Mon	364
John	Gar	233
John	Lin	116
John	Mon	356
John	Pul	142
John	Pul	143
John	Pul	143
Jos.	Gar	233
Samuel	Mon	367
Thomas	Pul	143
William	Pul	143
Zachariah	Pul	142
Eward, John	Bou	84
Ewatt, Henry	Bou	84
John	Bou	84
Ewel, Leroy	Mas	309
Ewen, Henry	Liv	157
Henry	War	243
Samuel	Fay	45
Ewes, Wm.	Adr	7
Ewin, Baker	Chr	115
Finas	Chr	116
Robert	Chr	113
Young	Chr	99
Ewine, Jane	Hrd	281
Ewing, Andw.	Adr	7
Charles	Gar	232
Catharine	Mer	318
Cheatham	Log	175
David	Way	361
Elinor	Fay	37
George	Way	361
Henrietta	Wsh	324
James	But	193
James	Hnr	368
James	Jes	37
John	Gra	241
John	Log	191
John	Pen	112
John B.S.	Log	196
Joseph	Sco	191
Mathew	Cum	169
Ewing, cont.		
Putman	Mon	373
Reuben	Log	185
Robert	Cum	169
Robert	Fle	84
Robert	Jef	15
Robert	Log	191
Robert	Mon	372
Samuel	Log	174
Thomas	Wsh	324
Urben	Log	195
William	But	193
William	Gra	237
Willm.	Sco	173
Ewings, John	Mas	270
Eylsbury, Jerra-miah	Chr	60
Ezel, Tho.	Bar	21
Ezell, Gellum	Chr	107
William	Chr	107

-- F --

Name	County	Page
Fagan, Henry	Mas	267
Michael	Wsh	321
Fagans, John	Mas	269
Obed	Mas	268
Fagen, James	Bra	146
Wm.	Bra	143
Fagin, William	Chr	57
Fagins, Giles	Bra	141
Faiket, Thos.	Cly	152
Fain, James	Fay	21
Fair, Edward	Mad	206
James	Lin	116
John	Mad	204
Faircloth, Jas.	Cly	154
Fairman, Richard	Mer	341
Fait, Henry	Jef	15
Peter	Jef	25
Faith, Henry	Bre	168
Nancy	Nel	29
William	Ohi	100
Falconbury, Jacob	Lin	116
Willm.	Lin	116
Falkner, Francis	Knx	90
John	Bou	85
Johnson	Hnd	325
Joseph	Fay	30
Lewis	Fay	21
Nelson	Fay	30
Saml.	Grn	263
William	Bre	167
Fallen, David	Bra	147
Fallenash, Polly	She	231
Faller, Jacob	Cal	7
Fallowell, Marcus	Wsh	322
Falls, Stern	Sco	170
Fandree, Vachal	Clr	146
Fann, John	Hnd	334
Fannin, David	Flo	98
Fanning, Michael	Mas	267
Fannon, John	Mon	354
Fant, Armstead	Mas	305
William P.	Sco	184
Fantton, James	Fay	48
Fard, James	She	237
Fardan, Abner	Mon	374
Farden, Wm.	Cum	183
Farel, John	Mad	205
Fares, Dudley	Mad	207
George	Mad	206
Micajah	Mad	206
Phebe	Mad	206

Fares, cont.
Thomas Mad 207
Faris, Absalom Cum 183
Alexander Mon 352
Elijah Wsh 321
Hanna Liv 153
Hezekiah Rck 159
James Cal 19
John Fle 61
John Jef 13
John Mon 367
John Rck 161
Major Wsh 321
Moses Rck 160
Saml. Cum 183
Farish, George Lew 101
Fariss, James Junr Lin 116
James, Snr Lin 116
Willm. Lin 118
Farley, Peggy Liv 154
Peter Gar 231
Thomas Hnr 359B
William Bou 85
Farlow, Clay Bar 41
Farly, Daniel Hnr 357
Daniel, Junr Hnr 358
John Hnr 357
Farman, Benjaman Fle 77
Farmer, Absolum Chr 56
Barnet Cum 166
Barnet War 255
Ben Cum 178
Benj. Bar 44
Benjamin Chr 56
Benjamin Chr 56
Benjamin Fra 127
Chas. Nic 56
Coonrod Log 166
Elias She 233
Elijah Hnr 363
Ezakel Cas 40
Fredrick Cal 18
Henry Pul 145
James Hrd 304
Jeremiah Hnr 359
Jerimiah Grp 273
Jessy Chr 73
Joel She 225
John Clr 129
John Log 169
John Log 195
John Nel 29
Joseph Pul 145
Joshua Grp 273
Nancy Nel 29
Nathan Chr 73
Otho Hrd 304
Stephen Knx 90
William Grn 258
Farney, Hudson Clr 129
Faror, John Fay 21
Farows, Thomas Hnr 361
Farquaim, James Cum 166
Farr, James Jef 31
John Bou 85
Farra, Amas Jes 37
Farrah, Daniel Mer 342
Farrel, Archibald Mad 206
Farrell, Robert Cum 183
Robt. Senr Cum 183
Wm. Cum 170
Wm. Cum 183
Farris, David Liv 153
Geo. W. Bar 35
George Knx 89
John Bar 52
John Knx 69
Farris, cont.
John, Jr Lin 116
John, Sr Knx 74
Paul Knx 88
Farrise, Aaron Fle 78
James Fle 87
John Fle 82
Farriss, Gilbert Lin 118
John Lin 116
John Lin 118
Johnson Lin 118
Jos. Grn 249
Farrnehell, Zachariah Cam 33
Farro, Robert Chr 54
Farrot, Tiney Fay 45
Farrow, Asa Fay 15
Ebenezer Fay 15
Elizebeth Mas 269
Henretta Fle 77
Isaac Mon 350
Thos. Fle 64
William Fay 45
Wm. Mon 374
Farrus, William Fay 31
Farthing, Wlliam Mad 206
Farthings, James Log 189
Fathergale, Thos. Bou 122
Faucett, Joseph She 201
Faughn, John Cal 8
Faught, John Hnr 362
Leonard She 208
Faulkener, Alexander Wsh 322
Betsy Wsh 322
Faulkner, James Hnr 366
John Gar 231
John Jef 30
Nichs. Sco 171
Peter Gar 230
Tho. Gar 230
Thomas Bre 160
Fauntleroy, William Chr 64
Fauquher, James Hnr 366
Fawler, Godrey Cal 6
Jacob Cam 33
Saml. Cal 10
Saml. Cal 12
Fazier, Joel Hrs 313
Feagle, Samuel Mad 206
Fear, John Mon 373
John D. Mon 372
Wm. Mon 374
Fearl, Lucrecy Bra 147
Fearley, Ignatious War 266
Paul War 266
Fearman, John Nic 56
Fearn, Samuel Gal 197
Fears, James Pul 145
Jesse Gar 230
Jno. Pul 145
Jonathan War 256
Wilm. War 256
Feather, Jacob Grn 249
Featherston, William Hnd 345
Featherstyle, Andrew Mon 384
Feavis, Edmund Cas 37
Edward, Sin Cas 39
Fee, John Bra 152
Feebeck, Fredrack Nic 55
Feemaster, John Acr 12
Fegley, James But 193
Feilder, John Est 1
Wm. Est 2
Fein , David Pul 144
Feirs, Denny Grn 247
Feland, Andrew Lin 116
Ann Lin 118
James Lin 118
Felix, John Fra 126
Wm. Hrd 296
Felkins, Jhon Pul 144
John Pul 144
Martin Pul 144
William Pul 145
Felkner, John Cly 152
Fell, John Log 179
Felps, Ambrose Pul 144
Ambrose Pul 145
Jno. Pul 144
Larcin Pul 145
Obediah Pul 145
William Gra 237
William, Senr Gra 237
Felton, Ezekiel Way 354
Felts, Archibald Log 177
Felty, John But 193
Femister, Jno. Pul 145
John Cum 167
Fenley, John Gra 242
Willm. Lin 116
Fenly, Mary Mer 316
Fenn, Peter Mer 317
William Mer 317
Fenton, Bartholomew Gar 231
Michael Mas 268
Richard Fle 79
Thos. Boo 59
Zacariah Lin 116
Fentrese, John Ohi 76
Fentress, Pleasant Bre 160
Valentine Bre 160
Fenwick, Benjamin Wsh 320
Cornelias Fra 127
Danl. Lew 104
Edward, Sr. Wsh 321
Henry Gra 238
Henry Wsh 321
Ignatius Sco 173
Joel Nel 28
John Gra 241
Richard Wsh 320
Thomas Wsh 320
William Fra 127
Ferce, Joel Jef 20
Fercron, Dixon Mon 351
Peter Mon 351
Fergerson, John Hop 372
John Ohi 96
Fergus, James Cum 171
Ferguson, Abraham Fay 47
Alexander Hrs 314
Andrew Knx 89
Becky Hnr 359
Bivion Fay 51
Bryant Fay 21
Champn. Cum 185
Clemont Bou 85
Danl. Hnr 358
David Bou 86
David Hrd 286
David Mon 369
Henry Fle 70
Jacob Jef 31
James Liv 158
James Sco 174
Jessee Bou 85
Jessee Bou 122
John Bul 177
John But 193
John Fay 21

Ferguson, cont.
  John Hrd 281
  John Jef 15
  John Jef 24
  John Mon 348
  John Mon 378
  Jno. Hrd 286
  Jonathan But 193
  Joseph Nel 28
  Joseph Wsh 322
  Joshua Wsh 321
  Kinder She 242
  Larkin Sco 174
  Martin Liv 155
  Nathaniel Fay 30
  Paul But 193
  Peter Chr 115
  Priscilia Fay 21
  Richard Bul 177
  Richard Flo 98
  Richard Jef 27
  Richard Liv 145
  Robert Fay 21
  Saml. Jef 25
  Thomas Fay 21
  Thomas Knx 71
  Thomas Mon 378
  William But 193
  William Flo 98
  William Flo 98
  Wm. Mon 384
Ferigo, John Mer 316
  Robert Mer 316
  William Mer 341
Ferman, William Clr 129
Fermon, Hambleton Mon 351
  James Mon 351
  John Lew 95
Fermster, Samuel Mon 384
Fern, Hugh Nic 56
Feron, John? Hrs 321
Ferquer, Wm. Jef 24
Ferratt, John Mul 400
Ferrel, Daniel Jes 38
  Ezekiel Bou 86
  James Clr 129
  John Boo 59
  Peter Clr 129
  Thomas Clr 129
Ferrell, Chs. War 263
  Isaac Sco 193
  John Cum 173
  John War 255
Ferren, Bethuel Mas 267
Ferrier, Joseph Sco 180
Ferril, Roger Bou 86
  Wm. Cas 41
Ferris se Pharis
Ferry, James Gra 239
Fersise, John Fay 51
Fersithe, Abraham Mon 371
Ferviel, Peter Est 8
Fesler, George Clr 129
Fetheringill, John Jef 14
  Mary Jef 31
Fetherkile, George Nel 28
  Nichls. Nel 28
Fetters, Daniel Mas 266
Fetty, Rachel Wsh 322
Feul, Benjamin Mer 316
Fewell, James She 229
  John Jef 15
  Nathaniel She 198
  Spencer She 215
Fewil, Henry Chr 104
Fichlin, Joseph War 269
Fichus, Adam Hnd 327
Fickland, Daniel Fle 78
  Jarrott Jes 38
  John Jes 38
Ficklen, Judith Mas 266
Ficklin, Thos. Sco 173
Fiddler, Jas. Nel 27
Fidler, Martin Bul 177
  Sarah Bul 177
Field, Aquilla Ohi 68
  Barnett Ohi 84
  Benja. Jef 31
  Benjamin Ohi 69
  Diana Bou 86
  Ebanezar Nic 55
  Ezekiel H. Bou 68
  Henry Bul 177
  Henry R. Ohi 96
  Joseph Wsh 320
  Larkin Bou 122
  Reubin Ohi 73
  Robt. Bar 31
  Robt. Bar 45
  Sarah Ohi 96
  William Mas 267
  William Nic 56
  Willis Bou 122
  Zacharias Clr 128
Fielder, George Nic 56
  George W. Wsh 320
Fielding, Joseph Cas 38
  Wm. Bar 31
Fields, Abraham Jef 13
  Abraham Sco 184
  Abner Jef 14
  Ezekel Hrd 295
  Ezekiel Jef 14
  Greenbury Mas 269
  James Bar 43
  James Mer 317
  James Sco 175
  John Adr 19
  John Bra 141
  John Cly 152
  John Jef 13
  Joseph Sco 168
  Joseph Sco 175
  Kizzy Sco 184
  Laben Bra 147
  Lansford Knx 87
  Lewis Jef 14
  Matthew Sco 186
  Patsey Knx 86
  Reason Sco 184
  Reason Sco 190
  Reuben Jef 14
  Richard Hrs 307
  Samuel Pul 145
  Stephen Pul 145
  William Mer 317
  William Pul 145
  Wm. Bra 143
Fife, John Bou 85
Fig, Celi Hrd 289
Figg, James She 210
  John Nel 28
  Robert But 193
  William She 210
  Wm. War 264
Figgins, George Bre 168
  Zachariah Clr 129
Fightmaster, Fred-
  erick Mon 370
  George Hrs 308
  George Hrs 308
  Phillip Hrs 308
Figins, Jarrat Mon 376
Figlin, John Sco 169
Fike, Elijah Log 166
  James Log 166
  John Log 166
Filer, William Fay 44
Files, John Ohi 98
Fillips, John Cly 154
Filly, Henry Liv 158
  Rogar Cal 9
Filpot, Thos. Pul 144
Filson, James Fle 65
  William Fay 60
Finch, James Chr 59
  John Nel 29
  Livinia Mas 268
  Wat Hrd 300
  William Bou 85
  William Bre 160
  William Woo 391
  Wm. Bar 38
  Wm. Cas 45
  Yelventon Mon 351
Fincer, Geo. Cly 158
  Issabal Cly 158
Findlay, Isaac Hrd 286
  Saml. Hrd 286
Findley, David Gar 231
  Saml. Gar 231
Findly, Saml. Lin 116
Fine, Jacob Jef 31
Fingle, John Fay 52
Fink, Henry Sco 176
Finley, Acy Chr 109
  Andrew Chr 63
  Dabney Chr 100
  George Hrs 313
  George Jef 14
  Isaac Jef 14
  James Hrs 324
  James Knx 76
  James Log 176
  James Wsh 320
  James C. Wsh 320
  John Chr 69
  John Chr 103
  John Jef 31
  John Jes 39
  John G. She 197
  John H. Jef 15
  Joseph Mon 377
  Michael Mon 362
  Richard Jef 15
  Saml. Sco 188
  Samuel Chr 114
  Thos. Hnr 356
  William Chr 64
  William Chr 82
  William She 197
  William C. She 217
  Wm. War 278
Finn, Evan Jes 38
  John Woo 382
  Martin Jes 38
  Peter Jes 38
  Peter War 270
  Richard Jes 38
  Scarlet Mon 350
  William Jes 38
  William, Jr Jes 38
  William, Ser Jes 38
Finne, Reubien Jes 39
Finnel, Achelles Gar 230
  Charles Gar 230
  Jas. Gar 231
  Jonathan Gar 230
  Nancy Gar 230
  Wm. Gar 230
Finnell, James Boo 59

Finnell, cont.
Robt. Boo 59
Finney, Abner Sco 184
George W. Sco 186
James Fle 66
James Sco 170
John War 263
Marget Fle 66
Morgan War 279
Wm. War 263
Finnie, Elijah Woo 381
James Woo 381
John Woo 381
John, Junr Woo 382
Finny, Joshua Mad 207
Fiper, Jacob Wsh 320
Fipps, Amus chr 76
Rowley Jef 14
Fips, George Pul 144
Firld, Joseph Bou 86
Firman, Aaron Bou 85
Firmon, Mary Bou 85
Thomas She 204
William Bou 85
William Bou 85
Fiscus, George Est 7
Fish, John H. Sco 188
Thos. Rck 159
Fishback, Alex Bra 141
Charles Jef 14
George Bou 86
James Fay 15
Jesse Bou 85
John Jes 37
John War 263
Joseph She 221
Wm. Jef 15
Fishel, M. John Fay 15
Fisher, Adam Mas 267
Adam Mer 316
Alexander Clr 129
Anthony Grn 250
Anthony Grn 261
Benjamin Mer 316
Bennett Mer 316
Calob Mer 316
David Bou 85
David Fay 15
David Jes 39
Elias Cas 39
Elias Mer 316
Elijah Chr 93
Elijah Mer 316
Henry Mad 206
Jacob Grn 250
James Fay 48
James Fay 60
Jas. Bar 34
Jas. Grn 251
Jeremiah Mer 342
John Bar 28
John Bre 163
John Clr 129
John Fay 15
John Fay 15
John Grn 250
John Mon 384
John Mul 407
Joseph Mer 316
Madox Fay 15
Margaret Bou 86
Matthias Lin 116
Merideth Hnd 344
Nancy Bou 85
Nathaniel Bou 85
Peter Grn 251
Peter She 210
Fisher, cont.
Rebecker Jes 38
Samuel Fay 48
Solamn. Bou 122
Spencir Chr 108
Stephen Mer 316
Stephen Mer 316
Thadues Lin 116
Thomas Fay 48
Thomas Gra 237
Trustum Mer 316
V. Suggon Fay 15
William Bou 85
William Bre 163
William Fay 59
Wm. Bar 34
Wm. Grn 250
Wm. Sco 178
Zachariah She 224
Fisher's Farm, M. Fay 59
Fishman, Ferdinand Jef 14
Fishwaters, John Hrs 322
Fisk, Abram Gal 188
David Gal 188
David Hnr 359A
Fistar, John Gal 197
Fitch, Joseph Lew 102
Salathiel Fle 81
Samuel Mas 301
Fitchjerrill,
Elijah Pul 144
Fitchpatrick, Jno. Pul 145
Thomas Mad 206
Kite, Jacob Bou 86
Jacob Nic 56
Peggy Bou 72
Fitsgerald, John Way 371
Fitsjarel, Silas Fay 44
Fitsjarrel, James Bar 35
Fitspatrick, James Nic 55
Fitsptrick, Dennis Fay 44
Fitsworth, Isaac Liv 157
John Liv 147
Peggy Liv 157
William Liv 156
Fitzerrald, Maryan Fra 126
Fitzgarrel, Isaam Bar 41
Fitzgerald, Barth-
olomew Mas 269
Benjamin Mas 266
Daniel Woo 375
Peter Mas 269
Thomas Mas 268
Thomas Wsh 320
William Flo 98
William She 228
Fitzgerel, James Mon 347
Fitzgerl, Jas. Gar 230
Laurence Gar 230
Fitzgerld, Jas. Fle 61
Fitzgibbon, John Sco 173
Fitzhew, Peter Log 166
Fitzhugh, Dennis Jef 26
John Log 173
Robert Log 173
Wm. Hnr 368
Fitzjarril, Ellis Woo 384
Fitzjerrald, George Boo 59
Jesse Boo 59
Fitzpatrick, Chs. Nel 29
Hugh Wsh 320
John Flo 98
John Flo 98
John Flo 98
Thomas Flo 98
Fizgerald, James She 233
Fizsimmns, Thomas She 233
Flack, James Mad 207
John Lin 116
William Lin 116
Flanagan, John Nel 10
Flanagin, James Mon 380
Wm. Mon 380
Flanerey, Daniel Liv 149
Elijah Liv 149
Elijah, Snr Liv 149
Flanigen, Peter Clr 146
Flanigin, Richard Pul 144
Flannagan, Patrick Wsh 322
Torrance Wsh 320
Flanry, Tho. Bar 21
Flarity, Barthw. Nel 28
Barthw. Nel 29
Bartt. Sr Nel 29
Edwd. Nel 27
Flathers, Benjamin Mad 206
Edward Mad 207
Flatt, John Bar 32
John Cum 182
Wm. Hrd 283
Flaughher, Christ-
opher Grp 274
Fleak, Christo. Nel 28
Fleetwood, Isaac Flo 99
Fleming, Enock Hnr 351
Geor. Mon 355
James Cam 25
James Fay 15
James Fay 15
James Fle 68
James Mad 206
James Mer 342
John Fay 21
John Mas 269
John D. Fle 81
Leonard J. Woo 387
Mary Mas 267
Stephen Mas 269
Thos. Hrd 299
Wm. H. Mon 355
Flemming, James Hnr 368
Flemon, Joseph Fay 44
Flernoy, Laurance Fay 21
Fletcher, Abraham Mad 206
Ambrose Knx 79
Anne Mon 376
Edward Gra 237
Elias Cum 169
Geo. W. Bar 35
George Mas 269
James Jes 37
James Log 166
James Log 184
James Mad 206
James Mon 350
Jas. Gar 231
Jilson, Mon 372
John Adr 7
John Chr 70
John Chr 77
John Clr 128
John Knx 64
John Knx 78
John Mad 205
John Mas 268
John Mon 381
John Pul 144
Joseph Lin 116
Martha Liv 148
Mercy Mad 207
Robert Fay 15
Robert Liv 148
Spencer Cum 169
Thomas Chr 71

Name	County	Page
Fletcher, cont.		
Thomas	Mon	376
Thos.	War	252
Verdimin	Knx	64
William	Knx	85
Flever, Jno.	Pul	145
Flickner, John	Gar	231
Flim, Robert	She	228
William	She	228
Flin, Arthew	Grp	273
John	Way	363
Peter	Mad	206
Flinn, Benjamin	Mas	267
John	Way	356
Patrick	Log	179
Stephen	Bar	34
Flint, John	Cal	13
John	Cal	19
John	Jes	37
Martin	Lin	116
William	Mas	268
Flippen, John	Bar	24
Flippin, James	Bar	26
Tho.	Bar	25
Wm.	Bar	26
Flonor, Anna	Mon	381
Flood, Joshua	She	214
Flooty, John	Clr	129
Flora, David	Mas	268
Robert	Mas	268
Robt.	Bra	151
Flore, Saml.	Jef	13
Florea, John	Woo	397
Florence, William	Woo	397
Wm. Senr	Woo	383
Flory, Jacob	Rck	161
Floures?, John	Fle	77
Flournoy, David	Sco	178
Francis	Pen	107
John F.	Cam	31
Samuel	Mer	316
Flowars, Micajah	Cly	160
Flowers, David	Mas	268
Edwd. Cum 170		
Thos.	Cum	180
Williams	Mad	205
Floyd, Abraham	Pul	144
Benjamin	Lin	118
Charles	Jef	14
David	Gal	188
Enoch	Mad	207
Geo.	Gar	231
Henry	Hnd	330
Henry H.	Hnd	329
James	Mad	205
John	Gar	229
John	Gar	231
John	Hnd	329
John B.	Woo	385
Jonathan	Mad	204
Levi	Woo	388
Mathew	Pul	144
Nathaniel	Hnd	330
Nathl.	Jef	13
Saml.	Gar	231
Singleton	Lin	118
Thomas	Gar	229
Thomas	Pul	144
Willm.	Lin	116
Flualen, Henry	But	193
Flurnoy, Mathes	Fay	41
Matthew	Fay	34
Flush, John	Log	170
flutee, Cuff-a free man of colour	Clr	129
Flynn, Armstrong	Clr	128
David	Clr	129
Flynn, cont.		
John	Clr	128
Mary	Clr	129
Michael	Clr	129
William	Clr	128
Foaly, John	Chr	90
Foard, Daniel	Chr	56
Jessy	Chr	55
William	Chr	56
Foare, Daniel	Chr	110
Foart, Jessy	Chr	92
Jessy	Chr	101
Michajah	Chr	100
Foddery, Joseph	Clr	129
Fodge, John	Cum	166
John, Senr	Cum	168
Fogle, Jacob	Pen	108
Joseph	Nel	29
Foibles, Joseph	She	227
Foister, John	Hrs	318
Samuel	Hrs	317
Folbert, James	Hrs	307
Folding, John	Adr	7
Foley, Bayless	Gal	188
Caty	Fay	46
David	Fay	21
Elijah	Fay	21
Elijah	Knx	74
Henry, Senr	Fle	75
James	Est	1
James	Hop	37
James	Mas	266
John	Fay	21
John	Fle	74
Moses	Pul	145
Owings	Fle	74
Richd.	Hop	371
Spencer	Knx	74
William	Fay	21
Wsley	War	262
Wm.	War	262
Folie, James	Mas	269
Folks, John	Mad	207
Folley, John	Liv	156
Folli, Richard	Hnr	352
Follice, Isaac	Jef	14
Jacob	Jef	14
Follis, Isaac	Mer	316
Folliss, Peter	War	275
Followell, Abraham	Wsh	319
John	Wsh	319
William	Wsh	319
Folson, Samel.	Fle	64
Foly, Thomas	Knx	79
Fonnoy, Abner	Lew	104
Fontain, James	Jef	26
Peter	Jef	14
Fontaine, Aaron	Jef	14
Edone Henry	Jef	26
Fontleroy, John	Mer	317
Fooks, Benjn.	Bou	85
John	Nel	28
Foot, John	Mad	204
For, Thomas	Pul	145
Forbes, Alexander	Ohi	85
John	Bou	85
John	Rck	166
Morgan	Grn	249
William	Rck	166
Forbis, George	Fay	45
George	Pul	145
James	Bar	30
James	Bar	54
James	Grn	249
John	Bar	27
John	Bar	52
Jonathan	Lin	116
Forbis, cont.		
Joseph	Clr	129
Robert	Bar	34
Forbiss, Montgomery	Lin	116
Forbus, Isaac	Hnr	357
Robert	Hnr	357
Samuel	Way	352
Forbush, Andrew	Mad	207
Gracy	Mon	384
Isaac	Mad	207
Robert	Mad	207
Samuel	But	193
Forbuss, Elexr.	Adr	7
Ford, Abner	Hnr	364
Absalom	Woo	385
Bailey	Sco	176
Bartlett	Mer	316
Benjamin	Fay	45
Charles	Bou	86
Edward	Bou	122
Edward	She	242
Egbert	Cly	151
Elisha	She	213
Elizabeth	Grn	246
Elizabeth	Wsh	322
Frederick	Gar	231
Hezekiah	She	213
Jacob	Fay	15
Jacob	Mad	206
James	Woo	378
Jarrett	Hnr	364
Jesse	Liv	158
Jno.	Nel	28
John	Bou	85
John	Cal	10
John	Hnr	364
John	Jef	14
John	Lin	118
John	Mad	206
John	Pen	115
John	She	212
John	She	214
John	Woo	377
John G.	Nel	28
Jonathan	Mer	342
Joseph	Flo	98
Joseph	Liv	148
Joshua	Gar	230
Josua	Bar	49
Laban	Mad	205
Lemuel	Woo	398
Lewis	Sco	170
Lewis	Wsh	322
Phillip	Liv	147
Rebeckah	Knx	84
Robert	Mon	371
Robert S.	She	204
Robt.	Hnr	365
Saml.	Hnr	360
Samuel	Way	360
Sarah	Mad	206
Stephen	Mad	205
Timothy	Gar	231
Warner	Hnr	365
William	Bou	122
William	Cal	5
William	Fay	41
William	Hnr	359B
William	Log	193
William	She	237
Fordan, John	Bou	85
Forde, Benjn.	War	264
James	War	252
Patrick	Gar	199
Fore, Jesse	Hnr	358
John	Hnr	352

Fore, cont.
John She 198
Joseph Hnr 368
Joseph She 220
Joseph She 222
Joseph She 227
Julias Hnr 363
Little B. Hnr 354
Peter Hnr 353
Silas Hnr 368
William P. Hnr 362
Foredise, Syrus Jef 13
Forehand, Enamiah Mul 397
Jarvis Mul 391
Lambert Mul 405
Foreman, Archer Jes 39
Ezekiel Mas 267
Jacob Liv 155
James Clr 128
Joseph Mas 267
Josh Nel 27
Samuel Mas 269
Thomas Mas 267
Thos. Nel 27
Forest, Grisham Hrs 314
Forester, William Hnd 337
Forewood, Wm. Jef 13
Forgason, Henry Hrs 320
John Mul 399
William B. Mul 385
Forgerson, Thos. Lew 99
Forgey, Hugh Bou 85
Forguson, Hugh Fra 126
John Fle 63
Nancy Bar 53
Forker, Thomas Bre 160
Forkner, Benjamin Chr 84
Forquer, George Fle 92
James Fle 92
Forqueran, John Bou 85
Forrest, Ila Hnd 342
Joel Bar 53
Richard Wsh 321
Thomas Wsh 320
Thomas Wsh 321
Zephaniah Wsh 321
Forrister, John Knx 63
Forsee, William Jra 126
Forsithe, Matthew Mer 316
George Clr 129
Forster, Abner War 265
Cornelius War 261
Drury War 279
Jeremiah Fle 84
John War 247
John War 252
Saml. Fle 63
Saml. War 253
Samuel Fle 84
Wilm. War 252
Forston, Charles Woo 393
Forsyth, John Gar 230
Thomas Gar 231
Forsythe, Benjamin Bou 86
David Jef 31
Isaac Bou 85
Elial Lin 116
Jacob Pen 112
James Jef 31
Jas. Lin 116
John Pen 105
Joseph But 193
Margaret Jef 31
Robert Pen 113
William But 193
Fort, Andrew Mon 368
David Liv 159

Fort, cont.
Francis Mon 364
Frederick War 254
Peter Mon 361
Wm. Cal 8
Forth, Josiah War 268
Fortin, Thomas Mon 363
Fortner, Henry Est 4
Jessee Cly 160
Lewis Log 193
Michael Pul 144
William Hrs 308
Fortnor, Robert Pen 108
Forts, Sally Sco 173
Fortune, Vincent Clr 129
Fortuneberry, Jas. Hrd 297
Fortuny, Conrad Lew 99
Fosith, John Nic 55
Fossett, Cornel-
ious Mon 378
Foster, Alexander Bre 166
Alexander She 201
Anthony Nel 29
Arther Fle 74
Asa Bou 122
Barnett Ohi 84
Bartley Nel 42
Charles Way 360
Cosby Gar 230
Edmd. Nel 27
George S. Chr 58
Harrison Nic 56
Henry Fay 46
Henry Mon 376
Isaac Flo 98
Isaac Sco 183
James Bou 85
James Liv 152
James Mon 360
Janes Bar 30
Jeremiah Mon 363
Jessee Bou 122
Jobe Grp 269
John Bar 51
John Bou 85
John Bou 85
John Chr 58
John Clr 129
John Mad 206
John Nel 28
John Nel 29
John Way 356
Joshua Mas 266
Leanna Jes 38
Mark Flo 99
Michal Cum 179
N. Fle 66
Nathaniel Mon 363
Priestly Mas 266
Rhode Nic 55
Robert Pul 145
Saml. Boo 59
Samuel Liv 153
Sarah Cam 24
Thomas Bou 85
Thomas Hrs 318
Thomas Hrs 320
Thomas Jef 14
Thomas Mul 407
Thos. Nel 27
Thos. Sco 182
William Clr 129
William Clr 129
William Hnr 353
William Lin 116
William Nel 28
Wm. Way 363

Fotner, Jonas Mon 369
Fouch, James Mon 381
William Fle 69
William Fle 74
Foudray, Samuel Fle 62
Foulers, John Fle 64
Foulger, John Clr 129
Robert Fle 75
Fousher, John Nel 28
Fouson, William Fay 47
Foust, Lewis Way 361
Fout, Bazel Fle 83
Fouts, Benja. Fle 70
Fowke, Roger Mas 268
Fowler, Alexander Mad 207
Allen Way 354
Ann Mad 205
Arther Hnd 340
Benjn. Boo 59
Charles Hrs 314
Edwd Hrd 304
Electius Wsh 321
Elija Cam 33
Elisha But 193
Eliza Grn 246
Isaac Knx 89
Jacob Mad 207
James Mon 351
Jams. Nic 56
Jas. Hrd 292
Jeremiah Mad 205
Jesse Knx 88
John Clr 129
John Est 4
John Fay 12
John Gar 230
John Jes 38
John Wsh 322
John W. Bul 177
Joseph Est 4
Joshua Jef 15
Luke (see also
Towler) Nic 62
Mordica Cal 15
More Bou 86
Moses Mas 305
Peter Way 355
Richard Mad 205
Richard, Jur Mad 205
Robt. Boo 59
Samuel Wsh 321
Stephenson Liv 159
Thomas Fle 78
Thomas Wsh 319
Thomas Wsh 321
William Chr 60
William Nel 29
Zakh. Nel 28
Fowntin, Edward Chr 71
Josiph Chr 84
Peter Chr 85
Fox, Abram. Adr 7
Andrew Nel 29
Benjamin Clr 129
Benjamin Knx 74
Claibourne Mas 268
Daniel Hop 379
Daniel Hop 379
Gates Cas 43
George Nel 28
Henry War 264
Isham Mad 205
Jacob Nel 28
James Cal 12
James Hop 380
James Mon 360
James Nel 28

Fox, cont.
  Jeremiah Hop 379
  Jessy Mon 360
  John Adr 7
  John Hrs 321
  John Mad 205
  John (Saml's Son) Mad 207
  John Mon 360
  John Way 368
  Jonathan Cly 157
  Noah Hop 380
  Richd. Woo 395
  Samuel Mad 205
  Samuel, Jur Mad 204
  Titus Hop 380
  William Clr 129
  Wm. Pul 121
Foxwirthy, Wm. Fle 83
Foxworthy, John Mas 299
Foy, Frederick Pen 106
  James Liv 148
Fraikes, Daniel Hrd 292
Frail, James Cam 32
Fraim, Archibald Bul 177
  William Bul 177
  William Clr 129
Fraizer, James Hrs 313
  John Hrs 314
  Wm. Hrs 317
Fraker, Michael War 253
Frakes, Conrod Hrd 292
  Hanna Hrd 293
  John Bou 85
  John Hrd 302
  John She 210
  Joseph Mon 371
  Nathan Bou 85
  Nathan Mon 382
  Peter Gra 244
Frale, Jonathan Log 174
Fraley, Daniel War 275
  Elizt. War 275
  John War 275
  Willm. War 275
Frame, George Bou 86
  James Bou 85
  Jeremiah Bou 85
  John Mon 360
  Samuel Bou 85
  Sarah Wsh 321
  William Bou 85
  Wm. Mon 374
France, Michael Mul 393
Frances, James Bou 122
  John Cas 48
  Thomas Bou 122
Franceway, Norad Hnd 337
Francis, Evan Jes 42
  Henry Pul 145
  Henry Way 369
  John Way 369
  Morgan Bou 69
  Robt. Gar 230
  Samuel Way 362
  Thomas Mad 244
  Thomas Sco 184
  William Bou 85
  Wm. Sco 179
Franciscoe, John Woo 380
Francum, Elender War 275
Frank (afree man of colour) Clr 129
Frank (freeman) Fay 15
Frank, George Bre 164
  John Fay 21
  John, Junior Bre 159
  Jos. Hnr 366
Franklin, Absolum Chr 101
  Claybourn Mer 317
  Edmund Mer 317
  Elijah Way 353
  George Fay 39
  James Fle 61
  James Hop 380
  James Mer 316
  James Wsh 320
  Jas. Bar 36
  John Bar 40
  John Flo 98
  John War 257
  John, Jun Bar 35
  John, Sen Bar 35
  Joseph Mas 268
  Owen Hop 374
  Reubin Clr 129
  Saml. Cal 18
  Tho. Hop 380
  Stephen Fay 49
  Thos. Cum 185
  William Hop 374
  Wm. Way 353
  Zephaniah Mas 268
Franks, John M. Pen 111
  Peter Bar 22
Fransisco, John Log 188
Fransiscoe, Andrew Woo 377
Fransley, James Jef 13
Frary, James Fay 21
Frasier, Alx. Cly 149
  James Jef 31
  John Cly 149
Frawner, John Woo 381
Frayly, Christan Bar 48
  Edward Bar 49
Frays, Frederick Bre 157
Frazer, Alexander Hnd 342
  Elizabeth Jes 38
  George Fay 30
  George Hrs 313
  George War 247
  James Bar 29
  James C. Log 161
  Jeremiah Jes 37
  John Fle 75
  John Hnd 342
  John Log 166
  John Log 186
  Joseph Fay 30
  Lewis Grp 272
  Michagia Grp 272
  William Hnd 342
Frazier see Phrazier
Frazier, Aaron Mas 269
  Alexander Fay 15
  Alexr. Cal 9
  Alexr. Jef 13
  Andrew She 200
  James Fra 126
  James Nic 55
  John But 193
  John Cam 24
  Joseph Chr 112
  Moses Mas 267
  Robert Fay 15
  Robert Mer 316
  Samuel Mas 267
  Sarah Flo 98
  Solomon Flo 98
  William Clr 129
  William Flo 98
  William Mas 266
  William Nic 55
  William Sco 190
Frazur, Squire Mas 269
Freaks, Henry Gar 229
  Wm. Bra 146
Frebet, Augustus Lew 95
Frederick, Andrew Jef 14
  Augustus Jef 13
  George Jef 13
  George Jef 14
  John Jef 13
  John Way 371
  Jno. Hrd 288
Fredrick, Joseph Hnr 359B
Freeland, Jacob Mas 267
  John Mas 268
  Robert Mon 382
Freeman, Aaron Knx 70
  David Mer 316
  Edward Mad 246
  Elisha Gar 231
  Geo. Cly 150
  George Woo 377
  Gollop Mad 206
  John Adr 7
  John Bar 28
  John Knx 88
  Jonathan Mad 205
  Margaret Fra 126
  Moses Nel 29
  Richd. War 263
  Richd. (mulatto) Woo 379
  Samuel Mad 205
  Thomas She 224
  William Clr 129
  William Mad 204
  William (Sam's son) Mad 205
  Michael Cal 6
Freeze, James Jef 14
French, David Jef 13
  Elisha Hrd 293
  Henry Jef 13
  Henry Mer 316
  Hugh Adr 7
  Ignatius Hrd 282
  Igns. Nel 27
  James Hrd 281
  James Mas 266
  James Mon 348
  James Mon 350
  John Mas 267
  Joseph Hnd 341
  Joseph Hrd 281
  Mason Adr 7
  Noah Boo 59
  Ralph Hrd 293
  Robt. Cal 14
  Rodolphus Wsh 320
  Siman Chr 107
  Stephen Hrd 293
  Thos. Hrd 292
  William Hnd 341
  William Mad 207
  William Nel 29
  Wm. Cal 14
  Wm. Cal 18
  Wm. Mon 372
Fresh, Benjn. Lin 116
  Francis Gal 188
Fretwell, Agness Bou 86
  John Chr 86
Frew, John Log 184
Friar, Richard Chr 92
Friat, Robert Chr 97
Friddle, Jacob Bul 177
Friend, Andrew Hrd 293
  Chas. Hrd 290
  Cinderella Bou 122
  Jacob Grp 276

Friend, Jacob She 201
Jesse Hrd 293
John Bou 85
John, Jr Bou 122
Friends, Andrew Grp 271
Frier, David Clr 129
James Gal 188
Robert Mad 207
Wm. Cal 8
Frila, Martin Hnd 346
Friles, Beverly Ohi 95
Frisbey, Isaac Mad 206
Fristoe, Daniel Chr 103
John Mas 305
Richard Mon 358
Frith, Thomas Gar 231
Fritsjarel, Jessy Fay 60
Fritts, Michael Clr 129
Valuntine Est 8
Fritzlin, George Woo 399
Frizel, Evan Jef 31
Frizzle, Arch Lew 103
Jacob Lew 100
Jason Log 176
William Log 175
Frogg, Arthur Cum 173
Leuricia Cum 179
Strother Cum 181
Wm. Cum 182
Frogget, Wm. Bar 52
Frogguo, Andrew Hnr 359B
Froman, Abrm. Hrd 297
Absalom Bul 177
Jacob Woo 381
Jacob, Jr Bul 177
John Nel 28
Joseph She 235
Sarah Wsh 322
Frord, Mordica Bra 151
Frost, Eli War 267
Jas. Way 358
Jedediah War 266
John Cum 176
Simeon, Jr Jes 38
Simeon, Ser Jes 38
Stephen Hrd 300
Stephen, Jur Jes 38
Stephen, Ser Jes 38
Frowman, Solomon Mas 301
Fruit, James Chr 79
Thomas Chr 65
Frutley, Hinry Jef 13
Fry, Abraham Hrs 310
Barbery Jes 37
Benjainaild Hrs 312
Benjamin Bou 85
Benjamin Bul 177
Betsy Fay 49
Easter Fay 21
Edward Mer 343
Elijah She 214
Felty Way 369
George Boo 59
George Clr 129
Henry Fay 49
Henry She 214
Henry Way 358
Isaac She 220
Jacob Bou 86
Jacob Hrs 310
Jacob Nel 28
Jacob She 227
James, Jr Bou 85
James, Senr Bou 85
John Cas 41
John Fay 21
John Log 175

Fry, cont.
John Mer 316
John Nic 55
John Way 369
Joseph Fay 49
Joshua Mer 342
Martin She 214
Michl. Way 369
Peter Way 368
Thomas Mer 316
William A. Jes 37
Wilson Way 359
Fryar, Bennett Fay 58
Fryatt, Edmond Jes 38
Frye, Abraham Jef 14
James, Junr Log 181
James, Senr Log 181
Fryer, Daniel Cly 157
John Gal 188
Robert Fay 21
Walter Pen 106
Fryerea, John Nel 10
Fryman, Henry Nic 55
Phillip Nic 55
Frymiller, John Fay 46
Frymire, John Bre 165
Polly Bre 165
Wm. Bre 168
Frymon, Phillip Hrs 318
Fryrear, Fras. Nel 27
Jerh. Nel 27
Fuckes, Andr. Nel 27
Fuel, Rodias Est 5
Spencer Cam 32
Fugate, George Hop 373
James Bou 85
Martin Pen 112
Mary Bou 86
Reubin Mon 354
Townsin Gar 230
William Bou 86
Fuget, Ben Cly 159
John Log 176
Jonathan Cly 159
Zacheriah Cly 159
Fugit, Joseph Flo 98
Martin Cly 159
Randal Flo 98
Fulcher, John Bar 26
Richd. Bar 26
Thomas Mas 268
Fuler, Wm. Bra 153
Fulkerson, Abraham Jes 38
Adam Ohi 81
Frederick Liv 151
Fulkerd Gra 243
Fulkerd Ohi 79
Jacob Nel 28
John Gra 243
Peter Gra 243
Philip Nel 28
Philip Nel 29
Phillip Ohi 74
Phillip Ohi 79
Richard Liv 147
Fulks, Elizabeth Knx 81
Zabril Knx 81
Fullalove, Anthony Mad 206
John Mad 205
Oswald Mad 205
William Mad 205
Wm. Jur Mad 205
Fullar, John Chr 57
Mical Grp 271
Fullenwider, Jacob She 241
Fuller, Aleg. Hop 373
Henry Cam 24

Fuller, cont.
Joseph Nic 55
Nathan. Bra 153
Rachel Hop 374
Wm. Bar 41
Wm. Bra 149
Fullove, William Jes 38
Fulsom, James Grp 274
Fulton, Andrew Hnr 359B
Hugh Fle 84
Hugh Mas 269
Joseph Mas 266
Isaac Fle 63
Samuel Mul 408
Samuel Nic 55
Funk, Abraham Hnr 355
Gabriel Lin 116
John Jef 14
John Nel 27
John Pul 144
Joseph Wsh 321
Peter Bou 122
Peter Jef 14
Funkhouser, Christr. But 193
Isaac But 198
Funston, Paul Bou 122
Fuqua, David Grp 271
Henry Hnd 335
John Hnd 334
John Mon 377
John She 242
Joseph Hnd 345
Joseph She 230
Mary Grp 270
Moses Grp 270
Moses, Junr Grp 271
Thomas Mon 377
William Grp 271
Fuquay, Henry Bul 177
Isom Bul 177
Furbin, Jaems Log 177
Furbush, Robert Log 161
Robert Log 166
William Log 166
William Log 184
Furgason, James War 250
John War 250
Jos. War 249
Furgeson, David Bou 85
Furguson, Arther Bar 24
Caty Bar 37
James Nel 28
John Nel 29
Tho. Bar 32
Furhee, Danl. Nel 27
Furlow, Robert Fle 70
Furnace, James Gal 188
Furney, Elizabeth Gar 231
James Hrs 307
James Hrs 309
John Hrs 307
Sary Hrs 307
Willm. Hrs 307
Willm. Hrs 308
Furr, Sampson Fle 69
Stephen Woo 390
William Fle 79
Futral, Daniel Chr 97
Nathan Chr 105
Sarah Chr 98
Shadrick Chr 98
Futhey, Benjamin Fay 15
Fyfe, Abijah Mas 269
James Mas 267
James, Junr Mas 266
Jonathan Mas 267

Fyfe, cont.
  Thomas Mas 269

-- G --

Gabbard, Mathias Lin 117
Gabberd, George Lin 117
Gabbert, John Cas 38
  Michal Cum 183
  Thomas Cas 42
Gabbertt, Jacob Lin 117
Gabert, George Mer 313
  John Mer 313
  Michael Mer 313
  Peter Mer 313
Gable, Jos. Hrd 299
Gabraiel, Stephen Log 174
Gabriel, John Log 167
Gadbury, Saml. Cas 40
Gadd, Thomas Rck 162
Gaddis, Jacob Cum 184
  Rees Cam 29
Gaddy, Silas Hrd 287
  Wm. Hrd 287
Gaden, Adam Pul 148
Gades, Whitfield Cas 41
Gadess, Thomas Cas 42
Gadman, William Nic 54
Gaff, Fransis Pul 148
Gaget, Ann Jes 58
Garland, Thomas Mad 208
Gain, Henry Hrs 320
Gainer, John Fay 59
Gaines, Daniel Fay 36
  John Clr 130
  Joseph Jes 41
  Katy Fay 36
  Robert Woo 396
  Thomas Fra 128
  Thomas L. Jes 40
  William Fra 128
  William Woo 396
Gains, Abner Boo 59
  Benjamin Bou 123
  Charles Hrs 311
  Francis Grp 275
  Franciss Lin 117
  George Boo 59
  Henry Bar 40
  Nathaniel Gra 243
  Richard Bar 40
  Richard Lin 117
  Richard H. Mer 342
  Richd. Sco 171
  Strawther Mer 315
  William Lin 117
  William Mer 314
Gaitay, John Jef 12
Gaither, Cornelius Mas 265
  Edward B. Wsh 343
  Greenly Nel 31
  Hart Nel 10
  John R. Bul 178
Gaitskill, Henry Clr 130
Galaher, Isaac (B) Fle 91
Galasby, Mary Mer 314
Galaspy, Alexander She 230
  John Fay 56
  John She 230
  Polly She 230
  Richard Way 374
  Simon Mon 380
  William She 230
Galaway, Elijah Bra 142
  Robert Mon 352

Galbraith, George Mas 264
Galbreath, Bin Nic 54
  Wm. Nic 54
Gale, James Fra 129
  John Gal 186
  Josiah Fra 128
  Matthew Sco 185
  Robert D. Fra 129
  Robert F. Woo 395
Galey, Benjamin She 212
  David Jes 40
  Hugh She 229
  James She 220
  Saml. She 223
  Samuel She 213
  William She 219
Galewood, John She 224
Galkin, John Way 364
Gallaghar, Mary Mas 263
Gallagher, Jno. Fle 63
Gallaghu, Miles Bou 70
Gallaher, Isaac Fle 81
  Susanah (B) Fle 91
Gallaspie, Martin Clr 130
Gallaway, Archi-
  bald Hnd 333
  John Mad 208
  John Wsh 315
  Obediah Hnd 333
  Robert Wsh 314
Gallghar, John Mas 264
Galligar, Charles Mas 303
Galliher, Jas. Fle 66
Galling, Frederick Gra 238
  John Gra 237
Gallion, Nathan Fra 129
  William But 194
Gallop, Enoch Clr 130
Galloway, Daniel Grn 261
  David Hrs 309
  Edmund Hnd 347
  Francis Hnd 333
  James Mer 314
  James She 207
  John Bar 31
  John Hnd 333
  John Ohi 101
  Mary She 233
  Pleasant Hnd 332
  Saml. Sco 181
  William ohi 91
  Zacheriah Ohi 101
Galusha, Elijah Cal 7
Galy, William Jes 39
Gambell, James War 270
  Thos. Cly 149
  Wm. War 270
Gambill, James Cly 154
  James Liv 153
Gamble, John Cam 28
  Joseph Chr 63
  Josias Bou 86
  William Nel 10
Gamblin, James Hop 377
Gambold, Aaron Wsh 316
Gambrel, James Mul 401
Gambril, Paris Gal 187
  William Mul 392
Gamel, Thomas Log 185
Gamell, Reuben Hnr 359
Gammel, James Cum 165
Gammon, Richard D. Grp 271
Gammons, Stokes Mon 380
Ganes, Elizabeth Fay 58
Gannon, James Wsh 314
Gano, Isaac E. Fra 130
  Richd. M. Sco 190

Ganoe, Danl. Sco 188
Gant, George Hnd 344
  John Mer 314
  Robert Fle 89
Gapp, Wm. Grn 262
Garbreath, Danul Chr 108
  John Chr 108
  Tortle Chr 108
Gardener, Abigail Mon 364
  James Mon 364
  John But 194
  John Archer But 194
  Jos. Nel 32
Gardenner, Jonia Fle 77
Gardiner, Clement Wsh 316
  Clemt. Nel 32
  Fras. Nel 30
  Raphael Wsh 316
  Richd. Nel 30
  Thomas Wsh 319
Gardner, Aaron Fle 65
  David Way 369
  Geo. R. Mad 209
  Henry Way 368
  James Mad 209
  Jno. Hrd 290
  John Clr 130
  John Fay 16
  Joseph Grp 276
  Neigent Fay 16
  Nichs. Fle 65
  Thomas Clr 130
  Thomas Clr 130
  William Mad 210
  Wm. Bar 32
  Wm. Hrd 284
Gargile, William Liv 155
Garison, Mason Log 167
Garland, Ambrose Flo 99
  Anderson Lin 117
  James Rck 163
  Robt. War 253
Garman, Adam Cum 167
  Isaac Cum 167
  John Cum 166
  Leonard Cum 167
  Nancy Cum 167
Garner, Charles War 260
  Churchhill Clr 130
  Daniel War 269
  James Woo 384

Garner, Jesse W. Clr 146
  John Bou 86
  John Jes 40
  Jona. Clr 130
  Joseph Mon 347
  Mary Jes 41
  Palla Pul 147
  Robert Fle 75
  Sally She 205
  Thomas Knx 75
  Vincent Pul 121
  William Bou 86
  William Pen 106
  Wm. Hop 373
Garnet, Andrew Hrs 320
  Edmund Boo 59
  Elijah Boo 59
  Hezekiah War 266
  Larken Hrs 320
  Leonard Fay 21
  Oliver Adr 8
  Robt. Boo 59
  Susanah Fay 54
Garnett, Ann Woo 401
  Benjamin She 207

Garnett, cont.
George Sco 189
James Clr 130
John Gal 186
John, Sr. Bar 30
Lewis Fay 38
Richard Bar 30
Thomas Jes 41
Waller Gal 186
William Woo 383
Zachariah Jes 40
Garnsey, David Fra 130
Garr, John Mer 315
Laurence Mer 315
Garrad, Henry Hnd 348
Samuel Hrs 310
Garrard, Daniel Bou 87
Daniel Cly 156
Henry Mul 403
James, Sr Bou 87
Jas. Senr Bou 86
Joel Cly 151
Nimrod Mon 350
Sary Hrs 311
Thomas Mul 403
Thos. & John M. Bou 87
William Mul 397
Wm. Jef 31
Garret, Bodtry Pul 146
Edmund Bar 38
Elijah Pul 148
Ignatious Grp 276
Prisley War 271
Thos. Cum 182
Garrett, Ambrose Jef 31
Amos War 266
Elijah Jef 31
Hugh Woo 382
Isaac She 206
J. Thomas Fay 16
Jacob Gar 228
John Gar 228
John Mad 211
John She 232
John Woo 383
Larkin Woo 383
Loving Hnr 359
Robt. Lew 104
Russell Gar 228
William Woo 383
Wm. Jef 31
Garretts, Edmand Jes 39
Garrick, Wm. Fle 63
Garris,Benjamin O. Chr 81
Marthy Chr 73
Sharpe Mul 388
Sikes Mul 392
Garrison, Baley Mer 315
Edmund Bar 27
Elwell Fay 39
Geo. Bar 32
James Hnd 340
Jas. War 249
John Log 174
John M. War 265
Mark War 267
Saml. War 265
Thomas Hnd 331
Garrit, Franciss Lin 117
Garrot, Curtis Mas 301
Daniel Chr 61
Henry Chr 104
Lemuel Chr 78
Garrott, Elimelech Flo 99
Henry, Jur Jes 39
Henry, Senr Jes 39
Lewis Clr 130
Garrott, cont.
Thomas Fay 34
Garth, David She 222
John Sco 172
Gartner, Leonard War 255
Gartney, Hugh Chr 114
Richard Chr 113
William Chr 114
Garton, Ann Hrs 309
James Hrs 309
James Wsh 314
Uriah Wsh 314
William Chr 82
Garver, Hannah Bar 54
Garvin, Archibald Gar 199
David Bar 53
John Cas 38
John Gar 229
John Mul 406
Thomas Chr 76
Garvis, John Mul 406
John Pul 147
Garvy, Job Fra 127
Garwood, Joseph Mon 350
Gary, John Cal 11
Gasaway, James She 233
John She 219
Sam. She 233
Saml. She 207
Gash, Michael Mas 263
Thomas Mas 265
Thomas Mer 315
Gaskins, Isaac Liv 151
John Liv 148
Gaslin, Samuel Log 177
Gasper, Elizabeth Clr 130
Peter Clr 130
Gass, David Mad 207
James Clr 130
James Mer 343
John Bou 123
Sarah Mad 207
Gassage, Mary Cly 157
Gassaway, Benj. Bar 30
Nicholas Bar 36
Saml. Bar 30
Gasten, James Pul 146
Gastineau, Job Pul 147
Gastinue, Charls Pul 147
George Pul 147
Job Pul 147
Gasway, Nicholas She 218
Gatch, Benjamin Bul 178
Frederick Bul 178
Gately, Jemima Cal 10
Elias Wsh 319
Elijah Gar 227
George Mul 402
Jacob Bar 49
Jacob Jef 30
James Mer 315
James Mas 264
John Jes 39
John Mul 402
Joseph Sco 183
Michael Mul 398
Philip Mul 388
William Mas 264
William Mer 315
Wm. Bar 49
Gatewood, A. Robert Fay 16
Anne Hnd 336
Hnery Fay 36
Hugh L. Gal 187
James Clr 130
James Jes 40
Gatewood, cont.
James Jef 12
John Fay 31
Larkin Fra 129
Leonard Jef 12
Peter Fay 36
Peter Sco 187
Sally Hnr 356
Richard Jes 39
Robert Jes 40
Thomas S. Jes 40
William Hnr 356
Williamson War 249
Gather, Thomas She 209
Gathright, Samuel She 198
Gathritt, John She 221
Gatliff, Aaron Knx 88
Charles Knx 86
James Knx 73
Moses Knx 73
Gatril, Hetty Nic 55
Gatson, William Clr 130
Gatten, Saml. Nel 31
Sylvester Bul 178
Gatton, Basel Bul 178
Joseph Bul 178
Thos. War 244
Gauf, Calob Mas 313
Gauge, Thomas Grn 256
Gaugh, George Nel 30
Isidere Nel 29
Phillip Pen 105
Gault, David Fle 81
Edward Mas 266
Wm. C. Jef 24
Gaunt, Reuben Gal 197
Gausney, James Jef 31
John Jef 31
Wm. Jef 31
Gautier, Nicholas Log 191
Gay, Alen Liv 153
Alexr. Lin 117
James Clr 130
John Woo 380
John, Esqr. Lin 117
Samuel Chr 53
Samuil Chr 53
Thomas Lin 117
Gaykin, John Jef 12
Gearhart, Peter Cum 167
Thos. Cum 174
Geater, John Jef 13
Wm. Jef 11
Gebbins, Jonathan She 215
Gee, James Cum 175
Jesse Cum 175
John Bar 50
John, Jr Cas 48
John, Sin. Cas 48
Mark Cas 37
Richard She 222
Robert Cas 47
Robert Jes 41
Geer, Ranson Cas 40
Geers, William Fay 52
Gehr, George Adr 8
Geiger, Frederick Jef 13
Frederick Jef 12
George Jef 13
Jacob Jef 31
Gelispie, William Fay 37
Gellaspie, James Fay 12
Gellum, Henry Chr 53
Genings, Charles Hnd 345
Genkins, Hamilton Fay 21
James Fay 36
Richard Fay 20

Genney (free woman) Fay 15
Gent, John Bar 38
  Tho. Bar 38
Gentle, John Cum 183
  Mary Cum 183
  William Mas 264
Gentree, Saml. Bar 48
Gentry, Bartlett Mad 209
  Blackston Bul 177
  Brightly Mad 208
  David Mad 208
  David Mad 208
  Eligah Cly 151
  Elizabeth Mad 210
  Henry Bul 177
  Isham Lin 117
  James Ohi 102
  Jesse Cum 175
  John Jef 12
  John Lin 117
  John Mad 209
  John (Stumpy) Mad 208
  Joseph Ohi 102
  Josiah Mad 209
  Martin Bul 177
  Martin Mad 209
  Martin, Jur Mad 209
  Matthew Ohi 88
  Nathaniel Pul 146
  Nicholas Bul 177
  Pleasent Fay 21
  Richard Mad 211
  Richard Pul 148
  Richard, Jur Mad 208
  Samuel Ohi 88
  William Ohi 89
  Wyatt Jef 12
Geoghegan, Ambrose Hrd 303
  Denton Hrd 303
  [illegible] Hrd 303
George, Alexander Chr 84
  Alexander Chr 97
  Andrew Cal 4
  David Jes 39
  Dolly Way 359
  Edward Hnr 365
  James Cal 12
  Jas. Gar 229
  Jenny Flo 99
  John Cal 10
  John Clr 130
  John Jes 40
  John Mer 315
  John Way 358
  Joseph Woo 395
  Leonard Sco 191
  Moses She 201
  Nicholas Clr 130
  Reuben Bou 87
  Richd. D. Fle 63
  Robt. Jnr Gar 228
  Robt. Snr Gar 228
  Sally Fra 127
  Whitson Clr 130
  William Woo 387
  Wm. Adr 7
  Wm. Mon 363
Geougg, James Pen 108
Gerald, James Mon 358
Gerard, Mansel Way 355
Gerdener, David Knx 73
Gerral, David Mer 314
Gerrard, William Fra 130
Gerrsan, John Fle 61
Gerton, Elijah Knx 75
  Elijah Knx 82
Gerven, Samuel Fle 75
Gesford, Joel Cas 43
Gest, John Fay 21
  Joseph Bar 49
  Joseph, Jr Bar 49
  Nathaniel Fay 31
  Sarah Fay 36
  Tho. Bar 44
  William Fay 21
  Wm. Bar 44
Geter, Fielding Woo 398
Ghaston, Hugh Knx 85
Ghobson, William S Grp 269
Gholson, Thos. Gal 187
Gholston, James Cum 165
Ghost, John Flo 99
Gibbins, Morgan Woo 390
  William She 216
Gibboney, Peter Jes 40
Gibbons, Arthur E. Wsh 316
  Elizth. Cum 185
Gibbs, Anne Way 368
  Benjamin Wsh 316
  Eletha Wsh 319
  James Lew 101
  James She 241
  Jeremiah Gar 229
  John Clr 130
  John Log 191
  John War 268
  John Way 356
  Jno. H. Nel 30
  Julius Sco 170
  William P. Wsh 316
Gibons, Elenor Hop 372
Gibsen, William Nel 10
Gibson, Alexander Sco 184
  Archd. Way 362
  Archibald Flo 99
  Barnabas Knx 82
  Catharine Lin 117
  Catherine Lin 117
  David Gal 186
  David Ohi 87
  Elisha She 211
  Ezekiel Flo 99
  Garrot Knx 71
  George Way 362
  Giddeon Ohi 88
  Isaac Knx 64
  Jacob Bar 35
  James Hnr 366
  James Knx 64
  James Knx 74
  Jesse Liv 148
  John Gal 186
  John Knx 71
  John Liv 148
  John Mer 314
  John Pul 147
  John Sco 169
  John Sco 180
  John Sco 184
  John H. Fra 127
  Jordon But 194
  Jordan Ohi 87
  Julius Mer 315
  Mary Ohi 99
  Nathan Mer 313
  Robert Mas 263
  Thomas Jes 40
  Thomas Pen 111
  Thos. Hrd 287
  Valentine Knx 65
  William But 194
  William Cly 150
  William Fra 129
  William Knx 85
Gibson, cont.
  William B. Wsh 319
Giddens, Reuben Flo 99
Giddings, George Clr 130
Gier, Margaret Mad 207
Gifford, Elisha, Jr Mas 264
  Elisha, Senr Mas 264
  Jacob Gal 187
  Pickle Lew 98
Gilaspie, Wm. She 242
Gilbert, Anthony H. Log 161
  Benjamin Jes 40
  Benjamin Ohi 83
  Charles Log 188
  Elijah Way 359
  Ezekiel Jes 42
  Henry Fay 60
  Isaac Mad 210
  Isham Lin 117
  James She 204
  John Cly 152
  John Lin 117
  John Wsh 317
  John, Junr Ohi 78
  John, Senr Ohi 78
  Joseph Way 359
  Joshua Way 359
  Mary Lin 117
  Samuel Mad 210
  Samuel, Jur Mad 208
  Simon Mad 208
Gilbreath, Hugh Adr 8
  Jas. Hnr 364
  John Adr 8
  John Hrs 305
  William Hnr 364
Gilchrest, Robert Hnd 331
Gilcreese, Robert Wsh 318
Gilehan, Clemins Wsh 316
Gilen, Daniel Mon 378
Giles, Absolam Rck 166
  Henry Sco 180
  John Hrd 304
  Lucinda Lin 117
  William Fle 67
Gilham, Mark Log 192
Gilka, Charles Mon 358
  Charles, Senr Mon 358
  Steward Mon 358
  Wm. Mon 358
Gilkerson, James Jef 12
  Robert Woo 380
Gilkeson, William Fle 86
Gilkey, Edward Grp 272
Gilkie, John Adr 8
Gilkison, John Fle 81
  John, Jur Fle 87
  Thomas Mer 314
  William Mer 314
  Wm. Fle 65
Gilky, David Wsh 319
  James Chr 55
Gill, Aaron Pul 146
  Benjamin Fay 21
  Catesby Fra 130
  Edward Bar 55
  Edward Mas 264
  Elexr. Adr 7
  George Hop 371
  George Pul 146
  George She 215
  James Grn 250
  James Mas 266
  James She 214
  James She 214
  John Grp 278
  Mary Hop 374

Gill, cont.
Matthew Wsh 314
Peater Mon 351
Reuben Bra 152
Richard Gar 227
Richard Pul 146
Richard Pul 147
Saml. Gar 227
Samuel Mon 352
Spencer, Jr Woo 396
Spencer, Senr Woo 400
Thomas Jef 31
Thomas Mon 352
William Gar 227
William Hnd 330
William Hop 374
William Pul 147
Wm. Bar 34
Gillaland, Adam She 197
Gillam, John Bra 153
John Fay 36
Polly Fay 36
Thomas Fay 43
Gillaspie, George Fle 89
John Grn 250
John P. Liv 156
William Liv 156
Wm. Fle 83
Gillaspy, James Nic 54
Gilleland, Jonathan Bar 43
Robert She 211
Gillerland, John Log 167
Gilles, William Wsh 317
Gillespie see Galasby
Gillian, Wm. Cal 16
Gillihan, Wm. Bar 26
Gillilan, Margaret Pul 148
Gilliland, Daniel She 197
Jas. Bar 42
Jas. Hrd 297
John Bar 43
Robert She 198
Thomas She 198
Thos. Hrd 284
Gillis, Joseph Knx 83
Joseph, Sr Knx 63
Gillispie, David Mad 208
Gabriel Mad 210
James Mad 208
Lewis mad 209
Gillitt, Samuel Woo 390
Gillock, James Bar 34
John Bou 86
Lawrence Bar 42
Wm. Bar 42
Gillom, John Sco 181
Thomas Sco 181
Gillott, Jonathan Lin 117
Gillum, Daniel Hnr 357
Gilman, Austin Gar 228
Timothy Jef 12
Gilmon, John War 244
Joseph Cal 16
Patrick War 244
Gilmoor, Elexr. Adr 8
Tom Adr 8
Wm. Adr 8
Gilmoore, John Chr 108
Gilmore, Andrew War 244
George Jef 24
George Lin 117
George Nel 30
James Cal 19
James Lin 117
James Mer 314
Gilmore, cont.
James Pul 148
John Jef 31
John Mer 313
John Pul 146
John Pul 147
John Pul 148
Joseph Log 187
Mathew Mon 364
Paddy Mon 358
Richard Mon 376
Richd. War 244
Robert Mas 264
Robert Pul 148
Robt. Boo 59
Saml. Jef 12
Samuel Pul 148
Thomas Chr 99
Wm. Mon 381
Wm. Nel 30
Gilmour, David Hrd 301
Alexander Hrd 301
Gilpin, Eli Mas 263
Joseph Clr 130
William Woo 386
Gilson, Edward Way 355
Samuel Way 359
Gilstrap, Nancey Rck 165
Gilstrop, Bright Way 352
Giltner, Abraham Bou 123
Barnett Bou 123
Francis Bou 123
John Bou 123
Michael Bou 123
Gimblin, Joseph Jef 13
Gimison, George Hrs 311
James Hrs 305
Gimlen, David Cum 176
Molly Cum 176
Saml. Cum 176
Gimmsion?, Samuel Hrs 323
Gin, James Nel 31
Ginings, Isaiah Mad 210
John Mad 210
Robert Mad 210
William Mad 211
ginkins, Downing Mer 314
Ginn, Benjamin Mas 264
Elizebeth Mas 264
James Mas 263
Laurence mas 266
Thomas Mas 264
Thomas She 234
William Lew 101
Ginnings, Eleanoh Hrs 312
Gintree, George Bar 48
Gipson, Cammel Mon 356
Henry Chr 78
Hugh Chr 76
George War 274
Jacob Cas 48
Jacob War 272
James Clr 130
James Mon 355
James Mon 357
James War 268
James War 276
Joel Chr 57
John Chr 75
John Chr 55
John Chr 111
John Pul 148
John War 269
John War 276
John War 276
John Woo 381
Joseph War 278
Gipson, cont.
Martin Pul 148
Mary War 274
Nathan Chr 78
Nicholas Chr 72
Randolph War 274
Samuel Mon 356
Samuel Mon 365
Susannah Chr 111
William Fay 21
William Pul 148
Wm. Mon 378
Girdlar, James Pul 146
Girley, Daniel Hrs 317
Gish, Christian Mul 393
John Mul 393
Gist, David Clr 130
Henry C. Log 195
James Clr 130
Jesse Log 167
Mordicai Clr 146
William Wsh 317
Githens, Edward Knx 74
Gitral, Dennis Way 373
Gitthens, Henry Nic 54
James Nic 54
John Nic 54
Gittings, Kinsey Wsh 317
Gittner, Jacob Fay 58
Givan, James Wsh 316
William Wsh 315
Givans, Alexander Fle 72
Given, Eleazer Hop 373
James Nel 33
Jas. Lew 95
Johnston Fle 86
Saml. Nel 30
Givens, Alen But 194
Alexr. Lin 117
Dixan Liv 155
George Lin 117
George, Jnr Lin 117
James Lin 117
James Lin 117
James Liv 147
John Lin 117
John Liv 153
Robert Lin 117
Robert, Jnr Lin 117
Samuel Hnd 332
William Fle 6-
William Hop 381
William Liv 153
Willm. Lin 117
Gividon, Joseph She 238
Givin, Thos. Nel 31
Givins, James D. Bou 87
Martha Mer 315
Samuel Bou 87
Givvens, George Hrs 314
John Hrs 313
Glacken, William Mad 210
Gladark, Jas. W. War 262
Gladdish, Richd. War 253
Gladwin, John Mul 403
Glanton, Burwel Woo 386
John Woo 380
Glasbrook, Jorden Bar 43
Richd. Bar 42
Susana Bar 51
Glascock, Cena Nic 55
Enoch Bre 159
George Bre 158
Gregory Bre 159
Horton Bar 50
Majck. Nel 31
Peggy Nic 55

Glascock, cont.
Peter Bre 159
Thomas Bre 159
Glascon, Thos. Nel 32
Glasebrok, Clifton Cas 46
Glasgo, Robert Chr 87
Glasgow, John Mad 208
Samuel Mad 208
Thos. Nel 32
Glass, Belfry Sco 171
Benjn. Sco 171
David Nel 31
Fleming Sco 187
Frances, Junr Liv 154
Frances, Senr Liv 154
George Fle 83
James Chr 89
James Fle 82
James Nel 31
John Hnr 352
John Sco 171
Jos. Jef 30
Jos. War 248
Michael War 252
Royal Bul 178
Saml. Sco 173
Thomas Jef 29
Thomas Sco 187
Thomas J. Bou 123
William Nel 31
Wm. Sco 170
Glasscock, Charnet Cum 176
Daniel Mas 266
Fielding Cum 176
Jesse Hrd 283
John Mas 265
Glasscok, George Fle 76
Glaves, Michael Pen 113
Glazebrook, Wm. Bar 36
Glazebrooks, James Mer 315
Gleavs, William Chr 109
Gleen, Auhebel Fle 71
Isaac Mas 266
Glen, Adam She 206
Celia She 199
David Ohi 90
John Hrd 300
Joseph Jef 30
Simion Nic 54
Glenn, Andrew Mul 398
Henry Mul 408
Hugh Mad 211
James Log 182
James Mas 266
James She 240
Jerh. Sco 168
John Gal 197
Martin Mad 209
Moses Mul 396
Robert Mas 265
Robert Mul 408
Thomas Mas 263
William Ohi 101
William Woo 382
Wm. She 240
Glidwell, Robt. Cum 182
Glinn, Benjamin Pen 106
Jeremiah Pen 110
Joseph K. Pen 114
Nehemiah Lin 117
Glisner, Nichols Nel 10
Glissen, Patrick Log 167
Glisson, Henry Log 167
Gloheart, John I. Mul 396
Glore, Adam Cam 28
Michael Boo 59
Saml. Boo 59
Glore, cont.
Solomon Jef 12
Glover, Chestley Mon 361
David Ohi 99
Ezekiel Jef 31
Job Bar 39
John Fay 21
John Fle 64
John Fra 130
John Mas 300
John A. Clr 130
Jonsa Mas 264
Mary She 204
Reubin Liv 156
Samuel Mon 352
Stephen Nel 32
Uriah Nel 32
Uriah She 215
William Liv 151
Wm. Jun Bar 40
Wm. Jur Bar 47
Wm. Sen Bar 40
Zacheriat Mon 368
Glovier, John Mad 208
Goad, Gabrel Cas 45
Goalley, Wm. Nel 30
Goan, Edward But 194
Goar, Benjmin Mon 368
John Mon 368
Goard, Lewis Chr 81
Peter Chr 81
Goare, Ashford Chr 93
isaac Chr 74
John Chr 76
Joshua Chr 78
Joshua Chr 100
Thomas Chr 78
Thomas Chr 100
Goatley, John Wsh 318
Peter Wsh 318
Gobel, Phebe Gar 229
Goben, James Hnd 328
Goberne, William Clr 130
Gobil, Abraham Grp 274
Gobils, Ephraim Grp 271
Gobin, James Jef 12
John She 220
Joseph Hnr 355
William She 199
Wm. Jef 12
Goble, Ben Hrd 291
Jno. Hrd 292
Gocum, Mathias Way 355
Godard, Michael Sco 173
Thos. Sco 178
William Cal 13
Godby, John Pul 147
William Pul 147
Goddard, Abbott Fle 74
Jesse Fle 86
John Fle 67
John Way 370
John, Senr Fle 77
John, Ser Fle 67
Joseph Fle 86
Wm. Fle 66
Godfry, John Mer 315
William Mer 314
Godley, John War 279
Godman, Martha Mer 313
William Hrs 314
Godmon,Zachariah B Pen 108
Godsey, Gilvert Nic 55
Godsil, T. Hnr 354
Goen, John (Freeman of colour) Jes 40
Micajah Bou 87
Goff, Andrew Mad 208
Elijah Grn 256
Elisha Pul 146
John Lin 117
John Pul 146
John Pul 146
Thomas Clr 130
Goggen, William Gra 241
Goggin, John Mad 210
Robert Mad 210
Wm. Cum 170
Goggins, Tom Adr 7
Goghagan, John Nic 54
John, Junr Nic 54
Gohagen, Michael Bou 86
Goheen, James Log 168
Gohiggins, Anthony Fay 20
Goin, Isaac Log 167
Isaiah Knx 83
Jacob Jes 39
Going, Faney Liv 159
Isaac She 228
Jas. Gar 228
Jeremiah Gar 229
John Liv 159
Mary Liv 151
Goings, Wm. Rck 159
Goins, James Clr 130
Golaphir, Martin Cal 11
Gold, Robert War 264
Golden, Abraham Mas 301
Edmond Knx 82
Hardin Mad 209
John Pen 106
Stephen Knx 83
Goldin, Jesse Mad 209
William Mad 208
Goldman, George Jef 11
John Jef 11
Martin Jef 11
Goldsberry, John Gar 228
Jona. Gra 241
Mack Gar 229
Goldsby, James Grn 264
Tarlton Jef 12
Goldsmith, John Cas 38
John Hrd 282
Saml. Hrd 299
Goldson, Benjamin Way 373
Wm. Gar 226
Goldston, Anthony Way 353
John Way 353
Goliher, John Log 166
Golleher, James Liv 150
Joseph Liv 150
Richard Liv 150
Thomas, Junr Liv 150
Thomas, Senr Liv 150
Goloher, Charles Mer 313
John Mer 314
Golsmith, Saml. Cas 37
Golt, John Log 192
Golthony, Wm. War 259
Gonce, George Nic 54
Nicholas Nic 54
Gonzales see Gunsaulus
Gooch, Dabny Lin 117
Gideon Mad 211
J. Charles Mas 263
James Jes 39
James War 269
Linas Lin 117
Matthew Liv 147
Thomas She 206
Thos. Lin 117
Willm. Lin 117

Good, Benjamin Lin 117
Edward Chr 87
Elisabeth Lin 117
Robert Chr 85
Thomas Chr 54
Goodall, John Bar 41
John War 248
Peter C. Bar 19
Tho. Bar 31
Goodding, Cornelius Fle 65
David Fle 66
Goode, Charles Hnr 358
Danl. Grn 260
John Chr 85
John C., Cas 46
Joseph Cas 48
Rebecca Hnr 359
Robert War 248
Saml. War 251
Timothy Cas 37
William Clr 130
Wm. Cas 39
Gooden, Daniel Mon 363
Elizabeth Mon 375
Enoch Mon 379
John She 237
Partrich Mon 376
Samuel Mon 363
Thomas She 237
Goodin, Alexander Knx 83
Alexander, Sr Knx 85
Hezekiah Knx 87
Isaac hrd 281
John Knx 65
Joseph Bar 54
Joseph Knx 83
Lewis Bar 46
Samuel Hrd 303
Thomas Knx 91
Thomas Knx 91
Thos. Hrd 296
Gooding, Eliza. and son Fle 64
Isaac and mother-Elizabeth Fle 65
John Fle 61
Richard Way 373
William She 235
Goodings, David Lew 104
Goodknight, Abraham She 224
Goodler, Jno. Nel 33
Goodlet, Ebenezer Log 185
Goodlett, Adam Nel 33
Adam Sco 175
James Sco 186
John Nel 10
Goodloe, George Clr 130
Henry Hop 380
Sarah Mad 209
Vivian Woo 380
William Mad 209
Goodlow, Thomas Fay 51
Goodman, Abraham Bar 29
Alexr. Bar 29
Amos Bar 33
Amos Jef 12
Anderson Bar 25
Andrew (see also-Andrew, Goodman Adr 8
Ansle Adr 8
Chas. Bar 26
Elijah Pul 146
Elisha But 194
Geo. Bar 25
Harden Bar 29
Goodman, cont.
Jacob Bar 39
James Fra 127
Jesse Adr 8
Jessee Bar 24
Joab Jef 13
John Bar 25
John Bar 29
John, Jr Bar 46
Kenneth Bar 24
Philip Mad 211
Saml. War 248
Steph. Hrd 287
Wm. Bar 24
Wm. Bar 29
Goddner, Jacob Gal 186
Goodnight, David Fay 49
Edmund Mer 313
Isaac War 255
Jacob Lin 117
John Mer 313
Michael Mul 390
Peter Mul 391
Tho. Gar 229
Goodpasture, Abraham Mon 366
Cornetious Mon 365
Jacob Mon 366
Joseph Mon 369
Goodrich, James Fra 129
James, Jr Fra 129
John Mad 208
Goodson, William Log 177
Wm. Junr Cum 173
Wm. Senr Cum 173
Goodsum, James Wsh 319
Wilfred Wsh 316
William Wsh 319
Goodwell, Tabitha Chr 112
Goodwin, Daniel Mon 379
Danl. Gal 187
Elijah Gal 186
James C. Fay 29
Jessy Chr 86
John But 194
John Chr 86
John Pen 117
Jos. Gal 186
Julius C. Pen 113
Samuel Chr 86
Tho. Bar 29
William Mas 265
Goodwine, James She 202
John Nel 32
Goolman, Abm. Clr 130
Charles Chr 130
Isaac Clr 130
Jacob Clr 130
Goose, Wm. Jef 11
Wm. Jef 32
Gossey, John Est 3
Peter Est 5
Gootee, Sarah Wsh 318
Gopp, Leonard Grn 257
Goram, John Sco 191
Sanford Bou 87
Goran, Galddin War 253
John H. War 253
Gordan, Freeman of Colour Jes 41
James Fay 36
Jonathan War 251
Gorden, Archibald Mer 314
Betsy Mer 314
James Fle 85
Jawel Grn 264
Jesse Adr 8
Gorden, cont.
John Gar 227
Randolph Mon 365
S. Wm. Gar 229
Theobald Nel 30
Thomas Mer 315
William Fay 52
Gordin, Benja. Clr 129
John Clr 129
John Clr 129
Judy Clr 129
Laurance Hnr 362
Rodman Hnr 358
William Clr 129
Gordon, David Mad 210
David She 223
Elisha Fay 15
Elizebeth mas 263
Geo. Hop 373
Hugh Wsh 318
James Liv 149
John Gal 187
John Hop 375
John Liv 150
Jonathan War 243
Lewis Mas 263
Noah Hrd 292
Samuel Log 193
William Gal 187
William Wsh 318
Wm. Hop 375
Gordwen, James C. Fay 11
Gordy, John Mas 265
Gore, Benjamin F. Jes 41
Henry Fra 130
James Bar 54
John Cal 20
John Mad 246
Jonathn. Nel 30
Mannon Bar 54
Sarah Fle 76
Thomas Cal 19
William Fra 128
William Gra 241
Goreforth, Thomas Jes 39
Goreham, William Log 169
Gorge, Abner Hrs 308
Abraham Hrs 308
Gabriel Hrs 309
Gorham, George Fay 41
John Fay 60
Thomas Log 196
Thos. Log 181
Gorin, Henry Chr 111
John Bar 19
John Chr 111
Gorman, Danl. Nic 54
Mary Bra 146
William Grp 271
Gorril, James Log 194
John Mon 379
Gorsuch, Benj. Bra 151
Gorton, Eleanor Wsh 319
Jeremiah Wsh 317
Thomas Wsh 317
Gorum, Alexdr. Bou 86
Gosay, James Gra 240
Gosbene, Peter and-sons Fle 66
Gosee, James Ohi 104
Gosh, John She 222
Gosley, Saml. Hnr 354
Goslin, Joseph Bar 27
Nathan Fle 78
Gosline, William Fle 92
Gosnel, Wm. Hrs 313
Gosney, Benjn. Cam 24

Gosney, cont.
Fredk. Cam 27
Richard Clr 130
Wm. Cam 29
Goss, Kinshon Lin 117
Nathaniel Pul 147
Gossage, Charles Mas 263
Gossam, Wm. War 243
Gosser, Peter Gar 229
Gosset, Nancy Pul 147
Reuben Pul 147
Gossett, Jacob Mon 378
Wm. Cal 19
Gossit, Reuben Pul 147
Gosso, Mary Fay 45
Got, Jessee Bar 49
Gotherman, James Fay 15
Gott, John D. She 218
Jonathan War 253
Peter She 230
Richard She 219
Robert She 212
Robert She 219
Sutton War 243
William She 228
Goud, John Adr 7
Goude, Flemg. Adr 8
Robert Adr 8
Gouge, Nicholas Adr 8
Thos. Hrs 308
Gough, Charles Wsh 318
Cornelius Sco 179
James Sco 173
Jaems Woo 380
Jeremiah Wsh 318
John B. Sco 173
John B. Wsh 319
Jonathan But 194
Michael Fay 16
William But 194
Gow, William Mas 264
Gowben, William Gal 186
Gowin, Anester Mad 211
Francis Mad 211
Gilbert Jes 40
John Mad 211
Joseph Mad 211
Manoah Mad 211
William Mad 211
Grable, David Bul 178
John Bre 169
Jona. Hrd 299
Saml. A. Mul 405
Grace, Allen Cal 6
Betty Way 367
Cany Chr 79
Greenberry Chr 79
Henrey Chr 79
John Hnr 351
John Way 370
John Way 370
Nathaniel Chr 65
Thomas Fra 127
Gracy, John Cal 7B
Graddy, Jessee Woo 402
John Mul 396
Linfield Adr 16
Grady, Benjamin Fay 21
Lewis Hop 377
Rachel Fay 16
Thomsen Jef 11
William Fay 21
Younger Cam 32
Gradyn, Linfield Adr 12
Grafford, Benjn. Bou 86
Thos. Bou 87
Graft, David Nel 29
Graft, cont.
Jacob Nel 32
Grafton, James She 220
Grag, John Pul 147
Wm. Cal 19
Grage, Mathwe Cam 32
Gragg, Abner Fle 85
Bennet Adr 8
Joseph Nic 55
Samuel Mon 367
Solomon Fle 85
Gragston, Richd. Bra 146
Graham, Amos Wsh 316
Arthur Bou 123
Bernard mas 263
Catharine Wsh 315
Charles Log 169
David Fra 130
David Wsh 315
David Wsh 316
Eli Log 191
Elizabeth Gar 227
Enoch Gar 229
Ephm. Cum 173
Flora Chr 108
Francis Fra 129
Francis Wsh 315
Geo. W. Fra 130
George Wsh 316
James Fle 72
James Hnd 327
James Lew 97
James Lew 104
James Lew 104
James Mer 314
James Mer 314
James Nic 54
James She 226
Jas. Gar 227
Jas. Lew 97
John Fra 128
John Flo 99
John Gar 229
John Hnd 329
John Jes 40
Joseph She 210
Levi Log 191
Luke Gar 227
Moses Liv 149
Richard Mas 263
Robert Chr 108
Robinson Fra 130
Samuel Hnd 335
Samuel Mer 314
Samuel Mer 314
Rho. Gar 229
Thomas Chr 113
Thomas Knx 86
Thomas Log 169
Thomas Lgo 192
Thomas She 217
Thomas She 217
William Fay 39
William Fra 129
William Lew 100
William Log 169
William She 235
William Wsh 315
Willm. But 198
Graives, Thomas Clr 130
Gramer, William But 194
Grant, Adam Wsh 317
Daniel Bou 87
Elijah Sco 181
George Bou 87
George Wsh 317
Jacob She 222
Grant, cont.
James Mad 264
James Sco 168
John Bou 87
John Mer 313
John Sco 174
John Sco 184
Jonathan Mas 263
Mosis Chr 112
Peter Mas 303
Robert Bou 123
Robert She 231
Rowling Mon 370
Sqr. Cam 26
Thomas Bul 178
Thomas Jef 31
William Fay 57
William Bou 87
William Bul 177
Wm. Boo 59
Grantham, John Hnd 342
Grason, William Hnd 340
Grass, Danl. Hrd 298
Henry Hrd 304
Grasty, John Chr 93
Gravat, Salley Grn 253
Graves, Absolem Boo 59
Anthony Liv 160
Asa Mon 371
Bartlet Cam 26
Bartlet Fay 41
Benjamin Fay 46
Benjn. Woo 380
David Bou 86
Edmund She 235
Edward Boo 59
Eleanor Wsh 318
Frances Fay 45
Frances Grn 246
George Fay 51
George Wsh 315
Howes Fay 46
James Boo 59
James Fay 33
James Fay 52
James Fra 128
James Rck 162
Jeremiah Boo 59
John Boo 59
John Fay 41
John Fay 41
John Fay 51
John Pul 147
John She 227
John Woo 401
John Wsh 315
John Wsh 318
John D. Fra 129
John S. Mul 390
Jos. Senr Boo 59
Joseph Boo 59
Josiah Fay 22
Leonard Mer 314
Patrick Liv 160
Pegy Fay 52
Philip Mul 395
Polly Fra 127
Reuben Boo 59
Richard She 215
Richd. Cum 170
Samuel Fay 41
Stephen Sco 188
Thomas Bou 86
Thomas Fay 60
Thos. Cum 170
William Rck 163
William Wsh 314

Graves, cont.
William Wsh 314
William Wsh 315
William B. Fay 36
Williamson Cly 149
Wm. Gar 228
Wm. War 271
Gravet, John Mad 208
Gravit, George S. Fra 128
John Clr 130
Thomas Fra 128
Gray, Abner Chr 81
Alexander Mas 265
Andrew Mon 382
Archibald Mer 315
Ben Hrd 285
Calis Way 354
Charles But 194
Daniel Chr 69
Daniel Chr 101
Daniel Hnd 339
David Jes 40
David Nel 30
David Nic 54
David Nic 55
Francis Hrs 311
Garrard Nel 30
Garrat Cal 3
George Fay 21
George Jef 24
George Sco 189
Isaac Fle 66
Isaac Mas 265
Isaac Mon 354
Isaac Nic 54
Isac Chr 93
James Bou 87
James Bou 87
James Bou 123
James Chr 99
James Chr 109
James Fle 88
James Fle 90
James Jef 25
James Mer 315
James Mon 355
James Nic 54
James She 218
Jane Chr 109
John Cal 3
John Chr 69
John Fay 21
John Mas 265
John Mas 265
John Mas 265
John Mer 315
John Mer 315
John War 272
John Wsh 314
John D. Gal 187
John F. Jef 24
Jona. Hrd 285
Jonas Hrd 303
Jonathan Woo 392
Joseph Mon 355
Joseph She 209
Joseph War 256
Jos. War 259
Jno. Hnr 363
Leaven Mad 210
Lydia Hrd 285
Mark Cly 158
Mathew Mas 265
Miles Chr 59
Nathl. Boo 59
Oliver Cal 8
Patrick Jes 40

Gray, cont.
Presley Gal 186
Richard Fay 36
Robert Chr 82
Robert Chr 87
Robert Mer 315
Robert She 235
Robert She 236
Rowland Way 361
Russel Hop 378
Samil Fle 90
Samuel Mer 314
Samuel She 236
Sanford Nel 31
Sarah Fay 16
Stephen Nel 29
Thomas Chr 66
Thomas Mad 208
Thomas Mon 359
William Bou 87
William Bou 87
William Bre 157
William Cal 3
William Chr 64
William Chr 67
William Gal 187
William Hrs 311
William Hrs 314
William Nel 32
Willis Knx 90
Wm. Cal 10
Wm. (mulatto) Woo 389
Wm. F. Fra 130
Grayham, Alexr. War 281
Andrew Bul 177
Andrew Log 161
Aths. Nel 30
Christr. Nel 32
Edd. War 274
Edward Grn 265
Elias Jef 12
Freeborn Grn 264
Green War 267
Harbert Grn 266
James Bou 87
James Log 183
James Mon 372
James Mon 375
James Nel 32
Jane War 278
Jeremiah Grn 265
John Fle 74
Johnson Grn 252
Mathew Log 192
Peter Grn 257
Rachal Jes 41
Robert Fay 52
Robert Grn 264
Robt. Nel 30
Robt. War 268
Samuel Mon 381
Sarah Grn 254
Sarah War 248
Thomas Jef 12
Thomas Log 193
William Bul 178
William Fle 83
William Grn 261
William Grn 264
Willm. Lin 117
Grayson, A. (Agent for) Grp 275
Alfred W. Fay 48
Benj. Nel 10
Frederick, W.S. Bul 177
George W. Grp 276
John Jef 12

Grason, cont.
Michael Mon 357
Robert H. Grp 276
Tho. Hop 373
Wm. Bar 29
Grdonings, William Hrs 319
Greaham, Andrew Cas 40
James Cas 41
Greathous, Saml. War 255
Greathouse, David Hop 378
David Jes 39
Harman Jes 39
Harn. Nel 31
Isaac She 205
Isaac War 256
John, Jr Jes 39
John, Ser Jes 39
William Jes 39
Wm. War 255
Greedy, Ruth Nel 32
William Mul 395
Green, Adam Nel 29
Alex Log 165
Allen Adr 8
Andw. Sco 171
Augusta Hrd 299
Beal Mon 375
Ben Nel 30
Benja. Gar 229
Benja. Hnr 364
Benjamin Hnr 360
Betsey Cam 29
Betsey She 234
Catherine Bou 87
Charles Sco 173
Daniel Mad 209
Daniel Pul 148
David Liv 145
Davis Mul 398
Delphe Liv 156
Edward Adr 8
Edward Fay 28
Edward Log 168
Edward Woo 388
Elihu Mad 208
Elijah Knx 74
Elisha Hrd 299
Elius Cam 33
Ephram Hrd 291
Fielding Fle 62
Francis W. Jef 13
Fred Hnr 364
Fredrk. Nel 33
GEo. Cum 181
George Adr 8
George Knx 64
Harrison Log 173
Henry Est 2
Henry Jes 41
Henry Mer 314
Henry Sco 180
Henry Woo 391
Isaac Bre 159
James Cal 8
James Clr 130
James Fay 31
James Fay 49
James Fle 84
James Hnr 365
James Mad 208
James Mad 211
James Mer 313
James She 218
James, Jur Woo 383
James, Senr Woo 383
Jamima Mad 209
Jesse Log 170

Green, cont.
  Jesse War 256
  Jesse Cal 3
  Jno. Hnr 369
  Joab Mer 314
  John Cal 20
  John Fay 36
  John Gar 228
  John Jes 40
  John Mad 210
  John Mas 263
  John Mas 265
  John Mer 341
  John Woo 393
  Joseph Sco 189
  Joshua Bul 178
  Leonard Wsh 315
  Leven Nel 31
  Lewis Adr 8
  Lewis Knx 79
  Lewis Way 355
  Liberty Grn 246
  Liberty Grn 255
  Loveren Bra 149
  Martin Mad 209
  Mathias Fay 60
  Nathl. Boo 59
  Paul Woo 384
  Peter Hnd 343
  Peter Wsh 315
  Polly Mer 313
  Rebecka Fay 12
  Reynolds Way 352
  Richard Fle 69
  Robert Bou 86
  Robert Cum 179
  Robert Jes 41
  Robt. Way 354
  Samuel Cal 7
  Sarah Woo 377
  Tho. Bar 35
  Thomas Chr 101
  Thomas Clr 130
  Thomas Log 168
  Thomas Pul 147
  Thomas She 197
  Thomas E. Wsh 316
  Thos. Boo 59
  Wile Hnr 363
  William Fay 36
  William Fle 62
  William Fle 66
  William Mad 209
  William Woo 379
  William, Jur Mad 209
  Williss Lin 117
  Wm. Adr 8
  Wm. Bar 40
  Wm. Bra 149
  Wm. Boo 59
  Wm. Way 352
  Wm. Way 358
  Zach. Gar 227
  Zacheriah Mon 362
  Zackh. Nel 31
Greene, John Pen 115
  Joseph Grn 259
  William P. Pen 116
Greenwalt, John Hrd 282
  Lewis Hrd 298
  Luke Hrd 298
Greenewault, David Hrd 282
Greenfield, Thomas G. Chr 112
Greenham, Wm. Cal 7
Greenhelgh, Jno. C. Mad 210
Greening, James Clr 129
Greening, cont.
  Reubin Clr 129
  Robert Clr 129
Greenslate, John Grp 273
Greenstreet, John Grn 249
  Peter Grn 257
Greenup, Christopher Fra 130
Greenwell, Alben Nel 30
  Eliza Nel 32
  Ignatius Sco 185
  Jas. Hrd 298
  Jno. Nel 32
  John Nel 29
  John Wsh 314
  Joshua Nel 32
  Mary Wsh 315
Greenwill, Henry Nel 33
Greenwood, Bartly Lin 117
  Elender Mer 315
  Henry Mer 313
  John Jes 40
  Nimrod Mer 313
  Phillip Hnr 362
  Thomas Bre 168
Greer, Amos Bar 35
  Amos War 259
  Aquila War 259
  George Fra 129
  Isaiah War 259
  James Cal 20
  John Bar 41
  John War 259
  Laurence Nel 30
  Saml. Nel 31
  Solomon Bar 35
Greffith, John She 236
Gregg, David She 227
  James Bou 87
  John Bou 87
  Joseph Sco 175
  Sammuel Fay 39
Greggs, Amos Sco 177
  Saml. Sco 176
Gregory, Abram Woo 389
  Asa She 205
  Beverley Knx 87
  Edward Way 366
  Fleming Way 366
  Byrd Ohi 96
  Godfrey Wsh 317
  Hiram Way 362
  James Mon 377
  John Bou 87
  John Woo 381
  John Wsh 317
  Joseph War 279
  Leroy C. Wsh 317
  Lewis Pen 112
  Mesech Way 357
  Mordaci Way 366
  Richard She 198
  Richard Wsh 314
  Smith Wsh 317
  Stephen Nel 31
  Thomas Cal 9
  William Wsh 315
  Wm. Nel 31
Greives, John Ohi 103
Grenald, John Nel 30
Grenard, William Mas 265
Grenaway, John Ohi 95
Grenup, John Sco 186
  Saml. Sco 186
Grenwell, Bennet Sco 172
Gresham, Benjamin Fay 59
  Job Lin 117
Gresham, cont.
  John Lin 117
  John Mad 208
  Nancy Fra 127
Grey, Benjamin Ohi 75
  Daniel Ohi 97
  Willm. Sr Nel 31
Greybill, John But 194
Greyer, James Sco 176
  Robert Sco 173
Greymoyr, Fredereck Bra 152
Greynoyr, Fredereck, Sr Bra 152
Grider, Henry War 243
  Jacob, Jun Bar 48
  Jacob, Sr Bar 48
  Martin Liv 155
  Michael War 251
  Nelly Gar 228
  Tobias Gar 228
Grier, Aquila War 259
  Henry Bre 157
Griffay, John War 270
Griffen, Elias Jes 41
  Fountain Hnd 346
  Gorden Mon 370
  Jasper Jes 41
  John Pul 147
  Richard mon 349
  Richard, Senr Mon 349
  Soloman Rck 164
  Tary Mon 349
  William Hnd 325
  William Liv 145
Griffeth, Alexr. Hop 380
  Greenby Nel 32
  James Bra 151
  James Mas 299
  Jesse Sco 173
  Paris Sco 189
  Thomas Sco 179
  Wilibee Fle 81
Griffett, Isaac Sco 179
Griffey, Bartlett Jef 11
  James Fra 128
  Joseph Fra 128
  Joseph Jef 12
  Samuel Jef 13
  Susanna Fra 128
  Thos. Cam 29
Griffin, Aaron Cum 176
  Alexander Fay 45
  Anthony Mon 349
  Anthony War 276
  Elijah Bul 178
  Gabriel Nic 54
  James Bul 178
  James Pul 149
  James Wsh 315
  Jesse Cum 181
  John Bul 178
  John (see also Griffith) Cam 30
  John Sco 190
  Jno. Pul 146
  Margaret Woo 385
  Rachel War 273
  Reson Bul 178
  Robert Bou 87
  Robert Hrs 321
  Soloman Pul 146
  Spencer War 249
  Squire Pul 146
  William Pul 146
  William Pul 148
  William She 218

Griffin, cont.
William Sco 180
Wm. Sco 169
Zachariah Knx 86
Griffing, Aaron Bou 69
Ebener Cam 30
Jeramiah Cam 30
John Cam 27
Phoebe Cam 30
Thos. Cam 26
Wm. Cam 30
Griffith, Abel Boo 59
Abel Bou 87
Benjamin Mas 264
Benjamin She 233
Caleb She 205
Ely Chr 88
George Chr 100
Isaac Mad 207
Isaac Sco 177
Jackson She 233
Joel Bou 86
John Boo 59
John Bou 86
John(see Griffin) Cam 30
John Cam 32
John Chr 88
Josiah Hrs 324
Martin Nic 54
Mary Bou 86
Mason Mas 265
Patrick Hrs 321
Patterson Est 2
Phileman Liv 147
Remus Ohi 68
Robert Bou 87
Samuel Hrs 318
Sarah Bou 87
Thomas Hnr 353
Thomas Mad 209
William Bou 87
William Chr 88
William Chr 88
William Chr 104
William Fle 76
William Liv 157
William Pul 146
William She 233
Griffiths, Joshua Ohi 96
Griffy, Elijah Hnd 337
Grigg, Aron Bra 142
William Pen 116
Griggs, Clem Clr 129
John Clr 129
John Mas 265
Minus Clr 129
Samuel Clr 129
William Clr 129
Willm. War 275
Grigory, Jeremiah Cal 11
Joseph Jef 11
Peter Fay 36
Thomas Knx 74
William Knx 87
Grigs, Sarah Bra 152
Grigsby, Aaron Mul 399
Baylis Bou 123
Benjn. Bou 123
Charles Ohi 77
Enock Nel 32
James Wsh 318
John Cly 153
John Nel 31
Joseph Wsh 318
Lewis Clr 130
Reubin Ohi 79
Samuel Mul 403

Grigsby, cont.
Smith Nel 31
Thos. Cly 153
Grigsly, John Mul 397
Grim, Andrew Bou 87
Frederick Bul 177
Grimel, Charles Fay 21
Grimes, Andy Jef 13
Avory Bou 123
Benjamin Fay 20
Charles B. Fay 21
Christian Bou 86
Edwd. H. Bou 123
James Fay 21
James Log 189
Jane Bou 123
Jesse Pul 148
John Clr 130
John Hnd 337
John Jef 12
John Mon 373
John A. Mad 244
Jonathan Clr 130
Joseph Mon 378
Leonard Hnr 356
Malinda Fay 21
Margarett Linn 117
Nathaniel Fle 68
Nicholas Bou 123
Noble Mas 266
Polly Fay 58
Robert Knx 80
Silvester Bou 123
Stephen Hnd 341
William Fay 38
Wm. Mon 358
Grimis, Lebra Way 353
Grimsly, David Bar 36
Grinald, Jas. Grn 247
Richard Grn 246
Robert Grn 260
Grindstaff, Henry Gar 227
Jacob Gar 227
Michael Knx 86
Grinstead, Leonard Fay 15
Robert Fay 16
Grinsted, Henry Bar 46
Jessee Bar 46
John Bar 19
John Bou 86
Philip Bar 36
Rihd. War 260
Grisell, Andrew Log 191
Henry Log 191
Grisham, John Lin 117
Uriah Rck 165
Griskill, John Grn 265
Grisom, John Bar 38
Grissam, David Sco 189
John Adr 8
Grissum, William Mer 315
Gristly, Benj. Nel 32
Gristy, Clemt. Nel 32
James Nel 30
Griswell, Elam Cam 31
Elum Cam 26
Wm. Cam 31
Gritton, Jesse Mer 315
John Mer 313
John Mer 315
William Mer 313
Groffe, John Jef 12
Gromer, William Mad 210
Groom, Abram Est 1
Abram Est 4
Jacob Est 6
Groomer, Fred Jnr Gar 227

Groomer, cont.
Frederick Gar 228
Jacob Gar 228
John Gar 227
Grooms, H. Elijah Fay 15
Isaac Bou 86
John Fay 15
Moses Bou 86
Moses Mon 384
Nancy Fay 16
Richard Clr 130
Robert Clr 130
Robert Fay 16
Sally Clr 130
William Bou 86
Wm. She 240
Groover, Benj. Bra 147
John Mas 264
Grooves, Edward Fle 82
Fredrick Mas 264
Grose, Jacob Fle 81
Gross, Abraham Cum 181
David Cum 182
Jacob But 194
Jacob Way 363
John Cum 182
John Cum 186
Joshua Liv 155
Peter Cum 182
Tywelt Cum 184
Grosshart, Adam Jef 12
Grosvenor, Richd. Nic 54
Ground, John Jef 27
Robt. War 256
Groves, Charlotte Hop 371
Daniel Mul 406
David Bre 168
Edward Fle 83
Fredrick Cal 18
Geo. Cum 168
Jacob Mul 402
James Cal 8
John Fle 68
John Hop 372
John Log 188
John Mon 380
Jonothan Mul 398
Jonathan Mul 402
Joseph Mul 401
Peter Mul 392
Robert Pen 116
Solomon Mul 389
Grovier, Jonathan Lew 95
Grubb, Christopher Knx 71
Jacob War 247
John Fra 129
John War 248
Philip War 248
Thos. War 281
Grubbin, James Wsh 315
Grubbs, Higgason Mad 211
Humphry Fay 36
Isaac Chr 83
James Boo 59
Thomas Mad 210
Grubs, Daniel Fay 15
John Bar 37
William Fay 21
Grugett, John Mad 244
Grugin, Paul Fra 128
Grundy, Gardum Bul 178
George Wsh 314
John Wsh 318
Peter(free man of colour) Bul 178
Robert Wsh 316
Samuel Wsh 316

Grundy, cont.
  William She 203
Gruwell, Isaac Hrs 319
  John Woo 380
Gryder, Fredk. Adr 8
  John Cum 171
  Martin Cum 170
Grymes, George Woo 391
Guardeen, Henry Ohi 102
Gudgel, Jacob Fra 128
Gudgen, Andrew Mon 358
Gudshall, Abram Woo 396
  Andrew Woo 396
  John Woo 384
Guelky, John Nel 31
Guess, Jesse Mad 210
  John Mad 210
Guest, Joshua Hnd 339
  Nathaniel Hnd 339
Guffen, Andrew Bra 151
  George Bra 151
Guffey, Ephm. Jr Way 353
  Eph. Sr Way 353
  Henry, Jr Way 351
  Henry, Sr Way 351
  John Way 353
Guffy, Alex Log 171
  Joseph Sco 169
Guier, John Mad 210
Guild, Samuel Hop 375
Guilky, Allen Nel 30
Guill, John Sco 179
Guilmore, James Adr 8
Guin, James Gal 187
  Thomas Clr 130
Guinn, Benjn. Sco 175
  Isom Gar 228
  Matthew Mad 209
  Moses Bou 86
Guire, Phillip Chr 102
Guiton, Samuel She 200
Gullaspey, Wm. Lew 102
Gulley, Jno. Mad 210
  Thomas Mad 210
Gullihugh, Ann Ohi 87
Gullion, Elijah Gal 186
  James Gal 187
  Jeremiah Gal 187
  Joseph Gal 187
Gully, Drury Gar 227
  Robt. J. Hop 374
  Wm. Gar 227
Gum, Jacob Hrd 288
  Jessee Bar 21
  Shepherd Hrd 297
Gumm, Charles Grn 248
  Elijah Grn 256
  John Grn 248
  Will Cly 157
Gumsly, Nelson Cam 28
Gun, James Pul 146
  Joseph Jef 12
Gunn, John Way 355
  Thos. Way 370
  Wm. Way 369
Gunnel, Richd. Sco 183
Gunner, Ruthy Hrs 317
Gunsaulus, James Nic 55
  Thos. Nic 55
Gunsules, Joanna Mas 305
Gunter, Hawky Bar 36
Guntreman, John She 202
Guntriman, Jacob Chr 69
Guntryman, Henry Bul 178
  Henry Bul 178
  Peter Bul 178
Gurden, David Adr 8
Gury, William Mad 211
Gust, William (freeman) Fay 15
Guthary, Jesse Hrs 322
Guthree, Wm. Hnr 359
Guthrey, Alexander Fra 128
Guthrie, Adam Nel 31
  Benjn. Woo 387
  Daniel Lin 117
  Elenor Mad 209
  Geo. Cum 180
  Hannah Cum 177
  James Cum 180
  James Fra 129
  James Jef 12
  Jas. Gar 228
  John Mer 314
  John Woo 382
  Richd. Gal 187
  Thos. Jr Woo 380
  Thos. Senr Woo 381
  Wiliam Woo 381
Gutrey, Daniel She 228
  Daniel She 228
Gutridge, William Fle 89
Gutrie, Levi Adr 8
  Steph. Adr 8
Gutry, Bevery. Adr 8
Gutthrie, William Mer 315
Gutt[illegible], Aaron Mer 314
Guttry, Alexander Mas 263
Guy, Benjn. Adr 8
  James Jes 40
  Richd. War 266
  Robert Jes 40
  William War 266
Gure, Henry Cly 152
Gwartney, Michaga Hrd 284
Gwartny, Anthony Hrd 288
  John Hrd 301
Gwathmey, John Jef 29
  Owen Jef 28
Gwathnery, Temple Jef 27
Gwin, Andrew Wsh 317
  Arthur Grn 264
  Thomas I. She 221
Gwinn, Johnson Woo 385
  Joseph Woo 381
  Robt. Jr Woo 389
  Robt. Senr Woo 388
  Saml. Woo 388
Gwyn, Joseph Cum 186

-- H --

Hack, Jonathan War 245
  Joseph War 245
  Philip War 245
Hackell, James She 209
Hacket, Martha Mon 369
  Peter Way 358
  William Fay 45
Hachete, Sarah Hnr 356
Hackett, Bazel Mad 212
  Jacob Mad 212
  James Woo 393
  Peter Mad 212
Hackler, Rose Knx 67
Hackley, Elizabeth Mon 359
  Francis Fra 132
  Coodridge Fra 132
  James Nel 37
  Joseph Lin 119
  Lott Mer 313
Hackley, cont.
  Richard Lin 119
  Robt. D. Hrd 295
  Saml. Hrd 290
Hackly, Hunt Lin 119
Hackman, Abraham Wsh 306
  James Lin 119
Hackney, John Woo 387
Hackwith, Jeremh. Flo 100
  John Flo 100
Hadden, Elisha But 194
  Hugh But 194
  James Log 189
  Samuel But 194
  William But 194
  William But 194
Haddon, Agness Fra 133
  John Fra 133
Haddox, Coleby Cly 159
  Saml. Cly 159
  William Cly 159
Haden, Abner Hrs 309
  Jno. Lew 104
  John Grn 252
  Turner Sco 175
  William Log 181
  William Log 187
  William Log 192
Hadin, Noah Mer 313
Hadley, John Adr 8
Hadsn, Jonathan Lew 97
Hafford, Maliga Chr 61
Hagaman, Simon Jef 9
Hagan, Arther Bar 49
  Arther R. Bar 49
  Benit Nel 39
  Clemt. Nel 35
  Edward Nel 33
  Enock Nel 34
  Henry Nel 33
  Henry Wsh 313
  Hezk. Nel 35
  Hugh Mad 249
  Igns. Nel 34
  James Nel 33
  James Nel 39
  John C. Nel 34
  Jonas Bar 49
  Joseph Nel 34
  Nicholas Nel 34
  Ranlf. Nel 35
  Rolf Nel 35
  Saml. Bar 52
  Samuel Mad 215
  Sarah She 222
  Thomas Wsh 310
  Walter, Jr Nel 35
  Wilford Nel 39
  Wm. Bar 49
  Wm. Bar 52
Hagans, David Clr 131
Hagar, David Jes 43
Hagard, David Mon 349
Hagen, Alexd. Clr 131
  Bazl. Nel 38
  Benj. Nel 33
  Chs. Nel 40
  Henry Jef 29
  Henry Nel 38
  Lucy Mul 387
Hagerman, Aaron Jef 9
  Gilbt. Nel 37
Hagerty, John Fay 59
  Maland Mon 368
  William Bou 91
Hages, James Wsh 311
Hagewood, Buckner Chr 112

Name	Co.	Page
Haggard, Bartlett	Clr	131
Benjn.	Rck	161
Dabney	Clr	131
David	Clr	131
Jas.	Gar	222
David	Mad	249
Edmund	Mad	247
Elizabeth	Clr	131
Henry	Rck	161
James	Clr	131
John	Clr	131
John	Clr	131
John	Rck	161
Martin	Clr	131
Nathaniel	Clr	131
Nathl.	Clr	131
Pleasant	Clr	131
William, Jun	Mad	249
Haggart, John	Fay	16
Haggarty, John	Clr	132
Robert	Clr	132
Haggerdy, ...	Mer	313
Haggon, John	Mer	315
Haggin, James	Mer	341
Hagle, John	Flo	100
Hahn, Christn.	Nel	9
Peter	Nel	35
Haiden, Elijah	Bar	41
Hail, Benjamin	Pul	151
Daniel	Chr	66
Hirum	Chr	101
Jessy	Chr	60
John	Mad	250
John	War	255
Levy	Mer	313
Thomas	Mer	313
William	Chr	62
Hailey, Abner	Bra	148
Haines, Christopher	War	260
Hezekiah	War	253
John	War	255
Petter	Mas	260
Richard	She	198
Wm.	War	255
Hainis, John	She	198
Hainleyson, John	Mon	347
Hains, Andrew	Mad	213
Evan	Mad	250
James	Lin	119
Jos.	Boo	60
Joseph	Mer	313
Michael	Bou	91
Michael	Mer	313
Hair, Daniel	Log	193
Jonas	Lew	97
Haislip, Thomas	Cal	13
Haisty, Clem	mon	370
Clem	Mon	375
Elizabeth	Mon	370
John	Mon	370
Wm.	Mon	370
Haithman, Geo. Jr	Bou	124
Geo. Sr	Bou	124
Hajan, Nancy	Bar	49
Hajght, Partrick	Cas	39
Hake, Simon	Pul	152
Halaway, Samuel	Log	195
Halbert, Noah	Hrs	307
Thos.	Nel	33
Thos. Jr	Nel	40
Halcell, Rezin	Clr	132
Halcombe, Caleb	Cal	13
Jonathan	War	282
Halcumb, Josiah	Log	169
Halderman, David	Bul	179
Hale, Abraham	Fle	72
Adam	Bou	92
Hale, cont.		
Benjamin	Cal	4
Benjn.	Grn	254
Caleb	Hop	375
Charles	Bou	92
Durham	Grn	249
Hesikia	Cal	9
Jesse	Mer	316
Job	Mer	316
John	Liv	150
Joseph	Flo	99
Joseph	Wsh	309
Laban	Pul	151
Malan	Mon	367
Nathaniel	Cal	18
Peter	Flo	99
Philip	Nel	38
Polly	Mer	316
Smith	Woo	389
Squire	Hnr	359B
Stephen	Pul	151
Thos.	Grn	246
William	Liv	151
Hales, James	Knx	66
Haleshouser, Jno.	Nel	35
Haley, Barneby	Rck	161
Bartlett	Lin	119
Benjamin	Fay	49
Benjamin	Fay	50
Benjn.	Lin	118
Edmund	Mer	315
George	Rck	166
Henry	Bar	30
James	Fay	43
John	Fay	20
Radel	Fay	41
Richard	Hrs	312
Robert	Mer	315
Susana	Fay	17
William	Fay	50
Half, Lucy	Mon	373
Halfield, John (see also Hatfield)	Bul	178
Halford, Thomas	She	239
Halfpenny, John	Clr	131
Hall, Aaron	Mon	358
Abel	Nel	34
Adam	Adr	9
Adam	Way	358
Alexander	Fay	21
Alexander	Fay	38
Andrew	Lin	118
Ann D.	Wsh	314
Ansel	Wsh	314
Anthony	Knx	85
Anthony	Pul	150
Arther	Nel	33
Arthur	Mon	351
Asa	Bul	179
Asa, Jr	Bul	179
Austin	Bul	179
Benjamin	Log	195
Bingam	Nic	52
Burbage	She	218
Caleb	bou	88
Carter	Wsh	310
Clayborne	Woo	392
Cornelius	Bar	45
Cornelius	Nic	52
Christopher	Wsh	305
Clark A.	Ohi	92
Clifton	Bul	179
Daniel	Hrs	314
David	Bul	179
David	Fra	133
David	Mad	250
David	Mer	313
Hall, cont.		
Drury	Hrd	303
Edward	Log	188
Edward	Clr	132
Edward	Log	164
Edward	She	211
Edward	Way	358
Edwd.	Bar	36
Elisha	Mas	256
Elizabeth	But	194
Francis	Bou	91
Francis	She	216
Garlen	Log	165
George	Fay	30
George	Mer	316
George	Way	373
Green	Mon	351
Henry	Grn	253
Henry	Hrs	314
Henry	Log	195
Henry	Mer	316
Hethy	Rck	164
Hezekiah	Cly	160
Jacob	Cly	160
James	Adr	9
James	Bar	40
James	But	194
James	Cal	15
James	Cum	176
James	Gal	196
James	Jef	9
James	Knx	81
James	Nic	52
James	War	250
Jane	Fay	50
Jas.	Way	363
Jenny	Sco	186
Jeremiah	Fra	135
Jno.	Hrd	293
John	Bar	53
John	Boo	60
John	Bul	179
John	Chr	63
John	Fay	21
John	Gar	223
John	Fay	22
John	Gar	224
John	Hnr	366
John	Hrs	307
John	Jef	9
John	Jef	11
John	Lin	118
John	Lin	121
John	Log	171
John	Log	179
John	Mad	247
John	Mer	313
John	Sco	193
John	Way	373
John	Way	374
John	Wsh	310
John	Wsh	314
John, Jr	Bou	123
John, Jr	Bul	179
John, Senr	Sco	189
Joseph	Bou	124
Joseph	Cum	176
Joseph	Cum	178
Joseph	Lin	121
Joshua	Bou	123
Joshua	Hrs	308
Joshua	Hrs	321
Josiah	Gar	223
Kinchan	Knx	67
Laurence	Bou	91
Levi	Grn	264
Lewis	War	246

Hall, cont.
Lewis War 246
Lowder Liv 150
Mahlon Bou 89
Mary Nel 9
Maze Clr 131
McCajah Est 8
Micajah Log 181
Michael R. Fay 30
Michl. W. Bar 40
Mingo Ohi 85
Moses Fle 87
Moses Nic 53
Moses She 207
Moses She 217
Nathan Jef 10
Nathan Jef 23
Nathaniel Bou 179
Neal War 260
Palmer Bar 34
Peter Clr 131
Philip Bou 91
Philip Hrd 292
Randolph Gar 220
Ransom, Junr Log 164
Richard Hrs 311
Richd. Gar 223
Richmond Mon 352
Robert Bou 91
Robert Bou 91
Robert Hrd 304
Robert Nic 53
Rose But 194
Sally Gar 223
Samuel Hrs 314
Samuel Nic 52
Samuel Pen 109
Simian Bul 178
Simmian, Jr Bul 179
Stephen Bou 70
Stephen Clr 132
Stephen Log 190
Sylvester Bar 39
Sylvester Nel 35
Theophilus Bou 124
Thomas Bar 40
Thomas Fay 47
Thomas Lew 104
Thomas Nel 40
Thomas Pul 152
Thos. Boo 59
Washington Sco 170
Will W. Bou 81
William Bou 124
William Bul 178
William But 194
William Chr 64
William Clr 131
William Fra 135
William Gra 241
William Grn 250
William Hnr 366
William Log 163
William Log 165
William Log 188
William Mad 250
William Mer 314
William Nic 53
William Pul 150
William Pul 153
William Sco 190
William, Jn Log 164
William, W. Log 161
Winny Bar 52
Wm. Bar 36
Wm. Cum 178
Wm. Gar 226

Hall, cont.
Wm. Knx 64
Wm. Mon 351
Wm. Way 351
Wm. Jnr Gar 223
Wm. Snr Gar 224
Wyatt Log 184
Hallack, Benjn. Bou 123
Hallaway, James Jes 45
Haller, Eliza Hnr 360
John Mas 263
Lewis Bou 68
Thos. Hnr 359B
Hallet, M. Winslow-
V. S. Fay 16
Halley, Benjn. Mon 351
Francis Mad 215
Jno. Mad 215
John Clr 131
Joshua Mon 347
Halloway, Samuel Mas 306
Halmes, James Senr She 209
Halsal, Ben Cum 177
Thos. Cum 175
Halsell, William Clr 133
Halsey, Joseph Cly 151
Halston, James She 227
Halton, Samuel Log 170
Haly, Coleman Gar 223
Halyard, John Clr 132
Ham, David Ohi 70
Drury Lin 119
Elijah Jes 44
George Mad 215
Jacob Bou 91
Jacob, Jr Bou 91
John Bou 91
John Mad 213
John, Jr Bou 91
Joseph Fle 62
Matthew Mul 400
Michael Bou 90
Nathan Log 164
Nathan Log 170
Peggy Mad 215
Peter Bou 91
Samuel Fle 68
Stephen Mad 248
William Mad 215
Wm. Bra 143
Haman, John Flo 99
John Pen 105
Hamar, James Cam 25
Hambaugh, Hy Nel 39
Hambey, John R. Jes 45
Hamblen, George She 228
Hambler, William Mer 314
Hambleton, Archi-
bald Mon 351
Charity Bou 91
Chas. Sco 167
Danil. Fle 81
James Chr 105
James Woo 391
James M. Hnd 336
John Bou 88
John Chr 83
John Chr 104
John Lin 121
John Sco 189
Polly Bou 124
Robert Bou 88
Robert Jes 45
Saml. Bou 90
Samuel Knx 79
Willm. Lin 118
Wm. Mon 352

Hamblin, Benjamin Hnr 357
Hambrick, Gilson Mas 260
Jesse Sco 176
John Log 182
Yelverton Bar 21
Hambright, James Log 169
John Log 172
Hambruk, Enock Bar 41
Hamburgh, John She 231
Hamby, Susana But 194
Hamed, Jonthn. Nel 33
Hamel, Francis Grn 247
Hamelton, Dav. Hnr 369
David Bra 151
Edward Bra 151
Elizabeth Bra 151
George Fay 55
James Fay 17
John Boo 59
John Bra 142
John Fay 16
John Way 361
Robert Fay 54
Wm. Boo 59
Hames, John Mer 316
Thos. Hrs 319
Hamey, Jno. M. Nel 9
John Nel 36
Saml. A. Bou 90
Selby Bou 90
Hamill, Robert Gal 197
Hamilton, Abner Bar 52
Allen Wsh 313
Allen Wsh 313
Andrew Bre 165
Andrew Bre 169
Andrew Mad 247
Andrew Mon 365
Andrew Woo 377
Anthony L. Liv 158
Archebald Fra 130
Baxter Mer 314
Benja. Flo 100
Benjn. Hrs 310
Charles Way 364
Chas. Cas 39
Clement Wsh 313
Daniel Fle 87
David Hrs 313
David L. Liv 158
Elisabeth Way 371
Elizebeth Mas 257
George Bul 178
George Ohi 89
Hance Cal 20
Henry Gar 224
Henry Mad 247
Isabel Mon 352
Isabella Bre 169
Isham Wsh 313
James Adr 9
James Clr 132
James Hnr 357
James Hrs 311
James She 216
Jas. Nel 33
Jesse War 263
Jno. A. Fle 63
John Adr 9
John Bar 25
John Bou 123
John Hrs 313
John Hrs 313
John Liv 158
John Log 174
John Mad 214
John Mon 353

Hamilton, cont.
John Nic 52
John War 274
John Woo 377
John Woo 377
John Wsh 313
Joseph Liv 148
Joseph Liv 152
Joseph Mas 259
Leonard Wsh 313
Leroy Clr 132
Margaritte Hrs 321
Matthew Wsh 303
Mordica Liv 149
Nancy Hrs 323
Nathaniel Bre 162
Patrick Liv 158
Pattrik, Jn Cly 158
Patrick, Sr Cly 158
Robert Bar 49
Robert Fay 31
Robert Fra 130
Saml. Bra 146
Samuel Bre 169
Samuel Fra 133
Theophilus Mer 315
Thomas Mad 247
Thos. Nic 53
Tom Adr 8
Vance Hrd 289
Walter Wsh 310
William Ohi 79
William Liv 158
William Wsh 313
Willm. Bou 123
Woods M. Liv 159
Wm. Cal 10
Wm. Mon 354
Hamlett, Thos. Fle 63
Hamlin, Dant. Knx 73
George Knx 72
John Knx 82
Hamlong, George Bra 151
Hamm, Willm. N. War 278
Wm. War 265
Hammack, Daniel Mad 215
Ephraim Mad 216
Lewis Mad 215
William Mad 215
Hammands, Absam. Adr 9
Tom Adr 8
Hammel, John Bar 46
Hammer, Frederick Knx 69
George Knx 88
John Clr 131
Hammerley, James Pen 107
Hammet, Jesse War 269
Samuel Mas 256
Hammett, Reubin War 251
Susanna Wsh 306
Willm. War 246
Hammilton, James Pul 152
Jas. Nel 39
John Fle 89
Hammit, Jno. Bar 37
Hammock, Wm. Cal 13
Hammon, Huston Jef 8
Hammond, Charles Woo 392
Christopher Cal 7
Ezra Woo 392
George Lin 121
Jemi Nel 35
Jno. Gal 186
Job Log 185
John Fle 83
John Fle 88
John Sco 178
Hammond, cont.
John War 257
John Woo 393
Lewis Sco 187
Mary Woo 393
richd. Bra 142
Solomon Jef 28
Thomas Log 163
Wm. Hrd 292
Wm. Lew 98
Hammonds, Charles Mas 262
James Sco 190
John Adr 9
John Adr 9
John Lin 121
Hammons, Isaac Knx 88
James Cas 42
Joseph Bar 35
Obediah Knx 92
Hammott, Elijah War 252
Hamner, Henry Mer 314
James Mer 314
Hamons, Edmun Cas 43
Hampton, Benjamin But 194
Benjn. War 264
Charles Clr 132
David Hrd 293
David, Jr Clr 131
David, Sr Clr 131
Elijah Bar 46
Ephraim Jef 11
George Clr 131
George Lin 119
James Fra 134
James Mas 262
James War 259
Jesse Clr 131
Joel Cam 27
Joel War 260
John Clr 146
John Fra 134
John Log 186
Jon. War 259
Jonathan Clr 132
Lewis Woo 380
Martha Jes 45
Oliver Jef 30
Preston Pen 114
Stephen Jes 41
Thomas But 194
Thos. Bra 150
William Fra 134
William Mad 248
Hamrick, William Fle 81
Hams, John Log 179
Hamton, Antonia Grp 271
Han, Peter Jef 8
Hanback, William Fay 52
Hanby, Isaac Chr 56
Jerramiah Chr 56
Samuel Chr 56
Wm. Bra 153
Hancock, Anny Gar 224
Benjamin Way 351
Bennit Cal 13
Francis Gar 224
George Mad 212
George Mas 301
Jesse Way 351
John Cal 7
John Fra 131
John Jef 30
Jos. Nel 34
Joshua Hnd 345
Micajah Hnd 338
Obed Woo 391
Rachel Mas 301
Hancock, cont.
Simon Adr 8
Simon Hnr 357
Stephen Mad 216
Thomas Fra 134
William Jes 43
William Woo 384
Wm. Jef 30
Wm. Way 372
Hand, Ephraim Bou 89
John Pen 109
Monica Wsh 305
Robert Bou 91
Uriah She 236
William Liv 145
Handby, Handy Jes 45
Handcock, John Adr 8
Willm. Adr 8
Wm. Adr 12
Handley, Alexander Wsh 313
James Wsh 313
John Ohi 69
John Wsh 309
John, Junr Ohi 98
Samuel Mul 391
Samuel Ohi 99
Handly, David Hnr 356
Jessee Cal 4
James Bar 53
Jessee Bar 40
Handy, Willm. Adr 9
Wm. Sco 185
Hane, David War 244
Hanee, Richard Bou 89
Haner, Harman War 273
James Wsh 303
Hanes, Ephraim Pul 150
Frederick Mul 390
Frederick Mul 397
George Nic 52
James Pul 152
Josiah Ohi 83
Thomas Pul 151
Haney, Abner Clr 132
David Cam 31
Richd. Clr 131
Richd. Clr 131
William Clr 131
William Pul 150
Hanger, Margt. Boo 59
Hanie, Samuel Mon 347
Hanigin, B. Edward Fay 17
Hankins, Fielding L. War 275
John Hop 376
Wm. Hop 377
Hanks, Abner Gal 185
Absalam Clr 132
Elijah Woo 383
Fielding Mon 348
Fleetwood Jef 30
George Fra 132
George Mon 348
George Woo 393
John Chr 81
John Hnr 365
John Mon 357
John Woo 396
Pitman Fra 132
Polly Mon 382
Thomas Chr 81
Turner Fra 132
William Gra 240
Wm. Hrd 286
Wm. Mon 360
Hanley, Darby She 210
John Adr 9
John Mon 349

Hanley, cont.
John Pul 150
Nelson Fay 53
Thos. War 250
Hanly, David War 257
Hann, John Gar 226
Hanna, Abraham She 200
Adam She 206
Brice Hop 377
David Mas 256
Ebenezer Flo 99
Edward Mas 309
John H. Fra 135
Rebecca Mas 305
Saml. Flo 99
Thomas She 213
William Mas 261
Wm. Lew 95
Hannah, Andrew Sco 176
Elizabeth Log 184
Hugh Chr 102
James Mer [illegible]
John Log 192
John Mer 341
John Way 368
Robert Grp 270
Saml. Bou 91
Stephen Mer 315
Willm. Lin 119
Hannerson, Easter Jef 10
Hannis, Henry She 219
Hannon, John Mon 375
Hannum, Jonathan Log 187
Richard M. Log 192
Hansberry, William Chr 116
Hansbraugh, Sarah She 208
Hansbrough, Enoch She 210
George She 240
Joel She 208
Joseph She 212
Peter Log 194
Peter She 207
William She 199
Hanse, William Mas 258
Hansell, Laurence Lin 121
Hansford, Chs. Nel 34
Thomas Pul 152
Thos. Pul 153
William Pul 152
Wm. F. Bou 90
Hanson, Samuel Clr 146
William Fay 17
Hanspiger, chris-ley Jes 42
Henry Jes 42
Michael Jes 44
Paul Jes 44
Hant, Robert Pul 150
Hanway, David Bou 124
Hany, James Log 163
James Pul 150
Happy, Benjn. Bou 89
Elijah Fay 21
James Bou 89
James Fay 24
John Fay 16
Hapwood, Martha She 239
Harbaugh, Philip Mas 257
Harbe.., Mary Mer 313
Harber, Joseph Chr 62
Joseph Chr 87
Judith Woo 393
Harberry, Elisha Chr 86
Harberson, ... Mer 314
Andrew Mer 313
George Jes 45
Nancy Mer 315
Harberson, cont.
Samuel Hnr 356
Harbert, Baley Mer 313
John Cam 27
Matthew Mer 314
Thos. Cam 31
William Wsh 305
Wm. Nic 52
Harbeson, Samuel She 241
Harbin, Allen Wsh 313
Harbinson, Archibald Mon 357
Harbolt, Leonard Jef 11
Harcourt, John Bou 69
Hardan, Cuthbert Bar 51
Jacob Cam 32
Hardaway, Richd.B. Hrd 289
Hardcastle, Jas. War 246
Harden, Daniel She 214
Geo. Gar 226
Henry Fle 71
John She 224
Nathan She 197
Hardenbrook, John Mer 314
Hardest, Harry Gra 240
Hardester, Uriah Boo 60
Hardesty, Benjn. Bou 124
Caleb Nel 33
Charles Wsh 309
George Wsh 313
John Wsh 305
Joseph Wsh 307
Samuel Fay 17
William Nel 38
Willm. Nel 39
Hardick, John Mad 250
John Mer 315
Hardin, Abraham Grn 258
Absolam Liv 149
Bailey Wsh 311
Benjamin Liv 159
Benjamin Wsh 312
Benjamin Wsh 312
Benoni Wsh 312
Charles Clr 132
Daniel Bre 156
Daniel S. Wsh 312
Davis Mad 244
Elihu Nic 53
Elijah Mas 259
Enos Fra 133
George Jef 30
Henry Bre 164
Henry Jef 11
Henry Jef 30
Henry Wsh 312
Isaac Bre 165
James Chr 85
James Fra 133
James Lin 118
Jamima Mad 249
Jepthah Mul 385
Joab Liv 155
John Grn 245
John Grn 260
John Liv 155
John Wsh 312
John Wsh 312
John Wsh 312
Joseph Liv 159
Josiah Mad 249
Lydia Liv 152
Margt. Nel 39
Mark Fra 135
Mark Wsh 312
Martin Hnr 351
Martin Wsh 312
Martin Wsh 312
Hardin, cont.
Martin Wsh 312
Martin D. Fra 135
Martin S. Wsh 312
Moses Wsh 311
Nathl. Hop 372
Nicholas Hop 371
Nicholas Ohi 83
Patsy Clr 132
Rebecca Jef 11
Richard Fra 132
Robt. Gar 221
Robt. Wsh 312
Samuel Chr 59
Thomas Est 1
Thos. Grn 246
Vingelist Fra 133
William Wsh 311
William Fay 32
William Fay 60
William She 219
William, Jr Bre 158
Wm. Jef 30
Wm. Senr Bre 163
Zephiniah Jef 11
Harding, Alexander Adr 9
Henry Adr 9
Josn. Adr 8
Nichs. Adr 8
Willm. Nel 34
Hardister, Henry Fay 47
Hardisty, Benj. Sr Bou 123
David Mad 213
Henry Mad 214
Thomas Clr 132
William Bou 123
Hardman, Edward Fra 136
Jacob Clr 132
Hardon, John Nic 53
Sarve Hrs 318
Save Hrs 317
Hardridge, Wm. Bar 36
Hardus, David Bar 43
Hardwick, Charey Cas 44
Charles Mon 350
Christo. Hnr 360
Christopher Mon 348
David Mon 372
Elizh. Adr 9
George Grp 273
Henry Bou 88
John Adr 9
John Bou 88
John Mon 382
Robert Hnr 358
Samuel Mon 350
Samuel Mon 355
William Jes 42
Hardy, Andw. Clr 131
Ashford Jes 46
Charles Chr 86
Curtis Bar 42
David Bul 179
Henry Sco 189
Isam Bar 40
Joseph Gal 185
Mary Clr 132
Saml. War 275
Samuel Mas 262
Thomas Bar 40
Willm. Sco 173
Hare, James Way 358
John Jef 11
Nathan Gal 184
Haregrove, George Chr 97
Hargan, Michael Hrd 303
Harget, Peter Mas 257

Hargett, Daniel Fle 62
Hargey, Catharine Fay 16
Hargrave, Hezikiah But 194
Samuel But 194
Hargraves, Seth Log 161
Hargis, Abriham Chr 83
Abriham Chr 116
Isaac Chr 101
Jame Pul 149
William Chr 92
William Chr 101
William Log 169
Hargro, Juda Mon 376
Hargrove, Joseph Mer 314
William Mer 314
William Mer 314
Harick, Walter Fay 30
Harid, Joel Chr 89
Hariford, George Way 358
Harin, William Hrs 307
Haris, F. George Pul 149
Harison, Charles Way 370
Hariss, Elizabeth Hrs 310
Harisson, Rubin Chr 69
Tunis Chr 69
Harken, Danl. Nel 38
Harker, Richard Hrs 323
Harkins, Samuel C. Liv 160
Harkley, Jno. Hrd 298
Harl, John Mas 261
William Mas 258
Harlan, James Wsh 309
John, Junr Bar 47
Harland, Barton Cum 167
David But 194
Elija But 194
George But 194
John But 194
Joshua Bra 142
Thomas Jef 31
Harler, Archd. Clr 132
Harley, Daniel Lin 119
Harlin, Aron Bar 50
Elihu Bar 49
Ezekiel Gra 240
Jacob Bar 47
Jahu Chr 109
James Bar 49
James Mer 315
John Bar 47
Joshua War 264
Nathaniel Mas 257
Saml. Bar 44
Silas Mer 315
William Mer 315
Harlow, Anderson Bar 40
Clebon Bar 31
Jessee Bar 34
John Adr 8
John Log 173
Michl. Bar 34
Randal Bar 34
Sherwood Hnr 360
Susanna Mon 372
Walter Gar 225
Wm. Bar 30
Harmah, Joseph Bou 90
Harman, Benskin War 274
Geoe. Adr 9
George War 274
Harry Hop 374
Isaac Adr 8
J.G. Nel 38
Jesper Bou 124
Micajah War 274
Michl. Hop 378
Peter Bou 124
Harman, cont.
Robert Fle 77
Valentine Bra 145
Willm. War 273
Harminser, Mary Grn 249
Harmon, David Pen 108
Fison Bou 89
Henry Way 368
Isaac Hnd 333
Jacob Knx 73
Jacob Mon 354
James Hnr 362
John Mon 353
John Pul 149
John Pul 151
Kezia Liv 160
Nat. Hnr 352
Peter Mer 314
Philip Mon 348
Saml. Bra 152
Saml. Cal 12
William Fle 73
William She 219
Harmond, George Log 163
Harned, Eneas Hrd 298
John Nel 38
Jona. Senr Hrd 298
Harness, Jacob Bou 90
Peter Cum 176
Peter Mon 374
Richd. War 249
Harney, Hyram (see Hyram, Harney) Nic 53
Mills Nic 53
Roland Nic 53
Thos. Nic 53
William Fay 55
Harnit, Benjamin Chr 70
Harod, Wm. Gal 185
Harp, Abraham Fay 48
Bostion Fay 55
Boston Fay 32
Conrod Fay 50
John Fay 55
John Nel 35
Mary Wsh 304
Susan Log 162
Tobias Knx 85
Harper, Absolom Bar 52
Adam Woo 379
Asa Cum 182
Charles Fle 66
Elizabeth Woo 379
Frederick Mul 395
Hance Bar 33
Henry Lin 119
Henry Woo 380
James Grn 257
James Mon 368
Jas. Way 371
Joel B. Bar 25
John Adr 9
John Log 181
John Mon 348
John Woo 379
John Wsh 311
Joseph Cas 44
Lydia Cum 182
Margaret Woo 377
Marton Bar 24
Mathew Bar 33
Merriday Wsh 311
Michael Woo 380
Nathan Mul 394
Pleasant Wsh 311
Richard Cam 32
Stephen Flo 100
Harper, cont.
Thomas Chr 74
Thomas Mon 368
Turner Mad 249
William Cal 14
William Fle 70
William Woo 379
Wm. Cas 37
Wm. Lew 103
Harpole, Jacob War 257
Harrald, Robert War 250
Harrard, James Fay 27
Harrell, Ann Nel 40
Isaac Nel 34
Isaac Nel 34
James Nel 40
Margery Nel 35
Harrid, Baily Pen 113
William Pen 110
Harril, Cado Chr 96
Harmon Chr 106
Harrilson, Eikle War 247
Heral War 266
Harriman, John mad 216
Harrington, Anthoney Mad 247
Drury Liv 154
John Liv 154
Joseph Lin 119
Merich War 278
Nathl. War 253
Nathl. War 253
Harriott, Ephraim Bou 88
John Bou 88
Harris, Abigal Mul 387
Agnes Mad 212
Ann Fra 136
Archibald Chr 58
Aron Nel 37
Arthur She 227
Benja. Bar 48
Benjamin Bar 46
Benjamin Knx 63
Benjamin Pul 153
Betsey Cas 43
Buckner Liv 155
Caleb Gal 185
Charles Cam 24
Charles Grn 264
Charles Hrd 299
Charles Wsh 304
Christopher Mad 248
Daniel Bou 88
Daniel Jes 45
Danl. Sco 183
David Hop 379
David Mad 216
David Woo 379
Edward, Junr Mas 306
Edward, Senr Mas 306
Electurous Mon 376
Elijah Clr 133
Elijah Sco 170
Elisha Wsh 305
Enoch War 247
Foster Mad 212
Francis Bar 19
Francis Bar 21
Francis Est 1
Frederick Mer 313
Geo Cam 25
George War 258
Gillum War 245
Gravis War 261
Henry, Jur Mad 214
Henry, Sen Mad 216
Higgason War 257

Name	County	Page
Harris, cont.		
Hosea	Sco	183
Isaac	Ohi	95
James	Cam	32
James	Gra	241
James	Jes	44
James	Liv	153
James	Mer	315
James	She	216
James	War	255
Jashua	She	238
Jeremiah	Gar	223
Jessee	Ohi	98
Jno.(Robt's son)	Mad	216
John	Bar	49
John	Clr	131
John	Cum	165
John	Flo	100
John	Fra	134
John	Gar	224
John	Knx	87
John	Liv	148
John	Mad	248
John(Jon'n's son)	Mad	250
John	She	204
John	She	223
John	She	224
John	She	234
John	Woo	398
Jonathan	Gra	241
Jonathan	Mad	250
Jonathan	She	229
Joseph	Cam	30
Joshua	Clr	132
Lewis	Jes	44
M. K. Jr	Nel	36
Macaijah	Nel	35
Mahu	Gra	242
Margaret	Mad	216
Melatto	Gar	220
Mordica	Fay	16
Moses	Adr	9
Nathan	Hrd	297
Nathanell	Bre	161
Nathaniel	Chr	53
Nathaniel	Jes	42
Nathaniel	Woo	379
P. James	Flo	100
Peggy	Bar	52
Phiby	Hnr	363
Randle	Hrs	308
Randolph	Fay	30
Richard	Mul	400
Richd.	Way	371
Richmond	Gar	222
Robert	Bar	41
Robert(W.head)	Mad	213
Robert	Mad	213
Robt. Junr	Log	177
Robt. Senr	Log	177
Rolen	Mul	392
Sarah	Mul	404
Sarah	Nel	37
Saml. Jr	Bou	69
Saml.	Hrd	290
Saml. Senr	Bou	68
Saml. P.	Mad	250
Samuel	Fay	55
Shearwood	Mad	249
Thomas	Knx	81
Thomas	Mad	248
Thompson	Mad	248
Thos.	Cam	28
Thos.	Hrs	321
Tira	Jef	9
Tyree	Gar	226
Walter	Nel	37

Name	County	Page
Harris, cont.		
Webber	Clr	132
West	Liv	148
William	Est	1
William	Jes	44
William	Mad	249
William	Mer	316
William	Mul	390
William	Mul	404
William	Sco	193
William	She	229
William B.	But	194
William C.	Log	188
William H.	Chr	87
William, Cpt.	Mad	248
Wm.	Cum	177
Wm.	Hrd	292
Wm.	Mon	365
Zachariah	Mul	404
Zakh.	Nel	33
Zepheniah	She	214
Harris E, William	Mad	212
Harrise, Joseph	Fle	64
Samuel	Fle	61
Harrison, Andw.	Clr	131
Binj.	Nel	40
Burr	Nel	37
Cuthbert	Wsh	310
Cuthburt	Bul	178
Daniel	Clr	132
David	Chr	90
Davis	Gal	185
Dominick	Mas	260
Edward P.	Fay	21
Elexonder	Fay	51
Ezekiel	She	229
Geo.	Bar	37
George	Bou	124
George	Grp	271
George	Mas	259
George	Nel	35
Greenberry	She	237
Grove	Nel	37
Henry	Woo	383
Hirem	Mon	375
Hirum	Clr	132
James	Bar	43
James	Cly	149
Jane	Fay	25
Jessee	Bar	49
John	Adr	9
John	Bou	124
John	Gar	225
John	Hnd	332
John	Knx	83
John	Liv	154
John	Mad	212
John	Ohi	103
John	She	220
John	She	225
Joseph	Fle	80
Joseph	Sco	192
Joshua	Cum	165
Joshua	She	228
Luke	Woo	383
Mary	Fay	21
Micajah	Mon	384
Michl.	Adr	9
Peyton	Cum	166
Richd.	Cam	28
Robert	Hrs	319
Robert	Mer	316
Robert C.	Fay	49
Ruben	She	225
Saml.	Cum	173
Samuel	Mas	257
Sarah	Mas	257

Name	County	Page
Harrison, cont.		
Susannah	Pen	115
Thomas	Fle	79
Fle 85		
Thomas	Wsh	310
Thomas E.	Fay	38
Thomas G.	Wsh	310
William	Fra	132
William	Gra	239
William	Log	182
William	Pen	115
William	She	234
Wm.	Adr	8
Wm.	Way	358
Zetheniah	Mul	392
Harriss, Alexr.	Grn	251
David	War	276
Elisha	Cly	150
George	Fay	16
Gilliam	War	245
James	Bul	179
James	Cly	152
John	Bul	179
John	War	245
Nancy	Fay	16
Nathaniel	Bul	179
Richd.	War	271
Simmian	Bul	179
William	Cly	150
Wm.	War	261
Harrissen, Fealding	Chr	97
Harrisson, Jessy	Chr	100
John	Chr	82
Josiah	Chr	103
Harrnin, Jackson	Fle	70
Harrod, Benja.	Hnr	361
Edward	Mad	214
James	Bou	124
John	Hnr	361
John	Sco	180
Samuel	She	217
Wm.	Bra	145
Harrow, James	Mon	359
Robert	Mon	361
Harrss, Jessee	Bul	179
John	Bul	179
Harry, Charles	Clr	132
Susanna	Mad	247
Harryman, Job	Jef	9
Harsha, James	Ohi	76
John	Ohi	82
Joseph	Ohi	81
William	Ohi	81
Harshfield, Henry	Bre	169
John	Bul	179
Harsin, Garrett	Grp	273
Hart, Aaron	Hrd	300
Anna	Hnd	331
Beasley	Pul	151
Benjn.	Mon	372
Charles	Mad	216
Charles	Mer	316
Charles	Mer	316
Charles	Way	371
Childers	Pul	151
David	Fle	81
Elenor	Fay	17
Elizabeth	Liv	150
Ezekiel	Jef	10
George	Log	163
Hardy	Cly	150
Henry	Bul	178
Henry	Log	163
Henry, Jr	Bul	178
Isiah	Hrd	300
Jack	Lin	119
James	Knx	82

Hart, cont.
John Bar 27
John Fay 22
John, Esqr Fle 79
John Hrd 304
John Hnd 331
John Knx 63
John Mad 212
John Mer 314
John Mon 373
Josiah Clr 131
Lucas Chr 73
Michael Fay 54
Moses Hrd 303
Nathaniel Mas 262
Nathaniel Woo 399
Nathaniel G.S. Fay 12
Richard Bul 178
Richard Hnd 346
Richard Mad 215
Richard Mon 382
Richrd. Fle 91
Robert Hop 374
Simian Jes 42
Solomon Hop 374
Susana Fay 16
Thomas Mad 250
Thos. Hrd 303
William Jef 26
Wm. Mon 373
Harte, John War 263
Harter, Conrod Fay 49
George Bou 91
Henry Bou 91
John Bou 91
Hartgrove, James Pul 152
John Pul 152
Hartley, Eliza Nic 53
George Fle 87
Hartman, Peter Mad 215
Hartmon, Abraham She 210
Jonathan She 240
Hartness, Robert Sco 178
Hartsack, Saml. Nic 53
Hartsock, Daniel Bra 147
Isaac Bra 148
James Bra 144
Harvard, Nathaniel Bre 160
Harvell, John Cas 44
Harvey, Charity Mas 256
Charles Bar 29
Cornelius Log 187
Danl. Adr 8
Eliza Bar 47
Isaac Adr 9
Jno. Bar 50
Jno. Hrd 296
Job Adr 8
Joel Chr 100
John Hop 374
John H. Hnd 338
Joseph Bar 30
Norris Mad 250
William Mad 250
William, Jur Mad 249
Willm. Lin 118
Harvie, John Boo 60
Wm. Boo 60
Harvy, John Chr 77
Harwood, Geo Cam 24
James Sco 182
Hase, Charles Pul 153
Isaac Pul 152
James Mer 316
Samuel Pul 153
William Pul 151
Hasel, Ignatiais Grn 262
Hasel, cont.
Jetson Grn 262
Haselwood, Joseph Cas 46
Randal Mad 249
Hash, Joseph Grn 250
Philip Grn 250
Thos. Grn 250
Hasher, John Grn 265
Hashfield, Martin Jef 10
Haskins, Aquila Wsh 309
Creed Adr 9
Jesse War 244
Joseph R. Wsh 307
Lucey Hnd 334
Hasleridge, Lucy Clr 132
Haslerigg, William Clr 132
Haslet, Samul Nic 52
Hasleton, James Chr 74
Haslett, William Fle 61
Wm. F. Fra 135
Haslin, George Lin 119
Joel Lin 119
Hass, John Fay 22
Hassel, Anthony Fay 38
Hasson, James Grp 278
Hastings, Abraham Cum 177
Danl. Cum 177
Henry Cum 177
Will She 225
Haston, Saml. Bar 27
Thomas She 238
Hastuter, Joseph Fay 16
Hastutler, Crist-ian She 216
Hasund, John Mer 314
Hasty, Archabald Pul 150
Robert Pul 150
Thomas Bou 124
Hatchell, Berriman Wsh 310
Parish War 265
Hatcher, Archibald Ohi 76
Edwards Grp 270
Henry Grn 255
John Flo 100
Samuel Mon 351
Samuel Mon 382
Uriah Chr 107
Hatchet, Tho. Gar 226
Hatfield, Benj. Bra 146
Edwd. Nel 39
Eli Way 354
Henry War 279
John Bul 178
John Hrd 300
John Mon 365
John War 266
John Way 351
Mansfield War 267
Martha Flo 99
Milley Way 362
Peter Bra 146
Peter Mon 355
Reubin Knx 67
Standly Knx 73
Thomas Bul 178
Whitely Nel 38
William Nel 33
Wm. War 267
Hathaway, Jonathan Mon 380
Phip Mon 382
Hathhorn, James Bar 26
Robert Bar 26
Robert Jef 30
Robert Jef 31
Wm. Jef 10
Hathman, Benjn. Mad 214
James Est 5
Hathman, cont.
Jonathan Mad 215
Joseph Mad 216
Thomas Jef 9
Hathorn, David Fay 40
Francis She 220
Hathr, Michl. Bar 21
Hathway, Danl. Cam 29
James Cam 29
Hatler, Philip Bar 29
Wm. Bar 29
Hattan, Adam Est 2
Wm. Est 2
Hatton, Ephram Mon 352
John Mon 352
Reuben Mad 213
Robert C. Fra 136
Thomas Fay 17
Thos. Fle 64
Hauck, John Cly 153
Haun, Anthony Mer 342
Tanner Fay 47
Hauners, Ichabod Gra 242
Hause, George Nel 34
Jacob But 194
John Jef 8
Leonard Bou 90
Peter Jef 8
Hauser, Nicholas Bar 49
Haut, Daniel Mul 405
John Mul 405
Hauts, Christopher Wsh 309
Thomas Wsh 343
Havelin, Benj. Nel 9
Haven, James Cal 18
Havens, Benja. Fle 64
Joel Fle 66
John Fle 67
Haverin, Robert Wsh 310
Havesin, James She 237
Haw, Edward Fay 16
James Pen 110
John Bar 31
John R. Bra 141
Rudeff Bar 30
Haward, Archebal She 239
Hawdeshal, Jacob Bar 31
Hawel, James Bar 54
William Hrs 324
Hawell, Merit Hrd 283
Hawes, Lambkin Bra 144
Hawey, Aaron Wsh 304
Hawk, Federick Grn 245
George Wsh 308
Michael Wsh 308
Nicholas Wsh 308
Hawkens, Saml. Nic 54
Hawkersmith, Henry Sco 174
Hawkins, Abner She 201
Abraham Mad 212
Abraham Mad 214
Abraham Mer 313
Andrew Mer 313
Anthony(freeman) Fay 16
Arculous Fra 131
B. John Gar 223
Benjamin Cal 20
Benjamin Chr 54
Benjamin Jes 41
Charles (free man of colour) Jes 43
Claburn She 226
David Hrd 294
David, Senr Hrd 295
Eleazer Hnr 353
Elijah Jef 11
Elijah Mad 213

Hawkins, cont.	
Elisha, Jr	Fra 131
Elisha, Senr	Fra 131
Francis	Mer 313
George	Jes 44
George	She 223
Giles	Jes 44
Gregory	Mon 359
Harmon	Cal 20
Henry	Jef 9
Henry	Mon 360
Henry S.	Pen 113
Isaac	Mon 381
Isam	Bar 37
James	Mon 356
James	Mon 381
James	Woo 389
James	Wsh 309
Jameson	Boo 59
Jane	Chr 101
Jehue	Bar 35
Jehue D.	Bar 35
Jesse	Jes 44
Jno.	Hrd 287
Jno.	Hrd 295
John	Bar 35
John	Boo 60
John	Est 2
John	Fay 56
John	Hnr 355
John	Jes 41
John	Jes 43
John	Mad 212
John	Mer 313
John	Mad 214
John	Mon 359
John	Pen 109
John	Sco 187
John	Sco 190
Jos.	Boo 60
Jos.	Hrd 295
Joseph	Fay 17
Joseph	Pen 108
Lewis	Bra 143
Lucy	Log 161
Martin	Sco 191
Mary	Mon 381
Matthew	Cum 175
Moses	Hnr 359
Moses	Jes 43
Moses	Woo 395
Nathan	Chr 69
Nathan	Mer 313
Nicholas	Mad 250
Philip	Mad 247
Philip	Sco 169
Reuben	Fra 131
Richard	Jes 41
Thomas	Jes 44
Thomas	Mon 365
Thomas	Pen 112
Thomas L.	Fra 133
Thos.	Nic 52
Thos. W.	Sco 191
Warner	Fay 16
Weedin	Gar 226
William	Chr 85
William	Fra 131
William	Woo 392
Willis	Woo 395
Willm.	Sco 173
Wm.	Mon 360
Wm.	Mon 381
Wm. Junr	Fra 131
Wm. Senr	Fra 131
Zadock	Pen 111
Hawks, George	Grn 256

Hawks, cont.	
Lewis	Jes 43
Matnew	Grn 256
William	Grn 256
Wm.	Grn 261
Hawley, Absolam	Nel 33
Haws, Alexander	Mas 258
Azareel	Flo 100
Isaac	Jef 30
John	Flo 100
James	Sco 171
John	Ohi 71
John	She 208
Robert	Flo 100
Saml.	Flo 99
Samuel	Flo 99
Samuel	Ohi 71
Thomas	Gal 184
Hawthhorn, Joseph	Hnd 348
Robert	Hnd 339
Hay, Adam	Hnd 334
Adrain	Rck 159
Daniel	But 194
Jams	Est 9
John	But 194
John	Fay 22
John	War 243
Kinnard	Lin 119
Michael	Hnd 334
Peter	Log 181
Robert	Wsh 313
Volentine	Hnd 344
Walter	Nel 35
William	But 1[illegible]
William	War [illegible]
William	Wsh 31[illegible]
Haycock, Daniel	Fra 13[illegible]
Haycraft, Jas.	Hrd 295
Joshua	Gra 243
Saml.	Hrd 304
Hayden, Belemus	Bou 89
Benjn.	Bou 90
Charles	Wsh 311
Elisha	Log 161
Elisha	Log 168
Enoch	Bou 90
George	Bre 158
James	Wsh 311
John	Mad 216
Lot	Bou 90
Saml.	Log 168
Samuel	Mad 211
Samuel	Mon 347
Thos.	Bou 92
Wm.	Gal 185
Haydon, Barnabus	Fle 72
Bazil	Wsh 311
Ben	Hnr 367
Ben	Hnr 367
Edward	Bul 178
Elizabeth	Wsh 305
Ezekiel	Jes 43
Francis S.	Fra 136
George	Wsh 305
Henly	Bou 89
Henry	Wsh 307
James	Fra 133
James	Hnr 359B
James J.	Jes 43
Jeremiah	Clr 132
John	Hrs 307
John	Way 357
John	Wsh 313
Joseph	Wsh 306
Lewis	Wsh 305
Samuel	Clr 133
Samuel	Wsh 311

Haydon, cont.	
Thomas	Jes 45
Webb	Fra 134
Wilfred	Wsh 311
William	Jes 43
William	Wsh 306
Wm.	Clr 131
Hayes, Andw.	Adr 9
Charles	Gar 222
Charles, Jnr	Gar 222
Gabriel	Adr 8
George	Mon 348
Isaac	Adr 9
James	War 252
Joseph	Chr 64
Josiph	Chr 78
Nina	Gar 222
Samuel	Jes 42
Thomas	Chr 54
Walter	Bou 91
Hayly, Benjn.	Lin 119
Haymaker, Eliza	Jef 30
Hayman, Philip	Mon 360
Haynes, Abm.	Gal 185
Charles	Ohi 89
Christopher	Liv 147
John	But 194
John, Junr	Ohi 90
Levy	Lew 95
William	Ohi 89
Hayns, John	Ohi 89
Havron, John	Mon 377
[illegible] Adam	Fay 43
[illegible]	Cum 185
[illegible]	Bar 43
[illegible]	Bar 48
[illegible]	Mad 215
[illegible]	Nel 40
Charls.	Cal 11
Charrity	Clr 131
Elias	Mad 248
Elijah	Hnd 335
Ezekiel	Bre 160
George	Jef 9
George	Mul 392
Henry	Bar 55
Hercules	Hrd 303
Hugh	Lin 121
Isaac	Wsh 306
James	Fle 88
James	Gra 237
James	Wsh 310
Jane	Knx 89
Jeramiah	War 252
Jeremiah	Mon 367
John	Clr 131
John	Flo 99
John	Gra 237
John	Jef 9
John	War 256
John	Way 371
John	Wsh 311
Jonathan	Knx 73
Joseph	Bar 47
Joshua	Knx 68
Joshua	Knx 68
Justin	Wsh 311
Peter	Jef 9
Peter	Mad 212
Peter	She 218
Polly	Bar 43
Richard	Cal 11
Richd.	Bar 48
Robt.	Grn 245
Saml.	War 255
Samuel	Mad 213
Starky	Wsh 307

Hays, Thomas Nel 40
Thos. Fle 88
William Fay 36
William Hrd 303
William Lin 121
William Wsh 306
William Wsh 310
William Wsh 311
William H. Wsh 343
Willis Knx 85
Wm. Bar 43
Haythorn, James Bou 90
Haywood, Barbary Mad 212
George Jef 11
Jno. Hrd 291
Wm. Jef 10
Hazard, Henry H. Woo 384
John Woo 392
Martin Grn 256
Hazel, Caleb Hrd 292
Hazle, Aaron Lew 104
Abraham Lew 101
Daniel Gra 241
Peter Hrd 292
Hazlerig, Graham She 200
William Bou 88
Hazlerigg, Ely Mon 357
John Bou 123
Joshua Mon 357
Hazelton, Nathan Wsh 309
Hazlewood, Benjn. Lin 118
Cliff Liv 157
John Pen 107
Hazlip, Robt. Hrd 283
Hazlo, Richd. Grn 254
Head, Alexr.Spence Jef 10
Anthony Jef 30
Benja. Jef 31
Benjn. Sco 174
Bigger Ohi 92
Bigger Wsh 307
Bigger I. Wsh 304
Cecilus Ohi 93
Cutht. Nel 39
Edwards Liv 160
Francis Nel 36
Hadly Hnr 359B
Henry Bul 178
Henry Pul 150
Henry Wsh 305
James Hnr 359A
James Wsh 304
Jesse Wsh 343
John Nel 37
John Sco 174
John Wsh 309
Milly Fra 134
Richard Nel 9
Tras. Nel 39
William Fra 134
William Ohi 93
William Wsh 343
Zachuah Hnr 359A
Headdy, Thos. Nel 42
Headen, Oliver Fra 133
Headley, James Fay 21
Headrick, Walter Hrd 289
Heads, Mary But 194
Heady, Elijah Nel 39
Gilbert She 229
Jacob She 234
James Nel 37
Stillwll. Nel 35
Thos. Nel 37
Thos. Nel 39
Heap, William She 237
Heard, Raphael Wsh 305
Hearn, Andrew Fra 135
Isaac Fra 133
Hearndon, George Log 162
Hearne, Clemont Bou 91
Heart, Israel Pul 151
John Pen 117
Nicholis Pen 116
Heartlow, Abraham She 202
Heater, John Lov 160
Heath, George Wsh 309
John Lew 100
William Fay 51
William Fra 136
Heather, William Mer 313
Heatherley, John Knx 73
Heatherly, Leonard Mad 249
Nathan Mad 212
Heathhorn, Thomas Mer 342
Heathorn, Andrew Cal 19
Heaton, Cally Lin 118
John Knx 76
John Lin 119
Heavenhill, Geo.Jr Nel 34
Wm. Nel 34
Heavens, John Jes 43
Heaveron, James Bra 147
Thos. Bra 143
Heavin, Jas. Way 354
Heck, Daniel Bra 150
George Bra 143
Godlove Bra 152
Henry Mul 393
Henry Mul 394
Jacob Bra 142
John Bra 142
Heckersmith, Coon-rod Log 173
Hecklin,Rebecca Fra 135
Hedden, Daniel She 208
Elisha She 208
Heddington, Abel Fay 16
Heddleston, David Bou 90
David Jr Bou 90
Hance Bou 90
James Bou 90
Jane Bou 90
Wm. Bou 90
Heddy, Abraham She 219
David Cum 177
Elias She 208
Isaac She 236
John She 214
Samuel She 208
Samuel She 214
Simon She 217
Hedge, Charles Bou 88
James Bou 89
Jonas Mon 376
Hedger, Johnathan Hrs 316
Joseph Cum 172
Joseph Mer 316
Rheubin Hrs 320
Stephen Clr 132
Thomas Mer 316
William Woo 400
Wm. Cum 172
Hedges, Enock Bou 88
Jackson Hrd 281
James Ohi 86
James Ohi 97
Jno. Nel 41
John Bou 124
John Bra 142
Jonathan Sco 175
Joseph Bou 124
Joseph Bul 179
Josiah, Junr Ohi 97
Hedges, cont.
Josiah, Senr Ohi 97
Peter Ohi 84
Saml. Boo 60
Samuel Mer 315
Sarah Bou 124
Solomon Grp 271
William Ohi 97
Hedgess, Benjamin Hrs 314
Hedington, Labin Bou 92
Saml. Bou 89
Zebulon Hrs 315
Hedlston, Alexr. Nic 53
Hedrake, Rachel Clr 132
Hedrick, Abaham Fle 76
George Lin 121
Jacob Fle 72
Jacob, Senr Fle 89
John Fle 74
Jos. Gar 224
Joseph Fle 79
Michael Fle 63
Michael Pul 150
Nicholas Fle 72
Nicholas Fle 89
Peter Gar 224
Phillip Fle 79
Hedruk, Jacob Fle 84
Hedspeth, Joel Log 163
Lemuel Hrd 286
William Log 163
Heely, Michael Mul 399
Heete, Elisha A. Way 374
Heeth, Phillip Pul 153
William Pul 153
Heffington,Stephen Log 188
Hefiller, Philip Mul 389
Hefington, David War 276
Stephen Log 163
Thomas Log 163
Thomas, Jr Log 163
Thos. War 276
Heflin, Elija Fle 63
Reubin Mas 258
William Bou 91
Heflon, Daniel Log 194
Hegdon, Erasmus Bul 179
Heidleson, William Mas 305
Heiftin, William Nel 40
Heighten, Josiah Mon 384
Heines, Jno. Lew 104
Heizer, Nathan Grn 259
Helderbrand, Jno. Lew 103
Hellard, John Mad 212
Helleny, Benj. Way 358
Helm, Benjamin Fay 16
Benjamin Hrd 281
Chas. Hrd 295
Geo. Cum 172
Geo. Hrd 303
H. Samuel Mas 262
Henry Cum 172
John Bre 168 Bre 168
Meridith Mas 257
Meridith, Senr Mas 262
Tho. Hop 377
Thomas Woo 400
Thos. Hrd 303
Helmes, James Knx 65
John Pul 153
Helms, Charles Grn 260
George, Jr Lin 119
George, Snr Lin 119
John Knx 81
Jonathan Knx 83
Joseph Lin 118
Marcus, Lin 119

Helms, cont.
Marius Lin 118
Moses But 194
Peater Mon 364
William Grn 260
William Mas 261
Wm. Jef 10
Helphinistine, Phil-
lip Fle 89
John P. Fle 83
Helpman, John Nic 53
Helsley, Jacob Mul 397
John Mul 389
Helt, Nicholas Ohi 102
Helton, Andw. Bar 32
James Knx 84
John Knx 84
John Wsh 309
Shadrick Knx 84
Thos. Nel 38
William Nel 33
Helvy, Charles Mas 262
Hemingwaye, Samuel She 201
Hemphill, James Jes 45
Hence, John Chr 56
Henceley, Benjman She 232
William Fra 131
Hench, John Chr 111
Hencock, Benjamin Bou 124
Thomas Knx 71
Henden, Taylor Sco 173
Henderson, Abraham Mad 248
Alexr. Bou 88
Alexr. Fle 69
Alexr. Gar 222
Alexr. Rck 159
Alexr. Sco 186
Bennett War 276
Charles Ohi 68
Chas. Bou 91
Cornelius Lew 101
Daniel Mad 216
Danl. Est 2
Danl. War 270
David Fle 76
DAvid Mad 247
Edward Jes 44
Edward Knx 77
Elender Fay 59
Elizabeth Fay 59
Hugh Log 196
Isaac Chr 65
J. Hnr 368
James Chr 106
James Fay 39
James Grp 276
James Hnr 361
James Liv 149
James Mas 259
James Sco 167
Jas. Gar 223
Jas. Jnr Gar 222
Jeremiah Mad 248
Jessee Bou 90
Jessee Bou 91
Joel Chr 70
John Bou 91
John Cal 7
John Clr 132
John Fay 49
John Gar 225
John Mad 249
John Mer 314
John Mer 315
John Mon 370
John Rck 162
John War 270

Henderson, cont.
Jones Sco 185
Joseh Boo 59
Joseph Bar 30
Joseph Hop 371
Joseph Mad 212
Joseph Mad 248
Joseph Rck 163
Martha War 277
Michael Log 196
Nat. Cal 19
Nathan Mas 257
Peter Bar 27
Richard Hrs 313
Robert Grp 276
Robt. Est 2
Robt. Gar 223
Saml. Bou 88
Thomas Lew 100
Thomas Sco 190
Thomas War 270
Thos. Boo 60
Thos. Bou 124
William Hnr 366
William Mad 248
William Mer 313
William Woo 395
Willm. T. War 276
Willson Mul 396
Wm. Bou 88
Wm. Rck 159
Hendley, John Fay 35
John Fay 38
Phantley Mul 400
Hendmon, [illegible]shel Ohi 71
Hendon, E[illegible]r Hnr 363
Hendraks, Andrew Mad 211
Isaac Mad 216
James Mad 214
John Mad 214
Hendrek, Obidiah Bar 31
Hendren, Elijah Gar 221
Taylor Sco 184
Hendrick, Abraham War 282
Benjn. War 260
Bird War 259
Danl. Bar 42
Harrison Ohi 73
James Mer 313
Jo W. Bar 29
John War 244
Jon. War 261
Robert Bre 162
Robert K. Fay 21
Scpt. Nel 38
Thomas War 244
Rhos. War 268
William Mer 313
Hendricks, Abraham Fay 51
Abraham War 276
Daniel Pen 106
Edwd. Sco 167
Enock Fle 73
Fredk. Bou 91
George Pen 105
Henry Sco 171
Henry War 276
Henry War 276
Jacob War 277
James War 277
Jno. Hrd 294
John War 273
John War 277
Jos. War 260
Margaret Knx 88
Michael Pen 111
Phillip Pen 107

Hendricks, cont.
Rachel War 272
Samuel Pul 149
Samuel Pul 152
Tobiah Hrd 297
Wm. Hrd 294
Hendrickson, Isaac Adr 8
James Adr 8
John Adr 8
Joshua Knx 84
Leonard Wsh 309
Simeon Wsh 304
Simeon Wsh 309
Hendrie, Moses Log 165
Hendrikson, John Knx 75
Nicholas Fle 88
Hendrix, Abraham Mon 375
Abraham Mon 380
Catharine Woo 384
Coonrod Woo 381
Elijah Gra 242
George Hrs 320
George Mon 380
Jacob Mon 368
Jacob Mon 378
Jacob Woo 388
John Log 163
Joseph Hrs 317
Moses Mon 379
Noah Mon 378
Peater Mon 356
Philip Mon 356
Rhudy Hnr 359A
Hendrixson, Danl. Lew 97
Oke Lew 99
Hendron, Doven Mad 216
Enus Mad 215
John Mad 215
Nimrod Mad 215
Hends, John Lew 98
Henecock, John Bou 124
Hening, James But 194
Michael But 194
Henley, Osburn Mon 384
Henline, George Mad 213
John Mad 213
Henly, Thomas Hnd 334
Hen[illegible]an, Samuel Ohi 80
He[illegible]n, William Fra 131
Henning, Ezekl. Nel 40
Saml. Jef 11
Henny, James Bou 88
Henrey, John Chr 81
Henrickson, John Cum 179
Henry (freeman of
colour) Clr 133
Henry, Alexr. Hop 375
Belfield Grn 255
Benjamin Hrs 311
Benjamin She 206
Daniel Grn 246
David Bou 90
David Wsh 310
Evan Clr 132
George Bou 89
Hugh Bou 89
Jacob Sco 180
James Liv 160
James Pen 108
Jesse She 197
Joel Woo 399
John Clr 132
John Fay 23
John Fay 38
John Hrs 322
John Lin 121
John Mas 256

Henry, cont.
John Nic 52
John She 199
John T. Sco 167
Joseph Hnr 365
Joseph Hop 374
Joseph Way 364
Mary Fay 23
Mathiah Way 364
Moses Est 1
Noah Mon 350
Robt. Gar 223
Robt. Grn 262
Samuel Fle 84
Samuel Mer 314
Samuel She 202
Samuel, Junr Liv 159
Samuel, Senr Liv 159
Thomas Fle 78
Thomas Hrs 322
Will. Gar 220
William Bou 90
William Fle 89
William Fay 17
William Hop 375
William Liv 158
William Log 176
Wm. Hrs 322
Wm. Sco 173
Zachariah Woo 387
Henrylider, Frederick Jef 10
Michael Jef 10
Michael, Sr Jef 10
Henseley, Clifton Sco 186
Hensley, Ann Jes 44
Benjn. Mon 356
Daniel Flo 100
Elijah Mon 369
Foster Hnr 355
James Flo 100
James She 217
John Hnd 334
Joseph Mon 362
Nicholas Woo 385
Thomas Hnr 356
William Flo 100
Wm. Mon 365
Hensly, John Lin 118
Henson, Benjamin Bul 178
Gilie War 268
James Cly 155
Jno. Mad 247
John Bra 152
John Cly 151
John War 278
John War 278
Joseph Cas 43
Luke Bou 91
Mary War 274
Paul Cly 150
Paul Cly 154
Richd. Cly 150
William Mad 247
Henthorn, Adam Boo 60
Henton, Benja. Fle 82
Giles Hnr 360
Sam. Fle 76
Vachel Fle 79
Zeckia Fle 85
Heny, Wm. Gal 185
Herald, Ferney Adr 9
James Hnr 361
Herberison, David She 223
Herbert, Jas. Lew 99
Jeremiah Wsh 310
Herbinson, David She 224
Hercules, John Hop 377
Herd, Elisha Hrs 322
John Cal 18
John, Jnr Gar 226
John, Snr Gar 226
Willis Jef 9
Willis Jef 30
Herdiman, George War 246
Here, Elisha Hrs 317
Herendon, Thomas Woo 387
William Woo 380
Herghus, William Nel 36
Herin, Isaac Cal 19
Herinder, Travis Fle 89
Herington, Saml. Bou 124
Herkins, James Chr 80
Herley, Isaac She 206
Herman, George Ohi 101
Jacob Gar 226
Samuel Ohi 86
Hermond, John Log 165
Hern, Clayton Mad 215
Jacob Gal 185
John Mad 212
Mary She 223
Waller Mad 212
William Mad 216
Herndon, Benjn. Cam 30
David Sco 186
Elisha Fra 131
Elisha Log 179
Henry Sco 192
James Log 168
James Sco 186
James She 224
Jermiah She 221
John Cal 14
John She 224
John Knx 75
John Log 168
John Sco 177
John Sco 178
Joseph Sco 187
Richardson Knx 84
Susannah Fay 44
Thomas Sco 186
Thos. Hnr 351
Wm. Clr 132
Herod, James Hnd 340
John Hnd 331
Herold, Wm. Cal 11
Heronimus, Frances Clr 133
Henry Clr 133
Herral, Noah Gra 240
Herrald, James She 238
Herrand, Ann Mer 315
Herrel, James Gra 237
Richard Bre 159
Herrell, Enock Flo 100
William Flo 100
Herren, Daniel She 225
Denness Cas 41
Isaac Pul 153
Isaac She 240
John She 218
Herrenden, John Clr 132
Herrenton, Jabes Jef 10
Herril, Jacob Cal 16
Herrin, Alexander Chr 82
Ephram Chr 70
Joseph Chr 73
Levey Cas 42
Nathan Chr 73
Reuben Hop 373
Saml. Nel 36
Shadrick Pul 149
Thomas Gar 226
Herrin, cont.
Thomas Pul 149
William Chr 73
William Nel 36
William Pul 149
William Pul 153
Wm. Hop 373
Herring, Agnes Nel 41
Edmd. Sco 174
Herrison, Peter Cum 165
Herrold, John But 194
John She 238
Herrom, Saml. Hop 372
Herronimus, Benja. Clr 132
Hervey, Robt. Adr 8
Hes, Saml. Bra 151
Hesen, John Cam 28
Hesler, Jacob She 238
John Mas 261
John H. Fle 66
Michael Hnr 356
William Mas 258
Hess, Apollis She 217
Henry Fay 30
John War 257
Hessin, William Lin 118
Hester, Frances Bar 31
James Hop 375
John Fle 84
Robert But 194
Wm. Hop 372
Hetford, Josiah Cal 16
Heth, David Mas 261
Hether, Thomas Wsh 303
Hetherington, James Liv 149
Heton, John Fle 78
Hevren, James She 235
Hewett, Wm. Sco 190
Hewil, Elizabeth Chr 103
Hewit, William Cal 6
Hewlett, Martin Hop 381
Hewlitt, Jas. War 261
Hews, Peter Fay 54
Heydon, Stanls. Nel 40
Hiatt, Benjamin Mas 262
Elisha Mas 260
Ezebell Rck 164
John Gar 224
John Mas 258
Jonathan Jes 43
Jonathan Mas 301
Polly Gar 221
Reuben Gar 226
Stephen Mas 262
Thomas Mas 259
Wm. Gar 221
Hibbard, Jediah Cly 154
John Cly 160
Hibberd, Lemuel Knx 77
Samuel Knx 80
Hibbs, Christiana Hrd 295
Isaac Hop 371
Isaac Joshua Nel 38
John Nel 35
John Nel 37
Jonah Liv 160
Jonathan Nel 38
Jos. Hrd 295
Joseph Bre 160
Joseph Nel 38
Mathew Hop 376
William Nel 38
Hibler, Daniel Bou 88
Joseph Bou 88
William Bou 88
William Bou 88
Hickason, Thos. Grn 260

Name	County	Page
Hickele, Robert	Fle	64
Hickenbotom, Andrew	Way	373
Hickerson, Hezekiah	Log	168
John	Log	174
Joseph	Wsh	304
Peter	Log	172
Samuel	Mad	247
William	Wsh	304
William	Wsh	304
Hickeson, Ezekiel	Cum	174
Hickey, Thomas	Nel	9
William	Fay	57
Hickland, Hugh	Cum	178
Hicklin, Hugh	Mon	370
Jonathan	Woo	379
Polly	Bou	88
Thomas	Woo	379
Wm.	Bar	25
Hickling, Charles	Mon	369
Hickman, Benj.	Fra	135
Benjamon	Hrs	318
Danl.	Gal	185
Davd.	Bou	124
Elizebeth	Mas	259
Jacob	Lin	119
Jessee	Bar	37
Jessee	War	269
Joel	Clr	133
John	Lin	119
John	Mas	260
John L.	Bou	90
Lewis	Fay	38
Paschal	Fra	136
Pheby	Fay	38
Reuben	Cas	42
Richd.	Clr	133
Saml.	Cum	170
Sarah	Mas	258
Thomas	Bou	91
Thomas	Fra	136
William	Fra	130
Willm.	Bou	88
Wm. Senr	Fra	134
Hicks, Absolum	Chr	85
Daniel	Clr	131
Demsey	Pul	152
Francis	Clr	131
Henry	Cly	154
Isaac	Cal	15
Jacob	Way	351
James	Chr	108
James	Hnd	336
James	Mer	315
Jas.	Way	351
John	Gar	225
John	Jes	46
John	Mad	214
John	Sco	171
Jos.	Jar	220
Joseph	Mer	342
Lucy	Pul	151
Michael	Log	181
Moses	Fay	30
Richard	Chr	84
Richd.	Cum	180
Robt.	Cly	153
Saml.	Log	180
Samuel	Jes	42
Sarah	Gar	225
Sherwood	Hnd	347
Tabitha	Pul	151
Thomas	Grn	253
Thomas	Jes	43
Thomas	Jes	45
Thomas	Jes	55
William	Hrd	304
Hicks, cont.		
William	Woo	379
Willis	Chr	62
Wm.	Cal	15
Wm.	Gal	185
Wm.	Gar	224
Hickson, Berjaman	Fle	89
Mary	Pul	150
Hicky, Daniel	Fay	57
Simon	Fay	17
Hide, Ezechal	Chr	86
Jessee	Cly	150
Hieatt, Lewis	Woo	398
Hiet, James	Mad	247
John	Mad	247
Joseph	Mad	216
Hiflins, Gustavous	Mon	371
Hifner, Conrod	Jes	44
Peter	Jes	44
Higbee, John	Fay	21
Joseph	Jes	41
Obediah	Fay	30
Peter	Jes	41
Vincent	Jes	41
Higdon, Francis	Gra	241
Ignatius	Wsh	305
James	Gra	238
John	Nel	40
Joseph	Bar	31
Peter	Wsh	305
Leonard	Nel	34
Thos.	Nel	34
Thos.	Nel	39
Higganbotham, Emanuel	Gar	223
Higgans, Rachel	Way	374
Higgens, John	Chr	72
Higginbotham, James	Jes	42
Higginbottom, Og.	Cum	170
Higginbottum, Ralph	Fay	16
Higgins, A...	Mer	313
Aaron	Hnd	335
Azeriah	Fay	60
G....	Mer	313
Isaac	Hnd	342
James	Mon	371
Jessa	Mon	371
Jessy	Chr	72
Jeter	Mon	371
John	Clr	132
John	Grp	269
John	Mer	341
Jomima	Chr	74
Levi	Fle	74
Mosis	Chr	73
Peter	Pul	149
Richard	Fay	17
Samuel	Mas	256
Thomas	Mon	371
William	Chr	73
William	Fay	31
William	Flo	100
William	Mas	306
William	Mer	341
Wm.	Bar	34
Wm.	Cum	170
Wm.	Mon	363
Wm.	War	246
Higginson, George	Hnd	331
Higgs, Rodam	Hnr	367
High, Mark	Bar	48
Micheal	Fle	70
Highbaugh, Geo.	Hrd	284
Highfiell, Jeremiah	Pen	110
Highland, Deninan	Bou	89
Highlander, George	Jes	44
Highshoe, Wm.	Hnr	363
Highsmith, James	Log	163
Highton, Rebeka	Bou	89
Hightower, Geo.	Cam	27
Goerge	Jes	42
Jane	War	252
John	War	253
Leroy	Est	4
Nancy	Mad	214
Richard	Jes	43
Stith	Mad	213
Higins, John	Mon	381
John, Senr	Mon	381
Moses	Mon	372
William	Fay	47
Higton, Peter	Nel	39
Hikes, George	Jef	10
Jacob	Jef	11
Hilborn, William	Grn	253
Hildred, Peter, Jr	Cal	7
Hildreth, James	Bou	123
John	Bou	92
Joseph	Bou	124
Hildrith, Willm.	Bou	88
Hildritt, Squire	Nic	54
Hile, Christopher	Sco	184
John	Sco	182
Palser	Sco	183
Hileleets, Jane	Bar	45
Hiler, James	Jes	41
Hiles, John	Sco	170
Hiley, Matthey	Fay	15
Hill, Abner	Mad	214
Abraham	Bou	91
Andrew	Liv	157
Atkison	Nel	37
Charles	But	184
Charles	Gar	221
Charles	Nel	34
Clement	Bar	50
Clement	Wsh	306
David	Liv	157
David	Mad	249
David	Way	355
Dempsey	Log	192
Edwd. Junr	Cum	166
Efram, Junr	Liv	157
Elijah	War	280
Elizabeth	Clr	131
Ephrim, Senr	Liv	157
Ezekiel	Bou	89
Ezekiel	Pen	107
Fergus	She	240
Francis	Cum	178
Frederick	Wsh	309
Gabrl.	Adr	9
Garland	Clr	132
George	Mul	399
Halcut	War	272
Henry	Hrd	291
Henry R.	Mad	214
Herman	Mas	261
Humphry	Est	4
Humphry	Est	4
Isaac	She	203
James	But	194
James	Chr	75
James	Fay	20
James	Grn	258
James	Nic	52
James	Sco	171
James	Sco	177
James	She	216
Jesse	Gar	220
Jno.	Hrd	300
Joel	Mad	214
Joel, Jr	Mad	214

Hill, cont.
John Bra 147
John Chr 57
John Clr 132
John Hrs 317
John Knx 81
John Lin 121
John Mul 387
John Nel 37
John Nic 52
John Pul 151
John Pul 152
John War 274
John Wsh 309
John, Jnr Gar 221
John, Snr Gar 221
John B. Nel 39
Joseph Fay 20
Joseph Fle 83
Joshua Mon 374
Josiah Liv 153
Leonard Clr 133
Margret She 203
Moncreffe Bou 88
Moses Hrd 291
Nancy Gar 220
Nathan Mas 261
Olive Cum 165
Pricilla War 263
Reason Mad 215
Reuben Cum 172
Richard Hrs 317
Robert Bou 90
Robert Fay 52
Robert Hnr 352
Robert Liv 158
Robert Mas 259
Rosel Gar 222
Ruebin Way 359
Russle Hrs 319
Saml. Cal 11
Solom. Fle 64
Susanah Fle 62
Thomas Fay 16
Thomas Fay 53
Thomas Log 162
Thomas Log 165
Thomas Mad 250
Thomas Mon 353
Thomas Mon 353
Thomas Pul 152
Thomas Pul 152
Thomas War 244
Travis Hop 378
Warren Bou 89
Westel War 244
Wiley Mul 401
William Bre 159
William But 194
William Mad 249
William Pul 152
William She 207
William, Jr Log 175
Willm. Lin 118
Willm. War 245
Wm. Hrs 319
Wm. Hrs 320
Wm. Way 355
Wm. C. Mon 359
Zacariah Lin 118
Zadock Hrd 297
Hillacos, Coonrod Fle 90
Jacob Fle 69
John Fle 81
Hiller, Samuel Lew 101
Hillhouse, David Liv 159
James Liv 159
Hillhouse, cont.
Robert D. Liv 159
Hilliard, Bartlet Grn 255
Hillick, Alexr. Nic 53
Hillingsworth, John Log 175
Hillion, Alexr. Cal 14
Hillis, Aba. Fle 91
Abraham Fle 80
James Bou 124
James Fle 80
John Cum 168
William Fle 79
Hillman, Benjamin Ohi 72
Danl. Mas 259
Henry Mas 259
John War 270
Hilmon, Benjamin Hnr 360
Hills, James Sco 173
Hilor, Cornelius Pen 114
Hilour, James Log 194
Hilton, Alexander Bul 178
Arthur Knx 80
B. Rhodrick Flo 100
Benja. Flo 100
Daniel Wsh 310
Jesse Flo 100
Joseph Nel 39
Luke Woo 388
Nathl. Bar 52
Peter Knx 80
William F. Bul 178
Hinch, Joseph Cal 8
Saml. Jef 9
William Bul 178
Hinckle, Nathan Cum 170
Hincle, Jane Bou 89
Hind, Elisha Fle 62
John Knx 68
Hindes, Samuel Fay 22
Hindman, Robert Fle 87
Robt. Adr 8
Robt. Bar 29
Susan Bou 90
Wm. Bar 29
Hinds, Alexander Jes 43
Hannah Way 369
James Bar 34
James Mon 363
Joseph Way 369
Joseph Way 370
Levy Way 354
Saml. Bar 34
Samuel Way 366
Hine, Thomas Clr 131
Hardy Mul 395
Hines, Henry War 250
Isarel Jes 46
James Pul 149
John Pul 149
John War 251
Joseph Chr 63
Joseph Knx 76
Thomas Clr 132
Thomas Pul 149
William Jes 46
Wilm. War 250
Hinkle, Charles She 214
Jacob Jef 25
John Jef 26
Michael Pul 149
Nelley She 227
Windle Jef 30
Hinkson, John Hrs 312
Samuel Hrs 312
Hinman, Jeramiah Hrs 321
Wm. Hrs 321
Hinnis, Henry Bou 123
Hinsely, Francis Gar 222
Hinsley, Robt. Hop 375
Hinson, Robert Fay 34
Robert Fay 50
Hinston, Henry Cum 182
Hinter, Mesheck Wsh 304
Hinton, Asher Sco 184
Ezekiel Nic 52
Hardy War 273
James Sco 167
Jeramiah War 265
Jesse War 276
John Hrd 304
Solomon Sco 183
Thomas Pul 153
Thomas She 235
Thomas Woo 393
Vachel Bre 163
Will She 229
Wm. Sco 184
Hiott, Gideon Hnr 361
Meshack Hnr 261
Shed Hnr 361
Hippard, Wm. Gar 225
Hipsley, Amos Ohi 72
Hirely, John Mer 135
Hirendon, Wm. Grn 252
Hirn, Edward Gal 184
Hirons, Samuel Hrs 323
Hirts, Richd. Fle 67
Hise, George Mer 315
Nancy Log 183
Hisel, Benjamin Mad 248
Thomas Mad 249
William Mad 248
Hiser, Philip Bou 70
Hisle, Samuel Clr 132
Histerly, John War 268
Hitch, John Mer 313
Joseph Pen 116
Saml. Bar 51
Thomas Pen 105
Wiseman Nic 53
Hitchcock, Asel Bou 90
Isaac Cly 152
John Cly 153
Hitchcraft, Thos. Bou 123
Hite, Abraham Jef 8
Andrew Jef 9
George Fle 84
Henry Clr 131
Joseph Jef 8
Thomas Mer 314
William Mer 314
Wm. Jef 10
Hiter, Charles Woo 388
richdy. Log 183
Hites, Peter Adr 9
Hitford, John Cal 3
Hitoure, Austin Cal 5
Hitt, Aaron Mas 261
Charles Fle 90
Elias Jes 43
Eliza Hnr 355
Jackey S. Bou 89
Martin Bou 90
Nathan Woo 400
William Fle 92
Hix, Greenberry Bar 49
John Est 9
Hixon, Nathaniel Mas 260
Thomas Mas 262
Hizer, Caleb Mas 261
Jacob Mas 260
Hoagland, Mary Gal 186
Hoahe, Cornelias Hnr 351
Hoback, Peter Bar 37

Hobb, Wm. War 261
Hobbs, Bazil Jef 11
Eli Nel 36
Ezekiel Bul 178
Hinson She 200
James Hnr 369
James She 200
Jesse Wsh 304
Job Ohi 100
John Nel 33
Joseph Fra 133
Joshua Nel 36
Joshua Nel 37
Joshua Nel 37
Joshua Nel 37
Nathl. Nel 36
Thomas Nel 40
Vachel Bul 178
Zachariah Wsh 308
Hobday, John Pen 116
Hobs, Nichs. Hrd 296
Hobson, Jonathan But 195
Thomas War 271
Zacheriah War 280
Hockaday, Edwd. Clr 132
Isaac Clr 132
James Mad 215
John Grp 269
Hocker, George Lin 121
John Lin 118
Nicolas Lin 121
Nicholas Mad 212
Nicholas Ohi 73
Philip Lin 121
Phillip Lin 121
Phillip Ohi 75
Phillip, Senr Ohi 76
Saml. Lin 119
Saml. Snr Lin 118
Samuel Mer 314
Weaver Lin 119
Weaver Ohi 74
William Lin 121
Hockersmith, David Jes 46
Eave Fay 21
Edward Log 192
George Mad 244
Jacob Fra 133
John Mad 249
Michl. Fra 132
Hockins, Saml. Grn 254
Hockinsmith, Jacob Est 8
Hodge, Abner Lin 118
Alexander Chr 60
Amose Cas 39
Benjamin Liv 148
Edmond War 244
Emasey Cas 39
George Chr 68
Henry, Junr Liv 152
Henry, Senr Liv 148
Joseph Mul 402
Nathan Clr 131
Robert Liv 147
Samuel Chr 68
Thomas Liv 150
William Bou 69
Willm. War 258
Wm. War 267
Hodgers, Andrew War 258
Hodges, Benjamin Mer 316
Betsy Nel 41
Daniel Fay 47
Debby Mon 376
Dreury Cly 150
Drury Hop 371
James Cly 150
Hodges, cont.
James Knx 86
Jesse Mad 213
Jno. Nel 36
John Adr 9
John Log 194
Saml. Adr 9
Samuel Log 165
Shadrack Cly 152
Thomas Mer 316
William Mer 315
Wm. Cas 38
Wm. Mon 384
Wm. War 263
Hodgins, Isaac Grn 264
Jno. Hrd 284
Sarah Hrd 284
Hodgson, David Knx 63
John B. Fra 134
Hoeback, Isaac Hrd 292
Jno. Hrd 293
Michl. Hrd 293
Hoff, Aaron She 234
Luke She 222
Hoffman, Barnet Cum 184
Ezekiel Cum 175
Jno. hrd 289
Hofford, Jessee Cal 18
Hog, Achilis Bar 26
Gobson Bar 26
Obediah Bar 26
Obediah Bar 27
Rubin Bar 26
Wm. Bar 26
Hogan, Betsey Gar 219
Daniel Grn 245
Danl. Cum 179
Danl. Nel 36
David Knx 78
Elijah Boo 60
Elizabeth Gar 220
James Grn 247
James Sco 179
Jas. Gar 224
John Grn 259
John Log 181
Proser Grn 258
Teberah Knx 80
Thos. Sco 177
William Knx 78
William Knx 81
William Mad 211
Zach. Gar 220
Hoge, Solamon Mon 366
Hogg, Anderson Lin 121
Andrew Cas 46
Davy Adr 9
Elijah Ohi 76
James Flo 99
Milburn Wsh 304
Robert Hrs 312
Stephen Bre 162
Stephen Flo 100
Susannah Pen 112
Hogge, Elizabeth Mon 350
Hoggins, Solomon Bou 91
Hogin, Hunphry Chr 109
Thomas Chr 79
Walter Chr 109
Hoglan, Abrm. Grn 262
Dorsey Nel 34
Isaac Grn 246
James Nel 35
Leny Nel 35
Hogland, Aron Hnr 359A
James Hnr 363
John She 240
Hogland, cont.
Martin Fay 59
Moses Hnr 355
Rebecah Fay 53
William Fay 59
Hoglar, Abr. Nel 33
Hoglen, Levy Hrs 308
Hoglin, James Mul 396
Okey Fay 30
Hogman, Benjamin Mas 258
Hogshead, Jos. War 262
William Fra 132
Hogue, ... Mer 314
.... Mer 314
Hohamer, Henry Grn 260
Hohimer, George Gar 222
Hoke, Adam Jef 10
Andrew Jef 8
Conrad Jef 8
George Jef 8
Jacob Jef 20
Peter Jef 10
Hokins, Thomas Hrs 311
Holacost, George Fle 66
Holaway, John Fay 50
Holbert, Henry Lew 102
Isack Lew 97
James Woo 398
Jno. Lew 102
Colby Sco 178
Henry Grn 247
Randal Flo 100
Zachh. Sco 178
Holcom, Mark Gar 223
S. Elbert Gar 226
Jeramiah War 282
Holcraft, George She 238
Holcum, Charles War 277
Preston War 277
Holden, James Sco 182
John Sco 169
Holder, Alston Knx 88
Gary Mon 366
Gary Mon 366
John Clr 133
John War 270
Shadrack Hop 372
Wm. Bar 27
Holderby, John Hop 377
Holderman, Jacob Cas 47
Jacob Hop 374
Holding, William Sco 183
Willm. Jur Sco 183
Holdren, Jacob Cas 41
Holdson, Enoch Jef 30
Hole, John Way 354
Holefield, Isaac Chr 83
Holeman, Daniel Mad 213
Danl. Woo 385
Edward Woo 391
Edwd. Gal 185
Isaac Hrs 308
Isaac Woo 392
James Cam 30
James Log 168
James Log 185
John Cal 18
John Log 174
Joseph Mad 213
Joseph, Jr Mad 214
Reuben Fay 22
Richard Mer 313
Thomas Mer 316
William Hne 363
William Mad 213
Holesclaw, Henry Nel 34
James Nel 33

Name	County	Page
Holeton, John	Woo	383
Holey, Berriman	War	260
Holiday, Moses	Gal	185
Zach.	Adr	9
Holiman, Tandy	Est	6
William	Hop	381
Holins, James	Bar	44
Holis, Benjamine	Bra	144
Holkum, Solomon	Knx	90
Hollace, Hudson	Mad	213
Holladay, Ben	Est	5
George	Clr	131
James	Clr	132
John	Cas	38
John	Clr	131
John	Mad	216
John A.	Bar	34
Stephen	Clr	131
Wm.	Nic	53
Wm.	Way	354
Hollan, Harpey	Gar	222
Wright	Grp	275
Holland, Allin	Mad	250
Benja.	Fle	71
Britton	Bar	38
Edward	Woo	380
Ephm.	Sco	186
Henry	Wsh	308
John	Cal	6
John	Cum	169
John	Gal	184
John	Grn	247
John	Mer	314
John	Mon	352
Jonas M.	She	228
Pheby	Bou	91
William	Cal	3
William	Sco	191
Wm.	Bar	28
Wm.	Bar	34
Wm.	Mon	352
Holler, Francis	Nic	53
Hollet, Mary	Rck	164
Solomon	Cum	183
Hollett, Thomas	Wsh	306
Holley, Henry	Clr	132
Richard	Clr	132
Samuel	She	213
Thompson	Nic	53
William	Clr	131
Hollice, Andrew	Jef	10
Catharine	Jef	10
Fielding	Jef	10
John	Jef	10
Vincent	Jef	10
Wm.	Jef	10
Hollida, Charles	Mon	381
Holliday, Jos.	Gal	185
Polly	Mas	259
Hollidy, William	Hrs	311
William	Hrs	311
Hollin, Baswell	Chr	83
Baswell	Chr	98
John	Chr	98
John M.	Chr	116
Milly	Chr	74
Hollingshead, James	Ohi	92
Hollingsworth,		
Robert	She	198
Susannah	She	198
Hollinsworth,		
Beasley	Cly	150
Isaac	Cly	157
Jas.	Cly	155
John	Cly	157
Joseph	Jef	9
Will	Cly	157
Hollis, John	She	219
John	She	226
Nancy	Jef	11
Sally	She	231
Hollman, Daniel	Hrd	303
Hollowman, David	War	272
Elisha	War	275
Hollowmon, Willson	Mul	395
Holloway, Geo.	Bou	123
George	Woo	389
Jacob	War	244
James	Bar	36
James	Cas	42
John	Hnd	337
Jonathan	War	244
Labourn	War	266
Robert	Fra	133
Robt.	Bar	36
S. Thomas	Mer	343
Selia	Mer	313
Soloman	War	266
William	Pul	149
Holly, James	Cal	6
Hollyman, John	Hnd	330
Mary	Fay	30
Holman, Andrew	Sco	175
James	Gra	239
Jesse L.	Gal	184
John	Gra	239
John	Knx	88
Holmes, Alexander	Bou	88
Andrew	She	214
Bryan	Mul	393
Charles	Mul	393
Daniel	Bou	90
Elias	War	250
Forgus	Fra	132
Hugh	Woo	398
Isaac	Ohi	95
James	Nel	9
James	Pen	115
James L.	She	214
Jesse	She	206
John	Fay	41
John	Lin	121
John	Mon	359
John	Way	370
John, A.	Woo	402
Lewis	She	213
Moses	Jef	9
Nicholas	Bre	160
Robert M.	Jef	24
William	Bul	178
William	Fay	41
William	Knx	86
William	She	200
Holms, Isaac	Fra	132
Joseph	Cal	4
Robert	Fay	16
Saml.	Adr	8
Wm.	Bar	45
Holody, Boswell	Hrs	316
Holoman, Blake	Liv	151
Holrel, Edward	Wsh	313
Holsclaw, Abner	Gar	226
Benja.	Gar	224
Elijah	Gar	226
Henry	Bar	47
Jacob	Gar	224
Jacob	Gar	225
James	Bul	179
Kelly	Jef	32
Holsehouser, J.	Nel	39
Holsel, Polley	War	245
Holsey, Betsy	Adr	9
Elizabeth	Cly	150
Jacob	Log	181
Holstead, Daniel	Fay	16
Holston, Absolom	Bar	52
Holt, Benjn.	Jef	9
Berryn.	Adr	9
David	Hrs	324
Dazwell	Knx	71
Drury	Knx	71
Elisha	Mad	212
Franciss	Lin	121
Isaac	Jef	9
Henry	Mad	215
Jehu	Wsh	306
John	Jef	9
John	Pul	151
John W.	Bre	163
Josh.	Adr	9
nancy	Wsh	308
Peter C.	Hnd	329
Polly	Gar	221
Rachel	Jef	8
Tapley	Wsh	308
Thomas	Hrs	312
Thomas	Pul	151
Thos. P.	Hrd	286
Ziba	Gal	186
Holtclaw, Henry	Bar	51
Jas.	Bar	51
Richd.	Bar	54
Holton, Catherine	Fra	134
Elijah	Mas	257
Jesse	Mas	257
John	Mas	262
John	War	249
Sarah	Mas	258
William	Mas	259
William, Senr	Mas	258
Holtsclaw, Amaseah	Lin	121
Archibald	Fay	47
Benjn.	Lin	119
John	Mad	216
Holuns, Jacob	Bar	45
Homer, John	Mad	214
Homerly, Garnett	War	270
Homes, James	Cum	176
John	Hrs	321
Honey, John Jr	Bou	90
John, Sr	Bou	90
Honke, Adam	Clr	132
Honn, Joseph	Mon	352
Joseph	Mon	359
Honne, George	Mer	313
Honore, J.A.	Jef	25
Honscer, Jacob	Nic	53
Hooberry, Jacob	Mer	314
Jacob	Mer	315
Richard	Mer	314
William	Mer	313
Hood, Andrew	Grp	273
James	Bar	28
James	Fle	83
Jesse	Adr	8
John	Fle	84
John	War	259
Joseph F.	She	238
Lewis	Clr	132
Lukkus	Clr	131
Mary	But	195
Massea	Grp	269
Robert	Grp	269
Samuel	Fle	84
Tho.	Bar	28
Thomas	Grp	269
William	But	195
Hoofman, Benjamin	Fay	20
Hook, John	Bra	141
Thomas	Bou	90
William	Mad	211

Hooke, George Fle 84
Hooker, George Hop 375
Robert Hop 375
Hooks, Phelix Way 368
Hoomes, Saml. Gar 224
Hoomis, Edwd. Gar 224
Hoopengarnen, Coonrod Bul 178
Hooper, Dempsey Hnd 339
Enock Hnd 335
James Hnd 335
Hootan, Wm. Clr 131
Hooten, Thomas Mad 249
Hooton, Elijah War 275
James Bra 144
John Mad 211
John War 279
Joseph War 265
Willm. War 270
Hoots, Peter Cum 179
Hoover, Andrew Jes 45
David Jes 41
David Jes 42
George Ohi 74
George Woo 388
Henry Woo 398
Jacob Jes 42
John Mas 259
Lawrence Sco 172
Moses Jes 42
Moses Jes 44
Peter Lew 104
Hoozer, Sampson Pul 151
Hope, Geroge Clr 132
James Log 183
Michael Mer 136
Richard Mer 314
S. Log 182
Hopewell, John Jef 10
John Nel 34
Thos. Hrd 297
William Bul 178
Hopewood, Christr. Lin 119
Hopkens, Samuel Sr Hnd 344
Hopkins, Anny Gra 242
Cyntho Nel 40
David Fle 68
Dennis Way 355
Edmund Hnd 328
Elihu Nic 52
Elijah Cum 182
Elizah. Adr 9
Ephriam Jes 43
Esick Bou 88
Ezekiel Bou 89
Ezekiel, Jr Bou 89
Francis Mon 351
Francis mon 370
Gardner Flo 99
George W. Bou 90
George W. Log 195
Hazard Bou 89
Henry She 220
Henry She 241
Jacob Fle 86
Jenethen Bou 89
Jno. Grn 263
John Boo 60
John Bou 90
John Gra 244
John Mul 400
John Nel 37
John Sco 169
John, Sr Bou 90
Richd. Boo 60
Richd. Sco 179
Robert Clr 132
Hopkins, cont.
Robert Woo 378
Saml. Bou 89
Saml. Cum 184
Samuel Hnd 327
Samuel Hrs 316
Samuel G. Hnd 337
Ste. Gar 224
Thos. Hrs 316
William Flo 99
William Woo 383
Wim. Nel 38
Wm. Mon 351
Hopper, Anderson Chr 100
Elijah Chr 71
Gilliam Pul 150
James Mad 216
John Chr 72
John Fay 47
John Mad 247
John Mas 260
John Mon 376
Joseph, Sr Mad 214
Joshua Adr 9
Mary Mad 247
Moses Mad 216
Nancy She 204
Patterson Chr 100
Rolley Pul 150
William Knx 87
Wm. Adr 9
Wm. Mon 359
Hopson, Henry Chr 58
Henry Chr 85
John Chr 82
Nevil Chr 85
Samuel Mon 350
Wile Grn 265
William Chr 32
William Chr 85
Hopton, Nathan Log 177
Hopwell, John Nel 37
Hopwood, James Mon 356
John Mad 215
Hord, Elias Mas 263
Edward Bou 124
Edwin Mas 258
James Jes 46
Jesse, Junr Mas 260
Jesse, Senr Mas 262
Thomas Mas 258
William Mer 341
Horine, Henry Jes 42
Jacob Jef 9
Jacob Jes 42
Saml. Nel 9
Horn, Aaron Mad 213
Christopher Knx 79
Daniel Bou 89
Edward Knx 86
Frederick Flo 99
Jacob Bou 89
John Bou 89
Jonas Bou 89
Mathew Est 9
Peter Bou 89
William Est 9
William Mad 248
Hornacre, John Fay 16
Mary Mon 358
Hornback, Abraham Hrd 301
Abraham Mon 374
Abraham Ohi 90
Daniel Ohi 87
Danl. Bou 123
Danl. Hrd 291
David Ohi 89
Hornback, cont.
Jacob Mon 374
James Clr 132
Jas Gra 237
Jas. Hrd 290
John Bul 178
John Cly 152
Michael Bou 89
Michl. Bou 124
Saml. Bou 123
Samuel Bul 179
Solomon Bul 179
Hornbaker, Harmonius Bou 88
Hornbrucle, Wm. Log 174
Hornbuckle, Hiram Mul 402
Richd. Mas 261
Thomas Mas 261
Wm. Fle 79
Horne, Abriham Bul 179
Horneback, Soloman Clr 133
Hornebuckle, John Log 174
Horner, Wm. R.B. Fra 136
Hornes, Donnald Fle 74
Hornsby, Joseph She 201
Thomas She 222
Horpoll, John War 257
Horrel, Cleved. Adr 8
Wm. Adr 8
Horrell, Plus P. Nel 42
Horril, James Pul 150
Horrin, John Hop 371
Horseley, Levi Bre 159
Horseman, William Fay 38
Horsey, Charles Fay 16
Horsley, Elijah Boo 60
James Grp 277
John Boo 60
Mathew Grp 277
Nancy Boo 60
Talor Grp 277
William Est 1
Horton, Adan War 278
Anthony Bre 168
Benja. Gar 225
George Log 167
Hugh Mad 250
John Hnd 347
Jos. Boo 59
Reubin War 268
Saml. Sco 185
William Bou 88
Hortt, Jno. Hnr 352
Hosack, James Liv 152
Hosen, Majhar Nic 52
Hosey, Daniel Log 178
Hosick, Alexander Liv 152
Alexander Liv 152
William Liv 152
Hoskins, Achillas Hnr 355
Charles Bre 159
George Bul 179
George Knx 79
Hugh Nel 38
Hoskins, James Fay 30
James Gra 241
Jas. Gar 225
Jeremiah Bul 178
Jery. Nel 38
John Bul 178
Joseph Bul 178
John Knx 77
John Knx 79
John Mad 248
Ninian Knx 78
Reuben Knx 78
Robert Jef 10

Hoskins, cont.
Samuel Mad 213
Thomas Knx 90
William Mad 214
William Mer 316
Wm. Gar 224
Hoskinson, Bazaliel Lin 119
Hugh Bre 159
Hugh Nel 33
Hosley, James Jef 30
Hoss, Michael Log 169
Hostell, Robert War 262
Hostley, Wm. Gar 221
Hostutler, Abraham She 208
Christian She 217
Hostutter, Adam She 229
Barnabas Bou 70
Jacob Nel 38
Hotsman, John Bar 28
Hott, Joseph Bou 71
Houchen, Frances War 249
Houchens, Charles War 249
John War 249
Hough, Charles Ohi 89
Joseph Bul 179
Moses Bul 179
William Bul 179
Houghten, Charles Mas 258
William Mas 258
Houghton, Aaron Mas 257
Elijah Mas 260
Joab Mas 260
Houk, Guilla Bra 141
Hourigan, Patrick Wsh 306
House, Andrew Bou 88
George Bou 88
Jacob Cum 184
James Pul 151
James Pul 152
James Pul 152
John Boo 60
John Clr 132
Joseph Mon 380
Mathias Gar 226
Matthias Log 161
Michael Gra 243
Nimrod Hrd 284
Simion Mer 316
William Bre 165
Wm. Mon 381
Houseman, John B. Ohi 85
Sousana Mul 404
Houser, Jacob Mas 261
William Mas 261
Housewort, Henry Fay 22
Housley, Cathrn. Nel 9
Robert Nel 9
Houston, Abigail Nel 35
Alexr. Nel 40
Anthony Sco 177
Benj. Nel 36
James Bou 88
James Bou 89
James Nel 9
Jno. Nel 34
John Mas 261
John Nel 36
John Nel 37
Joseph Lew 98
Joseph Nel 33
Joseph Sco 188
Peter Bou 88
Robert Hrs 311
Robt. Hrd 295
Robert Sco 186
Saml. Nel 36
Wm. Cal 14
Houtchens, Chas. Hrd 283
Houton, John Fay 42
Jonathan Hop 373
Houts, Cristofer Liv 160
Jacob Wsh 304
John Wsh 304
Houx, Frederic Log 186
Jacob Log 188
John Log 188
Houzer, Abraham Jr Jes 42
Abraham, Ser Jes 42
Jacob Jes 42
John Jes 42
Hovis, Wm. Adr 9
How, Abraham Mas 259
Christopher Bou 124
David, Sen Fle 79
James Grp 272
John Fle 83
John Fra 134
John W. Grp 269
Robert Boo 59
Howaid, Christo. Bar 25
Howard, Adron Knx 84
Andrew Knx 84
Ann Nel 39
Benjamin Knx 80
Benjn. Mad 213
Charles Bou 88
Charles War 243
Charles War 244
Charles Wsh 308
Clement Mad 216
Cornelius Hnd 342
David But 195
Diana Ohi 82
Edward Wsh 305
Elijah Bou 88
Elizth. Nel 39
Ellender Fle 77
Ely Mon 380
Geor. Mon 384
George Hnd 331
George Hrd 302
Gideon Nic 52
Gideon Nic 52
Henry Nic 52
Henry War 256
Isaac Woo 384
Isbell Est 7
Ignatious Mad 216
Jacob Nic 52
James Bou 90
James Cly 158
James Knx 80
James Mon 366
James Nel 34
James Woo 394
James Wsh 310
James, Sr Knx 79
Jarimiah Cas 43
John Bar 43
John Bra 145
John But 195
John Fay 60
John Jef 10
John Liv 150
John Hrd 303
John Knx 80
John Mas 258
John Mon 363
John Nel 36
John War 264
John Sr Bra 145
Joseph Jef 30
Joseph Nel 37
Julius Knx 82
Howard, cont.
Leroy Woo 384
Lindsey But 195
Littleton Ohi 79
Mark Ohi 103
Mary Mas 256
Mathew Bou 91
Mathew Hrs 313
Merradith Chr 53
Mordica Jes 42
Neal Est 5
Paris Bou 91
Peter Way 353
Philip Clr 132
Portman Way 353
Richd. Hrd 290
Robert Mas 309
Sally Bra 152
Samuel Liv 151
Stephen Bar 24
Thomas Bou 124
Thomas Knx 78
Thomas Mad 249
Thomas Mon 363
Thomas C. Mad 244
Thos. Bra 147
Thos. Nel 35
Vincent Woo 394
William Chr 88
William Knx 78
William Wsh 310
Willm. Nel 39
Willm. Nel 40
Willm. War 276
Wm. Bar 33
Wm. Bar 44
Wm. Jef 28
Wm. Jr Nel 36
Howcheler, Rebecha Bar 43
Howdeshill, Joseph Wsh 306
Howe, David Sur Fle 80
Jno. Hrd 289
Joseph Fle 61
Joseph P. Mon 369
Robert Fle 75
Samuel Fle 82
Samuel Mon 363
Samuel Nic 52
Samuel, Sen Fle 73
Thomas Mon 384
Howel, Daniel Bra 152
David Mon 376
Isaac Mon 378
James But 194
James Pul 153
John Log 191
John She 220
Polly Bar 38
Saml. Bar 38
Teakle Log 176
William Chr 77
Wm. Bar 38
Howell, Charles Nel 9
Chas. Hrd 293
Danl. S. Nel 9
James Hop 379
Jas. Hrd 292
Jas. Hrd 293
Jno. Hrd 293
Jno. Senr Hrd 293
John Jes 46
John Log 169
John Ohi 76
Lewis Hop 377
Nat. Hrd 293
Richd. Hrd 298
Saml. Hrd 300

Howell, cont.
Stephen She 219
Thomas Log 173
Thomas Log 177
William Jes 45
Howerton, George Nic 53
Obediah Gra 237
Howey, Jos. Hrd 299
Joseph Hrd 302
Moses Hrd 290
Howlet, John Boo 60
John Bul 178
Thos. Boo 60
Wm. Boo 60
Howley, Dennis Fra 132
Howorth, Laurence But 195
Hows, Jas. Way 356
Howser, Tho. Bar 49
Howsley, Marmaduke Ohi 70
Howsman, John Chr 81
Howson, John Mas 261
Hoxy, William Chr 103
Hoy, Joseph Hnd 340
Thomas Log 163
Thomas Log 194
Wm. Mon 357
Hoylen, Moses Bul 179
Hoyt, Fitch Liv 149
John Gal 186
Hubard, Jesse War 245
Miller War 243
Hubart, Jane Gar 222
John Gar 222
Jos. Gar 221
Wright Gar 221
Hubbard, Armstd. Nel 9
Asa K. Mad 250
Austin Nel 9
Benjn. Mad 247
Daniel Mad 250
Elisha Wsh 307
Eppa Bul 179
George Mad 250
Gilbert Mas 257
Hezekiah War 257
James Cly 156
James Wsh 307
John Fay 17
John, Jr Mad 211
John, Jr Mad 214
John, Sen Mad 214
Jos. Grn 246
Moses Cly 156
Peter Grn 245
Susannah Bou 88
Thomas Mad 247
Thomas Mas 262
Thomas, Jun Mad 247
Thos. Nel 36
Zebulon Cal 12
Hubbell, William Fra 135
Hubble, David Pul 153
Hubbord, Eli Way 363
Hubbs, Jacob Jef 9
Hubnuh, Richard Fle 86
Hucaby, Robert Way 361
Hucal, Elizabeth Clr 132
Richard Clr 131
Huchens, Aaron Mer 314
Huchings, John Cas 46
Thoms Cas 46
Huchinson, Carter Cam 30
Huchison, Benjn. Hrs 309
George Hrs 308
Huckabe, Joshua Lin 121
Huckaby, Tho. Bar 28
Huckrirr., Charles Hrs 323
Huckley, John She 203
Huckstept, John Jes 46
Samuel Jes 43
Hudder, Bartholemew Way 353
Huddleston, Thomas She 225
Hudgings, Daniel Lin 118
Hudgins, Medly Lin 121
Hudgius, William Grn 258
Hudlin, Benjamin Mas 256
Hudnut, Richard Fle 91
Hudson, Abram War 278
Barnett Ohi 74
Benja. Gar 225
Chas. Bar 51
Daniel Pul 151
Drury Grn 257
Drury War 271
Edward Ohi 97
Henry Pul 151
James Fay 38
Jesse War 277
Jno. Hrd 298
John Cum 173
John Fay 38
John Fay 44
John Mad 248
John Pul 151
John War 277
John Woo 397
Joseph Fay 16
Joshua Jes 43
Joshua War 279
Lewis Pul 149
Martin Mad 235
Martin Ohi 72
Mose Liv 149
Ob[illegible] Sco 177
Oratio Gar 220
Robert Pul 149
Rolly Woo 397
Rubin Fay 19
Sandy Pul 149
Simon Mad 247
T. Joseph Fay 17
Thomas Ohi 72
William Bou 124
William Cly 149
William Fay 38
William Ohi 75
William E. Ohi 74
William P. Ohi 103
Wm. Hrs 322
Hudspath, John War 267
Thos. War 267
Hudspeth, Ann War 261
George War 261
Hue, Samuel Hrs 311
Huey, Saml. Boo 59
Hueye, Anna Liv 154
Huff, Aquilla Bre 164
Benjamin Bre 167
Cornelius Wsh 307
Danl. Cum 185
Jesse Bre 156
John Bra 141
John Fra 134
John Mon 351
John Mon 359
John Mon 380
John Way 357
Jonathan Wsh 306
Leonard Cly 155
Mary Mer 316
Peter Mer 315
Reuben Bre 158
Richard Mer 316
Huff, cont.
Robert Fra 134
Saml. Cum 185
Samuel Mer 316
Thomas Mer 313
William Flo 99
Wm. Cum 183
Huffard, Danl. Sco 176
David Sco 176
George Woo 393
John Woo 382
Huffakre, Christopher Way 367
Isaac Way 352
Jacob Way 370
John Way 358
Huffer, Jacob Jes 44
Huffman, Ambros Bar 47
Ann Clr 132
Cornelius Bar 47
George Bre 162
George Nel 38
Henry Bar 47
Henry Gar 220
Henry, Jnr Gar 221
Jno. Jnr Gar 220
John Bou 123
John Gar 220
John Gar 220
John Gar 225
Julius Bar 55
Mary Gar 220
Michael Gar 225
Michl. Bou 123
Solomn. Boo 60
Teter Bar 55
Wm. Gar 199
Wm. Gar 220
Wm. Gar 226
Huffstuttar, John Log 161
Huffstutter, George Bou 90
John Bou 89
Hufft, Joseph Knx 82
Hufman, Armsted Bar 47
Fredrich Pen 112
George Hrs 319
Henry Hrs 319
Jacob Grp 272
James Cam 32
Peter Hrs 322
Petre Nic 53
Hufmon, Jacob Hrs 320
Phillip Hnr 361
Hufner, Valentine Nel 34
Huft, Abraham Mas 262
Hugan, Alexr Jef 27
Hugart, John Mon 367
Hugeon, Thos. Cam 30
Huggans, John Way 355
Moses Way 355
Huggard, John Adr 8
Huggens, Edward Jes 45
Henry Hnd 337
Hugh (free negro) Fay 30
Hugh, John Nel 37
Lewis Nel 35
Willm. Nel 35
Hughbank, Thomas Fle 86
Hughbanks, Herington Fle 77
James Fle 71
James Fle 77
John Fle 67
Laurence Fle 77
Thos. Fle 78
William Fle 78
Hughes, Abijah Woo 382

Hughes, cont.
Abner Jef 8
Absalom Gar 222
Absalon Mon 367
Amsterd Clr 131
Bathsheba Bou 91
Charles Chr 93
Chesse Jef 10
David Bou 88
David Chr 92
David Cum 169
David War 271
Edward Wsh 307
Fetter Jef 26
Franciss Lin 119
Gabriel Lin 119
George Bou 89
Isaac Gar 222
james Bou 88
James Bou 91
James Fle 87
James Liv 148
James Log 192
James Mas 256
James Wsh 343
James J. Liv 150
James William Fle 73
Jas. Gar 222
Jesse Jes 41
John Bou 89
John Bou 91
John Cal 6
John Cal 11
John Fra 131
John Hnd 346
John Jef 8
John Jef 10
John Jes 44
John Jes 44
John Jes 46
John Log 169
John Nel 37
John Way 369
John Wsh 307
Joseph Liv 150
Joseph Jes 45
Joseph, Jr Jes 45
Joseph, Sr Jes 45
Joshua Clr 132
Mary Cam 32
Mary Hnd 341
Mason Bou 91
Nathaniel Chr 107
Nathaniel Fay 21
Peter Fay 33
Ralph Hrd 286
Reuben Lin 119
Richard Fay 24
Robert Bou 88
Robert Fle 63
Robert Jef 11
Robert F. Liv 151
Samuel Jes 44
Thomas Bou 68
Thomas Fra 136
Thomas Jes 45
Thomas She 212
William Bou 88
William Fay 21
William jes 45'
William Jes 45
William Liv 150
William Ohi 87
William Wsh 306
Willm. Jnr Lin 119
Willm. Snr Lin 119
Wm. Log 168

Hughes, cont.
Wm. Mon 384
Wm. Nic 53
Wm. Way 355
Hughlet, John Mas 257
Hughs, Allen B. Fle 82
Andw. Boo 59
Anne Mad 248
Blackey Adr 12
Cornelius Boo 59
Edd. War 268
James Mon 380
Jesse Mul 395
John Mul 394
John Nel 37
John Pul 152
John S. Mad 213
Kinsey Bou 124
Margaret Mon 352
Samuel Mad 216
Thomas Fle 82
Thomas War 245
Thos. W. Boo 60
Wm. Mon 370
Hughston, John Fay 34
Robert Fay 30
Hughy, Ephraim Gar 226
John Mas 259
Hugly, Chs. Hnr 352
Lewis Hnr 352
Huhbanks, Wm. Fle 82
Hukel, Daniel Fay 54
Hukin, John Fay 52
Hukins, Abiah Mas 258
Daniel Mas 258
Hulan, Ambrose Est 6
John Est 6
Peggy Est 6
Huler, Josiah Nel 39
Hulet, Richard Fay 47
Hulets, Benjamin Fay 48
Hulett, John Jes 43
Polly Jes 43
Samuel Mul 392
Hulin, Thomas Mad 214
Huling, Janathan Cam 33
Hulit, John Jef 30
Hull, Archibald Bou 89
Garsham Hnd 332
George Bou 89
Jacob Fay 16
John Fay 16
John & sis-in-law-
Imaly Tows Fle 87
John Mas 261
Reuben Grn 258
Samuel Mas 261
Hulot, West Fay 48
Hulse, Alasons Jes 46
James Mon 350
John Clr 133
Nathan Clr 132
Paul, Jr Clr 133
Paul, Sr Clr 132
Richard Mon 350
Hults, Robert Bre 166
Human, James Mon 353
Humber, C. Charles Gar 199
Humble, Michael Hnr 353
Michael Mer 315
Noah Bou 89
Paul Hnr 353
Robert Woo 384
Uriah Bou 91
Uriah She 241
Hume, Elzaphan Boo 59
Geo. Cam 26

Hume, cont.
George Mad 248
John Cam 29
John Cam 29
John Clr 131
John Mad 250
Reuben Mad 249
William Mad 249
Wm. Cam 29
Humes, Enoch Bar 19
Gabriel Bou 124
Jane Jef 8
Mary Mer 315
Prue Pen 110
Sarah Pen 110
Stripling Pen 109
Humphey, John Bar 27
Humphrey, Benjamin Ohi 80
Daniel Ohi 90
David Cas 42
John Bou 91
John Cas 38
John Hnr 354
Owen Mon 381
Rauley Wsh 304
Wm. Bou 124
Humphreys, Cornel-
ius Gar 223
George Log 166
John Jef 11
Jonathan Fay 38
Humphries, Benjn. Sco 177
Charles Fra 135
Elijah Jef 25
Patrick Mad 250
Saml. Cum 182
Thomas Bou 90
Humphris, Absolum Chr 91
James Chr 74
John Fle 75
Reuben Hnr 369
Saml. Jur Fle 75
William Fle 75
Humphriys, Charles Fay 17
Humphrus, George Pul 151
Humphry, Geo. Hrd 288
Jno. Hrd 284
Jno. Nel 36
Mary Hnr 368
Saml. Nel 40
Samuel Hrd 301
Susan Nel 40
Thomas Hrd 301
Thos. Nel 40
William Hrd 301
Humphy, Horiner Hnr 355
Hunamaker, Lewis Cam 25
Hund, Dudley Mad 212
Hundley, Anthony Wsh 307
Anthony Wsh 308
Archd. Hrd 292
Charles Wsh 308
Elisha Wsh 308
Jesse Wsh 306
John Wsh 308
William Wsh 305
Hungate, Charles Mer 316
Charles Wsh 307
Charles Wsh 308
Job Wsh 308
John Mer 316
John Wsh 308
Joseph Mer 316
William Mer 313
Hunley, Eliza Jes 41
David Fay 52
Jas. Gar 225

Hunsacke, Andrew Mul 387
Hunsacker, Abraham Mul 388
George Mul 398
Isaac Mul 399
Samuel Mul 387
Hunsinger, Adam Mul 396
George Mul 394
Jacob Mul 392
Jacob Mul 400
Hunston, Willm. Lin 119
Hunt, Ambrose Grn 248
Daniel Mul 404
Enoch Clr 131
Ephraim Adr 19
Ewel Mon 379
Gasham Mul 391
George Fay 22
Graham Mul 404
Henry She 221
Isaiah Ohi 99
Israel Fle 70
James Bar 30
James Bar 53
James Mon 375
Jenney(free woman) Fay 17
Jerima. Fle 64
John Bra 141
John Fay 47
John Fle 61
John Flo 99
John Flo 100
John Fra 132
John Mer 315
John Mul 404
John War 271
Jonathan Bar 27
Jonathan Fay 52
Jonathan Mul 400
Laborn Grn 248
Mashack Fle 73
Mosis War 274
Owen But 194
Polly Fay 48
Ralph Ohi 100
Reuban Fle 71
Richard Lin 119
Roberson Mon 350
Simeon Grn 248
William She 210
Wilson Fay 21
Wilson Fay 47
Wilson Jes 43
Hunter, Absalom Woo 399
Alexander Way 361
Alexander Way 361
Alexr. Nel 38
Charles Chr 99
Charles S. Woo 393
Daniel Lin 121
Daniel She 227
David Hnd 342
David Log 185
David War 280
Dolly Chr 115
Elift. Nel 36
Francis Knx 88
George Fay 24
George Lin 119
Henry Jes 46
Henry She 216
Henry She 226
Henry She 227
Jacob Jes 46
James Gal 185
James Log 182
Jas. Jef 29
Hunter, cont.
John Fay 41
John Fra 135
John Gar 223
John Jes 42
John Jes 46
John Log 176
John Mas 259
John Mas 262
John Nic 54
John She 216
John She 226
John Way 361
Joseph Jes 46
Joshua Way 364
Judith Way 370
Mary Woo 398
Rachel Fay 24
Reubin Hnd 334
Richard Fay 24
Robert Hrd 302
Robert Knx 79
Robert Sco 173
Saml. Gar 225
Samuel Chr 63
Samuel Jes 46
Samuel She 216
Samuel Woo 394
Thomas She 216
Thos. Bou 124
Titus Grn 249
Tobias Fle 87
William Fra 135
William Jes 46
William Lew 100
William Log 185
William Nel 40
William She 217
Wm. Way 374
Zachariah Mer 315
Huntsman, George Lin 119
John Mad 249
Huntsucker, Joseph Chr 74
Huphines,Christian Log 190
Hupp, George Wsh 307
William Wsh 307
Hurd, James Cum 174
James Knx 71
Sally Cum 174
William Knx 72
Hurde, George War 249
Hurley, James Bou 90
James Mon 359
Hurndon, Elija Cam 26
Huron, Elijah Mas 256
Hursh, George Nel 40
Hurshman, George Bou 123
Hurst, Fielding Hnr 353
Henry Fle 63
Henry Fle 88
Henry Sco 167
Herman Mas 257
James Fle 75
James Sco 167
James Wsh 303
John Adr 8
John Bra 143
John Fle 65
John Mas 257
John Mas 262
John Sco 169
John Wsh 344
Jonn. Adr 8
Landy Fle 75
Nathaniel Mas 260
Peter Fay 50
Sarah Mas 262
Hurst, cont.
William Fay 42
William Fay 56
Wm. Adr 8
Wm. Adr 9
Hurt, Akery. Adr 9
Chas. Adr 9
James Bar 36
Jas. Gar 223
John Cal 19
John Cum 167
Little G. Mad 213
Little B. Jur Mad 212
Moses Way 356
Nathan Adr 8
William Mad 213
Willm. Adr 8
Willm. Adr 9
Wm. Gar 221
Husband, John Hnd 344
Husbands, George But 194
Harmon Chr 104
Veasy Wsh 307
Husbans, William Chr 63
Huse, James Mer 315
John Hrs 305
John Mer 315
Stephen Mer 313
William Mer 315
Huser, David Chr 112
Huses, Daniel Chr 114
Husgh, Richrd. Fle 83
Thomas Fle 83
Husk, Charles Cum 180
Isaac Hnd 333
Jesse Cum 177
John Hnd 332
Michl. Hnr 361
Richard She 219
Valentine Ohi 94
Hussy, Christopher Cal 7
Huston, Abel Grn 257
Abner Nel 39
Anny Lin 119
Archabald Lin 121
Archd. Boo 60
George Jef 9
Isaac Hrd 283
James Chr 78
James Fay 53
James Gra 237
James Hnd 329
Jesse Hrd 283
John Bul 179
John Chr 68
John Ohi 90
Joseph Bre 160
Joseph Bul 179
Stepheson Lin 118
William Bul 179
William Fay 17
William Ohi 90
Wm. J. Jef 28
Wm. Hrd 286
Hutchcraft, John But 195
Hutcherson, David Grn 246
Hutty B. Grn 246
John Log 177
Mathew Grn 252
Molly Jes 45
Nancy Jef 9
Robert Clr 131
William Log 194
Hutcheson, Jno. Grn 264
John Bre 161
John Cas 42
Joseph Bre 159

Hutcheson, cont.
Joseph Cum 175
Lewis Cas 40
Thos. Grn 263
Hutchings, James Lin 118
Jesse Clr 146
Hutchingson, Saml. Bra 150
Hutchins, John Cum 166
Thomas Sco 188
Hutchinson, Archibald Fay 44
Alexr. Boo 59
Daniel Bra 143
David Bra 143
John Sco 176
John Sco 188
Saml. Boo 59
Hutchirson, Hiram Jef 9
Hutchison, Andrew Bou 124
Bobert Pen 114
Charles Gar 221
James Bou 91
John Gar 219
John Gar 225
John Hrs 309
John M. Bou 88
Joseph Lin 121
Peter Bou 91
Philip Gar 225
Robert Log 177
Saml. Bou 88
Samuel Log 177
Tho. Gar 221
Thos. Lin 121
Will, Jr Bou 89
Will, Sr Bou 89
Wm. Grn 263
Hutchuson, Saml. Bou 90
Huter, George war 267
Huton, Wm. Bra 151
Hutsil, George Bou 124
John Bou 123
Susanna Bou 124
Hutson, David Mon 358
Isaac Cal 13
Isaac Log 164
James Adr 9
Moses Fra 134
Samuel Way 355
Thomas Mon 358
Wm. Way 355
Hutspeth, Peter Mul 401
Hutterback, Benjn. Bou 89
Harmon Bou 89
Hutton, Alexander Mon 380
Benjamin Fle 79
James Fra 132
John Nel 36
Joseph Hrs 310
Samuel Fra 131
William Grp 270
Hyatt, Benjn. Lin 118
John Lin 118
Snedrick Nic 53
Willm. Lin 118
Willson Lin 118
Hyde, Snedrach Hnr 363
Hyden, Richard Knx 71
Hyitt, Frederick Lin 119
Hynes, Isaac Gra 244
Joseph Way 371
Thos. Nel 36
William Pul 149
Wm. Way 351
Wm. R. Nel 9
Hyram, Harney (see Harney, Hyram) Nic 53
Hysong, Peter Fle 79
Hyton, James Hrs 308

-- I --

Igo, Jacob Log 186
Thomas Mon 365
Igou, John Mad 246
William Mad 246
Igue, Joshua Cly 153
Iler, Daniel Ohi 88
John Gar 217
Iles, Thomas Mon 375
Iliff, John Flo 100
Imler, William Mul 399
Imnan, Edmund Wsh 301
Inabnett, Jacob Pul 154
Indicut, Aron Hrs 313
John Hrs 312
Joseph Hrs 315
Joseph Nic 51
Moses Hrs 314
Samuel Hrs 323
Thos. Hrs 314
Thos. Hrs 314
Ingard, Jonas Lew 97
Ingle, Joseph Hrs 318
Inglebright, John Ohi 83
Ingledove, William Pul 154
William Pul 154
Ingleman, Sim... Lin 122
Ingler, David Mul 404
Ingles, Thomas Bou 125
Peter Nic 51
James, Senr Bou 125
James, Jr Bou 125
Boon Bou 69
Ingles see Ungles
Inglish, Francis Gle 70
William Fle 70
William, Jur Fle 70
Ingram, Giffeth Log 164
Isaac Log 165
Jacob Log 165
James Log 181
James Log 177
James Hnd 338
Jas. Way 370
Jerry Adr 9
John Adr 9
John But 195
Joseph Log 164
Moses Cal 4
Nancy Cal 15
Saml. Sco 179
Samuel Log 165
Wiatt Hnd 328
Zadock War 265
Ingrams, Thomas Mon 371
Ingrim, Isaac Pul 154
John Bar 48
Ingrum, Arthur She 217
Arthur She 208
Ebenezer Knx 78
Saml. Bou 125
William Knx 71
Inloe, Joseph Nel 43
Inlow, Benja. Bar 25
Henry Bou 125
Jesse Nic 51
Inman, James Mul 398
Willm. Lin 122
Inmon, Elisha Jr Knx 69
Elisha, Sr Knx 69
Inmon, cont.
Thomas Knx 69
Wm. Mul 394
Inmore, Jesse War 265
Innes, Harry Fra 137
Hugh Fra 137
John Fay 17
nathl. Sco 170
Innis, Jas. Gar 217
Innman, Henry Gar 218
Inscho, Joseph Bra 149
Saml. Bra 149
Inson, Nathaniel Log 179
Instone, John Fra 138
Inyard, John Lin 122
Silas Hrd 299
Irby, Charles War 278
Isham War 278
Phillip Log 179
Willm. War 274
Irchminger, Philip She 217
Ireland, Alexr. Jef 7
Alexr. Sco 180
Andrew Bou 92
Andrew Sco 179
James Mas 252
John Sco 180
John R. Sco 180
Saml. Hnr 367
Saml. Hrd 285
Wm. Hrd 285
Irons, Jonathan Bul 179
Irven, Andrew Nic 51
David Bou 125
Wm. Bra 150
Irvin, Abraham Wsh 303
George Nic 51
James Adr 9
Jane Fay 17
Laurance Fay 17
Thomas Mul 407
William Hnr 364
Irvine, Alex Grn 265
Alexander Jes 47
Benjamin Mad 245
Christopher Mad 246
David Bou 92
David Bou 70
David C. Mad 245
Fras. Cum 184
James Jes 48
Jesse Log 193
John Bou 92
John Mer 316
John Fay 24
John Fay 22
John Clr 146
John Jes 47
John Cum 184
John, Senr Cum 184
Robert Fay 22
Samuel Mad 244
Stephen M. Bou 92
William Jes 47
William Mad 246
Wm. Cum 184
Irvins, Walter Hrs 318
Irwin, Ben Hrd 296
Isaac Hrd 296
Jas. Hrd 296
John Ohi 102
John Ohi 81
John, M.C. Woo 390
Joseph Bul 180
Mary Gar 218
Richard Wsh 301
Sterling Gar 217

Irwin, cont.
Thomas Gar 218
William Bul 180
William Fay 43
William Grn 249
William Ohi 81
Irwine, Jno. Nel 44
John Nel 44
Joseph Nel 44
Isaac, Rutledge Adr 3
Wm. War 254
Isaacs, Godfree Cly 155
Jesse She 213
John Wsh 300
Saml. Bar 33
Isacks, William Pul 154
Isbel, Daniel Mad 245
George Chr 112
Henry Chr 94
Henry Mad 245
Henry Grn 245
James Grn 261
Joseph Chr 96
Thomas Chr 94
Isbell, Henry Jes 48
Thomas Cas 42
Willm. Adr 9
Isgrig, Daniel Hrs 313
Wm. Hrs 313
Isham, Aret Cly 152
GEo Cly 152
Nicey Bou 92
William Bou 92
Ishmael, John Nic 51
Thos. Nic 51
Ishenial, Benjaman Fle 70
Isler, Jacob Wsh 344
John Ohi 79
Peter Nel 9
Isnogle, Christa. Boo 60
Isom, William Wsh 300
William Wsh 300
Ison, Charles Gar 218
Jacob Cal 13
Jacob Cal 11
Jacob, Junr Cal 11
Jacob, Jur Cal 13
James Gar 218
John Cal 13
John Gar 218
William Gar 218
Israel, Joseph Cam 28
Itson, George Log 165
Ivens, Abraham Bra 150
Saml. Bra 149
Tho. Bra 147
Ivers, James Mon 371
Ivins, Caleb Sco 179
David Mul 391
John Bou 125
Robert Sco 182
Samuel Mer 316
Izard, Nicholas Fay 22

-- J --

Jack (free negro) Fay 32
Jack, James Nel 44
John Gal 183
John Pul 154
Joseph Nel 43
Negro Gar 217
Robert Gra 240
Robert Lew 104
Jackerson, Abner Jes 47
Archer Jes 47
David Jes 48
Jarrott Jes 47
John Jes 48
Jackett, John Way 367
Jackman, Elijah Mer 316
Jane Lin 122
John Cly 157
JOhn Cum 172
Joseph Wsh 303
Mary Cum 171
Thomas Mer 316
Wm. Junr Cum 171
Wm. Senr Cum 172
Jackmon, Hannah Gar 219
Jackon, Thos. Fle 87
Jacks, John Bou 93
Richard Mad 246
William Mad 246
Jackson, Alexander Mas 298
Alexr. Sco 184
Archibald Hrs 324
Archibald War 246
Benjn. War 268
Burnell War 248
Charles Jef 7
Christopher Ohi 76
Colby Sco 169
David mad 246
Dempsey Fle 66
Ebenezer Woo 389
Elijah Cum 178
Ephraim Lin 122
Ephram War 272
Ezekiel Cum 174
Ezekl. Nel 43
Federick Bar 24
Frances F. Clr 133
Francis Woo 389
Francis She 221
Gabril Knx 80
Garnet Knx 80
George Mon 371
George Ohi 102
Henry Bra 144
Hezekiah Cum 176
Hugh Gal 183
Isaac Bar 49
Isaac Bul 180
Isaiah Bul 180
Isral Chr 60
Jacob Fle 82
James Clr 133
James Fle 88
James Knx 80
James Woo 389
James Wsh 301
James R. Bra 146
Jas. Way 365
Jesse Mul 408
Jno. Nel 44
John Bou 125
John Bra 148
John Bra 153
John Bul 180
John Cum 175
John Cum 178
John Fay 42
John Fle 66
John Fra 138
John Jef 8
John Knx 88
John Lin 122
John Lin 122
John Liv 158
John Mas 255
Jackson, cont.
John Mas 306
John Nel 43
John Pul 154
John Pul 155
John Sco 189
John She 209
John War 250
John Way 364
John Woo 400
John Wsh 300
John Wsh 301
John Wsh 303
John B. Bul 180
John C. Fra 137
John, Jr Bou 125
Jonathan Bra 144
Joseph Bou 92
Joseph Bou 93
Joseph Pul 155
Joshua Hrs 313
Josiah Clr 133
Lee War 247
Leroy Mul 401
Levi Way 361
Levy Way 363
Lewis (freeman) Fay 17
Madra Bou 93
Mary Ohi 80
Michal Lin 122
Mordica Gal 183
Moses Gal 184
Nathan Hop 378
Rebecca She 232
Reuben Fra 137
Reuben Liv 159
Robert Woo 387
Ruben Bar 51
Sam L. Log 184
Saml. Bra 148
Saml. Fle 61
Saml. Gar 218
Saml. Jef 7
Saml. Nel 41
Saml. Nel 43
Samuel Liv 157
Samuel Mas 256
Samuel Mul 399
Simon Sco 172
Thomas Bou 125
Thomas Mas 298
Thos. Bou 93
Thos. Bra 149
Thos. Fle 88
Thos. Way 365
Vincent Nel 44
Will D. Bou 69
William Bou 92
William Bou 93
William Fle 72
William Fle 70
William Wsh 300
William Wsh 300
William Wsh 303
Wilm. R. War 273
Wingate Mon 353
Wm. Adr 9
Wm. Bra 148
Wm. Fle 88
Wm. Hnr 353
Wm. Mon 361
Wm. War 267
Jaco, Theodore Sco 184
Jacob, Arnold Cal 10
Jacobs, Bennett She 212
Gilson Mas 253
Harrison Clr 133

Jacobs, cont.
Henry Liv 151
Isaac Clr 133
James She 231
Jeremiah Nel 43
John Clr 133
John Fle 83
John Mas 253
John Sco 183
Joshua Mad 244
Mordica Mas 253
Morris Mad 245
Nathaniel Log 192
Nicholas Wsh 302
Richard Mas 254
Samuel Log 187
Samuel Mas 254
Samuel She 223
Sarah Mas 253
Thomas Mad 245
William Fle 65
William Flo 95
William She 206
Zacheriah Bou 93
Jacoby, Frederic Bou 125
Jacob Bou 125
John Bou 125
Ralph Bou 125
Jacoway, Archabald Knx 71
Jacs, John Log 183
Jains, Mary Flo 100
Jamason, Elizabith War 267
Jamerson, Alexander Jes 46
George Jes 47
Henry Log 172
Robert Log 189
Sally Log 185
William Jes 47
William, Jr Jes 48
William, Sr Jes 48
James(free negro) Fay 30
James, Benjamin Mon 363
Berryman Mas 254
Charles Jef 7
Daniel Fra 138
Daniel Hnr 359
Daniel Mul 397
David Cal 7
Foster ohi 82
George Mad 244
George Mul 392
Gideon Hop 378
Henry Pul 154
John Bou 92
John Fle 61
John Fle 86
John Mad 246
John Pul 154
John Pul 155
John She 240
John Wsh 300
John B. Bou 92
John, Jur Mad 246
John, Junr Ohi 79
John, Senr Ohi 77
Jos. Cly 152
Joseph Nel 44
Martin She 241
Mary Bul 180
Newman Way 371
Patsey War 256
Philip Log 170
Robert Mad 246
Samuel Flo 97
Samuel Mer 317
Samuel Mul 399
James, cont.
Tabias Mon 360
Tho. Bar 46
Thomas Hnd 342
Thomas Hnr 369
Thomas Mas 254
Thomas Mas 255
Thomas Nel 44
William But 195
Willis Log 182
Wm. Cas 43
Wm. Jef 7
Wm. Sco 171
Jameson, David Fle 74
Elizabeth Mad 244
Garrard Bar 46
Henry Fra 138
James Lin 122
John Fay 55
John Fle 74
John Mon 360
John Nel 44
Margaret Mad 244
Robert Chr 84
Robert Mad 244
Robt. Bar 32
Thomas Mon 359
Thomas, Senr Mon 360
Wm. Mon 355
Jamison, David Bou 93
David Bou 93
George Bar 32
James Gra 240
James Mon 359
Jas. Bar 54
Jas. Way 368
Jno. M. Bou 93
John Bar 54
John Bou 93
John Bou 93
John Chr 87
John Gra 241
Martha Cum 171
Saml. Bou 69
Saml. J. Bou 93
Samuel Gra 241
William Clr 146
Janes, Benjamin Wsh 303
Jas. Way 359
John War 251
John Wsh 303
John Wsh 303
Lydia Flo 95
Peter War 251
Polly Clr 133
Thomas Wsh 303
William Flo 96
Wm. Mon 375
January, B. James Fay 17
Ephram Jes 47
John Jes 48
John Pul 154
Samuel Mas 302
Thomas Fay 17
Jaquess, Isaac Hrs 324
John Hrs 314
Jarboe, Ann Wsh 300
George Nel 43
James Wsh 301
John Wsh 300
John Wsh 302
John Wsh 302
John R. Wsh 302
Joshua Wsh 300
Robert Grn 258
Walter Wsh 302
Jarman, John Mad 246
Jarman, cont.
Thomas, Jur Mad 245
Jarral, Isam Bar 46
Jarrard, Joel Bre 167
Thomas Bre 167
Jarratt, Danel Cal 9
Thomas Cal 9
Jarrel, James Fra 137
Jarrell, Whitfield Bou 93
Jarret, Joel Bre 157
Nathaniel Mon 372
Jarrett, David Liv 150
Samuel Bre 167
Jarves, Daniel Fle 78
Peter Knx 88
Jarvice, Solomam Fle 80
Jarvis, Edward Grn 260
Edward Mul 403
Eliphalet Grn 256
Jabes Adr 9
John Grn 256
Robert Hrs 307
Thomas Pul 154
William Mad 245
William Pen 110
Jasper, Abraham Pul 155
Andrew Pul 155
John Pul 155
Nicholas Pul 155
Jasup, Anna Bou 125
Jay, John Bar 36
Jazuns, Jesse Adr 9
Jeane, Berry Adr 8
Jeans, Berry Adr 9
David Adr 9
David, Sr Adr 9
John Jef 8
Joseph Jef 8
Samuel Mas 254
Wm. Adr 9
Jeater, Elijah Jef 8
Jefferas, Patsy Bar 52
Jefferies, David Hrd 286
Thos. Hrd 286
Jeffers, Anne Mad 244
henry Mon 376
Wm. Gar 217
Wm. Gar 218
Jefferson, J. Jestener Mas 255
James Mas 254
Samuel Mas 255
Jeffery, James Chr 86
Jeffres, James Grp 272
Rebecka Mad 245
Ambrose Fra 138
Anderson Wsh 302
Gowen Jef 8
James Wsh 302
Jeffry Grn 251
John Wsh 344
Moses Nel 44
Nathaniel Wsh 302
Robert She 215
Swepston Hnd 345
William Wsh 302
Jeffs, James Wsh 344
Jefreys, John Fay 53
Jefryes, John Jes 47
Thomas Jes 46
Jell, Jesse Nel 42
Jellison, James Fra 138
Jemason, Elizabeth War 251
Wm. War 255
Jemerson, Abraham She 239
Jemison, Isaac She 217
Margaret Mon 353

Jemmersen, Riley Log 175
Jenes, W. Read Pul 155
Jenings, James Bre 161
James, Sr. Bre 162
James Chr 88
John Chr 87
John Chr 87
Lewis Chr 89
Jenkens, Wm. Cas 40
Jenkins, Amos Mul 401
Barth Cal 4
Charles Jes 48
Edwd. Nel 43
Edwd. Way 373
Ezekiel Jes 46
Ezekiel Jes 47
Henry Sco 174
Ignatius Hrd 281
James Wsh 302
Jno. Hrd 290
Jno. Hrd 291
Jno. Hrd 292
John Bre 167
John Hrd 301
Joseph Bar 42
Margt. Nel 43
Murwood Fay 29
Norris Nel 43
Richard Wsh 302
Thomas Woo 381
Thos. C. Sco 174
Walter Mas 256
Will C. Bou 93
William But 195
William Hrd 302
William Knx 86
Wm. Sco 171
Jenning, Patsey Mon 369
Jennings, A. Alexr. Gar 219
Augustine Gar 219
Diana Gal 183
Elnathan Jef 27
Haslet Nel 43
James Chr 88
Jesse Gar 218
John Gar 219
Johnathan Gal 184
Joseph Cas 46
Lewis Nel 43
Osias Gar 217
Stephen Ohi 86
Thomas Mon 352
Wm. Cas 48
Wm. Jnr Gar 219
Wm. Snr Gar 219
Garrat Cal 16
Jenny (free woman) Fay 29
Jentry, David Cly 151
John Chr 89
Moses Clr 133
Richd. Adr 9
Robt. Adr 9
William Way 362
Jeppison, Jurdan Fay 53
Jeremiah, Thomas Mas 254
Jerome, Battis Flo 96
Jerrald, Elisha Cam 31
Jerrell, Demsey Liv 149
Jerrigan, Felix Cal 17
Jeter, Benjn. Grn 252
Jett, Elijah Wsh 302
James Nic 51
John Bra 144
John War 254
Joseph Pul 154
Mary Mad 246
Porter Bra 148
Jett, cont.
Presley Jef 8
Stephen Mad 246
Jevidan, John Gal 1[illegible]3
Jewel, Bazil Fra 1[illegible]
Chas. Bar 29
John Bar 53
Jonathan Fay 39
Seth Nel 41
William Fra 138
Wm. Bar 41
Wm. Bar 53
Jewell, David Jef 7
Enock Nel 44
George Gal 184
Jesse Nel 44
John Jes 47
Joseph Cum 170
Sanford Nel 43
Smallwood Jef 7
Thos. Cum 170
Will. She 226
Jewit, John Mon 361
Jhonson, Lewis Fle 61
Jiles, John Bar 36
Jimason, John War 268
Willm. War 268
Jimerson, Samuel Knx 86
Jimison, Alexr. Gar 218
Josiah Log 181
Thos. Jnr. Gar 217
Thos. Snr Gar 217
Jimmisan, Andrew Hrs 313
Jinken, Rachel Bra 145
Jinkens, Elijah Mon 362
Welliford Hop 371
Jinkins, Abel She 201
Andrew Hrs 324
Ann Bar 48
Barth, Jur Cal 9
David Bar 45
David Gar 218
Jacob Bar 45
James Bar 30
Jeremiah BAr 45
Jonathan Gar 218
Martha But 195
Mary Nic 52
Mathue Cam 29
Nancy Bar 43
Nathaniel Cal 17
Philip, Jr Bar 30
Philip, Sen BAr 19
Shadrick Cal 8
William Fay 43
Wm. Bar 42
Wm. Cam 29
Wm. Junr Bar 42
Jinnings, Daniel Mer 341
Israel Clr 133
James Clr 133
James Clr 133
Thomas Pul 154
William Mer 317
Job, Thomas She 227
Jobson, Jonathan Fay 34
Joe (freeman) Fay 21
Johes, Thomas Senr Mon 383
Johis, Francis Mon 383
John (freeman) Fay 24
John, Abm. Sco 186
Daniel Sco 186
David Log 163
John Mas 254
Jonathan Sco 181
Johnes, John Mer 317
Johns, Elizabeth Gar 217
Johns, cont.
George She 211
Henry Hrd 300
Jacob Cly 159
James Jes 46
Thomas Flo 96
William Jes 47
Johnsan, John Cly 150
Johnsay, Joshua Hrd 284
Johnson, Aaron Knx 68
Adam Sco 191
Alexander Liv 156
Andrew Boo 60
Andrew Bou 93
Andrew Cam 30
Andrew Flo 95
Andrew Hrd 283
Andrew Sco 168
Andrew, Jun Pul 154
Andrew, Sr Pul 154
Anson Jef 8
Arter FLe 63
Bailey Sco 187
Benja. Flo 95
Benjaman Fle 68
Benjamin Chr 115
Benjamin Fay 22
Benjm. Bou 93
Benjn. Boo 60
Benjn. Mon 355
Benjn. C. War 281
Benone Fay 22
Catey Mad 245
Cave Boo 60
Charles Chr 62
Charles Sco 186
Clement Wsh 300
Daniel Fra 137
Daniel Gal 184
Daniel Knx 83
Danl. Hrd 284
David Chr 83
David Fra 137
David Hrd 283
David Knx 72
David Knx 80
David Lew 102
David Mon 379
Delmus Chr 75
Dianna Clr 133
Duglis Chr 91
Ebenezer Fle 71
Eleaser, Jr Lew 102
Eleaser, Sr Lew 102
Elias Flo 95
Elisha Bul 180
Elisha Hrd 292
Eliza Jef 7
Ephraim Bul 180
Francis War 281
Gabl. Sco 170
Gabriel J. Jef 29
George Flo 95
George Jef 8
George Mon 359
Henry Mad 245
Henry Wsh 301
Hugh Chr 84
Hugh Mad 244
Hugh Mon 356
Ignatius S. Wsh 301
Isaac Fay 22
Isaac Grn 254
Isaac Hnd 336
Isaac Hrd 283
Isaac Jes 47
Isaac Mad 245

Johnson, cont.		
Isaac	Sco	167
Isaac	Sco	167
Isaac	Sco	182
Isaac	She	231
Isam	Nic	51
Isham	Grn	254
Jack	Hrd	293
Jacob	Fle	92
Jacob	Flo	96
Jacob	Hrs	321
Jacob	Hrs	322
Jacob	Mon	371
Jacob	Sco	180
Jacob	Sco	182
James	Chr	114
James	Clr	133
James	Fle	92
James	Gal	184
James	Grn	262
James	Hnr	367
James	Jes	47
James	Jes	47
James	Knx	76
James	Lin	122
James	Liv	160
James (Scarlet's-son)	Mad	244
James	Mad	246
James	Mon	354
James	Mon	371
James	Nic	51
James	Nic	52
James	Pul	155
James	Pul	155
James	Sco	187
James	Sco	190
James	Sco	193
James	She	228
James, Jun	Mad	246
James M.	Chr	53
James W.	Fay	22
Jandy	War	261
Jedediah	War	264
Jeptha	War	257
Jeremiah	Gal	184
Jesse	Hrd	285
Jesse	Mad	245
Jessy	Chr	86
Jno.	Lew	96
Jno.	Lew	98
John	Bou	93
John	Bou	92
John	Cal	11
John	Chr	57
John	Chr	67
John	Chr	67
John	Chr	114
John	Clr	133
John	Cly	158
John	Fay	12
John	Fay	30
John	Flo	95
John	Flo	95
John	Gal	184
John	Gal	197
John	Hnr	366
John	Hrs	324
John	Knx	71
John	Lew	98
John	Mad	244
John	Mon	348
John	Nic	51
John	Nic	51
John	Ohi	101
John	Sco	175
John	She	221

Johnson, cont.		
John	She	237
John	War	256
John A.	War	273
John J.	Sco	186
John M.	Gal	184
Jonathan	Nic	51
Jonathan	Sco	175
Jsoeph	Bou	92
Joseph	Fle	72
Joseph	Knx	75
Joseph	Sco	169
Laban	Hrs	315
Larkins	hnr	365
Laurance	Hnr	365
Levi	Sco	170
Lewis	Boo	60
Luke	Lin	122
Luke	Lin	122
Macum	Chr	57
Majar	Mad	245
Marcus	Ohi	103
Margaret	War	280
Martha	Hrd	289
Martin	Clr	133
Mary	Fay	22
Mason	Nic	51
Mat	Hnr	366
Mathew	Hrd	282
Matthew	Mad	244
Matthew	Sco	168
Meredith	War	280
Meridith	War	266
Michael	Knx	72
Michal	Cum	183
Michall	Lin	122
Moses	Bul	179
Moses	Lin	122
Mosis	War	256
Nathan	War	244
Neel	Cam	31
Nelly	Bou	92
Patrick	Flo	95
Patrick	Flo	96
Peter	Fle	92
Philip	Clr	133
Philip	Mad	245
Phillip	Bul	180
Pitway	War	264
Pleasant	Cly	157
Prissilla	Grp	275
Rebecca	Hrs	319
Richard, Capt	Mad	245
Richd. M.	Sco	193
Robert	Bul	180
Robert	Knx	76
Robert	Mad	244
Robert	Pul	154
Robert, Jr	Fra	138
Robert, Senr	Sco	193
Robt.	Boo	60
Robt.	Hrd	297
Robt. Jur	Sco	193
Sally	Mad	246
Saml.	Boo	60
Saml.	War	244
Saml.	War	273
Saml.	War	279
Samuel	Bul	179
Samuel	Jes	46
Samuel	Mon	374
Sanford,	Hnr	365
Sarah	Est	8
Sarah	Mon	350
Scarlet	Mad	244
Simpson	Fay	22
Smith	Lew	102

Johnson, cont.		
Susanah	Boo	60
Thomas	Adr	9
Thomas	Jef	7
Thomas	Knx	79
Thomas	Knx	79
Thomas	Knx	80
Thomas	Liv	150
Thomas	Mad	244
Thomas	Mon	355
Thomas	Sco	175
Thomas, Sr	Hnr	365
Thos.	Cly	154
Thos.	Flo	95
Thos.	Hrd	295
Thos.	Hrd	297
Thos.	Hrd	303
Thos.	Sco	175
Thos.	Sco	187
Thos.	War	280
Torgis	War	256
William	Bou	93
William	Cal	7
William	Chr	57
William	Chr	72
William	Chr	72
William	Chr	85
William	Chr	86
William	Clr	133
William	Fay	22
William	Flo	96
William	Gra	241
William	Hrs	312
William	Knx	74
William	Knx	81
William	Lin	122
William	Mad	245
William	Mad	246
William	Sco	193
William	Wsh	301
Willm.	Sco	169
Willm.	Sco	180
Willm.	Sco	182
Wm.	Hrd	284
Wm (man of colour)	Jef	30
Wm.	Mon	355
Wm.	Nic	51
Wm.	War	249
Yerles	Sco	186
Zachariah	Wsh	344
Zepha	Cal	18
Johnsten, David	She	203
Johnston, Abrm	Nel	43
Absalon	Cal	12
Adam	But	195
Alexander	Est	5
Alexander	She	240
Andrew	Cas	47
Anthony	Mas	254
Archibald	Mon	255
Arthur	Bar	32
Arthur	She	219
Asa	Grn	254
Baily	Mas	254
Barton	Bar	38
Benjamin	Mas	255
Benjamin	Mul	391
Benjamin	She	200
Charles	Gar	218
Charles	Mas	253
Coart	Mas	253
Daniel	Cas	47
David	Fra	137
David	Log	178
David	She	203
David	Woo	387

Johnston, cont.
Edward, Junr Fle 89
Edward, Senr Fle 89
Edwd. Gar 219
Elias Cas 46
Elijah Fle 89
Elizabeth Hnd 330
Elizabeth Woo 387
Francies Hnd 334
G. John Mas 306
Geo. Cum 173
George Log 180
George Nel 44
Henry Bar 21
Henry Mas 255
Henry Nel 42
Henry Woo 395
Hugh Mas 254
Isaac Bar 46
Isaac Fra 137
Isaac Woo 394
Jacob Cas 42
Jacob Cas 46
Jacob Mul 389
James Bou 70
James Bra 149
James Clr 133
James Fle 87
James Fra 137
James Fra 138
James Log 191
James Log 194
James Mer 342
James Mas 254
James Mas 256
James Ohi 84
James She 210
James She 215
Jerry Grn 266
Job Gar 219
John Bar 24
John Bra 146
John Bre 167
John Cal 16
John Cas 47
John Gar 219
John Gar 219
John Grn 254
John Grn 262
John Hrs 311
John Hrs 312
John Mas 255
John Mas 255
John Mas 306
John Nel 42
John She 203
John She 207
John D. Woo 390
Jonathan Mas 253
Joseph But 195
Joseph Cas 48
Joseph (negro) Hnr 359B
Lanty She 236
Leond. Nel 44
Lydia She 234
Martha Mer 342
Math Nel 44
Mathew Bar 38
Mathw. Nel 43
Moses Ohi 76
Nancy Nel 44
Nathan Log 162
Nelly Bou 93
Peter Nel 43
Peter Nel 44
Peter She 210
Philip She 206

Johnston, cont.
Philip She 242
Ralph But 195
Robert Bou 125
Robert Mer 317
Robert Mer 317
Robert Nel 43
Robt. Bar 29
Rueben Way 374
Sam. Bou 125
Saml. Nel 42
Saml. Way 351
Samuel Lin 122
Samuel Mer 317
Semela Hnd 334
Shabah Log 186
Soloman Cas 46
Susanna Bar 43
Tho. Bar 43
Thomas Bou 93
Thomas Log 196
Thomas She 217
Thomas Woo 396
Thos. Bou 125
Thos. Cum 167
Thos. Hnr 359B
Thos. Nel 44
Thos. Way 351
Thos. Jr Hnr 365
W. John Gar 218
William Fra 136
William Fra 136
William Grn 266
William Log 196
William Mas 254
William Mas 255
William She 209
William Woo 390
William S. She 217
Wm. Cum 175
Wm. Cum 182
Wm. Gar 219
Wm. She 236
Zachariah Cas 46
Johson, John Grp 270
Joice, George She 215
Thomas Jef 7
Joiner, Jonathan Liv 158
Rebecca Cly 146
William Chr 61
Jolley, Boling War 249
David Nic 51
Stephen War 249
Jolliff, James Bar 54
Richd. Bar 54
Jolly, Peter Pen 115
Jolson, Thomas Cas 42
Jones, Abraham Bar 27
Abraham Fay 46
Abram War 267
Alexander Pul 155
Alice Jef 7
Allen Adr 9
Allen Cas 44
Allen Mas 253
Allen Mer 316
Ambrose Flo 95
Ambrose Lin 122
Ames Chr 70
Amos Lew 98
Andrew Cal 15
Andrew Lew 99
Andrew Liv 156
Aquilla Hrd 289
Arther Cas 48
Balaam Wsh 301
Bartholemew Log 185

Jones, cont.
Benjamin Bou 93
Benjamin Cal 7B
Benjamin Hnr 353
Benjamin, Ser Rck 163
Benjn. War 245
Bernard Hrd 286
Briton Chr 111
Catharine Fay 22
Caty Jes 47
Charity Log 185
Charles Adr 9
Charles Bou 93
Charles Bul 179
Charles Cum 178
Charles Hnr 367
Charles Mon 369
Charls Cal 8
Charls Cal 10
Claybourn Cum 178
Daniel Hnd 328
Daniel War 252
Danl. Hnr 364
David Cal 8
David Cum 185
David Est 8
David Fay 35
David Grn 249
David Hop 378
David Lin 122
David Mad 245
David Mer 317
David Nel 43
Drury Nic 51
Dumas Hrs 314
Edmond Knx 90
Edward Jef 7
Edward Jef 8
Edward She 198
Elija Fle 63
Elijah Bar 27
Elijah Bar 42
Elijah Grn 249
Elijah Knx 86
Elijah Rck 163
Elisha Fle 63
Elizabeth She 240
Elizabeth War 243
Ellender Fle 76
Elliot Way 366
Enoch Grn 249
Erasmas Fra 137
Even Lin 122
Ezekiel Pul 155
Felding Hnd 328
Fleming Bou 92
Fleming Cum 178
Foster Mad 244
Frederick Chr 80
Gabriel Mad 244
Gabriel Ohi 91
Gaden Bou 93
George Bul 179
George Cas 38
George Gal 183
George Gar 217
Geo. W. Hrd 286
George Hrs 310
George Sco 175
George Way 372
Gorey Hrd 295
Griffeth Mas 254
Haden Mer 317
Hampton Hnd 334
Hansell War 265
Henry Cal 8
Henry Cal 12

Jones, cont.
Henry Chr 91
Henry Hnd 334
Henry H. War 256
Hudson Cam 30
Hugh Fle 70
Hugh Mas 253
Humphrey Mad 246
Ignatious Fle 64
Irvine Mad 246
Isaac Bou 125
Isaac Cly 157
Isaac Cly 159
Isaac Grn 253
Isaac Hrd 285
Isham Mon 373
Israel Hnr 359B
Iven Hrs 309
Jacob Bar 22
Jacob Bou 93
Jacob Bou 93
Jacob Nic 51
James Adr 9
James Bou 125
James Cas 42
James Chr 89
James Cum 179
James Fle 69
James Fle 75
James Gra 238
James Knx 71
James Mas 253
James Mer 317
James Mer 317
James mer 342
James Nel 43
James Ohi 92
James Pul 155
James Pul 155
James Sco 176
James She 229
James War 247
James, Esqr Rck 159
James, Jur Rck 164
James W. Bou 69
Jams. Adr 9
Jane Cum 166
Jane Fay 29
Jas. Way 353
Jas. Way 365
Jesse Mas 256
Jessee Cal 12
Jiles Clr 133
Joanna Mas 253
John Boo 60
John Bou 93
John Bul 180
John Cal 14
John Cal 19
John Cas 37
John Chr 89
John Cly 157
John Est 8
John Fay 17
John Fay 38
John Fle 69
John Fle 82
John Fle 85
John Flo 95
John Gal 183
John Gar 217
John Gar 218
John Grn 248
John Hnr 359A
John Hrs 322
John Jef 7
John Jef 7

Jones, cont.
John Jef 8
John Jef 8
John Knx 67
John Knx 78
John Knx 80
John Knx 90
John Lew 95
John Mas 253
John Mer 317
John Mer 317
John Mer 317
John Mer 317
John Mon 351
John Mon 379
John Nel 42
John Nic 51
John Pul 155
John Pul 155
John Sco 172
John Sco 179
John She 221
John She 240
John War 258
John War 265
John Way 369
John A. Cal 11
John Cr. Fay 22
John H. Sco 191
John R. Wsh 301
John, Jnr Gar 217
John, Jun Cas 42
John, Snr Lin 122
Jolly Cal 19
Jona. Hnr 368
Jonas Gal 184
Jonathan Cas 39
Jonathn. Cum 185
Jos. Sco 193
Joseph Bou 125
Joseph Est 3
Joseph Gal 183
Joseph Jes 41
Joseph Mon 383
Joshua Mad 244
Joshua Pen 115
Joshua Pul 155
Joshua She 220
Joshua Way 361
Joshua T. Way 356
Josse Bul 179
Juramiah Chr 97
Lemuel Cum 176
Leonard Wsh 301
Levi Fle 76
Lewis Bou 93
Lewis Chr 85
Lewis Fle 77
Lewis Hrs 309
Lewis Pul 155
Lowry She 222
Lunsford She 208
Martin Gal 183
Martin Wsh 300
Mary Chr 90
Mason Ohi 91
Mathew Clr 133
Mathy Clr 133
Maza Hrs 311
Michael Cas 46
Michall Bar 22
Mordecai Log 193
Morgan Grn 245
Moses Cly 154
Moses Hnr 359A
Moses Mer 317
Moses Nic 51

Jones, cont.
Mosias Mad 245
N. Josephus Mas 253
Nancy Flo 96
Peggy Bul 179
Peter Mul 391
Peter Mul 400
Peter Sco 179
Philip Gra 238
Philip War 254
Phillip Log 173
Price Jef 8
Rachal Chr 65
Randolf Fle 80
Randolph Fay 29
Rebecca Clr 133
Redmon Wsh 301
Richard Chr 92
Richard Hnd 348
Richard Liv 154
Richard Mon 359
Richard C. Fra 136
Ricd. Log 171
Richd. Gar 217
Richd. War 265
Robert Adr 19
Robert Fay 47
Robert Fra 137
Robert Grn 255
Robert Jef 8
Robert Knx 90
Robert Mad 246
Roger Fay 35
Ruth Cly 153
Saml. Cas 42
Saml. Grn 264
Samuel Cal 5
Samuel Chr 85
Samuel Clr 146
Samuel Fay 48
Samuel FLe 81
Samuel Mer 317
Samuel B. Chr 85
Stafford Sco 179
Stephen Cum 176
Stephen Fle 81
Stephen Fle 89
Stephen Fle 92
Stephen Knx 87
Stephin Fle 81
Sturdy Wsh 301
Susanna Jef 25
Tarlton War 254
Tholby Hnr 365
Thomas Bou 70
Thomas Bou 125
Thomas Bre 168
Thomas Cal 3
Thomas Chr 65
Thomas Clr 133
Thomas Gra 238
Thomas Gra 239
Thomas Hnd 331
Thomas Hnr 354
Thomas Knx 66
Thomas Mas 253
Thomas Mas 256
Thomas Mon 353
Thomas Ohi 92
Thomas Rck 161
Thomas Sco 179
Thomas She 229
Thomas E. Cas 40
Thomas (I) Gal 184
Thompson N. Ohi 95
Thornton Mer 317
Thos. Adr 9

Jones, cont.
Thos. Fle 61
Thos. Hnr 359B
Thos. (A) Gar 183
Thos. Jr Bou 125
W. Thomas Mas 253
Walter Log 183
Wiley Way 364
Will She 221
William Bou 92
William Bou 92
William Bou 93
William Bou 125
William Bre 167
William Bul 179
William Cal 6
William Cal 10
William Chr 65
William Cly 156
William Fle 76
William Flo 95
William Flo 95
William Fra 137
William Gra 242
William Grn 252
William Hnd 345
William Hnr 369
William Hop 378
William Jes 47
William Knx 76
William Knx 90
William Lin 122
William (Foster's-Son) Mad 244
William Mad 245
William Mas 255
William Mas 300
William Ohi 97
William Pen 109
William Wsh 300
William B. Fle 81
William, Sen Mad 245
Willm. Sco 170
Wherton Bou 125
Wm. Bar 36
Wm. Bar 24
Wm. Bar 43
Wm. Cal 15
Wm. Cas 44
Wm. Cum 178
Wm. Grn 248
Wm. Hrd 285
Wm. Jef 7
Wm. Jef 8
Wm. Mon 353
Wm. Way 370
Wyatt Wsh 301
Zachary Pul 155
Zadock Cas 38
Jonette, John Sco 176
Jonson, David Hrs 321
Janes Hrs 321
John Hrs 320
Wm. Hrs 320
Jonston, Ann Fay 55
James Fay 42
James Fay 59
John Fay 59
William Fay 55
Johnstone, Nelson Pen 116
William Pen 116
William, Sr Pen 113
Jordan, Adam Ohi 101
Adam Ohi 104
Archibald Hnd 348
James Ohi 84
John Jef 7

Jordan, cont.
Nancey Rck 163
Wm. Hrd 292
Wm. Hrd 303
Jorden, Saml. Bar 19
Jordin, William Grp 276
Jordon, George Fra 137
Jerard Fle 63
John, Junr Fay 17
Samuel Bre 161
Sharshall Clr 133
Thomas Mas 255
Thos. War 280
William Fle 86
Wm. War 280
Joseph, Eli Bre 164
Jesse Wsh 300
Jona. Hrd 291
Reson Cly 155
Uriah Bre 166
Wingate Fay 12
Josephs, William Flo 96
Joslen, Bejamin Cas 37
John Cas 44
Jas. Gar 219
Jost, Christian Flo 105
Jouitt, Matthew H. Fra 138
Jourdan, Ganett Mer 317
Peter Mer 317
Peter Mer 317
Jourdin, John Chr 87
Jourdon, Patrick Mer 317
John Log 167
Journey, Wm. Hrs 317
Joyce, Thomas Jef 25
Jud, Sally Fay 22
Juda, Samuel Mon 350
Judd, Daniel Mas 255
Daniel Mas 255
James Mas 255
John Adr 9
John Mas 256
Rolund Adr 9
William Bou 93
William Mas 255
Judge, Nancy Hrs 311
Judient, Samuel Flo 95
Judkins, David Cam 33
Joel Bou 125
Judy, free woman Fay 17
Judy, David Clr 133
Henry V. Clr 133
John J. Clr 133
Martin Clr 133
Winepark Clr 133
Juell, Peter Clr 133
Juet, David Bou 93
Juett, William Hrs 321
Jump, John Pen 109
John Pen 111
Marget Pen 115
Thos. War 271
William Pen 115
Junkin, Noble Boo 60
Junkins, James Bou 93
Jurdain, David Mul 394
Jurdy, Frederick Fay 59
Justice, Ezra Flo 95
Justin, George Flo 95
James Cam 32
Jno. Lew 104
John Flo 95
John Flo 95
John Flo 96
John War 273
Simeon Flo 96
Simon Flo 95

Justice, cont.
Simon Flo 96
Wade Flo 96
William Flo 95
William Flo 95
Juttle, James Way 374
Juvinall, David Nic 52

-- K --

Kafferty, James Mon 380
Kalion, Jacob Fle 73
Micheal Fle 73
Kampton, Kyser Jef 26
Kanaday, John Way 357
Jos. Boo 60
Kanatyer, Palser Way 374
Kandle, William Mas 251
Karr, George Mad 243
Henry Mad 243
James Mad 243
Robert Liv 156
Thomas Mad 241
William Liv 156
William Mad 243
William, Sr Mad 243
Zelfey Hop 378
Kates, Ephram Chr 83
Joshua Chr 115
Kaughey, Thos. Hrs 323
Kavanaugh, Charles Mad 243
Philip Mad 243
William Mad 243
Kay, John Fay 22
John, Jr Jes 48
Robert Fay 22
Kaye, August Jef 27
Kays, Geo. Bar 46
George Gar 216
John Gar 216
John Gra 241
William Gra 241
Wm. Bar 46
Kealough, James Mon 365
Keams, Danl. Nel 45
Kean, C. Joseph Gar 199
James Nel 45
Patrick Nel 45
Keas, Isaac Clr 133
James Clr 133
Keath, Abner Mul 401
Alexander Mul 401
Gabrial Mon 366
Henry Mul 401
James Mul 395
John Mul 395
Oney Mad 241
Uriah Mon 366
William Mul 389
William Mul 395
Keathley, John Mon 374
John Mon 374
John, Senr Mon 374
Keaton, Abraham Mon 347
Barnet Mon 358
Hezekiah Fra 139
John Mon 362
John Mon 373
Joseph Mon 362
Joseph Mon 373
William Hnr 353
Kecton, William Flo 96
Kedall, Aaron Mas 252
Kee, Henry Mad 241
Zachias Hrs 318

Keff, Reuben Mad 241
  Thomas Mad 241
Keel, Fredrick Cal 5
  Isaac Ohi 75
  Jacob Ohi 70
  James Mer 317
  Jesse Ohi 70
Keele, Abraham Wsh 298
Keeler, David Hop 373
Keelin, Ambrose Mad 242
  Leonard Mad 242
Keeling, Benjamin Wsh 299
  Benjn. Adr 10
  James Wsh 299
  John Chr 56
  John Wsh 299
  Thomas Wsh 299
  William Wsh 299
Keen, benjn. Sco 167
  Flemmer Lin 123
  Francis Fay 29
  Franciss Lin 123
  John Cum 183
  John Fay 29
  John Lin 123
  Joseph Hrs 208
  Nathl. Grn 266
  Nicholas Cum 183
  Oliver Fay 29
  Rachall Lin 123
  Sampson Cum 183
  Sanford Fay 29
Keenam, William Sco 178
Keenan, Hugh Boo 60
Keene, charles Sco 182
  Hilly Sco 178
  Hopewell Sco 175
  Mary Sco 177
  Richd. H. Sco 167
  Richd. L. Sco 167
  Saml. Sco 182
  Vachel Sco 177
Keener, Abriham Chr 109
Keeney, James Pul 156
  Joseph Cly 151
  Moses Pul 156
  Peter Pul 156
Keenon, Elizatth. Bou 70
Keens, John Cam 30
  Joseph Cam 30
Keer, John K. Gal 183
Keete, Georg. Fle 90
Keeth, Anderson Grp 269
Keeting, Wm. Jef 30
Keets, Thomas Fra 139
Keewood, Berry Knx 63
Kehoon, James Adr 10
Keiney, William Fle 74
Keir, Michael Hnr 355
Keiry, Henry Cum 165
  Nathaneel Cum 169
  Wilson Cum 169
Keiser, John Fay 17
Keisinger, Andrew Hrd 292
  Isaac Hrd 283
  Jacob Hrd 286
  Jacob, Senr Hrd 285
  Jos. Hrd 285
  Solm. Hrd 300
  Solo. Junr Hrd 285
Keith, Adam Nic 51
  Alexr. Hrd 298
  Alexr. Sco 173
  EDward Bou 95
  George Fra 139
  Isaac (B) Fle 91
  Jacob Hrd 284
Keith, cont.
  Jacob Nic 51
  Jarret Bou 94
  John (B) Fle 91
  John Ohi 92
  Jona. Hrd 292
  Phillip Nic 51
  Richard Bou 95
  Thomas Mas 252
  Walter Bou 94
Keithly, Joseph Bou 95
Kele, Robt. Cam 31
Keler, John Hrs 323
Kelfos, Frederick Jef 6
Kell, Jane Liv 159
Kellam, George Bre 162
Kellar, George Mer 342
  Isaac Fra 139
  Jacob Jes 48
  John Jes 48
  Valuntine Mer 317
Keller, Abm. Jef 17
  Abraham Bou 94
  Andrew Pul 156
  Benjamin Ohi 73
  Devault Pul 156
  George Gra 237
  John Gra 237
  John Jef 6
  Jos. Hnr 352
  Joseph Jef 7
  Samuel Ohi 78
Kelleson, Wm. Cas 43
Kelley, Andrew Ohi 100
  Beal Log 164
  Daniel Adr 10
  Daniel Jes 49
  David Ohi 90
  Elias Way 357
  Henry Fay 17
  James Hrs 323
  Jas. Lew 95
  John Flo 96
  John Flo 96
  John Jef 6
  John Jef 7
  John Pul 157
  Martin Grn 253
  Polley Mad 243
  Robert Jes 49
  Salley Flo 96
  Thomas Flo 96
  Thomas Jef 28
  Thos. War 249
  William Bou 94
  William Log 164
Kelli, Alexandre Grp 270
Kellingbarger, Joseph Bre 165
Kelliss, C. M. Hnr 359
  Cleon Hnr 368
Kellsy, Henry Lew 97
Kelly, Andrew Mad 241
  Anne E. Hnd 332
  Anthony Fle 85
  Beckham Lin 123
  Benjamin Chr 109
  Betsy Wsh 299
  Charity Mad 242
  Charls Cal 8
  Daniel Cal 18
  Daniel Fra 138
  Danl. Bar 43
  Danl. Hnr 362
  Eleanor Gal 183
  Elijah Gra 241
  Elizabeth Fay 12
Kelly, cont.
  Emanuel Mon 364
  Francis FLe 69
  Fredck. Nel 45
  Fredrck. Nel 46
  George Ohi 96
  George Way 355
  Gideon Hrd 300
  Griffin Sco 167
  Henry Mas 251
  Henry Mon 361
  Isaac Lin 123
  Jacob Hnr 368
  Jaems Bou 215
  Jaems Fle 69
  James Hnr 362
  James Sco 171
  Jane Mad 241
  jas. Bar 37
  Jiles Bar 50
  Jno. Lew 95
  John Fle 90
  John Gal 183
  John Hnr 361
  John Hnr 362
  John Pul 156
  JOhn Way 353
  John Wsh 298
  John Wsh 299
  John, Jnr Gra 241
  John, Senr Gra 241
  John, Sr Hnr 362
  Jonathan Knx 86
  Joseph Clr 133
  Joseph Fle 67
  Joseph Fle 78
  Joseph Pul 157
  Joshua Hrd 300
  Josiph Chr 110
  Mary Mon 377
  Mathew Grn 245
  Matthias Knx 86
  Mordicai Clr 133
  Moses Bou 95
  Nicholas Wsh 298
  Peter Cal 15
  Reubin Lin 123
  ruth Fay 44
  Saml. Bar 32
  Saml. Hnr 362
  Samuel Clr 134
  Samuel Mad 242
  Samuel Pul 156
  Thomas Chr 84
  Thomas Fle 89
  Thomas Wsh 299
  Thos. Nic 51
  Veland Mas 252
  Vincen Fay 41
  William Bou 68
  William Bou 125
  William Mas 251
  William Mer 318
  William Mer 318
  William Nel 9
  William Nel 46
  William Sco 191
  William L. Mer 342
  Wm. Lew 95
Kelsey, John Bar 26
  Wm. Bra 152
Kelson, Andrew Adr 10
Kelso, Charles Hrs 313
  Jane Cum 174
  Thomas She 217
Kelsoe, Hugh Mon 384
  John Mon 364

Kelsoe, cont.
  Joseph Mon 367
  Wm. Mon 384
Kelsy, James Bar 25
  Thomas Mas 251
Kelton, Thomas Liv 157
Kelvy, Thomas Mas 306
Kemmel, Philip But 195
Kemp, Edwd. Cal 19
  Hardin War 259
  John Way 365
  Marshall Adr 10
  Reubin Hrd 288
  Thomas Cal 19
Kemper, Benj. Gal 183
  Enoch Gar 216
  Henry Gar 217
  Jaems Fle 89
  Joel Hnr 358
  John, Snr Gar 216
  Jonathan Gal 183
  N. Geo. Gar 216
  Wm. Gar 216
Kenada, George Log 194
Kenaday, Andrw. Nic 51
  David Nel 51
  Robert Nic 51
  Wm. Way 356
Kenady, David War 275
  John Woo 388
  Philip Woo 381
Kenatzer, Mary Way 367
Kenchiloo, Coonrod Bar 36
Kendall, Eli Nel 46
  George Gal 183
  Hek. Nel 45
  James Gal 183
  Jerh. Nel 45
  John (C) Gal 183
  John (T) Gal 183
  Reubin Nel 46
  Thornton Nel 45
  Thos. Nel 45
  William Gal 183
  William Mas 251
  Wm. Nel 45
  Yelbert Gal 183
Kendle, Dicey Pen 106
Kendrich, Alex Cas 38
  Turner Cas 43
Kendrick, Austin Cas 40
  Benjn. Bou 95
  Benoni Sco 176
  John Lew 101
  Wm. Bou 95
Keneda, John Log 189
Keneday, John Pen 114
  Sarah Pen 114
Kenedy, Daniel Bul 180
  David Bou 94
  Elliott Mas 251
  Henry Nel 45
  James, Sr Bou 94
  Jas. Jr Bou 94
  John Way 363
  nancy Nel 46
  Thos. Nel 46
  William Bou 94
  William Liv 160
Kenerly, Ew. Hnr 368
Keney, Jesse Pul 156
Kenkaid, George Hnd 327
Kenly, John Mad 241
Kennada, John Pul 156
Kennady, Charles Chr 92
  Charles Chr 93
  Charles Woo 382
Kennady, cont.
  Charls. Flo 96
  James Chr 74
  James Chr 92
  James Chr 102
  Jane Bre 158
  Joseph Woo 382
  Michael Chr 99
  Mosis Chr 110
  Nely Chr 57
  Peter Chr 93
Kennedy, Andrew Mad 242
  Arthur Mad 242
  Danl. Hrd 288
  David Gar 216
  Easter Bou 125
  Eli Bou 125
  James Cam 27
  James Cum 185
  James Liv 159
  Jas. Gar 216
  Jno. Hrd 289
  Jno. Nel 45
  Jno. Senr Hrd 288
  John Cly 158
  John Hop 372
  John, Freeman of colour Jes 48
  John Mer 318
  Joseph Cam 24
  Joseph Mad 242
  Moore Jef 26
  Peter Hrd 303
  Robert Jef 6
  Robt. Hop 373
  Thos. Bou 125
  Thos. Gar 217
  Walter Fra 139
  William Clr 146
  William Jes 48
  Zakeriah Liv 158
Kennely, John Cum 179
Kenner, Lodham Mas 252
Kennerly, Philip Log 180
Kennett, Dixson Bou 72
  Press G. Pen 117
  William Bou 94
Kenney, Jesse Hrs 324
  John Cas 41
  Saml. Hrd 290
  Thos. Cas 41
Kenniday, John Fay 29
  Milly Fay 29
  William Fay 20
Kennison, John R. Bul 180
Kenny, David Fay 56
  James Bou 94
  James Chr 103
  James, Jr Bou 94
  John Bou 94
  Mathew Fay 52
  Moses Bou 94
  Thos. Sco 172
Kenser, Federick Pul 156
Kent, David Fay 33
  David Fay 53
  David Fay 53
  Henry Chr 69
  Henry Fay 53
  Isaac Adr 10
  William Fay 29
Kenton, John Mas 251
  Nancy Mer 317
  Nancy Mer 318
Kenworthy, Thos. Way 357
Kenyon, Robert Mas 252
Keown, Elizabeth War 245
Keown, cont.
  John War 251
  Nathan War 264
  Thomas War 245
Kephart, Abm. Jr Hnr 359B
  Abm. Sr Hnr 359B
  Polly Hnr 359B
Kepler, John Nel 46
Keplinger, Jacob Sco 191
Kerby, Alexander Jes 48
  Elisha Mad 242
  Eward Jes 49
  Francis Jes 49
  George Mad 243
  Hawkins Jes 48
  Henry Jes 49
  Jesse Mul 397
  Joel Mad 241
  John Mad 241
  John, Jesse' son Mad 241
  John Woo 389
  Nancy Mas 251
  Richard Bou 95
  William Mad 241
Kerchavill, James Cam 26
Kercheval, Jno. Nel 9
  John Mas 252
Kerchervall, George She 212
Kerechavell, John Log 175
Kerkindal, Mathew Bar 48
  Richd. Bar 48
Kerkindall, Jessee Cal 5
Kerley, William Mad 243
Kerlin, James Hnr 351
  Peter Hnr 351
Kermas, John Pul 157
Kerms, Aram Adr 10
Kernal, Elijah Log 186
Kernall, Fleming Hop 372
  Patrick Hnd 335
Kernine, Adam Hnr 368
  Richard Hnr 368
Kerns, Abraham Bou 94
  Adam Cum 171
  John Hrs 320
  Ralph Cum 172
  Robert Bou 95
  Simion Bou 94
  Wm. Hrs 320
Kerr, Armstrong Lin 123
  David Sco 180
  James Log 193
  James Pul 156
  John Log 185
  John Log 191
  Moses She 221
  Robert Mas 251
  Thomas Mas 251
  W. Jr Hnr 355
  William Pul 156
  Wm. Sco 193
Kerrich, Benja. H. She 237
  Hugh Fay 22
Kerrick, Edward Fay 29
Kerry, Robert Pul 156
Kersey, Clayborn Jes 49
  John Jes 41
  Lettia Jes 41
Kertley, Elijah Boo 60
  Elijah Rck 163
  Frances Fay 50
  Jeremiah Boo 60
  Mary Boo 60
  Robt. Boo 60
  Wm. Boo 60
Kertly, Jonithan Grn 262
  Simeon Bou 95

Name	County	Page
Kessik, Henry	Fle	77
Kester, John	She	199
William	She	199
Kesterson, John	Pul	157
Meridy	Pul	157
Wm.	Pul	157
Ketcham, Daniel	She	215
Ketchim, James	Wsh	298
Keterson, William	Pul	157
Keth, William	Nel	45
Kethler, Daniel	Bra	142
Lewis	Bra	142
Keton, John	Bou	94
Kevill, Thomas	Cal	3
Key, Elijah	War	267
Hugh	Way	351
Isaac	Mas	251
James	Bou	94
James	Mas	251
James, Sen	Mas	251
Jesse	War	266
Price	Clr	134
Simon	War	267
Thomas	Jef	6
Thomas	Mas	251
Keys, John	Chr	61
John, Junior	Chr	61
William	She	216
Keysucker, George	Jef	7
Kezee, Benjamin	Flo	96
Richard	Flo	96
Keziah, Saml.	Rck	163
Kibby, Amos	Grp	273
Joseph	Wsh	298
Moses	Grp	276
Kid, Elias	Knx	74
James	Chr	86
Milly	Knx	83
Philip	Fay	54
Richd.	Gar	216
Kidd, Andrew	Liv	153
Dave, free negro	Fay	38
Edmond	Fay	55
John	Liv	153
Philip	Fay	34
Kiddleston, Jno.	Hrs	324
Kiddy, Peter	Lew	101
Kidwell, Drury	Mad	242
Hezekiah	Wsh	299
John	Mad	242
Jonathan	Mad	242
Jonathan, Jur	Mad	242
Matthew	Cum	176
Thomas	Mad	242
Vincent	Mad	242
William	Mad	242
Wm.	Bou	94
Kieth, Zepheniah	Bou	94
Kiethley, Jacob	War	261
Roland	War	261
Kiger, ...b	Hrs	307
Kiggins, John	Clr	134
Kiging, Patrick	Fay	22
Kilabru, Kinchen	Chr	61
Kilbourn, Henry	Pul	156
Kilbreath, Alexander	Hrs	311
John	Mon	367
John	War	270
Kilbreth, Joseph	Jef	6
Kilburn, Elisha	Gar	216
Kilby, Henry	Mer	318
Kile, Adam	Mas	252
Benjamin	Fay	54
Patrick	Mer	318
Thomas	Mer	317
Kilgore, Benjn.	Cam	28
Kilgore, cont.		
Hugh	Cal	10
Jane	Cal	10
John	Hnd	333
Johnston	Hnd	333
Jonathan	Cal	10
Joseph	Mas	251
mary	Mas	252
Obed	Hrs	323
Saml.	Cal	10
Kilgour, David	Lew	100
William	Nic	51
Kilgy, Thomas	Cal	8
Kill, Wm.	Jef	6
Killam, Asa	Hrd	284
Killbreath, Alexr.	Lin	123
Killen, Robt.	Hrd	294
Killer, Wm.	Jef	30
Killin, John	Bul	180
Killion, John	Cal	5
John	Mon	363
Wm.	Cal	7
Killough, John	Sco	174
Killum, Peter	Bou	94
Kilpartrick, David	Mon	362
James	Mon	352
Kilpatrick, David	Mer	317
Hugh	Mad	241
James	Mer	318
Joseph	Hrd	282
Saml.	Fle	69
Kilwell, John	Way	355
Kimberland, Abraham	Hnr	351
John	Hnr	361
Sarah	Hrd	299
Kimberlin, Danl.	Hnr	366
John	Wsh	298
Kimble, Fedk.	Grn	245
Harmonius	Gra	240
Kimbrel, Duke	Mad	243
Green	Mad	243
Jackson	Mad	243
Kimbro. James	Lin	123
Kimbrogh, Elizabeth	Bou	72
Kimbrough, Eliza	Nic	51
John	Nic	51
Richd.	Nic	51
Robert	Nic	51
Wm.	Hrs	313
Kimer, Nicholas	Bra	152
Kimes, Jacob	Bou	94
Stephen	Bou	94
Kimly, Andrew	Mul	400
Kimmel, Philip	Mul	405
Kimmell, John	Hnd	339
Kimper, John Jnr	Gar	217
Kinard, Jonathan	Mas	251
Joseph	Mas	251
William	Mas	251
Kincade, Joseph	Bar	45
Kincaid, Andrew	Lin	123
Andrew	Mon	354
Andrew, Junr	Mon	355
Archibald	Mon	354
David	Grn	256
David	Mon	358
Geor.	Mon	356
James	Mad	241
James	Rck	163
John	Clr	133
John	Mad	241
John	Mas	252
John	Mer	317
John	Mon	354
John	Mon	379
Kincaid, cont.		
Robert	Clr	133
Robt.	Hrd	285
Thomas	Mon	361
Thomas	Mon	361
Thomas	Mon	374
Kincart, James	Nic	51
John	Nic	51
Samuel	Nic	51
Kincheloe, Joseph	Bre	169
Lewis	Mul	404
Peter	Mul	398
Stephen	Mul	393
Thomas	Bre	169
William	Mul	393
Willm.	Nel	45
Kinchelow, Ambros	Bar	28
Elias	Nel	45
Nimrod	Bar	42
Kinchilow, Adam	Bar	29
Kindal, Ben	Hrd	285
Kindall, Davis	Hnr	352
Reason	Hnr	363
Kindar, Peter	Hnr	359A
Kinder, George	Jef	6
George	She	241
Peter	Bre	158
Peter	Mad	243
Samuel	Mad	243
Wm.	Way	353
Kindle, Elijah	Fra	139
George	She	225
Jesse	Bou	95
John	Hrs	320
John	Hrs	322
Joseph	Bou	95
Lewis	Hrs	320
Lewis	Hrs	322
Roughly	Fle	69
Rowley	Jef	6
Rowsey	Jef	6
Smith	Bou	94
Sterne	Pen	113
Thomas	Jef	6
Willis	Jef	6
Wm.	Jef	30
Yelly	Gra	241
Kindler, Jeremiah	She	212
Kindreck, Rheubin	Hrs	322
Kindred, Bartholomew	Jes	48
DAvid	Mad	241
Edward	Clr	134
John	Mad	241
John	She	225
martin	Mad	243
Nathl.	Mad	241
Peter	She	240
William	Mad	241
Kindrick, Jacob	Mas	252
William	Wsh	299
Kines, Jacob	Bou	94
Kiney, Isaac	Bra	143
King, Aaron	Mad	242
Abner	Nel	45
Alexander	Bul	180
Barnett	Nic	51
Benjamine	Bra	151
Benjn.	Bar	39
Braxton	Hrs	318
Charles	Cly	157
Cornelius	Nel	46
Daniel	Hrs	316
Daniel	Nel	45
Daniel	Ohi	85
David	Clr	134
David	Mas	251

King, cont.
Edmund Gra 239
Edward Gar 216
Elijah Hnd 325
Elisha Flo 96
Elizabeth Chr 114
English Cas 40
Ezekiel Knx 73
Gabriel Mas 251
George Gar 216
George Mer 318
Harbert Lin 123
Henry Bar 49
Henry Bou 94
Henry Jes 48
Hilsman Knx 76
Ibzan Mer 317
Isaac Knx 70
Jacob Est 9
Jacob Jes 48
James, Esqr. Pen 117
Jas. Gar 216
Jeremiah Est 1
Jeremiah Jes 48
Jessee Bou 94
Jessey Est 6
Jno. Hrd 288
Joel Mad 242
John Bou 125
John Bra 145
John Bra 147
John Bra 152
John Clr 134
John Cum 180
John Fay 41
John Knx 67
John Lin 123
John Mer 317
John War 270
John Wsh 299
John B. Hrd 300
John E. Cum 165
Josep Nel 45
Joseph Est 3
Joseph Est 6
Joseph Hrs 318
Majer Est 6
Michael Mad 243
Nancy Mon 365
Nathaniel She 209
Nelson Bul 180
Nicholas Bar 39
Osborn She 209
Peter Nel 46
Polly Knx 76
Richard Fle 69
Richard Hrs 316
Richd. Cum 180
Robert Gal 183
Robert Hrs 316
Robert Hrs 318
Robert Lin 123
Robt. Adr 10
Samuel Bou 94
Samuel Flo 96
Samuel Pul 157
Seth Bul 180
Smith Gal 183
Smith Mon 347
Spencer Knx 77
Thomas Hnr 362
Thomas Jef 7
Thomas Knx 71
Thomas Mas 251
Thomas She 209
Thomas She 213
Valentine Bul 180

King, cont.
W.H. Grn 265
Weathers Bul 180
William Clr 134
William Fay 59
William Jes 48
William Mad 242
William Mas 251
William Nel 46
William Nel 46
William Pul 157
Wm. Bra 149
Wm. Cas 47
Wm. E. Nel 45
Zachariah Est 6
Zachariah Knx 64
Kingcaid, Archbd. Bou 94
Kinght, William Fle 77
Kingkaid, William Log 164
Kiniley, Beverly Mon 355
Kink, Daniel Wsh 298
James Wsh 298
Kinkade, Andrew Cam 25
Hugh Hrs 312
John Hrs 312
John Jes 49
Archibald Woo 400
Kinkead, Guy Woo 377
James Woo 377
John Woo 377
John Woo 400
Joseph Woo 400
Saml. Cal 7
William Woo 377
Kinley, James Wsh 298
Kinmon, David Pen 109
David, Sr Pen 109
John Pen 109
Kinnard, Joseph Mad 241
Kinnday, William Pul 156
Kinnerson, David Jef 7
John Jef 7
Kinnett, Anna Wsh 299
Joseph Wsh 298
Joshua Jef 6
Kinney, Joseph Woo 383
Matthew Fay 33
Polly Mer 318
Richard Woo 382
Kinning, William Hrs 312
Kinny, Edwd. D. Sco 172
Richard Mer 317
Kinsey, Jesse Wsh 298
Thomas Chr 81
Kinslow, James Hrs 310
James Hrs 312
Kiper, Frederick Gra 240
Jacob Gra 240
Kiphart, Jno. Hnr 359A
Kiplinger, John Bou 94
Philip Bou 95
Kirby, Asa War 257
Charles Pen 105
David War 257
David War 262
Enoch Pen 105
Isaiah War 257
Jesse War 257
Leonard War 257
Nancy Bou 95
Robert Bar 26
Saml. War 257
Saml. War 273
Soloman War 257
William Pen 109
Wm. War 257
Kirck, Daniel War 279

Kirckham, Henry War 255
Jos. War 255
Saml. War 255
Kirckwood, Margar-
et War 268
Kircland, Charles Cas 42
Kirk, Anthony She 225
Benjamin Mas 252
Garret Knx 89
George Mas 252
Hiram Hop 380
James Mon 365
Jesse Bou 180
Mathew Mon 365
Nathl. Fle 82
Richard Mas 251
Robert Liv 147
Thomas Mas 251
Thomas Mas 251
Thomas She 225
Vincent Bou 125
William Bou 94
William Mas 251
William, Jun Mas 251
Kirkindolph, Solli-
man Chr 75
Stepin Chr 72
Kirkland, John Mer 318
William Log 191
William Mer 318
Kirklin, Thomas Chr 116
Kirkman, Elijah Chr 71
George Chr 78
Thomas Chr 78
William Chr 72
Kirkmon, James Chr 72
Kirkly, Willis Lin 123
Kirkpatrick, Ann Lin 123
Elijah Cum 176
George Hrs 315
George Hrs 323
Hugh Fle 82
Hugh Mas 251
Jas. Boo 60
Jas. Bou 94
John Jef 6
Jos. Bou 125
Joseph Jef 30
Moses Cum 175
Robert Chr 109
Saml. Bou 125
Sarah Cum 176
Tho. Bar 53
Thos. Bou 125
Wm. Cum 175
Wm. Hrs 324
Wm. Jef 7
Wm. She 239
Kirkwood, Hugh Hop 371
James Liv 152
Wm. Jef 26
Kirns, Peter Sco 181
Kirsy, Jno. Grn 261
Kirt, Nicholas Bar 44
Kirtland, Shadrick Chr 95
Kirtley, Benja. Fle 61
James Grn 245
John Sco 192
Jonathan Grn 246
Rebbecca Woo 378
Thomas Grn 246
Wm. Grn 246
Wm. Grn 250
Kirtly, John Bar 35
Pleasant Grn 261
Kise, William Fay 60
Kiser, Adam Fay 52

Kiser, cont.
Frederik Hnr 359A
Frederick, Jr Hnr 359A
Jacob Bou 95
Jacob Fay 60
John Bou 95
John Bra 147
John Hnr 359A
Kishlor, Francis Hrs 318
Kisiah, Fedric Pul 157
William Pul 156
Kison, Jacob Grp 275
Kissinger, John Lin 123
Kister, Lewis Jef 7
Kitcham, John She 198
Joseph She 238
Kitchen, John Bul 180
John Knx 72
Kitchin, Anthony Wsh 298
Kitchins, James Pul 156
John Pul 156
Kite, Ezekial Mul 387
James Grp 275
Kitely, Abraham Mad 242
Kittinger, Jacob Mul 389
Martin Mul 394
Kitlan, John Chr 101
Kitral, Samuel Chr 96
Kitson, James She 218
Kitts, John Chr 105
Joseph Cam 32
Kivill, Benjamin Cal 10
Kleet, Fredk. Cam 28
Kliglesmith, Michl. Nel 45
Klingman, Henry War 258
Knab, Harry Hrd 289
Knap, George She 211
John She 201
Joseph Grp 276
Joshua She 211
William She 211
Knapp, Henry Clr 134
Knaus, Henry Mas 306
Knave, Joseph Log 164
Joseph Log 186
Joseph, Senr Log 164
Kneal, John Mad 243
Knetzer, Andrew Mas 252
Georg Mon 382
Kneu, Peter Hrs 316
Knew, Peter Hrs 320
Knewkum, John Mad 243
Knight, Anne Hnd 345
Charles Mas 252
Isaac Hnd 327
James Fle 80
James Jes 48
Jas. Gar 216
Jno. Hnr 351
John Chr 72
John Fle 80
John She 209
Jonathan Chr 81
Shearwood Mad 241
Shedrick Hrs 313
Thomas Chr 81
Thomas Fle 80
William Hnr 360
Wm. Hrs 317
Woodson Mas 251
Knighton, Amon Mul 390
Jesse Mul 401
Knokes, Abraham Mad 242
Knoll, Becky Cum 186
Knot, Henry Hrd 294
Knott, Bazle Nel 46
James Nel 46

Knott, cont.
Jeremiah Wsh 299
Joseph Mas 251
Joseph Wsh 298
Thomas Wsh 298
Knotts, Jonathan Nel 46
Knowlen, James Pen 111
Knowles, William Mas 252
Knox, Abner Mer 317
Benjamin Jes 49
David Bou 94
David Mer 317
George Grp 274
Hugh Hnd 346
James Fra 138
James She 224
John Hrd 300
John M. Bou 94
Joseph Mas 252
Robert Fra 138
Samuel Bou 94
Samuel Log 175
Stokely Log 188
Thomas Clr 134
Thomas Wsh 298
Thos. Sco 176
William Bou 94
Knuckles, Wm. Jef 7
Koffman, Abraham Wsh 299
Kogar, Nicholas Way 363
Kooker, Jacob Liv 155
Koon, Benjamin Chr 58
Koons, John Fra 139
Kopp, Jacob Mas 252
Kouns, Jacob Grp 272
John Grp 273
John Grp 275
Kreak, David War 258
Krickbaum, Jacob Jes 49
Krickle, Francis Fay 17
Krusor, Michiel Nic 51
Krylick, Jacob Cam 24
Kumaway, William Est 9
Kunce, George Knx 73
Kurkum, Henry Nel 46
Kusee, Jesse S. Bre 159
Kuth, Jno. Hrd 298
Kuykendall, Josiah But 195
Mathw. But 195
Moses But 195
Kuykendoll, Simon Hnd 340
Kuykindall, Jacob Jef 30
Kylander, Philip Bra 147
Kyle, Jacob Bou 95
John War 257
Kyler, Jos. Gar 216

-- L --

Labon, Nicholas Woo 390
Labree, Richd. Jr Sco 187
Lacefield, Abby She 229
John Bar 53
John Cum 168
Lacewell Chr 79
Thomas She 229
Wm. Bar 42
Lacewell, Daniel Hnd 338
Lacey, Edward Jr Liv 156
Edward, Senr Liv 153
Joshua, Senr Liv 153
Robert Liv 153
William Liv 153
William Nel 47

Lachey, Alex Mad 238
Lackey, Andrew Est 8
James Cum 181
James Mad 237
Nathan Clr 134
Saml. Mad 239
Thomas Mad 237
Thomas, Jun Mad 237
William Mad 237
Lackland, Aaron Clr 134
John, Jur Sco 190
John, Ser Sco 190
Lacky, Alexander Flo 105
Gabriel Lin 125
Wm. Gar 215
Lacog, John Grp 269
Lacre, Elizabeth She 207
Lacsa, John Lin 123
Michall Lin 123
Lacy, Barberry Jef 5
Benjamin Chr 68
Burley Log 178
David Chr 68
Elijah Woo 380
James Flo 105
Jepthy Chr 81
John Flo 105
Mark Mon 363
Mosis Chr 81
Thomas Cal 15
Walter Mas 253
William Chr 68
Wm. Mon 360
Wm. H. Cal 5
Lad, Benjamin Chr 59
Benjamin Chr 90
David Chr 86
Ladamore, Hugh Hrs 315
Ladd, Jacob Bou 126
Janes Bou 96
Laferay, James Bra 149
Laferday, Bary Hnr 351
Lafever, Peter Cam 33
Lafferty, Alexr. Cum 167
John She 205
Peggy Mon 373
Saml. Cum 167
Laffollet, Isaac Hrd 291
Jesse Hrd 291
Jos. Hrd 291
Uzel Hrd 290
Laffoon, Reatherford Hop 378
Lafidy, John Mer 319
Laflin, Zachariah Hrs 307
Lafollet, Jacob Hrd 296
Lafoon, James Fay 23
Laforce, Robinson Clr 134
William Woo 391
Lafourse, Jane Clr 134
Lahue, John Gra 240
Laid, John Log 178
Thomas Gal 191
Lail, Peter Fay 23
Lain, John Flo 105
Tilman Bar 44
Lainer, Henry Mul 407
Lair, Charles Hrs 312
David Gar 214
George Gar 214
Jas. Gar 214
John Hrs 312
John Hrs 323
Mathew Bar 35
Wm. Adr 10
Wm. Hrs 312
Wm. Sr Adr 10

Laird, Saml. Cum 172
Lardeman, Jacob Fay 59
Lake, Abr. Adr 10
  Daniel Hrs 312
  Ignatius Sco 184
  Joseph Hrs 309
  Ralp Wsh 297
  Thos. Adr 10
Lakey, Joel Knx 69
Lam, Adam Chr 72
  John Chr 72
Lamair, Willm. War 275
Laman, Daniel Grn 262
  Danl. Grn 263
  Isaac Grn 262
  John Grn 263
  Rudy Grn 262
  William Nel 48
Lamar, James Fle 78
Lamasters, Elijah Mon 357
  Isaac Mon 356
  Richard Mon 369
  Thomas Log 178
Lamb, Benjamin Cas 39
  Ceney? Cal 16
  Daniel Mer 342
  Edward Hrs 324
  George Cal 7
  George Fle 77
  Jac Hnr 367
  James Bou 96
  James Cas 38
  James Liv 153
  Jas. Gar 213
  Jesse Liv 155
  Jessee Fay 29
  John Bar 35
  John Cas 41
  John Hop 380
  John Mer 318
  Jonathan Fay 29
  Jonathan Mad 238
  Joseph Fle 80
  Longshear Cal 17
  Matthew Mad 238
  Moses Bou 126
  Peirce Mas 253
  Peirce, Junr Mas 254
  Richard Mad 238
  Richard, Sen Mad 237
  Samuel Hrs 311
  Thomas Grn 258
  Thomas Mad 238
  Thos. Cas 38
  Travies Cas 39
  William [illegible] 252
  William [illegible] 100
Lambers, David War 278
Lambert, Abrham Nel 48
  Benjamin Fay 41
  Courtland Mer 319
  Garrard Nel 48
  George Mad 238
  Hugh Knx 77
  James Bul 180
  James Mad 238
  Joel Hnd 343
  John Wsh 295
  Lewis Hnd 336
  Matthew Mad 238
  Moses She 231
  Rivers War 274
  Ruth Sco 176
  Shadrach War 252
  Sterling Mer 319
  Thos. Bra 147
  William Mad 238
Lambkin, James Woo 387
Lambton, Benj. Adr 10
Lamkin, Jno. Hrd 286
  John B. Woo 388
Lamkins, George Liv 149
  Samuel Liv 149
Lamme, James Bou 126
Lamons, Robert Nel 47
Lampkin, Daniel Jes 50
  George Wsh 296
  William Chr 79
  William Wsh 296
Lampkins, James Chr 57
Lampton, Clary Gar 214
  Henry Nel 48
  James Clr 134
  John Clr 134
  Joshua Clr 134
  Mark Jef 26
  Wm. Jef 29
Lamtin, Samuel Bou 126
Lancaster, Adam Log 166
  Christena Chr 75
  Henry Boo 60
  Henry Chr 60
  Jeremiah Wsh 296
  John Wsh 295
  Joseph Mon 378
  Joshua Wsh 295
  Moses Hnr 365
  Raphel Hnd 328
  Rheubin Cam 30
  Rhubin Hrs 307
  Richd. Hrd 288
  Susan Log 164
  Thomas Bou 72
  Thomas Pen 112
  Thos. Lin 125
  William Pen 106
  Willm. Lin 125
  Wm. Bra 150
Lance, Coonrod Mon 359
  George War 246
  Martin Bar 49
Lanceford, Augustin Chr 79
Lanchaster, John Jes 49
Lanckford, Thos. Bou 95
Land, Aaron Log 164
  Henry Cal 18
  Henry Jes 50
  Henry Liv 152
  James Mad 239
  John Mad 239
  Thomas War 276
Landcaster, Betsey Mad 240
  Delaney Mad 240
Lander, Charles Bou 95
  Henry Bou 95
  Henry Clr 134
  Jacob Bou 96
  Jacob Clr 134
  John Clr 134
  William Clr 134
Landers, Abm. Hop 376
  Caty War 279
  Felix Cas 45
  Jacob War 279
  James Wsh 296
  John War 279
  John Wsh 293
  Nathl. Nel 47
  Will She 229
Landess, John Wsh 295
Landis, Daniel Mul 407
  John Mul 392
Landiss, John Adr 10
Landreth, James Log 183
Landreth, cont.
  John Log 176
Landrum, James Sco 183
  Thomas Clr 134
Landsan, Wm. Mon 353
Lane, Adran Bar 49
  Amos Boo 60
  Benjamin Clr 134
  Daniel Cas 47
  Daniel Jef 5
  Daniel C. She 215
  Dutton Adr 10
  Dutton Gal 183
  Edward Fra 140
  G. James Mas 306
  Gerrard But 195
  Isham Mad 240
  James H. Mon 351
  Jesse She 211
  Jno. Hrd 300
  Joel Clr 134
  John Adr 10
  John Clr 134
  John Hnd 339
  John Log 195
  John Mas 256
  John Mon 351
  Joseph Lew 96
  Larkin Gar 215
  Letty Mon 353
  Moses Bar 25
  Moses Nel 47
  Robt. Bar 49
  Robert G. Mon 376
  Samuel Knx 64
  Sharred Gar 214
  Tarlton Gar 215
  Tho. Bar 27
  Thomas Mon 367
  Thomas She 198
  Thos. Way 358
  William Knx 78
  William, Jr Clr 134
  William, Sr Clr 134
  William N. Clr 146
  Wm. Hrd 300
Lanehart, Isaac Mad 238
Laney, Abraham Lin 125
  John Lin 125
  Joseph Lin 125
  Joseph, Snr Lin 125
  Peter Lew 101
  William Bou 126
Lang, Henry Hrd 300
  William She 220
Langdon, James Pul 157
  John Pul 157
  Joseph Rck 162
Langford, John W. Liv 149
  Margret Gar 215
  Nancy Rck 165
  Nathan War 245
  Polly War 248
  Stephen Rck 159
  John War 264
Langhorne, Maurice Bou 68
Langlen, James Pul 156
  Samuel Pul 156
Langley, Elisha Mul 388
  James Wsh 293
  Jeremiah Mul 408
  John War 272
  John Wsh 293
  Mathew Mul 399
  Thos. Nel 48
Langly, John Chr 95
  Marget Wsh 296

Langore, Wm. Hnr 364
Langsdon, Charles Bul 180
Royal Bul 180
Langsferd, Nichls. Nel 48
Langstin, Ragden Log 194
Langston, Abraham Bou 126
Jacob Cal 4
Jeremiah Way 367
John Log 192
Lanham, Elias Ohi 72
James Mad 240
Rachel Ohi 85
Stephen Mad 240
Thomas Mad 239
William But 195
Lanhaster, Robert Fay 29
Lankford, Larkin Fra 140
Robert Woo 383
Warken Pul 157
Lanly, Peyton Log 170
Thos. Log 170
Lanman, Griffen Jef 6
John Bre 163
Nathan Wsh 295
Lann, Andrew Mon 378
Lanning, Joseph Bar 25
Lannton, Nathan Chr 96
Lannum, Ashom Wsh 293
Clement Wsh 295
Zachariah Wsh 297
Lanpkin, Astin Chr 57
Powers Chr 79
Lansby, James Woo 382
Lansdale, Richd. Nel 47
Wm. Mon 376
Lansdall, Francis Mon 375
Lantern, Jacob Mon 355
Peter Gar 215
Thomas Mon 372
Lanterman, Peter Fle 88
Lantz, Martin Boo 60
Lanxton, Absolum Chr 93
Lany, Aaron Log 164
Isaac Log 164
Samuel Chr 69
Lapsley, A. John Gar 215
James Mer 341
John Adr 10
Joseph B. Nel 47
Polly Gar 215
Lar, Jas. Way 364
Larage, James Hrs 320
Laramore, Abraham Mad 237
Larance, James Pul 156
Lard, Jno. S. Lew 103
Joseph Bar 33
Samuel Fay 41
Larenc, John Fay 50
Larew, John Bra 143
Peter Liv 148
Larimer, Edward Log 185
Larimore, James Grn 264
Richard Grn 261
Larinell, Robt. Hnr 369
Lariper, Joseph Way 364
Laris, Andrew Lin 123
Larker, John Mul 403
Larkford, Joy Pul 156
Larkin, Wm. Hrd 296
Larkins, Mark Rck 160
Larne, Saml. Grn 251
Larner, Patrick Nel 47
Larrance, Black - well Clr 134
Henry, Jr Clr 134
Henry, Sr Clr 134
John War 263
Larrance, cont.
Meridith Clr 134
Lartler, Benj. Nel 47
LaRue, Isaac Hrd 294
Jacob, Junr Hrd 298
Jacob, Senr Hrd 288
Jas. Hrd 294
Jos. Hrd 294
Samuel Hrd 302
Squire Hrd 294
Wm. Hrd 298
Lary, Denniss Bou 126
Dennis, Senr Bou 126
Lasby, Saml. Sco 174
Lasery, Joil Chr 98
Lasewell, Ezekiel Wsh 294
Patsy Wsh 294
Lash, Adam Hrd 299
Peter Hnd 328
Lashbrook, James Bul 181
John Mas 254
Thomas She 206
William Bul 180
William, Jr Bul 181
Lashby, Andrew Cal 4
Lashly, George Mas 254
Lasley, James Grn 250
Lasly, Daniel Cal 20
John Bar 28
Lassiter, Dempsy Clr 134
Lasswell, Benjamin Wsh 295
Jessee Rck 161
John Rck 161
John, Ser Rck 164
Joseph Rck 161
Laster, Vincent Pul 156
Lastler, Jacob Nel 47
Lastly, Benjamin Mas 254
John Nel 48
Mancah Grn 262
Lastten, Solomn. Nel 47
Lastter, Soloman Nel 48
Lastty, Abraham Bul 180
Laswell, Charnil Mer 319
Jesse Hrd 297
Laten, Robert Hrs 319
Thomas Hrs 319
William H. Fle 85
Later, David Sco 176
Latham, Elijah Chr 74
James Hnd 332
Jeremiah Cal 6
John Bou 95
John Bra 153
John Log 161
Richard Mas 253
Lathroms, Sampson Bul 180
(freeman of colour)
Lathum, Baswell Chr 68
Latimer, John Mer 318
Samuel Mer 318
Latimore, William Pen 107
Latley, Andrew Lew 104
Latta, Alexander Gal 183
Matthew Woo 378
Lattimin, Jacob Grn 245
Lattimore, Frances Bar 30
Laughlen, William Lew 100
Laughlin, Benj. Bra 147
Henry Mad 238
James Cal 14
John Bou 95
John Cal 11
John Knx 65
John Knx 69
Joyn W. Fay 38
Sarah Bou 95
Laughlin, cont.
Thomas Knx 64
Wm. Bou 95
Laughlon, Anthony Cal 5
Lauhan, Henry Bar 35
Laural, Thos. Adr 10
Laurance, Argus War 282
James Chr 97
Laurel, Francis Sco 181
Laurence, David Bar 33
David Wsh 294
Henry Log 186
Hugh Lin 123
Isaac, Sr Fle 83
James Bar 22
James Fle 75
James Nel 47
Jesse Log 188
Jno. Bar 50
Jno. Nel 48
John Cam 25
John Lin 123
John Mas 253
Thomas But 195
Willm. Lin 123
Wm. Gar 199
Laurince, Hender- son Gar 215
Laurison, George Est 1
Lause, Jerimah Mer 318
Thomas Mer 318
Lauson, David Knx 65
Nathan Knx 65
Laveasten, Wm. Grn 257
Laveluy, William Nel 48
Lavender, John Mad 238
Lavet, Augustus Fay 18
Lavill, Joseph Jef 29
Law, Barney War 276
Holmon Knx 66
Jesse Hnr 356
Joel Hnr 357
John Way 372
John, Jr Log 180
John, Sr Log 180
Sary Bar 51
William Pen 113
William War 276
Lawe, David Lew 102
Lawell, Abraham Bou 126
John Hnr 359
Lawfield, Andrew Grn 245
Lawler, Bennett She 217
David Fra 141
Lawles, Theofilous Grp 277
Augl. Adr 10
Lawless, Benjn. War 252
Bird Wsh 293
Henry Pen 107
Jesse Adr 10
John Pen 107
Wm. Way 356
Lawman, James Bre 169
John Bre 163
Lawrance, Peter War 271
Benjn. Fef 6
Jacob Log 180
Lawrence, John Fra 140
Levin Jef 31
Oliver Gal 184
Saml. Jef 5
Samuel Fra 139
Lawry, Andw. Bar 31
James Cal 14
Sephia Cal 18
Stephen War 260
William Grp 272

Lawry, cont.
Wm. Bar 45
Laws, George Sco 185
John Bou 96
John Knx 90
Robert Sco 191
Thomas Jef 6
Thomas Knx 91
William Pul 156
Wm. Jef 6
Lawson, Berry Mer 319
David Log 187
David Lin 123
Jacob Fle 86
James Mad 237
Jas. Gar 215
Jas. Hrd 300
John Wsh 297
Joshua Wsh 296
Nathan Wsh 297
Olaron Pul 155
Peter Log 194
Richd. Sco 171
Robert Pen 112
Thomas Grp 271
Thomas Hnr 359B
Travers Flo 105
Walter Mad 244
Wm. Adr 10
Wm. Hnr 365
Zachariah Wsh 292
Lawsoson, Thomas Pen 116
Lawyers, Benjamin Log 196
Lax, Robert Mad 238
Robert, Jun Mad 238
William Mad 238
Lay, Benjamin Fay 29
Bird War 265
Daniel Bou 95
Elizabeth Fay 39
Frances Mad 239
Francis W. Fay 23
George Fay 29
George Fay 39
Jesse Knx 63
Jesse Knx 67
Joel Knx 83
Silvester Fay 29
Stephen Fay 23
Stephen [illegible] 39
Layell, Abner [illegible] 13
Layne, Abraham Flo 105
James Flo 105
James Flo 105
James Lew 99
Joseph Hnr 369
Samuel Flo 105
William Hnr 356
Lays, Samuel Flo 105
Layson, Isaac Bou 96
John Bou 96
Robt. Bou 96
Layton, Daniel Fay 18
James Mas 253
Jer Gar 213
John Gar 214
Spencer Bou 96
Susanna Gar 214
Thomas Liv 154
William Fra 139
William Pen 115
Wm. H. Fle 70
Layweil, Peter Fay 50
Lazell, Wm. Cal 11
Lazier, John Bou 96
Lea, John Hrs 318
John Woo 399

Lea, cont.
Nancy Jef 5
Leach, Bazel Bra 153
Enoch Nel 47
Henry Sco 186
Jerh. Sco 182
John Bar 33
John Mon 367
John Ohi 74
John Sco 170
Joseph Cal 18
Joseph Sco 184
Leonard Ohi 81
Marshall Sco 169
Marshall Sco 187
Simeon Fay 49
William Chr 76
William Chr 116
William Ohi 74
William Ohi 81
Willm. Sco 170
Leachman, Sampson Mer 318
Leadford, James Mon 382
John Mon 361
Leags, Chas. Bar 45
League, Richard Mer 318
[illegible] James Bra 150
[illegible] Bra 150
Leake, John Wsh 297
Richard Wsh 293
Leamons, Jacob Mon 362
Leaper, Samuel Hrs 322
Lear, Abraham Bou 96
Elizabeth Pen 112
Jacob Bou 70
Jesse Jes 50
Thomas M. Bou 126
Lease, George She 206
Henry She 235
James She 235
Nathan She 220
Leasure, John Gar 215
Jos. Gar 215
Nathan Gar 215
Leat, Hened Log 168
Leatch, John W. Lew 98
Leather, John Sr Cam 28
Leatherer, Joshua Sco 168
Leatherman, David She 208
Frederic Bul 180
Jacob She 208
Michael Jef 5
Leathermon, Chrst. She 223
Peggy She 234
Leathers, Charles Fra 140
John Cam 25
Joshua Cam 25
Mary Jef 6
Moses Jef 6
Nicholas Fra 140
Paul Hnd 327
William Nel 47
Leaton, Walter Wsh 293
Leauy, William Fay 17
Leavel, James Woo 397
Leavit, David Fle 62
Leavitt, Ignatious Mon 354
Leavy, Hugh Hrs 309
Lecky, John Clr 134
Lecoumpt, Charles Hnr 362
Ledan, Jno. Nel 47
John Nel 48
Ledbetter, Ephram Chr 61
Millington Log 194
Ledford, Joseph Fay 23
Ledington, Ephriem Knx 63
Lee, Abner Ohi 90

Lee, cont.
Alexr. Fle 83
Ambrose Lin 123
Andrew Knx 64
Ann Hrs 305
Anna Pul 156
Anne Mad 237
Archar Chr 107
Archibald Chr 105
B. John Pul 157
Barton Lew 95
Barton Lew 104
Benjamin Mas 255
Charles Grn 266
Charles Nel 47
Charles Nel 48
Charles Pul 155
Charles Pul 155
Citon Pul 155
Daniel Mas 302
Drury Pul 155
Edward Gra 242
Edward Mas 254
Elizabeth Woo 379
Frances Woo 391
Gasham Gal 183
[illegible]ham, Jr Gal 184
[illegible]rge Lin 123
[illegible]nry Mas 254
Henry Nel 48
Isaac War 280
James Bar 38
James Cas 43
James Fle 69
James Pen 105
Jas. Way 357
John Bul 180
John But 195
J[illegible]hn Cum 181
John Fle 70
John Gal 196
John She 197
John War 280
John N. Fle 65
Joseph Hnr 366
Joseph Sco 174
Joshua Grn 252
Josiah Jes 41
Ludwell Jes 50
Miller But 195
Nathan Gal 196
Obidiah Pul 155
Peter Mas 306
Peter Pul 156
Philip Log 188
Philip Wsh 296
Piety Chr 109
Richard Lin 123
Richard Mad 238
Richd. Hop 376
Rowland Jef 5
Saml. Adr 10
Samuel She 200
Shadrach Cum 181
Stephen Mas 253
Tarlton She 231
Tho. Bar 48
Thomas Fay 59
Thomas Gra 241
Wilford bul 180
William But 195
William Est 7
William Grn 266
William Lew 100
William Log 161
William Nel 47
William Pul 155

Lee, cont.
William Pul 157
William She 197
Willis A. Fra 140
Willis D. Fle 91
Wm. Grn 260
Wm. Lew 96
Wm. Way 358
Leear, Bradford Pul 157
Leebow, Daniel Knx 72
Isaac Knx 72
Leech, Benjamin Mas 254
Edward Lin 123
Jerh. Adr 10
John Pul 156
Joshua Mas 255
Reubin Lin 123
Saml. Adr 10
Walter Mas 252
Leechman, George Mas 255
Leechmon, Leonard she 236
Leek, James Sco 173
Walter Mas 253
Leeneard, Henry Fay 17
Leeper, Andrew Fle 71
Andrew Fle 87
Anna Bar 50
James Fle 69
John Hop 372
Robert Liv 156
Wm. Bar 52
Leer, David Bou 96
Leeright, Miner Hrd 300
Lees, Joseph Mad 244
Randolf Fle 66
Leeson, Thomas Fle 91
Leet, Delitha War 249
Lefevar, Abram Way 359
Lefever, Andw. Way 372
Dad. Way 372
Jacob Way 372
Leflar, Christor. Mad 239
Lefler, Jacob She 241
Lefon, Richard Jes 49
Leforce, Randol Sco 180
Ranoy Fay 50
Saml. Sco 180
Leforgee, Jesse Fle 77
Leforges, Lewis Fle 86
Lefter, Peter She 241
Legate, William Hnd 337
Leger, Coonrod Chr 74
Legett, Stephen Mon 378
Wm. Mon 379
Legg, Ambrose She 210
Isaac She 211
John Lin 123
Jonathan She 210
Legranch, Aron Nel 48
Legrand, George Wsh 294
Jon. O. War 259
Lucy War 259
Peter Fay 23
William Wsh 297
Legrans, Peter Mer 320
Legraves, Joseph Knx 87
Leich, Asa Flo 105
William Cal 10
Leighton, Wm. War 262
Leister, James Flo 105
Wm. Adr 10
Leisure, Abraham Jef 5
Leitz, John Bou 69
Lelcher, Thos. H. Nel 48
Lemair, Young War 265
Leman, Jno. Nel 47
Robert Nel 47
Lemar, John Cal 7B
Luke Cal 7
Samuel Bre 162
Lemarr, John Mas 255
Lemars, Leonard Bra 149
(see also Sellars)
Lemastens, Abm. Hnr 354
Abraham Hnr 359
James Hnr 359
Reuben Hnr 356
Richard Hnr 357
Wm. Hnr 365
Lemaster,Archibald Gal 183
Richard Bul 181
Lemasters, James Hnr 368
James, Junr Hnr 352
James, Sr Hnr 352
John Flo 105
Lemastes, Hugh She 212
Lemen, James She 202
Lemmon, Abrm. Hrd 287
John Sco 169
Joseph Mon 375
Robert Sco 177
Thomas Sco 186
William Sco 190
Wm. Sco 181
Lemmons, Abraham Log 180
John Nel 48
Lemon, James Fay 18
James Fay 58
Lemuel Bul 180
Wm. Boo 60
Lemons, David Hrs 308
Jacob Gra 242
James Bra 149
Robert Hrs 316
Wm. Hrs 316
Wm. Hrs 316
Lemuel, Harvey Hop 375
Lenafelter, Micheal Hrs 318
Lendsey, Nevil Hnd 327
Leneare, Saml. Nel 47
Lenner, Isham Pen 108
Lenox, John Bou 96
Lent, William Nel 47
Lenthecum, Thos. Nel 48
Lents, Jacob Nel 48
Jacob, Jr Nel 48
Leonard, Boley Fay 32
Fulton Hrs 320
Patrick Cam 25
Robert Fay 45
Whitehead Fay 23
Wm. Bar 54
Leper, James Adr 10
Lesear, David Cas 42
Lesher, Mary Nel 41
Lesley, James Jes 51
John Flo 105
Joseph Mon 367
Robert Flo 105
Leslie, Aaron Hrd 283
Alexr. Hrd 303
Lester, Abraham Cum 172
Danl. Cum 172
James Gal 184
John L. Gal 183
John Jr. Gal 197
Thos. Cum 172
Wm. Cum 172
Lestlie, Benjn. Nel 47
Letcher, Benja. Gar 213
Stephen Mer 319
Stephen G. Mer 341
Letchworth, Joseph Fay 54
Leton, John Grp 273
Lett, Randol Log 192
Leucas, Robt. War 243
Leumden, Reuben She 232
Levaugh, Abram War 256
Level, Ezekiel Mas 253
James Bar 36
James Mad 240
John Jes 49
Joseph Hrs 310
Levell, Stephen Lin 123
Leveridge, John Mad 238
Levers, William Nel 48
Levery, William Log 178
Levesty, John Mul 391
Levi, Coleman War 263
Elias Mas 252
Judas Mas 252
Levil, Edwd. Gar 214
Levill, Lewis She 206
Leville, Robert Fay 52
Levin, Richd. Hrd 292
Levinsher, John Woo 381
Levingston, David Bra 144
David Bra 146
James Jes 50
Jesse Jes 50
Levon, Jacob Mul 398
Levy, Abraham Hrs 309
Isacc Hrs 309
Levyman, Abraham Bar 41
Lewallen, Samuel Ohi 102
Lewallin, Clabourn War 244
Jacob Ohi 73
Wm. War 272
Lewallyn, Abednigo Hop 376
Mesheck Hop 376
Lewellen, Isaac Nel 47
Steely Jes 50
Lewes, Elizabeth Mul 402
Lewis, Aaron Log 184
Abijah Nel 47
Abner Knx 84
Abraham Mad 238
Abraham She 238
Adam Mad 238
Alexander Fra 141
Alexander Hrs 314
Andw. P. Bar 36
Ann, free woman of-colour Jes 50
Anna Cal 17
Aron War 251
Asa K. Clr 134
Asariah Chr 79
Azariah Wsh 294
Benj. Way 360
Benjamin Cum 166
Benjamin Flo 105
Catherine Cum 181
Catherine, Senr Cum 182
Charles Flo 105
Charles Pul 156
Charles L. Liv 158
Charles M. Grp 276
Daniel Nel 48
Daniel Pul 155
David Cam 33
David Gar 213
Edward Grn 256
Elizabeth Fay 39
Exum War 245
Fielding She 218
Fielding Woo 392
Francis Mas 255
Gabl. Log 178
Gabriel Fle 71

Lewis, George Wsh 296
Gidian Bar 45
Heckter Fay 50
Henry Fra 140
Henry Jef 5
Henry K. Chr 53
Hugh Liv 152
Isaac Chr 99
Isaac Log 182
Isaac She 234
Isaac She 236
Isaac O. War 251
Isaac Wsh 295
Isaiah War 272
Izaah Chr 64
Jacob, freeman Fay 17
Jacob She 237
James Bar 26
James Cly 155
James Cly 157
James Cly 157
James Fle 67
James She 207
James Woo 390
Jas. Bar 45
Jeremiah Grn 250
Jesse Nel 47
Jesse She 233
Jessee Fay 23
Jno. Hnr 364
Joab War 276
John Bou 126
John Bra 149
John Bre 162
John Cal 7B
John Cly 157
John Fra 140
John Gal 184
John Gar 213
John Gar 214
John Jes 50
John Knx 86
John Liv 155
John Mad 240
John Mer 319
John Mer 320
John Pul 155
John Woo 392
John Wsh 294
John Wsh 294
Jonathan Gar 214
Joseph Bar 36
Joseph Bra 142
Joseph Mad 239
Joseph Mer 319
Joseph Nel 8
Joseph Pul 157
Joseph She 233
Joseph She 237
Joseph F. Cum 165
Leonard Pul 155
Lilburne Liv 160
Martha Bou 126
Mary Fay 23
Mary Wsh 295
Messenger Cly 151
Nath. Cly 157
Nathl. Mad 238
Neriah War 276
Nicholas Lew 100
Nicholas M. Jef 29
Peter Hrs 320
Polly Chr 67
Randolph Liv 158
Richard Gal 183
Richard Mer 319
Richard Pul 157

Lewis, cont.
Richd. Cum 165
Robert Chr 80
Robert Lew 98
Robert T. Cas 48
Robert W. Jef 29
Robert W. Mer 319
Saml. Cal 17
Saml. Gar 215
Samuel Fra 141
Samuel Hrs 321
Samuel Pul 155
Shadrick Chr 72
Shadrick Jes 50
Sml. Lin 123
Solomon Sco 177
Stephen Mas 255
Steven Clr 134
Thaddious Lin 125
Thadeous Cly 157
Thomas Flo 105
Thomas Hrs 308
Thomas Jef 6
Thomas Jes 49
Thomas Log 193
Thomas Mas 252
Thomas Mas 255
Thomas, Sr Nel 48
Vencent Nel 48
William Clr 134
William Cly 150
William Fay 23
William Fra 140
William Jes 49
William She 237
Silliam, Col. Jes 49
Wm. Jef 5
Wm. War 255
Wm. Way 364
Lewiss, F. John Lin 125
Lewman, John FLe 76
Noah Fle 66
Lewright, John Bul 181
Leyman, John Ohi 91
Liasson, John Bou 95
Liburn, Richd. Sco 187
Licester, John Mer 319
Peter Mer 318
Lidick, Elizabeth Bou 126
Jacob Fay 58
Lidy, Michael Jes 51
Liech, James Cal 14
Lifton, Uriah Mas 255
Ligget, John Clr 134
William Ohi 79
Liggett, Esther She 209
John She 225
Light, Sally Grn 248
Lighter, Elizabeth Jef 6
Henry Jef 6
Lightfoot, Deastin Pen 111
Edward Jef 6
Edward B. Pen 114
Goodrich Pen 114
Goodridge Mer 319
Henry T. Wsh 294
John Nel 48
John B. Pen 105
Phillip Adr 10
Phillip Pen 105
Robert Pen 111
William Pen 114
Wm. War 268
Likeings, Jos. War 264
Wm. War 264
Likens, Isaac Mon 360
Likes, James Fle 75

Likes, cont.
Melakia Fle 75
Lile, James Grn 264
Jas. War 279
Liles, Peter Cum 174
Widow Cum 174
Lillard, Abraham Liv 145
Ann Mer 318
Daniel Mer 319
Ephraim Fra 139
James Mer 318
John Liv 145
John, Junr Fra 140
John, Senr Fra 140
Joseph Mer 319
Mason Liv 145
Thomas Fra 140
Thomas Mad 239
Lilley, John She 234
Wm. Mon 347
Lilly, Armiger Bou 96
Gabriel Woo 399
Jno. Nel 48
Joshua Hrs 313
Pleasant Nic 51
Susannah Bou 96
Thomas Nel 48
Thos. Jr Bou 96
Thomas, Sr Bou 96
Limeback, Daniel Clr 134
Limebaugh, Danl. Nel 8
Limes, Joseph Way 370
Limeson, James S. Grp 278
Lin, Bery Chr 94
David Cal 18
Linam, David Jef 5
Joseph Bou 96
Molly Bra 148
Linch, Benjamin Pul 156
Daniel Mon 360
Michel Bra 145
Nancy War 274
William Pul 156
Lincoln, Josiah Wsh 296
Mordecai Wsh 294
Thos. Hrd 299
Linder, Abraham Hrd 302
Danl. Junr Hrd 284
Daniel, Senr Hrd 302
Jacob, Junr Hrd 298
Jacob, Senr Hrd 302
Joseph Cum 181
Lindley, John Hop 378
Joseph Mas 254
Lindon, Ben Cly 159
Lindsay, George Hrd 302
John Fle 82
Lindsey, Abraham But 195
Abraham Ohi 85
Amos Log 189
Christopher Clr 134
Colep War 248
Daniel Ohi 85
James Bou 95
James Hnr 360
James Hnr 365
James Log 90
Jesse Gal 184
John Fra 142
John War 253
John B. Cam 33
Joseph Woo 400
Mark Way 366
Martha Hnr 356
Richd. Cam 25
Saml. Grn 249
Thomas Mas 252

Lindsey, cont.
Thos. Jr. Cam 25
Thos. Snr Cam 32
Vachal Fra 141
Walter Grn 247
Lindsy, John Hnr 360
Line, James Log 173
Timothy Log 173
Linear, Bird War 262
Collins War 261
Linebargar, Frederick Lin 123
Linebough, Thos. Log 184
Linegar, Elizabeth Mon 382
Linehard, Thos. Bou 126
Lines, Abrum Log 173
Liney, Charles Way 371
Lingen, Joseph Nel 48
Lingingfelter, -
George Fay 29
John Fay 29
Valenstine Fay 29
Lingonfelter,
Jacob Jes 49
Link, Christian Pul 156
Henry Adr 10
Jacob Bou 126
Joseph Clr 134
Linkhorn, Thomas Fay 23
Links, Nancy She 229
Linley, Jacob Chr 56
John Chr 56
Thomas Chr 55
Linn, Adam Chr 102
Alexr. Lin 125
Andrew Mas 253
Armiger Bou 96
Charles Chr 96
Ebenezer Mas 252
Edward War 273
Elexander Fay 55
Fanney Cas 41
James Ohi 100
John Pen 109
John Sco 186
Ruben Chr 96
Wm. Cas 45
Linna, George Mon 370
Linnise, Charles Est 8
Linsey, Allin Q. Fay 20
Ann Sco 185
Anthony Sco 186
Archibald Chr 68
Calip Chr 96
Carlton Chr 98
David Hrs 310
Henry Sco 171
James Chr 84
James Chr 97
James Sco 171
John Lin 125
Joseph Fay 43
Joshua Chr 97
Nathaniel Fay 20
William Fay 43
Linthicum, Thos. Cas 42
Thos. Cas 46
Wm. Cas 46
Linticum, John Bul 180
Linton, Moses Nel 47
Linvill, Lewis Bra 144
Morgan Clr 134
Linville, Elijah Mon 376
Isayas Mon 382
Jno. Hrd 297
John Mas 256
Wm. Jur Rck 163

Linville, cont.
Wm. Snr Rck 163
Worldly Rck 163
Liny, Henry Way 371
Lion, Ezekiel Mer 319
Hesikiah Grp 274
James, freeman Fay 18
John Mer 319
Joseph Bar 39
Joseph Mer 319
Samuel Mer 319
Stephen Mer 319
Lions, Umphra Hrs 312
Lipler, Geo. Hnr 364
Lips, Thomas Pul 157
Lipscomb, Nathan Mad 237
Lipscum, Andrew Cam 26
Geo. Cam 26
Lipscumb, John Cam 24
Lipsey, John Gar 214
Lipsy, Thomas Pul 155
Lisby, Henry She 228
Lisk, Geo. Hnr 351
William Hnr 362
Lisle, Danl. Grn 260
Lister, Carnelius She 238
Ebenezar Way 373
Elias Mer 318
John Way 373
Jonathan Bou 96
Joseph Way 373
Litcher, William Fra 141
Litchworth, Benjn. War 268
Litel, Robert Fay 52
Litel.., ... Hrs 305
Liter, Abraham Bou 126
Henry Bou 126
Henry, Jr Bou 126
Jacob Bou 126
John, Jr Bou 126
John, Senr Bou 126
Lewis Bou 126
Literal, Joseph Mer 318
Litherland, James Jef 5
John Jef 5
Litle, Henry Fle 72
Jacob Jef 5
Liton, James Pul 157
Litral, John Chr 100
Litret, Richard Fay 23
Litrey, John Gra 237
Litsey, James Bre 159
Litsing, Anthony Wsh 296
Randal Wsh 292
Susanna Wsh 296
Litt, Joseph War 255
Littele, John -
Sillers Log 164
Litteljohn, John Grp 270
Littell, James Log 164
John Mas 253
Littelton, Burrell Log 175
Litten, burton Knx 65
Caleb Bou 96
John Bou 95
Solomon Knx 80
Litteral, John Cum 168
Silas Cum 168
Litterrell, Thomas Knx 82
Little, Abraham Fle 88
Abraham Fra 139
Amos Hnr 363
Charles Mul 390
Edmond Jef 29
Elizabeth Mer 318
George Ohi 99
Henry Fle 90

Little, cont.
Isaac Flo 105
John Jef 5
John Ohi 96
Jonas Ohi 100
Jonas War 248
Michael She 213
Philip Sco 174
Saml. Log 171
Samuel Fle 80
William Fra 142
William, Junr Liv 148
William, Senr Liv 148
Wm. Bar 38
Wm. Jef 27
Littlejohn, Chals. Cas 40
John Mas 253
John Sco 177
Morris Nel 48
Saml. Lin 125
William Wsh 294
Littlepage, Epper Mul 388
James Mul 392
John Mul 388
Littleton, John Fle 67
Savage Hop 377
Wm. Hop 377
Litton, Michael Bou 96
Littrel, Richard Cas 44
Richd. Adr 10
Thos. Adr 10
Littrell, Abner Gar 215
Lively, Cannon Bar 41
Gilliam She 216
Richard Wsh 297
Shadrick Mas 253
Livers, Judith Wsh 295
Robert Nel 47
Robert Nel 48
Samuel Wsh 297
Thomas Wsh 296
Livesen, Samuel Bou 126
Livingston, Barny Hrd 288
Robert Liv 150
Sarah Woo 389
Liviston, Richd. Way 365
Liwis, James Cly 149
Lizen, Peter Fay 23
Lizenby, Wm. Woo 398
Lizon, James Hnd 327
Lloyd, Joseph Nel 47
Nancy Bou 96
Loathers, Jno. Nel 46
Lobb, Chapman Grn 252
Reuben Grn 252
Wm. Gar 215
Loch, John Hnd 327
Lochhart, Enoch Hnr 359A
Lochridge, James Mon 369
James Nic 52
John Nic 51
Robert Woo 377
Wm. Nic 51
Lock, Abraham Knx 90
David Bar 32
Jacob Bar 35
James Bar 35
John D. Jef 29
Peter Gal 184
Richard Mon 381
Richd. Jun Bar 35
Richd. Sen Bar 35
William Bou 95
Lockard, Arcd. Pul 156
Lockart, Charles Hrs 309
David Log 165
James Hrs 310

Lockart, cont.
Levy Mer 319
Locke, Nancy She 240
Samuel Hnr 356
Lockeman, Nicholas Mul 408
Locker, John Way 358
Locket, Andrew Pul 157
Archabald Pul 156
Elijah Cum 165
Jesse Bre 169
Joseph Pul 156
Wm. Way 360
Lockett, Benja. Clr 134
Francis Hnd 344
James Jes 50
Lockhart, David Log 192
Elisha Fra 139
James Chr 64
James Mas 256
Silies Jes 50
Lockit, Josiah Pul 157
Lockly, John Fay 50
Lockman, Vincent Mer 318
Lockmane, John Clr 134
Lockridge, Andrew Wsh 293
Joseph War 258
Robert Fle 70
Lockwood, Jacob Grp 271
John Fay 18
Samuel Pen 105
Lodowick, Chist Nel 48
Lodywick, Christopher Mer 320
John Mer 320
Loe, Jesse Lin 123
Jesse Lin 125
Lofferty, Thomas Clr 134
Loffland, Smith Log 194
Loftin, Easter Liv 153
John Jef 24
Sarah Liv 153
Van, Junr Liv 153
Van, Senr Liv 152
Loftis, George Chr 59
Loftiss, William Fle 85
Lofton, Isaac Mer 320
Logan, Archibald Fay 17
Archibald Jes 50
B. David Lin 125
David Fay 17
David Fay 43
David Lin 123
David Nic 51
George Fay 43
Hugh Hnd 331
Hugh Fay 33
Hugh Fay 54
Hugh, Jnr Lin 123
Hugh, Jnr Lin 123
Jugh, Snr Lin 123
Isaac Bar 42
James Cum 171
James Cum 179
James Fay 43
James Fle 62
James Hop 372
James Jes 50
James Knx 73
James Lin 125
James She 221
James, Snr Lin 125
John Fay 23
John Gar 214
John Knx 84
John Mad 240
John Mas 253
John She 240

Logan, cont.
John, Senr Mas 254
Joseph Bra 142
Joseph War 277
Joshua War 277
Nath. Cly 156
Patrick Jes 49
Robert Lin 125
Sally Fra 141
Saml. Log 180
Samuel Hrs 323
Samuel Log 165
Samuel Mad 244
Samuel Mas 254
Thomas Mer 319
Timothy Gar 214
William Bou 95
William Fay 43
William Lin 123
William, Jr Knx 74
William, Sr Knx 85
Willm. Sco 170
Wm. Bar 51
Wm. Bra 144
Wm. Jef 29
Wm. Mon 353
Wm. Sr Bra 144
Wm. B. Bar 31
Login, Charles Hnr 364
Mathew Chr 99
Logsden, Edward Mad 239
Joseph Mad 240
Logsdon, Edward Jr Mad 239
Elisha Mad 240
James Mad 239
John Bar 33
John Mad 237
Joseph Gra 241
Joseph, Redhead Mad 240
Peter Mad 240
Tho. Bar 33
Logstan, William Est 8
Logston, Henry Hrd 291
Jas. Hrd 295
Thos. Hrd 283
Thos. Hrd 286
Wm. Hrd 283
Wm. Hrd 285
Lohr, Christian Bou 96
Lohrage, William She 239
Loljen, Hugh Pul 156
Lollard, Jacob Cum 174
James Cum 178
Reuben Cum 178
Lollen, John Hnr 355
Loller, James Adr 10
Lomack, Elijah Bar 29
Lomax, Tho. Bar 41
London, Oliver Hnr 354
Robert, Jr Hnr 356
Robt. Sr Hnr 362
William Hnr 354
Lone, Margarel Clr 134
Loner, Jacob Nel 47
Loney, Rebcah Fay 60
Long, Aaron She 212
Abner War 254
Adam Fay 32
Adam Fay 53
Alexr. Sco 181
Anderson War 243
Andrew Hrd 286
Anne Bou 96
Benjamin Fra 141
Benjamin Mas 255
Benjn. War 270
Brumfield War 269

Long, cont.
David Mad 239
Edmund Mad 239
Edmund Mer 318
Edwd. Cum 185
Eliakum Bou 95
Elisha Fay 42
Elisha Sco 189
Eliza Hnr 361
Frances Fay 49
Gabrel Chr 115
Garrard Woo 402
Griffin Cal 12
Isac Fay 39
Jacob Hnd 332
James Pul 155
James War 254
James Woo 401
Jesse Mer 318
Jno. Hrd 303
Jno. D. Mad 239
Joel Way 359
John Chr 54
John Chr 73
John Fra 140
John Hnd 332
John Log 194
John Mad 239
John War 246
John War 256
John Way 369
John Wsh 293
John, Junr Woo 399
John, Senr Woo 398
John S. Log 181
Joseph Chr 67
Joseph Mon 365
Lawrence F[illegible] 140
Levi [illegible] 293
Mary Woo 394
Michl. Hrd 298
Nicholas Sco 189
Nimrod Log 191
Nocholas Fay 42
Polly Cum 179
Polly Fay 45
Reuben Woo 399
Richd. War 269
Robert Mon 365
Robert Sco 171
Robert She 227
Saml. Hnr 366
Samuel Fay 18
Samuel Mul 390
Samuel Nic 52
Samuel She 215
Solomon Cum 185
Thomas Fay 45
Thomas Fra 142
Thomas Jef 27
Thomas Wsh 294
Thomas Wsh 297
Thomas P. Fra 141
Thos. S. Log 181
William Chr 57
William Fay 29
William Fay 39
William Fra 141
William Hnd 339
William Knx 81
William B. Woo 400
Wm. Cum 180
Wm. War 243
Longdon, Beverly Sco 170
Edward Hrs 311
John Bar 55
Thomas Fay 44

Longley, Jno. Lew 103
Longly, Jno. Lew 104
Thomas Mas 252
Thomas, Jun Mas 255
William Mas 255
Longmore, Sarah Bou 95
Longnecker, Andr. Bou 96
Peter Bou 96
Loocke, Thos. Cas 48
Loofbourrow,
Thos. V. Fra 142
Looney, Jonathan Mer 318
Loots, Jacob Nel 48
William Nel 48
Loper, Peter Nel 48
Lorance, William Mad 240
Lord, Thos. Bra 146
Loring, Fredk. Bou 69
Lorton, Robt. Cum 175
Lot, George Ohi 86
Lotchridge, John Mon 353
Lotsprick, William Fay 18
Lott, Aaron Mul 395
Abner Clr 134
Batholomew Mul 396
Elisha Fra 140
Jessee She 204
John Wsh 293
John Wsh 293
Richard clr 134
Solomo Mul 395
Louallen, saml. Jef 29
Louden, Will Bou 96
Wm. Bou 96
Louderback, Abram Woo 382
Margaret Fra 141
Peter Hrs 314
Loudon, David Bou 126
John Hnr 366
Lough, Jacob Bar 49
John Cum 176
Thomas Cum 176
Lougherry, Alexr. Woo 399
Loughlen, Robert Hrs 307
Lourey, Jeremiah Jef 5
Loury, James Chr 113
Lousley, George D. Fle 81
Lovangood, George Nic 51
Love, Andrew Liv 147
Charles Fay 33
Charles Pen 108
David She 242
Edmund Bar 27
Elizabeth Fra 141
Esther Cal 20
James Knx 83
James Liv 152
James She 226
John Boo 60
Leonard Bra 142
Mary Fay 48
Matthew Jef 5
Samuel Bou 126
Samuel Mon 361
Tho. Bar 48
Thomas Pul 157
Thomas Pen 108
William Bou 126
William Bre 158
William Liv 147
Loveall, Jonathan Way 357
Stephen Way 357
Zachariah Way 357
Lovel, Gerreard Mer 319
Rheubin Hrs 323
Lovelace, Andrew But 195
Archd. But 195
Lovelace, cont.
Benj. Nel 47
Elias But 195
Zedh. Nel 47
Loveless, Anne Mad 237
John Cam 27
Reason Bul 180
Reason Bul 181
Selvinus Bra 151
Lovelis, Jno. Pul 157
Lovell, George Bou 126
James L. War 276
John Log 188
Willm. War 276
Lovers, Joseph Hop 374
Loving, Gabriel Hop 380
Isaac Jes 50
John Hop 380
John War 253
John War 257
Lovitt, Edward Knx 72
Lovlace, George Mul 398
Vatchel Mul 402
William Mul 400
Low, Charles Fay 32
Charles Fay 47
Hannah Mer 320
Isaac Nic 51
Jas. Way 367
John Clr 134
John Pen 108
Ralph Log 173
Richard Bul 180
Thos. Way 370
Thos. War 371
William Hrs 315
Lowderback, Andy Nic 51
Lowe, Calip War 259
David War 259
Edward Wsh 294
Eleanor Gal 183
George Nic 51
Isaac War 259
Isaac War 259
Samuel Wsh 294
Thomas Wsh 294
Wm. War 259
Lowell, Andrew Hrs 305
Lowens, Francis Jes 49
Francis, Jur Jes 51
Lowery, Gersham Jes 49
William Hrs 314
Lowlin, John Way 374
Lowman, John Fay 18
Joseph Jef 29
William Mad 240
Lowness, Henry Clr 134
Lownsdale, James Mas 255
Lowrey, Abraham Fay 44
James Fay 17
John Fay 25
Overton But 195
Robt. She 232
Saml. Sco 168
Samuel Chr 113
Wm. War 267
Lowry, Enoch Mad 237
James Fay 18
James Grp 273
John Fay 44
John Grp 272
John Jes 49
John Mad 239
John Sco 167
John Sco 183
Lucretia mad 239
Melvine Jes 50
Lowry, Melvun Grp 272
Nathan Mad 240
Robert Jes 50
Thomas Bre 169
Thomas Log 194
William Fra 141
William Mad 239
Wm. Bre 169
Wm. G. Fle 82
Lowstutter, Peter Boo 60
Loyd, Charles War 277
D. Richard Mas 255
Frethias Liv 157
James Mad 239
James Nel 48
Jas. Way 358
John Gar 215
John Nel 48
Nichl. Way 352
Robert Bou 95
Samuel Mad 239
Simeon Mas 254
Susanah Bra 151
Thomas Sco 192
Thos. Cum 169
William Wsh 297
Lucas, Abraham She 201
Abrm. Hrd 290
Bennet Bre 161
Charles War 243
Conelus Hrd 288
Elijah Boo 60
Elijah Sco 176
Henry Wsh 297
Ignatius Wsh 296
Joanna Fra 141
John Cas 41
John Chr 74
John Hop 371
John Ohi 80
John Sco 177
John She 204
Latitia Fay 18
Richd. Cly 149
Robert Mas 256
Samuel Mas 306
Sarah War 243
Stephen Sco 184
Thomas, Senr Sco 183
Thos. Sco 177
William Sco 183
Zachariah Fay 18
Zachariah Wsh 295
Luce, Abner But 195
David Mul 389
John Mul 400
William Mul 400
Luchie, N.T. Hnr 354
Luckett, Benjamin Wsh 296
Henry Wsh 295
Hezekiah Wsh 293
James Nel 47
Saml. M. Jef 6
Samuel Fay 24
Luckie, Willm. Lin 123
Lucky, James Mad 239
Jesse Flo 105
Joseph Bou 95
Robert Bou 95
Robert Bul 180
Lucus, Betsy Nel 41
Charles Bou 96
Charles D. Chr 55
Edmond Bra 148
Engram Liv 150
Jeremiah Liv 150
Jesse Mer 319

Lucus, cont.
Lenda Nel 47
Richd. Sco 174
Wm. Bra 153
Lucuss, Willm. Lin 125
Lucy, free woman Fay 18
Lucy, free negro Fay 32
Lucy, Cadwellade Chr 97
Isham Chr 104
Luggette, James Sco 186
John Jur Sco 186
John, Senr Sco 186
William Sco 186
Luke, John Sco 186
Lukens, Peter Fle 78
Luker, John Nic 52
Lumpton, Wm. Jef 6
Lunceford, Nancy Chr 116
Nelly Lin 123
Roadhan Lin 125
Luncy, Dad. Lew 101
Luney, David Lew 103
Lunsford, Bazel She 238
John Mas 255
Moses Mas 255
William She 226
Lursten, Thos. Adr 10
Lurton, Jacob Jef 6
James Mas 254
William Mas 254
Willm. Sco 169
Lurty, Robert Mas 253
William Mas 255
Lush, John Cly 157
Wm. Hrd 291
Lusk, George V. Liv 153
Hugh Hrd 303
John Clr 134
Saml. Cly 153
Wm. Gar 213
Luster, Abner Flo 105
Edwd. Gar 214
Fownten Chr 58
Jesse Mer 320
John Grp 274
Noah Bul 180
Vinson Pul 156
William Chr 93
Lutes, Henry Mad 240
Lutley, Merrit Log 195
Luttel, William She 207
Luttrel, George Sco 185
James She 214
John Sco 178
Joseph Sco 172
Joshua Sco 183
Robt. Gar 213
William Jes 50
Luttrol, Jonathan Sco 172
Lux, William She 204
Lycan, David Flo 105
Jeremiah Flo 105
John Flo 105
Lykens, Wm. Mon 363
Lykins, David Cum 186
Lyle, David She 228
Jane Fay 42
Joel R. Bou 69
John Bou 69
John Clr 134
John Fay 59
Peter Clr 134
Robert War 249
John War 249
Wm. War 250
Lynch, Alexander Wsh 295
David Mad 240
Lynch, cont.
Dings Pul 157
Edward War 247
Edwd. Hrd 283
Jerry Hrd 300
Milly Nel 47
Joseph Nel 46
Patrick Sco 177
Lyne, Milly Fra 142
Thomas Woo 391
Lynem, Margrate Jes 50
(free woman of colour)
Lynich, Cornelius Bou 96
Lynn, Adam Woo 386
Edley Hnd 334
Elizabeth Cam 30
Elizabeth Jef 5
James Jef 5
James Log 164
John Hnd 334
Patrick Mad 240
Pitts Log 164
Samuel Jef 5
William Hnd 334
William Mul 400
Lynsey, Jno. Nel 47
Lynville, Moses Grn 266
Lyon, Charles Mas 255
David Bar 50
Elizabeth Mas 254
Henry She 197
Hezekiah Jef 29
James Rck 161
Jas. Cly 154
John Adr 10
John Adr 10
John Bar 55
John Bou 126
John Wsh 297
Joseph Mon 382
Lawson Woo 383
Mathew Cal 7
Noah Mon 370
Saml. Jr Bou 96
Samuel She 197
Sarah Bou 126
Stephen Rck 159
Thomas Wsh 297
William She 197
Zachariah She 197
Lyons, Henry War 248
Hugh Bul 180
James Bra 145
John Fle 75
Jonethan Fay 23
Joseph Fle 79
Stephen Cam 26
Thomas Gar 214
Lytle, John Gar 214
Nathanel Fle 74
Robert Gar 199

-- M --

Maccaun, James Fay 18
Macconnell, James Jef 27
Maccoun, Ann Fay 28
James T. Fay 28
Maccy, James Lin 125
Mace, John Bou 98
Machir, John Mas 306
Mack, Daniel Wsh 288
Mackay, Alex. Mad 231
Alexander Wsh 289
MackCee, James Hrs 310
Mackentire, James Grp 271
Mackey, James Nel 40
James She 234
John Lew 98
Mackintire, Robt. Bou 97
Mackleroy, Peggy Jef 8
Macky, David Chr 94
James Cum 180
John Adr 11
Maclewain, Elizabeth Hrs 320
Macklin, Hugh Fra 147
Macollee, Thomas Flo 103
Macomson, Andrew Hrs 310
Thomas Hrs 310
Wm. Hrs 310
Maconison, John Hrs 310
Macum, Joseph Hnd 338
MadCalf, Thomas Fay 53
William Fay 54
Maddan, Susan Nic 55
Madden, Charles Mas 262
Elisha But 195
James But 195
Jeremiah Fle 71
John Bou 127
John Bou 127
John Fle 71
Joseph Fle 69
Walter Wsh 291
Maddens, Live Fle 80
Maddik, Nathl. Mad 229
Maddison, James But 198
Maddon, Dennes Grp 274
Nathan Grp 274
Maddox, George Flo 104
John Ohi 81
John Woo 393
John W. Hnd 346
Nelson Woo 389
Smallwood Mer 342
Stephen Hnd 338
Thomas Hnd 337
Maddus, George B. Fle 82
Madison, George Fra 149
John Fra 150
John Liv 156
John H. Cal 9
Maria Jes 51
Madkin, Joseph Sco 176
Madkins, Danl. War 259
Madole, John Log 195
Madrill, Adam Pul 153
George Pul 153
Maffett, George Fay 28
William Nel 42
Wm. Mon 353
Maffit, Henry Nic 53
William Nic 53
Maffitt, Thos. Nic 53
Mafield, John Knx 73
Micajah She 213
Micajah She 219
Magahe, Wm. Mon 380
Magarah, James Liv 155
Magbee, James Bou 100
John Bou 100
Henry Mad 233
Magee, Humphrey Mad 234
Ralph Mad 233
Wm. War 259
Magers, James Mas 261
Mageshion, Barna Mon 373
Maggard, Samuel Knx 85
Maggot, Jacob Bar 54
Magill, Hugh Lin 127

Magill, cont.
James Lin 127
John Fra 145
William Lin 127
William, Jun Lin 127
Maglone, Hugh Fay 18
Magner, John Bou 98
Willm. Bou 98
Magness, Joseph War 251
Magowan, W.Stewart Fay 18
Magruda, Nathaniel She 238
Magruder, Josiah She 220
Magrue, George Bul 181
Maguire, Edward Fay 44
Mahall, Timothy Fra 145
William Fra 142
William Fra 143
Mahan, James Knx 65
James Log 176
James War 275
Thomas Knx 76
Thos. Bou 98
William Woo 388
Wm. Grn 248
Mahany, James Bar 26
John Bou 98
Mahead, Samuel She 236
Mahett, John Fle 67
Mahhan, Alexr. War 251
Mahin, Elizes. Fle 85
John Fle 80
Maholen, William Mad 231
Mahon, Alexander Fay 28
Alexr. Cum 179
David Cum 170
John Mer 321
Peter She 201
Rane Bre 162
Mahoney, Henry Wsh 293
James She 215
William Wsh 293
Mahony, Jas. H. Sco 190
Mahorna, Milburn Bul 181
Mahorney, Dennes Fay 34
Mahue, Walter Fay 44
Mahurin, John She 214
Othenile She 208
Steph. Hrd 285
Maiart, John Fle 78
Maiden, Benjamin Gra 239
Main, John Jef 29
Mainer, Steven Hrs 319
Mainor, Christophr Flo 103
James Flo 103
Lewis Flo 103
Mains, Tho. Bar 49
Maiz, Robert Grn 258
Majers, Robert War 260
Major, James Fra 149
John Fra 148
Lewis R. Fra 148
Thomas Fra 149
Majors, Alexr. Log 177
George Fra 142
James Hnd 338
John Fra 144
Littleton Fra 142
Peggy Fra 142
Thos. P. Fra 151
Makem, John Hnd 347
Makenison, James Fle 84
Makim, Ellender Mer 324
Makimson, Joseph Bre 168
Makin, Robert Bre 163
Saml. Fle 63
Makinny, Enock Adr 10
Malady, John Boo 61
Malcolm, Jas. Bou 97
Malery, Henry Fay 18
Henry H. Bou 99
Rodger Fay 49
Samuel Fay 49
Malin, Elizabeth Mer 323
Isaac Hnr 360
Job Ohi 68
John Hop 377
Mallary, John Hrs 321
Mallett, Thomas Flo 104
Mallonce, William Mad 236
Mallory, Charles Sco 182
George Sco 180
Joseph Sco 186
Malohon, Charles Wsh 288
James Wsh 288
Malona, James Hrs 309
John Cly 159
Malone, Ben She 236
Catharine Hrs 309
Daniel Liv 158
Drury She 207
James Woo 377
John Gar 199
John Woo 378
John Wsh 291
John, Jr Woo 378
Jonas War 249
Saml. Bar 40
Simon Wsh 291
Simon Wsh 291
Tho. Hop 371
William Grn 260
Winn Bar 54
Malot, Elias Jef 6
Hiram Jef 8
Malott, Joseph Mad 236
Maloy, Gillim Cum 182
John Jef 5
Malrey, James Chr 104
John Chr 100
Thomas Chr 100
Thomas Chr 104
Malroy, Josiah B. Liv 153
Malry, William Bou 127
Malvin, James Log 179
Man, Benjn. Cam 24
Christopher Bra 143
Francis Hrs 317
George Chr 78
Peter Bra 148
Sarah Mas 265
Manes, Josiah Bar 21
Peter Boo 63
Mangan, Henry War 273
Mangham, John K. Log 193
Manifee, Richard Mon 363
Spencer Bou 100
Manihon, Jacob Pen 109
Manin, John Clr 135
John Nic 55
Meredith Nic 54
Samuel Nic 54
Maning, Hardy War 243
Manion, Ambrose Mad 234
Edward Mad 232
James Mad 235
Thomas War 245
Mankins, Peter Flo 103
Walter Flo 103
Manley, D. Joseph Fay 18
Gabl. Bar 29
James Mon 358
John R. Bar 28
Jonathan War 259
Jonathan War 259
Manley, cont.
Richd. War 261
Thos. War 259
Manliff, Mary Sco 179
Manlove, Bartholow Fay 42
Manly, Ephraim Gra 243
Mann, Andrew Chr 116
Beverly Mer 324
David Mer 324
Henry Bou 99
Jackson Mer 325
Jacob Nic 54
James Bou 97
James Woo 394
John Chr 116
John Grn 259
John Nic 55
John T. Pen 114
Joseph Grn 258
Josiah Mer 324
Mary Grn 259
Moses Grn 259
Peeter Nic 54
Richard Pen 105
Robert Cum 171
Samuel Flo 104
Thomas She 236
William Flo 103
William Grn 250
Mannen, John Hnd 343
John Mas 256
Mannifee, James Lin 125
Mannin, boaz Flo 104
Manning, Ambros Bar 25
Ambros Bar 37
James Bar 25
John Sco 169
Wm. Sco 185
Mannon, Elijah Cal 17
Mannors, Milendia Cas 38
Manor, Moses Flo 103
William Flo 103
Mansfield, Anns Fay 45
Jas. Bar 42
Mans, Jonas Hrs 319
Mansfield, Samuel Fay 48
Wm. Bar 42
Manson, John Nel 8
Manspile, Sally Lin 127
Mantfont, John Hnr 356
Mantiloe, James Bar 30
Manuel, Fleat Fay 48
Thomas Fay 48
William Fay 32
William Fay 48
Maple, Benjamin Mas 260
George Lew 95
John Jef 7
William Bou 128
Maples, Thomas Liv 145
Mapin, Jane Mon 374
Mar, M. Henry Mer 323
Maraman, Ann Nel 40
Jno. Nel 46
John Nel 37
Maratta, Mathias Nel 42
Marble, Peter Hrs 318
Marcason, John Jes 54
March, George Boo 61
Jacob Clr 135
John A. Fra 150
Laurance Fay 23
Rudolph Mad 235
Marchel, John Bra 141
Marcum, Abner Grn 253
Archd. Way 359
John Grn 253

Marcum, cont.
John Way 359
Marvil Way 359
Wm. Bou 128
Marcus, James Ohi 93
Mardis, James Cam 25
Nathan Jef 6
Rowly Jef 5
Mareme, Zaks. Nel 46
Marell, Wm. Nic 55
Margan, Benj. Nel 45
Margatta, Martha Nel 38
Margroves, Jessee Cal 17
Marhal, John Cam 27
Marier, Jonathan Mon 354
Maris, John Jef 29
Mark, Robert Mon 377
William Bou 99
Marker, John But 195
Timothy Sco 171
Markey, Jonas Bou 127
Markland, Matthew Mad 237
Marklin, Richd. Boo 61
Marks, Benj. Nel 38
Benjamin She 236
Benjamin She 240
Jacob Nel 46
Joanna Wsh 289
Richard Fay 18
Sarah Nel 38
Marksberry, Isaac Gar 213
Jno. Gar 211
Lucy Gar 208
Saml. Gar 208
Wm. Gar 208
Markum, Edm. Way 355
Lewis Sco 170
Thos. Grn 253
Markwell, George Jef 7
John Jef 7
Marlin, William Fra 146
Marlow, Rueben Way 365
Thomas Knx 90
Thomas Way 373
Thos. Hrd 293
Thos. Way 363
Marple, Bennett Wsh 292
John Wsh 291
Marquell, Jas. Fle 63
Landy Fle 63
William, Jr Fle 63
William, Sen Fle 63
Marquells, John Fle 63
Marquill, Henry Fle 88
Marquis, Robert Mad 233
Thomas She 205
William She 205
Wm. Kid Bul 181
Marrel, John Adr 11
Marrikle, George Fle 67
Marion Fle 67
Marrs, Hugh But 195
Hugh Log 178
Isaac Log 166
Isaac Log 178
James Hrs 310
James Jes 51
James Log 178
James Log 193
William But 195
William Log 178
Mars, Saml. Bar 48
Samuel Fra 143
Samuel S. or L. Fra 143
Marsback, Docr. Bou 127
Marsh, Beal Bou 97
Jesse Jes 52

Marsh, cont.
Richard Fay 18
Richard Fay 18
Thomas Jes 54
Thos. Nic 55
William Clr 136
William Jes 54
William Mad 228
William Sr Clr 136
Wm. Bra 142
Marshal, Elizabeth Wsh 289
George Mad 233
Hugh Bar 26
Jno. Grn 263
John Bar 42
Jos. Grn 263
Lewis Log 195
Mary War 253
Robert Fay 35
Robt. Grn 263
Saml. Bar 26
Saml. Bar 46
Samuel Bou 127
Stephen Pen 117
Thos. Grn 262
Thos. Grn 263
Marshall, Alexander Mas 257
Archd. Nic 56
David Bou 99
David Nic 56
Eliza Hnr 363
George Nel 38
George Sco 182
George She 212
George She 228
George She 232
Hubard Mon 357
Hugh Bra 145
Hugh Nic 53
Humphrey Fra 149
Isaac Nel 40
Isaac Nel 45
James Boo 61
James Woo 384
Jane Gar 212
Jane Nel 41
Jessee Rck 159
John Boo 61
John Hnr 359
John Mas 260
John Mas 262
John Mer 321
John Mon 358
John J. Fra 150
Josiah Log 192
K. Alexander Mas 262
Lewis Hnr 361
Lewis Woo 398
Mark Hrd 282
Martin Bra 141
Maryan Hnr 361
Ralph Nic 53
Rebecca Fra 145
Robert Fay 43
Saml. Grn 251
Saml. Nic 53
Sarah Gar 212
T. John Lin 128
Thomas Mas 256
Thomas Mas 306
William Hnd 345
William Jes 52
William Mas 259
William Nel 42
Willm. Lin 128
Willm. Nel 38

Marshall, cont.
Wm. Sco 171
Wm. Sco 175
Wm. Sco 181
Marshawn, Abraham Fay 20'
Marshel, Bennet Hnd 328
James Fay 44
Thomas Knx 81
James Hrs 318
Marstenson, Chrystopher Hrs 320
Marston, William Fra 146
Martain, Hennery Cas 38
Reuban Fle 75
Marten, James Hrs 320
Moses Pul 151
Nelson Pul 151
Martheny, Richard Mer 324
Martial, Wm. Cam 26
Martin, Aaron Sco 178
Abner Cal 19
Abner Hop 375
Abner She 227
Alexander Hrs 311
Amos Nel 40
Andrew Mer 325
Ann Jef 7
Austin Clr 135
Azeriah Est 3
Ben Hrd 286
Benj. She 231
Benjamin Fay 46
Benjamin Jes 53
Benjamin Way 363
Benjn. Sco 175
Charles Pul 153
Chas. Bar 31
Christopher Clr 135
David Fay 24
David Flo 104
David Gar 212
David Liv 150
E. Mary Gar 208
Edmund Mas 302
Edward Hrs 315
Edward Hrs 323
Edward Lin 127
Edward She 214
Elijah Gal 185
Elizabeth Mul 389
Enoch She 220
Esabel Fle 64
Frederick Hrd 286
French Fle 78
George Bra 145
George Clr 135
Gideon War 247
Harry Clr 135
Harry Fra 149
Harry Mas 258
Hartwell Grn 250
Henry Liv 149
Henry Mul 387
Henry C. Fay 51
Hosea Fra 144
Hugh Mul 385
Hugh Mul 392
Hutson Mul 387
Isaac Knx 89
Isabella Nel 40
Jacob Hrs 311
Jacob Hrs 321
Jacob Mon 352
Jacob Sco 187
Jacob, Jur Sco 187
James Bar 32
James Bar 49

Martin, cont.
James Chr 111
James Fra 148
James Hop 376
James Jes 54
James Liv 151
James Log 169
James Mer 321
James Mul 385
James Nic 53
James Ohi 97
James Sco 178
James She 216
James She 223
James She 231
James Woo 388
Jane Bou 98
Jane She 238
Jas. Gar 212
Jas. Way 355
Jas. G. War 252
Jeremiah Mas 262
Jesse Bul 181
Jesse Cum 177
Jesse Knx 83
Jesse She 237
Jno. Pul 149
John Adr 11
John Bar 25
John Bou 99
John Bou 99
John Clr 135
John Clr 135
John Clr 135
John Clr 135
John Clr 146
John Cum 174
John Hrs 320
John Jef 26
John Lin 125
John Lin 127
John Liv 151
John Log 165
John Mad 235
John Mas 260
John Mon 368
John Mul 392
John Nic 53
John Ohi 92
John She 205
John She 223
John She 231
John She 237
John Way 355
Johnson Pul 149
Jonas Hrs 320
Jos. She 231
Joseph Bar 32
Joseph Cam 31
Joseph Hrs 315
Joseph Mas 259
Joseph Sco 178
Joseph She 216
Joseph She 220
Joseph She 231
L. John Fay 18
Larken She 226
Leodice Bre 162
Leonard H. Bar 45
Lewis Cal 16
Lewis Ohi 88
Lewis She 231
Lewis Woo 379
Linza Hop 374
Littleton Bre 162
Luther Bul 181
Martha War 273

Martin, cont.
Martin Mul 402
Miab Nic 52
Micajah Mas 302
Moses Cly 154
Moses Jes 53
Moses Ohi 98
Nathan Clr 135
Nathl. Cum 168
Nathnl. Bar 44
Nicholas Jef 7
Nimrod She 210
Obadiah Lin 128
Obadiah Mer 325
Obediah Lin 115
Patey Liv 160
Peggy Grn 248
Peter Mer 320
Peter She 231
Peter War 275
Pleasant War 258
Reubin Ohi 78
Richard Flo 104
Richard Rck 161
Richard She 219
Robert Boo 61
Robert Bul 181
Robert Clr 135
Robert Mad 228
Robt. Hrd 287
Rubin Cal 12
Russell, Fra 144
Saml. Hrd 290
Saml. Way 369
Samuel Bou 98
Samuel Fay 22
Samuel She 209
Samuel Woo 378
Samuel Woo 394
Samuel L. Wsh 291
Sarah Clr 135
Sarah She 240
Sary Hrs 310
Silvanus Lin 115
Silvanus Lin 128
Stephen Bre 164
Stephen Bre 169
Tho. Bar 54
Thomas Fra 149
Thomas Hrs 310
Thomas Mul 402
Thomas She 201
Thomas She 216
Thomas She 219
Thomas Wsh 292
Thos. Cam 33
Thos. G. War 252
Thos. G. Jr War 252
Tobias Way 360
Tyree Mad 235
Valentine Fay 23
Wilfred Wsh 292
William Chr 68
William Chr 75
William Chr 108
William Chr 111
William Clr 135
William Clr 135
William Flo 104
William Flo 104
William Hnr 352
William Liv 150
William Liv 160
William Mad 229
William Mad 232
William Mad 236
William Mas 259

Martin, cont.
William Mas 259
William Mas 265
William Mer 321
William Mer 324
William Mul 387
William Mul 393
William Nel 39
William Ohi 92
William She 205
William She 220
William She 222
William Woo 385
William Wsh 290
William C. Knx 73
Wm. Bar 29
Wm. Bar 45
Wm. Cam 25
Wm. Cum 177
Wm. Gal 184
Wm. Grn 251
Wm. Hrd 298
Wm. Hrs 323
Wm. Lew 104
Wm. Mon 381
Zadock Knx 80
Martindrill, Thomas Pul 154
Martis, Ruby Grn 245
Marton, John Hnd 329
Marts, Jacob She 201
Marville, Eli Liv 158
Mary Nic 56
Mary, Caleb Flo 106
Marysfield, Elijah Log 177
James Log 177
John Log 177
Masden, John Bul 181
Masey, Alexander Fra 147
Benjaimin Hrs 309
Charles Fra 147
John Hrs 308
John Hrs 309
Robert Bre 167
Mash, David Hrs 324
Ezekiel Way 366
John Hrs 309
Johnathan Hrs 307
Johnathan Hrs 324
Samuel Hrs 324
Sarah Cum 171
Wright Cum 171
Wm. Hrs 324
Mashers, Zachariah Cam 32
Masner, Christian Jes 52
Mason, Andrew Cam 24
Andrew Wsh 289
Ann Fra 143
Benj. Nel 8
Benjn. Nel 42
Burgess Nic 53
Chas. Bou 97
Edwd. Gar 210
Elijah Gar 210
Elisha Gar 210
George Jes 53
George Nel 41
Hugh Cas 37
Isabella Mad 232
James Cas 37
James Knx 67
James Mon 375
James Ohi 81
James Wsh 289
Jno. Hrd 290
John Boo 61
John But 195
John Fay 46

Mason, cont.
John Gar 211
John Hnd 329
John Mad 232
John Mon 375
John Nel 40
John Way 351
John Way 374
John H. Ohi 77
Jonathan Jef 24
Joseph Bre 158
Levin Jef 8
Mathew Chr 81
Micajah Fay 29
Nimrod Fra 143
Peter Fay 29
Peter Sco 190
Reuben Way 365
Richard Cas 38
Robert Knx 67
Saml. Way 374
Thomas Jef 29
William But 195
William Lin 128
Wm. T. Nel 42
Massa, Caby Pul 151
E. Nicolas Pul 151
Massac, George Sco 178
Job Sco 178
Masse, James Lin 127
Massey, Joseph Knx 77
Thomas Knx 89
Thomas mon 375
Wm. Mon 375
Massie, David mas 307
Edwd. Cam 30
John Cam 30
Jonithan War 279
Silvester Mad 228
Thomas Mad 235
Thomas Mas 262
Willm. Sco 169
Massy, Burril Chr 87
Thomas Mer 324
Masten, Elijah Mas 256
Master, Saml. Nel 44
Masters, Curtis Mad 229
James Mad 232
John Woo 386
Joshua Wsh 292
Richard Mas 262
Samuel Mas 263
Samuel G. Log 183
Thomas Mad 229
William Mas 262
Masterson, Aaron Fay 41
Caleb Bou 98
Charles Nel 42
Charles She 213
Gutridge She 213
Hugh Nel 41
James Fay 56
James Pen 112
John Mas 261
John Sco 180
John She 211
John Nel 39
Sarah Gal 186
William Lin 127
Zakh. Nel 39
Mastin, Jacob Mad 233
John Fra 148
Thos. Junr Fra 147
Thos. Senr Fra 148
William Rck 166
Maston, John Fra 148
Matcheltree, George Cas 37

Mateir, Robert Mon 348
Mathene, John Jes 51
Matheny, Isaiah Hrd 293
Joshua Hrd 293
Michael Bou 97
Mickl. Hrd 287
Moses Bou 99
Mather, Richd. Hrd 290
Matherly, Isarel Lin 127
Samuel Lin 127
Mathers, George Fle 86
Given Nic 55
James Nic 55
Samuel Mon 377
Thomas Bou 99
William Nic 55
Wm. Nic 55
Mathes, Jobe Mul 403
Mathew, George Nel 46
Mathews, Burges Pul 154
Chechesr. Boo 61
Conrod, Jr Nel 42
Conrod, Sr Nel 42
Daniel Pul 149
Henry Bou 127
Henry Bul 181
Jacob Bou 127
James Bar 28
James Boo 61
James Pul 149
James Pul 154
Joel Jes 53
Joel Pul 153
John Bar 34
John Est 7
John, Jr Bar 19
Martin Hnd 335
Obadiah Pul 154
Peter Clr 146
Richard Grn 260
William Grn 256
Wm. Grn 248
Wm. Grn 261
Mathirs, Thomas Clr 146
Mathis, Daniel Gra 239
George Gra 239
Glover Clr 136
Hopkins Gra 240
John Clr 135
John Clr 136
Josiah Chr 106
Mary Gra 239
Nathl. Clr 135
Mathwes, George Nel 8
Matingly, James Bul 181
Matlock, Isham Wsh 291
John Wsh 291
Samuel Mas 265
William Wsh 291
Zacariah Cal 8
Mattocks, Edwd. Gar 213
Matocks, John Fle 86
Matox, Anna Bar 51
Matson, James Bou 127
Peyton Bou 127
Thomas Bou 127
Mattcks, Luke Pen 109
Mattel, Will Cly 152
Mattenley, Barton Bre 166
Zachariah Bre 169
Matterly, Barnard Bre 166
John Bre 156
John Bre 166
Richard Bre 166
Matterson, Francis Mad 229
Matthew, John Mad 229
Wm. Boo 61

Matthewes, Saml. Cum 177
Matthews, Benjamin Wsh 289
Benjn. Mad 231
Briscoe Jef 8
Burgis Pul 151
Daniel Hnd 335
David E. Fra 143
Edward Cas 41
Henry Jef 29
James Flo 103
James Knx 72
James Mer 325
James, Jr Jef 5
James, Sr Jef 5
Jas. Woo 377
Jeremiah Fra 146
Jeremiah Jef 5
John Jef 5
John Woo 377
Joseph Cum 169
Matthew Flo 103
Robert Sco 184
Will Bou 100
William Knx 72
William Mad 231
Matthis, Alexander She 224
Elizabeth She 208
Isaac Hop 372
James Hop 373
Jno. Hop 373
John Cam 31
John She 224
Wm. Cam 31
Mattingly, Barnett Wsh 292
Barton Wsh 289
Barton Wsh 292
Bazil Wsh 292
Bennett Wsh 292
Charles Wsh 292
Clement Wsh 289
Gabriel Wsh 291
Henry Mas 261
Ignatius Wsh 291
Jere Nel 42
John Wsh 287
John Wsh 289
John B. Wsh 292
Joseph Nel 45
Joseph Wsh 289
Joseph Wsh 291
Joseph Wsh 292
Joseph Wsh 292
Leonard Wsh 289
Leonard Wsh 292
Luke Wsh 292
Mark Wsh 291
Mary Wsh 292
Mary Ann Wsh 291
Philip Nel 46
Philip Wsh 287
Richard Mas 261
Townly Mas 261
William Wsh 289
William Wsh 291
Mattix, Benjmin Hrs 307
Edward hrs 323
Obyas Hrs 317
Mattocks, Elizebeth Mas 263
Wm. Boo 61
Mattox, Absolom She 238
Ann Gal 186
Dan Gal 184
David Gal 186
Hezakiah Cam 24
James Gal 186
John H. Lew 98
Michael Gal 184

Mattox, cont.
Nathl. Woo 395
Samuel Ohi 95
Shearwood Gal 186
Thomas Woo 377
William Mad 231
Willm. Lin 128
Wilson She 215
Wilson She 240
Wm. Bar 54
Mauldin, Tyre H. Liv 160
Maulding, Ambrose Hnd 330
Enneys Hnd 329
James Hnd 330
Morton Hop 381
Richard Hnd 340
West Log 183
Maunts, Elijah She 221
Maupin, Cornelius Mad 235
Dabney Cly 149
Daniel Mad 234
Gabriel Mad 229
Garland Mad 230
Garten B. Mad 236
Jessee Bou 97
John Cly 149
John Mad 236
John Mon 382
Perry Cly 154
Thomas Mad 232
Mauris, Christopher Mon 351
Daniel Mon 373
Daniel, Senr Mon 355
Isaac Mon 373
Jacob Mon 347
James Mon 373
John Mon 370
Moses Mon 351
Mausy, Geo. Bar 36
Mauzy, George Mas 259
Henry Gar 212
James Bou 97
John Fle 87
John Lin 128
William Bou 97
Mavely, John She 222
Maveo, Peter Boo 63
Maxey, Benjn. Mad 231
Boaz Gar 212
Edward War 264
Edwd. Hrd 285
Joel But 195
John War 250
John War 252
Nathaniel Mer 321
Philip Bar 34
Wm. War 250
Maxfield, David Way 362
George Fay 51
John Fay 51
John Way 363
Maxville, John Mon 380
Maxvills, Hugh Mon 352
Maxwel, Joseph Mas 256
Agnes Mad 232
Alexander Cal 9
Bazalell Gar 210
Chas. Sco 178
Danl. Cam 33
David Gar 199
David War 260
David Way 362
Elizabeth Bou 97
Jas. Log 170
John Cam 24
John Clr 136
John Fay 18
Maxwell, cont.
John Wsh 289
John C. Way 373
John G. Sco 185
M. Jas. Gar 210
Peggy Hrd 291
Robert Mul 385
Thomas Log 179
Thomas Mad 232
Thos. Grn 259
William Log 187
Wm. Cam 29
Wm. Log 170
Maxy, Caleb Cum 171
Ephraim Bar 34
Saml. Gar 209
Wm. Cum 178
May, Allen Hnr 363
Bennett Mer 323
Coleman Log 186
Deborah Mer 325
Francis Hnr 353
Gabl. Hnr 368
Gabl. Nel 41
Gidian Clr 137
Henry Mer 321
Henry Nel 38
Henry Nel 43
Humphrey Mer 320
Humphry Nel 38
Jacob Cly 156
Jacob, Jnr Lin 127
Jacob, Snr Lin 127
James Mad 230
Jesse Mad 230
Jno. Log 177
John Cal 12
John Flo 106
John Log 183
John Log 192
John Mad 230
John Mer 320
John Mer 320
John Nel 8
John She 208
John She 234
John L. Fra 150
John W. Nel 42
Joseph, Jr Log 179
Joshua Mer 323
Mary Fay 18
Nancy Lin 126
Nancy Lin 127
Nicholas Mon 367
Richd. Hrd 281
Roland Lin 128
Salamon She 235
Samuel Flo 106
Smith Nel 46
Stephen Nel 37
Stephen Nel 43
William Nel 37
Wm. Log 177
Mayben, Henry Chr 112
Mayberry, John Chr 94
Maybury, Joseph Mon 368
Mayer, Alexr. Hop 375
Mayers, Robert Fay 34
Mayes, George Liv 158
Mayfield, Elijah Jef 29
Geo. Bar 36
George Gal 184
Gidian Bar 48
Iaac Pul 150
Isaac Gar 210
Isaac Pul 152
Jas. Gar 208
Mayfield, cont.
Jno. Pul 151
Jno. Sen Bar 36
John, Jun Bar 36
Randolph Cas 37
Thomas Bar 19
Wm. Pul 151
Mayhall, Timothy Mas 263
William Mas 263
Mayhew, Alexr. War 275
Elisha Grp 269
Mosis War 279
Myra Grp 269
Mayho, Patsey War 256
Mayjors, David Jes 51
Maynor, Jerry M. Nic 53
Sarah Mer 322
Mayo, Danl. Cam 33
Mays, Abm. Jr Way 351
Abm. Sr Way 353
Frederick Cum 168
I. William Flo 106
James Hnd 331
James Hnd 339
Linsey Jes 55
Mosis War 269
William Flo 106
William Jes 52
William Knx 81
William Mer 324
William Woo 395
Wm. Junr Cum 168
Wm. Senr Cum 168
Wm. H. Fra 148
Maze, John Hrs 324
John Hrs 324
Samuel Hrs 324
Mc names see Mec..
McAchron, James She 215
John She 240
McAdam, Jacob Wsh 289
McAdams, Alex Nel 39
Danl. Hrd 290
Joseph Log 165
Saml. Nel 39
Saml. Nel 43
Wm. Bre 161
McAdora, Thomas Chr 89
McAdou, John Mas 258
McAfee, George Mer 324
Hannah Mer 325
James Mer 324
James Mer 325
John Fay 28
John Mer 323
John Mer 324
Robert Fay 28
Robert Mer 325
Robert B. Mer 320
Samuel Mer 324
William Wsh 290
McAins, George Bra 145
George Bra 150
Peter Bra 145
McAlexander, David Mad 237
McAlister, Allen Fra 145
Bartlett Fra 145
Charles Fra 145
DAvid Pul 153
Jemima Fra 146
John Pul 153
Zacheriah Fra 145
McAll, James Nic 54
McAllister, James She 208
Robert Mer 324
McAndrew, Bunyan Fra 147
McAnelly, John Mer 320

McAnnally, Henry Mas 260
Hugh Mas 259
Hugh, Senr Mas 259
McAntire, Josiah Wsh 289
McArdle, Edward Hrd 302
McArthur, Peter Sco 193
McArty, Thos. Nic 52
McAsham, John Chr 84
William Chr 89
McAtee, Elisha Wsh 287
Henry Wsh 290
Hezekiah Clr 135
John Fay 44
McAtenia, Thomas Fle 90
McBain, John Jef 25
McBath, Wm. Way 354
McBean, William Fay 18
McBee, Isaac Cum 168
Silas Hop 377
McBrayer, Ichobod Flo 104
McBrayers, Andrew Fra 144
James Fra 143
William Fra 144
McBride, Charles Fay 40
Daniel Hnd 344
David Lin 126
James Mad 233
John Flo 106
John Knx 63
John Lew 97
John Wsh 289
Lapsley Fra 144
Peter Nel 44
Samuel Fay 40
William Mer 341
McBrien, John Grn 265
McBrume, Wm. Jef 5
McCabe, John Cam 33
Josius Nic 52
Rutha Fle 92
McCable, Francis Jes 52
McCacron, William Nel 8
McCafferty, Adam Sco 168
Green Sco 190
McCaffry, Thoms. Nel 39
McCain, Isac Fay 45
James Hnd 342
McCaiver, Joseph Mer 343
McCaleb, Hugh Hrs 311
McCalester, Clarke Hnd 341
Eneas Hnd 336
Jesse Hnd 340
McCalf, Norris Rck 163
McCall, Bnej. Grn 262
James Jes 54
James P. Fay 19
John Clr 135
John Nic 52
William Fay 38
McCalla, Andrew Fay 18
John Bou 69
Jos. Sco 176
Robert Sco 185
McCallay, John Wsh 290
McCallie, Andrew Fay 28
McCallister, Danl. She 242
Frances Wsh 288
James Fra 149
John Wsh 290
McCally, Jane Bou 99
Joshua Fay 52
McCammel, Robt. Adr 10
McCammon, Matthew She 229
McCampbell, Andrew Jes 54
George W. She 210
James Jes 52
John Fra 142
McCampbell, cont.
John She 222
Martha She 222
McCamron, John Cly 150
William Cly 150
McCan, Elizabeth Fay 50
Flora Fle 87
Neal Fay 34
Neal Fay 52
Patrick Fle 66
Patrick Fle 88
Pleasant Clr 136
McCanacah, Rot. Nel 45
McCance, Thompson Chr 103
McCane, William Chr 54
McCanless, James [illegible] 108
McCanly, James Cam 26
McCann, James Bou 127
John Bou 69
Jos. Gal 184
Thos. Cas 41
McCannel, John She 228
McCardel, Henry Mas 306
McCardell, Jas. Nel 8
McCardie, Alexander She 199
McCargo, Radford Clr 135
McCarley, Moses Gar 212
McCarlin, Wm. Hnr 359
McCarmack, James She 226
McCarret, Tho. Hop 371
McCarrit, John Hop 371
McCarrol, Daniel Cal 5
McCarson, Betsy Mer 324
Daniel Mer 320
McCart, Edward Mon 361
Henry Clr 136
John Fle 61
William Clr 135
McCarta, James Log 178
McCarter, Henry Bra 143
Wm. Bra 143
Wm. Bra 143
McCarther, Jno. Nel 38
McCartney, Jos. War 281
Jos. Jur War 281
Joseph Jes 51
McCarty, Adam Pen 115
Augustine Mon 353
Billington Est 9
Charles Boo 61
Charles Chr 90
Cornelus Hrd 299
Daniel Mas 256
David Nic 52
Elijah Bar 50
James Clr 136
James Hrd 300
John Cal 7B
John Fle 85
John Jef 8
John Jes 55
John Log 180
Joseph Clr 136
Joseph Mas 263
Justin Wsh 288
Mary Jef 8
Nathaniel Pen 108
Nathaniel Pen 115
Sally Chr 115
Samuel Hrs 319
Samuel Pen 111
Thomas Hrd 304
Thos. Bra 147
William Chr 116
Wm. Bar 53
McCary, Martha Jes 51
McCashlin, Andw. Way 356
McCaskeys, Isaac Gal 185
McCaslin, David She 211
Jas. Jef 5
John Wsh 288
Mark Bou 98
Robert Wsh 288
McCaughan, John Chr 89
McCay, John Bre 168
William Nel 46
McCdole, James Nic 55
McCee, James Fay 54
Samuel Fay 54
McCegg, Robert Clr 137
McChan, Danl. Nic 53
McChandless, John Grn 252
Mary Grn 249
McChase, John Wsh 290
McChesny, Walter Cal 13
McChisney, Samuel Fay 18
McChristy, James Sco 178
McCine, John Boo 61
McCinney, David Fay 48
McCinny, James Fay 48
James Mul 402
McClain, Alexander She 218
Andrew She 235
Arche. Fle 74
Arter Nel 39
Chas. Nic 55
Danl. Sco 187
Duncan Nel 38
George Mad 233
Isaac Wsh 290
James Fay 27
James Lew 104
James Mad 231
John Mad 229
John Nel 39
Jonathan Mad 235
Mary Jef 25
Samuel Fay 45
Tho. Bar 51
Will. Nel 39
William She 201
Wm. Mon 362
Wm. Nel 39
McClaine, John Adr 11
McClanahan, James Log 195
Sarah Mad 230
William Jes 54
McClane, Alexander Liv 147
Daniel Pen 109
Elisha Liv 150
Geo. Hnr 367
James Chr 106
James Hnr 368
Jno. Sr Hnr 363
John Ohi 70
John N. Hnr 361
Joseph Chr 69
Mathew Gar 212
Mathew Ohi 82
Matthew, Junr Ohi 82
Nely Chr 80
Stat Gar 209
McClanehan, Elijah Fay 24
McClanican, Elijah Pen 108
McClannahan, Elizh. Bou 127
James Clr 137
Thos. Bou 128
Thos. Sr Bou 128
McClardy, Alex Log 186
McClary, Elizabeth Woo 387
Franklin Gar 209
James Fay 23
James Hnr 355

McClary, cont.
Saml. Gar 209
McClay, Thos. Boo 61
McClean, John Bra 153
John Hrd 303
McClearker, Felix Hrs 317
McCleaster, James Cam 33
McCleery, Samuel Wsh 288
William Wsh 288
McCleland, Alexander Mon 367
Daniel She 197
John Bar 34
John Fay 33
John Fay 46
Joseph Bar 35
William Fay 23
McClelin, James Clr 136
McClelland, Abraham Bre 164
Benjn. Sco 175
Hugh Bou 72
James Hnr 367
Jas. Bou 98
Jas. Bou 98
Molly Hnr 361
Robert Bul 181
Robt. Bou 98
Sarah Hnr 358
William Wsh 290
Wm. Bou 98
McClellem, Hance She 240
McClellen, William Clr 137
McClellin, John Bre 169
McClenachan, Robt. Grn 256
McClenahan, John Bra 144
McClendon, David Chr 70
Frederick Hnd 333
McClenehan, Joseph Cal 16
McClennan, Henry Fra 150
McClennin, John Chr 68
McClentic, James Bou 128
McCleskey, Alexander Liv 159
William Liv 159
McClewaine, Wm. Clr 136
McClintick, William Flo 104
McClintock, Alexr. Bou 71
Fanny Bou 100
Hugh Nic 54
Jos. Nic 53
Jos. Nic 53
Joseph Bou 71
Wm. Bou 99
McClosky, Joseph Nel 44
Michl. Fle 65
McCloud, John Clr 136
William Grp 270
McCluer, Alexander Pen 114
McClung, Saml. Bou 69
William Mas 260
McClure, Alexd. Clr 136
Daniel Rck 164
David Gra 242
David Hnd 331
Henry Fle 64
Holbert Rck 161
Hugh Cum 166
Italy Adr 11
James Adr 11
James Bou 99
James Bou 127
James Cam 33
James Fay 44
James Fra 143
James Hrs 308
James, Sr Bou 99
McClure, cont.
John Bou 97
John Fay 31
John Fay 39
John Hrs 307
Josiah War 261
Mary Mer 325
Moses Boo 61
Moses Hnd 331
Moses Rck 164
Moses, Jun Hnd 332
Mosis War 258
Nathl. Boo 61
Robert Chr 83
Robert Lin 128
Ruth Mas 264
Saml. Adr 11
Saml. Hnr 353
Samuel Fra 146
Sarah Mas 260
Than Mer 325
Thomas Chr 75
Thomas Ohi 94
Thos. Sco 170
Will She 221
William Mas 257
William Wsh 288
Wm. Hrd 298
McClurg, Charles War 254
McClurgh, Jas. Nic 52
McClusky, Peter Hrd 299
McClyd, James Cal 16
McCofe, Wile Grn 265
McColla, Christopher Jef 6
James Jef 6
Joshua Jef 6
Joshua Jef 7
Wm. Jef 7
McCollam, John Fle 74
McColester, James G. Log 167
McColgan, James Cum 175
John Grn 247
Wm. Grn 249
McColister, Jain Grp 277
Jas. Hrd 283
Mikel Grp 277
McColley, James Liv 145
McCollister, Anguish Liv 154
Archd. Hnr 353
Archd. Hnr 368
Colister Hnr 368
Daniel Liv 145
David Rck 166
James Sco 180
Joel Mer 324
John Chr 76
Sarah Fle 84
McCollum, Daniel Cly 150
Daniel Cly 155
David Cly 150
James Cam 24
Saml. Cly 151
Stephen Cly 150
Thos. Way 367
Wm. Cly 150
McColm, Jno. Hrd 284
McComas, James Lew 104
Patty Lew 103
Taylor Lew 103
McCombs, Hugh Bar 32
John Bar 36
Wm. Jef 8
McComes, John Chr 90
Martha Mer 322
McComnon, William Mul 399
McCon, David Boo 61
McConaha, David Bou 98
John Bou 98
McConel, John Grp 277
McConelley, Jacob Fay 40
McConice, Christo. Nic 53
McConnald, James Fay 28
William Fay 18
McConnel, Alexr. Sco 174
Edward Bou 128
Elizabeth Fay 39
Hugh Mas 257
John Bou 127
John Bou 128
John Mad 236
John Mul 406
Joseph Bou 128
Mary Bou 127
Mary Fay 39
Sampson Bou 127
Wm. Senr Bou 127
McConnell, Adam Jes 52
Archd. Clr 135
James War 275
Robert Jef 27
Saml. Bou 100
Thos. Bra 146
William Jes 52
McCool, Adam War 257
John Mer 322
William Ohi 93
McCorbin, John Chr 72
McCord, Charles Chr 59
David Mad 228
David Nic 52
David, Jr Mad 228
James Chr 57
John Fay 42
John Mad 228
John Nic 52
Joseph Clr 135
Michiel Nic 52
Robert Mad 228
William Chr 55
William Chr 62
William Nwc 52
Williams Mad 236
McCorde, John Fay 23
McCorkill, Margt. Boo 61
Wm. Boo 61
McCorkle, John Fle 88
John Grn 247
John Grn 258
Joseph Fle 79
Saml. Grn 258
William Fle 88
McCormac, James Bou 68
Robert Fay 18
McCormack, Daniel Lin 125
Eliza Nic 53
George Sco 167
Hugh Sco 179
James Mad 231
John Hop 372
John Lin 126
John She 241
Joseph Lin 126
Samuel Mad 231
Thos. She 233
Willm. Lin 125
Wm. She 233
McCormauck, Thomas Knx 73
McCormic, Andr. Nel 44
James Bra 146
McCormick, Elizabeth Gar 212

McCormick, cont.
George Hnd 333
George Mer 322
John Ohi 73
John Bra 143
McCorphin, John Chr 71
John Chr 71
Joseph Chr 71
McCoude, James Bou 128
McCown, Alex Nel 8
Andrew Nel 39
George Chr 73
George Lin 125
James Log 191
James Nel 8
James, Junr Cum 184
James, Senr Cum 184
John Cas 46
John Mer 324
Lawranc Nic 54
Moses Mer 324
Saml. Mer 323
McCoy, Alexr. Sco 189
Daniel Bou 100
Daniel Gar 211
Daniel Nic 55
Daniel She 207
Danl. Bar 30
David Fay 39
David Pul 150
Hugh Fay 41
James Mas 256
John Bou 97
John Bou 97
John Bou 100
John Bou 127
John Cal 20
John Flo 103
John Grp 270
John Liv 158
John Mer 323
John She 216
John War 249
John, Jur Boo 61
Martin Bou 99
Nancy Bou 127
Neal Fay 18
Saml. Fle 66
Saml. Rck 163
Samuel Flo 103
William Flo 103
William Hnd 327
William Mas 258
William She 201
Willis But 195
Wm. Boo 61
Wm. Cam 31
McCrab, Matt Hop 374
McCracen, John Fay 39
McCracken, John Mas 259
Samuel Log 192
Senica Fra 148
McCrackin, Elizbth. Bou 98
James Bar 37
William Hnr 366
McCracking, John Liv 154
McCraken, Charles Fle 83
John Fle 83
McCrakin, Jas. Gal 187
McCrary, Archibald Chr 105
James Jef 7
Martha Fay 51
McCraw, Cowither Mas 260
McCray, John Cly 151
Samuel Bou 127
William Pen 115
McCreery, Charles Ohi 68
McCreery, cont.
John Ohi 73
Wm. Gal 186
McCrery, Elijah Hnd 327
McCrocklin, Jesse Nel 43
William She 210
McCroclin, Lydia She 206
McCrory, James Bou 100
Samuel Clr 136
McCrosey, Andrew Bou 127
McCrosgey, Elijah Fay 35
McCrosky, James Fra 142
Jas. Sco 176
John Hnd 327
John, Senr Fra 145
Wm. Fle 85
McCrotlin, Jesse Nel 46
McCrury, Andrew Est 1
James Est 5
Wm. Est 5
McCubbin, Wm. Hop 375
McCuben, Niholas Grn 264
McCue, Edward Mas 261
John Nel 8
McCulla, James Lin 125
McCullam, James Hrd 282
Jno. Hrd 297
Richard Hrd 302
McCullaugh, Jos. Gar 208
McCullock, James Mon 365
John Fay 24
McCulloug, Alexr. Fle 88
McCullough, Archibald Fay 29
James Chr 65
James Fle 69
Lauson Fay 18
Will Cly 152
Wm. Fle 83
McCullum, Elth. Nel 40
Josh Nel 38
Macom Nel 44
Wm. Nel 44
McCully, Henry Bou 128
McCumprey, John She 223
McCumsey, William She 223
McCune, James Jes 53
John Bou 99
John Nic 55
Margaret Jes 53
Robert Nic 55
Robert Nic 55
Samuel Hrs 317
Sarah Jes 53
William Jes 53
Wm. Bou 99
McCunnon, Danl. Cam 30
McCurdy, Allen F. Fra 149
James Chr 64
McCurly, John Log 166
Thomas Log 192
McCurry, Lidia Bar 43
McCutcheon, Elizabeth Log 179
Hugh Log 194
James Log 165
Jas. Sco 171
John Log 194
Saml. Log 167
Saml. C. Log 194
William Log 165
McCutchin, Thos. Bou 69
McDade, Robert Fle 80
William Nel 39
McDaffa, Robett Hrs 318
Robert Hrs 318
McDahart, Alexandrew Hrs 317
McDanald, Allen Gar 208
Daniel Gar 209
John Gar 209
Mary Nic 53
Wm. Gar 209
Wm. Gar 210
McDanel, David Pul 149
John Bar 31
McDaniel, Aaron Mad 229
Alexr. Boo 61
Benj. Bra 151
Collins Gra 239
Cornelius Log 167
Cornelius Log 178
Daniel Pul 153
Duncan Log 185
Elias Ohi 92
Geo. Cly 153
George Mon 371
George Ohi 89
George Ohi 93
George Woo 402
Hezekea Fle 72
Hiram Liv 156
Hugh Adr 10
Hugh Pul 153
Isabel Jef 8
James Bul 181
James Jef 8
James Mad 235
James Ohi 94
Jesse Jes 53
Jinnings Bar 41
Jno. Lew 96
Jocephas Bul 181
John Adr 10
John Adr 11
John Bou 97
John Bra 142
John Gra 241
John Lew 97
John Log 186
John Log 195
John Mon 376
Joseph Ohi 94
Peter Bul 181
Reubin Mon 371
Samuel Mul 393
Spencer Pul 150
Spencer Pul 153
Stacey Cas 42
Thomas Fle 72
Thos. Cly 153
William Pul 150
William Pul 153
Wm. Grn 254
McDanield, Wm. Cas 39
McDaniels, Alexander Liv 154
Thos. Cas 37
McDannal, Archibald Chr 86
McDannald, Abner Mer 320
Clem Mer 320
McDannd, Pemberton Chr 112
McDannel, Alexander Hrs 323
Archibald Chr 98
Eli. Bou 98
Francis Hrs 314
Morgen Chr 99
Francis Bou 99
Robt. Bou 100
McDannell, Rowland Bou 99
McDannil, James Chr 91
James Chr 112

McDanold, Alexr. Nic 54
Edward Mas 260
Henley Mas 260
John Nic 54
Jos. Nic 54
M. Saml. Mas 264
Mordica Nic 55
Samuel Mas 260
Walter Mas 260
William Mas 258
McDavitt, James She 208
McDawel, George Cal 18
Rachal She 206
McDay, Hugh Adr 10
McDermot, Francis Way 372
McDerner, Daniel Jes 54
McDivit, Basil Woo 382
McDoel, Catharine Hrs 309
Jane Hrs 313
McDole, Daniel Bou 100
James Nic 55
William Nic 55
McDonal, John Fra 147
McDonald,... Nel 45
Aaron Jes 54
Alexander Wsh 288
Alexr. Nel 46
Alexr. Nic 56
Charles Fra 147
Danl. Nel 45
Elizath Nel 42
George Nic 54
Henry Fay 11
Henry Fay 30
Henry Fay 35
Isaac Hrd 287
James Fay 24
James Nel 44
Jas. Hrd 289
Jno. Hrd 291
John Grn 249
John Fay 24
John, Jr Fay 24
John, Junr Fay 28
John, Senr Fay 28
Jon. War 248
Joseph Nel 40
Joseph Wsh 288
Marshl. Nel 41
Mary Wsh 288
Neal Grn 261
Redm. Nel 41
Redn. Nel 45
Thomas Wsh 290
William Wsh 290
McDonell, Danl. Hrd 289
Jno. Hrd 296
McDonnal, Frances Clr 135
Hugh Clr 135
James Clr 135
James Clr 136
McDonnald, Mary Fay 18
McDonnel, George Lew 97
McDonough, Peter Sco 174
McDougal, Alexander Hrd 302
McDowel, Anguis War 260
Benjm. Adr 19
James Adr 19
James Bou 98
James Fay 43
John Bou 98
John Bul 181
John Chr 75
John Cum 186
John Fay 43
John War 261
McDowel, cont.
Josiah Bou 97
Margaret Woo 378
Mathew Pul 152
Robert Mon 356
William Chr 76
William Flo 103
McDowell, Alexander She 199
Alexr. Gal 196
Deborah Fra 151
Ephraim Mer 322
James Fay 32
James Mer 342
Jas. Gal 185
Jno. Hrd 303
Jno. G. Lew 101
John Bra 144
John Fay 31
John Log 170
Joseph Mer 322
Saml. Mer 323
Samuel Jes 52
Samuel Mer 321
William Mer 321
McDual, john Grp 274
McDugle, Robert Pen 116
McElhany, Patrick Lin 128
McElroy, Abraham Wsh 294
Daniel Mer 342
Equilla Cal 5
Hugh Hnd 329
Isaac Cal 8
James Wsh 288
James Wsh 291
James A. Wsh 288
Jas. War 277
John Cal 9
John Hnd 342
John Wsh 288
John Wsh 288
Samuel Wsh 287
Samuel Wsh 290
William Wsh 287
William Wsh 287
Wm. Cal 11
McElure, John Jes 52
McElvaine, William Log 167
McElvey, William Fra 150
McElwain, Francis War 262
Michael War 262
McElwee, Ann Lin 128
McEndre, Richd. Gal 185
McEntire, Frances Clr 137
McEntre, John Hnr 365
Reuben Hnr 365
McFadden, Conoly Mas 263
John War 264
McFaddeon, Jas. Gar 208
McFaddin, Elias B. War 273
Jacob Chr 102
John Chr 102
John Chr 111
John Chr 115
McFadgen, Jesse Knx 76
McFadin, Patrick Jef 27
McFall, Danl. Adr 11
Henry Adr 11
John Adr 11
Thomas Log 161
McFalls, John Hrs 311
Joseph Hrs 311
McFarland, Archd. Mas 258
Ben Cly 151
Benjm. Hrs 309
Charles Sco 179
John Ohi 84
McFarland, cont.
Joseph D. Ohi 83
Langford Sco 179
Levin Sco 167
Robt. Est 6
Walter Ohi 101
William Fay 45
William Ohi 83
William Ohi 101
Wm. Nic 53
McFarlin, Danl. Bar 39
Duncan Knx 63
George Knx 63
James Chr 86
Joseph Hrs 317
Robert Chr 86
Robert Fle 79
Walter mon 378
William Chr 67
McFarling, Benjamin War 287
McFarrin, Robt. Clr 135
Thos. Clr 135
McFarthige, Wm. Adr 10
McFartridge, John Woo 381
McFatrege, Abigal Mer 323
McFeartridge, Robt. Sco 189
McFeaters, Charles Fay 24
William Fay 28
McFern, Patrick Woo 380
McFersan, Josua Bar 43
McFerson, Aron Bar 43
Othnial Est 7
McFerran, John Bar 42
McFerren, James Fra 147
Thomas Mas 259
McFerrin, James Lin 125
John Mon 384
McField, Will Cly 154
McFrench, Saml. Cas 40
McGAfett, William Fle 87
McGannon, Darby Gal 187
McGara, Saml. Sco 179
McGaraty, Nicholas Cal 4
McGarvey, Andrew Nel 41
Andr. Nel 41
Jno. Nel 44
McGary, Danl. Hop 373
McGath, John Lew 99
McGaughey, Arthur Fra 143
Arthur Hrd 284
Daniel She 212
John She 205
John She 241
Saml. Jef 5
Wilson She 240
McGawn, David Way 358
McGe, William Chr 100
McGee, Asa Jef 5
David Clr 135
Hugh Chr 100
J. Hendrom Wsh 290
James Est 6
James Mer 322
John Fay 29
John Gar 210
John Mer 324
John Nel 43
John She 224
John Way 366
John Way 368
Joseph Mer 323
May Mer 325
Patrick Nel 41
Robert Mer 324
Saml. Woo 393
Samuel Gra 239

McGee, cont.
Thos. Nel 43
William Chr 84
William Mer 320
McGehe, Benjamin Chr 95
Charles Chr 82
Osburn Chr 104
William Chr 95
McGehee, Charles Mas 257
Henry Bar 53
McGeorge, Saml. Woo 389
McGholan, John Nic 56
McGill, Alexr. Bou 127
Andrew Cal 20
Daniel Ohi 86
David Nel 41
James Bra 150
John Lin 128
John Mer 324
Patrick Liv 145
Robert Mer 323
Rossund Ohi 87
Saml. P. Cly 154
McGillion, Eliza-
beth Fra 146
McGilney, John Gal 185
McGines, William Nic 54
McGinetry, John Fra 150
McGinnis, Green Mer 321
Hezekiah War 246
James Cam 33
Jesse Mer 321
John Bou 98
John Bou 98
John Mas 264
John Mer 321
John Mer 321
John Mer 323
John She 207
John, Jr Bou 98
Neal Mas 259
Patsy Mer 321
Richard Chr 114
Saml. Cam 28
Samuel Mer 321
Thomas Mer 321
Thomas Mer 322
Thomas Mer 323
Will Bou 97
William Mas 256
William Mas 259
Wm. Bar 29
Wm. Bar 40
Wm. Fra 144
McGiver, Edward Fay 32
McGlason, Matthew Cas 40
McGlasson, James Cum 169
Joseph Cum 169
McGlaughan, Jno. Hop 372
McGlaughlin, John Jef 7
William Grp 272
Wm. Jef 8
McGlaulen, James Mul 396
McGlochlin, James Chr 109
James H. Chr 110
John Mad 233
McGloclin, Edward Mon 369
McGlolan, John Nic 55
McGloling, Cornel-
ius Boo 61
McGlone, Owen Grp 277
McGlothlin, Fran-
cis Mad 235
McGlouglen, Mar-
gret Hnd 335
McGoffin, Beriah Mer 341
McGohan, Daniel Mas 260
McGohorn, Mark Mer 323
McGomery, Roberson Fay 31
McGonagle, Wm. Cum 169
McGongin, Charles Mas 256
McGouch, John Cal 16
Robert Chr 90
McGoughey, John She 240
McGounagol, Jos. Grn 259
McGowan, Charles Fay 23
James, Sen Fle 75
Mary Fay 18
McGowen, Alexr. War 248
Andrew War 248
James S. Mon 384
Nancy Mas 263
Saml. War 248
Saml. War 248
Samuel Log 194
Thomas Log 189
Wm. Mon 350
McGown, John Way 368
McGrada, Edward Cly 159
McGrath, Briant Jes 55
Robert She 240
Terrance Jes 53
McGraw, Isaiah Mas 260
John Cas 48
Richd. Woo 395
William Mer 320
McGready, James Hnd 335
McGreger, Wm. Hop 380
McGreggen, Ann Fay 18
McGrew, Alexander Hnr 353
John Hnr 352
Joseph She 199
M. Hnr 353
Moner Hnr 353
Robert Nel 46
McGriffin, Joseph Fle 70
McGruda, Richard Mas 257
McGruder, Aquila Jef 29
Enock Jef 29
McGrue, John Cal 12
Reed Ohi 72
McGuffey, James Cam 28
McGuffin, Samuel Bre 161
McGuier, William Mad 234
McGuin, Elizabeth Cly 159
McGuire, Allen Hnr 356
Arch Cly 158
Cornelius Flo 103
Daniel Mad 229
Dav Hnr 366
Elexr. Adr 11
Elijah War 274
Eliza, Sr Hnr 366
James Cly 158
James Flo 104
James Fra 143
James Grp 278
Jesse Hnr 366
John Flo 104
John Grp 275
John Mon 362
John Nic 53
John Woo 384
Jonathan Gal 186
Joseph Hnr 363
Lawrence Mer 320
Louisa War 270
Nathan War 278
Owen War 274
Samuel Flo 104
Squire Bar 38
Thomas Pul 151
Will Cly 158
William Clr 136
McGuire, cont.
William Flo 104
William Log 177
Zelic Hnr 355
McGuiwn, Wm. Nel 8
McGuown, John Knx 66
McHan, Joseph Mon 354
McHargue, Agness Knx 72
William Knx 72
McHarter, John Cas 37
McHattin, Will Bou 99
McHatton, David Sco 182
James Jef 5
Jane Nel 37
John, Jur Sco 191
John, Senr Sco 191
Robert Sco 168
McHattor, Saml. Sco 171
McHenry, Barnabas Wsh 287
Isaac Mad 230
Jas. Way 360
Joseph War 247
William Jes 53
McHitrett, Robert Hrs 309
McHolland, David Knx 82
McIlhaney, James Mon 357
John Mon 352
McIlroy, James Fay 51
Thomas Fay 54
McIlvain, Andrew Mon 364
Archibald Fay 35
Archibald Mon 384
Hugh Bou 128
James Mon 384
John Mas 262
Mary Mas 262
William Woo 380
McIlvany, William Chr 113
McIlwain, Thomas Lew 103
McIngtosh, Jos. War 260
McInny, John Pul 151
McInsy, Assa Pul 150
McIntire, Aaron Fle 78
Alexander Mon 352
Benja. Fle 68
David Bul 181
Elizabeht Mer 325
Isaac Fle 77
Jacob Fle 78
John Bou 98
John Fay 54
John Fle 90
Joseph Fle 92
Mary Hnr 361
Mary Hrd 294
Robert Jef 7
Robt. Grn 245
Thomas Wsh 288
William Bre 159
William Fle 71
McIntosh, Cornel-
ius Log 189
Daniel Fay 18
Elizebeth Mas 265
James Boo 61
James, Sr Boo 61
Joseph Lin 126
Nimrod Cly 160
Peter Cly 160
Rory Flo 104
Will Cly 159
McIntush, Wm. Mon 366
McIntyre, Alexr. Fle 71
McIntyrer, David Fle 66
McIsac, Isac Fay 51
McIsic, James Fay 40
McIver, Daniel Clr 135

McJilton, Thos. Cly 157
McJuineh, Daniel Cas 42
John Cas 43
Wm. Cas 42
McKadden, James Bra 148
McKalon, James Cal 8
McKan, Lanty Bra 149
McKann, Bartholomew Hnd 339
McKarty, James Adr 10
John Adr 10
McKay, Alexr. Bar 51
Alexr. Jef 5
George Wsh 344
Hugh Nel 41
James Mas 261
John Nel 41
Richard Nel 42
Tho. Bar 51
McKean, James Bra 149
McKeaney, John Grn 255
McKean, Joseph Bra 150
Robt. Hrd 290
McKee, Archibald Fay 22
David Hrs 310
David Jes 52
Gavin Fle 64
Gavin Fle 88
James Bou 71
James Bou 99
James Fay 33
James Hrd 301
John Bou 99
John Bou 99
John Clr 135
John Fle 88
John Fra 145
John Jes 52
John Mas 257
Joshua Clr 135
Joshua Clr 137
Lydia Mer 322
Matthew Knx 70
Pheby Fra 145
Rebecca Hrs 310
Robert Fle 81
Robert Fle 87
Robert Mon 353
Robert Woo 388
Saml. GAr 213
Samuel Fay 33
Thomas Chr 112
William Chr 113
William Fle 70
Wm. Adr 11
Wm. Gar 212
McKeenan, James Clr 136
McKendrick, Alex Fre 143
McKenley, John Nel 44
McKenney, Alexr. Bou 127
Daniel Lin 126
Geo. Cas 47
Wm. Cas 41
Abraham Lin 126
Collin Lin 126
Daniel Hnd 329
Francis Est 4
McKensey, Mordica Bra 143
McKenu, Thomas Fle 87
McKenzie, Richd. Gal 186
McKey, Alex Nel 46
Benjamin Knx 71
Elias Knx 66
John Knx 76
Matthias W. Knx 66
Saml. Jef 7
Uriah Nel 45
McKey, cont.
William Knx 75
McKim, joseph Bou 99
McKiney, Charles Bra 145
Dan Pul 151
David Pul 150
Jame Pul 151
McKinie, Lewis Fle 63
McKinley, George She 202
James Jef 8
James She 210
James She 236
John Fra 150
John Hrs 310
John She 215
Michl. Nel 40
Oliver Mas 260
William She 240
Wm. She 236
McKinly, Alexr. Lin 127
George Mas 259
James She 240
William She 203
McKinney, Alexr. Adr 10
Benjamin Fay 24
Chs. Lin 126
Daniel F. Wsh 287
Danl. She 204
Edmon Chr 58
Francis Bou 99
Garrard Bra 151
George Bou 98
Hampton Log 186
Haney She 200
Jas. Gal 186
Jas. Lin 126
John Chr 66
John Hnd 329
John Jes 52
John Wsh 290
John, Jr Woo 397
Joseph Jes 55
Mary Chr 66
Michl. Adr 10
Robt. Clr 135
Thomas Mer 321
William Fay 23
Willm. Lin 126
Wm. Adr 10
Wm. Gal 185
McKinnie, Andw. Fle 63
McKinny, Abenezer Lin 125
Alexr. Lin 127
Archabald Lin 125
James Lin 125
John Lin 127
John Mer 320
John Mer 320
John Mer 324
Micajor mer 321
Peter Mer 324
Robert Mer 324
Wildey Mad 229
William Hnr 366
William Mer 320
William Pul 154
Zany Lin 125
McKinsey, Collan Pul 154
John Bou 127
John Mad 229
Joseph Bou 127
Sanders Pul 152
Wm. Bou 127
McKinsy, Alexr. Lin 125
Lacy Pul 150
McKiny, John Mas 307
Lamkin Grp 276
McKinzey, Alexr. War 267
McKinzie, Alexr. Gar 210
Jno. Hrd 296
John War 262
McKitrett, Robert Hrs 309
McKittrick, John Wsh 287
McKneely, Jas. Gar 210
Michael Gar 209
McKnet, Samuel Mer 323
McKnight, Andrew Woo 379
James Chr 59
McKolister, Robrt. Pul 150
McKonel, James Woo 386
Jonathan Cas 38
McKown, Edward Jef 6
James Log 166
James Log 192
John Jef 32
McKoy, Wm. Jef 7
McKrary, Saml. Adr 11
McKubbin, Jas. Hrd 288
McKy, Saml. Nel 46
McLaghlan, John Hrs 309
McLain, David Gal 186
Edward Wsh 287
James Gal 184
John Mon 366
Polly mon 367
Samuel Mad 236
Samuel Woo 391
McLanahan, James Nic 52
Jas. Woo 378
William Nic 52
McLanglan, James Nel 8
McLarning, Hugh Adr 10
McLasby, Philip Mon 366
McLaud, Jesse Hnr 355
McLaughan, Jno. Gar 209
McLaughlin, Barnabas Mas 265
Daniel Mas 264
Elizabeth Mas 261
George Mas 261
George Pen 107
James Pen 107
James Wsh 291
John Cam 24
John Mas 262
John Wsh 287
John Wsh 287
Thos. Bou 100
William Mas 265
McLawthlin, Geo. Bou 128
John Bou 128
McLean, Alney Mul 385
Ephram Log 171
George Log 161
John Log 168
Robt. D. Mul 385
McLeary, Hugh Adr 10
Robt. Adr 10
Saml. Adr 11
McLease, Wm. Nic 54
McLees, David Grp 277
McLeis, Danl. Fle 72
Thomas Fle 72
McLelland, William Mas 302
McLemore, Gillum Rck 159
Sterling Rck 161
Wright Rck 162
McLinn, James Mas 257
John Mas 259
McLlain, Leonard War 259
McLlean, George War 259
McLlwain, Alexander Log 161
McLona, Daniel Hrs 308

Name	County	Page
McLure, Alexander	Woo	401
Greenup	She	223
James	She	216
John	She	205
Mathew	Mon	354
Saml.	Woo	384
Thomas	Mon	354
McMackin, John	But	195
William	But	195
McMahan, Abraham	Knx	88
Andrew	Grn	252
Archd.	Nic	53
James	Est	8
James	Hrs	321
Jams.	Est	8
Jesse	Mad	236
John	Chr	66
John	Clr	135
John	Grp	270
John	Nic	52
Joseph	Clr	136
Martin	War	256
Robert	Nic	56
Saml.	Est	8
Saml.	Mad	235
Thomas	Clr	136
William	Clr	135
William	Est	8
William	Log	195
McMahill, Thos.	Nic	54
William	Mas	259
McMahon, James	Hnd	325
Jno.	Hrd	296
Joseph	Cal	7
William	Mas	258
McMaines, Andrew	Fra	146
James	Fra	146
McMains, Abram	Woo	396
John	Woo	391
McManamy, James	Mas	263
Jas.	Boo	61
Saml.	She	197
McManaway, Wm.	Jef	5
McManes, Jas.	Way	373
Nancy	She	232
McManie, Isaac	Mon	362
McMannis, Charles	Bul	181
Henry	Gar	208
Mary	Nel	8
Patrick	Bar	46
William	Rck	165
McMeeken, William	Nel	46
McMerry, Jas.	War	244
McMichael, Barbarada	Mas	262
James	Fra	145
McMichel, Robt.	Bra	150
McMickens, Robert	Fay	28
McMickin, Jno.	Nel	8
McMickins, Robert	Fay	28
Samuel	Fay	59
McMickle, Jacob	Jef	8
McMillen, Francis	Cly	157
John	Wsh	290
Jos.	Gal	186
Mary	Bou	97
Nely	Chr	105
McMiller, Mary	Hrs	312
McMillian, Robt.	Sco	171
McMillin, John	Hrs	314
Littlebury	Log	172
Robert	Clr	136
Samuel	Hrs	322
William	Chr	76
William	Clr	135
Wm.	Gar	209
McMillion, Josh.	Adr	10
McMin, James	Pul	154
McMinimy, John	Woo	399
Wm.	Fra	146
McMirnd, Alexander	She	199
McMulin, James	Mon	358
McMullan, James	Fay	54
McMullen,Alexander	She	208
Danl.	Cum	177
James	Cum	178
John	Log	193
Samuel	Log	181
Wm.	Hrd	299
McMullin, Arthur	Mad	233
Jerr.	Lin	125
John	Hop	376
Lydia	Jef	5
Robert	Pen	112
Sina	Gar	208
Thomas	Bar	48
William	Fay	42
Archibald	Bre	164
McMunnigale, Barnett	Est	4
McMurday, Francis	Fay	28
McMurray, James	Wsh	287
John	Wsh	287
Robert	Wsh	290
McMurrin, John	Log	179
McMurry, Thomas	Fay	18
Thos.	Lin	127
Wm.	Cas	42
McMurtery, John	Mer	341
Samuel	Mer	323
William	Mer	323
McMurtey, Levy	Fay	59
McMurtry, Alexr.	Gar	211
James	Hnd	330
James	Hrs	310
Jas.	Hrd	289
Jno.	Gar	211
Joseph	Hnd	342
Robert	Jes	41
William	Sco	188
McMurtsy, Jas.	Bar	48
McNab, Andrew	Mon	369
Eias	Chr	96
James	Mon	369
John	Mon	353
Wm.	Mon	369
McNabb, William	Grn	252
McNair, Jane	Fay	24
McNairy, Alexander	Fay	24
John	Fay	24
William	Fay	24
McNalty, Joseph	Nic	54
McNan, Richard	Hnr	367
McNarey, Nancy	Fay	18
McNary, Hugh	Fay	35
John	Mas	260
McNay, Barbary	Bou	100
McNeal, Alexander	Mul	389
Archibald	Fay	34
Hector	Mul	386
McNeel, John	War	281
McNeely, George	Log	180
Saml.	Hop	372
McNeice, Jane	Hrs	317
McNeil, Danl.	Hrd	304
McNeill,Jonathan	Knx	66
McNeilly, Wm.	Adr	10
McNeily, David	Cum	171
McNemar, John	She	240
McNemor, Philip	She	203
McNett, Robert	Fay	18
McNew, Benjamin	Mul	394
Kizzy	Hnr	360
McNight, John	Mas	307
McNight, cont.		
William	Cal	5
McNolty, Janes	Nic	55
McNut, Francis	Mad	231
Joseph	Mad	230
McNutt, Alexander	Mas	264
John	Way	355
Joseph	Mas	263
William	Mas	257
McNutty, John	Mas	262
McOlister, Joseph	Pul	150
McOrmack, Adam	Nic	52
James	Woo	392
McOrmas, Steph	Pul	150
Mcoy, Moses	Fay	42
McParker, David	Grp	275
McPhaeters, Alexr.	Bou	127
McPhale, Neill	Log	167
Neill	Log	192
McPhearson, Jessa	Mon	351
Mark	Lin	128
McPhee, John	Fle	61
McPherron, Danl.	Log	180
McPherson, Alexr.	Boo	61
George	Log	166
Jehue	Bar	25
Jesse	Mul	402
John	Wsh	290
Mark	Boo	61
Moses	Fay	41
Thomas	Pen	107
McPike, James	Lew	101
McQuaddy, John	Woo	402
McQuaid, James	She	225
McQueen, James	Jes	53
John	Rck	159
Joshua	Mad	235
Joshua	Pen	107
Thomas	Pen	106
Uriah	Pen	107
McQuerrey, Elizabeth	Gar	210
McQuerry, Jos.	Gar	210
McQuerter, Isaac	Hnd	340
McQuiddy, James	She	223
Sally	Fra	151
Thomas	Fra	142
McQuie, Wm.	Gar	211
McQuirry, Rebecca	Gar	208
Wm.	Gar	208
McQuisten, Jane	Chr	76
McQuith, Marian	Fay	18
McRakin, Elizabeth	Woo	397
Virgil	Woo	384
McRea, Isaac	Fra	150
McReighly, Geo.	Lew	97
McReynold, John	War	275
McReynolds, Archibald	Log	195
James	War	275
Robt.	War	270
McRoberts, Andrew	Lin	127
Geo.	Lin	126
George	Lin	125
Isaac	Lin	125
James	Fle	74
John	Fle	75
John, Jnr	Lin	125
John, Snr	Lin	126
Margirak	Fle	86
Samuel	Fle	89
Thos.	Cly	151
McStet, Abednago	Fay	41
McSwain, Thomas	Mad	230
McTee, Benjamin	Mas	263
McTeer, Thomas	Mon	353
McTigers, John	Bra	145

Mculla, Jno. Pul 149
Robert Pul 149
Mcuddy, Isaac Woo 377
William Woo 377
McVay, Hugh Adr 10
John Fay 23
Langston Fra 150
Martin Jes 51
Sally Mon 359
McVeah, Jas. Hrd 292
McVey, Daniel Fay 18
McViers, Daniel Mon 379
McWain, George FLe 73
McWaters, Aron Chr 89
Mosis Chr 92
McWharry, Daniel Lin 127
McWherter, George - F. Log 161
James Cly 151
Robert Knx 66
Robt. War 258
McWhirter, Geo. Way 353
George M. Log 182
McWhriter, Elijah Cly 154
McWilliams, Agnis Mad 230
Andrew Mad 232
Andrew War 261
David Mad 230
David War 267
Elizabeth She 230
James Hrd 302
James Mad 236
James War 266
James, Jun Mad 230
John Clr 136
John Mad 232
John Mad 235
John, Jr Mad 236
Jon. War 261
McWilson, Perry Fay 54
McWthy, Elias Cal 6
Mead, Martin Chr 53
Moses Flo 104
Rhodes Flo 106
Robert Flo 104
Samuel Flo 104
Tho. Hop 377
Tho. Hop 378
Meade, David Jes 51
Richd. E. Grn 265
Meadows, Allen Way 355
Edward Knx 83
Isaiah Knx 69
Isom Knx 69
Israil Est 4
Jas. Way 358
Mary Nel 38
Thomas Bre 167
Thomas Knx 69
Thomas, Jr Knx 69
William Bre 165
William Est 4
Meads, Wm. War 248
Meady, William Wsh 289
Meains, George Bra 145
George Bra 150
Peter Bra 145
Meak, Thos. War 256
Meals, John Mad 245
Means, George Lew 96
George Wsh 287
Isaac Bar 44
James Chr 90
John Mon 355
John Mon 3[illegible]6
Josiph Chr 84
Robert Chr 90
Means, cont.
Samuel Chr 83
William Chr 84
William Chr 92
William She 212
Wm. Mon 356
Meanse, John Chr 90
Mearl, Peter Bra 149
Mears, Andrew Lew 98
Jas. Grn 255
John Grn 251
Moses Grn 251
Thos. Grn 251
Meater, Abednago Mon 379
Meaux, John G. Fra 144
Mecamish, Adam Mon 368
Mecarty, Elizabeth Mon 377
Mechim, Paul Hrd 285
Meclain, James Mon 354
Wm. Mon 354
Meclanihan, James Mon 362
Rogers Mon 362
Meclure, Andrew Mon 358
John Mon 355
Mecormic, Wm. Mon 382
Mecrary, Wm. Mon 367
Meculoc, John Mon 364
Medcalf, George Ohi 93
Wm. Fra 150
Meddak, Emanuel She 241
Meddaugh, James Grp 271
Medders, Jesse War 265
Meddice, Godfrey Jef 7
John Jef 25
Medley, George Mas 264
Ignatius Wsh 287
James War 272
John Nel 39
John Wsh 287
Joseph Ohi 95
Reuben Fra 146
Thomas Wsh 287
Medlock, Absolam War 261
Meeach?, Alexr. Nic 54
Meed, Abraham Knx 79
Meek, Bazil Jr Hnr 364
Isaac Hnr 364
James Chr 112
James Fay 58
James Woo 377
Jane Woo 377
Samuel Fra 146
Thos. Sco 169
Meeker, Forest Bou 98
Grove Bou 98
Meekes, Sudith Hrd 295
Meeks, Bazle Pul 152
Ben Hrd 285
David Pul 150
James Flo 106
James Grp 271
Jeremiah Pul 153
Nathan Pul 150
Nathan Pul 152
Prydy Hrd 300
Samuel Pul 150
Samuel Pul 151
Samuel Pul 152
Samuel Pul 152
Samuel She 202
William Flo 106
William Gra 239
William Pul 152
Wm. Hrd 285
Meekss, Bazil Hnr 363
Meese, Christian Pul 154
Christian Pul 154
Meese, cont.
Elizabeth Pul 154
Henry Pul 154
Thomas Pul 154
Mefford, Andrew Fay 42
Andrew Grp 278
George Mas 257
George Mas 258
Nathan Mas 265
Samuel Mas 265
Megaher, Danl. Sco 185
Megary, Daniel Mon 374
Meginis, James Mon 378
John Mon 378
Meglochlin, Hugh Mon 378
Meglothlin, Thomas Pul 154
Megowan, David Fay 18
Patrick Sco 172
Megruder, Archi- bald Bul 181
Meguns, George W. Mon 350
Mehorney, Richard B. Fra 147
Meichless, Freder- ich Mon 384
Mekee, Samuel Mon 374
Melay, Thomas Ohi 94
Meldrum, William She 209
Melear, Philip Mer 322
Meligan, James War 245
Mellender, Wm. Hrd 293
Melona, Robert Bul 181
Melone, Andrew Mon 365
Benjamin She 239
Isaac Cas 45
Jonathan Mon 360
Mary She 202
Thomas Mon 371
Melott, John Mas 264
Peter Mas 264
Thomas Mas 264
Melson, Peter Cum 171
Melton, Benjn. War 272
Charles Hrd 301
Daniel Jes 55
David War 272
Elijah Fay 28
Jacob Chr 107
James Cum 183
Jessee Bar 32
John Hrd 297
Michl. Hrd 297
Moses Nel 41
Moses Ohi 87
Richd. Cum 183
Stanl. Nel 39
Thomas Clr 136
Thos. Hrd 292
William War 272
Melvin, Abraham Log 180
George A. Mer 322
Peter Log 178
Whorton Log 181
Menix, Charles Flo 104
Menifee, Jarrott Sco 179
Mentan, John Fay 45
Mencdr, Jonas Liv 157
Menfield, Rachael Cam 27
Menzus, Saml. P. Woo 399
Mentelle, Waldemard Fay 18
Meradith, Dick (free negro) Fay 28
Lisha Fay 55
Samuel Fay 41
Meranda, James Bra 146
Rachel Bra 146
Saml. Bra 143
Mercen, John Wsh 292

Mercer, Carver Jef 24
Gean Way 366
George Wsh 287
George War 258
Howar Bar 26
John Cal 12
John Log 171
John She 202
John Way 357
Mary Cas 43
Nicholas Way 366
Nicholas Way 367
Richard Way 366
Samuel She 203
Merchant, John Woo 402
Mercy, John Mas 257
Meredeth, Robert Fle 85
Meredith, Absoum Nic 53
Danl. Adr 11
Edward Woo 400
James Hop 372
Saml. Hop 377
Will, Senr Sco 192
William Wsh 287
William, Junr Sco 192
William P. Woo 399
Meredy, William Mer 324
Mereman, Tras. Nel 46
Merewether, Thomas Wsh 287
Mericks, Henry War 275
Henry War 275
Merideth, David Log 193
John Bou 98
Joseph Fra 149
Meridith, Charles Gra 241
Joseph Gra 243
Thomas Bou 100
William Pul 152
Merit, Nathaniel Hop 374
Stephen Bar 28
Meritt, Archilus Bul 181
Meriwether, John Jef 5
Sarah Jef 6
Val She 205
Wm. Jef 6
Wm. Jef 6
Mermord, George Jes 52
Mernan, John Cam 27
Michael Cam 26
Merphe, James Wsh 287
Merrel, Dan Mas 263
Sarah Mas 263
Merrell, Sarah War 278
Timothy War 278
Merret, Arched. Boo 61
James Boo 61
Merrett, Ephraim Hnd 340
Merrick, John Mas 256
Merrifield, Rachel Wsh 294
Merril, Andrew Mas 257
Andrew Mon 347
Benjamin Fay 45
David Fay 43
Joseph Mas 262
Nicholas Mon 351
William Fay 42
Merrill, Andrew Est 6
Joseph Pen 117
Merriman, Noah Mad 235
Merrit, Richd. Gar 211
Ste. Gar 209
Thomas Mad 229
Merriwather, Charles Chr 112
Merriwether, Richd She 238
Merry, Owen T. Bar 32
Merryfield, Alexr. Hrd 293
Mersan, John Lin 127
Merser, Jacob Knx 88
Mershon, Andw. Gar 213
Cornelius Fle 81
Cornelus Fle 81
Cornelius Gar 213
Danl. Fle 86
Job Mer 322
Nathaniel Fle 81
Mertina, David Hnr 366
Earnest Hnr 363
Jona. Hnr 363
Mervin, Patrick Hrd 281
Meshew, Jesse Hnd 342
Mesinger, James Bou 128
Spencer Bou 128
Mesmer, Peter Fay 18
Mesoe, Mosis Chr 80
Messee, Lydia Mad 229
Messer, John Knx 67
Nathaniel Pul 152
Messic, Shellah Bou 128
Messuk, Samuel Jes 41
Mesuck, Abriham Chr 103
Isaac Chr 103
Mesy, Walter Pul 152
Metcalf, Eli Nic 52
Elisha Fay 24
Isaac Chr 57
John Jes 52
John She 239
Joseph She 197
Norris Chr 57
Thomas She 212
William Chr 55
William Chr 57
and Williams Bou 70
Metcalfe, John Bou 127
Thos. Nic 53
Metcalfes, William She 213
Metclf, Charles Fle 89
Metcalp, Igns. Nel 42
Metcap, James Nel 39
John K. Nel 43
Metts, Adam Hrs 311
Jacob Pen 112
Metz, Jac ob Mas 262
John Mas 264
Meuse, John Mer 324
Mevines, Pri Nel 8
Mews, Richard Pul 152
Thomas Pul 152
Meynard, Henry Cum 165
Mezinger, Joseph Sco 178
MGlothlin, James Bul 181
Mical, Robert Fay 48
Michael, Bennet Sco 181
Michaels, Benjamin Chr 93
Michals, David Chr 93
David D. Chr 93
Elizabeth Chr 93
James Chr 93
Micheson, Edwd. Cal 8
James Cal 7
Michum, Edmon Chr 68
Henry Cal 4
Jerramiah Chr 65
John Chr 65
Josiph Chr 68
William Chr 65
William Chr 70
Michuson, Edward Cal 10
Mickins, John Fay 53
Mickle, Elisha Way 352
Mickleberry, James Clr 135
Midcap, John Mon 351
Midcelf, John Clr 135
Middleton, Adam She 218
Charles Lin 127
Charles Lin 127
David She 220
Eth. Lin 126
Greeny. Adr 11
Hanh. Adr 11
Hanly Lin 127
Hawkins Gar 208
Jacob Woo 392
James Fra 145
James She 221
John Nel 40
John War 264
Martin Gar 208
Mattw. War 264
Robert Pul 153
Robt. Adr 11
Thomas Bul 181
Thos. War 243
William She 221
William C. Hnr 362
Midleton, Hennery Cas 44
Henry Lin 128
Robert Cas 43
Miers, Daniel War 247
Isaac Liv 155
Jacob Mad 231
Mies, James War 271
Mifford, Phillip Fra 147
Miflin, Wm. War 271
Migahhan, George Pul 152
Mikeswell, Jacob Bou 128
Peter Bou 128
Mikles, John Wsh 291
Miksel, John Hrs 323
Milam, Ambrose Mad 235
Benjamin Log 193
George She 215
Jarvis Mad 235
John Fra 143
Moses She 228
Stephen She 241
Milar, William Flo 106
Milburn, Andw. Way 370
John Wsh 288
Robert Wsh 288
William Pul 152
Milder, James Cly 159
Miles, Barton E. Wsh 291
Cyrus Nel 39
Daniel Bar 21
David She 233
Edwd. Hrd 288
Elisha Wsh 287
Evan She 234
Gabrile Hrs 308
Henrietta Gra 240
Henry Nel 44
Henry P. Wsh 287
Isaac Woo 395
Isaac Wsh 291
Isaac Wsh 292
James Fra 149
James Mas 261
Jere Grn 261
Jesse Bul 181
Jesse Wsh 291
John Bre 158
John Clr 146
John Fay 24
John Fra 148
John Jes 51
John Nel 44
John She 234
John Wsh 291
Joseph Nel 45

Miles, cont.
Morris Clr 135
Nathan Bul 181
Nathan Jef 7
Nicholas Nel 44
Reubien Jes 54
Richard Wsh 287
Samuel Clr 135
Samuel She 233
Samuel She 234
Thomas Bre 159
Thomas Nel 44
Wilford Cas 46
William Fay 35
William Fra 147
William She 238
William Wsh 291
Zepheniah Bre 159
Milfs, John Mon 384
Milhaney, Felix Mon 353
Milien, George Log 167
Miligen, Joseph Nel 41
Miligin, William Fay 47
Millar, Aaron Adr 11
Andw. Way 363
Charles Chr 116
Francis Chr 71
Frederick Way 370
Jacob Adr 10
James Chr 82
James Chr 109
John Adr 10
John Adr 11
John Chr 108
John Grp 273
Josh. Adr 10
Samuel Chr 110
Wm. Adr 10
Millbanks, John Sco 180
Millen, John Fay 28
Zakh. Nel 45
Miller, Aaron Clr 136
Aaron Fay 50
Aaron Fra 149
Abraham Clr 136
Abraham Hrs 317
Abraham Jef 5
Abraham Lin 126
Abraham Liv 158
Abraham Wsh 292
Abram Nic 53
Abriham Chr 89
Absalem Mul 389
Adam But 195
Adam Cum 180
Adam Gal 185
Adam Hnd 331
Adam Hrd 290
Adam Hrs 321
Adam Sco 168
Adam Sco 183
Adam War 245
Addam Hrs 317
Alexander Bre 163
Alexander Fle 65
Alexander Fle 83
Alexander Hop 381
Alexander She 217
Alexander Mad 244
Alexr. Hrd 292
Alexr. Lin 125
Alexr. Nel 40
Anderson Fra 150
Andrew Bre 158
Andrew Hrd 283
Andrew Log 176
Andrew Sco 177

Miller, cont.
Armstead Lin 125
Augustus Gal 197
Barney Bre 157
Benjn. War 245
Beverly Boo 61
Buckner Mer 322
Calab Log 177
Calob Mer 324
Caty Bou 128
Caty Fay 50
Charls Cal 6
Chris. Hrd 303
Christey Gra 242
Christian Nel 40
Christian War 279
Christley Bre 157
Christr. Cum 172
Coonrod She 208
Daniel Gar 210
Daniel Mad 229
David Gra 242
David Knx 74
Daniel Knx 76
David Lin 127
David Log 177
David Ohi 75
David She 216
David Wsh 292
David, Senr Gra 242
Edward Hrs 309
Edward She 235
Elijah She 221
Elizabeth Mon 356
Ephram Hnr 352
Ephram Hnr 358
Francis Jes 55
Francis She 211
Frederick Jef 29
Frederick Mad 231
Frederick Mul 387
Fredrk. Nel 42
George Cal 7B
George Clr 135
George Gal 185
George Knx 77
George Log 168
George Mul 387
George War 271
George Wsh 287
George S. Bou 71
George W. Sco 190
Hennery Cas 37
Henry Bar 19
Henry Bar 48
Henry Cum 184
Henry Fra 144
Henry Hrd 290
Henry Hrd 302
Henry Hop 381
Henry Nel 38
Henry War 269
Henry (A) Gal 185
Henry (I) Gal 185
Isaac Hrd 298
Isaac Hrs 323
Isaac Jef 5
Jacob Fra 144
Jacob Gar 209
Jacob Gra 237
Jacob Jef 6
Jacob Jef 29
Jacob Jes 52
Jacob Lin 126
Jacob Nel 38
Jacob Nel 40
Jacob Nel 42

Miller, cont.
Jacob Nel 44
Jacob Nel 46
Jacob Sco 168
Jacob War 245
Jacob War 271
Jacob Woo 382
Jacob, Jnr Gra 237
James Clr 136
James Hnd 339
James Liv 155
James Mon 356
James Nic 54
James, Jr Log 180
Jane Gar 199
Jane Knx 92
Jane Lew 95
Jane Mad 234
Jas. Hrd 295
John Boo 61
John Bou 97
John Bou 97
John Bou 127
John Bou 128
John Bra 147
John Bre 164
John Bre 168
John Cal 19
John Cum 172
John Cum 181
John Fle 81
John Fle 83
John Fle 86
John Gra 237
John Gra 240
John Hnr 353
John Hrs 309
John Jef 5
John Jef 6
John Jef 8
John Jef 8
John Jes 51
John Jes 55
John Lin 126
John Liv 154
John Log 166
John Log 179
John (Tavern keeper) Mad 230
John Mon 355
John Mon 358
John Mon 360
John Nel 38
John Nel 42
John Ohi 97
John Pul 149
John Sco 172
John Sco 183
John Sco 188
John War 247
John War 277
John Woo 389
John, Junr Gra 242
John, Senr Bou 98
John, Senr Mad 236
John, Sr Nel 37
John A. Bou 97
John A. Sco 193
John D. Ohi 74
Jos. Grn 256
Joseph Bou 71
Joseph Bou 99
Joseph Clr 135
Joseph Fay 54
Joseph Gra 242
Joseph Jef 6
Joseph Lin 128

Name	County	Page
Miller, cont.		
Joseph	Liv	153
Joseph	Mad	234
Joshua	Knx	78
Leonard	Bre	163
Leonard	Bre	169
Lewis	Mad	236
Little William	Mad	231
Luke	Hrs	309
Margara	Pen	106
Margaret	War	252
Martin	Knx	75
Mathew	Mon	366
Michael	Bre	164
Michael	Cl[illegible]	[illegible]7
Michael	Jef	32
Michael	Mad	236
Michael	War	271
Michael (I)	Gal	185
Michl.	Hrd	291
Mildred	Lin	128
Nicholas	Hrd	294
Nicholas	Nel	41
Pearson	Cum	185
Peter	Hnd	339
Peter	Hrd	287
Peter	Jef	6
Peter	Jef	6
Philip	Hrd	301
Phillip	Flo	104
Robert	Bar	40
Robert	Bou	98
Robert	Fle	86
Robert	Flo	106
Robert	Jef	6
Robert	Knx	75
Robert	Mad	245
Robert	Nel	8
Robert	Sco	186
Robert	She	216
Robert E.	Bou	71
Sally	Grn	246
Sally	Log	179
Saml.	Cly	159
Saml.	Hrd	296
Saml.	Nel	41
Samuel	Gra	242
Samuel	Jef	7
Samuel	Mas	302
Stephen	Bou	99
Stephen	Cly	159
Steven	Cal	7
Thomas	Lin	126
Thomas D.	Fay	24
Thos.	Fle	71
Thos.	Hrd	303
Tice	Cas	41
Weldol	Jef	7
Will	Bou	98
Will	Cly	159
Will	Gar	209
William	Clr	135
William	Clr	146
William	Fay	59
William	Fle	67
William	Hrd	301
William	Knx	92
William	Mas	265
William	Nel	43
William	Wsh	287
William, Esqr.	Mad	231
Willm.	Lin	127
Wm.	Bra	147
Wm.	Cum	184
Wm.	Flo	87
Wm.	Gar	210
Wm.	Mon	365
Miller, cont.		
Wm.	War	253
Wm. Senr	Bou	98
Millian, George	Hrs	319
Millican, John	Mad	234
Milligan, James	Mul	388
Patrick	Fle	74
Milliken, James	Log	177
Millikin, William	Log	177
Millin, Archibald	Chr	113
James	Chr	76
Robert	Chr	113
William	Chr	113
Millington, Charles	Log	169
Million, Alexander	Mad	234
Benjn. Jur	Mad	234
Benjn.	Mad	236
Benson	Mad	234
Daniel	Mad	234
Elzey	Mad	233
George	Mad	233
John	Jef	6
John	Mad	234
Robt.	Mad	234
Rodden	Mad	235
Travis	Mad	234
Millir, Daniel	Bre	168
Millirons, Michael	Flo	106
Millis, Polly	[illegible]	199
Millon, Saml.	[illegible]	360
Mills, Abraham	Jef	28
Absalom	Wsh	288
Adam	Log	194
Andrew	Bou	97
Anson	Clr	146
Archibald	Way	353
Baker	Way	367
Benjamin	Bou	97
Benjn.	Bou	68
Bernard	Wsh	287
Burrel	Hrs	322
Charles	Fra	147
Charles	Wsh	287
David	Jes	54
Edward	Fle	75
Edward	Mer	322
Ethelbert	Wsh	288
Evan	FLe	65
Francis	Wsh	292
Ignatius	Wsh	292
Jacob	Way	374
James	Nel	38
James	Nel	42
James	Ohi	77
Jas.	Way	362
Jehu	Way	353
Jno.	Nel	45
John	Chr	96
John	Chr	99
John	Chr	101
John	Log	176
John	Mad	235
John	Mas	258
John	Pul	152
John	Way	373
John	Wsh	287
Matha	Fle	67
Nicholas, Sr	Nel	40
Robert	Jes	54
Robert	War	258
Sally	Knx	74
Saml.	Jef	7
Saml. B.	Woo	381
Thomas	Fle	81
William	Pul	152
Wm.	Gar	211
Milner, Amos	Bra	152
Milner, cont.		
John	Bra	145
Mark	Hnr	359
Nicholas	Hrs	320
Vincent	Hrs	320
Milroy, John	Nel	43
Saml.	Nel	43
Milson, Jesse	Lew	100
Milspraugh, Danl.G.	Log	161
Milsted, James	Wsh	288
Milton, Francis	Wsh	292
John	Way	369
John	Way	373
Richd.	Nel	44
Mims, Gideon	War	281
Minach, James	Bou	99
Miner, Caliman	Lin	127
Elliot	Boo	61
Jacob	Cas	47
Joseph	Liv	149
Josias	Lin	128
Rufus	Fay	33
Rufus	Fay	55
Mines, Peter	Hrd	291
Mingis, Christy	Hrd	291
Mingo, Joseph	Way	368
Mings, Aaron	Wsh	288
Minish, Richard	Gal	184
Minnear, John	Fle	61
Minner, Elisha	Liv	148
Richard	Liv	147
Minnery, Charles	Bou	97
Minor, Alran	Gal	185
Anselm	Mer	321
George G.	War	243
George	Mer	320
Jerh.	Sco	172
John	Jes	54
John	Nel	42
Nicholas	Nel	42
Nicholas, Sr	Nel	40
Priscilla	Mer	321
Martha	Jes	54
Robert	Jes	54
Sarah	Pen	116
Thomas	She	236
Thos.	Cum	175
Waller	Pen	108
Minshall, Robert	Fle	78
Minter, Gabriel	Jes	53
Jane	Woo	384
John	Woo	401
Joseph	Jes	53
Thomas	Jef	8
William	Woo	392
Wm.	Hrs	322
Mintfort, Jno.	Hnr	368
Minton, Isaac	Knx	79
Mintor, William	Adr	19
Mires, Andrew	Pen	105
Christopher	Pul	154
Francis	Pen	108
Jacob	Cam	31
Jacob	Pul	154
Joseph	Pen	111
Nicholas	She	239
Peter	Mer	322
Phillip	Log	182
William	Pen	110
Mirt, Thomas	Way	364
Miry, George	Jef	25
Mise, Reuben	Mad	230
Milkill, Elizabeth	Mer	324
Mistleroe, Mary	Boo	61
Mitcalf, Benjamin	She	230
Mitchel, Adam	Grn	263
Alexander	Knx	63

Mitchel, cont.
Alexander Mon 378
Archebd. War 260
Aron Cas 45
Arthur Mas 302
Asa Liv 156
Benjn. War 265
Boswell Fay 49
Charles War 243
Edmond Woo 393
Elijah Bar 51
Ezekiel Nic 55
Frederic Bul 181
Frederich Woo 395
George Mas 264
George Mas 302
Goerge Woo 397
Giles Woo 385
Hiram Fay 18
Isaac Mas 265
James But 195
James Hrs 313
James Hrs 321
James, Junr Liv 147
James, Senr Liv 147
Jane Bou 127
John But 195
John Hnd 325
John Mad 231
John Mas 302
John Mon 361
John War 243
John D. Woo 399
Jos. War 260
Levan Mas 265
Lucrecy Bra 148
Martin War 264
Mathew Mon 355
Michael Woo 395
Mordica Knx 67
Moses Bar 27
Moses Bar 36
Nathaniel Bra 149
Nelly Gar 209
Nicholas War 260
Richard Fay 48
Richd. D. War 265
Robert Mon 361
Robert Woo 398
Robt. Grn 250
Robt. Grn 255
Robt. Hrs 313
Saml. G. Bou 97
Samuel Mon 370
Sandford Mas 257
Solomon Woo 295
Thos. Bar 38
Thomas Cam 27
Thomas Lew 95
Thos. War 270
William Bre 168
William Grn 256
William Liv 156
William Woo 396
William Woo 397
Willis War 266
Willis War 269
Wilm. War 264
Wyat War 270
Mitchell, Alex. J. Fra 150
Andrew Hnr 359
Anne Bou 99
Ben N. Nel 47
Benjn. Boo 61
Charity Log 195
Charity She 238
Charles Jef 5

Mitchell, cont.
Charles She 235
Cornelius Log 196
Daniel Wsh 288
Danl. She 242
David Cal 19
Elioeni Bou 97
George War 275
Harrod She 215
Henry Adr 10
Ignatius Mas 298
Isaac She 228
Isaac She 234
James Bou 97
James Clr 135
James Grn 250
James Hnr 351
James She 218
James B. She 219
James G. Bou 97
Jas. A. Nel 45
Jessee Bou 97
John Cal 7B
John Clr 137
John Gal 186
John Grn 251
John Hnr 360
John She 213
John Wsh 292
John A. Fra 149
Joseph Bou 98
Joseph She 197
Joseph F. Fra 143
Josh. Adr 11
Levin Jef 6
Obediah Ohi 77
Racheel Bou 97
Richard Log 176
Richd. Nel 41
Robert Bou 97
Robert Fra 144
Robert Mer 320
Robert She 223
Saml. Adr 11
Saml. Nel 41
Samuel Fra 146
Samuel Log 195
Samuel Log 196
Samuel She 234
Thomas She 217
Thos. Nel 38
Will Bou 69
William Bou 97
William Log 165
William Log 168
William Mer 323
William Wsh 288
Willis Sco 193
Wm. Adr 10
Wm. Bou 97
Wm. Gar 210
Wm. Grn 245
Wm. Hop 374
Mitchill, Thomas She 229
Mitchum, Dudley Woo 390
James Woo 385
Littlebury Cas 45
Wm. Cas 45
Mitchusson, Edwd. Cal 13
William Cal 4
Mitheson, John Cal 6
Mix, Enos Woo 395
Mixal, John Fay 57
Mize, Elizabeth Est 9
James Clr 135
Johua Est 9
Mizer, Jacob Jes 52

Mizner, John Mer 321
Mizs, William Est 4
Moak, Mary Mas 264
Moberly, Benja. Gar 213
Benjamin Mad 229
Benjamin, Jun Mad 237
Drury Mad 230
Edward Mad 231
Edwd. Gar 212
Ephraim Mad 229
Isaac Mad 233
Joab Gar 213
John Mad 230
Richard Mad 232
Samuel Mad 233
Mobley, Benjn. War 245
Clement War 251
Clement War 251
Elizabeth War 245
Isaiah War 251
John Hnd 334
Nathan Log 176
William Wsh 288
Mobly, Michael Cal 6
William Chr 76
Mochber, Margaret Mon 384
Mock, Andrew Bou 99
Jacob Bou 99
Joseph Bou 99
Ralph Bou 99
Ralph, Sr Bou 99
Randolph Mer 322
Mockabe, John Bra 147
Mockbe, William Bul 181
Mockbee, Stephen Mon 361
Modcalf, Charles Nel 43
Moderar, Robert Pul 150
Modril, John Ohi 101
Modrill, Robert Pul 152
Moffett, John Hrs 314
Moffit, John She 223
Robert, Jr Woo 377
Moffitt, James Woo 380
Robert Woo 378
Wm. Woo 378
Mofford, Daniel Bra 144
Daniel Bra 146
Isaiah Bra 146
John Bra 141
Mogan, Michael Nel 42
Mohhon, Dennis But 195
Molden, Equilla Pul 151
Margaret Bou 99
Moler, Isaac Nic 54
Joseph Bou 98
Lewis Bou 98
Moman, Hiram Mad 235
Monarch, Francis Wsh 292
Jno. B. Nel 46
Monaux, Joseph Wsh 292
Monboland, Daniel Fay 56
Monday, James Fay 45
Mintry Adr 11
Thomas Woo 381
Wm. Jef 23
Money, Adam Hrd 284
Henry Hnd 338
James Grn 264
Jos. Hrd 298
Monford, Martha Grn 255
Monical, Christor Nic 54
George Nic 52
Peter Nic 52
Monohon, John Mas 263
William Mas 263
Monroe, Alexander, Jr - Pen 117

Monroe, cont.
Alexander, Sr Pen 111
Danl. War 244
Danl. War 266
John Bar 19
John Fay 55
John Jef 6
John Pen 111
Johnston Bar 32
William Fay 24
William Pen 111
William Woo 388
Monson, George Hrs 313
Isaac Hrs 313
Samuel Hrs 313
Montague, Cave Boo 61
Clement Bar 31
John Sco 182
John Sco 190
Peter Sco 182
Thomas Fra 148
Thos. Sco 176
Thos. Sco 182
William Bre 166
Wm. Boo 61
Montell,Waldermare Fay 56
Montgomery, Alex Log 165
Alexander Chr 90
Allen Grn 255
Angus Sco 172
Ann Bul 181
Aylsey Grn 255
Barton Wsh 289
Bazel Wsh 293
Benja. Gar 212
Bernard Wsh 288
Elexander Fay 51
Wlish Nel 47
Ester Gar 211
Ezekiel Lin 125
Ezel. Adr 11
Frak. Adr 10
George Mon 366
George She 205
Hugh Grn 251
Hugh Log 165
Isaac GAr 212
James Clr 136
James Lin 127
James Mer 321
James Mer 342
James Mon 364
James Pul 153
James Wsh 289
Jas. Gar 211
Jas. Way 374
Jerimiah Cas 46
Jno. Hop 373
John Adr 10
John Adr 10
John But 195
John Fle 83
John Hnr 358
John Hrd 302
John Lin 126
John Mer 324
John Sco 190
John Wsh 288
John Wsh 289
Jos. (T) Gal 184
Joseph Mer 324
Joseph Mon 362
Joseph Way 367
Judith Log 164
Judith Log 180
Mary Mas 265
Mary Ann Wsh 292
Montgomery, cont.
Mima Liv 160
Nathn. Adr 11
Robert Chr 75
Robert Mer 321
Robt. Nel 45
Robt. (C1) Gal 186
Robt. (C2) Gal 186
Saml. Gar 212
Samuel Mon 365
Simp. Grn 261
Stephen Mer 321
Thomas Wsh 293
Thos. Lin 126
Thos. Nel 45
Thos. Sco 171
Ths. Nel 43
W. Nel 43
Will. Lew 100
William Bul 181
William Flo 106
William Hrd 281
William Wsh 288
Willm. Lin 126
Willm. Sco 182
Wm. Cum 180
Wm. Fra 148
Wm. Sco 174
Montgy, Alexander Hnr 359
Montjoy, Jarrat Mon 368
Moody, Alexander But 195
Alexr. Lin 127
Andw. Bar 35
Blanks, Jr Hnr 367
Blanks, Sr Hnr 362
Edmd. Cum 176
George Jef 29
James Knx 83
John Cum 175
John Hnr 367
Joseph Cum 176
Martin Pul 151
Richard Hnr 358
Thomas Jef 22
Thomas Sco 185
Thomas Wsh 289
Thomas, Jur Sco 185
Wm. Jef 8
Wm. Sco 185
Moon, Mordica Fay 31
Mordica Fay 41
Moone, Ann Jes 51
Mooney, Jacob Jef 7
Mauj. Fle 88
Moony, Sampson Fay 59
Moor, Abraham She 200
Barton Hrs 305
David Chr 83
Doratha Cam 29
Elinoor Lin 126
George Lin 127
Harbin Bra 142
James Hrs 318
Jesse Knx 89
John Nic 54
Jonathan Lin 126
Levy Bra 145
Mary Cam 29
Mordica Lin 127
Peter Bre 168
Saml. Lin 127
Samuel Lin 125
Samuel Lin 128
Simuns Nic 52
Thomas Hrs 311
William But 195
William Hrs 311
Moor, cont.
William Hrs 311
W[illegible]m Lin 126
Ze[illegible]iah Hrs 323
Moore, Aaron Woo 388
Adam Chr 73
Alexander Ohi 69
Alexr. Boo 61
Alexr. Fle 68
Alexr. Jur Boo 61
Alfred Hop 374
Ann Jes 54
Anne Bou 69
Anthony Clr 136
Asa Wsh 289
Benjn. Mad 233
Benjaim She 216
Benjamin Mas 258
BErnard Wsh 289
Betsey Bou 99
Butler Fay 28
Catharine Clr 136
Catharine Jef 24
Charles Adr 10
Charles Rck 163
Charles Sco 191
Christopher Flo 103
Clarke Sco 178
Collins Jes 51
Daniel Hnr 364
Daniel Jef 7
Daniel Lew 104
Daniel Mas 258
Daniel Mas 260
Danl. Hnr 362
David Chr 84
David Chr 111
David Fra 144
David Rck 165
David Way 374
David, Capt Mad 233
E. George Mas 260
Edward Nel 38
Elijah Mas 261
Elisha Cas 41
Elisha Log 191
Elizabeth Clr 136
Elizabeth Jef 6
Ell Nathan Fra 146
Evans Jef 6
Garsham Fra 146
George Adr 10
George Grn 249
George Grn 264
George Jef 8
George Mad 229
George Sco 173
George War 281
George Wsh 289
H.W. Mul 385
Harbin Wsh 289
Hector Jef 6
Henly Way 370
Henry Fay 19
Henson Wsh 289
Hugh War 258
Jacob Mon 354
James Boo 61
James Bou 99
James Fay 23
James Fle 90
James Gal 186
James Hop 371
James Jef 7
James Liv 158
James Mad 228
(Tho's Son)

Name	Co.	Page
Moore, cont.		
James (Geo son)	Mad	229
James	Mad	232
James	Sco	178
James	Sco	190
James	She	239
James M.	Mad	229
Jerimiah	Cal	17
Jessa	Mon	347
Jesse	Fra	144
Jesse	Hop	371
Jesse	nel	40
Jesse W.	War	255
Jno.	Hnr	363
Jno.	Hrd	295
Jno.	Lew	104
John	Bou	97
John	Bou	98
John	Bou	99
John	Bou	127
John	Bul	181
John	Chr	54
John	Chr	80
John	Chr	100
John	Est	3
John	Est	5
John (Long)	Fay	23
John (short)	Fay	23
John	Fay	24
John	Grn	250
John	Grn	251
John	Grn	259
John	Hnr	359
John	Jef	5
John	Jef	8
John	Jes	55
John	Lew	97
John	Mad	234
John	Mon	357
John	Mon	381
John	Sco	179
John	She	200
John, Revd.	Mad	236
John D.	Chr	85
John G.	Jef	7
John H.	Chr	108
Jos.	War	252
Joseph	Cal	17
Joseph	Fay	24
Joseph	Mad	231
Joseph	War	261
Joseph	Wsh	289
Joshua	Cas	37
Lambeth	Gar	211
Leavy	Jes	55
Levi	War	254
Lewis	Adr	11
Lewis	Est	6
Luke	Gar	209
Margaret	Mas	261
Martha	Wsh	289
Mary	War	254
Michael	Jef	29
Michael	Mon	377
Morris	Mul	388
Moses	Cal	6
Nathan	Est	8
Nathan	War	254
Nathaniel	Fay	23
Nicholas	Bou	99
Nina	Way	371
Obadiah	She	219
Obadiah	She	220
Obediah	Clr	136
Ostin	Chr	80
Patrick	Mad	230
Peter	She	211

Name	Co.	Page
Moore, cont.		
Philemon	Jef	8
Philip	Clr	136
Polley	Mad	228
Quinton	Bou	100
Reuben (D's son)	Mad	232
Reuben	Mad	237
Richard	Hnr	352
Richard	Wsh	293
Richrd.	Fle	85
Robert	Fle	78
Robert	Gal	185
Robert	Mon	351
Robert	Sco	175
Robert	Wsh	289
Robt.	Cam	27
Samuel	Chr	110
Samuel	Fay	28
Samuel	Fle	71
Samuel	Hnd	346
S Samuel	Hnr	362
Samuel	Mad	230
Samuel	Mas	259
Samuel	Mon	353
Sarah	Fle	78
Sary	Hop	378
Shadrick	Chr	92
Shadrick	Jes	53
Simon R.	War	257
Stephen	Mon	368
Thomas	Bou	97
Thomas	Cal	10
Thomas	Jef	5
Thomas	Jef	7
Thomas	Mad	228
Thomas	Mon	367
Thos.	Grn	257
Warren	War	254
Will	Hnr	352
William	Chr	67
William	Chr	76
William	Clr	135
William	Hnd	331
William	Mad	237
William	Rck	164
William	Sco	176
William	Sco	178
William	Woo	382
William	Wsh	289
William	Wsh	293
Wm.	Boo	63
Wm.	Boo63	
Wm.	Gar	213
Wm.	Hnr	362
Zebulon	Hnr	360
Moorehed, Armstead	Mul	388
Moorhead, Abner	Lin	128
Daniel	Lin	128
Mooris, Lewis	Nel	38
Moorman, James	Bre	156
James, Jr	Bre	158
James H. L.	Bre	166
John	Bre	162
Juda	Bre	163
William	Bre	165
Wm. Junior	Bre	158
Mooss, James	War	246
Moran, Edward	Bou	127
Elijah	Mad	232
John	Adr	11
John	Knx	88
John	Mad	232
Morbly, Edward	Rck	165
Mary	Rck	165
Morce, John	Fle	90
Mordock, Hans	Fay	60
Thomas	Fay	60

Name	Co.	Page
Mordock, cont.		
Thomas	Fay	60
More, Austin	Mer	325
Edmund W.	Gra	239
Ephrim	Knx	89
Henry	Pul	153
Isaac	Bar	46
Jacob	Mon	348
James	Bar	37
James	Bar	43
James	Cly	158
James	Knx	74
James	Nel	46
Jeremy	Bar	54
Jerimiah	Grp	271
Jesse	Knx	89
Joel	Bar	44
John	Bar	35
John	Bar	52
John	Cly	158
John	Knx	75
John	Mer	323
John	Mer	325
Joseph	Mer	325
Lawson	Mer	321
Levy	Knx	89
Lewis John	Mer	321
Moses	Knx	89
Saml.	Bar	44
Saml.	Cly	157
Samuel	Knx	65
Simeon	Mer	323
Thomas	Knx	88
Thomas	Mer	323
Will	Cly	158
William	Mer	342
William	Nel	43
Wilson	Cly	155
Wm.	Bar	52
Moredock, James	Bre	158
Morehead, A.K.	War	281
Armistead	Log	183
Charles	Log	193
Joel	Bou	100
John	Cum	167
John	War	280
Presly	Log	196
William	Fle	75
Moreheid, John	Boo	61
Moreland, John	She	213
Saml.	Bou	98
Susan	She	233
Thomas H.	Clr	135
William	She	215
Moren, Edward	Fle	83
Gabriel	Way	360
John	Fle	80
Moreton, Catharine	Nel	39
Saml.	Nel	8
Moretz, Cosper	Woo	390
Morfet, Susana	Fay	23
Morgan, Abel	Bra	152
Abraham	Wsh	290
Adonija	Pul	150
Agnes	Nic	52
Allin	Boo	61
Anne	Woo	395
Charles	But	195
Charles	Fle	92
Charles	Mul	388
Charles	War	276
Chas.	Nic	52
Daniel	Fra	145
David	Bou	97
David	Flo	103
Ellender	Ohi	70
Enoch	Cam	29

Morgan, cont.	
Evan	Fle 87
Garrett	Nic 56
Henry	War 272
Isaiah	Mad 233
Jacob	Hnd 331
James	Knx 65
Jas.	Hrd 291
Jesse	Hrd 304
Jessee	Cas 37
John	Bra 148
John	Clr 136
John	Flo 106
John	Gra 238
John	Hnr 359
John	Liv 155
John	Mon 382
John	Mul 402
John	Mul 40[illegible]
John	Mul 40[illegible]
John	Wsh 290
Jonathan	Cum 169
Joseph	Cal 13
Joseph	Mer 324
Lambeth	Bre 164
Leonard	Mul 391
Lewis	Sco 178
Mordica	Hnr 368
Mordicai	Clr 136
Morgan	Cum 169
Nat.	Bra 141
Nathan	Flo 106
Patrick	Wsh 290
Peter	Hnr 362
Philip	Wsh 290
Ralph	Mon 366
Reece	Bou 99
Saml.	Bou 98
Samuel	Bre 168
Samuel	Bul 181
Samuel	Jes 53
Samuel	Log 166
Sarah	Fay 23
Silas	Bar 38
Thomas	Mas 257
Thomas	Mas 259
Thomas	Ohi 71
Thos.	Gal 187
Tom.	Adr 10
Vincent	Wsh 290
William	Clr 136
William	Hnr 357
William	Knx 69
William	Mas 259
William	Mul 392
William	Nel 40
William	Nel 45
William	She 215
William	Wsh 289
William	Wsh 290
Willis	Mul 386
Wm.	Gal 185
Wm.	Hop 377
Wm.	Hrd 297
Wm.	Mon 380
Zadoc	Jef 7
Morgin, Lewis J.	Pul 150
Lewis S.	Pul 150
Morice, Abner	Grn 255
Morin, John	Bou 97
Morise,	Cas 43
Morison, Daniel	Hrs 310
Morning, Edward	Cam 32
John	Adr 11
Morras, Thomas	Chr 96
Morrel, Michael	Cam 28
Morris, Abriham	Chr 88

Morris, cont.	
Absolem	Jef 6
Ahijah W.	War 262
Amos	But 195
Benja.	Flo 105
Benjamin	Flo 104
Benjamin	Gra 242
Benjamin	Log 180
Colmore	Ohi 73
Daniel	Flo 104
Daniel	Gra 243
Daniel	War 262
David	Fay 40
David	Mas 257
David	War 262
Dickason	Bra 152
Edwd.	Log 177
Garry	Gra 238
[illegible]orge	Knx 75
[illegible]orge	Mad 236
Haman	Mad 232
Henry	Hrd 294
Henry	Log 196
Henry	She 226
Irwin	Gra 241
Jacob	Cal 20
Jacob	Chr 60
James	Chr 95
James	Clr 136
James	Mas 300
James	Pen 106
James	She 218
Jesse	Fra 150
Jesse	Mad 232
Jno.	Hrd 294
John	Fay 39
John	Fay 56
John	Flo 104
John	Fra 147
John	Gal 184
John	Gra 242
John	Jes 51
John	Log 196
John	Mas 300
John	Way 373
John H.	Gal 185
Joseph	Cum 168
Joseph	Fle 69
Joseph	Liv 148
Joshua	Nel 40
Mary	Flo 106
Morris	Bou 128
Morris	Nic 56
Moses	Cam 30
Nathaniel	Jes 52
Philip	War 262
Rachel	Jes 51
Richard	Bou 127
Richard	Log 167
Richard	Mer 323
Ruth	War 250
Sam.	Log 165
Saml.	Adr 11
Samuel	Clr 137
Samuel	Liv 148
Samuel	Log 180
Samuel	She 223
Sarah	Bou 97
Shadrach	Hnd 338
Thomas	Chr 102
Thomas	Mas 262
Thos.	Cam 24
Thos.	Nic 52
Warner	Mad 233
William	Bou 100
William	Chr 57
William	Clr 136

Morris, cont.	
William	Log 196
William	Mer 324
William	Woo 390
William, jr	Clr 136
William, Junr	Log 185
Zacheriah	War 257
Morrise, Joseph	Fle 89
Polley	Cas 43
Samuel	Fle 90
Morrison, Andrew	Liv 145
Archibald	Fay 45
Daniel L.	Ohi 71
David	Fle 66
Elizabeth	Jef 5
Ezra	Lin 128
Fredrick	Fle 85
Garin	Hrs 323
Hugh	Bou 128
Hugh	Jef 29
Hugh	War 269
James	Fay 18
James	Hnd 329
James	Hrd 282
James	Mas 302
Jane	War 267
Jas.	Bar 43
Jas.	War 269
Jess	Hrd 297
John	Adr 11
John	Fay 23
John	Fle 80
John	War 280
John O.	Bar 46
Joseph	Fle 80
Josh.	Adr 10
Mary	Mad 231
Mathew	Fle 74
Mitchel	Mad 232
Mortley	Mas 258
Nat.	Gar 211
Nathaniel	Fay 18
Patty	Mas 263
Polly	Hrd 290
Richd.	Bar 43
Robert	Fle 78
Thomas	Clr 136
William	Grp 276
William	Mad 231
Wm.	Bar 53
Wm.	Hrd 290
Wm.	Way 374
Wm. G.	Hrd 294
Morriss, Benjn.	Lin 127
George	Grn 265
James	Cly 154
John	Grn 248
John	Lin 128
John	Pen 112
Joseph	Grn 246
Judith	Grn 265
Martha	Sco 171
Wm.	Sco 168
Wm.	Sco 169
Morrisson, John	Chr 109
Morrow, David	War 268
Hugh	Log 178
Hugh	Log 191
James	Clr 136
James	Fle 81
Jesse	Log 195
Jno.	Bar 37
John	Bra 146
John	Clr 136
John	Hrs 315
John	Log 167
John	Log 180

Morrow, cont.
John Log 193
John Sco 173
John War 253
John Way 374
Matthew Way 374
Moses Log 193
Robert Bou 97
Robert Fle 73
Robert Mon 383
Robt. Hrs 315
Samuel Pul 151
Samuel Pul 154
Samuel Woo 398
Thomas Clr 136
Thomas Clr 136
Thomas Log 167
William Bul 181
William Log 177
William Log 192
Wm. Bar 37
Morse, Moses Fle 72
Mortamore, Famous Fle 78
Morten, James She 214
Morton, Archd. Clr 136
Armstridge Mon 373
Benjn. Mad 234
David Hnd 337
Elizabeth Cam 32
Elizabeth H. Log 187
George Mas 258
George She 214
George, Junr Mas 261
James Mon 373
Jehu Clr 137
Jeremiah Woo 394
John Clr 135
John Fay 24
John Grp 270
John Mad 234
John She 233
Josiah Grp 270
Levy Bra 152
Lucy Mon 347
Richard Clr 136
Richard Mad 230
Richard Ohi 77
Samuel Clr 135
Sarah Woo 394
Tho. Hop 377
Thomas Log 179
Thomas Ohi 76
Thomas Woo 394
William Fay 18
William Fay 56
William Woo 394
Mosby, Benja. Fle 82
Benjamin Clr 136
Daniel Boo 61
Edward Woo 385
John Sco 175
John Woo 396
Nicholas Woo 396
Robert Woo 386
Saml. Boo 61
Wm. Bar 22
Moseby, Ann Mer 322
Jesse Mer 323
Joseph Mer 322
Micajar Mer 321
Robert Mer 322
Samuel Mer 341
Wm. Adr 11
Moseley, Clement Sco 178
Daniel P. Mon 359
Jacob Sco 179
James Mon 370
Moseley, cont.
John War 255
Leonard Cas 41
Perin Clr 136
Susannah Sco 179
Thomas Mon 376
Mosely, Clemont Cal 9
George Nel 44
John Chr 58
John Chr 59
Joseph Chr 58
Pheby Chr 58
Moses, Andrew Way 363
John Knx 72
Joshua Knx 67
Milam Fra 143
Mosley, Elijah Ohi 94
John Jes 53
John Ohi 75
Robert Ohi 68
Thomas Ohi 68
Moss, Ebenezer Cal 14
Elijah Fle 82
Elizabeth Woo 386
Federick Bar 40
Fedrick Bar 27
Francis Fra 147
Henry Bar 44
James Cal 14
James Fle 72
James Hnr 369
James Jes 51
James Mas 302
Jarratt Cal 13
Jno. Grn 263
John Cal 5
John Hnd 327
John Mon 350
John War 245
John Woo 396
Lealey Boo 61
Mason Sco 188
Meredith Lew 98
Obed Cal 9
Ray Jes 54
Robert Woo 382
Thomas Bou 127
Thomas Chr 64
Thos. B. Sco 191
Tompson Liv 145
Triplett Liv 145
William Cal 15
William Fle 79
William Jef 53
William Jes 54
William Woo 396
Wm. Adr 10
Wm. Adr 11
Wright Adr 11
Mothershead, Charles She 207
George She 219
John Fra 144
Nathl. Sco 183
Wm. War 269
Motley, Edwin War 279
James War 279
John Adr 10
John Mon 347
John War 279
Mott, Caleb Liv 154
William Hnd 335
William Mad 231
Mounce, John Mon 369
John Way 363
Moulers, Joseph Mon 357
Mouller, John Mon 364
Mount, Amos She 218
Mathias Hnr 356
Mountjoy, Alvin Pen 117
Edmond, Sr Bou 97
Edwin Bou 98
George Bou 100
George, Jr Bou 100
John, Sr Pen 106
William, Esqr. Pen 112
Mounts, Thomas She 223
Mourning, Joshua Mad 235
Roger Grn 252
Wm. Bar 30
Mouser, Frederick Wsh 290
Mousten, Joseph Mer 320
Move, Daniel Fay 41
Frances Fay 44
James Fay 59
James L. Fay 52
John Fay 42
Martin Fay 49
Peter Fay 47
Rubin Fay 42
William Fay 57
Mowman, Jesse Hrd 300
Killy Hrd 298
Mowry, Adam Hnr 359A
Mowson, George War 271
Moxley, Daniel She 203
Samuel Fra 148
Thomas Clr 136
Moyer, Balsome Bra 146
John Bra 149
John Bra 149
John, Sr Bra 149
Moyes, John Wsh 288
Muazy, Peter Fle 87
Muck, Sarah Mad 236
Muc, Nicholas Bul 181
Walter Hrd 301
Mudd, Andrew Wsh 293
Elias Wsh 293
Francis Wsh 290
Henry Wsh 290
Henry L. Wsh 293
Hezekiah Wsh 290
Luke Wsh 290
Nancy Wsh 293
R.C. Nel 46
Richard Wsh 290
Thomas She 237
Thomas Wsh 290
William Wsh 290
William Wsh 291
Muffet, Benjamin Bre 169
Mugg, John Nel 41
Muir, James Clr 136
John Fay 38
Robert Clr 136
Mulan, Mary Way 366
Mulberry, Jacob Sco 181
James Sco 180
John Mon 380
John Sco 181
Mulder, Hugh Fay 28
Muldrough, Elizabeth Wsh 293
John Wsh 293
Mulhering, John Bou 99
Mulholm, Daniel Fay 18
Mulikin, John Fra 145
Mulkey, Philip Knx 76
Mulky, Hanner Pul 152
John Bar 49
Mullegan, James She 211
James She 211
Mullen, James Mas 264

Mullen, cont.
Jesse Clr 136
Thomas Mas 256
Mullens, Henry Rck 166
John Cas 45
Joshua Wsh 291
Terry Rck 166
Mullett, Nathan Flo 104
Mullican, James Cas 38
John Mer 324
Wm. Cas 38
Mulligan, Burton She 228
Wm. Hnr 368
Mullin, James Hrs 317
Samuel Nic 53
William Hrs 314
Mullins, Ambrose Flo 106
Ambrose Flo 106
Ambrose Flo 106
Beverly Gar 211
Booker Flo 106
Champ Rck 159
Fountain Pen 110
Gabriel Pen 110
Gardener Rck 159
John Flo 106
John Knx 87
John Mad 233
Joshua Flo 103
Matthew Mad 234
Reuben Pen 105
Richard Pen 111
Saml. Gar 212
Soloman Flo 106
Stephen Mer 321
Stephen Pen 109
Thomas Gar 211
Thos. Cas 45
William Est 1
William Flo 103
William Knx 84
Muluany, Sarah Wsh 294
Mumford, Richd. Bar 33
Willm. Lin 125
Muncy, John Knx 87
John, Sr Knx 84
Joshua Knx 84
Munday, Harrison Mad 233
Henry Mer 323
Reuben Fra 142
Reuben Mad 234
Stephen Mer 323
Muney, Joseph Mer 325
Munford, Richd. J. Hrd 286
Thos. Hrd 288
Munk, Malakiah Bar 36
Munns, John Bou 127
Munroe, Andrew Sco 172
John Mas 258
Munson, Allen Sco 167
Joel Nic 53
Wm. Sco 167
Munus, George Bou 128
Murdin, Edd. War 261
Murdock, Lewis Chr 67
Mure, George Fay 35
Samuel Bou 127
William Nel 44
Murfey, Felex Cas 39
Murley, Wm. Cum 179
Murnett, Isaac She 202
Muroe, John Sco 180
Murpey, Stephen Cas 46
Murphay, Jesse Fle 86
Marian Fle 86
Neal Fle 78
Murphey, Ann Fay 18

Murphey, cont.
Duncan Bra 152
Eady Mul 403
James Knx 72
James Mul 387
Jeremiah Fay 18
Jeremiah Mer 322
Jesse Mer 322
Jesse Mul 386
John Fay 24
John Hop 375
John Jef 6
John Mer 322
Philip Mul 399
Salley Knx 72
Spensor Mer 322
William Jes 54
William Mer 322
Wm. Lew 99
Murphy, Abraham Hrd 281
Charles Chr 102
Charles Mad 233
Charles Nel 39
Daniel Wsh 293
Gabl. Bar 44
Gabl. Nel 43
Gabl. Jr Nel 40
Gabril Lin 125
Hays Cum 169
Hez. K. Nel 45
James Chr 108
James Nel 45
Jas. Hrd 293
John Cly 154
John Flo 106
John Gar 208
John Lin 125
John Mad 232
John Nel 43
John Pul 153
John Woo 386
John, Jun Bar 35
John, Sen Bar 35
Joshua Sco 184
Kenelm Wsh 294
Leander She 226
Peter Adr 11
Richard Lin 125
Richd. L. Nel 44
Thomas Pul 149
Thos. Nel 43
W. George Nic 54
Will Pul 149
William Chr 100
William Lin 125
William log 191
William Mas 259
William Mas 306
William Pul 150
Wm. Bar 31
Wm, Jr Bar 31
Zachariah Clr 136
Zeph Nic 55
Murray, Barney Way 371
Charles Wsh 291
Edwd. Adr 11
Eli. Grn 248
Elizath. Cum 181
Fielding Jef 29
George Sco 181
Henry Grn 248
James Grn 248
James Log 178
James G. Fra 149
Jas. Gar 210
John Fra 148
John Wsh 344

Murray, cont.
Jos. Grn 248
Keaton Ohi 93
Michael Fra 146
Sarah Jef 5
Thomas Pul 152
Thomas Pul 153
William Chr 69
Wm. Cum 181
Murrel, Geo. Bar 41
Jesse Adr 10
Saml. Bar 41
Murren, John Sog 180
Murrill, George Lin 128
James Lin 128
Murrin, Michael Log 184
Murrow, Charles Hnr 359
George Hnr 357
George, Sr Hnr 358
James Hnr 358
James Mas 258
Joseph Mas 258
William Hnr 358
Murry, Catherine Fay 54
Darius Nel 41
James Fay 18
James Grn 265
James Hnd 327
James She 229
Jesse Nel 45
John K. Chr 115
Joshua Log 186
Keyton Bre 162
Leonard H. Bar 45
Nicholas Hnd 328
Samuel Flo 106
Thomas Flo 106
William Fay 28
Murtin, Wm. Bar 39
Murtle, Phebe Jef 5
Wm. Jef 5
Muse, George Fle 68
Isaac Pul 151
James Fle 86
Thomas Pul 149
Muset, James Bou 99
Musgrove, Aquilla Bul 181
Cuthburt Fay 42
Gilbert Mas 259
Samuel Mul 395
Musgroves, Saml. Mul 394
Mushett, John Pen 105
Music, Ephraim Mad 230
Jehoyada Bou 127
Musich, David Way 368
Musick, Cath Way 367
Jonathan Bou 98
Martin Way 373
Musoe, John Pul 154
Musslemon, David Hrs 321
Muster, John Fra 148
Muter, George Chr 70
George Woo 389
James Chr 70
William Chr 70
Myars, Benjn. Lin 127
Jacob Lin 127
Myaus, William Hrs 314
Mydiet, Micajah Cal 6
Myers, Abraham Ohi 91
Adam Mon 376
Alex. Bra 148
Barberry Jef 5
Charles Jes 52
Christopher Cum 183
Christr. Cum 185
Daniel Adr 11

Myers, cont.
Daniel Mon 363
David Lin 126
David Nic 54
Elias Clr 135
Elijah Ohi 80
Gasper Mon 357
George Mon 362
Henry Lew 103
Henry Mon 353
Henry Mon 363
Henry Mon 371
Henry Mon 377
Henry, Senr Mon 363
Jacob Cum 183
Jacob Gra 239
Jno. Lew 103
John Bul 181
John Bul 181
John Hrd 301
John Knx 73
John Mon 366
John Nic 54
Jonathan Clr 136
Jonathan Mon 363
Levi Ohi 103
Lewis Mon 363
Margaret Nic 54
Michael Ohi 78
Michael Ohi 91
Michall Lin 127
Solomon Mon 365
Susanna Mon 361
William Clr 136
Wm. Mon 362
Myles, Jesse She 207
John She 215
Richan She 240
Myres, Christian Wsh 293
Elizabeth Mas 264
Henry Mas 264
Heny Fle 90
Jacob Bou 128
Jacob Hnr 365
Jacob Wsh 291
John Cal 11
John Fle 89
Lewis Gar 211
Martha Fle 89
Michael Wsh 291
Polly Wsh 291
William FLe 65
William Wsh 291

-- N --

Nace, James Hrd 283
Nagle, John She 235
Nail, James Bou 101
Nailen, Isac Fay 43
Nailer, Geo. Gar 207
Paul Grp 277
Robert Hrs 315
T. Geo. Gar 207
Nailor, Benjn. Adr 11
John Jef 9
John Mas 307
Nicholas BAr 46
Nale, James Nel 37
Jas. H. Nel 36
John, Jr Nel 36
John, Sr Nel 36
Naley, Thomas Mer 326
Nall, Charles L. Woo 381
Nall, cont.
James Wsh 294
John Wsh 295
John Wsh 295
Lewis Sco 173
Martin Wsh 295
Richard Wsh 295
Wm. H. Woo 379
Nalley, Barney Nel 36
Francis Wsh 294
Nally, Mary Wsh 294
Raphael Wsh 294
Names, John Mon 354
Nance, Frederick Wsh 295
Hood Cum 175
James Cum 175
James, Senr Cum 175
John Hop 371
Moses Pul 148
Peter Mer 325
Nancy Nic 56
Nancy (free woman) Fay 18
Nancy Way 365
Naner, Free Jef 25
Nanny, James Mul 398
Uriah War 268
Nants, Zachariah Grn 264
Nantz, Harewood Ohi 84
Nany, Edmond Mul 404
Napper, Benjamin Mer 325
John Fay 24
Richard Nel 42
Rene Gra 237
William Nel 36
Wm. Sr Nel 35
Narsley, Christo. Gra 238
Nash, Arther Lin 128
Elizabeth Fle 67
Harman Jef 28
Iterbo Pul 148
Jeremiah Woo 394
John W. She 217
M. William Fay 18
Marvel, Jun Pul 148
Marvil, Cen Pul 148
Noble She 221
Nate, mary Hrs 323
Nation, Edward She 238
George She 231
Hezekiah She 202
Isaac Bar 32
John Mer 326
Joseph She 203
Labon Bar 32
Samson Mad 227
William She 218
Nations, Cristopher Chr 92
Nathan War 272
Natus, Fortrinatus Cam 30
Naught, Isaac Mul 388
Nancy Mul 403
Nave, Lenard Jes 55
Peter Jes 55
Naval, Knox Pul 148
Navel, Jas. Way 356
Navels, Enoch Way 355
Henry Way 356
Nawel, Archabal She 226
Nay, James She 222
Joseph Jef 28
Saml. Jef 28
Naylor, George Fay 25
John Pul 149
Samuel Fle 73
Neagly, David Hnd 343
Neal see Kneal
Neal, Abraham She 234
Neal, cont.
Barnett She 223
Benjamin But 196
Doras She 207
Edwd. She 229
Elijah Jes 56
George But 196
George Jes 56
John Boo 61
John Fay 20
John Nel 37
John War 266
John, Senr Boo 61
John, Sr Bou 101
Joseph Bou 101
Joseph Bou 101
Margarit Fra 151
Micajah She 219
Moses War 266
Nancy Fay 28
Samuel Bou 101
Samuel Ohi 102
Saml. Way 369
Stephen Fra 151
Tavner Bou 101
Thomas Bou 101
Thomas But 196
William But 196
William Fay 24
William Nel 36
William She 210
William She 222
William She 240
Wm. Boo 61
Neale, Christopher-
Jr Clr 137
Christopher, SR Clr 137
Daniel Sco 192
Jemima Sco 190
John Fay 18
Presly Sco 169
Rhoden Sco 173
William Hnr 367
Neales, Charles Fle 74
James Fle 83
Nealy, Isaac Pul 148
James Fay 59
Nearn, Mordecai Wsh 295
Neas, Henry Gra 238
Neasbit, Robert Hrs 311
Samuel Hrs 311
Sary Hrs 317
Neat, George Jes 55
John Adr 11
John Jes 56
Rudulft Adr 11
Neave, Jeremiah Fay 18
Neavis, John Gal 187
Neeal, Wm. War 266
Need, Jacob Fay 24
Neef, John Sco 176
Neel, Benjaimin Hrs 313
Charles Cal 10
Charles Pul 148
Isaac Pul 148
James Liv 152
James Wsh 295
Rachael Fra 151
Saml. Jef 9
Thos. Bar 25
William Cly 156
Wm. Way 359
Neele, William Log 180
Neeley, John Jes 41
Neely, David Log 190
Edward Log 165
Edward Log 190

Neely, cont.
George Log 166
Henry Hnd 342
James Log 165
John Log 195
John, Junr Log 165
John, Senr Log 165
Mathew L. Log 165
Richard Log 164
Thomas Log 165
Nefas, George Nel 36
John Nel 36
Neff, Adam Lin 128
Henry Mul 394
Negro, Nepton Log 178
Neighbours, Abm. Gra 242
Neil, Daniel Bou 101
Jacob Bou 101
Nancy Clr 137
William Bou 101
Neild, Daniel Mer 326
Thomas Mas 267
Neill, Arthur Knx 87
Ben Log 166
Charles Log 166
David log 166
James Log 179
John Knx 65
Lewis Hnr 368
Thomas Log 165
Thomas Log 190
Neiss, David Fra 152
Nekerves, Thomas Fay 18
Neley, David Fay 33
Nell, John Adr 11
John Cam 32
Nelsan, James Cly 150
Nelson, Alexander Sco 187
Andrew Gar 207
Bazil Wsh 295
Benjamin She 235
Emanuel Flo 103
Hadon Cam 30
James Fay 35
James Gra 240
James Mon 375
James Wsh 295
James O.B. Woo 392
Jesse Lew 102
Joel Cum 177
Joel Wsh 295
Jno. Hrd 292
John Bar 49
John Bou 101
John Jef 24
John Mon 372
John Sco 187
Joseph Fle 74
Josh. Adr 11
Margaret Bou 101
Rhoda Gar 207
Richd. Cam 27
Robert Log 179
Robert Sco 177
Robeson Hrs 322
Saml. Hnr 369
Susan Cam 27
Thomas Bou 101
Thomas Log 166
Thos. Bra 141
William Bou 101
William But 196
William Fra 151
Wm. Gar 207
Wm. Gar 207
Wm. Mon 374
Wm. Sco 180

Nemoe, David Cas 40
Nesbett, George Bou 101
Jeremiah Bou 101
John Bou 101
Joseph Bou 101
Nesbit, James Hop 379
James Mon 356
Nesbitt, Robt. Bou 101
Nesley, Philip Mer 325
Netherland, Benjamin Jes 42
Netherton, Abraham Jef 29
Henry Hnr 354
Henry Jef 29
Henry, Jr Hnr 366
John Hnr 355
John Jef 28
Jonathan Jef 9
Nethery, Robert Cum 172
Nett, Lawrence Jef 29
Nettles, Thomas Fay 24
Nevel, James Bar 29
James, Senr Bar 41
Joseph Bar 41
Wm. Bar 41
Neves, William Fra 151
Nevil, John BAr 41
Nelly Nel 35
Oswald She 227
Robert Woo 394
William She 237
Nevile, George Way 366
Nevill, John Hnd 342
John H. She 213
Marry Hnr 365
Nevit, Ann Nel 37
Joseph Nel 37
Mathew Nel 37
Richd. Nel 37
William Bre 159
Nevins, Henry Jes 55
New, Anthony Chr 107
Geo. W. Woo 379
Jacob Pen 108
James War 248
Jethro Gal 187
John Mul 390
John Ohi 71
Right Ohi 73
William Gal 187
Newberry, Henry Fra 152
Levy Bar 52
Newbold, David Sco 173
Newbolt, William Bul 182
Newboult, John Wsh 294
Newby, Bryant Mad 227
Edmon Pul 149
James Mad 227
John Mad 227
John Pul 148
Zachariah Mad 227
Newcom see Knewkum
Newcomb, Charles Fle 72
Daniel Fle 72
Daneil, Senr Fle 66
Thomas Fle 72
William Fle 88
Newcum, William Flo 103
Newdegate, Wm. Bra 151
Newel, James Bar 34
James Hrs 310
John Fay 18
Lewis She 229
Peter Grn 245
Robert Hrs 310
Samuel Pul 148
Wm. Bar 34

Newel, cont.
Wm. Hrs 311
Newellgate, John Nic 56
Wm. Nic 56
Newers, Alexander Mas 266
Newgent, Edward Lin 128
Thomas Fra 151
Newhouse, John Bar 34
Newkirk, Benjn. Jef 8
Elias, Junr
Elias Mon 380
Henry Mon 379
Isaac Bul 182
Jacob Jef 9
Peter Jef 9
Tunis Bul 181
William Bul 181
Newland, Abraham Mad 227
David Mad 227
Herod Bra 151
Joel Bra 151
John Clr 137
John Mad 228
John She 208
Lucy She 210
Patsey Mad 228
Wm. Jef 31
Newlin, Ezekiel Bar 51
William Flo 103
Newman, Elijah Clr 137
Edmund Bre 158
George Hrd 281
Henry She 207
Jacob Pul 148
John Fle 83
John P. Mad 228
Joshua Sco 187
Obediah Jef 9
Simon But 196
Simpson Hop 373
Thomas But 196
Thomas Fle 71
Thos. Nel 37
Jacob Hnd 346
Newneman, Geo. H. Jef 9
Newningham, Daniel Sco 187
Newport, Terady War 256
Newsom, Catharine Hop 371
Robert Hop 371
William Pul 138
Jonas Hop 371
Joseph Hop 380
Purson Hop 375
William Ohi 85
Newton, Archibald Wsh 295
Arnald Nel 36
Benjam Mer 325
Benjamin Ohi 80
Benjn. War 258
Elias Grn 259
Henry Fra 152
Ignatious Grn 260
Ignatius Wsh 294
Isaac Hnd 338
Isaac Knx 69
James Fra 152
James Gra 240
John Bou 101
John Fra 151
John Norman Wsh 294
Joseph Chr 80
Joseph Chr 82
Joseph Fra 151
Keneth Mon 367
Peter Hnd 338
Peter Jef 9
Reubin Hrd 296

Newton, cont.
Robt. Hop 372
Robt. Hop 376
Thomas Est 1
Wilfred Wsh 294
William Knx 68
William Knx 69
Niblick, Hugh Clr 137
John Clr 137
William Clr 137
Niccle, Henry Mon 356
Nichiel, Robt. Nic 56
Nicholas, Bolly Pul 148
David Mer 325
Edmund Bul 181
Eli Cal 17
Francis Way 370
Geo. Gar 207
George Chr 62
George Clr 137
Green Mer 325
James Chr 54
James Mas 266
James Mas 266
James Mer 326
James Nel 37
John Mas 266
John Mer 326
Joshua Clr 137
Julias Chr 62
Margery Mas 266
Nathaniel Chr 61
Pleasant Chr 63
Readick Cal 17
Robert Mer 326
Robt. War 258
Simon Mas 266
Thomas Chr 92
Thomas Log 176
Thomas Mas 266
Thomas Mer 326
William Chr 63
Nicholds, Abiel Bre 158
Frederic Bou 128
Nicholis, Simon Pen 112
Nicholisson, Robert Pen 110
Nichols, Amos Fay 45
Abner Sco 168
Betsey Mad 228
Cassandre Grp 273
Edmund Wsh 295
Frederic Fay 38
Isaac Sco 170
Isaiah Mad 227
Jah. War 261
James Cum 172
James Fay 45
James Mad 228
James Mul 396
James Nel 35
Jesse Hrd 286
John Cum 172
John Gra 242
John Mad 228
John Sco 172
John, Senr Fay 45
John F. Fay 34
John F. Fay 45
Jos. Hrd 296
Lewis Sco 169
Mrs Bou 101
Nathom Wsh 295
Nimrod Sco 168
Reason Mad 227
Thos. Sco 175
Valentine Gra 242
Nichols, cont.
Valentine Ohi 79
Will She 229
William Mad 226
Wm. Cal 16
Wm. Cum 172
Nicholson, Benjamin Jes 55
Benjamin Jes 56
Elizabeth Hnd 339
Jas. Gar 207
John Cal 13
Joseph Mad 227
Larkin Jes 55
Marmaduke Hnd 331
Peter Jes 56
Robert Nel 8
Thomas Jes 55
Thomas Jes 56
Thomas Knx 80
Thomas Mas 302
Thos. War 268
Thos. War 271
William Jes 55
Wm. Bra 151
Wm. Gar 207
Wm. Jr Woo 398
Wm. Senr Woo 398
Nick, John Pul 148
Nickason, Mary Bou 128
Nickeson, John Mad 227
Nickle, John Mon 348
Joseph, Senr Mon 348
Joseph Mon 348
Nickles, Isaac Flo 103
Thomas Flo 103
William Flo 103
William Wsh 294
Nicles, George Hrs 311
Nicolson, Jos Cly 150
Richd. Cly 150
Nicum, John Gar 207
Peter Gar 207
Susanna Gar 207
Niece, Elizabeth Mad 245
Nief, Francis Mer 326
George Mer 326
Henry Mer 326
John Mer 326
Niesbet, Nathan Nic 56
Thos. Nic 56
Thos. Nic 56
Niesbit, William Clr 137
Nifley, Philip Grn 252
Nifong, McDaniel Fay 57
Michael Mer 325
Night, Elijah Fle 63
Robt. Rck 165
Nithtingale, Mathew Cas 39
Matthew Cas 46
Nigly, George Chr 64
Nilson, James Grn 250
Moses Nic 56
William Log 176
Ninington, Tobias Fay 42
Nise, Moses Bar 38
Nivins, Jeremiah Mer 326
William Mer 326
Nivves, Daniel Nic 56
Nixon, Jonathon Jef 29
Scarlot Mul 406
Nixson, William Log 167
No, James Mer 326
Noah, George Fay 53
Noaks, George Lin 128
Noal, George Fay 33
Noale, Geo. Hnr 359B
Noble, A. J. Cly 154
Austin Nel 36
Daniel Clr 137
Doril Jes 56
Elijah Fay 18
James Cas 48
James Clr 137
John Clr 137
John Mon 378
Joseph Nel 36
Marke Cas 48
Nathan Cly 159
Peter Hrd 291
Susanna Mad 245
Thomas Cas 43
William Cly 159
Thos. Boo 61
William Fra 151
William Fra 152
William Hnd 344
Noblet, Joseph Way 358
Noblett, William Hnr 366
Noc, John Knx 90
Nocks, John Pul 148
Noe, Candon Clr 137
Daniel Fay 52
James Fay 36
Susanah Fay 37
William Grn 247
Noel, B. Little Gar 207
Elexr. Adr 11
Ephram War 276
Joel Lin 128
John Gal 187
John She 221
Loftus Fay 18
Lott Lin 128
Milly Gal 187
Moses Gar 207
Muscoe Gar 207
Olive Mad 227
Taylor Gar 207
Taylor Hrs 308
William Hop 371
William Wsh 295
Nofsinger, John Mul 387
Sousana Mul 393
Noil, Barnett Mer 326
Benjamin Mer 325
Dudley Mer 325
Nokes, George Ser Rck 165
John Rck 162
Thomas Rck 165
Nolan, Thomas Fra 152
Noland, Betsey Mad 227
Clarenda Mad 227
Francis Est 3
James Mad 226
Jesse Est 5
Jesse Est 6
John Mas 266
Leadstan Est 6
Leadston Mad 227
Mathew Fay 24
Matthias Fra 152
Nancy Mad 227
Phebe Mad 227
Smallwood Est 5
Stephen Mad 228
Thomas Est 7
Wesley Est 7
Wesley Mad 227
William Mad 227
Nolen, John Adr 12
John Hrs 324
Nancy Cas 43

Nolin, Nelson She 219
Noll, Martin Fra 152
Nolly, John Grn 263
Noon, John Jef 8
Noonon, Patrick Jes 56
Norcutt, John Lin 128
  Royd Lin 128
Norirse, John Nel 36
Noris, John Bra 147
  Joseph Bra 147
Normal, John Cam 29
  Benjn. Boo 61
  Caleb Boo 61
  Isaac She 203
  John Fle 80
  John Fle 85
  John Mas 307
  Joseph Grp 273
  Joseph, Junr Grp 273
  Lemuel She 199
  Thos. Way 356
Nornman, Caleb Hrs 313
Norrel, Patrick Grn 247
Norris, Barton Mas 266
  Enoch Hrd 301
  Ephram Hrd 299
  Ephram Jes 56
  Henry Nel 36
  Hugh Bar 29
  Jacob Mon 358
  James Log 183
  James Mas 266
  James Mas 266
  James, Junr Mas 266
  John Boo 61
  John Cal 16
  John Nel 37
  John Rck 166
  Joseph Mas 266
  Joseph Nel 36
  Joseph S. Sco 191
  Martha Bra 150
  Moses Clr 137
  Philip Nel 36
  Philip Nel 37
  Rhodias Nel 37
  Richard Mas 266
  Richd. Hrd 293
  Thomas Cal 17
  Thomas Hrs 312
  William Cal 12
  William Clr 137
Norrise, James Bra 144
  John Fle 70
Nortan, James Grp 274
North, Abijah Boo 61
  Abraham Jes 55
  John Chr 77
  John Knx 78
  Lot Boo 61
  Sidney Hnd 339
Northcott, Benja. Fle 75
Northcut, Benjn. Cam 26
  Benjn. Mon 367
  George Bou 101
  Hosy Mon 378
  John Hrs 322
  John Mas 266
  Wm. Mon 378
Northcutt, Archabal Cas 37
  Jereh. Bou 128
  Richard Cas 37
  Willm. Adr 11
  Wm. Bou 128
Norton, David Pen 116
  Elias Grn 246
Norton, cont.
  George Fay 18
  John Bou 101
  John Pen 113
  John F. Liv 156
  Samuel Bou 128
  Wm. Boo 61
Norturp, John Pul 148
Norvell, Hugh Lin 128
  James Jes 56
  Liendaman Jes 56
Norwood, Charles Woo 390
  James Fle 82
  Theophales Hrd 284
  William Ohi 95
Noslet, David Pul 148
  James Pul 148
Nothem, Rewben Nel 41
Nott, Bazel Nel 36
  Raphl. Nel 36
Nourse, Robert Log 185
  Sarah Nel 8
Novel, Thomas mon 371
Novington, John Jef 9
Nowell, Caleb Jef 9
  Edmond Jef 29
  Lipscomb Gar 207
  Major Jef 23
  Silas, M. Jef 31
Nowland, John Knx 89
Nowls, Abraham Bou 101
Nowper, Peyto Log 196
Nuckels, Andw. Bar 40
Nucum, Jno. Gar 207
  Nelson Gar 207
  Thomas Cal 11
  Wm. Jr GAr 207
Nucume, Wm. Gar 207
Nufas, Cornl. Nel 37
Nugent, Charles Fra 151
  John Bre 160
Nukirk, Cornelius Est 8
Numan, Isaac Mul 405
  John Mon 361
  John Mon 372
  Jonathan Jes 56
  Wm. mon 373
Numon, Henry Woo 382
Nun, Ira Liv 150
  Samuel Liv 150
  Walter Cum 167
Nunn, Ilui Bou 101
  James Log 183
  John Mul 400
  Richard Log 183
  Thomas Log 191
Nunneley, Anderson Pul 148
Nunnelley, William Jes 56
Nurse, William Mer 325
Nuttals, Price She 221
Nutter, David Sco 185
  Hewet Sco 178
  John Sco 192
  Thomas Fay 42
Nutterfield,George She 214
Nutgrass, Gray She 223
  Will She 223
Nymon, Elias Hrs 318

-- O --

Oakerson, Isah Fle 74
  John Fle 74
Oakley,Christopher Mon 368
Oakley, cont.
  Edmond Mon 368
  Fielding Cly 152
  John Flo 102
  Neldred Mon 368
  Nelley Mon 383
  Wm. Mon365
Oaks, David Mer 326
  Loban Log 186
Oar, William Fay 54
Oare, Samuel Chr 96
Oates, Bryan Mul 385
  Jesse Mul 385
  Jethro Mul 385
  Joseph Chr 113
  William Mul 388
Oatman, Mary Gar 208
Oats, Rodger Way 357
  Samuel (freeman Of colour) Clr 137
Obadiah Nic 57
Obanion, Andw. Gar 207
  Danl. Gar 207
  James Wsh 296
  Mary Wsh 296
  Wm. Gar 208
Obannon, John Woo 378
  Presley N. Log 182
  William Woo 378
Obanyon, John Sco 176
Obar, Ponston Knx 66
Obnint, Lewis Nel 35
Obrian, Ann Jef 30
Obrient, Sarah Woo 382
Obruce, Henry lew 102
OBryan, Ignatius Wsh 296
  Joseph Wsh 296
  William Wsh 296
Ockaman, Daniel Mon 357
OConner, Thos Nel 35
Odair, Hezikia Cal 15
  Zadock Cal 15
Odam, Lewis Ohi 99
  Willis Ohi 99
Oday, Joseph Log 185
Odear, Furniz Mer 326
Odel, Reuben Gal 187
Oden, Leonard War 250
  Richd. Gar 207
  Wm. Bra 148
Oder, Barnet Hrs 319
Odia, Barnet Hrs 320
Odle, Armsterd Mer 326
  James Mer 326
  John Mer 326
  Joseph Mer 326
  Street Mer 326
ODonald, Mary Wsh 296
Odor, Joseph Hrs 320
Oens, John Pul 147
Officer, James Sco 167
Offield, El[illegible] Mon 377
  Jane Mon 375
  Lemuel Mon 377
  Lewis Boo 62
Offolt, John Jef 30
Offult, Andrew Sco 185
  James Sco 192
Offutt, George H. Woo 379
  James Log 164
  Samuel Jes 56
  Thos. Sco 190
Ogan, John Mad 226
Ogbern, Henry Gal 188
Ogburn, Wm. Cal 14
  Wm. Cal 10
Ogden see Augden

Ogden, Aquilla Clr 137
Benjamin Hrd 281
Henry Bra 144
John Log 193
Materson She 219
Stephen Hrd 292
Winny Gra 242
Ogdon, David Cum 174
Francis Cum 174
Stephen Cly 159
Ogelton, Alex Log 186
Ogg, Thomas Hnr 355
William Mad 225
Ogle, Alexander Bou 102
John Grn 263
John Log 164
Margrd She 233
Oglesby, Constant Chr 101
Jesse She 241
Joseph Jef 28
Michael Jef 28
Nancy Jef 28
William She 227
OGlisby, William Chr 80
Jacob Chr 80
OGuin, John Hop 374
Oguon, Mary Nic 56
Ohara, John Grn 265
Ohare, Michael Flo 102
Oharra, Kean Woo 381
Oharrah, John Cal 7
OHaver, David Fay 60
David Fay 31
Oings, Jiaren Fay 52
Joshua Fay 46
OKelly, Abner Mad 226
Olanan, Susan Nic 56
OLaughlin, John Gal 187
Old, John Clr 137
Oldacre, Heny. Adr 11
Wm. Adr 11
Oldacres, Jacb. Adr 11
Oldfield, Elias Flo 102
Oldham, see Auldham
Oldham, Abner Mad 225
Conaway Jef 9
George Mad 225
George Sco 192
Hesekiah Est 6
James Mad 226
James She 201
Jesse, Sen Mad 226
John Gra 239
John Mad 226
John Est 6
John P. Bre 157
Moses Mad 226
Presley Mad 225
Richard Mad 226
Richard Est 6
Richd. Cam 33
Saml. Jef 9
Samuel Mad 226
Taply Bar 54
Tyree Mad 225
William Fay 47
Wm. Jef 9
Wm. Est 6
Zese Est 7
Oldridge, William Wsh 296
Saml. Nel 35
Olds, William Jes 56
Oliphant see Allifant
Oliphant, Wm. War 256
Oliver, Archibald Bou 102
Benja. Jef 9
Benjamin Fra 153

Oliver, cont.
Charles Fra 153
Elijah Fay 18
Isaac Clr 137
James Log 179
James Boo 62
Joel Chr 98
John Nel 35
John Lew 98
John Fra 153
John Woo 398
John Log 164
John Chr 67
John Log 185
Joseph Est 7
Josiah Chr 106
Joshua Chr 98
Martin Cal 6
Pleasant Fra 152
Presley Fra 153
Richard Clr 137
Richd. Boo 62
Samuel Bou 102
Shadrick Cal 16
Shadrick Cal 6
Thomas Fra 153
Thomas Jef 9
Thomas War 279
William Clr 137
William Fra 153
Willm. Lin 129
Wm. War 280
Oller, Geo Bar 33
John Bar 33
Olliver, David Jes 56
John Knx 77
John Nic 56
John Fle 76
Thos. Nic 56
Wilson Knx 72
Olquin, Danl. Hop 377
Omer, Daniel Jef 9
Onan, Clempson She 232
Dennis She 213
James Hnr 363
John She 237
ONeal, Arther Fay 40
Bennet Adr 11
Bernard War 245
Bryant Nel 35
Bryant She 232
Charles Boo 61
Danl. Fle 70
David Boo 61
Elenor Nel 35
Henry, Ser Fle 69
James Log 164
John Nel 35
John Nel 35
John Fay 52
John Rck 159
John Fle 76
John Adr 11
John Fra 152
Jonas Wsh 296
Joseph Jef 29
Joseph Mad 226
Lewis Fay 48
Robert Fay 28
Rodham Fay 42
Spencer Mul 390
Susannah Bou 102
Thomas Fra 153
Thornton War 275
William Gal 187
Wm. Boo 62
Oneel, Henry Bar 44

Oneel, cont.
James Fra 152
ONiel, Henry Bar 50
J. Arthur Mas 307
John Fra 153
ONeill, Hezekiah Liv 151
Onesby, James She 227
Onion, Eli Jef 30
Onstot, Nicholas Gar 207
Onstott, John Knx 88
Oram, Samuel Clr 137
Orander, Mathew Rck 162
Orange, Mercer(free-man) Fay 18
Orchard, Alexander Mad 225
Jas. Hrd 283
John Mad 226
William Mad 226
Irched, Isaac Bou 128
Orear, Benjamin Clr 137
Daniel Clr 137
James C. Clr 137
John Mon 366
John Mon 350
John C. Mon 349
Nancy Mon 350
Robert Clr 137
Wm. Mon 347
Oren, Samuel Clr 137
Orendorff, Christian Log 162
Organ, William Jes 57
Orgin, Joel Jes 57
Orkers, Henry Lin 129
Orlkins, John Nel 35
Orm, Nathaniel Bul 182
Phillip Bul 182
Susanna Bul 182
Orms, Ellee Adr 11
Mathew Bra 153
Moses Adr 11
Moses Lew 101
Phillips Adr 11
Watty Adr 11
Ormsby, John Ohi 88
Peter B. Jef 26
Stephen Jef 9
Orndorff, Christian Log 195
Orphin, Ransom Boo 61
Orr, Alexr. Jur Cal 14
Alexr. Ser Cal 14
D. Alexander Mas 267
Daniel Fra 152
Ellonar Hrs 319
George Bou 102
Hugh Log 161
James Hrs 319
Jno. Hop 381
John Sco 191
John Nic 57
Sarah Mas 267
William Fle 72
William Log 183
William Bou 102
Orrick, Andrew Fle 89
Wm. Hrd 289
Orrill, Benedict She 237
Orsbourn, Abner Nel 35
Dory Nel 35
Nichls. Nel 35
Walter Nel 35
Orsburn, Joseph Fle 73
Mary Fle 73
Orton, Edwd. Hop 374
Orvis, Hiel Log 191
Osborn, Levi Fle 66

Osborn, cont.
M. Hnr 364
Thomas Wsh 296
Walter Wsh 297
William Grp 270
Osborne, Danl. Hrd 288
Thomas Bou 69
Osbourn, Ephriem Knx 84
Jesse Knx 63
Nathan Knx 72
Peggy Knx 84
Solomon Knx 90
Osbourne, Elisabeth Flo 102
Edward Flo 102
Solomon Flo 102
Osburn, Benja. Bar 48
Benja. Bar 43
Benjamin Bul 182
Edward She 240
Eli Pen 109
Feilding Cam 30
Henry Bar 45
Jabous Hrs 322
James Fle 89
Jeremiah Fle 73
John Mas 267
John Bar 45
John Fle 89
John Bul 182
John Chr 76
John Pen 108
Jonathan She 204
Joseph Bar 45
Morgan Bra 152
Robt. Bar 45
Robt. Bar 45
Samuel She 203
Solomon Bar 45
William Fle 89
Wm. Bar 45
Ostin, George Clr 146
Ott, Federick Rck 159
Federick, Jur Rck 164
Henry Pul 147
Otwell, Francis Sco 188
Solomon Sco 188
Ouley, Peter Hrd 288
Wm. Hrd 289
Oulton, Jacob Mas 302
Ousley, Daniel Gar 208
David Gar 207
Elsworth Gar 207
Henry Gar 208
John Clr 137
John Grn 246
Nancy Clr 137
Thos. Hrd 287
William Gar 208
Wm. Gar 207
Outhouse, Isral Chr 92
Peter Hnr 356
Over, George Bul 182
[illegible], Ally Hrd 300
[illegible] Hrd 303
[illegible]n Bul 182
Robert Bul 182
Thompson Hrd 297
Thos. Hrd 299
William Bul 182
Overby, Henry Nic 56
Overdurff, Conrod Bra 142
Overfield, Mary Mas 267
Moses Nic 56
Overless, Coonrod Rck 161
Overlin, John Hrd 281
Overly, Jacob Fle 73

Overly, cont.
John Fle 88
Overstreet, Benjamin Mer 326
Gabriel Gar 207
Gabriel Jes 57
H. James Fay 18
Henry Woo 389
Henry Jes 57
James Mer 326
James, Jr Jes 57
James, Sr Jes 57
James R. Jes 57
Jas. Way 365
John She 204
Lewis Jes 57
Mitchel Mad 226
Richard Jes 57
Saml. Jef 28
Thomas Jes 57
Thomas Jes 57
Thomas Mer 326
Overten, William Gra 239
Overton, Bartlet Fay 44
Benjn. [illegible] 275
Beverly [illegible] 153
Jno. Hrd 300
Moses Gal 187
Patsy Clr 137
Reuben Boo 62
Samuel Wsh 296
Waller Fay 24
Overturf, Jacob Mon 362
Martin Mon 362
Owen, Abraham She 222
Aquilla Bul 182
Bird Hrd 284
David Rck 159
David, Jur Rck 164
David (J) Gal 187
David (T) Gal 187
Elisha Rck 162
Fleming Jes 57
Jesse She 231
Joseph Bar 33
John She 220
Morton Rck 162
Nat. Hrd 291
Owen Adr 11
Robert She 215
Robert Bre 166
Ruiban Hop 375
Samuel She 198
Thomas, Junr Bre 165
Thomas, Senr Bre 166
William Bre 166
William She 205
William Fra 153
William Jes 57
Wm. Hrd 297
Wm. Hop 376
Owens, Aaron Mas 267
Abram Woo 381
Armstead ESt 4
Aron Lew 100
Asael Lew 99
Barrister Mer 326
Bethuel Mas 267
Charles Sco 171
Daniel Flo 102
Eliz. Hrd 292
Elizebeth Mas 267
Elizabeth Jes 57
Enoch Way 364
Enock Jes 57
George Bra 143
George Bra 145

Owens, cont.
H. Log 164
Harroway Sco 181
Hezekiah War 260
Ignacias Clr 137
James BAr 32
James Sco 177
James Jes 56
James Woo 377
James Bra 142
James Bra 143
Jesse Cum 186
John Bar 32
John Lew 100
John Lew 100
John Mas 267
John Hnr 362
John Way 360
John War 255
John Way 352
John Cas 48
John Clr 137
John Clr 137
John Clr 137
John Cum 183
John Adr 11
John Sco 168
Joshua Log 164
Larance Clr 137
Levi Sco 168
Matthew Knx 65
Moses Knx 64
Nicholas Cum 184
Obediah War 260
Owen Sco 181
Owen Flo 102
Peter Way 364
Peter Log 189
Rachel Bou 102
Richd. War 282
Robert Bou 102
Robert Cum 185
Rueben Way 358
Saml. Adr 11
Samuel Jes 56
Samuel Clr 137
Samuel Pul 147
Samuel Mas 267
Tho. Bar 35
Tho. Sr Hnr 362
Thomas Clr 137
Thomas Flo 102
Thos. Bra 148
Thos. Bra 146
Thos. Sco 177
Thos. T. War 255
Wiley Liv 154
William Clr 137
William Jes 56
William Mas 267
William Pul 147
William Adr 19
Wm. Bar 32
Ower, John Adr 11
Owin, Joseph Hnd 327
Owings, Ely Mon 372
George Pen 106
George Mon 362
Henry Log 186
Isaac Jef 9
James Wsh 296
Mason Bou 128
Richard Pen 115
Richard Log 187
Richard Mon 384
Ruth Mon 361
Samuel Mon 357

Owings, cont.
Sophia Wsh 296
Thomas D. Mon 362
Owins, Barnett Mad 226
Barnett, Jr Mad 226
Benjamin Mul 393
Edmond Mul 391
George Cal 8
John Est 3
John Est 9
Nathl. Grn 265
Robert Chr 102
Thomas, Jr Hnr 366
William (Barnett's son) Mad 226
William Mad 226
William Cal 9
Owley, John Grn 259
Peter Bar 32
Peter Grn 260
Ownsby, Thos. Adr 11
Owsley, Anthony GAr 207
Wm. GAr 187
Owsly, Anthony Lin 129
Daniel Lin 129
Henry Lin 129
Thos. Jnr Lin 129
Thos. Snr Lin 129
William Lin 129
William, Snr Lin 129
Ouley, David Hrd 283
Oxier, Darcas Mon 351
Oxford, Saml. War 268
Oxley, Eleath Fay 60
Margrit Fle 73
Micagah Fay 60
Ozbern, Thomas Mon 379
Ozborn, Aberilla Sco 181
Benjn. Sco 191
Bennett Sco 180
James Sco 181
John Sco 181
Richd. Sco 178
Sarah Sco 181
Thos. Sco 167
Thos. Sco 177
William Sco 189
Wm. Sco 168
Wm. Sco 191
Ozborne, George Clr 137
William Clr 137
Ozburn, David Hrs 318
John Jef 24
Nicholas Rck 161

-- P --

Paca, John Log 196
Pace, Geo. Cly 149
James She 234
Jesse Knx 89
Jessee Rck 165
Joel Woo 393
John Clr 138
John Mad 225
John War 262
John Woo 395
Joseph Clr 138
Joseph Clr 138
Langston Cum 168
Murry Clr 138
Richd. War 272
Spencer Chr 73
Wm. Bar 50
Pacely, Robert Chr 86
William Chr 68
Pack, Benj. Way 365
Charles Flo 101
Phillip F. Hrs 307
Samuel Flo 102
Paddox, William Wsh 301
Padfield, William Chr 54
Padget, Daniel Nic 58
Timothy Bou 129
Zachariah Wsh 301
Padgett, John Mad 220
Mary Mad 223
William War 258
Padjet, John Bar 35
Padon, William Liv 152
Page, Aler. War 247
David Mon 367
Dillard Lin 131
Jesse Log 184
Joel Bar 54
John But 196
John Clr 138
John Cum 175
John Mad 221
Lindsey War 253
Robt. Adr 12
William Clr 138
William Mer 327
Paget, Edmund Mer 327
Kitty Hrd 294
William Mer 327
Pagget, James Jes 58
Paggett, Henry Jef 10
Jas. Jef 10
John Jef 10
Jonathan Jef 10
Thomas Jef 10
William Fay 57
Wm. Jef 12
Paggette, Ephraim Lin 131
Paggit, John Jes 58
James Mer 326
Pagitt, W.Williams Mas 270
Pain, Adam Grp 272
Bennett Mad 221
Elen Fay 28
George Hrs 324
Henry, Senr Fay 28
Henry C., Junr Fay 28
John Mad 220
Joseph Nel 35
Wm. Bar 40
Paine, Charles F. Woo 380
John Woo 390
Moses Woo 400
Painter, Jno. Hrd 283
John Bar 33
John Way 353
Joshua Lin 131
Pair, Charles Nel 34
Georg Mad 220
John Lin 129
John Lin 131
Palimon, Parsnenas War 251
Pall, James Nel 34
Pallard, Thomas She 204
Pallerson, Thos. Bra 151
Palmaterry, James Mad 220
Palmetur, William Fay 18
Palmer, Benjamin Hop 380
Charles Woo 382
Edward Chr 92
Henry Mer 341
Isaac Fra 156
Isaiah Hop 380
Jas. Gar 211
Palmer, cont.
Jno. Hop 375
John Bou 103
Joseph Clr 138
John Gar 211
John, Jnr Gar 211
John, Snr Gar 211
Jonathan Hop 376
Nixon Gar 211
Rolley Clr 138
Thomas Fra 156
Thos. Cam 26
William Clr 138
William Woo 393
Wm. Bra 151
Palmore, Reubin War 252
Pancake, Abraham Grp 270
Pane, John Bra 141
Philamon Way 373
Panel, Benjamin Chr 115
Pangbarn, Samuel Mas 268
Pangbern, Hampton Clr 138
Panibaker, Frederick Bul 182
William Bul 182
Pankake, Mary Bul 182
Pankey, Phillip Lin 131
Pannell, Jona. Hrd 284
Param, William Log 181
Paramore, David Bou 102
Paramour, Thos. Bou 103
Ezekiel Bou 103
Parce, Adam Wsh 297
Jacob Wsh 297
John Wsh 297
Lydia Wsh 297
Pard, John Wsh 296
William Wsh 296
Pare, John Grn 246
Paren, Josephas Hrs 311
Wm. Hrs 324
Parent, David Cal 9
Samuel Mas 307
Pariemt, William Fay 54
Parin, Archabald Lin 129
Paris, David Bul 182
David, Jr Bul 182
Joseph Bou 129
Robert She 221
Samuel Wsh 297
Stewart Bul 182
Parish, Abraham Bre 159
Anderson Bou 104
Benjamin Fay 18
Burrel Way 366
Carter Mer 327
Hezekiah Bul 182
James Woo 386
John Bou 102
John Bre 160
Jonathan Fay 50
Levi Mad 221
Lewis Fay 27
Littleberry Hrd 287
Merideth Clr 138
Nathanl. Bou 104
Nicholas Mer 327
Patsey Bou 104
Patsey Fay 37
Timothy Clr 138
Thos. Bra 150
William Mad 221
Wm. Cum 169
Pariss, John Bul 182
Park, Hugh Fle 65
John Fay 61
Robert Fay 39

Park, cont.
Willm. Adr 12
Parkam, Thomas Mad 224
Parken, John Fay 32
Parker, Abraham Bra 152
Absalam Hnr 365
Alexander Fay 17
Amy Mas 269
Aquilla Bou 102
Asher Lew 101
Charlotty Knx 85
Chas. Bou 103
David Cly 156
Edward Mon 368
Elizabeth War 265
Fielder Fay 43
Geo. Cum 181
Gilbert Fay 52
Hannah Bou 62
Henry Lew 101
Hutchison Fay 32
Hutchison Fay 43
Ibby Fay 46
Ichabud Gar 212
Isaac Cal 14
Jacob Clr 138
Jacob Mas 271
James Bou 129
James Mas 271
Jane War 250
Jas. Cly 156
Jesse Jef 10
John Bou 102
John Chr 56
John Cum 181
John Est 4
John Fra 155
John She 207
John She 220
John She 236
Jonathan Est 3
Jonathan Mad 223
Joseph Cam 27
Joseph Mad 222
Joseph Ohi 76
Lemuel Bou 102
Marshel Bra 148
Martin R. Wsh 297
Mary Gar 212
Mary Woo 398
Nathan Est 7
Nathaniel Chr 99
Nathaniel Chr 104
Nathl. War 246
North Fay 25
Peter Hop 376
Plesant Cly 154
R. Elizabeth Fay 18
Richd. Cam 32
Robert Cal 8
Rowld. T. Lew 104
Saml. Bar 38
Sampson Cum 166
Samuel Chr 66
Sarah Clr 138
Sarah Clr 138
Tho. Bar 35
Thomas Bou 129
Thomas Jef 10
Thomas Lew 101
Timothy Bou 71
Will Cly 157
William Est 4
William Fra 157
Winslo Lew 99
Wm. Cam 33
Wm. Cum 180
Parkes, James Hnd 340
John Mon 349
Thomas Fle 65
Wm. Cas 47
Parkey, Jno. Pul 144
Parkins, Jas. Hnr 367
Jno. Hnr 367
Joseph Hnr 367
Parkr, Ebenezer Est 4
Parks, Allin Mad 220
Amos Mad 220
Andrew Mul 405
Arther Fle 74
Asa Est 7
Charles Mad 225
Charles, Jr Mad 223
Ebenezer Mad 222
Eli Mad 221
George Nel 7
Hannah Fay 18
James Bou 103
James Bou 104
James Mad 225
James Nic 57
James Nic 58
James Sco 176
James, Esqr. Fle 71
Jesse Mad 221
John Lin 131
John Log 184
Joseph Bar 50
Moses Est 5
Moses Pen 109
Payton Gar 209
Peter Fay 25
Peterson Hnd 332
Reubin Lin 131
Richd. Mad 220
Robert Fra 155
Robert Grp 273
Samuel Lin 129
Samuel Mas 268
Soloman Fra 157
Timothy Mad 224
William Gar 208
Willm. Lin 131
Parkwood, Saml. Bar 41
Parmely, Efram Liv 152
Samuel Liv 159
Parmer, Edmend Fle 66
George Bou 103
Isaac Cam 25
James Bou 129
John Bou 104
John Bou 129
Philip Bar 26
Richard Hnr 362
Selvenus Cal 7
William Bou 104
Parmerly, John Way 364
John Way 364
Parmly, John Way 362
Parnul, James Rck 166
Parnull, Stephen Rck 160
Parr, Aron Hnr 362
John Adr 12
Smith Bre 168
Thos. Adr 12
William Bre 168
Parrado, John Clr 138
Parrell, John Hnr 364
Parrent, Esther Fra 154
John Fra 154
Phillip Hnr 368
Thomas Fra 154
Parris, James Clr 138
William Wsh 301
Parrish, Barret Cam 26
Benjamin She 220
Corbin Mer 327
Daniel War 260
Edmund Mad 225
Gilford Chr 87
James Chr 87
Jno. Mad 224
John Chr 112
John Cum 166
Jolly Mer 327
Nimrod Bou 103
William Est 3
William Log 196
Woodson Pen 110
Parrot, Armsted Knx 67
Richard Grn 247
Parrott, John H. Wsh 344
Joseph Rck 166
Rhodam Wsh 297
William Wsh 297
William Wsh 297
Parry, Gregg Mas 272
Parsley, John Adr 12
Wm. Adr 12
Parson, Joseph Bar 31
Parsons, Clement Wsh 297
Gabriel Flo 102
Isaac Bou 103
James Knx 74
James Wsh 297
Jesse Flo 102
Jesse Knx 63
John Flo 102
John Nic 58
Joseph Lin 129
Majr. Grn 263
Robert Knx 64
Sarah Flo 102
William Bou 104
William Flo 102
Partee, Lewis Liv 151
Parter, John She 221
Partin, James Mad 223
John Mad 223
Partlaw, Saml. Nel 34
Partlow, David Gal 188
Parton, Samuel Fay 42
Shelton Knx 66
Vinson Knx 91
Winston Knx 77
Parven, Thomas Bou 129
Parvin, Mark Jef 10
Pasinger, Gasper Bre 167
Paskil, Thomas Pul 146
William Pul 146
Pasley, Henry A. Hrd 290
Hugh Mad 225
Hugh, Sen Mad 224
Pasly, Thomas Bou 103
Pasmore, Augustin Mer 341
George Mer 341
Passons, Ezekiel Mon 362
Patchridge, Richard Knx 78
Pate, Benjam;in Bre 161
Edward Bre 161
Jeremiah Hrd 299
John Bre 160
William Bre 161
Pateete, Benj. Pul 145
Patersen, Archd. Mad 223
John (English) Mad 220
Thomas Mad 223
Paterson, Charles Mon 373
Frances Fay 54
Israel Mon 353
Jesse Mad 223

Paterson, cont.
John Mad 224
Joseph Fay 44
Richard Fay 51
Robert Fay 49
Samuel Fay 48
Samuel Fay 49
Thomas Mad 220
Thomas Mon 374
Wm. Mon 361
Pateson, James Cas 42
Patillo, Sarah War 253
Patison, James Jr Bou 103
Joseph Pul 144
Paton, James Bou 104
Joseph Bou 104
Joseph, Jr Bou 104
Peggy Bou 104
William Bou 104
William Bou 104
Patrich, Charles Fay 43
Patrick Nel 33
Patrick, Alexr. Woo 381
Charles Fay 31
Garrison Chr 92
James Flo 101
James Flo 101
John Bar 24
John Chr 101
John Clr 138
John Mad 221
Lucy Bar 39
Lydia Nel 7
Peter Nel 34
Polly Nel 32
Reubin War 251
Robert Jes 48
Saml. Nel 34
Sarah Clr 138
Sarah Lew 103
Thos. C. Nel 34
Patricks, John War 264
Patten, Elizabeth Mad 220
James Hrs 323
John Bou 129
John Log 191
Nathaniel Hrs 324
Thomas Log 185
Patterson, Abraham Bra 141
Armsted Mer 327
Arthur She 210
Carles Grn 260
Coleman Mer 326
Edward Bra 144
Elizabeth Fra 156
Frances Fle 84
George Bou 103
George Bra 148
George Hrd 281
Henry Mer 327
James Boo 62
James Bou 129
James Bra 146
James Log 179
James, Jr Log 179
Jas. Gar 210
Jas. Senr Boo 62
Jas. Senr Bou 103
Jno. Jnr Gar 210
Jno. Snr Gar 211
John Adr 12
John Bra 143
John Bra 146
John Bre 163
John Bul 182
John Cal 13
John Fay 25
Patterson, cont.
John Jef 12
John Mer 327
John Sco 190
Jonthn. Nel 41
Joseph Fay 25
Joseph Hrs 314
Joseph Mer 326
Josh. Adr 11
Mary Jes 58
Mattew Bra 141
N. Bra 141
Richd. Adr 11
Robert Fay 31
Robert Hrs 323
Robert Log 191
Saml. Gar 211
Samuel Fay 25
Thomas Hrd 302
Thomas Log 188
Thos. Bra 151
Wm. Adr 11
William Fay 31
William Fay 56
William Knx 75
William Mer 326
William Mer 327
William Sco 180
William She 209
William She 210
Wm. Bra 150
Pattie, John Bra 142
Sylvester Bra 152
Pattin, Joseph Hrs 319
Patton, Andrw. Fel 83
Benjamin W. Chr 53
Charles Cas 39
Charles Fay 25
Christopher Flo 101
David Gal 188
Ebenezar Bre 157
Felix Mon 372
George Clr 138
Henry Flo 101
James Clr 138
James Fle 80
James Flo 101
James Log 185
Jas. Jef 25
John Cal 7
John Chr 83
John Flo 101
John Gar 211
John Mas 273
John War 273
John, Jr War 273
Joseph Cum 183
Mathew Chr 53
Phillip Chr 71
Phillip Fra 155
Robert Pul 146
Roger Jes 58
Samuel Bre 166
Sarah Chr 71
Thomas Bre 166
Thomas But 196
Thos. Fle 63
Thos. Way 359
Will Bou 69
William Bre 157
William Chr 53
William Fle 69
William Mul 403
William She 198
William, Snr Lin 129
Patty, John Fra 157
Paul, Daniel Mas 271
Paul, cont.
Ephraim Hnr 364
Jacob Gra 237
John Gra 237
John Mas 270
John Woo 388
Michael Mon 375
Peter Fay 18
Samuel Lin 131
Pauley, Jno. Junr Hrd 295
John Hrd 299
Pavy, Sary Hrs 308
Pawel, Andrew Wsh 300
Ann She 236
John Wsh 300
Peter Wsh 300
Pawell, Mary She 228
Pawley, John Nic 58
Pawling, Henry Gar 209
Isicar Mer 327
John Gar 209
Sasanna Gar 212
Paxley, Elijah lew 102
Paxton, Hugh Grn 253
James Bul 182
James Fra 155
John Lin 129
Robirt Nic 57
Robt. Adr 12
Thomas Fra 155
Paydan, Adam Cam 25
Paydon, Lucinda Cam 27
Payn, Edmund Bar 47
Jessy Chr 59
Josiah Chr 73
Payne, Ambrose Gar 208
Bailey Sco 177
Vazil Wsh 298
Berry Fle 84
Charles Nel 33
Daniel Fay 39
Daniel Wsh 298
Dennis Bou 129
Duvall Mas 268
Elisha Knx 92
Elzee She 232
Enock Gal 196
James Fay 39
James Mon 374
Janothan She 198
Jas. Hrd 300
Jesse B. Hnr 360
Jessee Bou 103
Jilson Mon 350
John Bou 104
John Mer 327
John Sco 193
John She 236
John Wsh 298
John C. She 219
Jonathan Wsh 297
Jonathan Wsh 344
Joseph Knx 80
Joseph M. She 197
Labram Jef 28
Nathan Fay 40
Patrick Wsh 298
Reuben Gar 212
Reuben Mas 269
Reubin Lin 131
Reubin, Snr Lin 131
Richard Pen 110
Richard Wsh 298
Samuel Wsh 298
Thomas Bou 102
Travis Nel 33
Wafford Fra 153

Payne, cont.
William Fra 155
William Knx 79
William Mas 272
Wm. Bou 129
Wm. R. War 246
Zadock Fle 75
Zenus Sco 186
Payton, Charles She 218
Chas. Hrd 291
Daniel Gra 239
Elisha Gra 239
Gabriel Hrd 301
Jesse Mad 220
Joseph Bar 50
Lucy Cam 30
Martin Lin 131
Peggy Hrd 290
Randolph Lin 129
Sam. Nic 57
Stephen Nic 57
Stephen Nic 58
Stephen Nic 58
Thomas Chr 80
Thomas Mas 269
Thomas Mas 269
Thos. Nic 57
Valentine Lin 129
Wm. Mon 347
Yelverton Mad 221
Pea, John Jef 9
Peace, Joseph Grn 253
Joseph Knx 88
Pricilla Grn 265
Simon Grn 266
Peachy, Benjamin Mas 269
Peacock, Jacob Bul 182
James But 196
William Woo 399
Peak see Peaque
Peak, John Bar 52
John Nel 33
John She 222
John Wsh 301
John Wsh 301
Kalm. Nel 33
Patrick Hrd 299
Presley Boo 62
Presly Sco 193
Robert Wsh 298
Spencer Lin 131
Spencer Sco 193
Thos. Nel 34
William Wsh 301
Wm. Boo 62
Peake, Asa Cam 28
Daniel Fra 156
Francis Nel 34
Hekh. Sco 175
James Sco 172
Jesse Gal 188
John Bou 104
Thos. Sco 170
Thos. Sco 173
Wm. Sco 175
Peal, James Fay 45
Peanix, John Mon 354
Peaque, Patsy Pen 113
Pear, Joseph S. Hnd 334
Pearce, Benjamin Flo 101
Ephraim Cum 172
Francis Cum 186
George War 261
James A. Jef 9
Jesse Fle 83
John Bar 53
John Bou 129

Pearce, cont.
John Bra 144
John Fle 74
Leonard Nel 34
Philip She 200
Robert Woo 391
Samuel Fle 79
William Fay 54
William Fle 80
Pearcen, Joseph Mad 221
Pearcey, George She 238
Pearcy, George She 207
Hugh She 198
John She 237
Pearl, John Rck 162
Wm. Bra 145
Pearle, George Nel 33
Pearsall, Clement Wsh 298
Joseph Wsh 301
Richard Wsh 301
Samuel Clr 138
Pearson, Allen Fay 27
Israel Fay 43
John Bre 169
John War 274
Jonathan Fay 27
Joseph Grn 257
Meshack She 233
Moses Nel 41
Peter She 229
Robert Cum 184
Samuel Chr 81
Peart, Francis Woo 382
Peary, Thomas Mon 376
Pease, John Bar 32
Peast, James Fay 25
Peaveler, Libby Mon 354
Pebler, Michael Log 164
Peboth, Henry Fay 51
Pebworth, Robert Clr 138
Pecherer, Nancy Nic 57
Peck, Benjamin Mer 326
Benjn. Sco 184
Christian Jef 10
Christian Jef 11
Gasper Hrs 324
Jacob Mas 271
James Mas 269
James Mas 271
John Hrs 308
John Mas 271
William Mas 309
Zephh. Sco 184
Peckenpaugh, Henry Bre 167
John Bre 167
Peter Bre 167
Peter, Jr Bre 167
Pectol, Peter Bre 163
Pedcock, Horatio Hop 377
Pedd, Philip Bra 148
Peddcord, Thomas Mad 221
Peddes, Clifton Fay 47
Peddicord, Abel Mas 272
Emanuel mas 272
Jacob Mas 273
John Mas 272
John Mas 272
Nicholas Mas 268
Peden, Moses Bar 51
Pedigo, Edward Bar 52
Joseph Bar 52
Leah Bar 52
Levi Bar 51
Peebles, Abm. Gra 241
John Gra 241
John Mon 370
Peed, John Mas 271

Peed, cont.
Margaret Mas 271
Richard Mas 268
Peek, John Ohi 77
William Fra 156
Peel, Richard Liv 155
Thomas Liv 149
Peele, John Liv 156
Thomas, Senr Liv 156
Peers, Val Bou 69
Peet, Curtes Liv 145
Ransom Liv 152
Peevly, James Cum 178
Peg, Jno. Hrd 286
Martin Hrd 286
Saml. Hrd 285
Pegg, Paul Lin 129
Peggs, Joseph Hnr 354
Pehill, Alexander - P. Mer 342
Peirce, Jas. Gar 210
John Mas 268
John Mas 302
Stephen Mas 268
Peircell, Wm. Bou 103
Peirson, Isaril Fay 32
Jas. Gar 210
Pelfrey, William Flo 101
Pelham, Charles Mas 272
Tho. Bar 34
Pell, John Bra 147
Wm. Bra 146
Peller, Benjamin Log 181
Pells, Wm. Lew 97
Pelly, Benjn. Cam 28
Pelvin, Isaac Log 181
Pemberton, Bennett Fra 157
Elizabeth Fay 27
George Chr 88
George Way 362
George, Jun Chr 88
Henry Fra 154
Henry Hnr 354
Jessee B. Cal 8
John Clr 138
Lewis Clr 138
Reuben Hnr 354
Richd. Way 372
Stafford Fra 154
Stephen Fay 25
Thos. Lin 131
Tom. Adr 12
William Knx 67
Pemroy, Isaac She 240
Pen, Sally Liv 159
Penabaker, wyand Bre 164
Pence, Adam Sco 181
Adam Sco 189
Coonrod She 197
Emanuel Lin 129
George Sco 191
John Sco 173
Philip Jef 12
Pendagrass, Thos. Cas 39
Pendell, Thomas Fay 18
Pender, Thomas Ohi 72
Pendergrass, Edwd. Nic 58
Pendleton, Curtis Clr 138
Isaac Hnr 360
James Cam 27
John Adr 12
John Lin 129
Rice Clr 138
William But 196
Pendry, Ely Fay 59
Penex, James Lin 131
John Lin 131

Penington, Francis Chr 67
Isaac Chr 66
Jacob Chr 66
Peniston, John Jes 58
Thomas Jes 58
Penix, Charles Jes 58
William Jes 58
Willm. Snr Lin 131
Penkstaff, Andrew Fle 74
John Fle 74
Penland, Alexr. Fle 67
James Fle 67
William Fle 67
Penley, James Gra 240
John Flo 101
Penman, Jinny Lin 129
Penn, Benjamin She 233
Charles She 233
Eli Bou 129
George Bou 129
Joseph Bou 129
Saml. Sco 167
Shadrack Sco 167
Pennel, John Cas 45
Pearce Cas 45
Pearce, Sin Cas 45
Penney, Asa Hrs 311
Pennich, Edward Cas 44
Pennick, William Mas 268
Pennington, Abel Knx 85
Danl. Bar 44
Edward Log 182
Elizabeth Cas 45
James Knx 85
Jas. Gar 208
Jesse Cum 177
John Cal 15
Joshua Bar 44
Joshua Cum 177
Mary Log 182
Moses Bar 44
Partrich Cas 45
Ruben Bar 46
Simeon Bar 44
Stuart Bar 44
Timothy Bar 44
William Knx 86
Wm. Gar 210
Pennitentiary Fra 157
Pennrod, Sollomon Log 173
Penny, Ellinor Bar 47
Henry Ohi 100
James Ohi 100
John Fra 154
Thomas Ohi 100
Pennybaker, John Jef 30
Pennycuff, Jacob Way 360
John Way 362
Penrod, Alon Mul 390
Amanuel Mul 404
Catherin Mul 402
John Mul 389
Jonathan But 196
Samuel But 196
Samuel Mul 405
Solomon Mul 389
Pense, John Pul 146
Peoples, Rachel Clr 138
Saml. Bou 103
Thomas Fay 41
Pepper, Elijah Bou 104
Jesse Mas 272
John Mas 269
Jos. Hrd 289
S. Joseph Mas 269
Samuel Mas 268
Samuel Mas 270
Pepper, cont.
William Bou 104
William Fle 84
William, Junr Mas 268
William, Senr Mas 269
Peppins, William Liv 158
Perat, Volentine Mon 369
Percefull, James Hrd 281
Saml. Junr Hrd 294
Samuel, Senr Hrd 301
Perceveal, Timoy. Boo 62
Percivell, Susanah Lin 129
Perde, William Fle 61
Perdy, Alexdr. Bou 104
Isaac Bou 104
Perfect, John She 203
Pergram, James Mon 363
Perigo, Romeo Ohi 71
Perisfield, Valun-
tine Cly 154
Perit, Thos. Nel 32
Perkin, Aquilla Hrs 307
Perking, Edmond Mon 380
Perkins, Adam Cal 3
Benja. Gar 209
Benjamin But 196
Benjamin Mer 342
Chal.N. Cas 47
Christian Gar 210
Edmund Gar 209
Edward Mon 380
Elisha Bou 103
Jess War 260
Jas. Gar 210
John Bar 30
John Sco 178
Joseph Bou 102
Joseph Cum 173
Joshua Cal 3
Joshua Liv 155
Nancy Bra 152
Peter O. Log 179
Reuben Lin 131
Reubin Bou 103
Richard Fay 42
Richd. Adr 11
Saml. She 241
Simon Adr 12
Spencer Jef 10
Stephen Cal 8
Stephen Cal 8
Stephen Flo 102
Stephen Liv 152
Stephen Rck 159
Tho. Gar 210
Tom Adr 12
William Bou 103
Perl, William Cly 150
Permin, Giles Knx 75
Perrigim, Jacob Knx 71
Perrill, Henry Lin 131
William Lin 131
Perrin, Charles Gar 210
John Gar 211
John Mad 220
Lettuce Mad 221
Robert Mad 221
Samuel Mad 221
Perrine see Purryne
Perring, Wm. Mon 373
Perringar, Leonard Mer 342
Perrkins, Michael -
Jr Mad 222
Samuel Mad 222
Perry, Abraham She 231
Allen Woo 382
Bartlett Sco 170
Perry, cont.
Ben She 240
Benja. Sr Hnr 365
Benje. Jr Hnr 365
Benjn. Cam 25
Benjn. Sco 176
Benjn. Jr Cam 27
Daniel, Jur Fle 68
Daniel, Senr Fle 68
David Cam 33
Ebenezer Grn 254
Edmond Sco 170
Elijah Mon 376
Francis Mas 270
Franklin Woo 393
Geo. Cam 33
George Adr 12
James Log 176
James Sco 176
James Wsh 301
Jane She 208
John Cam 25
John Chr 111
John Flo 101
John Log 176
John She 218
Joseph Log 179
Larkin Sco 187
Lewis Woo 383
Obediah Cum 165
Randolph She 208
Richd. Grn 266
Robert Sco 182
Robert Woo 384
Roderick Woo 393
Samuel Fra 156
Silvester Jef 27
Tandy K. Woo 383
Thomas Log 176
Thomas Mas 270
William She 232
Perryman, Willm. Adr 12
Perseel, William Bou 103
Person, Abraham Rck 160
Persons, Amos Liv 156
Free Hnr 351
Pervis, Calvin Pul 146
Pery, Danl. Bar 31
Peter, Free Mon 349
Jesse Mer 326
Jonathan Wsh 302
Mary Wsh 302
Richd. Adr 12
Saml. Adr 12
Simon Hrs 310
William Wsh 298
William Wsh 301
Zachariah Wsh 298
Peters, Christian Mul 391
David Lew 104
George Jef 10
Henry Fra 155
James Woo 378
Jane Jes 58
John She 211
John Woo 397
Lewis Woo 378
Nathl. Woo 378
Nimrod Woo 378
Peter Hnd 330
Thos. Nel 34
Thomas Log 176
William Woo 378
Peterson, Garrett Wsh 298
Henry Wsh 298
James Fay 43
Jehu Lew 103

Peterson, cont.
  Peter She 199
Petett, Jerimiah Mon 370
  Mathew Mon 369
  Thomas Mon 370
Peticord, William Clr 138
Petigrew, George Log 177
  John Log 176
Petit, James Gal 188
Petman, James Log 188
Petree, Hozel Chr 114
Petroe, Philip Clr 138
Pettes, Thos. Grn 259
Pettet, George Mad 220
  Samuel Grp 278
  Stut Grp 278
Pettey, John Fay 28
  Joseph Gar 209
  Joseph War 243
Petticord, Higerson Ohi 75
Pettigroo, Mathew Chr 89
Pettit, Amos Pen 112
  Francis Cum 183
  John Fay 25
  Saml. Sco 185
  William Sco 192
Pettitt, Thomas She 233
Petty, Francis Clr 138
  Gaston Mer 326
  Harbin Mer 327
  James Woo 380
  Ralph Bar 39
  Ramsdail Clr 138
  Rhodam Wsh 298
  Thomas Clr 138
  Zachariah Mer 328
PettyJohn, Peter Adr 12
  William L. Chr 88
Pevihouse, John Way 367
Pew, Aquilla Gar 209
  Bethly Chr 104
  Gilbert Fra 153
  John Chr 64
  John Chr 64
  Jonathan Fay 18
  Joseph Bou 104
  Joseph Hrs 310
  Reuben Rck 164
  Richd. She 229
  Thomas Chr 64
Peyton, Augustey Cas 45
  Benjn. Woo 383
  Beuford Cas 37
  Cath H. Hop 381
  Charles Bou 102
  Charles Bou 102
  Daniel Flo 101
  Ephraim Wsh 299
  George Woo 394
  Hennery Cas 45
  James Cas 44
  James Wsh 301
  John Bou 102
  Joseph Bou 102
  Joseph Bou 103
  Lewis Wsh 301
  Philip Jef 10
  Rance Hnr 361
  Thomas Bou 102
  Thomas Woo 391
  Valuntine, Sr Bou 129
  Vinston Cas 45
  William Bul 182
Phafres, John Clr 138
Pharis, James Bul 182
  John Mon 351
  Samuel Bul 182
Phariss, John Grn 249
  William Grn 249
Phebe, (Free) Jef 11
Phebey (free woman) Fay 25
Phebus, Lewis Hrd 290
Phegley, David She 201
  Simon She 237
Phelps, Anthony Hrd 288
  Arington Jef 28
  Burgess Log 164
  Cary Adr 11
  Edmund Bul 182
  Guy Bul 182
  James But 196
  Jarrett mad 225
  John Bou 102
  John H. Cal 7B
  Josiah Mad 223
  Julan But 196
  Kessiah Mon 368
  Micajah Liv 157
  Nicholas But 196
  Philip Mad 222
  Richard Log 164
  Richard Ohi 72
  Smith Jef 28
  Tabitha Mad 224
  Thomas Clr 138
  Thomas Mad 223
  William Bou 103
  William Log 161
  William Log 196
  Zacheriah Mon 361
Phemister, Chas. Bou 103
Phigley, John She 235
Philbert, Wharton Clr 138
Philip, John Knx 63
  Prim Fay 40
Philips see Fillips
Philips, Aaron Mer 326
  Andrew Hop 371
  Arthur Log 167
  Charles Clr 138
  Conrord She 220
  Cornelius Way 359
  Dabner Mer 328
  David Mad 219
  Federich Mul 397
  Francis Grn 252
  Gabriel Mas 269
  Geor. Mon 352
  George Mas 268
  George Mer 326
  George Way 362
  Henry War 259
  Isaac Gar 208
  Jacob Mer 326
  Jacob Mul 393
  Jenkins Jef 11
  Joel Fra 155
  John Bre 168
  John Hnd 343
  John Mas 269
  John Mer 328
  John Mon 355
  John She 227
  John, Senr Mon 348
  Lott Grn 252
  Morris War 255
  Nicholas Mer 328
  Nimrod Clr 138
  Richard Jef 11
  Robert Gal 188
  Saml. Grn 247
  Saml. Hrd 294
  Saml. Jef 10
  Saml. Jef 28
Philips, cont.
  Sarah Gar 209
  Sarah Mas 273
  Stacia War 279
  Stephen Bar 41
  Thomas Bou 68
  Thomas Grn 256
  Thomas Jef 12
  William Grn 257
  William Mad 223
  William Mer 341
  William Woo 399
  Wm. Bou 129
  Wm. Grn 247
  Wm. Mon 347
Phillips, Aaron Wsh 299
  Benjamin Wsh 299
  Benjamin Wsh 302
  Burrell Liv 151
  Chals Cas 47
  Deonard Nkc 57
  Edman Grp 278
  Elijah Flo 101
  Jacob Fra 154
  James Adr 12
  James Adr 12
  James Adr 12
  James Cas 47
  Jaems Lin 129
  James Pul 145
  Jaems Wsh 299
  John Adr 12
  John Adr 12
  John Cal 12
  John Cas 47
  John Fra 154
  John Wsh 299
  John Wsh 302
  John, Junr Cum 173
  John, Junr Liv 151
  John, Senr Cum 180
  John, Senr Liv 151
  Joseph Jes 58
  Joshua Nic 58
  Lewis Lin 131
  Mark Liv 157
  Robert Jes 57
  Robert Liv 153
  Robets Jes 58
  Thomas Fra 154
  Thomas Hrs 317
  Thomas Wsh 299
  Thos. Log 175
  William Hrs 311
  William Jes 57
  William Wsh 301
  William Wsh 302
  Wm. J. Fra 157
Philpot, Mary Ann Grn 265
  Wm. Jr Grn 265
  Wm. Sr Grn 265
Philps, Samuel Mon 360
  Wm. Mon 360
Phipps, John Hnr 353
  Joshua Way 369
  William Bul 182
  William Ohi 69
Phips, Loch Log 187
Phirley, Richard Bar 40
Phirrin, Henry Log 180
Phrazier, Alexan-der Mon 377
Piatt, Jacot Boo 62
Picard, Peter Lin 131
Pickens, Isreal Liv 159
  James C. Liv 1[illegible]
  John Liv 15[illegible]

Pickens, cont.
John She 199
John War 274
Peggy Liv 159
William G. Liv 157
Williams Liv 159
Pickerel, Saml. Hrd 292
Wm. Hrd 292
Pickerell, Dennis Mas 273
John Wsh 301
Richard Mas 271
Richard, Senr Mas 271
Samuel Mas 272
Samuel, Senr Mas 272
Pickerill, Abel Mon 374
Pickering, Orange Mas 309
Picket, George Fay 11
George Fay 53
George Hrs 323
Henry Bar 25
John Bar 42
John Mas 268
Philup Cam 31
Wilson Hrs 323
Wm. Bar 31
Wm. Cam 30
Pickett, George Fay 25
John Jef 28
Thomas Clr 146
Pickleharmer, John Mon 354
Picklehimer, Henry Gar 211
Picklehymer, Abrm. Flo 101
Pickrell, Henry Fle 72
Wm. Fle 64
Pickrin, David Bra 150
Pierce, Absolom She 224
Daniel Mon 367
Elija Cam 33
George Grn 254
George She 226
James Grn 266
Jas. Hnr 369
Jesse Grn 252
Jesse Mon 372
Jno. Hrd 290
John Grn 252
John Knx 75
Joseph Fra 155
Lewis Mon 364
Mordica Mon 376
Reuben Pul 146
Thos. Grn 252
Wade Lin 139
Wm. Hrd 289
Wm. G. Hrd 290
Piercefield, Jeremiah Knx 78
John Knx 64
Percifield, Joseph Knx 82
Peter Knx 82
Piercy, Jacob Bou 103
George She 213
Pierman, Randal Hrd 298
Thos. Hrd 300
Pierpoint, Jeremiah Hrd 287
Piersall, John Clr 138
Pierson, Ben She 233
Benjamin She 216
Isaac Jef 11
Isham Mer 327
John Hop 372
John Hrd 301
John Sco 174
Shadrach Bou 103
Thomas She 242
Walter Jef 28
Pierson, cont.
William Mer 327
Piety, Thomas Bre 167
Pigg, Anderson Clr 138
James Nel 32
John Lin 131
John She 202
Lewis Cas 37
Lewis Fay 18
Moses Hrd 297
Mourning Hrs 321
William Cly 151
Willm. Sco 186
Pigman, Jesse Jes 58
Susannah Ohi 84
Pike, John Cas 46
John Wsh 301
Robert Mad 225
Samuel Bou 104
Tom Adr 12
William Wsh 299
Pilcher, Fielding Jes 58
Nancy Fay 27
Zacheriah Fay 27
Pile, Benjamin Wsh 299
Edward Bre 161
Thomas Adr 19
William Bre 161
Piles, Jno. Hnr 358
William Gal 188
Wm. Adr 12
Pilson, Richd. Way 361
Robert Bou 102
Pindle, Jacob Gra 244
Piner, Judith Lin 129
Willm. Lin 131
Pines, Larkin Sco 191
Ping, Jno. J. Pul 145
Jno. S. Pul 145
Thoms Pul 145
Will J. Pul 145
Will S. Pul 145
Pinion, Peter Chr 61
Pinkly, John Bar 26
Pinkney, Anthony Log 170
Pinkston, Danile T. Ohi 95
John Ohi 95
John, Senr Ohi 95
Shadrack Ohi 94
Pinkstun, Bazel Mad 222
Bazel, Jr Mad 222
Edward Mad 222
John Mad 222
Obadiah Mad 224
Sally Mad 222
Samuel Mad 222
William Mad 224
Pinnell, John Jef 28
Pinson, Aaron Flo 101
Allen Flo 101
Aron War 269
Henry Flo 102
Thomas Flo 101
William Flo 101
Zephaniah War 269
Pinter, James Pul 146
Pints, Arthur Sco 188
Piper, Alexdr. Bou 103
Asa War 269
James Bou 103
John Mer 327
Saml. Bou 103
William Bou 103
Winny Bar 53
Wm. Bar 50
Pipes, George Wsh 299
John Mer 327
Pipes, cont.
Sylvanus Wsh 299
William Wsh 320
Pippins, William Liv 147
Pirkens, Willm. War 247
Pirkings, Jesse War 246
Pirkins, Rubin Fay 41
Pirtle, George Wsh 299
Henry Wsh 299
Henry Wsh 299
Jacob Wsh 299
John Wsh 299
Pitcher, Elizabeth Jes 58
Morgan Est 4
Reubin Clr 138
Shadrick Jes 58
William Est 6
Pitchers, Thos. Boo 62
Pitchford, Danl. Bar 38
Ely Bar 38
Wm. Bar 38
Wm. Bar 38
Piteman, James Fay 33
Pitman, Ambrose Woo 384
Benjamin Liv 148
Berry Mer 327
James Fay 49
Jesse Est 8
John But 196
John Mad 225
Joshua Chr 113
Lewis But 196
Richard Knx 89
Thomas Knx 88
Thomas Mer 328
Pitmon, John Chr 114
Pitnal, Peter Cal 18
Pitt, Archibald Nel 34
Pittinger, Abram She 199
Pittman, James Nel 34
Jas. Nel 33
Joseph Nel 33
Pitts, Arch Nel 33
Benja. Hop 371
John Fle 86
John Log 163
John Mad 220
Joseph Fra 154
Josiah Sco 192
Robert Jef 25
Thomas Nel 34
William Fle 68
Wm. Lew 103
Younger Sco 173
Plain, Godfrey Fay 18
John Mul 400
Plank, Andrew Fle 81
Micheal Fle 81
Plaster, John Jef 11
Plasters, William She 233
Platt, Nancy Mon 361
Playe, Richd. Hop 371
Pleake, Matthias Mon 367
Pleasants, Edward Lin 129
Matthew Woo 388
Pledger, John S. Pul 147
Silas Pul 147
Jno. Pul 146
Pleger, Jno. J. Pul 147
John Pul 146
Plenath?, Elias Nic 57
Pliah, John Mon 368
Pliger, William Pul 146
Plough, Aldert Fra 154
Daniel Fra 155
Jerry Nic 58
Plowman, John Mad 223

Pluc, Nemiah Mon 379
Philip Mon 379
Plummer, Abiezer Wsh 300
Abraham Fle 71
Benja. Fle 67
Benjaman Fle 76
George Lin 131
Henry Cam 26
Hezekh. Lew 97
James Fle 67
Jeremiah Fle 69
John Jef 10
John Log 179
Joseph Fra 155
Joseph Log 165
Nancy Jef 9
Rachel Lew 95
Robt. Gal 196
Saml. Cly 159
Samuel Fle 67
Thomas Lew 95
Thomas K. Fle 82
William Fle 76
William Sco 183
Plunket, Willm. Hrs 308
Plunkett, Jesse hrs 321
Plunkitt, Caleb I. Clr 138
Poage, Alen Grp 270
James Grp 270
John Grp 269
John (Little) Mad 220
John Mad 221
Mary Grp 269
Poague, Robert Cum 170
Poe, Benjamen Bar 39
Brittain Mas 270
Edmund Fra 155
Edward Bra 141
John Bra 145
John Fra 156
Johnston Bar 39
Patrick Mas 270
Samuel Bra 141
Siman Chr 94
Simon Chr 95
Terry Chr 94
Virgil Fra 156
Wm. Bar 39
Poer, William Clr 138
Podigo, Elkin Bar 51
Poff, George Bou 71
Pogue, Elijah Fay 25
Henry Fay 25
James Wsh 300
John Cly 154
John Mas 269
John D. Fay 25
Joseph Sco 172
Robert Mas 268
Pohan, Wm. Jef 11
Poindexter,Gabriel Fra 153
Peter Jes 58
Robert Fra 154
Thos. Bou 102
William Fra 155
Pointer, Edwd. Gar 210
Jessa Mon 369
John Grn 250
Jos. Grn 250
Joseph Hnd 341
Samuel Fle 73
Tauzen Gra 239
Tho. Bar 34
Thomas Mon 364
Vincent Gar 210
Wm. Bar 34
Wm. Gar 210
Pointer, cont.
Wm. Grn 250
Wm. Mon 369
Points, Edward Pen 114
John Boo 62
John Cam 24
Luke Boo 62
Nathl. Boo 62
Poisel, Peter Bou 69
Poke, Edmund Bul 182
Ephm. Sco 181
Joseph Nel 34
Laden Lew 96
Poland, Wm. Hnr 363
Pole, David Nel 34
Polin, James Hnr 367
Polk, Charles Chr 84
John Boo 62
John War 266
Mosis War 266
Peggy Sco 185
Pollac, Zephiniah Bra 145
Pollack, Wm. Bra 145
Polland, Chattsen Hnr 365
Pollard, Absalom Gar 208
Braxton Pen 115
Elijah Jes 58
Elisha She 207
Greensville Gar 212
Henry She 198
Henry She 216
John Mas 271
John Wsh 302
Jos. War 260
Nancy Mas 271
Robert Jef 28
Samuel Mas 271
William Jes 57
William She 199
Pollett, Sovereign Mas 273
Polley, David Flo 102
Edward Flo 101
James Jes 58
Jesse Boo 62
Joseph Jef 11
Peter She 206
William Jes 58
Pollitt, Jonathan Fle 77
Pollock, James Bou 103
James Mas 270
John Fay 39
John Hrs 315
Joseph Lew 101
Josiah Mas 271
Layton Mas 273
Peter Jes 58
William Fay 27
Polluck, Georg Chr 111
Polly, (free woman) Fay 27
Polly (free woman) Fay 28
Polly, James Way 364
John She 238
Peter She 203
Polsgrove, Henry Pen 108
Jacob Pen 115
Polton, Isaac Mad 220
Poly, John She 231
Pompey Nic 57
Pond, Griffin Gar 211
R. Jos. Gar 211
Pondegrass, Jesse Jef 11
Pondexter, John Fay 25
Poo, Thomas Log 181
Pooke, Edmd. Nel 33
Pool, Andrew Grp 270
Elizabeth Wsh 300
Ezekiel Hnd 336
Pool, cont.
Henry Chr 59
John Bar 51
John Mas 273
Rachel Mas 273
Richard Hnd 328
Robert Bre 166
Saml. Cam 25
Samuel Hnd 328
Stephen Bre 166
William Bre 166
William Hnd 327
William Hnd 329
Poole, Anthony Clr 146
John Nel 33
John Nel 34
Wm. Jef 28
Poor, Drury W. Log 162
Jeremiah Mon 364
Wm. Mon 376
Poore, John Gar 209
Thomas Woo 381
Pope, Alemander Gar 208
Alexr. Jef 28
Benjamin Bul 182
Elijah Liv 154
George, Snr Lin 131
Humpy. Adr 12
John Jef 22
John Lin 129
Peter Hrs 319
Richd. War 275
Robt. Rck 160
Thomas Gar 208
Thomas Lin 129
William Gar 208
William, Jr Bul 182
Wm. Adr 12
Wm. Bar 42
Wm. Sr Jef 11
Worden Jef 29
Popham, Humphy Nel 34
Thos. Hrd 297
Popkins, John Mas 272
Poppuell, Isaac Adr 12
Porter, Andrew Hrs 308
Andrew Pen 107
Benjamin But 196
Benjamin She 239
Catharine Bou 69
Charles Hrs 313
David War 265
David War 269
Ebbin Sco 175
Edd. War 269
Edward Pen 111
Edwin Gar 208
Ephraim Woo 391
Ezekel Liv 151
Francis But 196
George Boo 62
George Log 164
Henry Mad 219
Henry, Jr Mad 220
Hezekiah Gra 242
Hugh But 196
Isan Fay 18
James bou 102
James Bul 182
James Fle 72
James Fra 156
James Hnr 369
James Hop 377
James Log 175
James She 242
James Mas 273
Jane Mas 270

Porter, cont.
John Boo 62
John Bul 182
John But 196
John Pen 116
John War 253
Joseph Bou 102
Joseph Fle 87
Joseph Pul 121
Josiah Bul 182
Michagia Grp 273
Nathaniel Fra 157
Nathl. Sco 179
Nicholas Jef 11
Nicholas B. Jef 11
Oliver C. But 196
Robert Bou 104
Robert Mad 225
Roland Mas 270
Saml. She 226
Samuel Fay 25
Samuel Liv 153
Solomon Mad 219
Thomas Bou 102
Thomas But 196
Thomas Liv 155
Thomas Mul 394
Watson Bou 72
William But 196
William Chr 62
William Fra 156
William Fra 157
William Knx 89
William Mas 302
William She 242
William C. But 196
Wilson Log 164
Wm. Mon 365
Porterfield, Jno. Pul 147
Samuel Log 163
Portlock, John Cum 167
Portman, Geo. Cas 42
John Cas 41
Portwood, Elizabeth Mad 224
Lewis hrd 286
Aaml. Mad 224
Posey, Fayatt Hnd 341
Humphrey Log 187
Humphry Chr 99
James Fra 154
John Hnd 341
Sarah Gar 211
Thomas Hnd 336
Thomas, Junr Ohi 68
William Hnd 335
Posten, Elias Bou 129
Eligah Bou 129
Postere, Andrew Bou 129
Postin, Samuel Clr 146
William Clr 146
Postlethwait, John Fay 17
Joseph Fay 18
Postlewait, Jonathan Mer 328
Wm. Jef 10
Postlewaite, Richd. Adr 12
Poteet, Job Ohi 70
Poten, Alex Grn 261
Potenga, Saml. Nel 34
Saml. Jr Nel 34
Poter, Saml. Nel 33
Poterfield, Alexander She 203
Potmesser, Jno. Hrd 292
Potoff, Andrew Jef 10
George Jef 12
Jacob Jef 10

Potoff, cont.
John Jef 11
Lewis Jef 11
Simon Jef 11
Sophia Jef 11
Pots, Fred Nic 57
Samuel Nic 57
Pott, David War 258
Jonathan War 251
Potter, Absalom Cal 17
B. John Gar 212
Benjn. Lin 129
Benjn. Mad 223
Benjn. Jnr Lin 129
Edward Flo 101
Federick War 257
Frederick War 257
George Log 161
John Knx 67
John Mer 326
Lewis War 256
Moses Lin 129
Nathaniel Gar 212
Reuben Mad 223
Richard Knx 83
Standford Clr 138
Thomas Knx 71
Thomas Knx 83
Thomas Lin 129
Thomas War 256
Thomas, Jr Knx 81
Thos. War 256
Uriah Knx 74
William Knx 70
Wm. War 258
Pottinger, William Wsh 302
Pottoff, Jacob Jef 10
Potts, Andrew Cas 40
Andrew Jef 11
Caty Mer 327
David Chr 105
David Mer 327
Henry Hrd 295
Jeremiah War 258
Jessee Ohi 91
John Bou 103
John Chr 94
John Chr 105
John Jef 11
John Jef 27
John War 253
Margret She 227
Polly Chr 94
polly Mer 327
Roger Ohi 99
Samuel Rck 165
Stephen Rck 165
William Jes 58
William Nic 58
William Rck 165
Poulson, John Gar 210
Wm. Gar 210
Poulter, Wm. Jef 10
Pound, Hezekiah Jef 11
John Jef 11
John E. Cal 12
Pounds, John Cal 5
Powe, Wm. Gar 212
Powel, Abraham Hrs 313
Colby Fay 42
Elias Adr 12
George Nic 57
Harrison Log 163
James Log 188
James, Senr Log 163
Jerry Nic 57
Jerry Nic 58

Powel, cont.
John Adr 12
John Nic 58
Joseph Bra 147
Joseph Grp 269
Linsey Cas 41
Nathaniel Log 163
Richd. Gar 210
Thomas Mon 380
Thos. Nic 58
Thos. Nic 58
William Log 183
William Mas 269
William Nic 58
Willoughby, Senr Log 188
Zinns Nic 57
Powell, Abd. Hop 377
Abram Boo 62
Ambrose Est 7
Ambrose Sco 188
Benj. Adr 12
Berry Mad 221
Cader Flo 102
Charles Mer 326
Charls Nic 58
Edmund Mad 224
Honor Sco 176
Jacob Flo 102
James Clr 138
James Clr 138
Jeremiah Mad 225
John Fle 73
John Log 173
John Mer 327
John Sco 169
Lazarus Hnd 345
Lewis Mer 326
Michajah Boo 62
Robt. Adr 12
Siman Est 7
Stephen Fle 89
Thos. Cly 158
Tuze Jes 58
William Mad 219
William Woo 392
William, Jr Mad 225
Willis Sco 181
Willoughby, Jr Log 171
Wm. Adr 11
Power, Chs. Nel 32
Elisabeth Fay 54
James Jes 58
James Mas 302
James Mon 375
John Fle 78
John Nel 32
Joseph Sco 185
Lewis Flo 101
Robert Fra 157
Robert Sco 191
Thomas Mon 377
Thos. Bra 151
Powers, George A. Fay 53
Henry Fle 89
Isaac Ohi 81
Jacob Grp 276
James Pen 105
John Bou 129
John Ohi 75
John Ohi 78
Joseph Fle 78
Joseph Mas 272
Joseph Sco 181
Richd. Sco 177
Robert Sco 180
William Liv 147
William Pen 116

Powers, cont.
Zillman Liv 154
Powets, Winney Gar 209
Powlas, John Fay 43
Powles, Daniel War 245
Powrs, John Fle 79
Poysey, Thos. Cam 29
Prail, William Fay 50
Prall, John Woo 378
Prat, Zephaniah Chr 65
Prater, Aaron Fay 25
Baruch Fay 25
Ester Fle 80
Henry Mer 327
Jno. Pul 145
Thomas Fay 25
Thos. Bra 149
Prather, Ashford Nic 57
Baruch Bou 103
Edward Pul 145
Fanny Jef 11
James Bou 103
James Bou 103
James Hop 372
James Mad 224
Jeremiah Bou 103
Jerry Nic 57
Jerry, Sr Nic 57
Jno. H. Mad 222
John Bou 103
John Bul 182
Jonathn. Bou 103
Philip Mad 222
Rachel Mas 270
Rezin Mas 268
Roz Mas 270
Tho. Hop 372
Thomas Fra 154
Thomas Mas 270
Thomas Jef 29
Thomas, Senr Mas 270
Walter Bou 103
William Mas 269
William Wsh 300
Wm. Bre 167
Prator, Archibald Flo 101
William Flo 101
Pratt, James Flo 101
James Lin 129
Thos. Cum 184
Wm. Sco 176
Prawl, Benjamin Mer 342
Praytor, John Mon 381
Wm. Mon 381
Preble, Wm. Sco 167
Preist, Peter Fay 55
Prenect, John Boo 62
Prentice, Daniel Mad 224
Prentis Wm. Way 369
Prentiss, Thos. M. Boo 62
Presser, Henry Boo 62
Preston, Daniel Chr 53
Enoch Gar 212
Frances Fay 34
Frances Fay 49
Isaac Flo 102
James Mul 400
Jesse Cum 169
Jiltson Gar 212
John Clr 146
John Cum 169
John Log 171
John Pul 144
Moses Flo 101
Nathan Flo 102
Patrick Mer 326
Robert Gra 239

Preston, cont.
Tolipher Gar 212
Walter Clr 138
William Rck 164
Prewet, Robert Fay 52
William C. Fay 51
Prewett, Bright Jef 10
Byrd Jes 58
David Knx 67
David Mer 327
Goldston Mer 326
Isham Mer 327
Jno. Rck 164
Joseph Mer 327
Matthew Mer 326
Prewit, Ann Fra 157
David Knx 69
Elijah Knx 69
William Knx 69
Prewitt, Elisha She 204
John Knx 69
Joseph She 204
Nathaniel She 227
Salley She 207
Samuel Knx 87
Stephen Knx 91
Susanna Clr 138
Priar, Susanna Jes 58
Pribble, John Bra 145
Saml. Bra 145
Price, Andrew Nel 36
Archibald Chr 82
Baidt. Nel 33
B. Pillemon Fay 55
Benjamin Way 373
Daniel War 247
Danl. Bar 51
Edmond Nel 7
Ervine Cal 11
Evans Fay 27
F. Andrew Fay 17
Francis Nel 7
Frederick She 209
Gifron Adr 12
Hansford Pul 144
Hatton Hrd 292
Isaac Lin 129
Isaac Sco 182
James Adr 12
James Cum 165
James Liv 147
James Liv 151
James Log 165
James Mon 382
James Pul 146
James Pul 147
James Sco 175
James C. Jes 58
Jesse Flo 102
John Adr 11
John Cas 40
John Clr 138
John Fay 18
John Fay 55
John Fle 64
John Fra 156
John Gar 211
John Grn 245
John Grn 256
John Jes 58
John Log 175
John Mul 402
John Mul 403
John Pul 146
John Sco 167
John Sco 182
John L. War 273

Price, cont.
John M. Gal 188
Joseph Pul 145
Josiah She 225
Larkin Woo 384
Mary Jes 58
Moses Fay 17
Moses Jes 57
Nathl. Cum 182
Peter Pul 146
Pew Fay 46
Pew Fay 55
Philemon Woo 377
Pugh Adr 12
Richard Fay 23
Richard Fra 157
Richard Nel 33
Richard Pul 144
Richard Pul 145
Richard Pul 145
Richd. Hrd 284
Robert Cas 43
Robert Nel 33
Robert War 244
Robert War 272
Robt. Adr 12
Samuel Fay 17
Samuel Pul 147
Shadrick Pul 146
Susannah Hrs 320
Thomas Fay 52
Thomas Fle 70
Thomas Flo 101
Thomas Flo 101
Thomas Pul 147
Thos. Hrd 284
Thos. Hrd 291
Veazy Mas 300
Veazy, Senr Mas 269
William Gar 208
William Grn 264
William Pul 146
William B. Fay 28
Williamson Fay 55
Willis Fay 31
Wm. Cas 40
Wm. Grn 264
Wm. Jef 9
Wm. Mon 353
Wm. Way 373
Wm. H. Adr 12
Prices Farm, Andrew Fay 56
Prichard, Betsy Sco 180
James Sco 193
John Sco 180
Thomas Knx 81
Pritchet, Isaac Mer 327
Pritchett, Ally Mas 273
Joseph Mas 273
Prickets, George Fay 30
Prics, Richard Flo 101
Prier, James Log 163
John Mer 326
John Mer 327
Jonathan Log 163
Priess, Danl. Grn 264
David Grn 264
Jonas Grn 264
Wm. Grn 266
Priest, Geo: Mon 377
John Grn 250
Laurance Hnr 359A
Revel Flo 102
Richd. Hnr 363
Rodeham Log 183
William Log 172
Wm. Pr Mon 348

Priestly, Wm. Cam 29
Priggmore, Samuel Flo 101
Prim, Joshua Cum 177
Primrows, Elias Hrs 313
Prince, Edward Jef 10
Elisha Liv 149
Elizabeth Cal 5
Enoch Liv 149
Francis Cal 10
Nancy Jef 23
Thomas Jef 11
Prine, James Mas 273
Joseph Mas 273
Pringle, James Hnr 361
James Jef 28
John Jef 10
Printess,Nathanile Fay 18
Printy, William Mas 272
Priscilla (free - woman) Fay 24
Prise, Bird Fay 55
Edman Grp 272
Samson Grp 272
Pritchard, Danl Hnd 354
Jas. Hnr 362
Jesse Mad 224
Obediah Fle 77
Pritchet, Jessa Mon 367
John Mon 367
John Mon 381
Philip Mon 377
Pritchett, Curtis Hnr 363
John Jes 57
Presley Mul 385
Wm. Nic 57
Pritichet, Philip Mon 347
Probius, Alexander Bul 182
Prockter, William Fle 68
George Fay 35
Procter, George Fay 52
John Fle 68
John Mad 220
Joseph Mad 222
Nicholas Mad 220
Richard She 222
William Mad 222
Wm. Bar 45
Proctor, Abraham Mas 272
Ben Log 192
Catlet Jes 58
Ezekal Jes 58
George Jes 58
Hezekiah Jes 57
Jacob Liv 151
James Rck 160
John Log 164
John Log 193
John, Jr Jes 58
John, Sr Jes 57
Mulingburge Jes 58
Thomas Log 192
Uriah Jes 58
William Jes 58
William Mas 272
William She 217
Proffit, Jessy Chr 62
Pleasant Mad 219
Prophater, Christn Bou 103
Proseer, Jane Fra 156
Prosise, Wm. Gar 208
Prosize, Geo. Rck 159
Proter, Brice War 273
Prouse, Thomas Mul 401
Province, Andrew Mad 221
Provo, John Way 368
Prowell, James Adr 12
Prudden, Daniel Ohi 71
Pruden, James Ohi 71
Pruet, Joel Hrs 313
Pruett, Dokes Hnd 347
Elijah Mad 221
Henry Mad 224
John Mad 221
Mosis War 270
Richd. Mad 223
Soloman Mad 221
Uriah Mad 224
Pruit, Archibald Wsh 300
Isaac Pul 146
John Wsh 300
John Wsh 302
Joseph Wsh 300
Joshua Wsh 300
Richärd Pul 146
Samuel Pul 146
Solomon Cum 179
William Wsh 300
Pruitt, Abram War 280
Beverly Hnr 367
Jno. Hnr 360
John Mad 223
Mosis War 280
Pruttsman, Jacob Nel 7
Pry, Elizabeth Woo 385
Jesse Hnd 332
John Hnd 332
John Hrs 320
Pryor, Jesse Wsh 302
John Bou 129
John Hnr 355
Joseph Bou 129
Joseph, Senr Bou 129
Patsy Hnr 358
Robert L. Bul 182
Saml. Hnr 356
Simon Bul 182
Thornton Bou 103
Pucket, Anna Pul 147
Jane Hnd 343
Nathaniel Mas 271
Timothy Bar 32
Puckett, James D. Cal 3
Puckitt, David Pul 146
Pugh, Geor. Mon 362
George Fra 155
Puket, John Fay 25
Puliam, Absalom Gar 209
Pullam, Barnabas Bar 46
Benja. Bar 33
Benjn. War 269
John War 280
Joseph Fay 52
Joseph War 269
Wm. War 263
Pullem, Geo Hrd 295
Jno. Hrd 294
Pulley, James Bou 129
Thomas Bou 129
William Woo 393
Pully, Deverex Mad 224
Pulliam, A. Jno. Car 209
Benja. Gar 209
Benjamin Fra 154
Benjamin Fra 157
Boswell War 266
Jennings Fra 156
Joseph Fay 18
Moody J. Woo 390
Nathan Gar 209
Nathan Gar 210
William Woo 391
Woodson Gar 209
Zachariah Fra 156
Pullin, Esher Nel 35
Pullin, cont.
John Hnr 356
John Hnr 367
John Sco 179
John War 266
Saml. War 255
Pulling, George Bre 159
Pullins, Loftus Mad 221
Pullum, Drury Mad 222
Gideon She 208
Gidion Mer 327
John Hnd 341
John Jef 28
Johnson Mad 222
Thomas Mad 222
William She 208
Pumroy, Francis Jef 12
George Jef 11
George She 199
Punnoy, Isaac She 240
Puntney, Samuel Log 187
Purcel, Jas. Hrd 289
Purcell, Ben Est 4
Dennis Nel 33
John Bul 182
Mary Nel 32
Thos. Nic 57
Purcely, Richard Chr 83
Purchiser, Michael Mas 270
Samuel Mas 268
Purcley, John Chr 80
Purdham, Tamor Mas 270
Purdon, Hezekiah Mad 224
Purdue, Ezekiel Way 351
Purdum, William Lin 129
Purdy, Aaron Wsh 302
Betsy Bou 104
Henry Wsh 302
Hugh Log 184
John Wsh 302
John Wsh 302
Samuel Pen 105
Stephen Wsh 300
William Wsh 300
Purkins, Anthony Mad 223
Dabney Mad 223
Garrett Fay 18
James Fay 25
James Log 165
James Log 185
Jessee Fay 25
Michael Mad 223
Richard Fay 25
William Fay 57
William Mad 219
Purkle, Jacob Cal 8
Marjaret Cal 8
Michall Cal 5
Purlee, John Way 363
Purnell, Wm. Nic 57
Purrine, Kenneth Fle 69
Purryne, Daniel Mas 272
Henry Mas 269
Pursel, Macum Chr 107
Pursell, Henry She 228
Pursley, Daniel Mad 223
Daniel She 211
John Lew 100
Margaret Mas 269
Thomas Mad 224
Pursly, Jas. Hrd 297
Purson, James Lin 129
Purtle, Uriah Gra 237
Purvines, Henrey Fay 18
Purvis, William Fle 76
Purviss, John Fle 76
Puryear, Wm. Jef 12

Pussley, Saml. Nel 33
Putman, Bazeal War 267
  Danl. K. Fle 70
  Ezekle War 267
  Henry Mas 268
  Hyrum Bar 49
  James Bra 148
  Sarah War 264
  Thos. War 268
  Wm. Bra 148
  Zechariah Mas 271
Putmon, James Pen 109
Putt, John Gra 240
  Samuel Gra 239
Putuff, John Fay 51
Pyburn, Richd. Hrd 294
Pyle, Joseph Chr 54
  Nicholas Chr 54
  Nicholas Chr 56
  Nicholas Chr 63
  Nicholas Chr 63
  William Chr 78

-- Q --

Quailes, Rogers Fay 32
Quaintance, James Fle 79
  William Fle 81
Qualls, Tuncil Pul 121
Qually, Patrick Fle 72
Quarles, Ambrose Fra 158
  James Woo 383
  Rodger Fay 60
  Tunstal Woo 383
  William Fra 158
Quate, David Chr 63
Queen, James Nel 32
  Richard M. Wsh 303
Queinton, Wm. Cas 43
Querry, Charles Jef 12
Quick, Abriham Bul 183
  Alexander Mad 219
  Andrew Bul 183
  Benjamin Bul 183
  David Gra 240
  Dennis Bul 183
  Jacob, Jr Est 6
  Jacob, Senr Est 6
  Jessee Bul 183
Quiet, James Bou 104
Quiggins, John Wsh 303
Quigley, Betsy Mer 328
  Lewis Nel 7
Quigly, James Bar 47
Quile, Henry (free-man) Fay 17
Quimby, Ephram Jes 57
  Rachel Jes 57
Quin, John Jef 12
Quinlan, Philip Mas 310
Quinn, Absalom Gar 212
  Francis Mad 219
  James Fle 63
  James, Jr Fle 67
  John Fra 158
  John Rck 164
  Joshua Fra 158
  Wm. Gar 212
Quinten, James Liv 152
Quinton, Philip Nel 7
Quire, William Fra 158
Quirk, Rebecca Nel 32
Quisenberry, James Clr 139
  Joel Clr 139
Quishingberry, John Mad 219

-- R --

R...., John Mer 343
Rabourn, George Pul 141
  Henry Mon 355
  John Mon 367
  Ralph Mon 367
  Wm. Mon 367
  Wm. Senr Mon 366
Raburn, David Fle 77
Rachals, Vallentine Chr 66
Rachel (free woman) Fay 17
Rachel Nic 58
Radacain, John Mon 352
Radcliff, David Gar 213
  John Gar 213
  Richd. Gar 216
Radclift, John Chr 80
Raddick, Whitman Cal 15
Rader, Alexander Bou 106
Radford, John She 236
  Richard she 237
  Robert She 208
Radikin, James Pul 144
  Joseph Pul 144
  Willim Pul 144
Radinour, Joseph Fle 76
Radley, Ichabod Hrd 281
Radman, David Wsh 344
  James Wsh 344
Radmon, Charles Hrs 311
Rafe, Abraham Sr Cas 42
Rafferty, Malem. Boo 62
Raffett, Samuel Mon 356
Raffety, Thomas Jr Log 163
Raffity, James Grn 246
  John Grn 245
  Richard Log 163
  Thomas, Sin Log 163
  Thos. Grn 263
  William Log 163
  Wm. Grn 245
Ragan, Mary Fay 56
  Robert Mad 218
Ragdal, Robert War 256
Ragen, Charles Mon 368
  John Mon 369
  Mary Fay 30
Rager, John Log 163
  William Log 164
Ragin, John Chr 59
  Spencer Fay 33
  Spencer Fay 56
  Thomas Chr 85
  Winifred Bre 159
Ragir, Burkett Log 188
Ragland, David Clr 139
  Edmond Clr 139
  Haley Hop 381
  James, Jr Clr 139
  James, Sr Clr 139
  Nathaniel Clr 139
  Robards Clr 139
Raglin, John Bar 37
  Richd. Bar 27
Ragsdal, Anthony Bul 183
  David Bar 30
  Wm. Bar 31
Ragsdale, Benjn. Log 179

Ragsdale, cont.
  Drury Mas 275
  Frederic Log 187
  Gabriel Mad 217
  Gadfrey She 228
  James Log 185
  Obediah Bra 149
  Patsy Wsh 309
  Peter Mad 217
  Richard Hnr 356
  Samuel Log 195
  Stephen Log 180
  William Log 185
  William She 227
Raifield, South Log 184
Railey, Bazil Wsh 307
  Charles Woo 375
  Henry Wsh 308
  Isham Woo 392
  John Wsh 308
  John Michael Wsh 309
  Jonathan Wsh 304
  Lydia Wsh 307
  Peter Wsh 308
  Randolph Woo 390
  Sarah Wsh 307
  Thomas Woo 394
  William Woo 392
Railsbacck, Edward Mas 275
  Daniel Clr 140
Raimey, Nathl. Nel 31
  Susan Nel 30
Rainbolt, Michael Knx 70
Rainbow, John Way 353
Raine, Nathaniel Bou 106
  William Log 180
Raines, Christo. Boo 62
  Walker Mon 372
Rainey, Abm. Sco 168
  Isaac Sco 179
  Jacob Sco 169
  John Clr 140
  Robert Pen 107
  Samuel Mon 366
Rains, Allen Knx 73
  Henry Knx 77
  John Knx 81
  Jonathan Knx 82
  Thomas Knx 73
Rainwater, Abraham Pul 141
Rainy, Wm. Hop 373
Raise, Benja. Fle 72
Raisor, Henry Mon 374
Raizor, George Grn 257
Raker, Michael Clr 139
Ralston, Andrew Hrs 307
  James Hrs 307
  John Bou 105
  John Hrs 307
  Wilm. Hrs 307
Ramage, James Liv 157
  Joseph Liv 158
Rambo, Enos Way 366
Ramer, Abram Gra 238
  Michael Gra 242
Ramey, Aaron Clr 139
  Daniel Flo 101
  Davis Mon 366
  James Clr 140
  Jesse Flo 101
  John Clr 139
  John Flo 101
  John Mon 368
  Rachel Clr 140
  Sinnet Fle 65
  William Flo 101
  William Flo 101

Ramey, cont.
Wm. P. Fle 65
Ramley, Henry Bra 152
John Gra 241
Rammage, John Liv 157
Josiah Liv 158
Ramsay, George Jes 55
Jno. Hrd 287
John Jes 56
Thos. Sco 171
Ramsdal, Wharton Hnr 367
Ramsey, Alexander Clr 139
Alexander Fle 73
Alexander Hnd 328
Archd. Nic 59
Bartholomew Bre 160
Benjamin She 222
David Fle 83
Enos Fra 160
Francis Rck 159
Geo. Hop 373
James Wsh 307
Jas. War 265
John Clr 139
John Gar 214
John Hnd 334
John Liv 148
John Liv 156
John Mon 377
Jonathan Liv 150
Josiah Liv 150
Larkin Gar 213
Obadiah Pul 143
Robert Hnd 334
Robert Mon 369
Sally Liv 149
Saml. Bar 43
Samuel Mas 302
Seth Woo 382
Stephen War 277
Thomas Gar 213
Thomas Jef 12
William Clr 139
William Hnd 335
William Liv 158
William H. Liv 154
Ramsom, Ignatious Mad 219
Ramy, Debby Mas 278
Henry Gal 189
John Gal 188
Randal, Michael War 262
Tho. Bar 39
Wm. War 262
Randales, Jno. Gar 214
Richd. Gar 214
Randalf, Moses Fay 41
Randall, John She 204
Randals, Benjn. Mad 218
John Mad 218
Nimrod Pul 143
Randel, Brice Fay 52
Randle, John Hrs 310
Randol, Joseph Bar 38
Moses Bar 38
Randolph, David Jef 28
Enoch Mer 329
Henry She 202
Hull Mon 352
James Mon 383
John Hnd 330
John Mul 397
Joseph Grn 261
Malichi Mer 329
Robert Mul 396
Thomas Mul 393
Thomas Mul 397
Wm. Jef 13

Raney, H. Wm. Gar 215
James Pul 144
James Wsh 304
John B. Wsh 304
Roger Wsh 306
William Mad 218
Rankens, Moses Nic 58
Rankin, Adam Fay 26
Adam Hnd 344
David Hnr 366
Jeremiah Woo 386
John Bar 49
John W. She 240
Mary Woo 386
Solomon Sco 171
Rankins, Adam Fay 17
Ben Lew 98
James Hrs 324
Jas. & sister Fle 66
John Clr 140
John Hnd 348
John Mas 276
Moses Mas 276
Reubin Bou 130
Robert Log 163
Robert Log 187
Samuel Fay 17
Thos. Hrs 314
William Fle 84
William Mas 279
Rannelle, David V. Sco 190
Ransal, Elizabeth Fay 42
Ransall, Presly Fay 56
Ransdal, Charles War 281
Jno. Hnr 367
Whorlan War 246
Ransdale, Christo.-C. Fra 162
Nancy Sco 174
Ransdall, Foxall She 213
John Mer 328
Nancy Mer 330
Sandford Mer 342
Wharton Hnr 351
Whorten Mer 328
Zachariah Mer 330
Ransom, Richard Mad 217
Rany, Mathew Chr 69
Wm. Hop 375
Raper, Thomas Pul 144
Rapier, Chas. Nel 32
Richd. J. Nel 28
William Nel 29
Rappelyea, John B. Fra 162
Rapperton, Wm. Adr 13
Wm. L. Adr 13
Raridon, Katharine Mas 276
Rasco, Rachal Chr 101
William Chr 100
Rash, David Hnd 335
John Clr 139
Richard Hnd 330
Stephen Clr 139
William, jr Clr 139
William, Sr Clr 139
Rasor, Harmon Hnr 361
Issabella Mer 342
Jac Hnr 361
John Hnr 361
Ratcliff, Chs. Nel 31
James But 196
Minor Sco 178
Ratcliffe, Joseph Woo 396
Thomas Woo 396
Ratherford, Geo. Gar 213
Ratlef, Daniel Grp 272
Ratleff, Alexander She 198

Ratleff, cont.
Charles She 233
Ratliff, Charles Hrs 311
Francis Fra 161
George Fra 161
James Flo 101
Jas. War 256
Jeremiah Flo 101
Joseph Mon 356
Richard Flo 101
Samuel She 214
Silas Flo 101
Stephen Flo 101
William Flo 101
William Mas 276
Wm. Bar 53
Zephaniah Mon 356
Rattey, Wm. Grn 249
Ratton, Tarlton Cal 7B
Raussau, James Pul 144
Ravencraft, John Mas 277
Ravenscraft, John Hrs 312
Thomas Hrs 312
Rawland, Anna Cal 10
Rawlings, Aaron Bre 158
Aaron Hrd 304
Edward Bre 169
Edwd. Hrd 296
Eli Hnr 366
Henry Wsh 308
Isaac Hrd 296
John Wsh 308
Jos. Hnr 366
Moses Bre 169
Nathan Fle 64
Nathan Hnr 369
Stephen Bre 163
Stephen Hrd 297
Thomas Fle 74
William Wsh 304
William, Jur Fle 73
William, Sen Fle 73
Rawlins, John Sco 188
Rawsey, Tho. Bar 31
Ray, Aaron Jef 13
Absalom Wsh 303
Andrew War 254
Baxter War 268
Benjamin ESt 4
Benjamin Wsh 303
Benjn. War 244
Charles Clr 139
Daniel Mer 329
Daniel War 254
Elijah Pul 143
Francis Nic 59
Francis Wsh 303
Isaac Pul 143
James Mer 329
James War 244
Jas. Bar 54
Jennings Gal 189
John Bar 43
John Cum 168
John Fra 158
John Gal 188
John Jef 13
John Mon 364
John War 263
John Wsh 303
John Wsh 303
John S. Wsh 303
Joseph Cum 176
Joseph Lin 131
Joseph Liv 157
Joseph Wsh 303
Joseph Wsh 309

Ray, cont.
Matthew She 212
Moses Gal 189
Nathaniel Lin 133
Nicholas Wsh 303
Polly Bar 50
Richard Clr 140
Richard Wsh 303
Robert Lew 98
Samuel Chr 89
Samuel She 211
Samuel Wsh 303
Stephen Wsh 304
Thomas Pul 140
Thos. Cum 176
Thos. Log 178
William Cum 175
William Gal 189
William Mer 328
William Pul 143
William Wsh 303
Wm. Way 364
Rayalty, Daniel Wsh 307
Thomas Wsh 307
Rayborn, Robert Mad 219
Susanna Mad 219
William Mad 218
Raybourn, Polly Fra 162
Robert Cum 166
Raybourne, Cornelius [illegible]
Rayburn, James [illegible]
John [illegible]
Rayder, Ruth [illegible]
Rayfield, Isaac Cum 180
Wm. Cum 180
Raymon, Andrew Bul 183
John Bul 183
Wm. Hrs 318
Raymond, Andw. Nel 28
Rayne, William Jes 55
Raynolds, James Fay 17
Rayns, Thomas Clr 139
Razor, Anthony Hrd 299
Jacob Hrd 297
Paul She 198
Peter Hrd 296
Rea, Samuel Mas 277
Reace, Anne Mad 218
David Hrs 323
Ephram Chr 107
George Hrs 316
Isaac Hrs 317
Isaac Hrs 323
Reach, Gabriel Gal 188
Read, Alsey Liv 151
Danl. War 263
Francis S. Lin 131
H. Stephan Fay 17
Handkerson, Jr Woo 400
Handkerson, Sr Woo 190
Harman War 256
James But 196
James War 272
James War 272
John Bar 49
John But 196
John Chr 82
John Woo 401
John, Junior Chr 82
Jonathan Bou 105
Joseph Mon 355
Moses But 196
Robert But 196
Saml. War 262
Samuel Fay 17
Wm. Mon 349
Wm. Mon 382

Read, cont.
Wm. Senr Mon 347
Reading, John Fra 158
John She 230
William Log 183
Readinghour, John Pen 107
Readman, Jno. Nel 31
John Bar 45
Joseph Fle 83
Ready, Willm. Lin 131
Reagan, Michael Pul 143
Reaidin, Hiram Hnr 365
Reams, Jas. Hrd 284
Robt. Hrd 285
Reamy, Elizabeth Fle 72
Enock Fle 86
Rearden, Nancy Woo 387
Reardon, Dennis Woo 383
Rease, Jehu Knx 85
Reatherford, Jas. Lin 131
Robert Log 189
Wm. Hop 376
Reaves, Daniel War 258
John Bar 52
John Grn 254
Miles Chr 104
Wm. Hrs 316
Reavis, Harris War 273
Isham War 258
Willm. War 258
[illegible]aviss, Mark War 273
[illegible]vle, Randolph Cam 31
Sarah Cam 32
Thos. Cam 32
Rebertson, John Cal 9
Records, Alexr. Boo 62
Charles Boo 62
Rector, Benjn. Nel 32
Daniel Mon 358
Enock Nel 28
Red, Dadley Log 181
John Jef 27
Mordica Jef 27
Redd, Agatha Woo 378
John She 213
Thomas Hrs 322
Thomas Woo 392
Thomas M. Woo 397
Reddick, William Cam 26
Reddin, Matthew Mad 218
Nehemiah Woo 396
Redding, Elij. Nic 59
John Lew 100
Joseph, Jur Sco 189
Joseph, Senr Sco 189
Rubin She 237
Timothy She 240
Willm. Sco 180
Wm. Nic 59
Reddirt, Jaems She 199
Reddy, Crawford Mad 219
Reder, Isaack Cal 10
Redick, William Nel 31
Reding, Felix Wsh 308
Saml. Bou 105
Redix, William Nel 28
Redman, Aaron Adr 12
Absm. Adr 12
Charles K. Fay 53
Chukesberry Fay 41
Frances Fay 54
Geo. Hrd 291
George Bou 106
Isaac Jef 25
Jno. Nel 29
John C. Fay 54
Levy Fay 41

Redman, cont.
Nancy Bou 106
Richd. Nel 30
Thomas Log 163
Thos. Adr 12
Thos. Nel 29
Washington Mad 217
William Clr 139
William Fay 41
William Nel 30
Wm. T. Bou 106
Redmon, Charles Hrs 323
Cjarles Mul 388
George She 239
Joseph She 202
Leadston She 239
Mary She 203
Thomas Mon 363
Thos. Hrs 314
Redmond, James Woo 384
Joseph Woo 390
King Woo 391
Redy, ishan Grn 262
Reece, Agness Bou 105
Isaac Bra 146
Reed, Adam Fle 69
Alex She 221
Alexander Est 5
Alexr. Jnr Gar 212
Alexr. Snr Gar 215
Andrew Chr 82
Andrew Mas 276
Armstead Fra 159
Barnard She 199
Benja. Fle 76
Benjamin Fay 17
Benjamin Knx 82
Benjamine Mer 343
Boos Cam 25
Caleb She 202
Daniel Chr 76
David Nel 31
David She 199
Edward Bar 32
Elijah Mer 330
Elizabeth Clr 139
Elizabeth Fle 75
Ellendey Cas 46
Frederick Bou 106
Gabriel Fle 76
George Bou 130
George Bul 183
George Grn 250
Henry Fay 17
Hensly Hrd 293
Isaac Fay 17
Isaac Hrs 307
Jacob Fle 79
Jacob Gar 199
Jacob Hrd 303
James Bar 47
James Clr 139
James Fay 53
James Fle 76
James Fle 79
James Fle 91
James Fra 158
James Grn 251
James Jef 13
James Jef 13
James Mer 328
James Ohi 73
Jane Lin 131
Jas. Bar 52
Jno. Hrd 283
John Bul 183
John Cas 42

Reed, cont.
John Clr 139
John Fle 69
John Fra 158
John Hnr 356
John Hrs 308
John Jef 13
John Knx 65
John Liv 155
John Mas 276
John Mer 329
John Mer 330
John Pul 143
John Wsh 304
John Wsh 308
John, Jr Bou 130
John S. Bou 130
Jona. Hnr 352
Jonathan Lin 133
Jos. Gar 235
Joseph Bul 183
Joseph Cas 37
Joseph Mas 278
Joseph, Junr Liv 155
Joseph, Senr Liv 155
Joshua She 201
Leonard War 277
Leonard, Junr Bar 32
Margarat Lin 133
Matthias Knx 67
Michael Grn 248
Nathan Wsh 309
Philip Hrd 293
Robert Hrd 302
Robert Jes 42
Robert Knx 85
Robert B. Liv 159
Saml. Gar 213
Saml. Sco 167
Saml. Sco 170
Samuel Clr 140
Samuel Fle 71
Samuel Knx 82
Samuel Wsh 304
Solomon Knx 75
Susannah She 197
Tho. B. Nel 7
Thomas Jes 55
Thomas Mas 276
Thomas Pul 142
Thomas She 202
Walker Mas 307
Walter Bre 168
William Bou 130
William Fay 17
William Fay 17
William Fay 59
William Knx 70
William Knx 85
William Liv 155
William Mas 275
William Nel 31
William She 201
Wm. Cum 173
Wm. Jef 13
Wm. Jef 27
Reedd, Susanna Wsh 307
Reeder, Amus Chr 82
Isaac War 272
Jehu Hnd 344
Joshua War 271
Lewis War 274
Reeds, Samuel Jes 55
William Jes 55
Reddy, Daniel Jef 12
Henry Jef 12
Jacob Jef 12
Reedy, cont.
Samuel She 231
Reeidman, Jeremiah Fle 74
Reel, Jacob Jef 12
John Jef 24
Reemer, David Boo 62
Reenns, William Mer 329
Rees, Abram War 246
David Cam 25
David Mas 307
Elizabeth Fay 17
Isaac Hnr 353
Jacob War 252
John Clr 139
John Cly 160
Thomas F. Hnr 358
Thos. Cam 27
Reese, Abraham Mas 275
Daniel Mas 275
Elisha Liv 147
Franky Clr 140
George Bra 142
James Bra 142
John Mas 307
Joseph Jef 14
Samuel Clr 140
Solomon Bra 153
Reeser, Frederick She 228
Josiah She 229
Reeve, Asa Fle 83
Reeves, Ann Jef 29
Austin Mas 276
Austin, Junr Mas 276
Benja. Fle 64
Benjamin Mas 278
Elijah Fle 63
Elijah, Senr Fle 75
George Mad 219
H. John Flo 101
James Hnr 365
Jerimiah Mad 218
John Mas 278
John Mas 278
Joseph Gal 188
Samuel Mas 278
Samuel Mas 278
Spencer Fle 75
Thomas Gal 188
William, Jr Mad 219
William Mad 219
Reevs, Benjamin H. Chr 110
James Chr 60
Marthy Chr 110
Regan, John Log 187
Regedu's, Mary Chr 66
Reid, Anderson Mad 219
James Mad 218
Jas. War 253
Jas. Way 371
John Mad 219
John, Capt. Mad 219
John, Cor. Mad 219
John C. Sco 174
Lewis Hnd 345
Thomas Mad 219
William Lew 104
William Mad 217
William (Cor's - son) Mad 219
Zachariah Mad 218
Reiger, Richard She 233
Reily, John Cam 26
John Cam 31
Thos. Cam 30
Reimel, Catherine Bou 106
Reins, John Mas 303
Uriah Way 351
Reives, Wm. Grn 248
Remkin, Hugh Fay 55
Remy, Archi Fle 61
John Cum 184
Renalds, James Lin 133
Robert Lin 133
Wm. Mon 376
Renberger, George Hrd 296
Rench, Michl. Nel 30
Render, George Ohi 80
Robert, Junr Ohi 80
Robert, Senr Ohi 71
Rendshaw, William Log 163
Renerson, Christopher Cas 45
Renfro, Isaac Rck 160
Joshua Bre 168
Lewis Rck 160
Mark Rck 159
Renfrow, Isaac Bar 28
Jessee Bar 29
John Bar 29
John, Senr Bar 28
Joseph Mad 217
Peter Mad 217
Renick, Alexander Woo 401
James Woo 380
Wm. War 255
Renicks, George Clr 140
Renix, William Bou 130
Renn, John Lin 133
Rennals, John Chr 91
John G. Chr 53
William Chr 91
Rennalls, John Lin 133
Rennard, Benjamin Pul 142
Rennells, Fowntan Lin 133
Joseph Lin 131
Renner, Adam War 251
Rennex, James Lin 131
Rennick, James Bar 29
John Fra 162
Saml. Bar 42
Renno. Aaron Cum 181
John Cum 181
Rennoe, Benjn. Bou 106
Zele Bou 106
Rennolds, Matthew Fra 161
Rennor, Jacob Rck 163
Renns, James Mer 329
Rennuk, Henry Bar 30
Wm. Bar 46
Reno, Jesse Mul 403
John Mul 397
Lewis Hrs 323
Lewis Mul 395
Renshaw, John Chr 57
Rentfro, Absolam Rck 164
John But 196
Joseph But 196
Mark But 196
Moses Gar 215
Peter But 196
Thomas Rck 163
William But 196
Wm. Gar 215
Rentfrow, Isaac Lin 133
John Liv 157
Renwick, Wm. Gal 188
Resor, Fredk. Sco 176
Michael She 215
Respess, Austin C. Bou 130
Thomas Bou 106
Retherford, Archibald Jes 57
Dudy. Adr 12
Josiah Liv 145

Retherford, cont.
Robert Chr 111
Shelton Jes 57
William Grp 271
Wm. Adr 12
Retzel, Peter Nic 58
Reveil, Michael Nic 59
Thos. Nic 59
Reves, Asa Fle 63
Asa, Jur Fle 92
Asa, Senr Fle 92
George Fle 92
Jabez Fle 92
Samuel Mul 392
Staca Cam 27
William Fle 92
Revess, Henry Hnd 342
Reviel, Joseph Nic 58
Revil, Ethedral Chr 84
Micajah Chr 84
Revis, Joseph Fle 81
Reymond, Francis Jef 28
Reymonds, Levi Mas 303
Reynalds, James Bra 142
Robt. War 258
Wm. Gar 214
Reyner, James Cal 17
Reynnolds, Drake Bou 130
Reynolds, Aaron Hop 372
Benja. Hop 376
Benjamin Mas 279
Charles Jef 28
David Bar 33
Daniel Knx 67
David Gar 215
David G. Jef 25
Edwd. Cum 170
Glover Way 367
Henry Adr 12
Henry Gar 215
Henry Gar 215
Isbal Gar 215
Jesse Jes 57
Jno. Hrd 286
Jno. Nel 30
John Cal 7B
John Cal 14
John Knx 72
John Mon 368
Joseph Mul 394
Mathew Pul 143
Mathias Bar 33
Moses Pul 141
Nancy Cal 14
Richard Mul 400
Richd. Bar 48
Saml. Bou 106
Saml. Gar 216
Sarah Bra 150
Tarlton Knx 71
Tho. Hop 376
Thomas Bre 159
Thomas(in the - hills) Jes 55
Thomas Jes 56
Thomas Knx 81
Thomas Mas 274
Thomas Woo 399
Vincent Woo 384
William Bou 106
William Pul 142
Wm. Bar 33
Wm. Bar 47
Rezier, Adam Nic 58
Rhea, Alexr. Hop 379
Archibald Grn 255
William Grn 257
Rheuby, James Mon 382
Joseph Hrs 322
Rhoades, Barney Nel 29
Bazl. Nel 31
Cors. Nel 30
Igns. Nel 30
Jacob Gra 241
James Nel 32
John Gra 241
Mathw. Nel 31
Rhoads, Daniel Mul 390
David Mul 390
Henry Mul 401
Heny Mul 389
Jacob Mul 390
Jacob Mul 400
John Mul 387
Solomon Mul 397
Thos. Nel 32
Rhoden, Thomas Fle 74
Rhodes, Benedict Wsh 304
Buchn. Nic 59
Elias Bre 166
George Fay 17
Jonas Mon 370
Sulus Nic 59
Rhodus, John Mad 217
Joseph Mad 217
William Mad 217
Rial, Sarah Bre 160
Rialtey, John Cas 39
Rian, Joel Fay 50
Ribelin, Wm. Mon 364
Ribertson, Littleberry Log 195
Ribble, Adam Nel 29
Joseph She 210
Rice, Abraham War 243
Anderson Lin 133
Andrew Gar 214
Andrew Jes 57
Andrew, Jnr GAr 214
Aron Fle 76
Bazil She 235
Benja. Gar 214
Benjamin G. Mul 390
Benjn. Cam 25
Benjn. Grn 253
Cabeb Fay 56
Caleb Fay 35
Cammel Mon 377
Charels, Sen Fle 61
Charles She 235
Claibourn Mul 386
Davenport Bou 105
David Hnr 355
David Jes 56
David Mer 329
David Mon 369
Dempsey Pen 105
Edmond Jef 13
Edmund Grn 260
Edwin Grn 252
Elias Bre 157
Elizabeth Nel 28
Elizabeth Woo 383
Ezekiel Wsh 304
Fisher Jes 56
Gabriel Gar 214
George Bou 105
George Hnd 337
Henry Mon 380
Hyram Bou 105
Isaac Clr 140
Jacob Bre 166
Jacob Jes 56
Jacob She 241
Rice, cont.
James Bra 146
James Jef 27
James Knx 88
James Log 191
James Mon 368
James Way 364
James H. Mul 402
Jas. H. Bar 22
Jasper Jes 41
Jefferson Jes 56
Jesse Mul 388
Jesse She 218
Jno. Hrd 299
John Bou 130
John But 196
john Clr 139
John Fle 76
John Grn 258
John Hnr 364
John Jef 32
John Jes 57
John Mer 329
Jonathan Bre 162
Jonathan Log 195
Joseph Mer 328
Joseph Mon 357
Joshua Boo 62
Larkin Mul 401
Lucinda Gar 216
Mary Bre 162
Mathews Lin 133
Michael Jes 57
Moses Cas 37
Nathan Mul 403
Nathan Ohi 92
Patrick Mul 387
Philip Bra 144
Randolphe Grn 252
Richard Woo 391
Rowlett She 218
Samuel Hnr 256
Sarah (Chs. widow) Mad 217
Sarah Mad 218
Shelton Mon 349
Simon Pen 111
Solomon Adr 12
Thomas Bre 164
Thomas Way 364
William Fle 76
William Fra 161
William Hnr 355
William Knx 89
William Liv 157
William Mer 329
William Mul 387
William She 236
Wm. Cam 27
Rices, William Fay 48
Rich, Jeremiah Cum 178
Jesse Cum 177
Obadiah Cum 177
Robert Cum 177
Saml. Hnr 364
Samuel Bou 106
Stephen Cam 32
Thos. Cam 30
Thos. Cam 32
Wm. Cum 177
Richard, Andrue Mon 353
Wm. Mon 352
Richards, Abrm. Lin 131
Burton Bou 105
David Gar 214
Elzaphen Mon 357
Felix Lin 133

Richards, cont.
Henry Mad 219
Hiram War 266
Isaiah Cum 182
Jacob Mas 277
James Grp 276
James Mad 219
John Cas 41
John Mon 352
John Nel 28
John, Snr Lin 133
Josiah Mon 363
Leonard Cas 39
Leonard Cas 44
Lewis Hop 372
Miriam Fay 57
Nathan Bre 160
Philemon Hnd 331
Robert Clr 140
Robert Clr 140
Robert Mon 363
Samuel Jef 27
Thomas Grp 278
William Bul 183
William Clr 140
Willm Lin 133
Wm. War 266
Richardson, Abednego Cum 183
Allen Fra 159
Amos Hrd 296
Amos Hrd 297
Archd. Mad 217
Benjn. Mad 217
Bradley Clr 140
Charles Pul 142
Daniel Hnr 356
Danl. Gar 214
David Jes 41
David Lin 131
David Pul 142
Dudly Bar 29
Ebenezer Hrd 297
Elijah Mad 217
Elizabeth Clr 140
Ezra Fra 161
Geo. Cum 180
George Wsh 305
Henry Mer 329
Isreal Gar 213
James Bou 130
James Jes 56
James Pen 111
James Pul 141
James She 214
Jesse Mad 219
Jesse Pul 142
John Cam 31
John Cum 173
John Est 7
John Fay 17
John Fay 57
John Lin 131
John Mas 276
John Mer 328
John C. Fay 57
John D. Fra 162
Jon. War 249
Jonathan Pul 141
Jos. Hrd 286
Joseph War 259
Joshua Pul 140
Joshua She 235
Landy Mer 329
Lewis Pul 142
Lucy Mas 275
Marquis Fra 160
Richardson, cont.
Mary Clr 140
Minor S. Pen 111
Nathan Est 3
Nath. Fra 159
Pearce Pul 141
Philip Clr 147
Richard (free negro) Fay 32
Richd. War 249
Richd. War 254
Richd. War 264
Robert Chr 70
Robert Pen 117
Shadh. Cum 180
Stephen Jef 12
Thomas Mad 217
Thomas Mad 219
Thomas Pul 141
Thos. Bou 130
Thos. Hrd 289
William Chr 70
William (Jno. R's son) Mad 217
William Mad 217
William Mad 217
William Ohi 87
Wm. Bar 33
Wm. Clr 139
Wm. Gar 213
Wm. Pul 142
Wm. Jnr Gar 213
Wm. H. Sco 189
Richasn., Augustus Cam 31
Richd. Way 366
Riche, John Mon 366
Richer, Charles Mer 329
John Mul 389
Richerson, Amos Nel 32
Frances Mon 373
Jas. Grn 255
Jno. Nel 32
Joseph Nel 32
Thomas Fay 55
Richeson, Thos. Gra 238
Wm. Gra 238
Richey, Abraham She 202
Crocket Cly 155
Jacob She 238
Jno. Sr. Nel 29
John She 203
Joseph She 202
Robt. Cal 19
William, Sr Bre 161
Wm. Gar 215
Wm. Jr Bre 161
Richie, Stephen War 243
Richison, James Fle 62
Jos. Grn 263
Joseph Way 372
Richmond, George War 271
James Hnr 357
John Knx 72
Levi War 271
Richton, Nathaniel Bul 183
Richy, Andw. Bar 37
Conls. Nel 32
David Mas 278
Jacob Mas 274
James Bar 46
James Hrs 308
James Fay 27
James, Jun Bar 37
Jas. Sen BAr 37
John Bar 33
Mary Hrs 319
Mary Hrs 320
Richy, cont.
Robt. Bar 46
Saml. Bar 50
Samuel Fay 27
William Mas 307
Wm. Bar 27
Rick, Joseph Lew 98
Ricke, Jorden Fle 77
Ricker, Adam Hrs 308
Rickerson, Margt. Nel 7
Rickets, Jonathan Bul 183
Peter Bul 183
Rulef Mas 278
Ricketts, Caleb Adr 12
Reubin Clr 139
William Mas 277
Zachariah Wsh 304
Rickey, Daniel Jes 57
Rickitts, John Fle 73
Rickles, William Fra 160
Rickmire, Cors. Nel 30
Ricks, Jonithan Chr 98
Richard Chr 97
Riddell, Lewis Boo 62
Wm. Boo 62
Riddle, Andrew Fle 85
George Pen 106
George, Jr Pen 114
Isaac Hrs 314
Isaac Pen 114
Jacob She 232
James Cum 173
James Est 8
James Fra 159
James Wsh 304
Jeramiah Hnd 332
John War 265
Marget Wsh 304
Moses Gar 214
Robt. Est 8
Thomas She 232
William Sco 186
Wm. Bou 130
Wm. Hrs 321
Rideck, Wm. Bra 152
Ridefott, Julius Way 366
Riden, Thomas Fay 38
Wm. Mon 367
Rider, Daniel Cal 7B
John War 271
Tho. Bar 44
Ridge, Amos Pul 140
Amos Pul 141
Charles Wsh 304
Elizabeth Wsh 307
John Wsh 304
Robertson Pul 141
Thomas Chr 102
William Wsh 304
Ridgel, John Cly 154
Ridgeway, Elijah Lin 133
John Bre 160
John Clr 139
Mary Lin 131
Ninian Clr 139
Osburn Lin 131
Rezin Clr 139
Saml. Lin 133
William Bul 183
Zachariah Clr 139
Ridgley, Frederick Fay 17
Ridgway, James Fle 81
John Bul 183
Joseph Bul 183
Joseph, Jr Bul 183
Joshua Fle 83
Saml. Fle 81

Ridgway, cont.	
Samuel	Bul 183
Ried, Henry	Cal 6
Jane	Cal 4
John	Mas 274
Rien, John	War 246
Rieves, James	Grn 245
Rievs, Burrell	War 258
Rife, John	Adr 13
Rifeong, Daniel	Fay 32
Riffe, Abraham	Cas 40
Christopher	Cas 37
Rigdon, James	Mas 274
William	Mas 275
Rigg, Clement	Mas 276
John	Mer 330
Jonathan	Fay 31
Peter	Fra 158
Rigge, John	Nel 31
Riggins, John	Mas 279
Jos.	War 281
Riggs, Bethuel	Cam 32
Charles	Knx 71
Charles	Wsh 308
Daniel	Chr 99
Edman	Jes 55
Erasmus	Bou 105
Hannah	Chr 99
Iram	Rck 162
Isaac	Mon 375
James	Mas 277
Janathan	Cam 27
Jas.	Cam 29
John	Cam 29
John	Wsh 308
Jonathan	Fay 45
Nathaniel	Mas 307
Samuel	Fle 86
Samuel	Lin 131
Sarah	Wsh 308
Silas	Mon 365
Silas	Rck 162
Thomas	Log 163
Thomas	Log 188
William	Wsh 304
Wm.	Lew 103
Zadock	Lin 131
Right, George	Mer 328
Hilrey	Fay 48
Jno.	Grn 264
John	Mer 329
John	Pul 141
Joseph	Bra 142
Joseph	Log 189
Joseph	Mon 351
Newton	Log 176
Samuel	Fay 26
Stephen	Mul 397
Thomas	Mer 328
Thos.	Grn 246
Thos.	Grn 264
William	Fay 51
William	Nel 31
Riglesworth, John	Fay 17
Rigley, Miles	Fay 17
Rigney, Harison	Cas 45
Jesse	Cas 45
John	Lin 133
Rigsby, Wm.	Gar 214
Riker, Samuel	She 201
Riland, Richd.	Nel 28
Riley, Abraham	Gra 241
Alexr.	Lin 131
Amos	Jef 13
Andrew	Log 166
Charles	Mas 307
E.	Hnr 358
Riley, cont.	
Edward	Bou 105
Edward	Mas 277
Eliphas	War 270
Elizabeth	[illegible] 105
Elizabeth	Ohi 71
George	Lin 131
Henry	Mas 276
James	Cly 160
James	Fay 25
James	Gra 238
James	Jef 13
James	Mas 274
James	Sco 184
James	War 273
John	Clr 139
John	Grn 247
John	Lew 102
John	Lin 133
John	Log 171
John	Mad 217
John	Mas 307
John	Nic 59
John	She 218
John	Wsh 305
Joseph	Wsh 309
Lewis	Wsh 305
Michel	Bul 183
Moses	Log 176
Ninian	Fay 25
Ninian	Fay 25
Patrik, Jr	Cly 160
Patrick, Sr	Cly 160
William	Clr 139
William	Mas 307
Rinehart, Daniel	Wsh 305
James	Wsh 305
Riney, Bazil	Wsh 308
Clement	Wsh 305
Jeremiah	Wsh 305
John	Wsh 305
John	Wsh 308
Jonathan	Wsh 305
Richard	Wsh 305
Robert	Wsh 305
Thomas	Wsh 308
William	Wsh 305
Wm.	Hrd 297
Zachariah	Wsh 305
Ringo, Burtes	Fle 68
Cornelius	She 203
John	She 203
Ringold, Cornel - ious	Mon 365
Cornelius	Mon 369
Henry	Mon 384
John	Mon 382
Joseph	Mon 365
Mager	Mon 369
Peter	Mon 365
Samuel	Mon 359
Wm.	Mon 355
Rings, Connel	Hnr 369
Cornes.	Nel 31
Rinker, George	Bra 148
Jonathan	Bra 148
Rion, Thomas	Bre 163
Rions, William	She 220
John	She 239
Ripley, Pleasant	Knx 90
Ripperdon, Freder- ick	Mer 329
Ripple, Michael	Mul 405
Rise, James	Grp 269
Joshua M.	Log 196
Rilk, William	Clr 140
Risley, Elihu	Bul 183
Risley, cont.	
James	Bul 183
James	Bul 183
Risller, Edmund	Log 188
Risly, Charles	Hnr 359B
Ristine, John	Gal 189
Lewis	Nel 30
Ritchee, John	Nel 30
Ritcherson, Isham	Grn 257
John	Grn 258
Thomas	Grn 257
Ritchey, Daniel	Liv 155
Esau	Nic 59
Gilbert	Nic 58
Isaac	Nic 58
James, Junr	Liv 157
James, Senr	Liv 157
John	Liv 157
Noah	Nic 59
Robert	Nic 59
Simson	Liv 157
Sollom.	NIc 58
Thomas	She 233
Wm.	Nic 59
Ritchie, Alexander - Sr.	Clr 139
Alexr.	War 263
George	War 263
John	Clr 139
John	Sco 167
Jos.	War 263
Robert	Bou 106
Saml.	War 263
Samuel	Clr 139
Stephen	Sco 191
Thomas	Woo 397
Ritchison, Amos	Gar 216
Ritchy, James	cum 168
John	Cum 168
Rite, Jaeb	Log 180
Jonathan	Bra 141
Ritter, Abraham	Bar 40
Abraham	Bar 47
Boman	Bar 47
Henry (free wo- man)sic	Fay 17
Henry	Fay 56
Isaac	Bar 46
John	Bar 47
John	Bou 130
Joseph	Bar 47
Marget	Bar 47
Richard	Mas 277
Rittinger, Abraham	Jef 28
Rittor, Michael	Hrs 307
River, Daniel	Bra 143
Wm.	Bra 150
Rivers, John	Log 166
John	Wsh 309
Joshua (freeman of colour)	Jes 57
Rix, John	Nel 31
Thos.	Nel 31
Rizener, Michael	Knx 80
Rizer, Jacob	Nel 7
Mats	Nel 7
Philip	Nel 30
Roach, Aimey	Mer 328
Briant	Chr 81
Charlotte	Mas 275
Henry	Mon 379
Isaac	Cas 39
John	Jef 31
Littleberry	Mer 329
Ruth	Nel 7
Thomas	Mad 219

Roach, cont.
Thomas Mas 277
William Woo 383
Wm. Cal 15
Road, Wm. Cal 17
Roads, Ephram Chr 92
James Nel 29
M. Nel 29
Thomas Bre 168
William Knx 91
Roaidin, Henry Hnr 365
Roan, Eliphalet Mad 217
Roarch, John Bar 39
Levi Bar 39
Martin Mul 386
William Mul 401
Wm. Bar 38
Roark, John Wsh 309
Robard, Daniel Jes 54
Edward War 253
William, Jr Jes 54
Robards, Edward Clr 139
George Clr 140
James Rck 163
John Bar 38
Phillip Jes 55
Sary BAr 38
Tho. BAr 41
Thomas Jes 57
William Clr 140
William, Jr Jes 57
William, Senr Jes 55
William, Sr Jes 57
Robb, Henry Jef 13
Henry Jes 56
Hugh Hnd 330
Joseph Fay 27
Joseph Mon 366
Michael Jes 56
Robt. Lew 102
Thomas Mas 278
Wm. Lew 104
Robbins, Abel Hnr 359
Absolam Hnr 355
Elender Cly 153
Nathl. She 242
Richard Wsh 309
Richd. She 242
Richd. She 242
Spencer Bou 105
William Hnr 355
William, Sr Hnr 359B
Robersen, William Chr 60
Benjn. Bou 130
Benjn. Mon 381
Elijah Mon 355
Isral Chr 59
James Bou 106
James Chr 67
John Chr 85
John Mon 361
John Mon 378
Lawson Mon 354
Mary Mad 218
Moses Fay 32
Nancy Chr 86
Richard Jes 55
Richard Mon 357
Robert Log 175
Sary Mon 373
Thomas Flo 101
Wm. Mon 356
Zakua. Fle 92
Robert, I. Peter Fay 17
James Fay 12
William Mas 275
Roberts, Aaron Way 357

Roberts, cont.
Abner Nel 30
Alexander Bou 106
Alexr. Jef 30
Ardemas Mas 300
Augustine She 238
B. Log 188
Benjamin Hnr 352
Benjamin Ohi 87
Benjamin She 213
Benjamin, Jr Hnr 352
Bernet Way 357
Catharine She 237
Daniel Mad 217
David Pul 141
David Pul 142
Deama? Nel 29
Edmund Ohi 90
Edward Fra 160
Edward Mad 217
Edward Mon 350
Edward Mad 218
Edward Mon 363
Elias Pen 117
Elijah Bou 106
Elisha Grn 262
Elisha Mad 219
Evan Cal 15
Frank Mon 359
Geo. Cam 27
Geo. Hnr 369
Geo. Jr. Hnr 362
George Mer 329
Gidean Pul 140
Greenberry Log 183
Henry Chr 64
Henry Hnr 352
Henry She 217
Henly Nic 59
Hez. Nic 59
Hizeriah Sco 176
Hiram Lin 131
Humphrey Pul 140
Isaac Cum 176
Isaac Mad 217
Iven Fay 52
Jacob Bul 183
James Chr 111
James Flo 101
James Fra 160
James Fra 161
James Hnr 366
James Hnr 367
James Jef 13
James Mad 217
James (Big) Mad 218
James Pul 142
Jane Cal 19
Jas. Hnr 362
Jes. Mon 382
Jesse Grn 256
Jesse Liv 157
Jesse Mer 329
Jesse Way 358
Jessee Cly 149
Jns. Chr 76
Joel Mad 217
Joel Way 369
John Cal 7B
John Cas 44
John Chr 109
John Fra 161
John Hnr 360
John Hnr 366
John Lin 131
John Lin 133
John Log 189

Roberts, cont.
John Mad 217
John Mon 350
John Mon 362
John Mon 381
John Mul 402
John Nic 59
John Ohi 93
John Pen 107
John Pul 142
John Pul 141
John She 217
John She 240
John Way 354
John, Sr Hnr 361
Joseph Bre 163
Joseph Hnr 358
Joseph Lig 178
Joseph She 222
Joseph, Jr Hnr 359B
Jos. Cly 160
Joshua Chr 110
Joshua Mad 218
Josiph Chr 114
Lewis Bul 183
Margaret Mad 218
Minor Fle 63
Moses Cly 160
Mourning Mad 218
Naaman Mad 218
Nancy Mad 218
Nathan Mad 218
Nathan, Jun Mad 217
Nehem Nic 59
Nelly Liv 159
Nicholas Mad 217
Peter Gal 188
Philip Mad 219
Richard Hnr 359B
Richard Nel 30
Richardson Wsh 305
Samuel She 237
Sandy Nel 31
Sarah Lin 131
Shadrick, Sen Pul 142
Shdrick Pul 142
Thos. Nic 59
Thomas Chr 89
Thomas Hrs 314
Will Hnr 367
Will She 224
William Hnd 343
William (Elisha's son) Mad 217
William Mad 217
William (Nathan's son) Mad 218
William Mad 219
William Mad 219
William Mer 329
William Nel 28
William Ohi 93
William Rck 162
William, Jur Rck 164
Willm. Sco 168
Wm. Cum 166
Wm. Mon 382
Wm. Way 354
Wm. Way 361
Robertson, Abner War 261
Alexr. Nic 59
Alexr. War 253
Allen Liv 153
Allin Bar 34
Basil War 244
Benjamin Fay 31
Benjamin Fay 49

Robertson, cont.
Benjamin Fay 49
Benjamin Hrs 321
Charles Fra 160
Daniel Liv 159
David BAr 54
David Liv 148
David Mul 386
Dencan Lin 133
Dudley Wsh 345
Edward Mas 278
Edward Pul 142
Elijah Mas 275
Ezekial Hnd 335
Fleming Wsh 306
Geo. Gar 199
Geo. Gar 216
George Cal 13
George Liv 155
George Liv 157
George Mas 275
George Mer 329
George Wsh 306
Griffin Hrs 312
H. Richd. Gar 215
Haleum Pul 142
Hosea Lin 133
Jacob Mer 329
James Bou 106
James Cal 4
James Fay 49
James Gar 213
James Hnd 341
James Liv 153
James Mad 218
James Nic 59
James Pul 141
Jeramiah War 253
Jno. Snr Gar 216
Joel Gar 213
John Bar 26
John Bar 40
John Bou 106
John Cas 40
John Fay 49
John Fle 69
John Gar 216
John Hop 371
John Hop 372
John Hop 376
John Hrs 321
John Mer 329
John Nel 30
Jos. Grn 257
Jos. War 258
Joseph Fay 49
Joseph Fay 54
Joseph Liv 154
Joseph Liv 159
Joseph Wsh 306
Lewis Fay 49
Littleton Hrs 311
Lucy Fay 48
Luke Lin 133
Mack Hrs 321
Mary Wsh 306
Michael Fay 44
Michael Hnd 334
Mills She 233
Milly Wsh 306
Nathan Fra 160
Nathaniel Mas 275
Pleasant War 272
Randolph War 274
Robert Mul 388
Robt. Gar 213
Robt. Hop 371

Robertson, cont.
Robt. Lew 102
Sam. Nic 59
Saml. Cal 20
Samuel Log 178
Samuel Mad 218
Samuel Ohi 75
Samuel Wsh 345
Samuel Wsh 305
Spencer Fay 55
Squire War 265
Stephen Fay 27
Sterling Wsh 306
Thomas Knx 66
Thomas Knx 85
Thomas Mer 328
Thos. Cas 43
Thos. Hnr 359B
William Fay 34
William Fay 46
Wm. Bra 141
Wm. Cal 6
Wm. Hop 373
Wm. Sr Bra 143
Robetson, Sarah Hnd 334
Robey, Hezekiah Bou 105
Hezekiah Wsh 309
Joseph Wsh 306
Robin, Nicholas Hrs 322
Robins, James Mon 361
John G. Chr 111
Joseph She 240
Roger Mas 279
Robinson, Aarchabald She 208
Andrew Sco 168
Andrew She 209
Archibald Mas 276
Benjamin Fra 161
Benjn. Bou 105
Benjn. Sco 178
Charles Mer 330
Cornelius Woo 391
Isaac Fra 161
Israel Mer 330
George Fle 64
George Fra 159
George Sco 170
George She 224
George Woo 396
Henry Nel 31
Horatio She 214
James Boo 62
James Bul 183
James Mer 328
James She 197
Jane Mer 328
Jas. Nel32
Jas. Way 368
Jesse Est 3
John Boo 62
John Clr 139
John Fra 159
John Mer 328
John Nel 28
John Sco 174
John, Senr Fra 159
John F. She 242
Jonathan Sco 170
Joseph Cam 24
Joseph Nel 31
Joseph She 212
Joseph She 225
Leonard She 205
Lewis Adr 12
Littleton Bre 161
Mathw. Adr 12

Robinson, cont/
Owen Fra 162
Payton Mad 218
Philip She 228
Richard Mas 274
Richard Woo 400
Robert Fra 159
Saml. Cum 175
Samuel Mad 219
Samuel Mer 330
Samuel Mer 341
Scarlet Sco 177
Stephen Boo 62
Thomas Clr 140
Thomas Mas 274
Thomas Woo 391
Thos. Adr 13
Toliver Sco 187
William Clr 140
William Clr 140
William Fra 159
William Fra 159
William Mad 218
William Mas 274
William She 223
Wm. Adr 13
Wm. Junr Fra 159
Wm. Senr Fra 159
Robion, John Fle 70
Robirson, Henry Mon 359
John Bou 130
Robison, Abner Chr 67
Danl. Hrd 294
David Pen 115
Geo. Hrd 300
James Pen 115
James She 238
Jesse Pen 115
John Fle 88
Samuel Hrd 281
Stephen Hrd 303
Thos. Grn 260
William Fle 83
William Log 179
Wm. Fle 88
Zachariah Pen 108
Roblens, Daniel Cly 153
Robnett, Enich Bou 130
John Bou 105
Joseph Bou 105
Joseph Bou 105
John Bou 130
Rachael Bou 105
Richard Bou 105
Zepheniah Bou 105
Roburts, Richardson Ser Rck 164
Roby, Barton Hrd 282
Roch, Reuben Fay 25
Roche, Walker Est 8
Rochester, Nathl. Knx 88
Rock, John Bar 29
John Mon 347
John Mon 361
Rockhold, Charles Knx 70
Rockwell, Henry Clr 140
Rodden, Barnabas Fay 25
Rodes, Elizabeth Sco 168
John Bar 30
Robert Mad 218
Rodgers, Asa Ohi 99
Edward Bul 183
George She 216
James Fay 51
Matthew She 199
Travis She 207
Rodjers, James Grn 258

Rodman, Esther Wsh 345
Rodmon, Hugh She 210
Rods, Elisha Cal 16
Roe, Athe Fle 68
Hezekia Cal 11
Jacob Mas 277
John Mas 303
Micheal Way 367
William Mas 274
Roebuck, Katharine Mas 277
Roff, Jonathan Mas 275
Nathaniel Mas 275
Rogan, Tas. Way 367
Roger (& negro) Hnr 351
Rogers, Andrew Fra 160
Andrew Nel 30
Andrew Nel 31
Ann Chr 106
Benjn. Sco 189
Bird Bar 51
Bargis Clr 140
Charles Mas 279
Charles Mon 355
Charles She 234
Coleman Mer 343
Daniel Chr 71
Daniel Gar 216
Daniel Nel 28
Daniel Nel 31
Edmund Bar 52
Elias She 233
Elijah Bar 31
Elijah Fra 161
Elizabeth Fra 160
Evan Mer 329
Ezekiel Bou 105
Isaac Hnd 333
Isabella Mas 278
George Fay 49
George Mas 277
George Way 373
Hambleton Bou 105
Hannah Fle 90
Harris Mad 217
Henry Fay 49
Hugh Cam 30
James Bou 105
James Bou 105
James Chr 66
James Knx 64
James Mon 377
James Nel 29
James Ohi 68
James, Sr Nel 29
Jane Nel 29
Jeremiah Fay 32
Jessee Bar 32
Jno. Hrd 296
Joel Chr 103
John Adr 12
John Bar 26
John Bar 42
John Chr 87
John Clr 139
John Fay 49
John Grn 259
John Lin 133
John Mas 274
John Mer 330
John Nel 29
John Ohi 101
John Pen 106
John Sco 175
John She 233
John C. Ohi 68
Jonathan Nel 30
Joseph Fay 45
Rogers, cont.
Joseph Hop 381
Joseph Nel 29
Joseph Sco 183
Joseph, Senr Fay 49
Lamiel Bou 105
Lasirus Chr 79
Lydia Hrs 309
Mathew Bar 52
Mathew Mas 307
Matthew Fay 17
Matthew Ohi 84
McNus Hnd 332
Oaddt Nib 378
Philip Hrd 301
Robert Chr 65
Robert Chr 87
Samuel Mon 359
Samuel Mon 374
Samuel Mon 382
Stephen Mon 372
Susan Bou 106
Thomas Bou 105
Thomas Clr 140
Thomas Mas 274
Turner Woo 389
William Bou 105
William Bou 105
William Bou 130
William Flo 101
William Mas 278
William Ohi 68
William Sco 172
William Wsh 309
William C. Liv 151
Wilson Cal 19
Wm. Adr 13
Wm. Cal 6
Wm. Hrd 290
Wm. Mon 377
Wm. Mon 377
Rogerson, James She 229
John Nel 30
Rohrer, Jacob Log 184
Rojers, Susannah Est 1
Roland, Archd. Cum 174
Gasper War 261
George Cum 166
George Gra 241
George Jes 56
George She 207
James Lew 95
Jesse War 280
John Cum 174
John War 279
Joseph War 278
Micajah Log 184
William She 207
Rolen, John Hrs 317
Roles, Robert Fay 27
Rolin, Robt. Adr 12
Rollens, Thomas Fay 27
Roller, Jacob Wsh 306
John Wsh 306
Rolley, William Grn 249
Rollins, Abner Bar 37
Asail Jef 13
Benja. Bar 37
Ezekiel Pen 113
James Log 194
Jane Jef 13
Jas. War 259
John Clr 139
Joseph Mas 275
Micajah Chr 61
Rachael Sco 177
Thomas Clr 139
Rollings, Thomas Fay 39
Rolls, Glaucester Nel 28
Hebron Mon 377
Jesse Nel 28
Larkin Hop 374
Rologary, William Hop 371
Roloson, Laureance Hnd 347
Rolston, David Chr 77
Mathew Bar 28
Mathew Chr 77
Joseph Bar 29
Vincent Mad 218
Wm. Bar 34
Wm. Mon 375
Roman, Thomas Wsh 306
Wm. Gar 213
Romans, John War 247
Philip War 245
Philip War 247
Romine, Christy Jef 12
James She 197
Peter Hrd 285
William She 197
Romino, Andw. Clr 140
Romjue, John Hnr 366
Ronamus, John Mad 218
Rone, Adam But 196
John But 196
Lifelit Jes 55
Roney, Geo. Cly 157
Hercules She 227
James Jef 12
James She 228
Joseph Pul 141
Joseph She 228
Patrick Wsh 307
Phebe Fay 40
Roof, Martin Hrd 281
Michl. Hrd 297
Nichs. Hrd 284
Rooks, Buckner Bre 166
Rooksberry, Jacob Jef 27
Roop, Nicholas Fra 158
Root, Daniel Knx 76
Roots, Philip Grn 252
Philip J. Sco 182
Roper, David Cum 180
David Pul 141
David Pul 142
Jesse Jes 56
Joseph Woo 395
William Jes 56
Wm. B. Fle 65
Rorar, Jacob Cal 9
Rorax, Reuben Grn 251
Rorrer, Chrisley Jes 55
Henry, Jr Jes 55
Henry, Sr Jes 55
Jacob Jes 55
John Jes 55
RoRust, Mathew Mas 278
Rosco, Rachal Chr 92
Rose, Benja. Gar 213
Benjamin Mer 329
Charles Mer 329
Elisha Cal 7
Francis Flo 101
Francis Jef 13
George Fay 26
James Fay 17
James Mer 329
Jesse Hrs 323
John Cly 159
John Jef 13
Jonathan Fle 70
Leroy Fay 26
Lewis Mer 329

Rose, cont.
Randle Gra 237
Robert Pul 140
Robt. Est 4
Samuel Ohi 68
Sarah Mul 398
Thomas Gra 242
Thomas Jef 13
William Hnr 352
William Pul 140
Williby War 278
Zekiel Fle 89
Roseberry, Wm. Cum 185
Wm. Jef 13
Rosebrough, Charles Mon 361
Charles Mon 3[illegible]
James Mon 37[illegible]
Wm. Mon 360
Rosemire, Frederick She 219
Rosier, Jacob Bou 106
Rosity, Timothy Gar 216
Ross, A. Isaac Gar 215
Alexander Mas 274
Alexander Gar 215
Allexander Nic 58
Andrew Gal 189
Andrew Woo 395
Angus Knx 71
Benja. Fle 67
Benjamin Log 188
Benjamin Mon 382
Clayton Log 186
Clemont Bou 105
Daniel Cas 43
Daniel Gal 189
Daniel Jes 55
Evan Ohi 85
Francis Mas 278
Gabriel Mad 217
George Bra 143
James Bou 130
James Bre 167
James Cam 25
James Fle 79
James Nel 29
James, Jr Bre 167
Job Way 359
John Adr 13
John Cal 3
John Fle 72
John Fle 67
John Log 185
John Log 196
John Mad 218
John Mad 218
John (John's son) Mad 218
John Mas 275
John She 211
John, Jr Est 3
John, Senr Est 3
Johnston Fle 80
Joseph Fle 80
Joseph Nel 29
Laurance Est 3
Lawrence Jef 12
Lewis Mad 218
Margarette Hrs 317
Peter Log 180
Peter Log 188
Peter Log 192
Philip Jef 28
Rheuben Jef 28
Richard Fle 85
Richard Mas 307
Robert Jef 12
Saml. Gar 215
Ross, cont.
Samuel Bou 105
Samuel Bou 130
Samuel Knx 80
Samuel Knx 81
Samuel Log 182
Samuel Log 190
Samuel Mad 218
Sarah Cum 185
Shapley Jef 28
Thomas Chr 75
Thomas Knx 63
Thomas Ohi 78
Thos. Cum 170
Thos. J. Rck 160
[illegible]lman Bou 105
[illegible]ravice Bar 29
Vincent, Jr Woo 400
Vincent, Senr Woo 398
Will She 221
William Chr 97
William Fay 17
William Fay 58
William Mad 219
Wm. Cal 17
Zachariah Knx 80
Zacheriah Fra 161
Rossan, Archilas War 280
Rossel, Jonathan War 264
Shadk. Boo 62
Rosser, Richd. Gar 214
Rosson, Daniel Hnd 342
Joseph Fra 159
William Fra 160
Roszel, Charles Fra 160
Rotherford, Jane Log 184
Rothwell, Kay Jef 27
Rotramel, John Log 184
Rouce, Daniel Cas 40
Rouglas, William Mer 329
Rounder, Jacob Hnr 357
Roundtree, Dudly Bar 34
Dudley Hrd 282
Henry Bar 36
Lavina Chr 56
Mary Bar 41
Richd. Bar 30
Saml. Bar 42
Rouner, Abraham Wsh 306
Joseph Wsh 306
Joseph Wsh 306
Rounsavall, Josiah Liv 151
Rountree, John Clr 139
Rouse, George Boo 62
Jacob Boo 62
Jacob, Jur Boo 62
John Boo 62
John Clr 140
John Fay 51
Lewis Boo 62
Michl. Boo 62
Moses Bul 183
Saml. Boo 62
William Nel 7
Rousseau, David Pul 144
Rout, Daniel Clr 139
George Clr 140
John Bra 143
John Gar 214
Roadham Woo 399
William Bou 106
Route, John W. Bra 148
Routen, Tho. Gar 216
Routt, William Pen 105
Roux, Jno. Hrd 294
Row, Beriman War 272
Edward Mad 217
Row, cont.
George Ohi 77
George, Junr Ohi 87
Henry Bou 130
Henry Mul 398
Jacob Bou 130
Jno. Hrd 286
John War 255
Rowan, Andrew Ohi 77
Francis Boo 62
Jane Bar 33
John Boo 62
John Nel 30
Stephen Ohi 76
Rowazee? Hnr 365
Rowe, David But 196
George But 196
James Hnr 360
John Chr 88
John Chr 97
Martin But 198
Reubin Mon 353
Wm. Adr 12
Rowel, Wm. Grn 249
Rower, Robirt Mon 370
Rowl, Ben Hrd 289
Jno. Hrd 291
Michl. Hrd 288
Rowland, Abraham Bou 105
George Jes 56
H[illegible]y Woo 401
Jacob Log 163
Jacob Log 195
John Mer 328
Reuben Wsh 306
Richd. Woo 397
Robert Mad 218
Robert Mer 328
Rowlen, James Bul 183
Samuel Bul 183
Rowlet, Philip Hrd 286
Rowlett, Daniel Fra 160
William Fra 160
Rowling, Elizabeth Liv 156
Rowls, Daniel Mon 356
Nathaniel Mon 356
Willis Hop 371
Rowman, Isaac Jes 57
William Fay 25
Rowntree, James War 254
John War 249
Thomas War 254
Turner War 254
Wm. War 249
Rows, James Mon 377
Robert Mon 348
Robert Mon 352
Rowtin, Elisabeth Lin 133
William Lin 131
Roy, Asa Pul 143
Enos Pul 143
Joseph Pul 143
Royal, Thomas Fay 27
Royall, Richard Jes 56
Royster, Charles Lew 98
John Jes 56
Royston, Wm. Gar 212
Rozel, Stephen Sco 186
Rozell, Ely Sco 192
John Sco 192
Rritchie, John Fle 77
Rroach, Baley Mad 217
Rrowntree, Jesse War 254
Ruark, Timothy Pul 141
Ruba, Charles Wsh 307
Charles Wsh 307
James Wsh 307

Rubard, James Mas 276
RuJohn Mas 278
John, Senr Mas 279
Ruben, Free Jes 12
Rubey, Thos. Fle 74
Rubison, Calza Nel 28
Ruble, Isaac Nel 28
Jacob She 220
Swinfield Mad 218
Thomas W. Mad 245
Ruby, David Ohi 68
Eli Bre 159
John Hop 376
Laurance Bul 183
Leonard Fay 55
Peter Hop 372
Rachiel Bou 106
Thomas Fle 75
William Bul 183
Rucker, Abner Woo 392
Ahmed Woo 394
Barnett Jes 55
Elizapun Grp 274
Elliott Woo 397
George She 207
George She 237
Isaac Jes 57
James, Jur Cal 9
James, Senr Cal 9
James P. Woo 394
Jeremiah Mad 218
Jerry Cal 10
John Cal 9
John Fay 27
John, Senr Woo 397
Joshua Fay 17
Joshua She 236
Michael Jes 56
R. James Mad 219
Reubin Grp 269
Robert A. Bre 162
Wict Grp 274
William Woo 397
Wisdom Mer 330
Ruckman, Jas. Bar 43
Ruckmon, Isaah Bar 43
Ruddell, George Fle 75
Lewis Bou 105
Ruddick, Elisha Knx 84
Ruddle, Abraham Bou 106
Cornelias Chr 75
Cornelias Chr 103
Cornelius Woo 378
Isaac Bou 106
James Bou 106
Stephen Bou 106
Rude, Eliz. Hrd 291
Isaac War 255
Thomas Gra 241
Thompson Hrd 284
Rudford, John Lew 101
Rudy, George Jef 30
Rue, Joseph Fay 26
Ruffett, Christopher Mon 357
Rufner, Henry Lin 131
Reubin Lin 131
Ruggles, James Pen 115
Rugland, Gideon Hrd 286
Ruglas, John Lew 97
Jonn. Lew 100
John Lew 101
Ruglass, Thomas Lew 98
Rule, Hyram Bou 106
Jaems Bou 106
John Bou 72
John Bou 105
Rule, cont.
Samuel Bou 105
Thomas Bou 106
William Bou 105
Ruley, Thomas Fay 26
Rulon, James Clr 140
Rumal, Charles Cam 30
Rumford, Jonathan Mas 277
Rumiels, Thomas Mer 330
Ruminge, Christian Log 181
Rumley, Thomas Fay 27
Thomas Wsh 309
Rumsey, Edward Chr 117
Runalds, Thomas Mon 347
Runan, Freeman Gar 215
Runckle, James Mad 217
Runels, Richd. Nic 59
Runey, William Woo 384
Runing, David Fle 63
Runion, James Fay 43
John Fay 60
Joseph Fay 60
Runnals, Amos Pul 144
Isom Pul 144
James Chr 57
Shadric Pul 144
William Pul 144
Wm. Pul 144
Runnels, Bowen Cas 44
Jessy Fay 54
Sillvaness Fay 50
William Bou 106
Runner, Michl. Nel 29
Runnion, Henry Flo 101
Joseph Mer 343
Runnoe, Charles Bou 106
Runnols, John Mad 219
Richard Mad 217
Thomas Mad 217
Runyan, Benjm. Mon 352
Jos. Gal 189
Peter Boo 62
Reuben Fra 162
Spencer Fra 160
Runyon, Absalom Mad 219
Daniel Mas 276
Enily Mad 219
John Mad 218
Martin Mad 218
Phineas Mad 219
Vincent Mas 277
Rupard, John Clr 139
Rupe, Barney Lin 133
Rupert, David Chr 60
David Chr 60
Rusell, Jas. War 264
Rush, Benja. Bar 49
Benjamin Cal 17
Elijah Mas 274
Conrod Jef 13
Grigsby Log 163
James Bar 49
Jno. Hrd 289
John Bar 38
John Pen 116
Martha Wsh 310
Patrick Fay 50
Peter Pen 114
Saml. Cum 181
Thomas Pen 114
Rushbrook, Robert Mad 245
Rusher, Andrew Bre 165
Henry Bre 162
James Bre 164
William Bre 164
Rushin, Noah Chr 102
Robert Chr 105
Rushing, Richard Liv 158
Rusk, Charles Pul 144
David Sco 171
Elam Nel 30
James Jes 56
James Sco 181
James Sco 185
John Sco 170
John Sco 190
Robert Jef 13
Russ, Nicholas But 196
Russel, Abslom Cas 43
Baly Chr 109
Buckner Bar 27
Daniel Cas 47
Dowel Chr 109
Ephram Chr 55
George War 256
James Bar 27
John Cas 46
John Sco 178
Nicholas Bul 183
Robert Fay 17
Robert S. Fay 33
Saml. Grn 258
Thomas Bul 183
Thos. Way 356
William Fay 55
Wm. Cas 43
Russell, Benjamin Ohi 82
Charles Wsh 307
Constantine Jef 13
Danil Nel 31
Ezekiel Wsh 307
George War 275
Hedgemon She 224
James Fra 158
James Liv 153
Jas. Way 365
John Flo 101
John Hnr 368
John Log 189
John Mul 404
John She 200
John She 219
John She 226
Joseph J. Lin 131
Joseph, Snr Lin 133
Levi Jef 13
O. Mary Fay 17
Rachel She 236
Robert Mer 330
Robert Wsh 309
Genl. Robert Fay 57
Saml. Nel 32
Samuel Mul 385
Sanders Lin 131
Thomas Log 185
Thomas Wsh 309
William Lin 131
William Mul 399
William Nel 29
William Wsh 309
Wm. Jef 12
Wm. War 255
Wm. War 275
Russil, Robert Chr 63
Russle, Andrew Pul 143
Free Mon 347
Rust, Geo. Hrd 287
Isaac Hnd 333
John Mas 274
Mathew Hrd 287
Nancy Mas 277
Ruth, Barberry Chr 60
Samuel Fay 20
William Fay 17

Rutherfad, Stephen Log 161
Rutherford, Benjamn. But 196
Isaac Way 359
Jessee Fay 26
John Fra 161
Joseph Fay 17
Joseph Fay 26
Reuben Flo 101
Susanna Fra 161
Ruthey(free woman) Fay 17
Ruthie, Neal Fle 76
Rutlage, Peter Hrs 319
Rutledge, Abraham She 200
Abraham W. She 232
Jacob Clr 139
James Hnd 336
John Sco 169
Joseph Clr 139
Joseph Clr 140
Thomas Hnd 327
William Hnd 339
Rutlige, John Clr 139
Rutter, Alexander Hrs 315
Edmund Wsh 307
James, Junr Liv 151
James, Senr Liv 151
John Jef [illegible]
Moses Fra [illegible]
William Hrs [illegible]
William Liv 151
Rutton, Isaiah Mas 274
Thomas Mas 275
Ryan, Betsy Nel 7
Harris Pul 143
James Wsh 307
John Cum 173
John Put 143
Joseph Knx 71
Michael Mas 276
Patrick War 263
Polly Cum 170
Richard Wsh 307
Winston Fra 159
Wm. Cum 170
Ryblane, Martin [illegible]
Ryle, James [illegible]
John Boo 62
Larkin Boo 62
Wm. Boo 62
Ryley, Edward Mer 328
Henry Gra 239
John Lin 133
Joseph Knx 79
Wm. Jef 12
Ryman, Joseph Fay 27
Rachel Fay 27
Rynearson, Abraham Mer 328
Barent Mer 330
Isaac Lin 131
Ryneasson, Tina Nel 28
Ryon, Benjamen Adr 12
Betsy Mer 328
David Mer 330
Edwd. Way 367
George Mon 374
John Hnr 351
John B. Clr 139
Joseph Adr 12
Joseph Hnr 363
Leonard Clr 139
Philip Clr 139
Philip H. Clr 139
Soloman Mer 330
Thomas Mer 330
William Bou 130
Winny Clr 140
Ryon, cont.
Wm. Way 360
Rysinger, George Jef 13
Jacob Jef 13
Martin Jef 21

-- S --

Sabastain, Sarah Mad 223
Wiley Mad 223
Sabastion, Samuel She 202
Sacre, Robirt Fra 167
Sacry, George Fay 26
James Fra 168
Saddler, Edwd. Gar 223
Jas. Gar 220
Jessee Bou 110
Pleasant She 228
Wm. Gar 221
Sadler, Edward Nic 60
John Mon 366
John Nic 60
Samuel Mon 366
Samuel Mon 370
[illegible]ell, Joshua Fra 164
[illegible]er, John Mon 360
[illegible]ser, Henry Fay 46
Jacob Fay 47
Sagasor, Jacob Hrs 320
Sage, Alex Hnr 358
Hennery Cas 46
Jesse Hnr 355
John Mer 330
Sagerser, Frederick Jes 49
Sail, Anthony Jef 14
John Hrs 313
Lewis Jef 14
Sailor, Conrod Fay 27
Sailors, Phillip Boo 63
Sain, Charles Grp 269
Saintjohn, Noah Pul 138
Saml. Pul 140
Saladay, Samuel Grp 269
Sale, Leonard Log 194
Robert Gal 189
Samuel Mer 333
Salesberry, Nathl. Way 371
Salisbury, Thomas Mul 386
Sallee, Jacob Jes 53
Joseph, Jr Jes 52
Joseph, Sr Jes 52
William Jes 52
Salley, George Fay 39
Henry Mad 222
John Pul 136
John Pul 140
Joseph Pul 138
Oliver Ohi 88
Stephen Mad 222
Wm. Pul 121
Sallier, James Chr 54
John Mer 333
Sallinger, Robt. Hnr 365
Sally Fra 168
Sally, see also end of S's
Edward Mon 367
George Fay 27
George Wsh 312
Isaac Adr 13
John Mer 334
Oliver Mer 334
Philip Wsh 310
William Wsh 310
Sally, cont.
Wm. Gar 220
Sallyar, Dunn Gar 224
Joseph Fle 90
Salmon, Jacob Boo 63
John She 220
Salmons, see also end of S's
Rowland Flo 102
Salsberry, Benj. Way 372
Nathl. Way 372
William Flo 102
Salseman, William Fay 25
Salter, Henry Mer 341
Jacob Mer 332
John Mer 334
Lambert Mer 332
Michael Gar 199
Salts, John Bra 152
Saltsman, Jacib Gra 241
John Grn 253
Peter Gra 243
Wm. Grn 253
Salyers, Benjamin Knx 80
Sam (freeman) Fay 27
Sames, James Clr 141
Sammar, David Jef 15
Sammons, James Mad 221
Thomas Grp 273
Thomas Rck 164
Sampels, Elias Jes 51
Sample, Andrew Woo 395
Charles Fle 64
Gilbert (living by himself) Fay 16
Jacob Woo 394
Mary Nic 62
William Hnd 342
William Woo 395
Samples, Aley She 235
Saml. She 232
Saml. She 232
Sampsan, William Lin 133
Sampson, Akeula Fle 82
Benjn. War 251
David Lin 134
Francis Mas 381
Isaac She 214
Jacob Mas 283
James Jef 15
John Mas 283
Richard Woo 389
Robert She 213
William Lin 134
Wm. Gar 223
Sampur, Joseph Hnd 328
Sams, see also end of S's
Lott But 196
Benjamin Mad 223
Samuel, Giles Fra 169
Giles M. Fra 170
James Jef 16
James Mad 226
Jesse Fra 170
John Fra 170
John Mas 308
John Sco 187
Josiah Clr 141
Larkin Fra 167
Lucy Woo 389
Reuben Fra 168
Reuben Fra 169
Robert Fra 167
Thomas Fra 165
William Fra 169
William Fra 170
Samuell, Nancy Hnr 368
Samuels, Anthony Jes 53

Samuels, cont.
John Mer 333
Mathw. Nel 27
Robert Bul 185
Robert Nel 24
William Bul 185
Wm. Nel 27
Sanberry, Benjamin Hrs 310
Sandafer, see also end of S
William Liv 153
Sandafur, Bennett Hnd 327
Richard Hnd 344
Sanders, see also end of S's
Ackley Fle 78
Benjamin Chr 105
Benjn. Mon 377
Betsey Mad 221
Christopher Clr 141
Clark Mas 303
Daniel Chr 102
David Chr 105
Elijah Pul 139
Elizabeth Chr 63
Francis Way 361
Garden Fay 59
George Fay 26
Gunnell Fle 71
Gunnal Fle 86
Gunnal, Jur Fle 87
Henry Fay 34
Hisb. Nic 62
Hugh Fra 168
Isaac Mer 334
Jacob Mad 225
Jacob Way 373
James Adr 13
James Chr 105
James Fay 40
James Fle 78
James Fra 162
James Jes 52
James Lin 135
James Mon 381
James Nic 62
Jeffery Log 194
Jno. Way 366
Joel Mad 225
John Fra 166
John Gar 221
John Hnd 333
John Mon 352
John She 204
Joseph Chr 105
Joshua Cam 29
Joshua Gra 243
Joshua Mas 285
Judith Hnr 368
Julius Fay 25
Kimbrow Fay 41
Lear Mul 387
Lecar Way 373
Lewis Chr 70
Lewis Fay 12
Mary Chr 70
Mirard Fay 27
Moses Fle 65
Oliver Fle 86
Phillip Chr 105
Rachel Mad 224
Rayman Fay 40
Sally Fra 168
Samuel Chr 105
Samuel Mon 377
Sarah Pen 105
Thomas Clr 142
Thomas Fra 166
Thomas Hnr 353

Sanders, cont.
Thomas Mad 222
Thomas (Geo'son) Mad 223
Thomas Mer 334
Wiley Mad 222
William Chr 105
William Chr 105
William Fay 34
William Fle 75
William Fra 165
William Mad 222
William Pen 105
William T. Chr 71
Wm. Mon 349
Wm. Mon 369
Wm. Mon 379
Zachariah Way 361
Sanderson, John Nic 62
Mary Nic 62
Robt. Nic 62
William Fay 50
Sandford, Alfred Cam 32
John Mer 334
Laurance Boo 63
Laurance W. Boo 63
Thos. Cam 28
Sandifer, Henry Mer 330
James Mer 334
William Mer 331
Sandifur, James Grn 245
Sandige, Hastin Grn 253
Sandridge, John Lin 134
Larken Lin 134
Patsy Mas 282
Sands, James Gra 239
Robt. Hrd 298
Sandsbury, James Mas 286
Sandusky, Anthy. Cum 185
Emanuel Cum 185
Jacob Cum 185
Jacob Wsh 312
John Wsh 312
Rebecca Wsh 312
Samuel Wsh 312
Sanford, Dan Sr Hnr 368
Danl. Jr Hnr 364
Henry B. Mon 381
James Woo 387
John Mad 222
Lace. Hnr 368
Sanner, Isaac Fra 167
Sansberry, Henrietta Wsh 310
Santee, Joseph Sco 167
Sapingfield, Mchl. Bou 108
Sapington, Sylvester Clr 141
Sapp, Anna Wsh 312
Benjamin Wsh 313
Betsy Adr 14
Calab Cas 43
Daniel Bou 111
Danil. Fle 88
Elias Wsh 313
Imanuel Grn 245
Jacob Wsh 313
James Wsh 312
John Wsh 312
Matthew Bou 111
Nathan Wsh 312
Theodorus Wsh 313
Sappington, James Mad 220
Sapsly, Robert Bar 34
Sarah(freewoman) Fay 32
Sarah Nic 59
Saran, Sollomon Hrs 307
Sare, Reuben Fra 167

Sargeant, John Cam 26
William Woo 390
Sargent see Serjeants
Sargent, William She 212
Sartain, Elijah Gar 199
Sarvers, John War 279
Sarvis, William She 220
Satalee, John Bou 108
Satchwell, Joseph Fay 54
Sattenfield, Solomon Bou 109
Saterfield, Eli War 255
Isaac War 279
James Cal 10
Saterwhite, Maan Fay 52
Satterfield, Jessee Bar 26
Satterly, Jacob Wsh 313
Satterwhite, John Fra 164
William Fay 16
Jno. Hnr 369
Saulsberry, Andrew Liv 159
Saulsbery, William Liv 159
Saulsbury, Jno. Lew 101
Saunders, Ann Grn 257
Anthy. Nel 7
Azariah Hrd 295
Charles Gal 190
Cristian J. Bul 184
Eleanor Wsh 313
Elizabeth Bul 185
Henry Grn 248
Henry, Jr Knx 69
Henry, Sr Knx 69
Jacob Flo 102
Jas. Grn 247
Jessee Bar 31
Jesse Hop 380
Jno. Hrd 284
John Adr 13
John, Sr Bar 31
John Bar 31
Jos. Hrd 284
Joseph Bar 28
Joseph Bul 184
Joseph Knx 69
Nathaniel Gal 190
Richard Woo 389
Saml. Gal 190
Saml. Grn 255
Sarah Ohi 95
Teakle Log 187
Thomas Bul 185
Saunderson, Robt. Woo 388
Sautherland, Frances She 200
Savage, Berry War 244
Hamilton Cum 177
Levin Cum 177
Mary Lew 95
Wm. Bar 19
Savary, Amos Hrd 290
John Bou 71
Savatier, Wm. Nic 61
Savern, David Gal 190
Saveteear, Wm. Bou 108
Sawyer, Chas. Junr Hrd 298
Chas., Senr Hrd 298
Sawyers, see also end of S
David Log 186
Jacob Sco 178
John She 211
Sayers, John Clr 141
John Rck 159
Saml. Cam 31
Saylor, Elizabeth Mon 354
Emanuel Mon 354
John Mon 354

Saylor, cont.
Joseph Knx 90
Solomon Knx 79
Scaaggs, Rich Adr 13
Scaags, James Adr 14
Sarah Adr 14
Scaggs, Henry Gra 241
James Gra 241
Martin Gra 240
William Gra 240
Wm. Grn 253
Scags, Henry Bar 53
R[illegible]d. Bar 53
Wm. Grn 261
Scale, Geo. Wolf Way 368
Scalf, John Flo 102
Scallions, John Way 373
Scamelhorn, Nat. Hrd 287
Scandland, Edmond Fra 164
Scanland, Gideon Woo 389
James Wsh 313
John Wsh 310
Reuben Gal 192
Robt. Gal 192
Walker Hnd 336
William Woo 389
Wm. Gal 190
Scantland, James Fay 55
Scarberry, Green Chr 77
Scarbrough, Wm. Rck 162
Scarce, David Woo 402
James Woo 385
James Woo 398
John Woo 385
Robert [illegible]
William [illegible]
Scarrot, John [illegible]
Scarveny, Jessy [illegible]
Scaton, George Bre 169
Scensibaugh, Adam War 262
Scharmahorne, Joseph Wsh 313
Peter Wsh 313
Schofield, Judy Fle 75
Scholl, Abraham Clr 140
Joseph Clr 142
Peter Clr 141
William Clr 142
Schoolcraff, James Pul 135
Schoolcraft, John Cly 150
Schooler, Benjn. Mad 223
Henry Clr 141
John Mad 223
John, Jr Mad 223
William Clr 141
Younger Fay 37
Schoolfield, John Bra 141
Schooling, James Wsh 313
Joseph Jef 16
Joseph Wsh 313
Schoonover, David Hrd 295
Schroeder, Emanuel F. War 251
Jon. G. War 251
Schuyler, Jos. Gar 222
Schwing, John G. Jef 26
Scissel, Jas. Gar 219
Scisses, Mathias She 233
Scobee, Daniel Clr 141
John Clr 140
John, Sr. Clr 141
Robert Clr 141
Stephen Clr 141
Scofield, Henry Sco 179
John Fra 163
John Sco 188
Thomas Sco 179
Scoggins, Allen Chr 75
Jonas Chr 75
Robert Chr 75
Scogin, George She 232
Wm. She 232
Scoler, Wharton Fay 51
Scomp, Henry Mer 341
John Mer 331
Sconce, Henry Bou 109
James Bou 109
Mary Bou 109
Nancy Bou 109
Robert Bou 109
Saml. Bou 109
Wm. Cum 178
Scool, John Mad 222
Scooler, Robert Fay 50
Scot, Andrew Fay 46
Arther Fay 47
Elizabeth Fay 42
John Grn 253
Samuel Fay 39
Thomas Fay 46
Scothorn, Nathan She 225
Scotson, James Woo 400
Scott, Abm. Sco 190
Absalom Cum 165
Achiles She 224
Adam Bar 37
Andrew Nic 61
Archibald Gal 19
Arthur She 208
Belitha Clr 150
Benjamin Cas 44
Benjamin Jes 53
Bob (freeman) Fay 16
Charles Clr 141
Charles Fra 170
Chimp Bar 47
Cosby Nel 22
Daniel Hnd 329
David Clr 142
David Grp 278
David Hrs 319
Early Fra 168
Edward Mon 363
Elijah Hnr 369
Elisha Hnr 351
Elizabeth Woo 380
Evan Mad 223
Francis Bar 51
Geo. Cam 28
Geo. Hnr 369
George Wsh 310
Grizet Jes 52
Henry Bre 165
Henry Cum 184
Hugh Adr 14
Hugh Woo 391
Jacob Cum 179
Jacob Way 364
James Cam 31
James Clr 141
James Clr 141
James Fay 48
James Gal 191
Jas. Gar 219
Jas. Gar 224
James Grn 266
James Hnd 344
James Jes 50
James Jes 53
James Lin 134
James Lin 135
James Mas. 280
James Nel 27
James She 219
Scott, cont.
James Wsh 313
James D. Bou 130
Jas. Hnr 367
Jeremiah Bou 111
Jessee Rck 160
Joel Sco 173
John Bar 26
John Bar 45
John Bou 107
John Cal 4
John Cam 31
John Cas 44
John Cum 179
John Fle 87
John Fra 163
John Gal 191
John Grn 250
John Hrs 321
John Jef 16
John Jes 51
John Jes 52
John Jes 53
John Liv 158
John Log 169
John Mad 223
John Mer 330
John Mer 333
John Mul 388
John Mul 396
John Nic 61
John Sco 187
John She 233
John She 238
John Way 364
John Wsh 310
John Wsh 313
John M. Fra 169
Jonathan Bou 107
Jonathan Gar 223
Jos. Gar 220
Joseph Bar 40
Joseph Chr 101
Joseph Fle 80
Joseph Hrd 301
Joseph Jef 15
Joseph Liv 154
Joseph Liv 154
Joseph Mad 224
Joseph, Senr Fle 72
Joshua Liv 156
Josiah Bou 109
Levi Hnr 368
Lewis War 281
Margerit Fay 42
Martha Gar 224
Martin Way 358
Mary Hrs 323
Mary Jef 28
Mathew Mon 374
Matthew Mad 223
Matthew Nic 60
Matthew T. Fra 169
Moses Boo 63
Moses She 223
Nancy Bou 131
Nancy Woo 383
Nathan Mul 394
Nathaniel Gar 219
Nathaniel Way 359
Obediah Cam 32
Patrick Bou 107
Pleasant Bul 184
Rebert Hrs 322
Richard Wsh 130
Robert Bou 107
Robert Bou 107

Scott, cont.
Robert Hnr 358
Robert Hrs 321
Robert Wsh 313
Rodeham Log 172
Sam Bar 47
Saml. Adr 14
Saml. Cum 184
Saml. Lew 102
Samule Bou 130
Samuel Chr 97
Samuel Chr 106
Samuel Jes 51
Samuel Log 196
Samuel Mas 282
Samuel Wsh 313
Samuel, Sr Bou 131
Sarah Mas 285
Stephen Hrd 292
Tabert Cas 37
Tho Bar 47
Thomas Bre 159
Thomas Chr 104
Thomas Fay 48
Thomas Grp 273
Thomas Jes 51
Thomas Jes 53
Thomas Jes 53
Thomas Knx 89
Thomas Lin 135
Thomas Mon 381
Thomas Mul 396
Thomas Nic 60
Thomas Nic 61
Thomas She 234
Thomas War 250
Thos. Adr 13
Thos. Cum 184
Thos. Grn 258
Thos. Nic 61
William Bou 68
William Bou 107
William Bou 130
William Cal 17
William Chr 100
William Fay 16
William Fay 26
William Fay 48
William Fle 80
William Flo 103
William Gal 191
William Hnr 368
William Jes 52
William Mer 330
William Nel 23
William She 225
William Way 375
William, B. Bou 110
Willm. Lin 135
Wm. Cas 37
Wm. Gar 220
Wm. Grn 254
Wm. Hnr 351
Wm. Hrd 295
Wm. Hrs 317
Wm. Hrs 321
Wm. Jef 18
Wm. Lew 102
Wm. Mon 349
Wm. Mon 355
Wm. Mon 363
Wm. Mon 367
Wm. War 260
Wm. Way 356
Wm. Way 371
Wm. Sin Cas 38
Scowler, Benjamin Fay 46
Scraggins, Charles Jef 27
John She 239
Scribner, Lewis S. War 280
Wm. War 264
Scrimsher, John Fra 166
Scritchfield, John Gar 223
Scrivner, James Est 7
Joseph Est 4
Thomas Mad 225
Scroeder, Jon. N. War 251
Scroggin, George Bou 111
George She 219
Jno. Jr Bou 111
John, Sr Bou 110
Jos. Bou 111
Saml. Bou 111
Wm. Bou 110
Scroggins, Henry Log 195
Robt. Bou 107
Thos. C. Woo 388
Scorggs, Ebinezir Fle 84
Scrogins, Joseph Fay 26
Scruggs, thos.Jur Sco 173
Thos. Senr Sco 173
Willm. Sco 172
Wm. Gar 218
Scrugham, Joseph Fay 26
Scrughan, Danl. Mad 221
Joseph Mad 221
Scrugs, Nathanill Cal 15
Scrutchfield, Arter Lin 134
James Lin 134
Nathl. Lin 135
Torry Lin 134
Scudder, Mary Mad 225
Scurlock, Thomas Woo 394
Sea, Coonrod Mon 359
John Mon 359
Wm. Mon 356
Seabolt, George Jef 18
Seaborn, Jacob Mad 221
Seal, James Mad 222
John Nel 24
Seaner, Philip Jef 18
Wm. Jef 18
Searcy, Allin Mad 220
Berry Fra 164
Charles Mad 226
Edmond Woo 402
Henry Fra 163
John Fra 163
John Gal 190
Leonard Woo 388
Richard Mad 221
Richard, Jr Mad 226
Richd. Woo 388
Saml. Mad 220
Searight, Willm. Bou 111
Sears, Christian Jef 27
Daniel Bou 108
David Log 162
Henry Bou 108
Jacob Bou 108
James Knx 91
Jesse Knx 67
John Chr 75
John Knx 65
John, Jr Bou 108
John, Sr Bou 108
William Chr 74
William Knx 88
Searse, James Log 161
Samuel Log 176
William Log 161
Searsey, Elijabeth Boo 62
Seas, Barnet Chr 86
Seat, Feterich Log 172
Seates, Joseph Chr 116
Seatherland, William Log 195
Seaton, Allen Way 363
George Jef 17
Isaac Way 364
James Jef 17
Kinner Jef 17
Mary Jef 17
Sarah K. Jef 18
Thomas Lin 135
William Bre 160
William Log 165
Seay, Allen Cal 11
Jacob Wsh 314
Leonard Fra 164
Samuel Wsh 314
Sebastian, Benjn. Jef 14
Benjn. Sco 168
Lewis Sco 168
Wm. Jef 14
Sebaum, Jacob Cly 156
Sebree, John Fra 167
Laben Woo 377
Reuben Boo 63
Richd. Senr Sco 172
Thos. Sco 177
Urial Boo 63
Wm. Boo 63
Seburn, Ralph She 200
Secrets, Charles - Junr Fay 26
Charles, Senr Fay 26
Secston, John Mon 372
Seddens, Wm. Bar 40
Seders, Bennet Bou 131
See, George Bou 108
George Log 179
Margaret Bou 108
Seears, Joseph War 280
Seego, James Knx 67
Seels, Barnart Boo 63
Seecrest, Jacob Fay 26
Seet, Charles Pul 136
Robert Pul 138
Seevers, Henry Fle 75
Segear, Benjamin Jes 53
Segraves, John War 267
Saml. War 266
William Knx 86
Selah, B. Jane Mas 283
Barbara Mer 331
Samuel Mas 308
Selby, Bartlet Bou 108
Charles Mad 220
Henry Bou 108
Isaac Nec 62
Jno. Hrd 295
John Bou 107
Josa. Adr 13
Majr. Bou 108
Richard Wsh 310
William Bou 109
Seldon, George Bou 71
Self, Charmick Fay 43
Edwd. Hrd 284
Henry Bar 48
Henry Fay 44
James Fay 43
Jno. Hrd 283
John Clr 141
John Cum 171
Ownsby Bar 27
Robert Cum 171
Thomas Grn 259
Selford, Jon. War 281

Sellars, Elizabeth Hrs 310
  George Bra 147
  Henry Hrs 309
  Jas. Gar 224
  John Bra 145
  John Woo 381
  Jonathan Mad 225
  Joseph Woo 398
  Leonard Bra 149
  Michel Bra 150
  Philip Bra 150
Seller, Ann Liv 151
Sellers, Ephraim Hnd 345
  Isham Hnd 338
  John Mer 335
  Lewis Hnd 337
  Samuel She 233
Selley, John Bou 111
Sellors, Isaac Hrs 307
  Rebecca Hrs 308
Selvy, James Adr 14
  Lingan Adr 14
Selyers, Samuel Mon 366
Semands, Manson Bou 130
Semonus, John Fra 165
Semony, Francis Bou 72
Semore, Claybourn Mer 331
Senate, Richard Mer 334
Senbner, Plesant War 244
Seney, David Adr 14
Senior, Bryant Cam 24
  John Cam 31
Sentany, John Mas 285
  Lewis Mas 284
Senter, James Lin 134
Sergant, Jas. War 248
Sergeant, Aaron Pul 138
  Johnson Pul 135
Sergent, James Pul 138
  Joseph Pul 140
  Stephen Pul 138
  Thomas Pul 138
  Thomas Pul 140
Serjeants, William Mas 281
Serjent, Dabney Fay 50
Serring, Saml. Cam 31
Servant, William Wsh 314
Sessions, Solomon But 196
Sessons, Jabob Chr 96
Settle, James Nel 22
  Joseph Nel 25
  Simon Bar 36
  Thomas Fra 168
  Thornton War 255
  Willis Bar 36
Settler, Elizabeth Bar 51
Settles, Elizabeth Bar 36
  George War 256
  Henry Hop 377
Seurloch, George Log 187
Sever, Enoch Hnd 336
Severe, Christopher Mer 334
  William Mer 334
Severs, John Mul 402
  Michael Mad 220
  Solomon Mul 389
Sevinng, Saml. Bar 53
Seward, John Mad 220
Sewards, Saml. Bra 153
Sewel, James, Jr Mad 224
  Jas. Mad 224
Sewell, Arington Mad 223
  Banford Jef 27
Sexton, Benjm. Mon 353
  Benjm. Mon 372
  George Cum 166
Sexton, cont.
  George Cum 265
  Isaac [illegible] 87
  Jacob Knx 66
  John Cal 5
  Josua Cal 4
  Lewis Cal 14
  Mesheck Cum 166
  Thomas Mad 224
  Wm. Mon 353
Seybold, Jesper Fle 69
  Jesse Wsh 314
  John Fle 82
Shackeford, Zachariah Cas 43
Shackeleford, John Cly 160
Shackelet, Benjamin Hrd 302
  John Hrd 301
Shackelford, Benjamin Chr 53
  Carter Fra 166
  Dolley Cas 43
  Geo. Mad 221
  Henry Knx 63
  James Cas 39
  John She 205
  John She 217
  Jerry She 214
  Richard Cas 43
  Richd. Boo 63
  Sterling She 217
  William She 218
  Wm. Cas 39
  Wm. Fle 90
  Wm. War 254
Shackels, Abrm. Hrd 291
  Jno. Hrd 291
  Richd. Hrd 291
Shackleford, Benjn. Adr 13
  Edmond Lin 133
  Ewd. Cly 154
  George Mas 281
  James Mas 281
  Jas. Gar 199
  Jas. Gar 222
  Saml. Lin 134
Shacklet, Blancet Hrd 296
Shad, John Mer 333
Shadbourn, Wm. Nel 6
Shadburn, Amos Jef 15
Shadde, John Gar 221
Shaddrick, Thos. Nel 22
Shadocks, Jno. Hrd 289
Shadowens, Wm. Pul 137
Shadower, And Grn 261
Shadrick, Benjamin She 232
Shadrock, Jno. Hrd 295
Shadwick, Isreal Fle 91
  John Grp 270
Shafer, John Boo 63
Shaffer, John Lin 135
Shain, Able Bul 185
  Edward Gra 239
  James Gra 239
  John Gra 239
  John Nel 25
  Thomas Gra 239
  William Bul 185
Shake, George Jef 14
  Wm. Cas 43
Shakel, Loyd Fle 73
  Mahald Fle 73
Shakleford, John Jes 52
Shaller, Jacob Bul 185
Shammet, Jonathan Pul 134
Shamril, Zachariah Chr 107
Shamwell, James Log 168
  Saml. Log 168
Shanan, Margret Nic 61
Shankland, Dad. Nic 61
  John Nic 61
Shanklen, Richard Bul 184
Shanklin, Alexander Log 193
  Andrew Mon 354
  Edward Chr 77
  Gordon Fle 87
  James Mas 280
  John Chr 114
  Josiph Chr 114
  Robert Jes 54
  Saml. Jes 52
  Thomas Fle 81
  Thomas Jes 54
Shanks, David Bou 107
  James Adr 14
  James Bul 185
  James Pul 136
  John Gra 240
  John Liv 148
  Robert She 238
  Samuel She 223
  Thomas She 223
  William Lin 135
  William She 214
  Zak Nel 23
Shannen, Samuel She 200
Shannon, Absalam Lin 135
  Alexander She 210
  David Hrd 284
  Elijah War 272
  Hugh Sco 173
  Hugh Sco 184
  Hugh Sco 190
  Hugh War 253
  James Bou 70
  James She 200
  John She 205
  John She 222
  Joseph Log 170
  Joseph Log 178
  Joseph Sco 186
  Joseph Woo 381
  Joseph, Sr Log 168
  Nathl. Sco 170
  Robert Jes 54
  Saml. Adr 13
  Samuel Fra 164
  Samuel Fra 165
  Samuel She 199
  Thos. Lin 135
  Thos. R. War 253
  William Hnr 359B
  William Mad 225
Shanon, John Fay 42
  John Nic 61
Shanscy, Wm. Sr Nel 27
Shaplaw, Thomas Bul 184
Shaptaw, John Bul 184
Shark, David She 227
Sharke, Abram Mer 333
Sharon, Hugh Sco 182
Sharp, Aaron Est 7
  Abraham Fra 164
  Abraham Log 169
  Adam Est 7
  Anthony Chr 84
  Benjamin Fay 38
  Benjamin She 218
  Benjn. Sco 183
  Charles Clr 142
  Ebenezer Fay 26-
  Edward She 225

Sharp, cont.
Elias Fay 37
George Fay 19
George Fay 25
George Hrs 312
George She 223
James Mul 390
John Adr 13
John But 197
John Fay 19
John Grn 263
John Pen 115
John She 225
John She 232
Lincefield Sco 184
Luke She 240
Moses Est 7
Moses Mon 357
Noah Fra 163
Richard Fay 34
Richard Fay 45
Richard Grp 273
Stephen Mon 356
T. John Nic 60
Thomas Log 192
Thos. Bra 149
Thos. Sco 175
William Sco 183
William She 215
Wm. Way 370
Sharpe, Soloman Mer 333
Sharper Fra 169
Sharram, George Nel 24
Sharrow, Christian Bou 131
Sharry, John War 278
William War 267
Shasteen, Elijah Mon 368
Martin Mon 368
Shateen, Jesse Way 371
Peter Hrd 283
Shatteen, Val She 242
Shauley, John Nel 25
Lewis Nel 23
Shaushe, Thos. Cal 18
Shavage, John Grp 272
Shaver, Abm. Way 366
Ben Hrd 300
Geo. Cam 30
Jacob Hrd 300
Jacob Jef 18
John Bou 110
Lewis Bra 150
Shavers, George Fle 76
Jacob Fle 61
Simon Fay 39
Shavor, James Mer 332
Shavour, Peter Mer 343
Shaw, Anna Cal 15
Archebald Fra 170
Daniel Mer 330
David Liv 157
David War 269
Francis She 206
Henry Fle 88
Hiram Fay 16
Jacob She 203
James Cam 28
James Mas 286
Joel Bar 22
John Bar 40
John Bou 109
John Bou 110
John Bou 110
John Bou 111
John Fay 23
John She 221
Jos. War 269
Shaw, cont.
Lenard Chr 105
Michl. Hnr 351
R. John Fay 17
Robt. Cam 24
Samuel Bou 110
Thomas Bou 110
Thomas Fay 16
Thos. Adr 13
William Chr 69
William Gra 237
Wm. Bra 153
Wm. Jef 15
Shawhan, Danl. Fle 86
John Bou 110
Joseph Bou 107
Shawler, Jno. Hrd 298
Shawn, Henry Log 172
Saml. Log 172
Shawuch, Isreal Fle 77
Shealds, Francis Nel 27
John Mer 333
John Nel 22
Mary Mer 335
William Mer 333
William Mer 333
Sheals, James Bou 108
Margarette Hrs 323
Rhody Hrs 317
Samuel Hrs 324
Thomas Bou 108
Shealy, David Junr Fay 51
David, Senr Fay 51
Shean, Sabastan Nel 28
Shearer, Jacob Jef 28
James Mad 226
Matthew Mad 226
Peter Bou 68
Reuben Gar 223
Saml. Nel 25
Thomas Mad 221
Wm. Gar 223
Shearley, Arge Sco 170
Benjn. War 259
Benjn. War 260
Edwd. Sco 172
Wm. Bra 148
Wm. Jef 14
Absolam Jef 27
Ezekiel Sco 173
Shearman, Charles Jes 18
Shdk. Bou 108
Shears, Joseph Fay 16
Shearward, Thos. Cas 37
Shearwood, Robert Jes 51
Sheats, Archibald Hrs 309
Sheby, Joshua Mas 282
Sheckles, Ely Mon 380
Sheehan, John Wsh 314
Sheehi, Jno. Hrd 296
Sheeks, David Way 373
Sheen, Jas. War 268
Sheene, Wm. Boo 63
Sheets, Benjn. Woo 388
Frederick Gal 190
Henry Fra 166
Martin Fra 167
William Woo 395
Sheffeild, George Est 6
Sheils, Parick Fay 40
Shekliff, Joseph Nel 22
Shelay, John Sco 178
Shelbourn, Augustin She 226
Dionysious She 220
John She 223
Robn. Nel 24
Shelbourn, cont.
Will She 226
Shelby, Evin Lin 134
Isaac Lin 134
James Fay 32
Joshua Mas 284
Moses, Junr Liv 156
Moses, Senr Liv 157
William Liv 152
Shelds, John Fay 16
Shell, Freeman Cum 182
Shelada, Caleb She 225
Shelladye, George She 206
Shellers, John Sco 173
Shelley, Jacob Bou 107
Jane Knx 74
Shelly, George Cal 16
John Cal 11
Shelman, Adam Bre 164
Lewis Bre 165
Martin Bre 168
Shelton, Abednego But 197
Asher But 197
Benjamin Log 190
Daniel Fay 26
David Mul 398
David Sco 174
Fielding Jes 53
George Woo 391
Gilbert But 197
Greenwood Fay 25
Henry Hrd 295
Jacob Gal 189
James Hnd 344
James Mas 282
James Mas 283
Jeremiah But 197
Jeremiah But 197
Jeremiah Lin 133
Jesse But 197
Jno. Hrd 295
John Jes 54
John Knx 66
John, Sr Jes 54
Joshua But 197
Medly Gal 189
Micajah Log 170
Nelson Hrd 287
Redrick Mul 397
Robert Woo 397
Samuel Mer 331
Stephen Jes 53
Thomas Mad 224
Thomas Mas 285
William Chr 55
William Clr 142
William Nel 23
Wm. Jef 16
Wyat Chr 73
Shelty, Wm. Cal 16
Shepard, Daniel Mon 374
Isabella Mer 331
Isaiah Mon 374
John Gar 218
John Grp 273
John She 236
Jonathan Mer 334
Margaret Mer 334
Saml. Cum 168
Saml. Sco 189
Thomas W. Clr 147
Shephard, John Woo 378
Shepherd, Adam Bul 185
Benjamin Lew 101
Chas. Lew 101
Christo. Hnr 355
George Mas 280

Name	County	Page
Shepherd, cont.		
Henry	Wsh	322
Isaac	Way	353
James	Hnr	354
James	Mad	226
John	Boo	63
John	Mas	284
John	Bul	185
John	Wsh	311
Joseph	Mas	282
Lucretia	Bre	163
Roland	Hop	376
Saml.	Fle	77
Solon.	Lew	99
Thos.	Hrd	288
William	Lew	99
William	Woo	379
Wm.	Lew	100
Shepler, Jno.	Hrd	291
Shepley, Richard	Fay	25
Sheppard, David	She	218
Sher, David	Adr	13
Sherl, Ambros	Grn	262
Jas	Grn	262
Jno	Grn	262
Sherly, Saml.	Cal	16
Samuel	Log	176
Sherrard, Jno.	Hrd	293
Robert	Log	182
Sherril, Wm. Sr	Grn	261
Sherrill, Elisha	Wsh	314
Sherrod, Samuel	Hrs	324
Sherrol, William	Mas	285
Sherwood, Moses	Clr	142
Shevely, Mary	Mer	335
Shevery, Sally	Fay	25
Sheward, Cornelas	Bra	153
Shewberb, Nicholas	Mon	372
Shewmate, John	Hrs	319
Steven	Hrs	319
Shey, Thos.	Cum	180
Shield, Jeramiah	War	268
Thos.	Nel	23
James	Gra	237
James	Jes	52
James	She	216
James	She	235
Shields, Jas.	Gar	216
John	Adr	14
John	Fra	165
Jonathan	Mas	282
Joseph	Grn	256
Page	Liv	147
Robert	Mon	371
Thos.	War	275
William	Bou	70
William	Fle	64
William	Ma[illegible]	[illegible]2
Shifer, Samuel	Fay	26
Shiffer, Jacob	Gar	220
Shiflet, Thomas	Mad	225
Shilds, John	Adr	14
Shiles, John	Fay	25
Shillers, John	Cal	14
Shingfield, Wm.	Bar	31
Shinglebower, Geo.	Gar	199
Shingleton, George	Way	356
Jonathn.	Bou	110
Ship, Ambrose	Grn	245
Edmond	Jef	15
Elijah	Clr	141
John	Grn	245
Joseph	Cal	5
Joseph	Clr	141
Thos.	Grn	245
Shiphd., William	Hnd	354
Shipley, Geo.	Bar	37
Shipley, cont.		
Robt.	Bar	31
Robt.	Bar	37
Shiply, Joseph	Bar	37
Noah	Mas	284
Rezin	Mas	284
Samuel	Lin	135
Thomas	Lin	135
Shipman, David	She	224
John	She	197
Wm.	She	241
Shipmon, Phebee	Bar	36
Shipp, Colby	Bou	110
John	Hrs	321
Laban	Bou	110
Richd.	Grn	246
Richd. Jr	Woo	377
Richd. Senr	Woo	377
Shipton, Jesse	Mad	220
Peter	Clr	142
Shirkliff, John	Wsh	311
Thomas	Wsh	311
Shirley, George	Adr	13
John	Adr	13
John	Adr	14
John	Lew	100
John	Nel	24
John, Senr	Log	178
Shirly, Danl.	Bar	54
Jas.	Gar	222
John	Gar	222
Nimrod	Bar	54
Robert	Bar	55
Tho.	Bar	50
Tho.	Bar	53
Tho. Senr	Bar	51
Shirril, Isaac	Way	364
Shirts, John	Hrs	317
Shirwood, John	Fle	83
Shitle, Martin	Bar	27
Peter	Bar	24
Shivaly, Jacob	Grn	247
Shivel, Frederick	Fay	16
Shiveley, Henry	She	205
Shively, Christian	Jef	15
Jacob	Jef	16
Michael	Grn	258
Philip	Jef	15
Shives, George	Cum	167
Shoalders, Abner	Chr	89
Dicy	Chr	99
Josua	Chr	102
Shoat, Augustus	Mon	371
Chrisr.	Way	360
Edward	Fle	75
Richard	Mon	371
Shock, Adam	Nel	23
John	Fay	58
John	Nel	23
Shockeney, Elija	Nel	25
Richard W.	She	213
Shockey, John	Fle	70
Shockley, James	Fle	77
Saml.	Bou	109
Thermal	Fle	90
Wm.	Fle	66
Shockly, David	Bar	52
James	Lin	134
Lemuel	Bar	52
Levi	Lin	135
Shockney, James	Bou	131
Shocky, Michl.	Nel	27
Shoemake, Fielding	Mer	332
Shoemaker, Adam	Ohi	96
Cornelius	Wsh	311
Evan	Grn	257
Hezekiah	Wsh	311
Shoemaker, cont.		
Jesse	Grn	265
John	Lin	135
John	She	236
John	Wsh	311
John, Jr	Bre	169
John, Sr	Bre	169
Thomas	Wsh	314
William	Wsh	311
Shoemate, Benja.	Hop	376
Daniel	Gar	221
Shofstall?, Jacob	Bra	144
Shofuen?, Robert	Grn	248
Shofun, Henry	Grn	251
Sholan, Kader	War	252
Shomaker, James	Knx	85
Leonard C.	Knx	85
Shoman, John B.	Mul	401
Shomate, Jessee	Bou	109
Shonie, Abraham	Mon	355
Jacob	Mon	355
Shook, George	Bul	184
Gabl.	Way	354
John	Fay	47
Shoots, James	Fay	47
John	Fay	47
Shopit, Michael	Chr	114
Shoptaw, Henry	Nel	24
Shore, Charles	Mon	364
John	Mon	347
Shores, Frederick	Cum	168
Gilbert	Fay	60
Matty	Mon	379
Susannah	Fay	60
Shoriden, Thomas	Fra	170
Short, Aaron	Grp	274
Abner	Wsh	311
Danl.	Sco	177
Ely, Jur	Sco	180
Ely, Senr	Sco	181
Flemming	Bar	34
George	Lin	135
George	Nic	61
Isaac	Wsh	314
Jacob	Sco	180
Jahu	Grn	264
James	Grn	264
James	Mer	333
John	Bou	131
John	Pul	135
John	Pul	137
John	Woo	392
Jos.	Grn	249
Josiah	Bar	27
Josiah	Mer	330
Joshua	Grn	255
Lannum	Bar	27
Needham	Bar	25
Obadiah	Sco	186
Pleasant	Clr	142
Purnel	Sco	180
Saml.	Hop	376
Samuel	Mas	282
Wesley	Pul	134
William	Cal	15
William	Grn	249
William	Wsh	314
Zach.	Gar	223
Shortridge, Andrew	Pul	140
George	Bou	107
George	Pul	140
John	Bou	107
John	Mon	376
Margaret	Grp	271
Saml.	Bou	131
William, Jur	Sco	191
William, Senr	Sco	191

Shote, Richard Est 7
Shott, John Fay 35
Shotten, Christo-
  pher Woo 378
Shotwell, Daniel Knx 88
  John Mas 300
  John, Junr Mas 300
  Nathan Mas 381
  William Mas 300
Shouce, John She 236
Showdy, Benedict Mas 281
Shoults, Christian Mon 369
  Elizabeth Mon 369
  Henry Mon 367
  John Mon 370
  Math Mon 367
  Pheby Mon 365
Shouse, Daniel Woo 393
  Henry Fra 163
  Henry Woo 393
  John Liv 153
  Saml. Woo 386
Shown, Peter Ohi 78
Shrader, Adam Jef 27
  Christopher Jef 27
  Jacob Jef 14
  Tobias Bou 130
Shrador, Jacob Jef 14
  Wm. Jef 14
Shrake, George Jef 32
Shrder?, Conrod Bou 69
Shreve, William Jes 54
Shrewsberry, Able Way 357
  Allen Gar 222
  Drewry Way 371
Shrewsbury, Nathan-
  iel Bre 164
Shrimp, George Jef 18
Shrioe, Matthew Fay 16
Shrite, John Clr 140
Shriveley, John Bra 148
Shriver, Peter Fle 61
Shrock, John Mad 245
Shrode, Henry But 197
  John But 197
  William But 197
Shropshire, Abner Bou 110
  Benjn. Bou 110
  James Fle 62
  James Hrs 308
  John Clr 141
  Jos. Bou 110
  Mary Clr 141
  Walter Hrs 307
  Wilm. Hrs 307
Shrosebury, Daniel Mon 355
  Thomas Mon 355
Shrote, Peter Jef 18
Shroupe, Adam Mas 283
Shrout, Gasper Mon 364
  Samuel Fle 62
Shuck, Carnelius She 239
  Cos. Hnr 351
  David Chr 74
  Jacob Wsh 314
  John Cas 37
  John She 210
  John Wsh 314
  John Wsh 317
  Philip Wsh 315
  Philip Wsh 318
Shuff, Isaac Sco 182
  Jacob Sco 185
  Jonathan Bou 110
Shuffe, Ephram Chr 7′
Shulas, Alex. Hnr 366
Shull, Frederick Knx 64
Shull, cont.
  Peter Mul 400
  John Knx 68
  Joseph Knx 73
  Philip Knx 90
Shults, Jacob Adr 14
  Joseph War 276
  Matthias Ohi 82
  Peter Bou 108
Shumake, John Chr 59
  Thos. Bou 131
Shumaker, Lakey Pen 110
Shumate, Nimrod Hrd 304
Shur, John Cal 7B
Shurley, John Log 178
Shurly, Armstead Mas 283
  Charles Cly 158
  Christian Mad 221
  Daniel Mas 298
  George Mad 221
  Toliver Mas 283
Shutherland, Fen-
  nel Cas 38
  Geo. Cas 38
  Owen Cas 38
Shutt, Henry Mul 402
Shuttleworth, All-
  en Wsh 320
  Susanna Wsh 322
Shy, Jesse Mer 331
  Samuel Bou 110
Sias (free negro) Fay 30
Sibert, Catharine Wsh 321
  John Wsh 321
  Peter Nel 25
Sibler, Henry Log 178
Sibley, Isaac Hnd 328
Siddens, James Bar 26
Sidebotans, Wm. Grn 260
Sidebotham, John Clr 141
Sidebottom, Joseph Hnr 353
  Peter Grn 256
  Susan Grn 264
Sidebottoms, Peter Pul 140
Sidener, Catherine Mon 367
  Frederic Bou 131
  Marten Bou 131
  Martin Clr 141
Sidner, Conrod Fay 57
  Frdrick Fay 58
  Henry Fay 58
  Jacob Fay 58
  John Fay 57
  Peter Fay 58
Sidwell, Cathe. Way 363
  Elisha Bou 131
  Hugh Bou 131
  John Bou 131
  Joseph Cum 181
  Nathan Mas 285
  Reuben Mas 286
  Wm. Cum 180
Sieles, Henry Bar 39
Sights, Jacob Hnd 341
Siglar, John Cly 149
Sigler, Jacob But 196
Sike, Jacob Jes 50
Sikes, Jesse Liv 158
  Sarah Grp 270
Silavant, Andrew But 196
Silby, Joseph Knx 86
  Thomas · Knx 87
Siler, Jacob Knx 74
Silkwood, Bazel She 238
  James Hop 379
  Solomon Hop 378
Sill, Adam She 231
Sill, cont.
  Register She 205
Sillin, Willm. War 247
Silor, Charls Cal 4
Silver, William Log 179
Silvers, Charles Cum 185
  Hugh Cas 48
  Jane Mer 332
  John Cas 48
  John Mas 282
  John Wsh 314
  Samuel Wsh 314
  William Pul 134
  William, Sen Pul 134
  Wm. Cas 48
Silvy, James Fle 76
  John Adr 14
  Sally Mer 331
Sily, George Gar 223
Simbrill, Francis Wsh 315
Simermon, Daniel Mon 369
Simions, Samul Hnr 352
  Will Hnr 352
Simkins, George Liv 157
Simmemon, Lawrence Jef 15
Simming, David Gra 238
Simmon, Nasa Bar 21
Simmons, Aron Jef 25
  Cephas Bul 185
  Chas. Bar 35
  Elisha Bar 39
  Isam Bar 44
  Jesse Bul 184
  John Hop 377
  John Log 191
  John Mad 220
  Jona. Hrd 300
  Jos. Hrd 296
  Joseph Bul 184
  Joseph Bul 185
  Leonard Mas 284
  Levi Bul 185
  Richard Bul 185
  Richard Bul 185
  Richard P. Bul 183
  Robert Bul 185
  Robert Mul 389
  Samuel Bul 184
  Sarah War 254
  Stasa Bar 39
  Thomas W. Bul 184
  Thos. Boo 63
  Verlinda Bul 185
  William Bul 184
  Wilm. War 248
  Wm. Bar 38
  Wm. War 254
Simms, Eleanor Wsh 315
  Frances Cas 42
  John Wsh 311
  John Wsh 315
  John Wsh 315
  Mark Wsh 310
  Martin Flo 105
  Rodolphus Wsh 311
  Samuel Wsh 315
  Thomas Wsh 315
  William Nel 24
Simons, Izabel (free
  woman) Fay 27
  Jno. Hrd 283
  John Cum 184
  John Way 371
  Joseph Liv 145
  Mark Hrs 305
  Mary Log 161
  Peter Chr 74

Name	Co.	Page
Simonton, Robert	Cum	178
Simpkins, Benjamin	Liv	157
Simpler, John	Bre	156
Simpson, Abraham	Fay	38
Agness	She	198
Andrew	Mon	380
Benjamin	Cal	19
Betsey	She	198
Charles	Gar	223
Christian	Way	367
Christian	Way	367
Ctherine	Fay	60
Elenor	Mad	220
Elijah	Adr	13
Elijah	Gar	222
Elijah	Log	177
Erasmus	She	240
Frances	Clr	140
Geo.	Gar	217
George	Hrs	313
George	Jes	50
George	Nel	26
Henry	Bar	50
Hugh	War	253
James	Cal	12
James	Chr	78
James	Clr	147
James	Gal	190
James	Log	181
James	Mad	222
James	Nel	26
James	She	212
James	War	253
James	Wsh	310
James	Wsh	315
Jas.	Way	351
Jas.	Way	369
Jesse	Gar	217
Joel	Log	169
John	Adr	13
John	Adr	14
John	Bar	27
John	Bou	111
John	Fay	60
John	Gal	191
John	Nel	26
John	Pul	137
John	Way	357
John	Wsh	310
John	Wsh	315
Joseph	Bou	107
Joseph	Mon	384
Joseph	Wsh	311
Josha.	Adr	14
Joshua	Way	373
Jothn.	Nel	7
Levi	Bou	107
Loyd	Wsh	315
Mary	Cal	15
Mary	She	198
Mattw.	War	253
Peter	Chr	76
Peter	Jes	50
Peter	Jes	54
Richard	Chr	78
Richard	Fay	25
Richard	Wsh	315
Robert	Fay	43
Robert	Jes	51
Robert	Mer	335
Robt.	Adr	13
Rueben	Way	364
Rueben	Way	373
Saml.	Adr	14
Saml.	Gal	192
Samuel	Jes	50
Solomon	Mas	283

Name	Co.	Page
Simpson, cont.		
Solomon	She	198
Thos.	Gal	192
Thos.	Nel	6
Thos.	Nel	24
Thos.	Way	369
Thomas	Cal	13
Thomas	Way	360
Walter	Nel	26
Water	Cam	31
William	Fay	26
William	Fay	43
William	Liv	151
William	Mer	334
Wm.	Way	367
Wm.	Way	368
Simrall, Wm. F.	Jef	28
Sims, Ann	Hop	373
Augustin	Cum	178
Benjamin	Nel	26
Edward	Gal	192
George	Cum	178
Ignatius	Nel	26
James	Cal	20
John	Chr	79
John	Cum	178
John	Mon	360
Joseph	Fle	84
Marmke.	Nel	26
Martin	Way	354
Mymaduke	Fay	41
Polly	Fay	57
Wm.	Cal	20
Starling	Knx	88
Wm.	Cum	178
Wm.	Gar	216
Simson, Barnet	Bou	131
Sinberry, Lewis	Mas	280
Sinclair see Cinclear		
Sinclair, Armstead	Sco	183
Danl.	Sco	175
Elexr.	Adr	13
Jas.	Sco	175
Robert	Sco	186
Sarah	War	263
Waugh	Bou	111
Sinclare, Palmer	Wsh	311
Sincleer, Wayman	Way	371
Sincler, Isaac	Way	370
Siner, Benjamin	Bre	162
Mathias	Bou	131
Singer, William	She	200
William	She	200
Singleton, Ann	Cly	151
Ben	Hrd	299
Christopher	Lin	133
David	Gar	220
Edmond	Jes	53
Jechonius	Woo	385
Jno.	Pul	140
John	Gar	220
John	Lin	133
John	Woo	395
Joshua	Lew	97
Manoah	Jes	53
Mary	Lin	133
Mason	Jes	52
Midleton	Rck	164
Phil	Cly	149
Phillip	Rck	164
Richard	Lin	133
Richd.	Cly	160
Thomas	Mad	224
William	Mad	224
Wm.	Gar	220
Sink, Daniel	Jef	18
Jacob	Jef	18

Name	Co.	Page
Sinkhorn, Andrew	Cas	47
Sinks, Jacob	Pen	117
Sinomon, John	She	226
Sinpers, Amos	She	238
Siper, Henry	Bre	167
Siple, Nathanil	Fay	41
Siry, John	Bar	50
Sisk, Barnabas	Hop	380
Pluright	Woo	402
Robert	Hop	379
Tho.	Hop	379
Tho.	Hop	379
Timothy	Hop	379
Sisney, Robert	Chr	66
Stevin	Chr	66
Sisson, Benja.	Gar	218
John	Jef	16
Vincent	Jef	17
Sisul, Samuel	Way	354
Sittle, John	Fra	164
Six, Abraham	Ohi	71
Jacob	Mon	382
John	Ohi	77
Jacob	Ohi	82
John	Mon	360
Sizemore, Edw.	Cly	151
George	Cly	153
John	Cly	151
Rhoda	Cly	155
Skaaggs, Archd.	Adr	13
Skaags, Henry	Adr	14
Skaggs, David	Grn	251
Eliza	Grn	253
Elizabeth	Grn	250
Henry	Grn	251
Henry	Grn	254
Henry	Liv	148
James	Grn	251
James	Grn	253
James	Grn	265
Jane	Grn	254
Jeremiah	Grn	253
Moses	Grn	265
Stephus	Grn	254
Thomas	Grn	249
Skan, Thos.	Boo	62
Skean, Elenaor	Jes	53
Skeen, Aron	Chr	64
David	Jes	51
Skeets, Josiah	Clr	142
Skeigs, Henry	Hrd	289
Jas.	Hrd	289
Skelton, Powel	She	230
Sketoe, Joseph	Mul	395
William	Mul	395
Skeys, Richard	Mad	225
Skggs, Daniel	War	257
James	War	246
Joseph	War	246
Skidmire, William	Hnr	365
Skidmore, Charity	Mad	225
Henry	Mad	221
John	Bar	46
John	Knx	63
Jos.	Cly	149
Joseph	Grp	273
Joseph	Grp	278
Joseph	Lin	133
Paul	Mon	371
Samuel	Grp	278
Thomas	Mad	225
Skiles, Henry	Bul	184
Henry	War	257
Jacob	War	251
Thomas	Nel	27
Wm.	War	262
Skilman, Christr.	Bou	107

Skilman, cont.
  John Clr 141
Skilsen, George Lin 134
Skinner, Clarke Est 8
  Coatland Est 8
  Cornelius bul 184
  Cornelius Clr 141
  Isaac Jef 16
  Jesse Hnd 341
  John Clr 141
  John Est 8
  John Mad 221
  Joseph Mad 226
  Leonard Ohi 78
  Richard Fle 78
  Richard Fle 83
  Richard Nel 27
  Theophilas Chr 97
  William Chr 98
  William Chr 105
  Wily Chr 97
  Wm. Hrs 320
  Wm. Hrs 322
Skirvin, Absolam Pen 109
  Clayton Woo 386
  John Pen 116
Slack, Jacob Mas 284
  John Mas 283
  John Mas 284
  John Wsh 316
  Randal Hrd 287
  Randolp Wsh 315
  Wm. Hrd 287
Slade, James Chr 83
  James Chr 106
Slades, Sary Hrs 318
  Wm. Hrs 318
Sladyen, John Mad 221
Slagle, John Wsh 345
  Peter Way 360
Slanderford, James She 211
Slaning, Robert Gra 242
Slankard, George Chr 98
  Henry Chr 98
Slater, Joseph Cum 180
Slaton, Dabney Bar 46
  Edwd. Hop 374
  John Adr 14
  John Hop 374
  Tyre Adr 14
Slatter, Josh. Adr 13
Slaughter, Austin Mer 332
  Cad Mer 335
  Charles Fra 164
  Elizabeth Knx 75
  Fanny Mer 331
  Francis Fra 163
  Gabriel Mer 335
  Geo. Senr Bou 131
  George Bou 68
  Harrison Mer 333
  James Mer 341
  Jas. Nel 23
  Jas. P. Nel 26
  Jesse Mer 334
  John Jef 17
  Mathew Lin 134
  Presley Chr 107
  Ransdale Jef 14
  Robert Mer 332
  Robt. C. Hrd 289
  Tho. Nel 25
  Tho. K. Bar 34
  Thos. S. Log 175
  William Hnr 359B
Slaves, John Mul 385
Slavin, John Gar 222
Slavins, Isaiah Mon 373
  Reubin Mon 373
Slayden, Arthur Woo 390
Slayton, Arthur Hop 379
Sled, Thomas Bou 109
Sleet, Drucilla Gar 217
  Finlason Gar 217
Sleett, Weden Boo 62
Sligar, David Bul 184
Slinker, Fedk. Grn 253
  Henry Grn 249
  Henry Grn 253
  John Grn 251
  John Grn 261
  Malinda Grn 251
Sloan, James Grn 257
  John Jef 26
  John Rck 159
  John She 231
  Joseph Hop 371
  Thomas Bre 158
Slockham, John Lew 100
  John, Jr Lew 98
Slocumb, Samuel Hnd 339
Slone, Archibald Bar 45
  James Flo 102
  James Pul 138
  John Bar 26
  Mary Flo 102
  Shadrack Flo 102
  Thomas Knx 84
  William Pul 139
  William Pul 140
Sloop, Joseph Nic 60
Sloss, John War 262
  Joseph Log 169
Slpaham, Richd. Hop 375
Sluder, David Cas 42
  Isaac Jes 54
Slusher, Jacob Flo 102
  Philip Knx 80
Sluss, Adams Clr 147
Smack, Godward Mer 334
Small, Benjamin Mas 282
  Catharin War 251
  Geo. Cly 149
  George Mon 355
  Henry Log 179
  James Mas 282
  John Bou 111
  John Log 162
  John Log 179
  John Way 363
  Mary Log 179
  Matthew Way 373
  Samuel Mul 396
  Thos. Way 355
  Wm. Way 373
Smalley, Abraham Cum 172
  Andw. Cum 171
  Joshua Bou 108
Smallwood, Elijah Cly 157
  John She 210
  Randolph She 203
  Samuel Hrd 281
  Samuel She 202
  William Mad 222
Smally, Andrew Mas 285
  John Nic 61
  Susanna Mas 283
  William Mas 283
Smart, Edmond Mon 352
  Elisha Mon 352
  James, Senr Fra 162
  John Fra 170
  Labourn War 246
  Richard Fra 162
Smart, cont.
  Samuel Mas 285
  Thos. L. Fra 162
Smawley, Joshua Chr 102
  Josiph Chr 115
Smawlwood, Bean Mon 354
Smedley, Aaron Bou 68
  Christopher Fay 16
  Samuel Fay 26
  Samuel, Junr Fay 27
Smeller, Paula Hop 371
Smelser, Peter Hrs 310
Smelsor, Steven Chr 79
Smelzer, Adam Bou 110
  Barbary Bou 110
  John Bou 109
  John Bou 110
Smethers, Andrew Mon 370
  James Ohi 91
  Joseph Mon 357
  Thomas Mon 352
  William Ohi 83
Smiley, David Hrs 314
  Henry Nel 24
  Henry Nel 27
  James Nel 6
  Jesse Nel 24
  John Cas 37
  John Fra 163
  Rachl. Nel 24
  Saml. Nel 7
Smily, Danl. Cum 168
  Jas. Way 374
Smiser, Henry She 228
  Michael She 227
Smith, A. Wm. Bar 50
  Aaron Fay 49
  Aaron Mul 402
  Abner Ary Mon 374
  Abra. Cas 37
  Abraham Bou 108
  Abraham Knx 63
  Abraham She 241
  Abram Nic 61
  Abriham Chr 91
  Abrm. Cal 5
  Absolom Bar 50
  Adam Jef 16
  Adam Nel 27
  Adam She 238
  Adrew Lew 103
  Alexander Jes 50
  Alexander Mon 377
  Alexr. Woo 385
  Ally Gra 240
  Ameriah Mon 366
  Amos BAr 31
  Amos Nel 25
  Andrew Fay 26
  Andrew Mad 225
  Andw. Way 362
  Ann Clr 147
  Ann Mas 303
  Anthony Mon 357
  Aquila Lew 101
  Archd. Bra 152
  Archd. Cam 25
  Armstead Nel 22
  Aron War 275
  Arther Lin 135
  Asa Gar 220
  Augustin Boo 63
  Augustine Gar 221
  B. William Mas 283
  Barnabass Log 193
  Bazil Wsh 312
  Becky Cum 185

Smith, cont.
Ben Nel 27
Benja. Fle 88
Benjamin Cal 18
Benjamin Fay 34
Benjamin Fay 45
Benjamin Ohi 97
Benjamin She 221
Benjn. Cam 26
Benjn. Log 180
Bennett Mad 221
Bent. Nel 6
Berryman Sco 182
Brooks Knx 74
Catharine Jef 27
Caty War 248
Charles Adr 13
Charles Cly 160
Charles Grn 252
Charles Hrs 312
Charles Hrs 313
Charles Lin 135
Charles Mad 226
Charles Nel 27
Chas. Coln. Bou 109
Chas. Nel 27
Christn. Adr 13
Cristopher Gar 217
Clemon Fay 46
Clifton Sco 176
Cols. Grn 261
Cooley Wsh 315
Cornelius Pul 134
Cristeney Bou 131
Daniel Bou 111
Daniel Hnr 357
Daniel Jef 27
Daniel She 215
Daniel J. War 249
Daniel J. Hnd 348
Danl. War 362
Darky Fay 45
David Bra 144
David Cal 18
David Cam 28
David Chr 112
David Fay 58
David Fay 60
David Grn 262
David Hrd 284
David Jef 15
David Mas 281
David Nic 62
David War 245
David War 257
David, Jr Pul 134
David, Sr Hnr 365
David, Sn Pul 135
Drury War 280
Ebby Mon 348
Ebenezer Cam 25
Edmund Gar 219
Edmund, Snr Gar 218
Edward Bre 165
Edward Pul 137
Edward She 217
Edward Wsh 316
Edward B. Wsh 316
Elexander Fay 53
Elias Gar 217
Elias Mul 407
Elias Nel 26
Elias G. Hop 374
Elihu Hrd 281
Elijah Bou 111
Elijah Fay 26
Elijah Mon 366

Smith, cont.
Elijah Rck 161
Elisha Liv 159
Elizabeth Pul 134
Elizabeth War 251
Ely Mul 386
Enoch Mon 381
Enoch, Senr Mon 372
Enoch Fay 16
Ephraim Log 189
Eunice Bul 185
Ezekle War 248
Federeck Bar 31
Fielding Fay 31
Fleming Cum 176
Foster Knx 89
Frances Fay 46
Francis Fay 17
Francis Grn 262
Francis Jes 53
Frederick Cum 169
Gabriel Gra 240
Gambol Gar 218
Geo. Cam 24
George Bra 142
George Cam 28
George Cum 185
George Fra 168
George Hnd 348
George Hrs 310
George Jef 14
George Jes 51
George Pul 136
George Rck 164
George She 206
George She 214
George She 221
George She 235
George War 271
George Woo 389
George, Junr Ohi 76
Geromiah Cly 157
Gidion Bra 152
Giles She 211
Godfrey War 243
Greenbury Fay 25
H. Lewis Fay 16
Hardy Ohi 97
Hawkins Bou 111
Henry Adr 14
Henry Clr 142
Henry Fle 90
Henry Gar 218
Henry Jef 17
Henry Knx 87
Henry Lew 96
Henry Lew 102
Henry Log 180
Henry Mon 357
Henry Mon 375
Henry Sco 175
Henry Sco 176
Henry She 201
Henry She 201
Henry Woo 392
Herrard Bar 50
Herry Cam 28
Hizahs Nic 60
Horace Mer 331
Horratio Nel 26
Howel War 271
Hugh Bar 36
Hugh Mer 332
Hugh Mer 332
Hugh Nic 62
Humble Mer 332
Humphrey Woo 388

Smith, cont.
Isaac Bra 149
Isaac Cal 17
Isaac Cam 28
Isaac Cas 47
Isaac Knx 74
Isaac Lew 96
Isaac Pul 135
Isaac Rck 164
Isaac Sco 176
Isabel Mon 357
Jabel Cly 154
Jackman Gra 241
Jacob Bar 25
Jacob Bar 26
Jacob Bar 43
Jacob Bou 107
Jacob Bou 108
Jacob Clr 140
Jacob Gal 192
Jacob Grn 251
Jacob Grp 269
Jacob Hrs 320
Jacob Jef 17
Jacob Jes 50
Jacob Jes 51
Jacob Log 184
Jacob War 245
James Adr 13
James Bar 38
James Bou 130
James Cal 16
James Cal 18
James Cam 24
James Cas 39
James Chr 78
James Chr 91
James Cum 167
James Cum 180
James Cum 186
James Est 5
James Gal 190
James Grn 247
James Hnr 356
James Hrd 300
James Hrs 311
James Jef 15
James Knx 87
James Knx 89
James Lew 100
James Lin 134
James Lin 135
James Log 161
James Log 176
James Log 179
James Mad 223
James Mul 402
James Mer 332
James Mer 334
James Pul 137
James Pul 137
James Sco 175
James Sco 189
James Sco 193
James Wsh 316
James, Jr Pen 112
James, Senr Fay 46
James, Sr Pen 109
James Arra Sco 169
James T. Knx 87
Jarret Lew 98
Jarrot Sco 172
Jas. Gar 219
Jas. Gar 221
Jas. Hrd 298
Jas. Mad 221
Jas. Nic 60

Smith, cont.
Jeramiah Cam 24
Jeremiah Cum 168
Jeremiah Knx 76
Jesse Cum 184
Jesse Gar 218
Jesse Hop 373
Jesse Lin 135
Jesse Mer 331
Jessee Cam 28
Jessy Bou 108
Jno. Bar 51
Jno. Hrd 298
Jno. G. Mad 224
Joab War 266
Joel Woo 389
John Adr 19
John Bar 38
John Bar 41
John Boo 63
John Bou 109
John Bou 109
John Bra 153
John Bul 184
John Cal 7
John Cal 13
John Cas 38
John Chr 54
John Clr 140
John Clr 142
John Cly 154
John Cly 156
John Cly 156
John Cly 160
John Cum 179
John Fay 42
John Fle 65
John Fle 85
John Fra 163
John Fra 165
John Fra 168
John Gar 217
John Gar 219
John Gra 242
John Grn 247
John Grn 250
John Grn 255
John Grn 255
John Grn 256
John Grn 263
John Hnd 330
John Hnd 339
John Hnr 354
John Hrs 312
John Hrs 315
John Hrs 317
John Hrs 318
John Jef 17
John Jef 17
John Jef 23
John Jef 25
John Jes 50
John Jes 52
John Jes 54
John Knx 72
John Knx 88
John Knx 91
John Lin 134
John Lin 135
John Lin 135
John Log 161
John Log 163
John Mad 221
John Mad 225
John Mer 332
John Mer 332
John Mer 334

Smith, cont.
John Mon 357
John Mon 361
John Mul 392
John Mul 402
John Nic 61
John Pen 108
John Pul 134
John Pul 137
John Pul 137
John Pul 137
John Sco 171
John Sco 171
John Sco 178
John She 219
John She 240
John War 260
John War 264
John War 270
John War 270
John War 280
John Way 354
John Way 359
John Way 364
John Woo 382
John Woo 391
John Woo 392
John Wsh 311
John Wsh 316
John, jr Mad 221
John B. Sco 171
John B. War 276
John I. Wsh 316
John K. Log 162
Jonathan Gal 191
Jonathan Gra 244
Jonathan Log 187
Jonathan Mas 308
Jonathan Pul 136
Jonathan Rck 166
Jonathan, Jr Knx 85
Jonathan, Sr Knx 85
Jonathn. Cum 171
Jos. Hrd 294
Jos. War 261
Jos. D. Grn 257
Joseph BAr 37
Joseph Bou 109
Joseph Bou 111
Joseph Bou 111
Joseph Cal 17
Joseph Cas 39
Joseph Cum 185
Joseph Fle 85
Joseph Mer 330
Joseph Mon 353
Joseph Mon 374
Joseph Sco 170
Joseph She 201
Joseph Woo 388
Josiah Knx 74
Jseph War 258
Judy Jef 14
Kitty Gar 220
Laurance War 260
Leroy Hnd 338
Leven Bou 130
Lewis Sco 176
Lewis Sco 180
Liberty Gar 224
Margaret Mas 282
Margaret Mas 308
Martain Cas 38
Martin Adr 13
Martin Bou 107
Martin Clr 141
Marry Fle 86

Smith, cont.
Mary, Fle 85
Mary Wsh 316
Meley Nel 28
Michael Cam 26
Michael Hrs 312
Michael Jef 14
Michael Mon 374
Michl. Bar 26
Milley Cum 167
Millington Log 187
Millington log 194
Mitchel Nic 61
Moses Grp 272
Moses Sco 176
Moses, Junr Cum 167
Moses, Senr Cum 167
Nancy Cum 167
Nancy Hnr 359A
Nathan Hnd 325
Nathl. Knx 66
Nathn. Boo 63
Neemiah Pen 110
Nelson Sco 169
Nicholas Bou 110
Nicholas Gar 224
Nicholas She 231
Nicholas Wsh 316
Nichos. Hnr 359B
Ooel Fay 25
Paul Hrs 324
Peter Bou 110
Peter Bul 184
Peter Gal 192
Peter Hnr 365
Peter Hrs 311
Peter Mon 369
Peter Rck 159
Peyton War 256
Philip Jef 18
Philip War 257
Phillip Jes 52
Phillip Way 361
Plesly Wsh 316
Polly Bou 111
Prudence Liv 154
R. Jer. Gar 219
Rachal Bar 51
Ralph Adr 19
Ralph Bou 111
Randail Grp 277
Randlee Cly 155
Rebecka Fle 75
Reuben Lin 133
Reuben She 211
Rhubin Hrs 311
Rice Fay 41
Richard Grp 277
Richd. Cly 150
Richd. Cly 152
Richd. B. Bou 108
Robert Cly 154
Robert Cum 168
Robert Hnd 328
Robert Liv 148
Robert Liv 151
Robert Mas 280
Robert Pul 135
Robert Pul 137
Robert Pul 138
Robert Sco 180
Robert She 221
Robert M. Grp 274
Robo. (N) Hnr 361
Robt. Jr Hnr 365
Robt. (Sr) Hnr 361
Rodes Sco 181

Smith, cont.
Rubin She 199
Sally Gar 223
Saml. Adr 13
Saml. Bar 50
Saml. Bra 153
Saml. Cal 19
Saml. Clr 150
Saml. Cum 169
Saml. Cum 176
Saml. Cum 181
Saml. Gar 219
Saml. War 263
Samuel Bul 185
Samuel Chr 81
Samuel Chr 108
Samuel Lew 104
Samuel Mon 363
Samuel Mon 373
Samuel Mon 375
Samuel She 238
Samuel Woo 387
Samuel Wsh 316
Sarah Hnd 345
Scarlet Lin 135
Simion Jes 54
Solomon Bar 45
Solomon Mer 331
Spencer Cal 18
Stafford Hrd 301
Stephen Cam 29
Stephen Liv 145
Stephen Log 195
Stephen Nel 23
Stephen Nel 23
Stephen Nel 26
Stephen Pul 138
Stephen Pul 140
Stephen She 205
Stephen Wsh 312
Susanna Woo 393
Tarrance Wsh 316
Temple Hrs 310
Theresa Wsh 316
Thomas Bou 110
Thomas Chr 57
Thomas Clr 142
Thomas Fra 166
Thomas Fra 168
Thomas Gra 242
Thomas Grn 255
Thomas Grp 277
Thomas Hnr 359
Thomas Jes 51
Thomas Mad 222
Thomas Mer 332
Thomas Mon 376
Thomas Ohi 90
Thomas Pul 134
Thomas Wsh 320
Thomas, Senr Gra 241
Thoms. Nel 25
Thos. Adr 13
Thos. Boo 63
Thos. Cly 154
Thos. Cum 167
Thos. Cum 168
Thos. Grn 250
Thos. Sco 171
Thos. War 260
Thos. H. War 261
Turner Adr 12
Turner Wsh 312
Usley Mad 220
Washington Hrd 282
Weathers Bou 110
Wethers Bou 131

Smith, cont.
Will Cly 156
William Cly 156
William Est 7
William Est 7
William Fay 25
William Fay 31
William Fay 45
William Fay 47
William Fay 53
William Fra 168
William Fra 169
William Knx 89
William Liv 145
William Mul 392
William Nic 62
William Ohi 93
William Pen 108
William She 208
William Woo 402
William Wsh 312
William Wsh 316
William Wsh 316
William Wsh 137
William, Jr Pen 115
William, Sr Pen 116
William B. Ohi 90
Williams Pul 136
Willm. Sco 168
Willm. Sco 171
Wm. Adr 13
Wm. Adr 14
Wm. Bar 50
Wm. Boo 63
Wm. Bra 153
Wm. Cam 32
Wm. Cas 48
Wm. Cum 167
Wm. Cum 168
Wm. Cum 169
Wm. Cum 173
Wm. Gar 219
Wm. Jnr Gar 219
Wm. Gar 222
Wm. Hrd 295
Wm. Jef 27
Wm. Lin 135
Wm. Mon 347
Wm. Mon 366
Wm. Mon 373
Wm. Mon 373
Wm. Rck 160
Wm., Colo. Rck 163
Wm. Sco 173
Wm. Sco 176
Wm. Sco 181
Wm. War 260
Wm. Way 354
Wm. Way 358
Wm. I. Bre 166
Woodson Grp 278
Zach. Gar 219
Zachariah Mer 332
Zadock Bou 130
Smither, Benjn. Woo 385
James Fra 166
Jno. Hrd 298
John Fra 168
Leonard Fra 166
Polly Fra 167
Reuben Jef 18
Robert Nel 25
Samuel Woo 384
William Woo 392
William Woo 397
Wm. Boo 63
Smithers, John Mon 378

Smithey, Fielding Fay 44
George Bou 107
Smithy, Thomas Mer 333
Smoch, John Bul 184
Smock, Abraham Mer 331
Abraham She 241
Barnett Mer 333
Henry Mer 334
Henry Wsh 317
Jacob Mer 331
James Bul 184
James Mer 331
Jeremiah Bou 131
John Mer 331
John She 201
Matthew She 238
Matthias Bul 185
Peter Wsh 317
Smoot, Alexanr. Jef 17
Armstead Hrd 297
Beaston Fle 75
Claburn Fle 72
George Fra 166
John Gra 241
John Hrd 297
Leonard Fra 165
Philip B. Bou 71
William R. Fra 165
Smothers, Daniel Wsh 317
Hugh Bar 25
James Wsh 317
Smuck, John Jef 17
Smullen, Louden Bou 111
Smuthers, William Fra 165
Smyth, Henry Way 372
Snack, Godliss Lin 135
Snap, George Nic 60
Laurence Grn 262
Lewis Hrd 302
Peter Nic 60
Samuel Nic 60
Snead, Achillis(Plantation) Fra 164
Achillis Fra 169
William Fra 164
Sneathen, Will Cly 155
Snediger, Moses Fle 73
Sneed, Alexander Mer 333
Charles Knx 76
Charles Pul 135
James Jef 15
John Grn 256
John Mer 331
Landon She 232
Mary Grn 265
Patrick She 215
Saml. C. Gal 192
Wm. Gar 223
Wm. Grn 265
Snelagan, Elendar Mon 364
Snell, Charles Hnr 359B
Cumberland Sco 175
Jacob Fle 86
John Jef 27
John Sco 187
Joseph Bou 109
Lewis Hrs 313
Louden Fra 166
William Sco 190
Snellen, Benjn. Mon 377
Snellenbarger, John Bul 185
Snelling, Alexander Bre 161
Anthony Wsh 320
Benjamin Bre 165
Enoch Bre 161
Hugh Bre 160
Jessee Woo 387

Snelling, John Woo 387
  William Nel 26
  Wm. Bou 131
Snelson, Mylard Mon 348
Snider, Adam Clr 141
  Andrew Fle 73
  Anthony Jef 16
  Anthony, Jr Jef 15
  Baltzer Fra 169
  Christopher Fra 170
  Christopher Mas 286
  Frederick Knx 69
  Harmon She 238
  Jacob Jef 16
  Jacob Knx 69
  Jacob Nel 27
  jacob, Sr Jef 18
  John Fle 92
  John Gra 242
  John Jef 16
  John Sco 177
  John Nel 26
  John She 234
  Jonas She 207
  Joseph Jef 18
  Peter Knx 65
  Shadrick Gra 238
  Simon Knx 69
Smiser, Jacob Jef 16
Snither, Jacob She 208
Snoddy, Furgus Bou 108
  John Bou 108
  John Gar 222
  John Mad 224
  Samuel Mad 225
Snodgrass, Benjn. Bou 108
  David But 197
  Hugh Wsh 317
  Isaac Cas 40
  John Hnd 333
  Joseph Bou 108
  Joseph Log 177
  Robert Wsh 317
Snodter, John Jef 16
  Thomas Jef 16
Snolke, John Nel 24
Snotgrass, ... Hrs 314
  John Hrs 318
  Robert Hrs 318
  Samuel Hrs 314
  Thomas Hrs 305
  Wm. Hrs 321
Snow, Aquilla Liv 152
  Benjamin Boo 63
  Frastin Lin 133
  George Est 6
  John Bar 40
  Leonard Lin 133
  Nicodemos Lin 134
  Saml. Lin 133
  Thomas War 269
  Willm. War 243
  Wm. Cum 173
Snowden, Jacob War 255
  James War 255
Snowdon, Charles Clr 142
  David Clr 142
Snyder, Adam Woo 389
  Joseph Wsh 317
Soap, Joseph Mon 348
  Joseph Mon 370
Soaper, Charles Bou 108
Sodouskey,Jacob Jr Jes 52
  Jacob, Sr Jes 52
Sodousky, Ephraim Jes 52
Sodowsky, Andrew Bou 109
Sohridge, Chs. Hnr 368
Solans, Peter Way 355
Soliman(freeman) Fay 16
Sollaman, Elisa-
    beth Fay 40
Sollody, Daniel Hrs 308
  Jasob Hrs 307
Solomon,Elijah Log 184
  Henry Way 374
  John Mas 308
  William Knx 84
Solyers, David Hop 373
Son, Michael Cal 16
Soper, John Jes 50
  John Jes 53
Sord, Henry Gar 220
Sorrel, Elijah Mon 375
  James Mon 366
  John Bar 38
Sorrell, James Fle 83
Sorrels, Elleanor Fra 169
Sorril, Redmom Pul 140
Soterfield, John War 273
Sotherlen, Jesse Bra 141
Souder, Solomon Bou 110
Souerkelser,George Hnd 345
Sourbright, George Fay 16
Sourds, Daniel Pen 107
Sourency, Jacob Mon 378
Sourincy, David Mon 360
Sously, Henry Bul 184
South, Ann Gal 196
  Benjn. Mon 373
  Henry Wsh 318
  John Fay 25
  John Way 358
  Samuel Mad 225
  Weldon bou 108
  William Mad 226
  William Wsh 318
Southard, Benjamin Ohi 79
  James Pen 110
  John Lin 133
  Larrance Pen 110
  Wm. Nel 25
  Zekiah Fle 78
Souther, Abram. Boo 63
  Henry Jef 14
  Henry Jef 27
  Jacob Jef 27
  Jessee Bar 51
  Joseph Bar 19
Southerland, Jno. Nel 25
  Philip Knx 71
  Wm. Lew 101
Southerlund, Santy Mad 220
Southerlin, Enos Lin 133
Southern, Boaz War 270
Southgate, Richd. Cam 33
Southren, William Mer 331
Southwood, Wm. Way 353
Soward, Fisha Flo 102
  John Sco 168
Sowards, Charles Mas 286
  Elijah Mas 309
Sowdar, John Jes 51
Sowder, David Rck 161
  Michael Rck 160
  Peter Rck 163
Sowdusky, Jas. Bou 109
  Thos. Bou 109
Sowel, George Chr 77
Sowsby, David, Jur Fle 71
Spaar, Saml. Grn 257
  Thos. Grn 257
Spadlin, Jas. Way 363
Spadon, John Jef 18
Spalding, Aaron Wsh 320
Spalding, cont.
  Benedict Wsh 317
  Benedict Wsh 317
  Bennet Wsh 320
  Chas. War 251
  Edward Wsh 320
  Henry Jef 14
  Ignatius Wsh 320
  James Wsh 320
  Jas. Nel 27
  Joseph Wsh 318
  Moses C. Fra 167
  Nancy Wsh 321
  Peter Nel 22
  Richard Wsh 317
  Richard Wsh 317
  Richard Wsh 321
  Sally Nel 25
  Stephen Wsh 319
  Thomas Wsh 320
  Wilson Fra 162
Span, Elizabeth War 277
Spangler, Danl. Woo 399
  John Fay 25
Spann, Aron War 280
  Jeramiah War 266
  Jesse Gar 222
  Solomon Gar 222
  Thos. War 266
Spark, Wm. Adr 14
Sparkes, Benjamin She 204
Sparks, Anthony Fra 166
  Catherine Bou 108
  Daniel Bul 184
  David Pul 134
  Elijah ESt 5
  Elijah Jef 17
  Elizabeth Fle 76
  George Est 5
  George Lew 99
  George Mer 334
  Henry Fra 166
  Humphrey Sco 173
  Isaac Est 1
  Isaac, Senr Est 1
  James Bou 107
  James Bou 109
  James Bou 131
  James Fra 165
  James Jef 14
  James Jef 18
  John Bou 109
  John Est 1
  Joseph Lew 95
  Martin Mad 220
  Mathw. Adr 13
  Matthew She 210
  Richd. She 224
  Robert Lin 133
  Samuel Bul 184
  Stephen Jef 15
  Thos. Hrd 297
  Walter Jef 17
  William Est 1
  Willm. Sco 190
  Wm. Bou 107
  Wm. Jef 17
Sparrow, Elias Log 187
  Henry Mer 331
  Peter Bar 27
  Thos. Hrd 297
Spars, James Lin 134
Spates, Robert Mas 281
  Samuel Bou 131
Spaugh, Henry Nic 59
  Jacob Nic 60
Spaulding,James Woo 402

Spaulding, cont.
  Robinson Woo 382
  William Woo 402
Spaw, Daniel Clr 140
Speak, Basil Adr 13
  James Nel 28
  John Adr 13
  John Jef 14
Speakmon, Thos. Bar 44
Speaks, Hezekiah Bou 110
  Joseph Hnr 353
  Joseph Mad 221
Spearman, Wm. Cum 174
Spears, Christian Bou 107
  Christina Lin 133
  David Lin 133
  George Grn 251
  George Jef 15
  Jacob Bou 109
  Jacob Lin 135
  Jane Jes 50
  John Fay 25
  John Grn 259
  Moses Cas 42
  Squire Hnr 368
  Thos. Grn 252
  William Grn 251
  William Pul 138
Speck, Jacob Cum 184
Speece, Frederick Bra 147
Speed, James Mer 331
  John Cas 41
  John, Jr Jef 16
  John, Sr Jef 15
  Lewis Jef 18
  Matthias, Jun Cas 38
  Matthias Cas 39
  Thomas Nel 23
Speer, Andrew She 228
  Andrew She 228
  Aron Hnr 353
  Ben, Junr Cum 179
  Ben, Senr Cum 179
  Henry Hnr 368
  John Cum 1[illegible]9
  John Hnr 353
  John K. Hnr 358
  Joseph Cum 179
  Richd. Cum 179
  William She 228
Speers, Jos. K. Hnr 365
  Levi Cum 177
  Robert Fra 164
  Thomas Flo 103
  Thos. Cum 179
  Wm. Cum 179
Spelerner, John Way 371
Spellers, Edward Log 189
Spence, James Mad 225
  John Ohi 87
  Jonas Lew 98
  Malice Mad 220
  Robert Liv 158
  Thomas Grn 247
  Wm. Mon 368
Spencemire, Phillip Cas 46
Spencer, Amasa Pul 135
  Barnard Pen 110
  Charles R. Jes 53
  David Jes 50
  Edward Gal 191
  Francis Pen 114
  George Nel 25
  Isaac Mas 282
  James Fle 92
  James Pul 138
  Jesse Knx 65
Spencer, cont.
  John Bar 37
  John Bou 107
  John Bul 184
  John Lin 133
  John She 216
  Joseph Pen 110
  Marry Fle 92
  Moses Bar 37
  Moses Jes 51
  Moses, Junr Bar 37
  Richard Hnd 328
  Robertson Wsh 317
  Saml. Bar 46
  Samuel Bre 161
  Sharp Nel 23
  Thos. Cum 169
  Walter Hnr 359
  William Bul 185
  William Liv 160
  Wm. Bou 131
Spensar, John Chr 86
Spensor, Jeffery Mer 334
Sperry, James Grp 275
  Samuel Grp 271
  Thomas Adr 19
Sphar, James Clr 141
Spicer, Cain Fra 168
  Elizabeth Fra 166
  Leanuel Cas 47
  Rauser Bou 109
Spiers, James Jes 53
  Joshua Fra 165
  Samuel Fay 26
  Spencer Flo 102
Spiker, John Clr 141
Spilers, Thomas Mon 380
Spill, Reding Liv 159
Spiller, Polly Bou 110
  William Fay 42
Spillman, Rot. War 269
  Thos. War 269
Spilman, Charles Gar 216
  Charles Gar 219
  Frank Cam 31
  James Grn 261
  James Woo 377
  Mary Gal 189
  Tho. Gar 216
  Thomas Gal 189
Spilmon, Benjamin Mul 398
  George Hnr 354
  Henry Hnr 355
  Jac. Hnr 354
  James Clr 147
Spilts, Joseph Grn 266
Spiner, Benja. Fle 85
Spink, Francis Wsh 321
  Ignatious Hrd 298
  Raphal Jef 27
  William Wsh 318
Spinks, Thos. War 245
Spires, Catherine Fay 25
  Greenberry Fay 26
  John Lin 133
  Willm. Lin 133
Spirlock, William Knx 87
Spoldwin, Aaron Cam 28
Spoon, Conrad Sco 176
  Jacob Clr 141
  Lucy Bou 111
Spoonanine, Fredk. Lin 135
  Henry Lin 135
Spooner, Gracy Fay 16
Spoonhoward, Hennery Cas 40
Spoonhouard, John Cas 38
Sportsman, Jacob Mer 332
Spotswood, Alexander Bar 46
Spradlin, Jas. War 260
Spraggens, James Cas 45
Spraggins, Jesse Lin 134
Sprigins, Nathanil Lin 133
Sprague, Ebenezer Woo 379
Sprake, Thomas Bou 69
Sprate, William Lin 134
Spratt, Andrew Mon 370
Spraul, Joseph Lin 134
Spray, Abner Ohi 100
Spriger, George Jes 54
Sprigg, Leven Nel 23
  Robert Liv 145
  Thos. Nel 27
Spriggs, Daniel Grp 271
Sprigs, David Bre 168
  Thomas Nel 23
Springate, John Mer 333
  William Mer 333
Springer, Charles Bre 168
  Charles Fra 169
  Edward Wsh 318
  Ezikiel Bar 49
  Gabriel Fay 40
  Gabriel Fra 169
  Isaac Wsh 320
  Jacob Jes 49
  John Bar 44
  John Jes 51
  John Wsh 318
  John Wsh 318
  Joseph Wsh 318
  Levi Wsh 318
  Nel Sco 171
  Robert Wsh 318
  Willm. Sco 171
Springston, Abraham Bre 162
Sprinkle, George Hnd 337
  Jacob Hnd 344
  John Fay 16
  Michael [illegible] 344
Spriougher?, Catherine Liv 160
Sprott, John War 259
Sproual, Joseph Lin 135
Sprouce, George Chr 70
Sproul, Alexr. Cum 170
  Oliver Mad 224
Sproule, Alexr. Grn 250
  Charles Fra 170
  Elijah Grn 258
  Jas. Gal 189
Sproull, James Hnr 351
Sprout, John Log 191
Spur, James Fay 26
  William Fay 26
Spurgen, Samuel Mon 384
Spurgeon, Isaac Cam 29
Spurgin, Betsey Bou 107
  David Bou 107
  James Bou 107
  Jeremiah Fle 83
  Moses Fle 82
  Saml. Fle 69
  Sarah Bou 107
  William Bou 107
  Wm. Bou 130
Spurling, William Chr 68
Spurlock, David Flo 102
  Jessee Cly 159
  John Cly 159
  John Flo 103
  Matthew Flo 102

Spurquier, Joseph Mas 286
Spurr, Daniel Fay 60
Spurrier, Aaron Gra 240
  Elisha Gra 240
  Jos. Hrd 285
  Richd. Hrd 285
Spurtsman, Peter Ohi 91
Squires, Caleb Fay 60
  George Adr 13
  George Adr 14
Squirs, Thomas Mad 223
Srance, Noolas Lin 133
Sreags, Abner Grn 259
Srieves, Wm. Grn 246
Srigby, Joseph Grn 256
Srineger, John Grn 248
Sriock, Friderick Fay 47
Sryock, John Fay 49
Stacey, Benjamin Cas 48
Stacy, Jno. Hrd 283
  Peter Cly 155
  Simon Flo 102
  Simon Pul 135
Stader, Ann Hrd 293
  Jno. Hrd 293
  Peter Hrd 293
Stadley, William Clr 141
Stafford, Absalom Flo 103
  Benjn. Jef 18
  Christopher Mas 281
  Gideon Sco 184
  Henry Gal 190
  John Gal 190
  Martin Gal 191
  Stewart Cal 9
  Thomas Jef 17
  Thomas Jef 17
  William Gal 192
  Willm. Sco 183
Stagg, Daniel Mer 334
  James Mer 332
  John Mer 332
Staggs, Daniel Mas 285
  James Fle 86
  John Mas 285
  Joseph Fle 86
  Joseph Mas 285
  Samuel Mas 280
Stagner, Barney Mad 220
  Jesse Mad 223
  John War 247
  John War 247
  Wm. War 247
Stagstill, Daniel Pul 135
Stahl, Simon Bou 69
Staiks, Joseph Chr 81
Stalcup, Aaron Cum 174
  Hannah Hnr 357
  Mark Liv 157
  Sevillien Flo 103
Staley, Adam Cam 29
  Flaty Fay 17
Staliard, Walter Nel 26
Stallcup, Margaret Wsh 321
Stallings, Henry Bul 183
  Hezekiah Wsh 322
  Joseph Wsh 322
  Samuel Bul 183
  William Wsh 318
Stallions, Ruben Chr 61
Stalsworth, Jessee Bar 32
Stambridge, William Mul 394
Stamp, Mildred War 266
Stampard, John Mon 382
  Richard Mon 382
Stamper, Jacob Pen 108
  Jesse Pen 108
Stamper, cont.
  Joseph Clr 142
Stamps, Wm. Bou 107
Stanbow, Jacob Chr 87
Stanclift, Joseph Mon 363
Standard, John Chr 114
  Thomas Chr 114
  William Chr 76
Standeford, James Jef 16
  Nathan C. Bou 68
Standerford, David She 220
  Job Pul 139
  Samuel Pul 139
  Skelton Pul 139
  Will She 222
Standiford, Agnl. Nic 61
  George Nic 59
  Jarrel Hrd 294
  Jno. W. Hrd 300
  Sarah Nic 59
Standler, Syphorus But 197
Standley, Jonathan Clr 141
Stanfield, John Cum 182
  Salomon Cal 11
  Saml. Cum 183
  Sampson Knx 76
  Thos. Cum 182
Stanford, James Woo 391
  John Chr 86
Stanley, Anderson Mer 331
  Jacob Log 190
  James Chr 81
  John She 214
  Joseph Flo 102
  Spencer Mul 387
  Thomas Log 172
  William Fay 16
  William Mul 386
  Wm. Cam 25
Stanly, Anderson Log 177
  Solomon Log 177
  Stephen Hnd 338
Stans, Saml. War 251
Stansberry, Benjamin Bul 184
  Josiah Mon 373
Stansbury, Benjamin Fra 162
  Saloman Cly 149
  Thomas Bul 184
Stansley, Jessey Gra 240
Stanton, Fleming Gar 221
  Mat Mad 222
  Richard Pul 135
  Thomas Cas 40
  Thos. Cas 43
  Thos. Gar 221
  Wm. Cas 41
Stanup, Robert Fay 55
Stap, John Adr 13
Staphenson, James - Jur Sco 169
  James, Senr Sco 169
  Willm. Sco 169
Staples, Edmund Log 187
  James Hnd 336
  Jas. Hnr 357
  William Hnd 336
Stapleton, Edward Knx 82
  George Fay 25
  John Bre 169
  Joseph Knx 75
  Thomas Knx 88
  William Knx 91
  William Mad 224
Stapp, Benjn. Adr 13
  James Adr 13
Stapp, cont.
  James Woo 383
  John Hnd 345
Star, Adam Clr 141
  Jeremiah Jef 16
Starca, Permela Cam 32
Stares, John Bre 166
Stark, Aaron Bul 185
  Abner Hnr 357
  Benjamin Hnr 357
  Daniel Bul 185
  David Hnr 357
  David Mas 280
  David, Junr Jnr 357
  Elisha Hnr 357
  Hannah Hnr 357
  James She 202
  James War 279
  Jeramiah War 279
  Jesse Cum 179
  Jesse War 279
  Jno. Hnr 357
  John Bou 107
  John Fay 16
  John Log 195
  John War 279
  John, Junr Hnr 357
  Jonathan Cum 179
  Phillip Hnr 357
  Raleigh War 279
  Reuben Hnr 359A
  Stephen Hnr 357
  Thomas Bou 107
  William Bul 185
Starkey, Stacy Fle 69
  James Bou 131
  Jessy Chr 73
  John Chr 71
Starks, John Fay 53
  Nancy Mer 341
  Rubin Chr 73
  Thomas Log 169
  William Bou 131
Starling, Thos. H. Woo 379
Starnes, John Liv 159
Starnetter, Joseph Jef 16
Starns, Frederick Mer 333
  John Rck 162
Starr, Christopher Jes 50
  Henry Jes 51
  Jacob Bou 107
  Jacob Bou 130
  Jas. Way 359
Starrett, Thomas War 251
Stass, John Adr 13
Stateler, George Ohi 91
Staten, John Cal 7B
  Joseph Wsh 321
  Obed Wsh 321
  Peter Wsh 318
  Thomas Wsh 319
Statin, Jehue Bar 27
  Martha Mas 286
Statler, Stephen Ohi 84
Staton, Barthw. Gar 217
  Geo. Hnr 359A
  George Hnr 359A
  George Hnr 359A
  George Mon 369
  Hannah Bra 141
  James Hnr 359A
  James Mon 367
  James War 250
  John But 197
  John But 197
  Peter War 264
  Reuben Mon 374

Staton, cont.
Reubin Adr 13
Samuel Mon 365
Thomas Mon 347
Thomas R. Hnr 359A
Thos. War 280
William Hnr 359A
William Hnr 362
Wm. Bra 141
Wm. Cas 44
Wm. Gar 217
Statton, Robt. Lew 103
St. Clair, Henry Mas 308
St. Clear, Mary Log 178
St. Cleer, Geo. Way 370
Isaac Way 371
Steagler, Benjamin She 203
Steal, Heny Mon 366
Henry, Junr Mon 349
John Mon 367
Nicholas Mon 382
Thomas Mon 354
Stealy, Christian Gar 221
Stean, Wm. Gar 224
Stearman, Foxhall Grn 251
S Wm. Grn 251
Stears, Wm. Hrs 323
Stedman, Thomas Fay 16
Steel, Archibald Clr 141
Christian Way 364
Hugh Bou 110
James Bou 110
James Bul 184
John Bou 109
James Ohi 101
John Fle 76
John Way 360
Jonah Bul 184
Joseph Bou 109
Joseph Bou 110
Laurance Hop 373
Martha War 268
Mosis Chr 53
Ninian Bou 107
Paul Adr 13
Robt. Cam 32
Samuel Chr 111
Samuel Fay 43
Ruben Fay 26
Samuel Knx 65
William Chr 63
William Gra 239
William Knx 87
William, Jr Bou 110
Willm. Adr 13
Wm. War 265
Wm. Senr Bou 109
Steele, Adam She 239
Andrew Jef 27
Brice Fay 31
David Clr 141
David Jes 51
Henry Woo 383
James Woo 391
John Hop 378
John Pen 106
John Woo 378
Jos. Gal 192
Joseph Mas 282
Richard Jef 29
Ruth Jes 51
Saml. Jef 14
Samuel Fay 11
Samuel Fay 26
Samuel She 218
Thomas Jes 51
Thomas Woo 378

Steele, cont.
Washington Hnr 354
William Fra 163
William Woo 391
William Wsh 321
Willm. Sco 185
Steeley, Hezekiah Jef 18
Steely, Hetta Pul 135
John War 244
Steen, Nathan Hop 372
William Mas 280
William Mer 331
Steene, Alexr. Fle 63
Steppleton, John Woo 389
Steers, Holliday Bou 111
Hugh Boo 63
Wm. Hrs 309
Steevenson, Wm. Nic 62
Steffer, Harmon Bou 130
Steger, John Woo 386
Stelton, Stephen Jes 54
Stemmins, Stephen Mer 330
Henry Wsh 319
Jacob Log 195
Stennet, Charles Wsh 319
John Wsh 319
Wm. Gar 224
Stenson, Joseph Mas 280
Mathew Cal 18
Step, Benjamen Adr 19
William Mer 333
Stepens, John Adr 14
Wm. Adr 14
Stepenson, James War 258
Stephans, Bela Fay 16
Stephen, David Hnd 334
John Fay 16
John War 250
Stephenann, Stephen Adr 14
Stephens, Allin Wsh 320
Benjamin Fra 166
Benjn. Boo 62
Benjn. Bou 110
Benjn. Log 187
Benjn. War 272
Charles Jef 17
Christopher Hnr 358
Daniel Fra 165
Daniel Mad 221
David H. Mul 403
Edward Jes 50
Elisha Pul 138
Francis Pul 138
Gilbert Knx 63
Henson Jef 17
Isaa War 252
Isaiah Pul 139
Jacob Mad 224
Jacob Mon 361
James Fay 46
James She 225
James, Sr Clr 140
Jas. Clr 142
Jesse Log 190
John Boo 63
John Boo 63
John Fra 168
John Mad 220
John Mad 224
John Mad 226
John Mon 359
John Pul 139
John Rck 162
John, Jun Mad 223
John G. Ohi 77
Jos. L. Bou 110

Stephens, cont.
Joseph Fle 75
Joseph Jef 16
Joseph Way 353
Joseph Way 356
Joshua Knx 70
Joshua War 261
Lewis Knx 71
Merriman Woo 382
Moses Knx 70
Natthaniel Lew 103
Nehh. Adr 13
Peter Way 353
Richard Mon 359
Richard Nel 24
Richard Ohi 74
Saml. Boo 63
Samuel Mas 280
Samuel Mas 286
Solomon Knx 70
Thomas Mad 246
Thomas Ohi 103
Thomas Pul 139
Thomas She 225
Thomas She 227
Thomas Wsh 321
Thos. Boo 63
Wifford Fra 165
William Fra 165
William Hnr 355
William Jes 52
William Ohi 78
William Pul 136
William Pul 138
William Pul 139
William She 224
Wm. Adr 13
Wm. Adr 14
Wm. Mon 380
Wm. Way 353
Stephensen, William Liv 159
Stephenson, Abraham Est 8
Alexdr. Bou 108
Andrew Liv 160
Andrew Mad 224
Benjn. Way 360
Edward Mad 224
Eliza Nic 61
George Bou 109
Hugh Log 192
James Jef 17
James Log 185
James Log 185
Jas. Bou 108
Jas. Gal 191
Jas. Log 170
Jas. War 251
Jas. Way 373
Jno. Way 366
John Bar 48
John Boo 63
John Lew 99
John Log 170
John Mad 222
John Mad 223
John Mas 280
John Ohi 89
John War 250
John Way 363
Jos. Nic 61
Joseph Mad 223
Joseph Mas 283
Joseph Mas 285
Joseph Mas 285
Nathan Mas 282
Phebe Mad 225

Stephenson, cont.
Robert Log 169
Robert Nic 61
Robert, Jr Log 169
Robt. Nic 61
Thomas Fay 31
Thomas Mad 223
Thomas Mas 282
Thos. Nic 60
William Knx 84
William Liv 149
Stephers, John Lin 135
Stephins, John Sr Adr 14
Seth Fay 41
Stepp, Achilles Sco 170
Elijah Adr 14
Ely Sco 170
James Cly 149
Joseph Adr 14
Joshua Adr 14
Reuben Mad 222
Wm. Adr 14
Steppe, Joseph Woo 387
Stepton, James Adr 14
Sterling, Elisha Way 361
William Mer 331
William Mer 332
Sterne, Charles Pen 117
Sterrel, Robert Bar 19
Sterret, Joel Grn 253
Stewart Hrd 297
Sterrett, John Sco 182
Steuart, Isaac War 259
Williby NIc 60
Stevens, Abraham She 218
Champ Cum 171
Delilah Cum 176
Edward Cam 24
James Cal 12
James Cam 24
James Nel 23
John Cal 8
John Cal 11
John Gar 221
John Gar 223
John R. Cam 24
Lewis Pen 106
Meshech Cum 182
Moses Cal 11
Molley Nel 23
Moses Cal 5
Robert Hrs 312
Saml. Cal 10
Tho. Gar 221
Thos. Cam 26
Vincent Hrd 294
William Fay 26
William Pen 106
William S. Fay 30
Wm. Cam 26
Stevenson, Aaron Sco 179
Alexr. Cal 9
Alexr. Cal 18
Arthur Log 180
Benjn. Woo 399
Charles Clr 141
George Clr 142
George Fay 53
Isaac Woo 398
James Cal 19
James Flo 102
James, Jr Woo 386
James M. Clr 141
Jas. Senr Woo 397
Jno. A. Hrd 288
Job Sco 190
John Clr 142

Stevenson, cont.
John Hrd 288
John Mer 333
John Pen 116
John, Junr Woo 386
John, Senr Woo 386
Margaret Woo 386
Nancy Hrd 288
Reuben Bra 151
Richards Grp 278
Saml. Log 172
Saml. Mer 333
Saml. Senr Woo 380
Saml. Senr Woo 400
Samuel Clr 141
Samuel Hrd 281
Thomas Fay 52
Thomas Woo 395
William Hrs 312
William Mer 333
William Sco 179
Wm. Cal 11
Wm. Jr Woo 398
Stever, Henry Gar 223
Stevert, Thomas Jes 53
Stevins, Samuel Chr 86
Wm. Cal 19
Stevinson, Mathew Cal 14
Steward, Annanias Sco 176
Archibd. Bou 108
Benjamin Woo 391
David Fle 80
David Mad 226
David Mon 364
Ezekiel Mon 354
George Mon 348
Henry Mon 364
Henry Mon 366
Hugh Bul 184
Jacob Mon 359
James Clr 141
James Fle 70
James Pul 136
James Sco 177
John Bou 107
John Mon 367
John Sco 176
Levy Mon 365
Mariah Pul 136
Richard Bou 107
Robert Pul 137
Robt. Hrs 314
Saml. Fle 66
Samuel Mad 226
Stephen Mon 348
Thomas Bul 183
Wm. Hrs 319
Wm. Hrs 319
Wm. (mulattoe) Woo 396
Stewart, Abel Bou 110
Agness War 250
Alex Mad 222
Alexander Fay 16
Alexander Knx 75
Alexander Ohi 73
Alexr. Jef 14
Allen Hnr 367
Andrew She 197
Asa Hnr 367
Ayres Liv 160
Charles Clr 140
Charles Pen 108
Charles Rck 163
Chs. Nel 26
Daniel Cly 156
Danl. Gal 191
Elinor War 250

Stewart, cont.
Elisha Gal 191
Elizabeth Jef 18
Hugh Boo 62
Humphrey Liv 147
Isaac Knx 75
Jacob Woo 394
James Cal 10
James Cal 12
James Clr 140
James Jef 14
James Jef 15
James Knx 87
James Mon 351
James Pen 115
James She 202
Jane Fay 43
Jane Nel 23
Jas. Gal 191
Jas. Lew 95
Jeremiah Bra 141
Jesse Pen 116
Jno. Hnr 368
Jno. Hrd 283
Jno. Nel 42
John Cly 152
John Fra 167
John Jef 18
John Knx 72
John Mad 222
John Pen 110
Jos. Nic 60
Joseph Knx 83
Lucy Fay 48
Mary Nic 61
Mary War 243
Mathew Grp 275
Matthew Jef 15
Nancy Jef 27
Peter Bra 143
Robert Fay 26
Robert Nel 25
Robert Nel 27
Robert Woo 383
Robt. Gar 222
Robt. War 255
Rot. War 263
Sally Jef 23
Tho. Gar 217
Thomas Jef 15
Thomas Rck 163
Thomas She 221
Thos. Cam 29
Thos. Cum 167
Washington Liv 157
William Clr 141
William Cly 149
William Fay 16
William Fay 16
William Fay 49
William Hrs 323
William Liv 153
William Log 182
Willm. War 255
Wilm. War 245
Wm. Hop 377
Wm. Hrs 324
Wm. Jef 14
Sthreshly, Thomas Fay 27
William Fay 27
Stice, Andrew War 253
Charles Gal 190
David War 254
Peter Gal 192
Robert War 253
Stickles, Isaac Bul 185
Stiff, Joseph Mon 380

Stifler, Adam Sco 174
Stigar, David Bul 184
Stiger, Peter Nel 7
Stiles, Jno. Hnr 369
John Fle 85
Rachel Bra 151
Richard Fle 85
Richrd. Fle 70
Stephen Wsh 320
Stilfield, John [illegible] 16
Still, John [illegible] 53
John War 262
Murphey D. She 210
Saml. Bar 45
Stillwell, Danl. Adr 13
Eli Nel 24
Elias Nel 27
Elijah Adr 13
John Mon 357
Joseph Cam 33
William Mas 284
Stilts, Federick Grn 250
Jno. Hrd 293
Stilwell, Daniel She 211
John She 211
John She 212
John She 216
John She 223
Joseph She 202
Joseph She 211
Stine, Jacob Lin 134
Jacob, Jnr Lin 133
Jacob, Snr Lin 133
Stinet, Reuben Gar 217
Stinnet, Benjamin Chr 72
Jerrusha Chr 72
Stinson, Birdit Bar 39
George Log 178
George Way 372
James Bar 45
Jas. Bar 44
Jas. Gar 217
John Bar 39
John Bar 45
John Hrs 324
Levi Bar 39
Richard Jef 15
Robert Hrs 324
Robert Knx 72
Robert Mon 380
Stip, Frederick Clr 141
George Bou 109
George, Jr Bou 131
John Bou 131
Michael Clr 141
Stipe, Frederick Jes 53
John Jes 54
Stipens, Warren War 252
Stiphenson, James Est 6
Stirett, John Bre 160
Stites, John Sco 190
William Pen 109
Stith, B. Baldwin Mas 308
Ben Hrd 299
Jno. Hrd 289
John Bre 163
Jos. Bre 158
Richard Bre 161
Richd. Hrd 299
Thomas Bre 167
Wm. Hrd 289
Stitis, Saml. Bra 147
Stitt, Hugh Bou 108
Stivers, Edward Clr 141
Edward Fay 25
John Est 1
Richard Mad 220
Stivers, cont.
Robert Fay 25
Ruben Fay 25
William Mad 226
Sto, Joel Kns 75
Robertson Knx 65
Stobuck, Andrew Log 176
Stockain, Nathan Log 169
Stockdon, John Mas 284
Stocker, Martha Mad 222
Stockey, George Jef 32
Stockstill, Danl. Way 362
Warnel Mad 222
Stockston, George Fle 65
Stockton, Elizth. Cum 185
Jesse Cum 185
Jessee Bar 50
John Cum 181
Joshua Fle 66
Margaret Cum 185
Michel Cum 185
Newberry Mad 224
Robert Bar 39
Robert Cum 177
Susana Bar 52
Thomas Bar 52
Thos. Bar 42
Thos. Cum 185
Wm. Cum 185
Stockwell, Jas. Fle 66
Jesse Hrd 293
John Nic 60
Jos. Boo 63
Micheal Fle 79
Micheal Fle 80
Michl. Fle 85
Samuel Fle 83
Wm. Bra 149
Stoddert, Ben Jr Gra 237
Stodgehill, Thomas She 234
Stodghill, Jacob Fra 167
John She 232
Stoe, Richard Chr 84
Stogdale, James Nic 60
Wm. Nic 60
Stogden, Claton Way 355
John Log 187
Mesheck Way 354
Stoghill, Sarah Way 370
Stogstill, Benja-min Pul 139
Richard Pul 136
Samuel Pul 136
Shadrick Pul 136
Shadrick Pul 140
Thomas Pul 137
Williams Pul 136
Stokely, Jacob Mon 363
Stoker, Edward Bou 109
Wm. Fle 78
Stokes, Absolam Liv 155
Anny Bou 108
Benja. Hop 372
Berryman Mon 372
John Chr 114
Jones Chr 76
Mathew Chr 77
Reding Hnd 334
Robert Mon 349
Robert Mon 370
Salley Cas 48
Sally Mon 372
Tho. Hop 372
William Mul 397
Young Chr 77
Stom, John Mul 385
John Mul 386
Stom, cont.
Leonard Mul 405
Stomp, christopher Grp 271
Stone, Alexander Chr 110
Balis Grn 248
Barton W. Bou 107
Benjamin Pul 134
Benjamin She 223
Benjn. Nel 23
Bennedeck Log 174
Bryant Nel 24
Caleman She 222
Catharine Woo 395
Christopher Gra 238
Danl. War 264
David Nel 25
Dudly Mad 221
Elijah Bar 44
Elisha Mer 331
Elizabeth Woo 395
Enock Nel 26
Erekiel Flo 102
George Fay 27
George She 205
Henry Fay 27
Henry Woo 375
Jacob Fay 26
Jacob Woo 395
James Bou 131
James Mer 332
James She 216
James She 217
James She 232
Jane Fay 27
Jas. Mad 220
Jas. Way 368
Jeremiah Pul 136
Jesse Bou 131
John Adr 13
John Cal 8
John Cal 15
John Cly 149
John Fay 26
John Knx 84
John Lin 135
John Log 172
John Nel 22
John Sco 180
Josiah Hnd 344
Josiah Mad 222
Josiah Nel 23
Levi Lin 135
Levy Chr 93
Levy Mer 332
Lvy Chr 98
Micajah Fay 43
Moses Gra 241
Nimrod Grn 247
Polly Gar 224
Richard Mon 354
Robert Mon 356
Rufus Sco 186
Smith Gar 218
Spencer Lin 135
Stephen Adr 13
Thomas Clr 142
Thomas Lin 135
Thomas Mer 334
Uriah Adr 14
Valuntine Mon 356
William Chr 53
William Fay 27
William Gra 242
William Log 168
William Nel 26
William Nel 27
William She 201

Stone, cont.
William, Jr Log 179
William D. Hrd 281
Wm. Adr 13
Wm. Adr 14
Wm. Mad 220
Wm. Way 363
Stoner, Jesse Nel 25
John Nel 24
Michael Way 360
Stonesifer, John Cam 28
Simion Cam 25
Stonesiffer, Abram Boo 63
Stonestreet,John D Jes 51
Stong, John Sco 189
Stonum, Fortunates Chr 104
Stoops, Phillip Nic 61
Stoots, John Adr 13
Stootts, Soln. Adr 13
Store, John Pul 134
Storey, Fras. War 265
Storkdell, William Sco 189
Storm, Conrod Gar 217
Isaac She 226
James Hnr 359A
John Gra 243
John Hnr 369
Peter Gra 242
Peter Hnr 369
William Gra 243
Story, Asa Sco 182
Isaac Way 362
John Cal 4
John Grp 276
John Mon 347
John Sco 181
John Woo 390
Joshua Way 362
Thomas Fle 89
Thomas Sco 190
Thos. Cam 28
Storry, James fle 86
Stots, John Cly 149
John Pul 136
Stott, Adam Bou 111
James Fra 164
James Knx 89
John Hop 379
Lewis L. Fra 163
Rawleigh Fra 163
Stephen Fra 164
Thomas Hnd 335
William T. Fra 163
Isaac Knx 80
John Pul 135
Reuben Pul 136
Thos. Adr 13
Wm. Adr 13
Stought, Michael Liv 154
Stoud, Lott Mul 396
Stout, Aaron She 211
Absalem Mul 386
Anthony Fay 42
Ben She 222
Benjamin Fay 16
Daniel Fra 169
Daniel Mas 303
David Fay 16
David Mas 281
David, Senr Mas 280
Elijah Fay 26
Elijah She 205
Elijah She 227
Ely Sco 175
Hezikiah Fra 163
Isaac Lew 103
Jacob Mer 330
Stout, cont.
James She 210
James She 213
Janathan She 199
Jediah Fay 60
Job Bra 152
John She 206
John N. Fle 79
Jonathan Mas 284
Joseph Mer 343
Joseph She 205
Margaret Fay 16
Peter Mad 224
Peter She 210
Philemon Sco 175
Reuben She 202
Saml. Lin 135
Unitince Hrd 289
W. John Fay 16
William She 205
Zebulon Mas 284
Stoute, Jonathan Bra 152
Stoval, Eliza Grn 261
Jessee Bar 41
Stovall, Drury War 280
Susanna War 279
Thos. War 280
Stoveall, Geo. Hrd 297
Heze. Hrd 298
Ralp Hrd 288
Stover, Jas. Grn 251
Stowers, Jeremiah Gal 190
John Gal 189
John Jef 16
Nicholas Jef 15
William Pen 111
Wm. GAl 192
Straden, Henry Grn 248
Strader, Francis Hrd 300
Henry Grn 255
Lewis Grn 264
Strahan, David Cas 39
David Fle 74
Samuel Fle 74
Straight, Leonard Nel 25
Strain, William Hnd 332
Strainey, Nichl. Sco 174
Strait, David War 269
Willm. War 280
Strakerson, John Fle 64
Stranbough, Michael Log 169
Strang, Charles She 207
Strange, Archr. Adr 13
Cornwell Bou 108
Jas. Hrd 291
Jeremiah Mon 350
John Jef 15
John Wsh 321
Nacy Hrd 291
Philip Hrd 298
Stephen Mon 349
Stephen Mon 350
Washington Gar 218
Wm. Gar 218
Stratan, William Log 186
Strather, John Log 174
Straton, Serardah Grp 273
Stratton, Aaron Lew 95
David Wsh 322
Harry Flo 103
Hiram Flo 102
John Flo 103
Owens Log 190
Richard Flo 103
Seth She 216
Solomon Flo 102
Stratton, cont.
Solomon Hnr 356
Taudy Flo 103
Thomas Flo 102
William Gal 190
William Hnr 355
William Log 190
Wm. Bra 143
Straughan, John She 233
Polly She 233
Straun, Saml. Log 174
Strauther, Wm. Log 174
Strawbey, Nicholas Bra 142
Strawby, Jacob Bra 146
Strawhan, Benjamin Mad 225
Jacob Mad 226
Thomas Mad 226
Strawn, Hazia Log 168
Strawther, Nelly Bou 131
Streat, Nathaniel Lin 135
Streman, Wm. Way 351
Street, Anthony Wsh 321
David She 231
Jacob Mul 389
James Fle 75
James Fle 84
James Hnd 338
Joseph Cum 171
Joseph M. Hnd 341
Josh. Adr 13
Samuel Wsh 319
Wm. Jef 27
Stribling, William Clr 141
William Clr 141
Strickland, James Liv 148
Strickler, John Sco 192
Stricklet, Jacob Lew 104
Peter Lew 103
Stricklin, Elisha Chr 79
Zacheriah War 258
Strider, Coonrod Log 170
Striner, Leanuel Cas 47
String, Jeremiah Bou 109
Stringe, Lawrens Mul 396
Stringer, David Pul 139
Edmund Bul 184
Edwd. Gar 218
Geo. Gar 216
John Bul 184
John Grn 246
Reuben Pul 137
Richard Bul 184
Ruben Bul 185
Thomas Bul 184
Thos. Gar 218
Wm. Gar 220
Stringfeller, - George Woo 379
Stringfield, James Bar 35
Stripland, Benjn. Sco 174
John Sco 174
Striplin, Nancy Clr 141
Strobridge, Jonathan Clr 141
Strode, Jairres War 254
James Bou 130
Jeremiah Fle 61
Jehu War 254
John Clr 140
Mary Clr 141
Stephen Clr 141
Wm. Cum 175
Stromatt, John Cal 14
Strong, Elizabeth Mer 343
John Cum 173
John Mad 245
William Cly 155

Strother, Benj. Nel 6
George Gal 190
James Mas 280
Joseph Jef 14
Saml. Bar 36
Stephen Jef 14
Wm. Jef 14
Stroud, Ansel Pul 135
Ansel Pul 138
Isaac War 254
Joseph Jef 30
Thomas P. But 197
Stroude, Samuel Mas 284
Samuel Mas 285
Thomas Mas 285
Strowd, Asy Chr 80
Isaac Chr 68
Levy Chr 65
William Chr 79
Strutt, Antony Adr 13
Strutton, Absolam War 258
Stuard, James Pul 139
William Chr 63
Stuart, Abriham Chr 80
Alexr. Bar 39
Alexr. Bar 39
Alixr. Bar 25
Chas. Bar 29
Elijah Chr 79
G. Robert Mas 285
Gravener Chr 102
Hugh Chr 70
James Cas 46
James Chr 72
James Chr 83
James Hnr 367
John Lin 135
John Mas 281
John Woo 387
Lazarus Bar 45
Mary Cas 43
Mary Lin 135
Nathaniel Lin 135
Peter Hnd 345
Quinten Chr 70
Richd. Bar 53
Sarah War 243
Solomon Mas 283
Stevin Chr 79
William Mas 281
Wm. Bar 21
Wm. Bar 45
Wm. Cas 47
Stubbins, Jona. Hnr 369
Joseph She 211
Saml. Hnr 369
Stubblefeed, William Mas 308
Stubblefield, Alexr Mas 286
Robert Mas 286
Stubbs, Denny Chr 61
John Hnd 345
Robt. Cam 32
Wm. Cas 38
Stublefield, Thomas Log 188
Stubs, Dennis Chr 88
Wm. Bar 27
Stucker, Jacob Sco 188
Jacob Woo 396
Michael Woo 396
Stuckey, Martin Jef 18
Samuel Bre 156
Wm. Mon 371
Studebaker, Jacob Mul 391
Stull, Andrew Jes 51
Jane Hnr 352
Stultz, George Adr 13
Stumaugh, Phillip Fle 102
Stump, David Mul 407
Frederick Boo 63
Lenard Hrs 311
Robert Nel 24
Stumph, George G. Wsh 321
Sturgeon, Jno. Hrd 295
John Nel 24
Nancy Hrd 294
Robert Jef 27
Samul Hnr 361
Simpson She 225
Thomas Jef 27
Sturges, J. Samuel Mas 286
Sturgin, Jas. Bar 32
Sturgis, Polley She 237
Sturgus, James A. Bul 185
Robert Mad 245
Sturman, Tho. J. Mad 245
Valentine Bou 109
Sturt, Barnot Mul 395
Daniel Mul 389
Ely Mul 400
John Mul 407
Jonothan Mul 401
Samuel Mul 400
Stuteville, Chas. Gra 241
Martin Gra 238
Richard Gra 240
Stutiville, James Gra 237
Stuward, Thomas Hrs 313
Stwart, Charles Grp 273
Stwert, John Jes 50
Styatts, Peter Mon 348
Stygall, George Rck 162
William Rck 162
Suart, Chas. Bar 39
Subblet, Lewis Jr Woo 397
Lewis, Senr Woo 386
Sublet, Benjn. War 245
Benjn. War 251
Chas. I. War 251
John Gar 223
Wm. GAr 221
Sublete, Jaems Hnr 354
William Hnr 354
Sublett, A. Phillip Lin 135
Abraham Pul 136
George Lin 135
Hilly. Adr 13
Robert Sco 187
William Sco 187
Sublit, Abraham Grn 257
Branch Grn 246
Field Grn 246
Field Grn 259
Mageret Grn 259
Suddath, Francis Mon 357
Suddoth, Henry Hnr 367
James Hnr 367
Lewis Hnr 367
Sudduth, Ann Clr 141
William Clr 142
Suduth, James Clr 141
Suel, Joseph Pul 137
Suetor, John Nic 60
Suffrett, John Jes 50
Sugan, James Bou 131
Sugars, Eli Cum 182
Sugg, Allen I. Hnd 338
Joel Ohi 82
Simon Hnd 334
Wila. Hnd 348
William Hnd 334
Suilivan, Cornelius Mad 225
Suilivan, cont.
Samuel Mad 245
Suit, Nathaniel Mas 282
Suiter, Geo. Gar 217
John Bar 50
Sulcer, William Hrd 302
Sulevin, Mary Lin 134
Menoah Lin 134
Sulivan, Bergis Far 30
Charles Cal 8
Claboon Cal 7B
George Fay 16
James Fay 26
Joseph War 265
Nathaniel Cal 9
Thomas Fay 16
William Fay 26
Suliven, Able Mul 394
Lewis Mul 395
Uriah Mul 396
Sullard, Samuel Flo 102
Sullards, John Flo 103
Sullavain, John Mas 280
John, Senr Mas 310
Lewis Mas 284
William Mas 284
Sullavin, Tho. Bar 48
Sullenger, Mary Woo 378
Sullens, Reuben Way 353
Sullinger, Gabriel Fra 167
James Hnr 366
Peter Liv 154
Thomas Gra 239
Sullivan, Dannis Hnr 354
James Knx 83
James Sco 176
James Woo 400
Jeremiah Hnr 354
Lewis Woo 385
Mary Clr 141
Nathl. Jef 15
Peter Flo 102
William Grn 260
Willm Sco 172
Sulovin, Clem Mer 334
Sulze, John Chr 108
Sumers, Obediah Grn 261
Sumerveal, Miha Nic 61
Summer, George Way 367
Summers, Able Way 371
Abram Way 364
Archibald Mon 381
Benjamin Bul 184
Caleb Boo 63
Charles Log 189
Charles Wsh 319
Cornileous Mon 348
Danl. Bou 111
Edward BAr 34
Elijah She 201
Elijah She 237
George Wsh 319
Isaac Wah 368
Jahu Fle 62
James Jes 50
Jeremiah Way 366
Jesse Wsh 319
John Bar 25
John Grn 264
John Wsh 319
John, Senr Mon 348
Levy Grn 255
Lewis Fle 91
Michael Mas 280
Michl. Nel 28
Moses Way 371
Mosse She 206

Summers, cont.
Nathan Log 174
Polly Jes 50
Richard Wsh 319
Richd. Way 366
Saml. Nel 26
Simon Way 367
Thomas Hrd 300
Thos. Way 368
Thos. D. Boo 63
William Fay 25
William Fle 69
William Woo 390
William, Senr Mas 280
Wm. Nel 26
Summervill, John Fle 79
Summett, Christo. Nic 60
George Nic 60
Summons, Wm. Way 370
Sumnars, Sollaman Chr 92
Sumner, John Flo 102
John Log 169
John Mul 389
Nazarius Log 187
Thomas Log 172
Sumners, John Fle 69
Sumpter, George Knx 74
Wm. War 250
Sunmons, David Jes 54
Sunrall, James She 240
Supinger, Christopher War 280
Surber, Henry Pul 134
Isaac Pul 137
Surist, Joseph Fle 86
William Fle 91
Surs, John Nic 62
Surseen, Lewis Pul 139
Susan Way 358
Suter, Jesse Fra 167
John Woo 379
William Woo 380
Sutfield, Richard Mer 341
Suthards, John Lin 135
Sutherlan, Jos. Gar 220
Sutherland, David Clr 142
Frederick Clr 140
George Knx 73
Isbal Gar 221
James Adr 13
Jaems Mer 331
John Clr 140
Jane Pul 138
Marey Cas 44
Mordicai Hnd 343
Rebeckey Cas 44
Thomas Clr 140
Walter E. Clr 142
Wm. Adr 14
Wm. Way 369
Suthvard, Peshant Cas 41
Sutphen, John Sco 181
Sutt, Christian She 201
Sutten, John Knx 74
Sutter, James Sco 167
Sutterfield, James Mer 335
Ned Mer 335
Suttle, Hannah Gra 239
Josef Nel 25
Suttles, Benjn. Grn 262
Joseph Bou 131
Judigh Grn 262
Wm. Adr 13
Sutton, Asy Chr 60
Benja. Gar 217
David Fay 16
David Jes 52
Sutton, cont.
E. Hnr 368
Ebnezer Nic 61
Edmond Lin 133
Ephraim She 234
Henry She 212
Isaac mer 341
James Hnr 367
James Lin 133
James Lin 135
John Gar 217
John Gra 239
John Jef 27
John Log 182
John Mad 220
John Mon 355
John She 229
John War 274
John Wsh 322
Joshua Lin 135
Nathnl. Bou 111
Oliver Fay 34
Oliver Fay 52
Richard Fle 66
Richard Wsh 322
Robert Sco 185
Rowland Bou 111
Samuel Mon 367
Temperance Sco 173
Thos. War 266
William Chr 60
William Sco 190
Willm. Sco 169
Wm. Adr 14
Wm. Fle 66
Wm. Sco 182
Wm. Way 370
Wm. W. Woo 398
Sutzer, Frederick Hrd 297
Swafford, Isaac Cly 150
Swaford, James Chr 71
Swagart, John Fay 25
Swagott, Anw. Bou 131
Swain, Collons Pul 138
Nathan Nic 60
Swaine, James Mas 286
Swalls, Isaac Mas 303
Swan, Edward Nel 24
George Fay 45
George Mas 281
Jacob Sco 184
James Log 193
James, Jr Log 170
John (free man of colour) Bul 185
John Sco 185
Thomas Hrd 281
William Liv 155
Swaney, Michael Ohi 91
Swango, Abm. Gal 191
Jacob Sco 178
Samuel Mon 362
Wm. Gal 191
Swank, Jacob Hrd 295
Joseph Hrd 303
Rosy Hrd 303
Swanson, John Nic 60
Maryan Way 372
Swarford, Abm Way 353
Jacob Way 353
Wm. Way 362
Swarringam, Wm. War 281
Swart, James Nic 60
Swartz, Henry Lew 104
Swayles, Wm. Cam 30
Swayne, Henry Bul 197
Sweany, John Mon 368
Swearagin, Andrew Mon 366
Swearengen, Elemilek Bul 184
Samuel Bul 184
Swearengin, Rachel Bul 184
Swearingan, Van Bar 34
Swearingen, Abijah Jef 18
Saml. War 244
Van She 206
Swearingim, Danl. Lew 99
Jno. lew 101
Swearins, David Hrd 284
Sweasy, William Nel 27
Sweat, Peter Lin 133
Benja. (B) Fle 91
Sweatman, Wm. Mon 378
Sweeney, Edmond War 252
Sweeny, Benjamin Wsh 322
Daniel Wsh 322
Joseph Wsh 319
Moses Wsh 322
William Wsh 319
Sweet, James Fle 71
Thos. Fle 91
William Fle 87
Sweeten, Lane Cly 156
Sweeter, William Cly 149
Sweetin, Asalem Cly 156
Sweeton, Moses Way 362
Sweets, Thos. Nel 7
Sweezer, Peter Ohi 103
Sweney, Gennet Fle 71
Swenney, John Hrs 311
Swerrengim, Othe Lew 99
Swerringim, Jno. Lew 99
Swetnan, George Sco 169
Swezey, Joseph Nel 26
Swidzer, Valentine Fra 167
Swift, David Bar 21
Jno. Senr Hnr 364
John Bou 109
John Chr 63
Tho. Bar 24
Swiggate, James Cas 37
Swim, Alexander Fle 77
Isaac, Sur Fle 87
John Fle 62
John, Senr Fle 72
Vinson Fle 87
Swindley, Jonathan She 223
Swiney, A. Tho. Gar 220
Swinford, Eastice Hrs 316
Hezakiah Hrs 317
James Chr 98
James Hrs 316
James Hrs 318
John Hrs 310
Joshua Hrs 318
Swingle, John Mon 351
Swingler, Jesse Jef 16
Swink, Leonard Pul 136
Swinney, Augustin Shw 226
Chals. Cas 38
Edmon Chr 116
Henry She 226
Job Cas 37
John Bou 109
John Gar 221
John She 226
Lewis She 226
Lindsay She 226
Michajah Gar 219
Moses Gar 222
Robert She 227
Shepperd Cas 37
Val She 241
Swinny, Daniel Pul 139

Swinny, cont.
  William Pul 139
Swiny, Moses Lin 135
Switzer, Abraham Mon 351
  Samuel Jes 54
Swolavan, Birges Fay 53
Swoop, David She 203
  George She 199
  Joseph She 202
Swoope, Charles Gar 219
  Saml. Gar 218
Swope, Benedict Gar 219
  Geo. Cum 186
  George Mon 374
  Jacob Lin 135
Sybert, Daniel Cly 154
Sydnor, William Hrs 311
Sykes, Drury Flo 102
Sylla(free woman) Fay 23
Sylvestil, Robt. Way 351
Symminds, John Wsh 320
Sympson, Geo. Cum 180
  Wm. Grn 256
Syms, Anthony Bre 156
  Anthony Bre 169
  Barnard Bre 158
  Calob Mer 334
  Nathl. Mad 220
  Randolph Mad 220
  Rebecca Bre 160
  William Mad 224
Sypes, George Hrd 293
Syson, John Jes 50
Sally, cont.
  Abraham Bra 143
  John Pul 134
Salmons, cont.
  Joel Clr 142
  Nathan Clr 141
Sams, cont.
  Joseph Fay 48
  Warren Cum 182
Sandafer, cont.
  Lowry Liv 153
  Mary Pul 135
Sanders, cont.
  Abraham Mad 225
  John Cly 160
Sawyers, cont.
  Charles Cum 186
  Robert Pul 135

-- T --

Tabb, John Mas 288
Taber, Amasa Bre 165
  John Bre 158
Tabir, Justice Bre 164
Tabler, Jacob Nel 22
  Peter Clr 142
Tabour, Isaac War 244
  Jacob War 279
Tacket, William Knx 74
Tackett, George Flo 103
  John Adr 15
  Lewis Knx 90
  Philip Knx 84
  Wm. War 270
Tadisman, George Wsh 329
Tadlock, Edward Bar 44
  John Mer 336
Taque, Geo. Hnr 351
  Jno. Hnr 351
  Nathl. Knx 66
Taque, cont.
  Robt. Hnr 352
Tahoof, Margaret Mer 335
Tailor, Alexander Hrs 310
  John Hrs 310
Talbert, Cyrus Nel 21
  Gazaway Sco 182
  Hendley Nel 22
  James Ohi 86
  Peter Pen 113
  William Nel 22
Talbot, David She 214
  Demoval Bou 132
  Edward She 213
  George Jes 49
  Isham, Sinr Hnd 336
  John R. Ohi 96
  Nathaniel She 213
  Nicholas Bou 132
  Nocholas Cum 183
  Paul Clr 143
  Presley Bou 112
  Rodham Clr 143
  Samuel Clr 143
  Thomas Jef 19
Talbott, Danl. She 222
  Daniel Bou 72
  Edmund Hnd 327
  Enock Hnd 330
  French Bou 132
  Hail Mad 226
  Henry Bou 113
  Hugh Bou 113
  Isham Fra 171
  James Mad 227
  James S. Boo 63
  John Bou 113
  John Hnd 345
  John C. Bou 132
  Saml. Bou 132
  Wm. Bou 72
  Wm. Bou 113
Talbutt, Joshua But 197
Talifero, Nicholas Bra 150
Talketon, Steven Chr 76
Talkington, Elizabeth Log 193
  Samuel Log 193
Tall, Jonathan Mon 375
Tallbot, Thos. Bou 132
Tall[illegible], Overnton Hrs 320
Tally, Claibern Mon 352
  Mary Jef 19
  Nelson Gal 193
Talmage, Thomas Jef 19
Talton, Jezine Hop 375
Tandy, Achilles Fay 50
  Gabriel Fay 15
  John, Jr Gal 192
  John, Sr Gal 192
  Mills Chr 100
  Moses Hnr 357
  Smyth Grn 246
  William Gal 193
Tankersley, John War 268
Tankersly, George War 277
  Joseph War 266
Tankesley, Charles Bre 166
Tanksley, Jos Gar 227
Tannehel, James Chr 72
Tanner, Branch Clr 143
  Catharine Mon 378
  Creed Hnr 358
  Edward Chr 113
  Edward She 214
  Ephrm. Boo 63
  Federick Bar 47
Tanner, cont.
  George Jes 48
  Ginings Mad 229
  James Mul 399
  Joel Grn 263
  John Boo 63
  John Mon 363
  John Mul 393
  Jonathan Mad 229
  Lucias Hnr 365
  Martin Lin 137
  Mathewq Hnr 358
  Richd. Boo 63
  Richd. M. Clr 143
  Saml. Hnr 366
  Samuel Boo 63
  Samuel Hnr 358
  Samuel Mul 392
  Samuel Mul 396
  Sarah Clr 143
  Semeon Boo 63
  Solkins Ohi 83
  William Mul 393
  William, Junr Ohi 83
  William, Senr Ohi 84
Tanneyhill, Josiah Fay 15
Tannon, Joseph Mon 363
Tapp, Isaac Clr 143
  John Mon 376
  John Sco 193
  Lewis Jes 47
Tar, [illegible] Jef 20
Tarb[illegible] David Fle 67
Tarence, David Sco 179
Targot, Dennis Grn 259
Tarleton, Charles Ohi 74
  Townsend Ohi 103
Tarley, John Bou 112
Tarlton, Caleb Sco 179
  Elizebeth Mas 288
  Jeremiah Sco 184
  Jerh. Sco 183
  Robert Ohi 70
  William Mas 288
Tarr, Charles Bou 113
  Jno. Hrd 292
  John Bou 132
  Lydia Bou 132
  William She 220
Tarrant, Carter Gal 196
  Reuben Gar 225
  Saml War 267
  Te[illegible] War 264
Tarr[illegible], John A. Jef 26
  Lewis A. Jef 30
Tarry, John Way 361
  Josiah Way 361
Tarter, Chrisley Pul 131
  John Pul 131
  Peter Pul 131
Tarven, George Bra 150
  Thos. Bra 145
Tarvin, George Fle 70
  Richard Cam 24
Tate, Benja. Hnr 361
  Isaac Grn 259
  James Hrs 322
  John Bou 132
  John Cam 26
  John Grn 259
  John Log 193
  Robert Pul 132
  Samuel Bre 169
  Samuel Pul 132
  Stephen Rck 159
  Thomas Fra 171
  William Clr 143

Tate, cont.
William Lin 136
Tatem, John Log 170
Tatman, Joshua Fle 79
Josshua Fle 81
Heahemiah Fle 82
Tatmon, John Mon 374
Tatum, Crafton Mad 228
John Mad 228
Nichs. Gar 227
Samuel Mad 229
Seth Pul 131
Taul, Arthur Fay 26
Benja. J. Clr 143
Levy Clr 143
Michl. War 357
Samuel Fay 26
Taumhill, Ninian Log 191
Taunihill Log 191
Tavin, Joseph Cam 24
Tawglle, Griffin Woo 383
Tayler, Argyle Woo 392
Chapman Woo 387
George War 257
Henry Woo 394
James She 203
John Lin 136
John Woo 392
Joseph Woo 382
Joseph F. Woo 399
Mosis War 250
Reddin War 250
Richard Woo 389
Robert Woo 381
Walter Lin 136
Wm. Jr Woo 394
Wm. Senr Woo 394
Taylor, Abram Log 185
Absalim Cly 151
Absalom Pul 131
Absolam War 248
Ariss Bou 113
Arnold Ohi 98
Arthur Log 186
Arthur Log 192
Asa Fay 34
Asa Fay 53
Baily Hnd 329
Bartholomew Bra 146
Ben Hrd 283
Benjamin Ohi 98
Benjn. Jef 26
Berryman Hrd 288
Chapman Log 196
Cleden Wsh 323
Colby H. Jef 27
Cranson She 242
Daniel Bul 186
Daniel Log 168
Daniel Log 179
Daniel War 246
David Hop 373
David Knx 90
David Mad 227
David, Jr Hnr 359
Dudley Gar 226
Edmund Cam 33
Edmund Log 180
Edward Chr 78
Edward Clr 143
Edward Mad 228
Edmund Mad 229
Edward Mas 288
Edwd. Hop 378
Francis Cly 157
Francis Jef 19
Francis Jef 19
Taylor, cont.
Francis Mas 308
Gabe Wsh 324
Geo. Fle 74
Georege Pen 114
George Adr 15
George Clr 142
George Fle 64
George Fle 85
George Nic 62
George Nic 63
George, Senr Fle 65
George, G. Clr 142
Giles Chr 80
Hardeman Jes 49
Harrison, Junr Ohi 77
Harrison, Senr Ohi 76
Henry Fle 66
Henry Fle 70
Henry Gar 227
Henry Ohi 78
Henry Ohi 88
Henry Wsh 323
Hubbard Clr 142
Isaac Cum 165
Isaac Hop 380
Isaac Hrd 285
Isaac Hrs 318
Isaac Nel 22
J. Caleb Mas 290
Jacob Mul 402
Jacob Hrs 319
James Fra 170
James Jef 19
James Liv 148
James Mad 226
James Mad 229
James Mul 396
James Ohi 74
James Sco 179
James Cam 31
James Cum 165
Jas. Gar 227
Jas. Hrd 285
Jas. Hrd 285
Jessa Mon 353
Jno. Lew 101
John Bar 32
John Bou 113
John Fay 15
John Fle 84
John Fle 84
John Gal 193
John Gar 225
John Grn 246
John Hop 378
John Lew 98
John Lin 137
John Lin 137
John Log 167
John Mad 228
John Mad 230
John Mer 335
John Mon 381
John Mul 395
John Ohi 70
John Pul 132
John She 207
John Wsh 323
John Wsh 323
John Wsh 323
John Wsh 327
John M. Fay 49
John P. But 197
John S. Wsh 324
John Y. Grn 256
Jonathan Gar 225
Taylor, cont.
Jonathan Hnd 336
Jos. War 249
Joseph But 197
Joseph Fra 172
Joseph Lew 101
Joseph Mad 230
Joseph Ohi 70
Joseph War 250
Joseph War 282
Joshua Fle 78
Joshua Fle 88
Joshua Fra 170
Joshua Fra 171
Joshua Nic 63
L. James Mas 287
L. John Nic 62
Larkin Est 8
Leonard Cas 48
M. Willis Wsh 324
Manuel Ohi 98
Mary Fay 60
Matthew Bou 113
Michal Cum 178
Moorman Gar 228
Mosis War 248
Nancy Gra 237
Nat Nic 62
Nathan Jef 19
Nathaniel Gra 243
Nicholas Fle 64
Pardon Ohi 103
Peter Log 185
Peter Mad 227
Philip She 206
Phillip Fay 15
Phillip Fra 172
Phillip Ohi 98
Polly Log 185
Ranson Fle 61
Reuben Jef 18
Richard Fra 172
Richard Mon 382
Richard Ohi 76
Richard, Jr Jef 26
Richard, Sr Jef 19
Richard, Sr. Jef 26
Right Log 191
Right, Jr Log 167
Robert Mas 308
Robert She 198
Robert, Sr Pen 112
Robt. Gar 226
Robt. Jr Pen 108
Robt. Lew 95
Roger Jef 26
Saml. Abr 51
Samuel Grn 259
Samuel Pul 131
Samuel Wsh 324
Samuel M. Clr 142
Sarah Mad 229
Sarah Mas 290
Sarah Mon 382
Septimus Hrs 323
Septimus Ohi 70
Simon Bou 112
Simon Ohi 104
Stark Fay 54
Stephen Bra 141
Stephen Knx 64
Talton Mad 229
Taply Nic 62
Tarply Fle 66
Tekel Fra 171
Tetel Log 185
Tho. Hop 374

Taylor, cont.
Thomas But 197
Thomas Gra 237
Thomas Jef 19
Thomas Lew 98
Thomas Log 176
Thomas Log 185
Thomas Log 186
Thomas Log 193
Thomas (little) Mad 230
Thomas (Big) Mad 230
Thomas Mad 246
Thomas Mer 336
Thomas Ohi 85
Thompson Jef 26
Thompson Nel 22
Thurston Clr 147
Tinwick Lew 101
William Bou 185
William But 197
William Clr 142
William Fay 54
William Fle 69
William Knx 79
William Mad 229
William (son of little Tom) Mad 230
William Mas 287
William Mas 308
William Mer 336
William Ohi 71
William Wsh 323
William Wsh 323
William H. Mer 335
Wm. Cum 176
Wm. Jef 20
Wm. Jef 26
Wm. She 242
Zachariah Jef 19
Zachariah Jes 49
Zachariah Woo 379
Zachy. Adr 14
Zachy. Adr 15
Taytor, Levy Chr 66
Nicholas Log 167
Teaford, Christn. Bou 132
Teag, Joseph She 229
Teagarden, George Fay 59
Teague, Able Hop 378
David Knx 74
Joshua Knx 66
Van S. Hop 377
William Chr 64
Tearley, Aron War 263
Benjn. War 267
Tears, William Chr 88
Teats, John Bul 186
Michael Bul 186
Tebbs, Samuel Mas 30[illegible]
William Mas 28[illegible]
Tedford, Gabral Chr 94
Simon Chr 93
Teel, Adam Mul 385
Tegarden, Bazel She 207
Tegey, Adam Lew 101
Teorey, George War 272
Telchener, Danl. Nel 22
Telford, John Bar 30
John Fay 15
Telp, John Boo 63
Tellett, Saml. Nel 21
Temple, Benjamin Log 188
Benjn. War 254
Geo. Cum 182
Jessee Bar 38
John W. Cum 173
Loyd Bar 38
Temple, cont.
Stephen Log 181
Thomas She 217
Templeman, Henry Fay 26
John Lin 137
Roy Nel 20
Templeton, George Way 353
James Cly 15[illegible]
James Knx 7[illegible]
John Chr 9[illegible]
Templin, Martha Lin 13[illegible]
Tenant, Richard Mas 287
Tenelly, George Jef 26
Tenley, Charles Nel 20
Tennasin, Robert Chr 85
Tennel, George Mad 230
Tennell, Danl. Nel 21
Hugh Nel 21
John Nel 21
Tennill, William Mad 231
Tennis, John Mas 289
Samuel Mas 288
Tennison, Asa J. Grn 255
Jacob But 197
Terbeville, James Mul 387
Terguson, John Chr 99
Terhoon, Garret Mer 337
Stephen Mer 337
Terhune, Abirk Sr Fle 72
Albert Fle 61
Barnet Fle 79
Danil Fle 88
Isaac Fle 72
Luke Fle 71
Terrel, Henry Gar 227
John Boo 63
John Gar 226
Jos. Gar 226
Mary Gar 226
Robt. Gar 227
Terrell, Henry Clr 142
John Jef 19
Peter Cal 6
Solomon Knx 75
Terrence, James But 197
Terress, Henry Fay 15
Terril, Archibald Woo 401
George Mad 231
Terrill, Edmund Mad 231
James Bou 112
John Bou 112
Presley Woo 387
Terrol, Robert Mas 290
Terry, Aaron Hrd 300
Champion Liv 158
Geo. Hop 378
Hannah Grp 274
[illegible]sper Hrd 282
[illegible]h Cal 14
[illegible]n Bou 112
[illegible]t Hnd 347
[illegible] Bar 52
Thomas Bou 112
Thomas Liv 157
Wm. Hrd 304
Teter, Geo. Jnr Gar 226
Geo. Snr Gar 226
Littleton Far 44
Parris Gar 227
Saml. Gar 227
Will Gar 227
Teterton, Thomas Mul 401
Tetrack, John Fay 26
Tetrick, Jos. Boo 63
Tevis, Jeremiah Mad 228
Katharine Mas 289
Nathanl. Mad 230
Tevis, cont.
Peter Mas 287
Robert Mad 227
Robert She 206
Thomas Mad 227
Tevott, John Mer 336
Tewell, Barton Mas 287
[illegible]as. Hrd 299
[illegible]n Mas 288
[illegible]ndford Mas 288
Thacker, Allen Gar 226
Benja. Gar 226
Edwd. War 277
Joel Fra 171
William Pul 131
Thaogmatin, Joshua Chr 77
Tharp, Abner Mas 289
Andrew Mas 286
Charles Wsh 323
Elihu Mas 290
Jacob Fle 67
James Wsh 328
John Bre 159
John She 233
Parra Wsh 324
Saml. Boo 63
Samuel Mul 400
William Wsh 323
William Wsh 328
Willm. A. Sco 168
Thartkeld, Ann Fle 90
Thatcher, Barthw. Bou 132
Danl. Cam 24
Jese Bra 142
John. Bou 132
Joseph Bra 152
Joseph She 222
Nancy She 208
Wm. Bou 132
Theobald, Thomas Jef 19
Theoblads, James Pen 112
William Sco 193
Theobles, Cl[illegible] Mas 287
Therlkill, Pe[illegible] Bar 30
Thickston, Abraham Bul 186
Elizabeth Bul 186
Jacob Mer 337
Joseph Bul 185
William Bul 186
Thirman, Joseph War 279
Willm. War 279
Thixton, Abraham Wsh 324
Thomas, Abraham Mad 230
Agnes Gal 193
Alexr. Nel 21
Alexr. Way 362
Anderson Pul 133
Ann Fra 172
Ann Wsh 322
Anthony Hrs 308
Anna Mer 335
Aron Bra 143
Benjamin Mon 383
Benjamin Nel 21
Benjamin Ohi 102
Benjamin Wsh 328
Bennett Jes 49
Bennett Wsh 324
C. William Mas 287
Charles Cum 170
Daniel Bou 113
Daniel Pen 106
Daniel Pen 107
David Bou 112
David Fay 54
David 48
David 289

Thomas, cont.
David Mas 289
David Mul 400
David She 200
Edward Nic 63
Edward S. Nel 21
Eli Bou 132
Eli War 262
Elias Mas 290
Elijah Way 362
Elisha Mer 343
Eliza Pul 133
Elizabeth War 262
Enos Wsh 328
Epraim Mas 287
Flemg. Adr 14
Francis Gal 193
Francis W. Bul 186
Geo Lew 102
George Bou 132
Gilbreth Lew 101
Harder Cas 37
Hardin Hrd 290
Harrison Cas 37
Henry Mas 289
Henry War 243
Henry Way 356
Henry H. Mad 226
Isaac Bre 161
Isaac Hrd 296
Isaac Jef 19
Isaac Mas 289
Isaac Mul 403
Isaac Nel 22
Isac Fay 45
Isl. Lew 102
Jacob Bra 141
Jacob Log 175
James Bar 43
James Chr 95
James Chr 97
James Clr 143
James Fle 86
James Fle 86
James, Capt. Mad 228
James Nel 6
James Ohi 73
James Pen 112
James War 260
Jas. Bou 113
Jas. Hnr 369
Jas. Hrd 283
Jesse Mad 227
Jesse Bar 24
Jno. Hrd 287
Joel Mon 378
John Bou 132
John Bra 149
John Bra 150
John Bra 150
John Est 8
John Gal 194
John Hrs 307
John Hrs 307
John Jes 49
John Jes 49
John Knx 64
John Lin 136
John Log 168
John Log 191
John Mer 336
John Mer 336
John Mer 337
John Pul 133
John She 204
John War 278
John Wsh 328

Thomas, cont.
Jonathan Jef 19
Jonathn. Nel 21
Joseph Bou 132
Joseph Hrd 304
Joseph Knx 69
Joseph Mad 232
Joseph Mer 335
Joseph Pul 133
Joshua Mad 232
Larken Mon 378
Lewis Mer 336
Lewis Wsh 328
Louis Nel 20
Marchant Cly 149
Martha Clr 142
Martin Log 166
Massey Ohi 104
Michal Fay 48
Moses Bou 132
Moses Hrd 297
Moses Mas 290
Nathan Boo 63
Nathan War 262
Nathaniel Mas 287
Notley Hrs 308
Oswald She 222
Pendleton Mer 336
Phillip Boo 63
Plummer Lew 98
Presley Bou 113
Randol Log 165
Redn. G. Nel 21
Reuben Cas 40
Reuben Hnr 369
Richard Bou 112
Richard Jef 27
Richd. M. Woo 381
Robert Adr 17
Robert Gal 193
Robert Mas 288
Robert Mon 357
Robert, Senr Mon 357
Roland Lew 99
Roland Lew 99
Ron Hnr 354
Rosil Bou 112
Saml. Bra 141
Samuel Bou 132
Samuel Chr 109
Sollomon Lew 99
Tapley Woo 385
Taylor Bou 72
Thomas Wsh 322
Thompson Mer 335
Thos. Bou 112
Thos. Senr Bou 113
Thos. P. Bra 150
Thruston Bra 150
Walter War 263
Westley War 263
William Bou 112
William Bre 163
William Chr 67
William Fle 90
William Rck 162
William She 222
William War 263
William Wsh 328
Wm. Cas 42
Wm. Gal 193
Zachariah Bar 31
Thomasbury, William Log 183
Thaomson, Joseph Sco 184
Reubin Bou 112
Saml. Sco 170

Thomason, cont.
Saml. Sco 172
Saml. D. Hop 377
Sandy Bou 112
Sarah Sco 174
Thomasson, John Cam 25
Thompkins, Christopher Grn 262
Gwin Fay 59
Murphry Bar 33
Nat. Nic 62
Thompon, Sally Nic 62
Thompsan, Jos. War 263
Thompsen, John Mad 231
Thompson, A.Nelson Lin 136
Abraham Mon 363
Adam Chr 60
Alexr. Lin 136
Alexr. Nic 63
Ambrose Wsh 325
Andrew Fle 88
Andrew Flo 103
Andrew Log 167
Andrew Mer 337
Andw Hop 373
Ann Wsh 324
Anthony Ohi 83
Anthony Woo 390
Anty. Lew 98
Archabald She 200
Archd. Mas 286
Archibald Mer 336
Arthur Mer 336
Asa Fay 50
Athr. Nel 21
Austin Wsh 325
Baliam War 277
Barton Bre 166
Bazil Wsh 325
Benard Wsh 325
Benjamin But 197
Bent Nel 20
Bowler Liv 148
Carter But 197
Charles Mas 287
Chas. Nel 21
Clifton Fay 50
Closs Cam 31
Daniel Nic 63
David Clr 142
David Gar 226
David She 205
David She 238
David Woo 379
Dickenson Way 363
Ealtren Nel 21
Ebenezer Mas 289
Edward Wsh 328
Edwd. Hrd 288
Edwd. Hrd 293
Elexander Way 368
Eli Bul 186
Elijah Bra 148
Elixtious Jes 47
Eliza Hnr 359A
Elizabeth Jef 19
Elizath. Nel 21
Elizabeth Wsh 325
Ephraim Wsh 325
Ephram War 277
Evan Mer 335
Foster Mer 335
Fulton Fay 39
Gabriel Wsh 325
George Bra 144
George Lin 136
George Mer 335

Thompson, cont.
George Mer 336
George Mer 341
George Mon 371
George War 258
George Wsh 324
Geprge Wsh 325
Gideon Chr 113
Henry Bul 186
Henry Nic 63
Hugh Bre 162
Hugh Mas 289
Igns. Nel 21
Igs. Nel 20
James Bra 151
James Bra 151
James Bre 163
James Bul 186
James But 197
James Chr 64
James Chr 81
James Clr 142
James Fay 53
James Flo 103
James Jef 26
James Jef 26
James Mer 337
James Mer 337
James Nic 63
James M. Chr 59
Jas. Gar 225
Jas. Hrd 298
Jeremiah War 257
Jesse Mad 231
Jesse Pul 132
Joel Chr 90
Joel Hnr 351
John Chr 60
John Chr 83
John Chr 103
John Chr 114
John Clr 142
John Clr 142
John Clr 142
John Fra 171
John Fra 171
John Flo 103
John Jef 19
John Mas 288
John Mas 290
John Mer 335
John Mer 336
John Mon 373
John Ohi 99
John Pul 132
John She 202
John War 280
John Wsh 323
John Wsh 325
John B. Mer 335
John B. Wsh 324
Jos. War 257
Joseph Cam 32
Joseph Clr 142
Joseph Mas 287
Joseph Mer 336
Joseph Mer 341
Joseph Mon 366
Joseph Mon 371
Joseph Mon 372
Joseph Ohi 92
Joseph Rck 162
Joseph Wsh 325
Laurence Fle 74
Laurence Wsh 325
Lawrence Mad 232
Leffard Mas 289

Thompson, cont.
Lexius Flo 103
Lovet Bra 146
Lucy(freewoman) Fay 15
Mary Mer 336
Mathy Clr 142
Matthew Lew 95
Matthew Lew 99
Matthew Lew 100
Meridith Rch 162
Molly Bou 113
Moses But 197
Moses Fle 86
Nancy But 197
Nathl. Woo 390
Peter Chr 116
Peter War 268
Phebe Cum 177
Raphl. Nel 21
Rawdon Cum 177
Reaves Wsh 325
Reuben Mas 289
Richard Flo 103
Richard Wsh 324
Richd. Nel 6
Richd. War 274
Richd. War 278
Robert Chr 115
Robert Chr 116
Robert Jef 19
Robert Jef 20
Sally Jef 20
Saml. Cam 27
Saml. War 273
Samuel Chr 62
Samuel Fle 61
Samuel Fle 82
Samuel Fle 89
Samuel Flo 103
Samuel Hrs 313
Samuel Log 195
Sarah Lin 136
Stephen War 277
Thomas Fay 27
Thomas Mas 290
Thoms Mon 363
Thomas Mon 378
Thomas Wsh 324
Thomas Wsh 325
Thomas Wsh 325
Thomas Wsh 328
Thompson Pul 132
Thos. Nel 20
Thos. Nle 22
Thos. Way 363
Thos. A. Bou 113
Uriah Bre 158
Walter Fay 41
William Chr 56
William Chr 84
William Fay 26
William Grn 253
William Hnr 351
William Liv 150
William Liv 152
William Mad 230
William, Revd. Mad 231
William Mul 405
William She 213
William Woo 382
William Wsh 324
William Wsh 328
William G. Fay 15
Willm. Lin 136
Willm. Nel 20
Willm. War 274
Wilm. War 274

Thompson, cont.
Wm. Bar 34
Wm. Bra 151
Wm. Bra 151
Wm. Cam 27
Wm. Gal 193
Wm. Jef 26
Wm. Lew 97
Wm. Lew 99
Wm. Lew 103
Wm. Mon 367
Wm. Mon 378
Wm. Nic 63
Woody Bar 53
Zachariah Bra 144
Thompsons, John Lew 99
Thoms, Arther Bra 141
Thomson, David Sco 170
George Hnr 351
Gilbert Sco 179
Harry(free man of colour) Jes 48
Henry Mer 337
Hugh D. Mon 384
James Cal 13
James Cal 15
Jarvis Sco 176
Jas. Hnr 359B
John Sco 170
John Sco 179
Joseph Jes 48
Leonard Way 357
Martin Sco 179
Peter Sco 180
Peter Sco 187
Polly Jes 48
Poyndexter Hnr 361
Richard Mul 402
Robert But 197
Robert Sco 169
Robert, Jur Sco 179
Robert, Senr Sco 178
Rodes Sco 189
Samuel Mer 335
Thomas Cal 7B
Washington Cal 12
William Hnr 355
William Jes 49
Wooddy Grp 270
Wm. Sco 176
Thorn, Anthony Jef 19
Henry Jef 19
John Hnr 361
John Woo 377
Nicholas Hop 377
Thos. Sco 182
William Mas 287
Thornbrough, Joel Fay 26
Thornburg, Isaac Mad 230
Thornbury, Elijah Mas 287
Thornhill, John Pen 115
Rheuben? Hrs 319
Thornsberry, Daniel Bul 186
Francis Gra 244
Samuel Bul 185
Thomas Mer 336
Thornsbury, Benj. Nel 22
Winna Bul 185
Zehcariah Mas 288
Thornton, Anthony Grn 257
Antony Nic 62
Antoy. Jr Bou 1[illegible]
Aron War 248
Benjn. Bou 112
Doctr. Chas. Bou 70
George Fra 171
George Jes 48

Thornton, cont.
George Lin 136
Henry P. Bou 112
James Woo 401
Joel War 248
John Pen 106
Josiah Cal 5
Luke War 244
Mark Cal 8
Patsey Gar 224
Peter Lin 136
Presly Hnd 344
Susannah Sco 170
Thomas Wsh 323
Thomas Wsh 328
Thos. Bou 112
William Clr 143
William clr 143
William Mas 288
Wm. Cal 15
Thoroughman, Charles Mas 290
John Mas 288
William Mas 286
William, Junr Mas 290
Thorp, David Hrd 286
Dodsen Mad 232
Jeremiah Mad 230
Jno. Hrd 287
Terry Hrd 299
Thomas Mad 230
Zachariah Mad 232
Thowe, Edward Woo 399
Thraelkill, Daniel Mer 335
George Mer 335
Thrailkell, Daniel Bra 148
William Mer 336
Thrailkile, Gabriel Mul 389
Thrailkill, Daniel Mer 337
George Sco 181
Jesse Sco 181
John She 215
Moses She 210
Wm. Sco 178
Thralekile, Aaron Mul 387
Thrash, William Hnd 340
Thrasher, Eli Bre 160
John Bre 164
John Pen 117
John, Sr Pen 106
Josiah Cam 24
Josiah Pen 106
Stephen Pen 106
William Pen 106
Wm. Cum 184
Threlkeld, John Fle 77
William Fle 65
Threlkild, Daniel Hnd 325
Thriet, Frederick Chr 104
Thrift, Charles Fay 26
Tabitha Fay 24
Throckmorton, Arc Nic 62
John Nic 62
Saml. Fra 172
Tho. NIc 62
Thos. Nic 62
Throlls, Isaac Nel 22
Throop, John Cal 7
Thruston, Ezekil. Bou 132
Thurman, Bazer Nel 21
Benjamin Pul 131
Betsy Nel 41
C. James Lin 136
Henderson Mad 232
John Grn 251
Livingston Wsh 345

Thurman, cont.
Nathan Cum 169
Philip Wsh 323
Richard Mad 232
Richard Wsh 329
Thos. Cum 182
William Clr 143
William Wsh 327
Wm. Cum 182
Thurmen, William Wsh 328
Thurmon, John Wsh 329
Mary Wsh 327
Thomas Wsh 329
William Wsh 329
Thurmond, Charles Wsh 329
David Lin 136
Elisha Liv 150
Henry Wsh 329
John Lin 136
Molly Lin 137
Phillip Lin 137
Willm. Lin 137
Thurston, Plummer She 238
Susanna Bou 132
Thomas Jef 27
Wm. Bou 132
Tiag, Joshua Liv 156
Tibbart, Thomas Fay 16
Tibbles, Richard Mas 289
Tibbs, Daniel Jef 26
Diskin Grn 262
William Ohi 98
William T. Fle 84
Tiber, Frederick She 220
Tibs, Danl. Grn 262
Jos. Hrd 303
Ticen, Macklin Sco 184
Tichenor, Jerod Ohi 71
Jonas Ohi 71
Peter She 201
Timothy Ohi 85
Tichner, Jacob She 199
Tidford, Josiah Cal 4
Tidman, Tho.? Hop 372
Tidwell, Edmon chr 78
William Hnr 356
Tietar, Robt.? Hnr 368
Tiffel, Charles Wsh 323
Tigart, John Wsh 323
Samuel She 221
Tiggs, Greenbury Mon 373
Tiler, Benjamin Fay 44
William, Senr Fay 44
Tilery, Thomas Mon 348
Tilford, Alexander Sco 192
Alexr. Sco 191
Alexr. Senr Sco 191
Andw. Adr 14
Elexr. Adr 14
Gabral Chr 96
James Mer 336
James Sco 188
John Adr 14
Nancy War 262
Robert Fra 170
Robt. Adr 14
Saml. Adr 14
William Lin 137
William Sco 191
Tilla, James Log 178
Tiller, James War 247
John Fra 171
Tabitha War 247
Tillet, Giles Bou 132
James Bou 132
John, Senr Bou 132
Tilley, Aron She 228

Tilley, cont.
Benjamin Jes 48
Henry She 236
James Jes 49
Lazerus She 235
Lazrous She 228
William Bou 132
Tillis, Jane Fay 26
Tillory, William Woo 396
Tilly, Moses She 215
Tilman, Edward Log 171
Francess But 197
Wiggins Log 166
Tilmon, George Chr 77
Tilson, Stephen Pul 132
Tilton, Peter Fay 15
Richard Mas 287
Robert Fay 31
Robert Fay 39
Timberlake, George Hrs 323
Henry Bou 68
John Mad 230
Joseph Mad 232
Oba Grp 275
Oba Grp 275
Philip Cam 28
Timberlick, William Mer 335
Timberman, Stophel Cum 184
Times, James Chr 91
Walter Chr 71
Timmins, Nimrod Mer 337
Timmirs, Toliver Hop 376
Timmons, Abner Hop 371
Elizabeth Hop 372
Geo. Hop 377
Moses Cal 7
Saml. Bar 38
Stephen Hop 377
Timpy, Barnard Fay 42
Tims, Hollis Chr 93
Tincher, Hamilton Est 5
Robert Mad 232
Samuel Mad 232
William Mad 232
William H. Est 3
Wm. Mon 373
Tindal, Elizabeth War 246
John Boo 63
John Lin 136
John Liv 157
John L. Liv 157
Tindall, William Lin 137
Tindel, Obadiah Chr 92
Tinden, James Fay 26
Tinder, Elijah Woo 392
James Woo 386
Tindle, Charles Jes 48
Edmund Cam 29
Moses Bre 163
William Bre 163
Tiner, Richd. Sco 193
Tingle, Jasper Fay 26
Kindal Hnr 367
L. Hnr 367
Thos. Hnr 368
Tinker, Anderson ESt 7
Tinley, Thos. War 274
Tinn, Richard Cas 37
Tinnell, Samuel Wsh 329
Tinney, Nathaniel Wsh 329
Tinsley, Isaac Fay 26
James Mul 401
Jas. Bou 112
John Fay 44
John She 213
Jona. She 231

Tinsley, cont.
  Joseph Grp 277
  Mary Wsh 327
  Ransom Clr 143
  Samuel She 208
  Starlin Bar 21
  Thomas Knx 65
  William Fay 35
  William Knx 78
  William She 213
Tinsly, Elijah Bar 37
  James Lin 137
Tipton, Electious Mon 348
  Jabes Mad 227
  James Knx 68
  John Est 5
  Michel Mon 382
  Moses Mad 228
  Samuel Mon 375
  Solomon Mon 382
  William Est 5
  Wm. Mon 382
Tirey, Joseph Clr 143
Tiroe, William Grp 272
Tipen, John Cam 31
Tirpin, Jacob Mon 372
Tisdale, Mary Cal 4
Tisdall, John Lin 137
  Willm. Lin 136
Tisdle, Richard Hrs 309
Titchener, Lewis She 199
Titford, Walter Cal 6
Titus Nic 62
Titus , Ebenezer Mad 228
  George Gal 193
  John Mad 230
  Joseph Mad 230
  Mary Bra 147
  William Mad 228
Tiver, Reason Bra 143
Tives, Robt. Bra 150
Tobias, a free Negro Mad 231
Tobin, Robert Wsh 329
Tod, Joseph Cam 33
Todd, Andrew Bou 70
  Andrew She 226
  Benjamin Log 162
  Benjamin(Clay's Overseer) Mad 232
  Benjamin, Jr Log 166
  Benjamin, Senr Log 166
  Benjamin, Sen Mad 232
  Benjn. War 244
  Benjn. Jr Mad 231
  Isaac Mad 227
  Jane Bou 112
  Jane Pul 132
  Jas. Cly 154
  John Bou 132
  John Fay 26
  John Jef 28
  John Mad 231
  John Mon 353
  John She 206
  John She 240
  John War 270
  Johnson She 228
  Jona Hop 374
  Joseph Hrd 281
  Joseph Mad 228
  Joseph Mon 369
  Joseph, Jun Mad 232
  Joseph, Senr Mad 232
  Joshua Mad 232
  Leven Bou 113
  Nancy Hop 371
Todd, cont.
  Peter Mad 226
  Richd. Sco 187
  Robert Fay 59
  Robert She 241
  Robert War 270
  Robt. Adr 14
  Saml. Cly 154
  Saml. Jnr Gar 199
  Samuel Gal 193
  Sarah Hop 371
  Thomas Est 3
  Thomas Fle 64
  Thomas Jef 27
  Thomas Mad 228
  Thomas Mad 230
  Thomas Woo 390
  William Fay 15
  William Fay 15
  William Mad 227
  William Woo 393
  William, Jr Mad 231
Todhunter, Jacob Jes 49
Toel, Michael
  Patrick Nel 21
Toewit, Tutman Sco 180
Tolan, Elias Mon 382
  James Mon 372
  Poterfield Mon 382
Tolar, Christopher Flo 103
  Robert Flo 103
Tolbert, Abner Cam 33
  Henson Hrs 324
  Hugh Hrs 313
  James Mul 396
  John B. Sco 183
  Reason Hrs 313
  Richard Lin 137
  Thomas Grp 272
Tolberts, John Mul 396
Tolbot, Charles Boo 63
Tolby, Isaac Cly 152
  Saml. Cly 153
Tolin, Marquis Adr 16
  Marquis Adr 16
  Peter Mon 370
  Porter Mon 350
Tolisman, Mathias Lin 136
Tolle, Jonathan Mas 287
  Jonathan, Junr Mas 290
  Reuben Mas 287
  Stephen Mas 288
  Stephen Mas 290
Tolly, John Mer 336
  William Mer 336
Tom, Free Mon 384
Tomberlin, Jas Bar 26
Tombs, Edward She 232
Tomelson, Ambrose Fay 52
  Eligah Far 52
Tomlin, Jesse Sco 191
  Joseph Adr 14
  Wm. Sco 170
Tomlinson, Archbald Mon 373
  George Mad 227
  James Mon 374
  John Sco 181
  William Sco 191
Tompkins, Edward Lin 137
  James Hop 375
  Joel Fay 20
  John Fay 26
  Robt. Hrd 285
Tompson, Clifton Fay 32
  H. James Lin 136
  James Fay 35
  John Fay 48
Tompson, cont.
  Robert Hrs 322
  Saml. Jr Log 174
  Thomas Log 187
Toncrey, Danl. Nel 6
Toney, Alexr. Bar 31
  Jessee Bar 31
  John (freeman) Fay 15
  Nowel Bar 21
Tong, James F. Ohi 78
  Joseph F. Ohi 80
  William Ohi 80
Tonkins, John Jes 49
Tonkley, Azrray Lew 98
Tool, Daniel She 237
  Dennis Nel 22
  James Mad 230
  Larence Hrs 314
  William She 216
  William She 237
Tooley, Charles Mad 231
  William Mer 336
Tooly, Geroge Mad 231
  George Mul 391
  John Mer 337
  Wm. Bar 46
Toombs, John Jes 49
Toon, Sanislaus Wsh 329
Toothman, John Boo 63
Tootle, Richard But 197
Topass, John Woo 380
Tope, Fredrick But 197
Torbitt, James Sr Woo 398
  John A. Woo 398
  Robert Woo 382
Torgason, Hugh War 271
Torgison, William Cly 160
Torian, Peter Chr 90
Tornes, Andrew Lew 97
  Martin Lew 95
  Martin Lew 99
Tornesy, John Mer 337
Tosh, John Bar 44
Totton, Jinny Gar 227
Totty, Wm. War 255
Toulman, Thos. Bra 150
Toulson, Thomas Flo 103
  James Bou 132
Tounsand, Thos. Log 171
  Tounson, Carrod Clr 143
Towler, Luke Nic 62
Towles, Thomas Hnd 344
Towman, Edwin Mer 336
Town, Bert Mon 365
Townhall, Wm. J. She 241
Towns, Henry Hnd 345
Townsel, Enoch Pul 132
Townsend, George Bra 143
  Jas. Way 353
  Joshua Bou 72
  Joshua Bou 112
  Oswald Mad 228
  Thomas Mad 228
Townson, Jacob War 271
  Moses She 225
  Nicholas Pul 133
  Roda Est 5
Tows, Imaly Fle 87
  (see also Hull, John)
  Imaly Fle 87
Towsan, Abednego Mer 336
Towsey, Lerah Boo 63
  Moses Boo 63
  Thos. Boo 63
Towson, Light War 254
Trabars, Elizabeth Fay 16
Trabue, Danl. Adr 15

Trabue, cont.
  David Jes 48
  Edward Woo 397
  Robert Adr 19
  Stephen Grn 264
Tracey, John She 213
Tracy, Charles Clr 143
  Erasmus Bar 31
  Geo. Jnr Gar 225
  Geo. Snr Gar 225
  Isaac Bar 25
  James Bar 38
  James Hnr 358
  Jerimiah Gar 224
  John Bar 38
  John Mas 288
  Michl. Bar 38
  Nathaniel Hnr 358
  Will Gar 225
  William Hnr 358
Trafford, Rebecca Mas 289
Trahoon, Stephen Hnr 362
Trail, Osburn Cam 31
  Solomon Log 167
Trailer, Agnes Clr 143
  George Cum 165
Trainer, Isaac Fay 26
Tramell, Thompson War 270
Trammell, Sampson Cly 160
Traner, John War 277
Tranver, Wm. Grn 263
Trapnel, Vincent Mer 336
Trapnell, Philip Mer 336
Trasenrider,Conrod Jef 32
  Frederick Jef 32
  John Jef 19
Traster, Michael Bou 113
  Will Bou 113
Trauber, Michael Log 188
Travelstreet, John War 271
  Wm. War 271
Travers, Charles War 273
  Henry War 273
  Jas. War 273
  John War 273
Travess, Thomas Log 167
Travice, John Jes 49
Travis, Arther Liv 152
  Daniel Liv 153
  Elizabeth Liv 153
  James Liv 147
  James Liv 153
  James Nel 21
  John Liv 152
  Mary Ohi 101
  Thomas Liv 150
Traviss, Benjamin Log 186
  Benjn. Log 191
Traw, Fredk. Sco 169
Traxel,Christopher Way 365
  Danl. Way 365
  Peter Way 365
Traxell, Jacob Way 362
  Peter Way 362
Traylor, Cary Fle 76
  Micajah Gar 224
Treacle, Stephen Mas 308
Treadaway, Joel Mon 347
  John Mon 347
  John, Junr Mon 347
  Wm. Mon 349
Trebble, Thomas Est 6
Trebe, James Fle 74
Treble, William Grn 255
Tredaway, Moses Clr 143
Tredway, Arur Chr 94
Tree, Robert Jes 48

Trent, Alexr. Bar 53
  Bryant Grn 249
  Susanna Bar 53
  Wm. Bar 53
Trevis, Wm. Cum 185
Tribbey, Jacob Fle 67
Tribble, Andrew Mad 228
  John Ohi 96
  Peter Mad 227
  Silas Mad 227
Tribby, John Mas 303
Tribey, Jason Fle 67
  William Fle 73
Trible, Samuel Clr 143
Tribue, Jane Bou 113
Trickle, Thomas Fle 78
Trigg, Allen Bou 112
  Daniel Jef 26
  Haiden Bar 55
  Simeon Mad 231
  Stephen Est 5
  Thomas Bou 112
  Thomas Jef 26
  William Fra 172
  Wm. Bar 55
  Wm. Jef 27
Triggs, Jessey Lew 95
Trimbels, William Fle 64
Trimble, David Mon 359
  David Mon 365
  Elisha Cam 27
  Elizabeth Bou 72
  Geo. Bou 132
  Isaac Bou 112
  James Bre 160
  James Fay 38
  James Liv 160
  James Mon 365
  John Fay 31
  John Jes 49
  John Liv 148
  Joseph Liv 148
  Robert Bou 69
  Robert, Senr Liv 148
  Thomas Fle 67
  William Clr 143
  William Log 181
  William Pul 133
  Trimdle, Bazil Bou 69
Trip, Reuben Log 167
  Stephen Log 174
  William Log 166
  Wm. Cal 19
Triplet, Elizebeth Mas 289
  Thos. Bou 132
Triplett,Frederick Jes 49
  George Nel 22
  Greenbury Fle 78
  Hedgeman Fra 171
  John Adr 15
  Laurance Fle 77
  Wm. Adr 15
Tripp, William, Sr Log 167
Trisler, Catharine Jes 48
  Henry Jes 48
  Jacob Jes 48
  Joseph Jes 48
  Peter Jes 48
Trissel, Wm. Lew 101
Trobridge, Davdi Clr 143
  Ebenezer Clr 142
  Isaac Clr 142
Trobridje, Joab Bar 34
Trosper, Elijah Knx 87
  James Knx 87
  Nicholas Knx 64
  Nicholas, Jr Knx 84

Trosper, cont.
  Robert Knx 73
Trotsail, John Ohi 97
Trott, Abraham Cas 45
Trotter, Elijah Lin 136
  George, Junr Fay 15
  George, Senr Fay 15
  James Bou 112
  James Cum 184
  James Fay 26
  James Sco 186
  John Grn 255
  John Lin 137
  Joseph Sco 172
  Nancy Bou 112
  Samuel Fay 15
  Sarah Bou 112
  William Fra 171
  Wm. Hrd 283
Troup, Geo. Sco 191
  Mary Rck 163
Trout, Daniel Gal 193
  Jeremiah Gal 192
  Wender Fay 42
Troutman, Abraham Bul 186
  Adam Fay 32
  Adam Fay 47
  Jacob Fay 47
  Leond. Bou 132
  Leond. Nel 20
  Michael Bul 186
  P. Hnr 368
  Peter Fay 47
  Jacob Fay 35
Trouver, Augustus Lew 98
Trover, John Log 194
  Leonard Cam 32
  Michael Log 167
Trower, John Mer 335
Troxall, Frederick Gra 243
Troxley, John Gal 193
Troy, John Fay 54
Troyman, James Sco 168
Truat, Obadiah Nel 21
True, Benjamin Mas 289
  James, Junr Fay 33
  James, Junr Fay 50
  James, Senr Fay 33
  James, Senr Fay 50
  Jno. Grn 264
  John Fay 26
  John Fay 50
  John Fay 51
  John, Junr Woo 387
  John, Senr Woo 386
  John P. Grn 264
  Larken Fay 16
  Martin Pul 133
  Mary Mas 290
  Robert Fay 26
  Robert Woo 387
  Thomas Clr 143
Tureaxe, Isaac Adr 14
  John Adr 12
Trueman, Henry Hrd 299
  Jno. Hrd 299
  Walter Hrd 301
Truet, Riley Bra 142
Truett, Job Liv 149
  Riley War 253
Truit, Thos. Way 366
Truitt, Ely Fle 79
  George Fle 81
  Jesse Hnr 368
  Joseph Fle 79
  Marry Fle 79
  Saxigotha Fle 79

Name	County	Page
Truitt, cont.		
William	Fle	81
Wm.	Lew	102
Trulock, Parker	Bou	112
Trulove, C. Will	Nic	62
Trumble, James	Liv	147
Trumbo, Jacob	Mon	375
John	Mon	375
Trumbow, Adam	Bou	132
Andrew	Bou	132
Geo.	Bou	132
Truman, Benjn.	War	244
Trumon, Andrew	She	233
William	She	237
Trump, Frederick	Lin	136
Trumun, Absolam	War	267
Trunells, Ivins	Bou	132
Trunnel, John	Bul	186
Trusdale, Nathan	Cam	29
Nathan	Cam	31
Trussel, Jilson	Bou	112
Nahum	Bou	112
Trussell, Sally	Log	167
Trustner, Peggy	Gar	225
Philip	Gar	297
Trvis, Flotin	Cam	32
Tubb, William	Grn	256
Tubman, John	Wsh	329
Silvanus	Wsh	329
Tubs, Jesse	Jes	49
Tuck, Happy	But	197
Tuckar, Edward	Hrd	313
Edward	Hrs	312
Wm.	Hrs	314
Tucker, Alexander	Hnr	355
Alexdr.	Bou	113
Aquilla	Bou	113
Archibard	Clr	142
Benjaman	Fle	72
Benjamin	Clr	142
Boothe	Hnr	359
Charles	Chr	101
Daniel L. or S.	Fra	171
Edward	Bou	112
Edward	Bra	149
Elias	Bou	113
Elijah	Bra	149
Henry	Cly	158
Henry	Hnd	329
Jacob	Hrd	291
James	Bul	186
James	Hnr	364
James	Wsh	327
Jesse	Mas	290
John	Bou	112
John	Bra	144
John	Bre	165
John	Wsh	327
Joseph	Wsh	327
Littlebury	Lin	136
Martin	Bar	39
Mary	Hnr	359
Matthew	Wsh	327
Nathan	Clr	142
Nathan	Hrd	288
Patsey	Bou	113
Peter	Gra	239
Peyton	Liv	154
Pleasant	Lin	136
Robert	Fay	26
Robert	Lin	136
Saml.	Fle	87
Samuel	Chr	68
Sarah	Hrd	284
Thomas	Bou	113
Thomas	She	203
Thos.	Bra	144

Name	County	Page
Tucker, cont.		
Truman	Wsh	327
William	Hrs	314
Wm.	Adr	15
Zacariah	Lin	136
Zacheriah	Bou	113
Tuckor, Edwd?	Cam	27
Tuder, Bloomer	Mad	228
Daniel	Mad	229
Henry	Bar	47
Henry, Sen	Bar	47
John	Bar	47
John	Fay	33
John	Mad	229
Kinsey	BAr	48
Oswald	Mad	229
Thomas	Fay	26
Valintine	Mad	229
Tudis, Sally	Knx	90
Tuel, William	Wsh	327
Tuggle, Henry	Pul	132
James	Pul	132
Thomas	Knx	67
William	Clr	142
William	Pul	132
William	Pul	132
William	Pul	133
Tuley, Wyet P.	Bul	186
Tull, Frederick	Hrd	282
Isaac	Bou	132
Jessee	Bou	113
John	Bou	113
Samuel	Boo	63
Samuel	Pen	110
Sammuel	Fay	39
Thomas	Fay	39
Tuller, James	Pul	133
Jno.	Hnr	353
John	Pul	133
Tulley, John	Lew	102
Tullis, Joel	Bre	160
Tully, Ireal	Fle	78
James	Fay	56
Saml.	Sco	188
Tuly, Elizabeth	Jef	26
John	Jef	19
Wm. F.	Jef	26
Tumbleston, Isaac	Bou	113
Tumblestone, Sarah	Sco	190
Tummelson, John	Pul	133
Tune, Henry	Sco	178
Tungate, Ephraim	Gar	225
James	Clr	143
Jas.	Gar	226
John	Gar	227
Mary	Gar	227
Rial	Gar	227
Tunhone?, Jacob	Fle	63
Tuning, Charles	Jes	49
Tunks, Alexy.	Jes	48
Tunnil, John	Bar	48
Tunstal, Leonard	Bar	25
John	Bar	25
Joseph	Bar	41
Tempel	Bar	47
Tunstall, Humphrey	Mad	231
John	Fra	171
Mille	Fra	172
Richard	Mad	227
Tunstell, Richard	Mad	231
Tunsy, Matthew	Sco	181
Tur, Samuel	Hnd	331
Turbow, Jacob	Adr	14
Tureman, Thomas	Mas	289
William	Mas	308
Turham, Joel	Jes	48
Turhoon, John	Mer	336

Name	County	Page
Turhoon, cont.		
John	Mer	336
William	Mer	336
William	Mer	336
Turk, Tom	Adr	14
Turley, Benjn.	Mad	231
David	Mon	367
James	Mon	368
John	Cum	173
Leonard	Mon	356
Samuel	Mon	365
Samuel	Pul	132
Stephen	Mad	231
Turman, John	Flo	105
Turnage, John	War	276
Turnam, John	Nel	22
Turnbow, John	Adr	14
John	Ohi	72
Turnbull, John	Cum	180
Turner, Action	Jes	47
Agnes	Sco	181
Alexr.	Woo	383
Andrew	Pul	132
Ann	Lin	137
Anne	Mad	227
Arthur	Woo	402
Bartlet	Woo	386
Berry	Knx	77
Calep	Lin	137
Charles	Mer	335
Cornelias	War	262
Derum	Gra	238
Edward	Cly	151
Edward	Fle	79
Edward	Mad	228
Edward	War	246
Elias, Junr	Hnd	345
Elias, Sinr	Hnd	345
Elijah	Hop	375
Elijah	Hop	379
Ezekil	Hrs	316
Francis	Hrd	298
Francis	Pen	114
George	Gal	193
George	Knx	83
George	Pen	113
Isaac (freeman)	Fay	15
Isaac	Gal	193
Isaac	Hrs	323
James	Bra	150
James	Chr	88
James	Fle	78
James	Grn	248
Jaems	Mad	228
James	She	236
Jesse	Mad	232
Jesse	Mer	335
John	Cly	149
John	Hnr	359
John	Knx	78
John	Mad	228
John(son of Jno)	Mad	229
John	Mon	352
John	Way	357
John, Jur	Mad	227
John, Senr	Hnr	359
John, Sr	Knx	77
John, Sr	Pen	105
John D.	Liv	145
Jos.	[illegible]	[illegible]98
Joseph	[illegible]	[illegible]2
Joseph	[illegible]	[illegible]4
Josh.	Adr	14
Larken	Cum	174
Lewis E.	Fay	26
Lewis	Fle	70
Molly	Lin	137

Turner, cont.
Nancy Mad 227
Nelson Jes 48
Philip Mad 228
Reuben Pen 117
Richard Bou 68
Robert Bou 112
Robert Bou 112
Robert Fle 64
Saml. Bou 68
Samuel Clr 142
Samuel Hnr 359
Saphire Liv 160
Sarah Mad 229
Smith Mon 352
Starling Mad 229
Thomas Adr 15
Thomas, Capt Mad 227
Thomas Mad 230
Thomes Mad 228
Vincent Fay 26
William Knx 86
Wm. Bou 112
Wm. Gar 225
Wm. Hrs 320
Wm. Mon 369
Wm. Way 372
Turney, Daniel Bou 113
Michael War 245
Peter Bou 112
Turngate, Nancy Fay 16
Turnham, David She 216
George She 216
Jno. Nel 21
Thomas Woo 390
Turnum, James Hrs 319
Turpen, James Pul 133
Moses Pul 132
William Hnd 346
Turpin, Aron Way 370
Champin Cly 157
Elijah Grn 252
George Woo 379
Henry Gra 239
Hezekiah Gar 228
Hugh Gar 225
Isaac Mon 371
James Mad 229
Jas. Gar 224
Jas.(mulatto) Woo 393
Jer. Gar 225
Jerh. Gar 226
John Mad 230
Josiah Ohi 88
Martin Pul 133
Mary Mad 232
Moses Pul 131
Nathan Bar 30
Nathan Hrd 283
Obediah Knx 85
Philip Gra 239
Solomon Mad 232
Solomon Pul 132
Solomon Way 367
Tho. Gar 228
William Mad 229
Wm. Adr 14
Wm. Bar 33
Wm. Gar 226
Wm. Mon 377
Turtle, John Knx 85
Tusdale, Solmn. Cam 27
Tutt, George H. Woo 382
Hansford Woo 382
Lewis Y. Woo 389
Richard Bou 113
Sarah Nel 20

Tutt, cont.
William War 276
Tuttle see Juttle
Tuttle, James Mas 288
Nicholas Way 370
Peter Cly 156
Peter Mas 299
William ESt 1
Tutwiler, John Mad 227
Twaits, Elizabeth Fay 36
Tweay, David Bra 147
Twedle, John Liv 149
Tweedy, David Bou 112
Twidwell, Silas Gar 228
Twiman, George Woo 397
Reuben Woo 377
Twitty, John Bar 43
Twyman, Wm. Bar 40
Tybott, John Fle 79
Tye, Elizabeth Knx 82
George Knx 63
John Knx 82
Joshua Knx 82
Tygart, James War 250
Jane War 250
John War 250
Saml. War 257
Tyler, Able She 238
Asa But 197
Charles Fra 171
Edward Jef 19
James But 197
John But 197
Moses Jef 19
Moses, Jr Jef 19
Peter War 250
Robert She 224
Robert She 236
William Gal 193
Wm. Jef 19
Tylor, Joseph Fle 72
Robert Jef 19
Tyman, Edward Cly 149
Tyre, Willm. Sco 191
Tyred, John Hnr 352
Tyree, Benjamin Mad 232
John Rck 161
Thomas Mad 229

-- U --

Ulery, Peater Mon 361
Ulien, Benjamin Grp 278
Ullet, John Grp 274
Thomas Grp 277
Umphrey, ... Grp 275
Umstead, Benjaman Fle 89
Underhill, Jas. Gal 194
Thos. Boo 63
Wm. Boo 63
Wm. Senr Boo 63
Underman, Saml. Nel 20
Underwod, Rheubin Mon 376
Underwood, A.Caleb Gar 228
Bennett Bou 114
Francis Jes 47
Francis Hrs 307
Hiram Grn 256
Jacob She 217
James Hnr 356
James Grn 264
Jesse Hnr 355
John She 221
John Fra 172

Underwood, cont.
John Mon 352
Joseph She 234
Josiah Mul 405
Matthew Ohi 85
Mildred Mon 362
Nathan She 204
Nathaniel Hrs 313
Reuben Jes 41
Sam(freeman) Fay 15
Saml. Cal 10
Samuel Chr 57
Thomas Chr 111
Wm. Grn 265
Wm. Grn 264
Wm. S. or L. Fra 172
Ungles, John Nic 63
Unsel, Henry Nel 6
John Nel 20
Unsell, Abraham Mul 405
Frederick Mul 398
Frederick Mul 387
Henry Mul 391
James Mul 387
Upchurch, Avey War 261
David War 267
John War 277
Updike, Major Fra 172
Upp, Jacob Hnd 337
Upton, Benj. Way 370
Benjamin Cas 40
Daniel Grn 264
Joseph War 264
Urby, Charles Log 173
Urtin, Peter Gar 228
Usery, William Pul 131
Usher, James Hnd 341
Luke Fay 15
Utles, John Fay 37
Utley, David Fay 46
John Jes 47
Murrel Log 166
Utly, Josiah Mer 337
William Mer 337
Uton, Levi Fay 60
Utqus, John Nel 20
Utridge, John Log 178
Utterback, Benjn. Woo 396
Charles Fra 172
Hamon Mon 357
Hankerson Boo 63
Jacob Woo 394
Lewis Woo 386
Martin Hrd 299
Nimrod Woo 396
Patsy Mon 357
Uttinger, George Jes 47
Uzzell, Elisha Mul 398

-- V --

Vail, Ganalian She 224
John Bou 133
Joshua Chr 77
Vails, Saml. Bar 45
Valandingham, -
George Fay 25
James Fay 25
Lewis Sco 177
Valentine, Henry Mas 291
Vallandingham,-
Richd. Gal 194
Richd. Clr 143
Valetes, Tho. Bar 44

Name	County	Page
Van, Reuben	Way	365
Vanarsdale, Corl.	Nel	20
Vanato, Benjamin	She	240
Vanatten, Ferdiand	Fle	77
Vanbiben, James	Grp	269
Vanbiber, Jacob	Grp	271
Vanbrik, John	Mer	338
Vanbrike, Barnett	Mer	338
Vanbuskirk, George	Est	7
John	Mas	291
Vancamp, Garret	Mas	291
Vance, Alexr.	Grn	249
Andrew	Hnd	335
Benjn.	Woo	400
David	Fay	39
David	Hrd	281
Elenor	Rck	160
Eliza	Jef	16
Handle	Woo	391
Jacob	Gar	228
James	Log	161
James	Log	181
James	Fay	59
James	War	281
James	Fay	39
James	Jef	14
Jane	Fay	40
John	Chr	75
Joseph	Sco	174
Patrick	Fay	59
Patrick, Jr	Fay	59
Robert	Fay	51
Samuel	Log	181
Samuel	Jef	18
Thomas	Hnd	332
William	Sco	167
Wm.	Grn	264
Wm.	Gar	228
Vancleave, Aaran	She	229
Aaran	She	229
Aaron	Wsh	331
Ben	She	242
Benjamin	She	240
Benjamin	She	229
Benjamin	She	230
James	Fra	173
Jesse	She	230
John	She	230
John	She	230
John	Wsh	331
Joseph	She	240
Ralph	She	230
Samuel	She	230
Vancleve, Abigail	Gar	228
David	She	198
William	She	229
Vandamiere, Thos.	Hrd	303
Vandaran, John	Hrs	310
Vandavander, Peter	Mas	291
Vandavaugh, Chas.	Bar	35
Vandaverd, Ashbury	Cas	39
Chal. Sin	Cas	43
Charl.	Cas	38
George	Cas	39
Vandebeck, John	Sco	182
Vandegraff, Jas.	Lew	103
Vandegraft, Abm.S.	Sco	175
Saml.	Bou	114
Vanderife, Cornelius	Mer	338
Horace	Mer	338
Vanderslice, Benjamin	Chr	106
Vandike, Garret	Mer	338
Henry	Mer	337
John	Cas	44
Peter	She	206
Vandike, Peter	She	205
Richard	Wsh	331
Thos.	Cas	44
Vandiver, Aron	Hnr	362
Aron	Hnr	364
Chs.	Hnr	364
George	Hnr	364
Henry	Mer	337
Henry	Mer	338
John	Hnr	354
John, Sr	Hnr	364
Peter	Mer	337
Thos.	Hnr	363
Thos. Sr	Hnr	354
Vandivere, Garret	Mer	337
Vandlingham, George	Mer	338
Vandvander, Abraham	Mas	291
Vandvert, Peter	Nel	20
Vandyke, Dominicus	Mas	291
Vaney, Sarah	Hnd	338
Vanhees, Fredrick	Fle	67
Vanhies, James	Mer	337
Vanhise, Abram	Mer	343
Cornelius	Mer	337
Isaac	Mer	337
John	Mer	337
Vanhook, Aaron	Pul	130
Benjamine	Pul	130
Rachael	Pul	130
Samuel	Pul	130
Sary	Hrs	322
Thos.	Lin	137
William	Pul	130
Vanhorn, Jessee	Cam	28
Vanhouser, Jacob	Way	357
Vanice, Peter	Mer	337
Vanist, Peter	Mer	337
Vankirk, Elizabeth	Mon	377
John	Hnd	334
Vankook, Abner	Nic	63
Archd.	Nic	63
Sam	Nic	63
Vanlandenham, Benj.	War	251
Wm.	War	251
Vanlandinham, Lewis	War	264
Vanlandingham, Geo	Fle	64
Jas.	Bou	114
Jno.	Fle	72
Susanah	Fle	89
Vanleave, John	She	229
Vanmatre, Abm.	Gra	242
Abrm.	Hrd	297
Isaac	Hrd	301
Jacob	Hrd	301
Jacob	Hrd	296
Jacob	Hrd	296
John	Gra	238
Vanmeter, Henry	Grp	271
Rebecca	Jef	31
William	She	208
Vanmiackle, Jobe	Chr	54
Vann, Absalem	Hnd	336
Vannoy, Jonathan	Knx	86
William	Knx	80
Vanosdall, Richrd.	Fle	88
Vanover, Henry	Gar	228
Vanpelt, John	Gal	194
John	Fay	27
Jos.	Gal	194
Samuel	Fay	15
William	Fay	27
Vanr, Mashac	Fay	25
Vansandt, Elisha	Fle	74
Vansant, Aaron	Fle	81
Vanscouh, Hiza	Nic	63
Vanskike, Robert	Mas	291
Vanskite, Josiah	Fle	82
Margrete	Fle	83
Reuban	Fle	80
VanSwearingen, - Thos.	Log	183
Vanter, Elliott	Gal	194
Vanters, Aron	Lin	137
Vantrice, James	Hnr	351
Vantriss, William	Lin	137
Vantruce, Fredreck	Fle	70
Vanttur, Gilbert	Mas	303
Vanusdale, Cornelius	Mer	337
Isaac	Mer	337
Peter	Mer	337
Vanusdall, Abram	Mer	337
Christop	Mer	338
Cornelius	Mer	337
Isaac	Mer	338
James	Mer	338
Lucus	Mer	337
Simon	Mer	338
Simon	Mer	338
Simon	Mer	338
Vanvacter, Benjamin	Hrd	303
Vanwencle, Joseph	Nel	20
Vanwincle, Alexr.	Nel	20
Vanwinkle, Abm.	Way	351
Benjamin	Mad	233
John	Way	372
Saml.	Cal	10
Vanzant, John	Log	195
Mary	Sco	181
Varble, Daniel	Hnr	359A
Danl.	Hnr	358
George	Hnr	354
George	Hnr	355
Henry	Woo	396
Henry	Fay	25
John	Fra	172
Philip	Fay	27
Vardamon, Prudence	She	200
Vardeman, Ham	Lin	137
Jeremah	Fay	47
Vardiman, Molly	Pul	130
Morgan	Lin	137
Vardimon, Thos.	Hnr	361
William	Pul	130
Varis, Isaac	Mer	338
Varn, Isaac	Hrs	312
Varnam, John	Bou	114
John, Jr	Bou	114
Varnarsdall, Cornelius	She	212
Varnel, Joseph	Cum	165
Varnell, Coonrod	Hrs	312
William	Cal	9
Varner, Adam	Mon	370
James	Hnd	339
John	Mas	308
Varnon, Benjn.	Bou	71
Vastine, Abraham	Pen	105
Vaughan, Abram.	Boo	63
Chesley	Wsh	330
Claiborne	Wsh	330
Daniel T.	Pen	109
Edmond	Fra	173
Henry	Grn	255
Joel	Wsh	330
John	Wsh	331
John	Fra	173
Luke	Wsh	331
Luke	Wsh	330
Nelson	Fra	173
Peter	Wsh	330
Philip	Grn	253
Prudence	Wsh	330

Vaughan, cont.
Reuben Grn 252
Saml. Cum 177
Samuel Wsh 331
Thos. Grn 255
William Bou 70
William Wsh 331
Vaughin, Joseph Fle 72
Vaughn, Allin Lin 137
Ann Chr 69
Benja. BAr 45
Benjamin Hnd 341
Daniel Woo 380
Edmond War 272
Elijah Clr 143
Elijah Clr 143
Elisha Lin 137
Enus Mad 233
Evans Mad 233
Hector Liv 147
James Chr 69
James Lin 137
Jesse Clr 143
John Hnd 341
John Woo 401
Josiah Chr 96
Mastin Chr 96
Nathanl. Mad 233
Obediah Bar 27
Robert Chr 96
Thomas Clr 143
Thomas Chr 69
Thomas Lin 137
Thomas Hnd 341
Thos. Nic 63
William Clr 147
Wm. Senr Bar 45
Wm. Cal 17
Vaughor, Abram Fay 15
Vaught. Jasper Pul 130
Vaun, James Adr 15
Vausln?, George Mer 338
Vawn, Abraham Fay 32
Cornelius Fay 24
James Fay 27
Molly Fay 27
Samuel Pul 130
Vawter, Edmond F. Woo 399
Jessee Woo 399
Richard Sco 185
William Woo 399
Vayles, Esther Wsh 331
Thomas Wsh 331
Veach, Daniel Hrs 314
Elijah Way 356
Janes Hrs 314
Jeremiah Jes 47
John Hrs 314
John Jef 16
Thomas Fle 78
Thos. Hrs 315
Veal, Thomas Gal 194
Veale, William Fay 37
Veatch, Amos Knx 70
Asa C. Woo 388
Benjn. Woo 388
Charity Woo 388
Elias Hnd 343
Isaac Knx 70
James Hnd 346
Oshy Woo 388
William Hnd 335
Vedon, Marnin Fay 59
Veech, Benjn. Sco 168
George She 205
John She 209
Veers, Nathan Hrd 289
Veluzat, Fraciss Lin 137
Venable, Dorcase Mad 233
James She 206
James She 224
Jos. War 266
Joseph Bar 29
Larken War 266
Rachal Bar 34
Wm. War 244
Venables, Benjamin Mul 385
VEness, John Fra 173
Venible, Abraham Fay 25
Venice, Isaac She 238
Tunice She 213
Vennable, Joseph War 265
Venor, Emanuel Bre 160
Venters, Arthur Flo 104
Ventioner, James Gal 194
Venyard, William Hrs 307
Verdin, Hugh Nic 63
Vergin, Dorsey Nel 20
Vermillion, Edward Mas 291
Vernaught, Peggy Bul 186
Vernon, Anthony Hrd 288
Wm. S. Jef 24
Vernosdal, Jac Hnr 363
Simon Hnr 351
Tho. Hnr 363
Vernoy, Frances Nic 63
Verser, Saml. Est 5
Vert, Nathaniel Clr 143
Wm. Mon 365
Vertner, John Mas 291
Vertrees, Jacob Gra 239
Vertreese, Eliza Hrd 304
Isaac Hrd 302
Jacob Hrd 290
John Hrd 302
Jos. Hrd 287
William Hrd 302
Vessage, Thomas Liv 154
Vessells, Charles Wsh 330
Delijus Wsh 330
James Wsh 330
James Wsh 330
John Wsh 330
William Wsh 330
Vest, Calip Hnr 359
Edwd. Gar 228
George Boo 63
John Boo 63
John Grn 260
Richard Hnr 257
Richard, Sr Hnr 358
Robert Lin 137
Squire Boo 63
Vettelo, Stephen Nel 20
Viale, John Fay 36
Vibbert, Geo. Cum 176
Vicars, James Mas 303
Joseph Way 358
Theophelus Cal 4
Wm. Way 359
Vice, Aaron Mon 379
Easom Mon 379
Edmond Mon 362
Elija Cam 26
John Mon 379
Mourning Mon 379
Nathanl. Cam 26
Wm. Mon 379
Vick, Stephen Mad 233
Vickars, Edward Pul 130
Vicker, Wm. Boo 63
Vickers, Edwd. Gar 228
James Mad 233
Joseph Mul 394
Vicory, Frans. Way 366
Victor, Hannah Bou 114
James Bou 114
Littleton Bou 114
William Bou 114
Vicus, Charles Chr 71
John Chr 68
Moses Cam 29
Vidiloe, Thomas Pul 130
Viers, Robert Lew 97
Vigle, Matthias Jes 25
Vigras, Zachy. ADr 15
Vigus, Jabez Fay 15
Vilate, Saml. Nel 20
Vilet(free woman) Fay 15
Villers, Mathew Bul 186
Villizet, Phila-delphia Mon 354
Vimount, Lewis Bou 71
Vincent, Barten Gra 240
David Mad 233
Ezekiel Mad 233
James Fay 15
Mary Fay 15
Peggy Mer 338
William Mad 233
Vincner, Geo. Cum 167
Vine, Abraham Jes 47
Vines, Benjamin Chr 115
John War 265
Willm. War 245
Viney, Abraham War 254
Vinsant, Garrard Bar 30
James Adr 15
Wm. Adr 15
Vinson, Eli Gal 194
Leven Fle 84
Vinsner, Elizabeth Wsh 331
Vinzant, John Sco 187
Violett, Augusta Woo 381
Edward Woo 380
Henson Woo 380
John Hnr 366
Thomas Woo 380
Virden, Manux Fay 33
Virgin, Febe (B) Fle 91
Kinza Grp 272
Razen Grp 272
Thomas Grp 276
Vise, Enock Grp 274
Morning Grp 274
Nathaniel Clr 143
Vittiloe, Daniel Ohi 101
Vittitow, Daniel Hrd 291
Wm. Hrd 294
Vivale, John Jef 25
Vivian, Isaiah Est 1
Vivion, Flavel Clr 143
Harvy Clr 143
John Clr 143
Milton Clr 143
Randal Clr 143
Smith Clr 143
Thomas Clr 143
Voight, W. C. Mul 385
Voinaada, Daniel Hnd 332
Voineada, Martin Hnd 348
Solomon Hnd 327
Vonn, Malice Gar 228
Voores, Albert She 239
Voorhies, Peter G. Fra 173
Voorhis, Peter Hnr 367
Vooris, Carnelius She 239
John She 238
Vorais, Garred Cas 44
Voris, Cornelius She 218
Court Mer 338

Voris, cont.
Jacob Mer 338
John Mer 338
Mariah Mer 338
Peter Mer 343
Vortress, Isaac Bre 159
Vorus, Garret Sco 170
Jaems Hnd 333
John Hnd 333
Votau, John Adr 15
Vought, Abraham Mul 407
Gilbret Mul 390
John Mul 407
Simon Mul 389
Voules, Mary Nel 20
Voulez, Thomas Nel 20

-- W --

W..., William Fra 177
Waats, Sarah Fay 55
Waddill, Granville Fra 178
Joseph Fra 175
Waddle, David Grn 256
Henry Pul 124
James, Ser Fle 71
James, Jur Fle 71
John Fle 71
John Pul 124
William Flo 104
William Mas 293
Waddleton, Wm. Cal 11
Waddy, Samuel She 215
Thomas Bou 115
Wade, Banister Cal 6
Caleb Hop 380
Dawson Mon 366
Dawson Way 366
Edmond Liv 155
Elisha Way 351
Greenberry Wsh 338
James Mon 362
Jeremiah Pen 114
John Clr 145
John Way 351
John Wsh 338
John Wsh 345
Joseph Adr 16
Joseph Mon 370
Joseph Way 361
Martin Bre 169
obediah Bar 45
Pierce Lin 139
Pierce Wsh 334
Richard Cum 168
Richd. Way 352
Robert Chr 107
Royal She 209
Stephen Bar 39
Tho. Hop 380
Thomas Clr 145
Thomas Mad 237
Tignal Bar 32
Willm. Lin 141
Wm. Adr 16
Wm. Bar 33
Wm. Way 366
Zach Hop 374
Wadkins, Daniel Grn 250
Henry Cum 172
James Cum 172
Joel M. Clr 145
Wadleton, Richard Cal 4
Warner Cal 5
Wadley, Samuel Log 162
William Hrd 282
Wadlington, Furdinand Chr 95
James Cal 11
James, Jun Cal 4
Mercer Cal 13
Thomas Chr 95
Wafer, James Cal 14
Wagennon, John Jes 44
Wages, Benjamin Knx 66
Francis Est 7
Wagganer, Jacob J. Pul 129
Waggle, John Jef 20
Waggoer, Henry Pul 129
Waggoner, Christ Nic 64
Daniel Bre 159
Dennis Bre 166
George Jef 20
Harvard Adr 15
Henry Pul 129
Jacob Liv 147
Jacob Pul 129
James Bar 54
John Adr 15
John Hnd 325
John Hop 375
John Liv 147
John Nic 64
Peter War 265
Reuben Adr 16
Reuben Adr 19
Richd. Bar 54
Thomas Sco 192
Zachariah Liv 147
Wagle, John jun Mad 236
John, Sen Mad 236
Wagnon, John Mul 399
Waid, John Grp 273
Waide, Daniel Hrd 281
Horatio Hrd 281
Wain, Benjn. Mon 372
Nathanl. Est 5
Waine, John Mon 375
Wainscot, Abraham - Junr Mad 236
Abraham Mad 236
Jos. Jur Sco 178
Wainscott, Isaac Hnr 360
John Sco 178
Josepn, Senr Sco 178
Richard Hnr 360
Wair, George Chr 110
Hugh Chr 111
James Chr 110
John Chr 110
Joseph Chr 110
Waits, David Hnr 361
Waitt, Miajah Fle 79
Wakefield, Jno. Nel 17
John Nel 17
Mathw. Nel 17
Ruth Nel 14
Wm. Bar 27
Wm. Nel 17
Wakeland, Mary Ohi 80
William Ohi 80
Waker, Jno. Senr Log 178
Waland, Joshua She 230
Walbert, John Cum 167
Walce, Frederic Fay 24
Frederick Fay 31
Walden, Abednago Woo 392
Benjamin Mad 241
Elijah Woo 378
Elisha Fay 24
John Gar 229
Walden, cont.
John She 229
Joseph Woo 395
Nathan Hnd 348
Thos. Sco 175
William Fay 52
Wm. Bar 36
Waldng, John Chr 91
Waldren, John Hnr 353
Waldrip, Elizabeth Chr 74
Joseph Chr 74
Waldron, David Bar 44
Waldrope, Younger Bar 33
Waldrup, Dickerson Chr 72
Ester Chr 73
John Chr 72
Wale, Martin Bre 169
Waler, Aggy Fay 48
Waley, James Fay 38
Walice, James Hrs 320
Walker, Abraham Liv 151
Alexander Hrs 323
Alexander Mad 239
Alexander Mer 339
Alexr. Sco 191
Andrew Fay 24
Andrew Pen 115
Arandolph Jes 45
Benet Nel 14
Benj. Way 365
Caly War 245
Charles Pul 125
Charles Pul 128
Clay Mer 339
Cupet(freeman of colour) Jes 45
Daniel Hrd 302
Daniel Nel 16
David Adr 15
David Adr 16
David Log 171
Edmund Fay 12
Eijah Chr 65
Elex Adr 15
Elexr. Adr 15
Elexr. Sen Adr 15
Elijah Gar 231
Elizabeth Gar 230
Ellis Way 365
Ephram Liv 150
George Jes 46
George She 201
Gideon Nel 19
Harrison Bou 116
Henry Fay 24
Henry Fle 80
Henry Gar 231
Henry Log 175
Henry Nel 14
Henry Woo 385
Henry H. Wsh 334
Howard Nel 18
Hush Mer 339
Isaac Hnr 352
Isaac W. Fay 24
Jacob Clr 145
Jacob Hnr 353
jacob W. Log 193
James Adr 15
James Adr 15
James Chr 104
James Chr 106
James Clr 145
James Fle 80
James Hnd 339
James Jes 44
James Mad 240

Walker, cont.
James Mas 292
James Mon 375
James Mul 394
James Pen 111
James Pen 114
James Pul 127
James She 212
Jane Adr 16
Jane She 200
Jas. Way 353
Jere Hrd 286
Jeremiah Cal 6
Jeremiah Way 365
Jesse Lin 139
Jesse Lin 139
Jesse Way 365
Jesse Way 365
John Adr 16
John Bar 42
John Bre 163
John Chr 71
John Chr 106
John Est 1
John Fay 30
John Fay 56
John Fle 69
John Fra 175
John Grn 257
John Grp 274
John Jef 5
John Hop 375
John Knx 75
John Log 191
John Mad 234
John Mad 245
John Rck 165
John Sco 189
John Way 359
John Wsh 334
Johnston Way 365
Joseph Fay 27
Joseph Hrs 310
Joseph Nel 14
Joseph Nel 14
Josh. Adr 15
Josh. Adr 15
Joshua Clr 145
Juda Mad 237
Lewis Wsh 338
M. D. Nel 18
Mary Cal 15
Mary Fle 80
Matthew Jes 46
Matthew Liv 150
Moses Jes 44
Moses Liv 150
Pathaney Mad 241
Philip Mer 339
Philip Wsh 336
Priscila Jes 46
Randolph Fra 174
Renelder Knx 72
Richard Chr 78
Richard Chr 78
Richard Hrd 302
Richard Wsh 333
Richd. Bra 152
Richd. Hrd 303
Robert Boo 64
Robert Bou 133
Robert Clr 144
Robert Fle 67
Robert Fle 71
Robert Fle 84
Robert Mer 339
Ruth Nel 17

Walker, cont.
Saml. Sco 188
Samuel Chr 106
Samuel Hnr 351
Sarah Flo 104
Stanley Hrd 292
Stephen Mad 238
Tho. Gar 231
Thomas Wsh 340
Travis Woo 396
William Bre 158
William Fay 58
William Fra 176
William Gra 239
William Jes 46
William Mad 238
William Woo 394
William Wsh 334
William, Senr Fle 67
Willis Grn 261
Winston Bou 115
Wm. Adr 15
Wm. Lew 97
Wm. Mon 356
Zepheniah Hnr 365
Walkins, Ambrose War 278
Gregory Bar 53
John Mer 339
Walkrupt, John Mer 338
Walkup, Samuel Mad 240
Wall, Allin Mad 241
Banister Hnr 362
Frances Cas 42
Gabriel Cas 42
Jacob, Sin Cas 42
James Hrs 313
James Lin 141
John Hrs 313
Luttle I. Cas 39
Lydia Mas 297
Manlove Bre 164
Reuban Fle 71
Robert Lin 139
Robert Ohi 99
Wallace, Aaron Jes 44
Alexander Fay 56
Allen Gar 229
Andrew Hrd 298
Andrew Lin 139
Benja. Hop 376
Caleb Woo 377
Charity Bra 152
James Fay 56
James Fay 56
James Hnd 340
Jno. Hrd 291
John Fay 53
John Nel 18
John Sco 179
John She 206
John War 250
John War 254
John War 282
John Wsh 339
Jonathan Cum 177
Joseph Jes 46
Joseph Woo 377
Joshua Hnr 361
Josiah Gar 229
Michael Gar 231
Oliver Liv 154
Patrick Boo 64
Robert War 258
Robt. Way 352
Thomas Fay 12
Thomas Fay 31
Thomas Fay 56

Wallace, cont.
Thomas Mas 296
Thomas She 236
Thos. Grn 258
Timothy Flo 106
William Fay 12
William Log 183
William Ohi 85
Wm. Bar 28
Wm. Bar 29
Wm. Gar 231
Wm. Jef 20
Wm. Nic 63
Wallase, John Fay 59
Wallen, Elisha Knx 65
James Cal 18
Waller, Benj. Gal 194
Cornelius Mas 294
Eben C. Gal 194
Edmond Woo 397
Evan Knx 90
John Bou 71
John Hnd 331
Mary Gal 194
Richard Mas 294
Richard She 206
Stephen She 209
Thomas Jef 21
Thomas Mas 294
William Hnr 359
William L. or S. Fra 179
Wallice, John Hrs 311
John Hrs 318
Joseph Cas 44
Robert Hrs 317
Wallingford, Jno. Fle 83
Jno. Lew 103
Joseph Fle 82
Richard Fle 78
Wallingsford, Benj. Mas 293
Joseph Mas 292
Mark Mas 293
Nicholas Mas 291
Wallis, Andrew Bou 114
Arthur Ohi 74
Charles Ohi 74
Colsten O. Mul 388
John Chr 59
William Chr 116
Walliss, Gracey Mad 239
Jane Mad 240
Josiah Mad 241
Samuel Mad 239
Samuel Mad 241
Samuel Mad 241
William Mad 239
Wallon, Agnes Bra 153
Walls, Edward, Fra 174
George Bou 133
Gareald, Hrs 314
Jessy Chr 91
John Bou 69
John Liv 152
Joshua, Revd. Bre 156
Moses H. Jes 47
Parum Chr 62
Richd. She 227
Saml. Sco 180
Samuel Hrd 282
Simon Mul 390
William She 201
Walsh, Anthony Hrd 288
James H. Pen 117
Walston, Charles Fle 69
Joseph Wsh 339
Josiah Fle 78
Obed Wsh 333

Walston, cont.
William Fle 77
Waltan, John Hrs 313
Walteis, John Gra 242
Walter, Clement Mas 294
Dempsey Hnd 330
John Bra 147
John Mer 339
Peter Mon 371
Thomas Jes 44
Thomas Wsh 334
Walters, Andrew Hrd 290
Barnabas Bar 32
Conrod, Junr Hrd 290
Conrod, Senr Hrd 287
Coonrad Bar 32
George Bar 30
George Flo 106
Jacob Bar 31
Jacob Gal 196
James Bar 31
Jno. Gal 196
John Knx 71
Richard Pul 128
Robert Knx 84
Stephen Jes 44
Thomas Jes 46
William Flo 106
William Jes 43
Walthal, Richd. Cum 169
Thos. S. Cum 165
Walton, Agnes Bra 153
Edward Mad 242
H. Josiah Mas 296
Henry Chr 62
Jacob Chr 54
Jobe Fle 74
John Fle 64
John Mas 297
Matthew Wsh 332
Robt. Bra 143
Thos. Hrs 313
William Fle 65
William Mas 297
Wm. Bra 143
Waltrip, Joseph Bre 165
Luke Bre 165
William Bre 165
Wamock, Richd. Adr 15
Wamsley, Wm. Boo 64
Wand, James But 197
Thomas But 197
Wane, Isaac Jef 21
Wann, Alexr. Way 364
Edwd. Way 354
Wm. Way 354
Wansley, Polley Mad 239
Wanthing, Thomas Pul 129
Wapon, James Fay 24
Wapshott, Graves Wsh 333
War, Thomas Clr 145
Warant, John Lin 139
Warburton, Reuben Wsh 332
Ward, Adam Log 176
Andrew Hrs 311
Andrew Hrs 315
Benjamin Chr 73
Benjamin Hrs 311
Beverly Boo 64
Charles Mas 291
Daniel Way 356
David L. Jef 20
Edward Ohi 102
Eli Hop 376
Elisha Wsh 333
Elizabeth Bou 115
Frederick Hnd 341
Ward, cont.
Isaac Mas 295
Ivin Sco 172
Jacob Sco 172
James Chr 112
James Grp 275
James Jef 22
James Log 175
James Mas 291
James Mul 396
James Wsh 333
Jerry Log 174
Jesse Bre 162
John Clr 147
John Gar 232
John Grn 248
John Grn 256
John Hrs 311
John Jef 22
John Jes 45
John Log 174
John Mas 295
John Mer 338
John Mer 340
John Mon 367
John Wsh 333
John R. Jes 47
Joseph Hrs 312
Joseph Hrs 312
Joseph Lew 98
Joshua Cum 174
Josias Fay 33
Laurance Fay 24
Margraet Jes 45
Mark Log 184
Mathew Mul 394
Michael War 278
Michal Liv 150
Nathan Wsh 333
Samuel Chr 64
Samuel Wsh 333
Sarah Flo 104
Solomon Flo 106
Washington Hnd 328
William Bou 133
William Lin 141
William Mad 238
William Mul 403
William Sco 169
William Sco 193
Wm. Mon 383
Wm. Way 356
Warde, Flan War 253
James War 278
Warden, James Mad 235
John Bar 51
John Lin 141
Joseph Ohi 69
Mark Log 166
Nathan Mad 242
Philip Log 185
William Mad 242
William Rck 162
Warder, Joseph Jr Bar 51
Joseph, Senr Bar 51
Walter Bar 51
Wardlaw, James Fay 24
Jos. War 257
Wardlow, Andw. Clr 144
Wards, Thomason Grp 278
Ware, Alexander Cam 25
Caleb Clr 145
Charles Fay 46
Danl. Cam 29
Dudley Pul 126
Dudley Pul 129
Edmond Fra 178
Ware, cont.
Isaac Cam 29
Isreal Cam 27
James Fra 179
James She 214
John She 200
Markham Mad 240
Nicholas She 200
Samuel Woo 401
Thomson Bou 133
Will She 228
William Fra 178
Wareford, Abram Est 8
Waren, Jacob Gar 232
John Gar 232
Michael Gar 232
Wm. Gar 232
Warf, Abraham Bou 115
Warfelt, Wm. War 266
Warfield, Caleb Mon 365
Elisha Fay 12
Garrett Hnr 362
Gerrard She 232
Lisha Fay 46
Peter Fay 23
Reason Knx 84
Shaderick Fra 177
Vachal She 233
Walter Fay 12
Warford, John She 237
Joseph She 226
Warhob, Mathw. Adr 15
Warhol, Joseph Adr 16
Wariner, Jacob Cas 42
Waring, Clement H. Grp 274
Francis Grp 278
James H. Grp 274
Thomas Grp 274
Thomas T. G. Grp 269
Warker, Jerry Cal 20
Warman, Hannah Hnd 333
Warmoth, John Mad 239
Thaddeus Mad 239
Thadius Gar 232
Thadius Gar 232
Warnell, John Eb Bul 186
Warner, George Mer 338
Jacob Lin 139
Jacob Mon 365
John Lin 139
John Mer 339
Moses Knx 68
Peter Lin 139
Samuel Mon 364
William Fay 60
William Mad 238
Warnix, Eliza Jef 21
Warnock, Jacob Boo 64
Warnold, Thomas Clr 145
Warnon, Jacob Hrs 317
Warr, James Bou 116
Warre, James Hrs 320
Warren, Burris Pul 126
David Bar 35
Gabriel Lin 139
Hardin Grn 254
Hardy War 253
Henryetta Bou 69
Hugh, Jr Grn 266
Hugh, Sr Grn 254
Humphrey Mad 241
Isaac Nic 64
Jack (freeman) Fay 25
James Adr 16
James Adr 16
James Mer 338
Joel She 205

Warren, cont.
John Mad 239
John Mon 363
John Pul 128
John Rck 160
John Woo 396
John, Senr Mon 363
John W. Wsh 340
Jos. Gar 232
Jos. Grn 251
Martin Adr 16
Robert Way 365
Robert Way 365
Rueben Way 353
Saml. Grn 265
Thomas Fra 177
Thomas Mad 241
Thomas B. Fay 42
William Grn 254
William Lin 141
William Woo 394
William, Jur Lin 141
Willm. Sco 190
Warrener, Jacob Adr 17
Warrick, John Fle 65
Warrin, Benjamine Pul 126
Benjn. Lin 141
Charles Pul 129
Charles J. Pul 129
David Pul 126
James Chr 70
James Lin 139
James Lin 141
James, Snr Lin 139
Joel Pul 126
John Clr 144
John Lin 139
John Lin 141
John Pul 126
John Pul 129
John, Jnr Lin 141
Peter Pul 126
William Chr 77
William Chr 78
William, Jnr Lin 139
Wm. Pul 125
Warring, James Grn 254
James H. Fle 82
Warson, John Pul 129
Wartton, Lincy Jes 45
Warwick, Wilson Woo 389
Wash, Benjamin Fra 174
Benjamin Wsh 333
Charles Bra 142
James Sco 167
John Cum 167
John Fra 174
Thos. Senr Cum 168
Washbourn, Benjamin She 201
Elias Bra 144
Henry War 264
Washburn, Delany Jef 22
James Jef 20
John Bra 148
Jonathan Fle 72
Jonathan Fle 87
Philip Wsh 334
Washer, George Nel 15
Washington, Beverly Log 188
John Jes 47
John Log 196
Wasson, Chas. Bou 115
Ebel Pul 128
Isbel Pul 127
James Mad 238
Wasson, cont.
John Bou 115
Robert She 198
Water, Peter Mer 339
Waterfield, John Fay 27
Waters, Barbara Fay 12
Chamels Jes 43
David Jes 44
Elijah Way 360
Elizabeth Jes 46
Enoch Knx 68
Ezekiel Knx 68
Izzoel(freeman) Fay 15
James Grn 248
James Jes 43
John Cas 37
John Est 6
John Knx 68
John, Jur Jes 43
John, Sr Jes 43
Joseph Cas 40
Joseph Fra 176
Josephas Bra 149
Judy Fay 15
Major Jef 31
Mary Jes 44
Mathew But 197
Perry Log 162
Philemon Wsh 334
Philemon B. Wsh 334
Pleasant Jes 43
Richard Fay 24
Richard Bul 187
Robert Cly 157
Salley Jes 43
Saml. Lin 141
Solomon Jes 43
Thomas Fra 175
William Bul 186
William Jes 44
Wates, Charles Nic 64
John Nic 64
Wathen, Harrvy Nel 19
Jerh. Nel 17
Thomas Nel 17
Wilford Nel 17
Wathens, Charles Nel 19
Watkin, Benedict Wsh 345
Edward Wsh 334
Henrietta Wsh 340
William Wsh 340
Watkins, Andrew She 242
Benjn. Woo 386
Chapman Knx 76
Evan, Jr Hnr 360
Evan, Sr Hnr 360
Francis War 268
George Cas 45
George Rck 162
Henry Woo 400
Isaac Hnr 360
Isaac She 241
Isaiah Gra 238
James Cas 46
James Gra 241
James Grn 245
James Wsh 334
Jas. Hrd 304
Jessy Hnr 360
Jno. Hrd 288
Joel Knx 87
John Bar 27
John Fra 174
John Fra 179
John Gra 237
John Hnr 360
Joseph Lew 98
Watkins, cont.
Joshua Pen 114
Lewis Grn 251
Luke Knx 76
Mary Bar 54
Molley Cas 47
Peter Mul 407
Pleasant N. Mad 245
Samuel Hrd 295
Sarah Fle 85
Shastan C. Clr 144
Thomas Fay 27
Wm. Bra 141
Wm. Hrd 284
Wm. Hrd 289
Wm. Lew 95
Wm. Lew 98
Wats, Andw. Bar 50
George Fay 39
John Bar 49
John Fay 40
Joseph Grn 256
Prudence Hrd 303
Watson, Abner Cum 175
Abner Fra 174
Abrahm. Nel 14
Amos Liv 148
Arthur Mas 291
Bashol She 209
Benja. Gar 229
Benjn. Mad 237
Daniel Bre 168
Daniel Hnd 343
David Chr 106
David Mad 242
David Wsh 338
David G. Fay 22
Elagar Fle 68
Eleanah Mas 295
Evan Mad 238
Gilbert Cal 4
Henry Nel 14
Henry Nel 17
Hezekiah Fle 64
Jacob Fle 73
James Bou 133
James Bre 168
James Cas 46
James Fra 179
James Nel 14
James Nic 64
James Nic 64
Jas. Hrd 295
Joab War 281
John Adr 15
John Bra 152
John Fra 175
John Gra 242
John Jef 21
John Mas 292
John She 208
John, Jr Mad 237
John, Sen Mad 236
Johnson Adr 15
Joseph Clr 144
Joseph Mad 242
Joseph Nel 16
Josiah Cal 7B
Josiah Cal 14
Josiah Cal 17
Michael Mas 296
Michael, Jun Mas 296
Obed Fle 78
Patrick Jes 41
Patrick Sco 184
Pearson Knx 90
Peter Hnd 338

Watson, cont.
Rachel Wsh 339
Rachl. Nel 15
Robert Bul 186
Robert Chr 95
Robert Chr 106
Robert Gra 239
Robert She 235
Saml. Bou 114
Saml. Jef 25
Saml. War 257
Saml. Jur Cal 13
Samuel Cal 6
Samuel Mad 241
Samuel Wsh 339
Shem Liv 148
Tarlton Hnd 338
Thomas Fay 24
Thomas Knx 70
Thomas Log 189
Thomas Log 196
Thomas Nel 16
William Chr 114
William Fay 24
William Hnd 338
William Mad 237
William Nel 17
William She 235
Wm. Jef 22
Zephaniah Mas 297
Watt, Gabriel War 248
James Fle 65
John War 248
Levy Bra 144
Watters, Ann Mas 296
Bailey Clr 145
Bladen Fay 15
Jno. Hrd 284
John Mas 295
Michael Mas 295
Watts, Benja. Bre 164
Bledsoe Fra 175
Charles Log 174
David Bar 40
David Fay 38
Drury War 270
Edmond Fra 173
Fielding Clr 145
Francis Bre 161
George Cly 152
George Flo 106
Jacob She 205
Jacob Wsh 334
Jeremiah Fra 173
John Boo 64
John Bou 133
John Clr 145
John Fra 173
John Way 351
John Way 359
John T. Clr 145
Johnson Boo 64
Joseph War 248
Julicus Clr 144
Nathan Boo 64
O. William Mas 309
Richard Wsh 333
Saml. War 248
Samuel Jes 46
Sarah Fay 27
Thomas Mad 236
Thomas She 219
Thomas She 240
Thos. Fle 73
Thos. Way 358
William Fle 73
William Fle 91
Watts, cont.
William She 222
William Wsh 333
Wm. Gar 234
Waugh, Henson Mas 303
Jacob Nic 63
Jacob Nic 63
John Mas 292
Waumock, Wm. Adr 16
Wawson, James Bou 114
Wm. Bou 114
Way, John Jef 21
Saml. Sco 172
Sarah Wsh 345
Thomas Grp 274
William Bou 116
Wayland, George [illegible] [illegible]8
Wayley, Elander [illegible] 150
Wayman, Harmar Cam 31
Moses Cam 31
Simion Cam 31
Solmn. Cam 31
William Fay 51
Waymon, Edmnd She 222
Wayne, Ephraim Mad 237
John Wsh 333
Judith Bou 116
William Wsh 332
Waysor, Jacob Jes 47
Wayward, Aaron Cam 25
Weagle, Jacob Mon 362
John Mon 356
Weagleswith, Thompson Hrs 323
Weaglesworth, John Hrs 311
Wm. Hrs 312
Weakley, Abrhm. Nel 14
John Wsh 335
Thomas She 231
Weaks, Elijah Bul 187
Wear, Dudley Gar 231
Henry Gar 233
Wearman, Wm. Grn 260
Weary, George Fay 15
Weather, Joseph Hrs 320
Weathered, Thomas Mad 241
Weatherford, Abel Lin 139
Elijah Lin 141
Geo. Cas 37
Harden She 241
Joel Cas 43
John Cas 46
Weatherhead, Robt. Bou 116
Weatherington, David Bra 146
John Bra 146
John Bra 146
Mark Bra 147
Thos. Lin 139
Wm. Bra 142
Wm. Bra 146
Weatherman, Simon Pul 129
Weatheroe, wm. Bar 37
Weathers, Abijah Gar 230
Benjamin Bul 186
Benjn. War 255
Chas. Bar 46
Daniel War 282
James Fay 35
James Lin 141
James Lin 141
James Wsh 335
Jno. Lew 102
John Gar 230
John Hnd 340
John Jes 44
Joseph War 256
Weathers, cont.
Mary War 256
Peter Jes 42
Peter Jes 46
Richd. Bar 36
Robert She 227
Thomas Mon 355
William War 255
William N. Bul 186
Weaver, Adam Bra 146
George Bou 105
George P. Fle 72
John Fle 69
John She 211
Littleberry She 198
Moore She 206
Peter Gra 243
Phillip Fle 87
Simon Fle 64
Susanna Woo 390
William Woo 389
Web, Martin Hrd 283
Mary Fay 47
Webb, Aden Clr 144
Allass Pen 105
Andrew, Jr Fle 66
Asa Hnd 340
Austin She 218
Benj. Nel 18
Benjamin Flo 104
Benjamn. Bou 114
Bevan Sco 188
Charles Nic 64
David Cly 153
Edwerd Boo 64
Eli War 247
Eligah Bou 133
Forrest Boo 64
Francis Adr 15
George Clr 14[illegible]
Isaac Bou 133
Jacob Adr 16
James Hnd 368
James She 209
James She 225
James C. Mon 373
James M. Bre 165
Jeremiah She 197
John Hnr 353
John Log 187
John Mon 372
John Nel 17
John She 199
Jonathan She 198
Joseph Bou 114
Lazerus War 247
Martin War 249
Massa Log 191
Merry Bar 32
Moses Bar 53
Moses Fay 32
Nehemiah Nel 6
Rheubin Hrs 307
Rheubin Hrs 316
Richd. Bar 29
Robt. Hnr 352
Saml. She 229
Samuel Flo 104
Thomas Log 165
Thomas Mas 291
Waller Hnr 353
William Clr 147
William Cly 153
William Flo 104
William Flo 106
William Hnr 369
William Log 165

Name	County	Page
Webb, cont.		
William	She	225
William	Woo	377
William, Sr	Hnr	353
Willis	Log	191
Wilm.	War	252
Winney	Bou	133
Wm.	Bar	34
Webber, Archibald	Jes	47
Augustus	Est	2
John	Jes	46
Jones	Est	2
Philip	Fay	25
Philip	She	234
Sarah	Jes	47
William T.	She	209
Weber, George A.	Fay	53
Webster, Achilas	Fay	25
Anny	Fay	55
Beverly	Fay	25
Beverly	Fay	55
Cornelius	Fay	26
Christopher	Jes	45
Daniel	Fay	25
Dudley	Fay	27
Edward	Fay	27
George	Gal	195
Henry	But	197
Henry	Fay	25
Isaac	Fay	27
Jacob	Fay	55
Jacob	Gal	196
James	Fay	25
John	Fay	25
Leroy	Fay	24
Martin	Fay	55
Natth.	Nic	65
Polley	Cas	47
Roy	Fay	56
Wiley	Fay	55
William	Clr	144
Wm.	Adr	16
Wm.	Cas	47
Weddington, Henry	Flo	104
Weddl, John	Pul	127
Weddle, DenCel	Pul	125
John	Pul	125
Weeb, Moses	Fay	59
Weed, James	Hrs	324
Weeden, Benjn.	War	244
Weedman, Christon	Gra	242
Weekley, Enoch	Sco	187
Jerh.	Sco	167
Stephen	She	236
Thomas	She	236
Weeks, David	Hop	377
Wees, Samuel	Knx	91
Weever, Valentine	Mad	242
Weigert, A.Phillip	Fay	15
Weir, James	Fay	12
James	Mul	385
John	Fle	84
Samuel	Mul	407
William	Hnd	342
William	Mul	408
Weisagar, John	Mas	297
Weiseger, Daniel	Fra	179
Welbern, James	Mul	390
Welch	Way	367
Ann	Fay	12
Betsey	Fay	51
George	Fra	179
George	Way	357
Henry	Hop	377
Henry	Jes	46
Hezias	Log	191
Jacob	Bou	72
Welch, cont.		
James	Cum	180
James	Fay	51
James, Jr	Bul	186
James, Ser	Bul	187
Jas.	Way	356
John	Jes	46
John	Mas	297
John	Nel	6
Jos.	Gar	229
Lewis	Hop	374
Michael	Bou	72
Nicholas	Log	188
Ozias	Log	172
Samuel	Clr	145
Samuel	Mas	297
Thomas	Log	196
Thomas	Mas	297
Thomas	Mon	354
Thos.	Est	3
Thos.	Lin	139
Thos.	War	275
William	Mas	293
William	She	235
Wm.	Way	368
Weld, Mosess	Hrs	320
Welden, Cornelius	Pul	126
Weldin, Abm.	Clr	144
Henry	Pul	124
Weldon, Grace	Wsh	334
Jacob	Bul	187
John	Lin	139
Vachel	Bra	141
Welker, Danl.	Jef	32
Weller, Christian	Log	184
Conrod	Nel	14
Daniel	Nel	16
Frederick	Log	183
Henry	Nel	6
Henry	Nel	19
John	Hnd	347
John	Nel	6
Margaret	Nel	14
Philip	Nel	18
Welles, Peter	Mon	350
Wellmon, Bennatt	Flo	104
Elisha	Flo	104
John, Sr	Pen	109
Joseph	Flo	104
Wells, Abraham	She	221
Abhm.	Nel	18
Andrew	Est	3
Barnet	Bar	42
Benjamin	Knx	64
Benjamin	She	204
Benjm.	Mon	373
Carty	She	210
Charles	Jef	20
David	Cum	170
David	Nel	19
Edmond	Mon	353
Edward	Mad	242
Edward	Mer	340
Elijah	Wsh	334
Francis	Mul	389
George	She	204
George, Jr	She	204
Haden	She	214
Hasten	Mon	373
Henry	Log	194
Henry	Mad	238
Henry, Sen	Mad	242
Isaac	Bra	141
Jacob	Bul	186
Jacob	Mer	340
James	Bou	114
James	Bra	153
Wells, cont.		
James	Clr	144
James	Wsh	335
Jesse	Nel	19
Jessee	Bar	30
John	Bar	47
John	Bra	147
John	Clr	144
John	Est	4
John	Flo	106
John	Grn	255
John	Knx	71
John	Log	176
John	Mer	340
John	Mon	373
John	Mul	399
John	She	209
John E.	Grp	272
Joseph	Fra	175
Joseph	Log	177
Joseph	War	256
Joseph	Way	355
L. B.	Hnr	360
Levy	Knx	64
Lewis	Chr	54
Lewis	Hrd	296
Mary	Clr	145
Michajah	Mul	398
Nathan	Bul	187
Nicholas	Mad	235
Patty	Rck	161
Philip, Senr	Grn	255
Rachel	Mas	292
Richard	Hnr	357
Richard	Mad	242
Richd.	Cam	28
Robert	Wsh	340
Robt.	Est	4
Saml.	Hrd	285
Saml.	Jef	21
Saml.	Jef	22
Samuel	Mon	370
Samuel, Jr	Jes	44
Samuel, Sr	Jes	44
Thomas	Bul	186
Thomas	Fle	77
Thomas	Hrs	322
Thomas	Log	171
Thomas	Mad	233
Thomas	Mas	296
Thomas K.	Mad	245
Thos.	Nel	16
William	Fle	69
William	Flo	106
William	Grn	255
William	Hrs	322
William	Liv	149
William	Log	165
William	She	204
Wm.	Bar	24
Wm.	Cum	173
Wm.	Jef	20
Yelberton P.	Jef	22
Welman, Saml.	Clr	145
Thomas	Mad	237
Welsh, Andrew	Jef	21
Elizabeth	Bar	19
James	Bar	47
James	Jef	20
James	Lin	139
John	Bar	45
John	Lin	139
John	Lin	141
Joseph	Lin	139
Robert	Jef	21
Robert	Jef	26
Saml.	Jef	20

Welsh, cont.
Tho. Bar 44
Thomas Mad 236
Wm. Jef 20
Wm. Jef 21
Welsher, John Lin 141
Joseph Lin 141
Welson, Eli B. Est 1
Joseph Bar 42
Ralph Est 1
Weltch, Wm. War 272
Welton, Michael Clr 144
Welty, Abraham War 278
Peter War 274
Weltz, Francis Bra 141
Wendle, Sarah Hnd 334
Wenner, Daniel Wsh 339
Wenset, James Nel 15
John Nel 14
Raphl. Nel 15
Raphl. Nel 18
Wenton, McCleland Way 369
Wentworth, Lebi She 200
Wersley, William Fay 12
Wesl, John Bar 46
West, Alexander Pul 128
Alexander Way 354
Amos Log 173
Amus Nic 65
Charles Chr 65
Charles Jes 47
Edward Fay 12
Ephram She 224
Frances Flo 104
Geo. Cam 27
Hessakiah Chr 77
Ievine Bou 71
Isaac Cum 186
Isaac Nic 65
Isaac Way 353
James Lew 104
James Log 194
James Mad 238
James Mas 297
James Mer 343
James Sco 168
James, Junr Log 174
James, Senr Log 174
Jams Lew 99
Jas. Hrd 285
Jeptha Chr 65
Jeptha Pul 126
Jeremiah Fra 176
Jesse Mad 240
Jesse Mas 293
John Chr 68
John Chr 77
John Fra 177
John Jes 46
John Log 174
John Mad 240
John Mon 358
John Nic 64
John, Jr Mad 240
Jonathan Mad 242
Jonathan, Jun Mad 234
Jos. Gar 229
Joseph Flo 106
Joseph Knx 88
Joshua Nel 16
Leonard Log 172
Littleton Mad 240
Littleton Way 367
Lynn Sco 190
Martin Nel 18
Matthew Log 174
Nancy Bra 152

West, cont.
Nancy Grn 258
Phillip Nic 65
Polly Mon 362
Reason Fra 175
Reuben Fra 177
Richard Chr 65
Richard Fay 49
Richard Log 172
Richard Log 175
Richard Mad 237
Richard, Jr Log 174
Richd. Bra 152
Roaland Jes 47
Rubin But 197
Saml. Way 370
Samuel Est 3
Samuel Mad 240
Simion Mas 292
Soloman Mad 235
Solomon, Jr Way 367
Solomon, Sr Way 367
Temple Chr 56
Thomas Chr 68
Thomas Mas 297
Thomas Mas 297
Thomas Nic 64
Thomas Nic 64
Thomas Pen 106
Thos. Cam 30
Thos. Nel 15
William Clr 145
William Fay 55
William Flo 104
William Fra 175
William Fra 176
William Fra 177
William Lin 139
William Log 174
Wm. Way 367
Westbrock, Demsy Mul 393
Elisha War 252
Westenman, Charles Pul 126
Wester, Fulgy Chr 98
Westerfield, Cornelius Mer 338
Isaac Mer 339
James Mer 339
James Mer 339
John Mer 339
Western, James Fra 177
Westfall, Cornelius Gra 240
Daniel Bul 186
Henry Bul 186
Hezekiah Bul 187
Jacob Bul 187
John Bul 187
Susana Hrd 303
Wm. Hrd 303
Westiman, William Pul 128
Westover, Samuel Bre 166
Westrope, William Pen 114
Wetherford, Jackson Mer 340
Wetherington, Ben Adr 16
Charles Ohi 94
Joseph Adr 16
Richd. Adr 16
William Fay 41
Wm. Adr 16
Wethers, James Fay 48
Mathew H. Fay 53
Wetherse, Wm. Bar 25
Wetherspoon, George Liv 149
Robert Fra 177
Wettell, George Nel 15

Wettell, cont.
Thomas Nel 15
William Nel 15
Wetty, David Bou 115
Mary Bou 115
Wever, John Pul 125
Micael Pul 125
Whale, John Hnr 358
Whalen, Henry Hrs 319
James Jef 19
John Hnr 359
Sollomon Hrs 319
Sollomon Hrs 319
Whaley, Edward Bou 114
James Fay 24
Lee Bou 116
Wm. War 266
Whaling, Patrick Nel 16
Whaly, John Mas 295
Thomas Mas 297
William Mas 294
Wharlton, Richd. Clr 144
Wharry, John Cam 33
Whealer, Joseph Mon 375
Whearett, William Jes 46
Wheat, Bazel Mad 234
Hesekiah Bou 133
James Adr 16
John Adr 16
John Grn 257
Joseph Bou 133
Samuel Lew 98
Zacheriah Bou 133
Wheatley, Arthur Bre 163
Benedict Wsh 338
Edward Wsh 335
James Wsh 335
George Nel 6
John Bre 168
John Wsh 332
John Wsh 335
Jos. Gal 196
Leonard Bre 166
Nicholas Cas 46
Thomas Wsh 339
Wheatly, John Mas 293
Robert War 282
Thomas Mas 292
Wm. Fle 84
Wheelar, Clament Hrs 315
Wheeldon, Jas. Gar 231
Jos. Gar 230
Wheeler, Arches. Adr 15
Benja. Gar 232
Benjamen Adr 16
Benjamin Mas 294
Benjn. Mad 237
Drummon Pen 108
Efram Liv 149
Francis Bar 28
George Jef 21
George F. Pen 115
Henry Liv 158
Ignacious Hrs 324
Ignatious Pen 109
James Flo 104
James Hnd 339
James Liv 158
John Adr 15
John Bar 28
John Hnd 337
John Liv 158
John Mad 234
John Mas 292
John C. Bul 186
John N. Pen 107
Joseph Bou 115

Wheeler, cont.
Joseph Way 370
Joshua Mad 235
Lawrence Mas 294
Levi Mas 294
Polly Mon 363
Preciller Mon 374
Stephen Flo 104
Tho. Gar 232
Thomas Bre 156
Unity Bou 116
Warren Fay 24
Wm. Gar 232
Wm. Jef 21
Wm. Nic 64
Zadock Wsh 335
Whelar, William Chr 62
Whelen, Hezakias Hrs 323
Wheler, David War 270
Whetsett, William - Junr Log 192
William, Senr Log 192
Whetten, Geo. Gar 229
While, Andrew Grn 258
John Fle 79
Solomon Grp 272
Whimon, Jacob Mul 389
Whip, Adam Jes 44
Whips, Elizebeth Mas 295
George Jef 22
John Jef 22
John Mas 296
John, Senr Mas 292
William Mas 292
Whisichar, Josiah Hrs 322
Whitacer, Elizabe Pul 126
William Pul 124
Whitacre, David But 198
Henry But 198
John But 198
Mark But 198
Mark But 198
Thomas But 198
Whitaker, Abraham Jef 12
Abraham She 209
Charles She 202
Elisha She 200
Elisha She 202
Henry Log 185
Isaac She 206
Jiles Pul 129
John She 216
John She 224
Joshu Way 354
Levi She 200
Mark Pul 127
Martha She 200
Prudance Pul 125
William W. Log 183
William W. Log 186
Whitamore, John Mad 240
White, Abraham Jef 20
Absalom Wsh 338
Ambrose Fra 176
Amos War 260
Andrew Fra 178
Andrew Mas 293
Annabel Fle 87
Anne Est 9
Aquila Mad 242
Archer Bar 49
Archibald Bar 49
Archibald Hrd 290
Arnald Mad 242
Arnet Fay 2.
Asa Mad 235
Bartholemew War 267

White, cont.
Benja. Gar 229
Benjamin Log 178
Bennet Mas 296
Benni Mad 236
Benson Nel 6
Brittin Bul 187
Brockman Sco 188
Charles Log 193
Charles Mon 368
Daniel Fay 12
Daniel Jef 20
Daniel Woo 396
Danl. Grn 260
Danl. Sco 187
David Gar 229
David Grp 271
David Mad 241
David Pul 125
David Pul 128
David She 199
David, Junr Hnr 369
David, Sen Mad 241
Dimpsy Chr 60
Durret Mad 240
Edmond Sco 176
Edmund Bar 29
Edward Pul 129
Eliza Bar 29
Elizabeth Mad 238
Elizabeth Mer 338
Francis Clr 145
Galin Mad 235
George Cas 48
George Jef 21
George Mad 234
George Nel 19
George Pul 125
George Pul 128
George Wsh 332
Hendrick Knx 65
Henry Adr 16
Henry Est 1
Henry Fay 37
Henry Hrd 286
Henry Jef 5
Henry Jef 21
Hugh Cly 157
Iliff Fle 67
Jacob Cam 24
Jacob Gal 197
Jacob Nel 5
James Bar 31
James Bar 36
James Est 7
James Grn 246
James Grn 251
James, Capt. Mad 233
James Grn 260
James Jes 45
James Mas 309
James Mon 361
James Sco 168
James She 239
James T. Cal 11
Jane War 264
Jeremiah Fay 35
Jeremiah Fay 47
Jesse Adr 15
Jesse Est 1
Jesse Fle 69
Jno. Grn 263
Jno. (N) Hnd 352
Jno. Hnr 353
Jno.(Nichs. son) Mad 239
Joel Mad 236
Joel Mer 340

White, cont.
John Adr 15
John Bar 41
John But 197
John Cly 158
John Fay 27
John Fay 47
John Gal 194
John Gra 237
John Hnr 354
John Hrs 311
John Jes 45
John Knx 70
John(Baldhead) Mad 234
John(David's son) Mad 241
John Mad 241
John Mon 362
John Mon 365
John mon 369
John Nic 64
John Sco 170
John She 197
John She 218
John War 260
Joseph Cam 28
Joseph Fay 15
Joseph Jef 21
Joseph Mad 235
Joseph Ohi 72
Joseph Sco 177
Joseph She 201
Joseph Woo 391
Karr Mas 293
Lafford Jef 21
Lambert Pul 128
Lemuel Ohi 98
Lewis Sco 175
Martin Jes 44
Mary Jef 9
Mases Log 171
Milley Jef 20
Mourning Log 175
Mussel War 250
Nathan Mad 235
Nathaniel Jes 45
Nicholas Mad 239
Peter She 225
Pheby Woo 380
Philip Fra 174
Pierce Mad 233
Pleasant Bar 50
Prestly Mer 340
Randolph Cas 47
Reason Gar 233
Richard Knx 69
Robert Log 176
Robert Mon 363
Robert She 232
Robt. Way 373
Sally Jef 20
Saml. Grn 257
Saml. Grn 259
Saml. W. She 225
Samuel Grn 259
Samuel Hnd 337
Samuel Hrs 322
Smith Hrs 307
Soloman War 267
Soloman War 267
Stephen Adr 15
Stephen Adr 15
Stephen S. Mad 241
Stuwart Hnr 351
Susan Woo 377
Susanna Bou 70
Thomas Bar 40
Thomas Cal 7

White, cont.
Thomas Chr 97
Thomas Fra 179
Thomas Jef 22
Thomas Mad 235
Thomas, Sen Mad 239
Thos. Adr 15
Thos. Cly 158
Thos. Cum 177
Thos. Hnr 366
Timothy Wsh 339
Trumon She 209
Walter She 197
Wesley Pul 124
William Bou 133
William Bre 163
William Clr 144
William Est 1
William Fay 31
Williams Fay 54
William Fra 178
William Grp 270
William Hnr 368
William Jes 44
William Jes 46
William Knx 78
William Lin 139
William Log 178
William Ohi 88
William Pul 125
William She 215
Willis Est 9
Wilm. War 264
Wm. Bar 45
Wm. Cal 12
Wm. Jef 24
Wm. Jef 30
Wm. Mon 369
Zephenia Fle 67
Witeaker, Thos. Boo 64
Whiteby, Joseph Hnr 363
Whitecar, James Hnr 359A
James Hnr 364
Jno. Hnd 352
Whitecotton, James Wsh 335
Whitecraft, John Mon 358
Whitefield, White Mer 340
Whitehause, Thomas Cal 9
Whitehead, John Gal 195
Jonathan Way 369
Joseph Wsh 335
Margrette Hrs 321
William Flo 106
Wm. Hrd 291
Whitehorn, Wm. Gra 241
Whitehouse, Benja. Mer 338
Thomas Mer 338
[illegible]er, Isaac Cly 153
[illegible]k Fay 27
Whitelaw, Nicholas Woo 379
Whitely, Wm. Nic 64
Thomas Pul 124
Whiteman, John Jef 28
Shardlow Fle 87
Whitemire, John Jes 43
Whitemore, Valuntine Mul 393
Whiten, Michael Wsh 335
Polly Pul 125
Robert Pul 125
Whiteneck, Abram Mer 340
Henry Mer 340
John Mer 340
Whitendon, John Fay 48
Whitenhall, George Mer 340
Peter Mer 340
Whitesett, John War 261
Whiteside, Caty Fay 52
James Mon 355
Joseph Hrs 312
Lewis Way 368
Ralph Mon 355
Robt. Way 368
Samuel Mon 348
Samuel Mon 352
Thos. Rck 159
Whitesides, Francis Chr 107
Isaac She 226
James Hnr 364
James Pul 125
Jane Lin 139
John Clr 145
John Hop 376
John War 250
John War 282
Joseph Hnr 355
Martin Hnr 364
Rebicat Mon 348
Saml. Hop 371
Saml. War 250
Saml. War 282
Will Cly 151
Wm. Hop 371
Whitesitt Wm. Clr 145
Whitfill, Barnett Wsh 339
Joseph Wsh 339
Whitham, James Clr 144
Whithurst, Peter Clr 145
Whitichar, John Hrs 318
Joseph Hrs 317
Whitiker, James Nic 63
Joseph Knx 86
Whiting, Thomas Woo 389
Whitinghill, John Ohi 79
Whitledge, Tho. Bar 42
Whitler, John Wsh 332
Whitley, Danl. Nic 64
James Wsh 332
Margret Pul 129
Reuben Grn 259
Sharp Liv 159
Whitlige, Lyna Bou 115
Whitlock, Charles Adr 16
Robert War 260
Thos. Cum 180
Whitlow, Britton Mad 237
Granville Bar 50
John Mad 237
Solon. Bar 50
Whitly, Andrew Lin 139
Soloman Lin 139
Tarlton Mer 340
Willm. Lin 139
Whitman, John Gar 233
Mary Gar 234
Richd. Hrd 287
Thos. Hrd 288
Wm. Bre 161
Whitmore, John Mul 393
Whitnal, Josiah Cal 16
Whitney, Elijah Chr 95
Hiram War 249
Jeremiah Bar 37
John Bar 37
John Fra 178
Saml. Gar 234
Thomas Fay 12
Whitsell, Jacob Boo 64
Whitsitt, Samuel Clr 145
William Clr 144
Whitson, Benjamin Hnr 357
Isaac Knx 86
Jerimiah Cal 13
Whitson, cont.
John Hnr 369
Ruth Jef 22
Whittacer, William Pul 127
Whittaker, John Fra 173
Wittedge, Overall Bul 187
Thomas Bul 187
William Bul 187
Whitten, Elijah Wsh 339
Noel Wsh 339
Robert Pul 128
Whittington, Woo 398
Benja. Woo 398
Joshua Woo 386
Littleton Woo 399
Whittle, John Cas 37
John, Sin Cas 38
Robt. Cam 30
Vinston Cas 38
Whitton, Easton War 273
Elijah War 273
Whitwell, Tho. Bar 37
Whitworth, Abraham Bre 167
Wm. Cum 178
Whord, Margaret Grn 260
Whorton, Eli Bou 116
George Jes 45
Joseph Bou 114
William Pen 116
Whoten, Reuben Knx 78
William Knx 77
Whte, Conyers Cam 26
Whylock, Wm. Adr 16
Whyte, Isaac Hop 372
Wiat, William Chr 114
Wiatt, Duglas Mon 359
Francis Mon 369
James Knx 79
John Cal 6
Samuel Knx 84
Thomas Knx 65
Woolford Fle 81
Wicker, Thomas Chr 87
Thomas Lin 139
Wickersham, James Sco 193
Wickershan, Sampson Mer 340
Wickham, Jesse Fra 179
Wickliff, Aronton Mul 403
Charles Fay 52
Charles Wsh 336
Moses Mul 407
Robert Mul 398
Wickliffe, Charles Fay 34
Chs. A. Nel 6
M.H.A.N. Nel 6
Wickling, Jerh. [illegible]84
Wickware, Alpheus [illegible]69
Saml. War 280
Wicliff, Robert Fay 46
Wicuff, Nicholas Mer 339
Widiner, George Fra 178
Widows, Peter Clr 145
Wien, Turner Hnd 341
Wier, John Clr 145
Saml. Hrd 283
Wiett, Joseph Lew 101
Wigenton, Henry Bou 133
Wm. Bou 133
Wiggengton, Elijah Nel 17
Wiggham, John Mer 339
Wiggington, Seth Nel 18
Wiggins, Abraham Sco 182
Archibald Mas 292
Archibald, Junr Mas 294
Archibald, Little Mas 294
Henry Hrs 320
James Hrs 310

Wiggins, cont.
John Nic 64
John Sco 168
John Sco 182
Jonas Sco 173
Joseph Mas 294
William Mas 292
Wm. Nic 64
Wigginton, John Log 181
Wiggs, Richard Bou 133
Wight, Isle Of Nel 18
William Wsh 336
Wigington,Pressley Hnd 341
Wiginton, Roger Boo 64
Wigrett, George She 224
Wigs, William Chr 79
Wilaby, Benjm. Mon 359
Wm. Mon 355
Wilbanks, Berriman War 261
Wilbourn, Edward Knx 86
Edwd. Cum 174
Gidean Bar 43
Joshua Bar 43
Robert Cum 174
Saml. Bar 43
Saml. Cas 40
Thos. Cum 174
Wilburn, Isaac Bar 42
Jas. Bar 43
William Mad 238
Zachariah Mad 235
Wilcockson, Danl. Clr 144
Jesse Clr 144
John Clr 144
Wilcoks, Ezra Hrd 292
Wilcox, Abraham Mul 397
David She 229
Edmond Cal 12
George She 224
Isaac She 220
John Cal 9
John Log 175
John She 224
Joseph She 231
Josiah Log 182
Ruth She 231
Thomas H. Bul 187
Wilcoxing, Benjan. Adr 16
Wilcoxon, Lewis Bul 186
Wilcoxson, Danl. Woo 386
George Grn 253
Lewis Pen 106
Wm. Grn 253
Wm. Mon 377
Wilder, Joab Knx 70
Joseph Knx 91
Sampson Knx 70
William Knx 70
Wilds, Benja. Gar 234
John, Jnr Gar 234
John, Snr Gar 234
Wile, Abraham Nel 15
Lewis Nel 17
Wileh, Thomas Fay 15
Wiles, Stephen Mul 390
Wiley, Abel Mas 294
Alex Mad 237
Aquilla War 251
Bartley She 234
Benja. Gar 232
Benjn. War 251
Christine Gar 231
Elijah Bra 145
Elijah Bra 146
George Sco 169
Henry She 218
Hugh Nic 65

Wiley, cont.
John Bra 146
John Mad 239
John Nic 65
John, Junr Nic 65
Joseph Sco 174
Joseph, Senr Sco 174
Robert Mon 361
Samuel Nic 65
Tho. Bar 44
Thomas Flo 104
Thomas Hrd 303
William Log 173
Wm. Gar 232
Wm. Mon 360
Zachar. Mad 239
Wilgoos, Asa Fay 59
Wilhelm, Alexr. Grn 257
Wilhight, Jessee Woo 385
Michael Woo 377
Wilhite, Achilles She 232
Elliott Jef 26
Evan Jef 26
Ezekiel Knc 90
Humphrey Jef 26
James Hnr 367
Jesse Jef 26
John Jef 26
Joseph Jef 26
Lewis Jef 22
Matthew Knx 66
Nicholas Mer 339
Sampson Mer 338
Simeon H. Jef 26
Simon Jef 25
Wm. Boo 64
Wilkens, Charles Fay 12
James Mul 406
Wilkenson, James Cas 41
John Cas 38
Talton Cas 37
Wilkers, William Mul 391
Williby Mul 391
Wilkerson, Benjamin Wsh 337
David Mad 240
Edmond Fra 178
George Nel 17
Henry Mon 348
Jane Jes 43
Jobe War 259
John BAr 30
John Clr 144
John Mon 347
John Mon 350
Joseph Clr 144
Nancy Mon 369
Newman Grn 252
Newton Grn 252
Presley Mad 246
Thomas Knx 77
William Mad 240
William Wsh 340
Wm. Bar 36
Wm. Clr 144
Wyatt Mad 235
Wildeson, John Gra 241
Wilkins, James Cas 47
James Chr 67
James Chr 67
James Chr 71
James Mul 392
John Chr 73
John Log 177
Michael Mul 392
Richard Log 175
Robert Mul 397

Wilkins, cont.
Samuel Liv 154
Solomon Gal 195
Steward Woo 386
Thomas Chr 71
Thomas Wsh 340
Willis Mul 393
Wilkinson, Charles Mas 296
Drury Adr 16
Jas. Hrd 286
Joseph P. Bre 166
Michael Ohi 91
Robt. Hrd 283
Wm. Cas 37
Wm. Hrd 294
Wilkirson, Martin Bar 43
Wilkison, James Mer 339
John Lin 139
Meredy Mer 340
Ste. Gar 232
Wilks, Mills Bra 149
Saml. Jef 21
Wm. Jef 21
Willamsen, Thomas Chr 55
Willard, Henry Bre 167
Willat, George Mas 293
Willbarger, John Bou 114
Willcox, Isreal Nel 19
James Mul 385
Isaac Nel 16
Phebe Nel 19
William Nel 19
Willer, Math Nel 16
Willert, James Fle 78
Willes, Henry Pul 128
Willet, Griffeth Nel 19
Richd. Hrd 299
Richd. Hrd 300
Willett, John She 240
Willey, Jacob Mul 393
Willham, Wm. Gar 233
Willhelms, Geo Bar 34
Willhite, Arron Lin 139
Joseph Lin 139
Lewis Lin 139
Willhoit, Lewis Fra 176
Sally Fra 177
Willhoite, John Fra 176
Tobias Fra 176
William, Barns Adr 12
James, Senr Cum 181
Jeremiah Jef 20
John Cly 153
John Mer 343
John Mer 343
Joseph Mas 293
Levi Woo 381
Wilkerson (Wyatt's son) Mad 242
Williams, Aaron Adr 16
Abraham Mas 295
Absolem Fra 174
Alex Nel 17
Alexander Fra 176
Alexander Wsh 322
Alfred Hnd 343
Alier Knx 74
Amos Bre 158
Amos Wsh 336
Andrew Fra 177
Anthony Hop 372
Archibald Mas 294
Arthur Cal 15
Atkins Adr 3
B. William Mas 295
Baily Hnr 352
Basel Fle 71

Williams, cont.	
Bat.	Knx 75
Bazel	She 212
Bazel	War272
Ben	Hrs 310
Benj.	Bar 42
Benja.	Fle 88
Benjamin	Jes 45
Benjn.	Bou 115
Benjn.	Bou 115
Benjn.	Mad 235
Bennett	Pen 113
Beverly	Mer 340
Burrel	Hop 375
Caleb	Fay 12
Caleb	Mon 348
Charles	Fra 175
Charles	Hrd 301
Charles	Jes 45
Charles	Knx 72
Charles	Sco 177
Chas.	Bou 116
Chas.	Bou 116
Chs.	Nel 16
Coaldin	Chr 58
Dan	Mad 237
Danl.	Adr 15
Danl.	Fle 77
Danl.	Grn 263
Daniel	Flo 106
Daniel	Grn 258
Daniel	Jef 25
Daniel	Mad 234
Daniel	Pen 105
Davey	She 231
David	Bre 163
David	Hrs 308
David	Lin 139
David	Lin 139
David	Mad 233
David	Mer 339
Edward	Fay 24
Edward	Gal 195
Edward	Mad 236
Edward	Ohi 87
Edward, Junr	Ohi 87
Eli	Grp 275
Eli	She 216
Elias	Liv 160
Elijah	Gar 229
Elijah	Lew 96
Elijah	ohi 75
Elizabeth	Jes 44
Evan	Jef 7
Evan	Ohi 72
Evan	Ohi 86
Federick	Pul 128
Frederick	Hop 375
Geor.	Mon 357
George	Cas 41
George	Clr 145
George	Fra 173
George	Mer 339
Geroge	Mer 339
George	Ohi 86
George	Pul 127
George	War 275
George	Wsh 336
Hannah	Hrs 313
Hanson	Fay 39
Harden	Cum 173
Henry	Mon 378
Henson	Fay 32
Hubbart	Bou 116
Isaac	Lin 139
Isaac	Wsh 336
Ivin	Nel 15

Williams, cont.	
J. J.	Mul 385
Ja.	Hnr 351
Jacob	Gra 240
Jacob	Knx 72
James	Bar 39
James	Bar 42
Jaes	Cas 45
James	Chr 68
James	Cly 160
James	Cum 173
James	Fle 72
James	Flo 106
James	Hrd 301
James	Jes 44
James, Maj.	Jes 47
James	Log 176
James	Log 180
James	Mad 240
James	Mon 361
James	Pen 108
James	Pul 128
James	Sco 179
James, Junr	Cum 181
James, Jr	Log 176
Jas.	Way 353
Jas.	Way 365
Jas.	Way 373
Jaspar	Nel 16
Jemy	Nel 6
Jeremiah	Jef 29
Jeremiah	Sco 181
Jerrard	Mas 296
Jesse	Log 175
Jesse	Log 176
Jesse	Log 191
Jesse	Pul 130
Jessee	Cal 19
Jessy	Mon 379
Jno.	Hnr 351
Jno.	Hrd 295
Joel	Grn 261
John	Bar 29
John	Bar 39
John	Bar 53
John	Bul 187
John	Bou 133
John	Cas 41
John	Chr 54
John	Chr 70
John	Chr 81
John	Clr 145
John	Cly 154
John	Cum 166
John	Cum 173
John	Cum 176
John	Cum 181
John	Fle 66
John	Fle 75
John	Flo 106
John	Flo 106
John	Fra 176
John	Gar 230
John	Hnd 328
John	Hnr 360
John	Hnr 360
John	Lin 141
John	Mad 234
John	Mad 235
John	Mer 338
John	Mon 356
John	Mon 359
John	Mon 368
John	Mon 370
John	Mul 392
John	Nel 15
John	Nic 65

Williams, cont.	
John	Pul 130
John	Sco 190
John	She 209
John	She 211
John	She 227
John	War 277
John	Way 374
John	Woo 383
John	Woo 401
John	Woo 402
John F.	Sco 177
Jonas	Bar 30
Jonathan	Hop 375
Joseph	Bou 116
Joseph	Cas 37
Joseph	Cum 180
Joseph	Cum 181
Joseph	Fra 174
Joseph	Lin 139
Joseph	Mad 233
Joseph	Mas 292
Joseph	Mon 349
Joseph	Mon 351
Joseph	She 240
Joshua	Flo 106
Josia	Gal 195
Josiah	Woo 388
Josiph	Chr 106
Katharine	Mas 297
Kelly	Nel 16
Langston	War 265
Laurence	Fle 82
Lemuel	Cum 168
Lewis	War 274
Lilburn	Fle 90
Luke	Knx 66
Margaret	Mas 294
Mary	Gal 195
Mason	Flo 106
Mary	Gra 244
Mary	Mer 338
Massa	Gar 233
Matthew	Mul 388
Mordica	Grp 269
Metcalf and	Bou 70
Morgin	Pul 124
Morgin	Pul 127
Moses	Mon 358
Nancy	Bou 116
Nancy	Lew 100
Nancy	Ohi 68
Nathan	Mon 362
Nelson	Wsh 337
Noah	Ohi 86
Noris	Pul 127
Noris	Pul 127
Original	Fay 22
Ohty	Bre 162
Philip	Mon 363
Philip	Pul 126
Phillip	Cly 152
Phillip	Hrd 298
Pope	Pen 114
Presley	Boo 64
Providence	Hnd 340
Rafh.	Pul 128
Rawleigh	Mon 369
Richard	Fra 176
Richard	Knx 77
Richd.	Cum 180
Robert	Cum 176
Robert	Log 161
Robert	Mon 375
Robert	Pul 126
Robert	Sco 183
Robt.	Cal 20

Williams, cont.
Roger Bou 116
Roley War 267
Sally Clr 145
Sally Fra 177
Sam Pul 127
Saml. Bou 115
Saml. Gar 233
Saml. Jef 21
Saml. Lin 139
Samuel Chr 56
Samuel Hnd 343
Samuel Log 191
Samuel Mon 384
Samuel Pul 128
Samuel Wsh 335
Sanford Bou 116
Shadrach Mad 236
Shedrick Fle 66
Simon Sco 170
Simon War 274
Simpson Gal 195
Smith Pul 127
Ste. Gar 230
Stephen Ohi 79
Stephn. Nel 17
Susan She 228
Susanna Clr 145
Tho. Bar 39
Tho. Hop 374
Thomas Fle 69
Thomas Gar 230
Thomas Hrd 300
Thomas Knx 77
Thomas Mas 309
Thomas Nel 16
Thomas Pen 111
Thomas Pul 126
Thomas Wsh 336
Thos. Hrd 294
Thos. Hrd 296
Uriah Chr 58
Walter Gar 229
William Chr 55
William Chr 69
William Clr 145
William Hnd 343
William Hnd 344
William, Mjr. Mad 235
William Hnr 352
William Log 190
William Mad 240
William Mas 293
William Woo 383
William, Sen Mad 237
William, L. Woo 393
Willm. Hrs 307
Winford Cal 18
Wm. Bou 133
Wm. Bre 162
Wm. Grn 260
Wm. Lew 102
Wm. Mon 374
Wm. Nic 64
Wm. War 266
Wm. Way 353
Wm. Way 368
Wm. M. Mad 237
Zealy Bul 187
Zed Mon 362
Williamson, Abm. Sco 168
Alexr. Hrd 294
Anderson Fay 35
Benja. Flo 104
David Fay 12
David Sco 185
Dawson Cal 13

Williamson, cont.
Elliott Jef 20
Federick Grn 248
Garret Fay 59
George Jef 21
Hamen Flo 104
Henry Jef 20
Jacob Grn 261
Jesse War 267
John Bar 33
John Log 196
John Nic 64
John Sco 171
John She 197
John She 198
John, Jun Fle 61
Jos. War 279
Juo. Flo 104
Lewis Sco 182
Patrick Gar 229
Ramy Gar 230
Richard Fay 60
Roger Sco 176
Samuel Fay 60
Samuel Pen 109
Tho. Bar 33
Thomas Sco 183
Thos. Lin 141
Turner Sco 183
William Fay 60
William Log 190
Wm. Fle 88
Willians, Elison Cam 28
Williby, Alexander Jes 43
Williford, Britten Mad 234
Elizabeth Mad 234
James Mad 234
John Knx 79
Samuel Mad 240
Willing, David Grn 257
Thos. Grn 263
Willingham, Isaac Hnd 332
Isham Hnd 333
Jarett Hnd 331
Jarrott Hnd 328
John Hnd 332
John Hnd 335
Thomas Hnd 328
William Hnd 333
Willis, Abner Fay 26
Britain Mul 402
Edmund Adr 15
Henry Wsh 339
James Chr 67
James Chr 73
John Cum 180
John She 239
John Woo 391
Joseph Mer 339
Lemuel She 223
Lewis Gra 237
Major She 218
Matthew Cum 179
Matthew Mul 392
Owen Gra 237
Robt. Adr 16
Smith Way 354
Thomas Pul 127
Thos. Cly 150
William Adr 16
William Hnr 356
William Jes 44
William Wsh 336
Wm. Adr 15
Wm. Adr 15
Wm. Bar 36
Wm. Cum 182

Willis, cont.
Wright W. Hop 375
Willison, James Cam 29
Williss, Drury Mad 235
Edward Mad 237
James Mad 236
James Mad 239
John Mad 238
Nancy Mad 242
Sterling Mad 236
William Mad 236
Willitt, John Wsh 336
Willmot, George Nel 19
John Bou 116
Willock, David Grn 247
Willon, Levi Fle 72
Willot, Charles Mas 297
Willott, Richard Mas 303
Willoughby, David Fle 69
Willowby, Andrew War 273
Anthony War 273
Wills, Aaron Nic 64
Andrew Fle 88
Barbary Mon 348
Betsy Mon 353
Daniel Mon 377
David Fle 74
David Nic 64
Elizabeth Mon 375
Frances Mul 403
Frederick Clr 144
George Chr 111
Isaac Clr 144
Isaac Fay 26
James Fle 66
James Fle 74
John Fle 74
John Nic 64
John Sco 175
Matthew Flo 106
Michael Mon 376
Nathan Nic 64
Philip, Jr Grn 255
Richard Clr 144
Samel Fle 66
Saml. Fle 73
Thornton Clr 144
Washington Clr 144
William Clr 144
William Hnr 357
Willis Chr 82
Willson, Abraham Lin 141
Catherine Lin 141
Elijah Mul 387
Fenelon R. Adr 15
George Bou 114
James Adr 16
James Bou 115
James Gra 239
James Mul 402
James, Junr Gra 243
Jno. F. Bou 115
John Cam 26
John Mul 407
Jolson Adr 16
Joseph Gra 239
Joseph Fra 239
Josiah Adr 16
Manson Mul 403
Mathew Lin 141
Matthew Hnd 328
Moses Adr 16
Moses Adr 16
Moses Adr 16
Nathan Adr 16
Robert Hnd 340
Thos. Adr 16

Willson, cont.
William Bou 114
William Gra 239
Wm. Cam 25
Willumson, Thomas Chr 59
Wilman, Christian Mas 309
Cornelius Fay 12
Wilmin, John Woo 378
Wilmore, James Jes 41
Jane Jes 44
Wilmot, Erasmus Gar 229
Richd. War 269
Saml. Gar 199
Wilmoth, James Hrd 281
Wilmott, Robert Bou 133
Wilmouth, Thos. Nel 16
Wiloughby, Willm Lin 139
Wilsen, Benjamin Chr 97
Wilson, Abner Fay 48
Abraham Mon 376
Absalom Woo 387
Agness Wsh 332
Alexander Grp 274
Alexander Mer 340
Alexander Mon 347
Alexander Mon 347
Alexander Woo 382
Alexander, Senr Fra 173
Alexr. Jef 21
Ambrose Hnd 330
Amos Fra 174
Andrew Mon 360
Andrw. Fle 88
Ann Fle 70
Archebald Fra 174
Armstead Fra 175
Augustes Fay 51
Bazaleel Gar 233
Ben Cum 180
Ben Nic 65
Benjamin Woo 379
Benjn. Bou 115
Catherine Bou 115
Charles Knx 68
Christo. Boo 64
Daniel Fle 75
Daniel Hnd 325
David Fay 27
David Fay 48
David Gal 195
David Hrs 310
David Knx 82
David Mer 340
David Mon 379
Drusilla Lew 103
Edward Clr 144
Edward Gra 239
Edward She 234
Elfon Bul 187
Eli She 224
Ephram. Bou 133
Francis Mer 339
Geo. Hrd 291
George Clr 144
George Gra 240
George Mon 347
George B. But 197
Hannah Wsh 335
Harris Flo 104
Henry Bou 115
Henry Nel 16
Henry, Senr Bou 115
Isaac Fle 87
Isaac Fra 177
Isaac Grn 258
Isaac Mer 340
Isaac Nel 18

Wilson, cont.
Isaac Nic 65
Isaiah Bou 133
Isra Bar 47
Jacob Bar 43
Jacob Clr 144
Jacob Bou 116
James Bar 30
James Boo 64
James Bre 165
James Chr 79
James Clr 144
James Clr 144
James Cum 178
James Fay 12
James Fra 175
James Fra 178
James Gal 196
James Grn 250
James Grp 272
James Hrs 314
James Jef 26
James Knx 83
James Hnd 337
James Lew 100
James Liv 158
James Log 162
James Mas 295
James Nel 18
James Nic 64
James Pen 117
James Woo 396
James Wsh 337
James, Jr Pen 111
James, Senr Boo 64
James, Senr Boo 64
Jane Nic 64
Janes Nic 63
Jarrod Clr 144
Jas. Hrd 286
Jas. Hrd 288
Jas. Lew 102
Jas. Jr Lew 102
Jeremiah Bou 115
Jeremiah Clr 144
Jeremiah Clr 144
Jeremiah Liv 150
Jeremiah Woo 394
Jesse Bul 187
Jesse Mas 295
Jessy Gra 239
Jno. Hrd 286
Jno. Lew 102
Joel Chr 95
John Bar 27
John Bar 43
John Bar 43
John Bar 47
John Bou 115
John Bou 115
John But 197
John But 198
John Chr 78
John Chr 98
John Chr 98
John Chr 105
John Clr 144
John Clr 144
John Clr 144
John Clr 147
John Fle 63
John Fle 82
John Flo 104
John Fra 173
John Fra 175
John (B) Gal 194
John Gra 239

Wilson, cont.
John Hop 372
John Hop 379
John Hrs 305
John Lew 103
John Liv 149
John Log 189
John Mad 234
John Mad 234
John Mas 295
John Mas 296
John Mer 340
John Mer 343
John Mon 347
John Mon 366
John Mon 368
John Mon 377
John Mon 380
John Nel 16
John Nel 18
John Nel 18
John Pen 114
John Pul 126
John Sco 193
John War 265
John Woo 384
John, Jur Sco 180
John, Sr Nel 18
Jonas Rck 162
Jonathan Clr 156
Jonathan Fay 51
Jonathan Gra 244
Joseph Bou 115
Joseph Knx 68
Joseph Mon 379
Joseph Nel 19
Joseph Rck 161
Joseph Sco 180
Joseph War 279
Joshua Bar 30
Joshua Fay 12
Joshua Rck 159
Joshua Rck 162
Joshua Woo 381
Joshua, Ser Rck 164
L. Tho. Bar 43
Laurence Woo 382
Lewis Fay 38
Loyd Grp 270
Martha Mer 339
Martin Wsh 337
Mary Log 190
Mary Nel 14
Mary Sco 193
Mathew Chr 66
Mathew Chr 112
Mathew Hrs 312
Michael Knx 76
Michael She 224
Moses Boo 64
Moses Cal 11
Moses Clr 144
Moses Jes 45
Moses Lew 100
Moses Nel 14
Moses Way 358
Nancy Gar 234
Nathan Mon 358
Nathaniel Bul 187
Nicholas Mul 397
Partrick Mon 347
Phillip Cly 151
Presley Mon 366
Pugh Grn 261
Ralph Pen 114
Reed Fay 45
Richard Knx 80

Wilson, cont.
Richard Log 185
Richd. Sco 187
Robert Bul 186
Robert Fay 12
Robert Fay 31
Robert Fay 42
Robert Fay 42
Robert Fle 88
Robert Hrs 315
Robert Jef 25
Robert Liv 149
Robert Mas 309
Robert Mon 369
Robert Nel 16
Robt. Gal 196
Sally She 204
Saml. Bou 116
Saml. Cum 168
Saml. Cum 178
Saml. Grn 255
Saml. Lew 96
Samuel Clr 144
Samuel Fay 25
Samuel Fle 67
Samuel Jes 46
Samuel Knx 87
Samuel Liv 149
Samuel Log 175
Samuel Log 196
Samuel Mon 366
Samuel She 198
Samuel She 200
Sanford Mon 366
Silas Bou 115
Singleton She 208
Solomon Mas 292
Stephen Rck 162
Tapley Fra 175
Tho. Bar 40
Thomas But 197
Thomas Fle 81
Thomas Gar 230
Thomas Hrs 310
Thomas Jes 45
Thomas Lin 139
Thomas Log 193
Thomas Mas 293
Thomas Mer 339
Thomas Mer 340
Thomas Pen 115
Thomas War 245
Thomas Woo 382
Thomas, Jr Pen 113
Thornton Hnd 329
Thos. Bou 115
Thos. Bou 115
Thos. Way 352
Thos. Way 372
Uriah Bou 115
Uriah Mon 379
Vance Mer 340
W. Jef 24
William Clr 144
William Grn 256
William Grn 259
William Jes 46
William Liv 150
William Log 166
William Log 186
William Mad 235
William Pul 125
William Sco 177
William Sco 188
William Sco 192
William Woo 382
William Wsh 332

Wilson, cont.
William L. Chr 107
Wm. Bar 26
Wm. Bar 47
Wm. Bra 144
Wm. Grn 250
Wm. Hrd 286
Wm. Hrd 287
Wm. Jef 21
Wm. Lew 96
Wm. Mon 347
Wm. Mon 366
Wm. Mon 370
Wm. War 258
Wm. A. Bra 151
Wm. G. Lew 96
Wiltcher, William Ohi 97
Wilton, John Grn 257
Wily, David Chr 63
James Hnr 360
John Hnr 355
John Hnr 358
Mathew Chr 85
Wilyard, Henry Bre 160
Wiman, Lucus Wsh 340
Wimberly, Hardy War 274
Wimer, Martin Fay 27
Win, John Cam 30
John Clr 156
Saml. Jef 21
Wm. Bra 147
Winam, Philip Jef 15
Winans, James Fle 83
Winborne, Henry Mad 234
Jesse Mad 234
Winchester, John Hrd 301
Richard Jef 22
Richd. Hrd 287
Winder, Thomas Bou 70
Winders, George Wsh 336
John Mul 396
Saml. Hrd 298
Windings, James Jr Pen 111
Winebruner, Cath-erine Fra 179
Winfield, Ann Nel 15
David Wsh 336
Winfred, Joshia Bar 26
Winfree, Fenny Cum 169
Winfrey, Hennery Cas 41
Phillip Adr 15
Wm. Adr 15
Winford, Novel Adr 15
Winfry, Charles Hnd 334
James War 274
John Adr 16
Thos. Adr 16
Wing, Chs. Mul 385
Margaret Mul 402
Wingard, George (freeman) Fay 27
Wingate, Cyrus Fra 177
Eunes Fay 24
Jacob Pen 110
John Fay 24
John Wsh 337
John C. Fay 32
Joseph Fay 12
Susanna Fra 177
Thos. Hnr 369
Wingfield, Henry Hnr 353
Jon. War 248
Wingo, James Grp 270
Winion, John Flo 106
Winins, Jacob Sco 172
Winkler, Adam Mul 394
Adam Wsh 335

Winkler, cont.
Daniel Mul 393
Daniel Mul 399
David Ohi 94
Henry Est 7
John Wsh 335
Winlock, Henry Grn 253
Joseph She 204
Winn, Adam Fay 24
Daniel Clr 144
George Fay 24
Harmon Way 372
James Clr 144
James Hrs 307
Jessy Fay 47
John Fay 24
John Fle 61
John Grn 251
John Mad 234
John, Junr Fay 24
John B. Mer 338
Joshua Bar 40
Joshua, Junr Bar 42
Mary Fay 24
Stephen Clr 144
Tho. Bar 28
Thomas Clr 144
Thomas Fay 24
William Fay 24
Winscot, Isaac Gal 197
Richd. War 246
Robt. War 246
Winscott, Abm. Gal 196
David Gal 196
Winset, Felix Nel 15
Nelly Nel 15
Wtephen Wsh 336
Winslow, Thomas Lew 101
Wm. Gal 196
Winston, John Cam 25
John J. Grn 255
Winters, Daniel Fra 179
Fredk. Cum 174
Jacob Sco 183
James Lew 98
John Mas 296
William Mul 403
Wm. Cam 32
Wire, David Clr 145
John Bre 166
Wirkman, Henry Chr 58
Wirkmon, Michael Chr 58
Wirt, George Sco 173
George, Jur Sco 173
John Sco 173
Wiruk, Nicholas Bra 146
Wisdom, Francis Adr 16
Francis Cum 167
Fras. Senr Cum 167
John, Jur Cum 167
John, Senr Cum 167
Thos. Cum 167
Tom Adr 16
Wise, Abnr. Gal 195
Abraham Mas 294
Adam Hrd 293
Amy Bul 187
Anna Nel 16
Caleb Bul 186
Daniel Gal 194
Daniel She 217
Henry Gal 195
Henry Grn 246
Jacob Bre 164
Jacob Nel 18
John Gal 196
John Mas 293

Name	County	Page
Wise, cont.		
Peter, Jr	Jef	20
Peter, Sr	Jef	20
Rhody	Mon	375
Tobias	Ohi	79
Wisehart, George	Hrd	282
Wiseheart, Henry	Nel	19
John	Nel	19
Wisely, William	Bou	116
Wiseman, Abner	Est	3
Abrm.	Hrd	303
James	Mad	242
John	Nel	18
Sally	Nel	15
Thomas	Nel	15
Wiser, Betsy	Mer	338
Phillip	Cas	45
Wishard, Abraham	Fle	84
Saml.	Fle	71
Samuel	Fle	71
William, Senr	Fle	71
Wishhard, William	Fle	70
Wisnam, Charles	Way	357
Wisner, George	Chr	74
Wisson, Wm.	Knx	67
Wisteman, William	Pul	128
Wistemon, John	Pul	127
Wit, John	Clr	145
Witehouse, Thomas	Jef	25
Withem, Peter	Cum	171
Witherington, Elizebeth	Mas	296
Jacob	Fle	89
John	Mas	293
Witheroe, John	Cum	177
Witherow, Samuel	Cal	4
Withers, Gideon	Hrd	295
James	Sco	192
John	Lin	141
Thomas	Woo	396
Wm. Junr	Hrd	299
Wm. Senr	Hrd	299
Withrow, John	Grp	274
John	Wsh	337
Joseph	Wsh	338
Williams	Wsh	336
Witly, John B.	Chr	78
Witson, William	Bou	133
Witt, Charles	Est	5
Elisha	Est	5
John	Log	[illegible]
Robert	Log	186
William	Est	5
William	Est	9
Witter, Samuel	Bre	158
Witts, Charles	Grn	249
Wize, David	Jef	21
Wm, Bishop	Hop	371
Wmson, Tho. Junr	Bar	33
Woby, Jerry	Gra	240
Woddle, Polly	Mer	339
Wodson, William	Pul	125
Woelson, Mikiel	Pul	129
Wolbanks, Reuben	War	257
Wolf, Andrew	Sco	185
Christ.	Nel	42
Conrad	Sco	168
David	Sco	168
Henry	Sco	191
Jacob	Hop	375
Jacob	Sco	169
Jacob	Sco	190
Jesse	Log	184
John	Bar	25
Michl.	Hop	376
Peter	Hrd	296
Wolfe, Athel	Jef	21
Wolfe, cont.		
Eliza	Jef	22
George	Jef	32
George, J.	Jef	32
John	Jef	21
Michael	Fra	174
Wollard, Saml.	Hrd	289
Wollitt, John	Jef	17
Wollum, Andrew	Knx	78
Wolsey, Joseph	Pul	127
Nathaniel	Pul	128
Richard	Pul	126
Richard	Way	357
Wolsy, Jacob	Cal	19
Wolton, George	War	243
Wolverton, Wilm.	Pul	125
Thos.	Pul	125
Womack, Abner	But	197
Wood, Abner	Fle	80
Abraham	Fay	27
Abram	Cas	38
Amos	Sco	171
Anderson	Bar	28
Andrew	Mas	293
Anna	Cal	17
Archibald	Hrs	320
Avary	Mul	404
Ba[illegible]zel	Log	191
Bartholimew	Chr	116
Bartholomew	But	198
Barthomew	Bar	43
Benjamin	Mas	295
Bennet	Log	175
Bruce	Log	161
Daniel	Clr	144
David	Mas	292
Edmond	Sco	189
Edmund	Cas	39
Eli	Mas	296
Elias	She	198
Ezeckal	Chr	63
Francis	Mad	234
George	Mas	309
George	Sco	190
Gideon	Fay	25
Henry	Mas	295
Henry	War	260
Henry	Wsh	339
[illegible]llby	Nic	65
[illegible]	Hrd	287
[illegible]	Mer	339
[illegible]es	Bar	31
James	Cal	10
James	Cal	12
James	Clr	145
James	Cum	185
James	Hrs	312
James	Mad	237
James	Mul	404
James	She	198
Jarimiah	Cas	39
Jenney	Mad	239
Jesse	Hrd	287
Jessee	Bar	44
John	Bou	116
John	Bou	116
John	Bou	116
John	Bul	186
John	Cas	38
John	Cum	183
John	Gal	196
John	Jef	20
John	Jef	25
John	Knx	88
John	Liv	156
John	Log	181
John	Log	184
Wood, cont.		
John	Mad	237
John	Mer	339
John	Mul	404
John	Nel	14
John	Nel	18
Jonothan	Nel	19
Joseph	But	198
Joseph	Fle	80
Lasareth	Mul	397
Lewis	Hrd	287
Malcolm	Bou	116
Matthew	She	233
Miller	War	259
Mises	Mas	291
Moses	Mul	394
Nathan	Bar	45
Nathaniel B.	Bul	186
Nicholas	Mas	295
Peter	Bar	28
Peter	Gar	230
Peter	Log	192
Rhoden	Sco	173
Richard	Fle	69
Robert	Clr	145
Robt.	Cal	8
Robt.	Cal	17
Robert	Log	176
Saml.	Bar	45
Samuel	Log	175
Samuel	Mad	239
Samuel	Mad	240
Stephen	Fay	24
Thomas	Lin	139
Thomas	Log	161
Thomas	Mad	240
Thomas	Mas	296
Thomas	Mer	339
Thomas	Mul	401
Thos.	Cum	185
Thos.	Sco	167
Tos. G.	War	249
Wiley	Mad	240
William	Clr	145
William	Log	192
William	Log	196
William	Mer	339
William	Ohi	94
Willm.	Sco	174
William	Sco	180
William (I)	Gal	195
Wm.	Adr	15
Wm.	Bar	45
Wm.	Bou	116
Wm.	Cum	184
Wm. J.	Bar	33
Woodall, Benjamin	Clr	145
Charles	Lin	141
Charles	Rck	164
James	Pul	129
Jehu	Lin	141
John	Lin	141
Overton	Gar	230
Willm.	Lin	141
Woodard, Asel	Bra	148
Busttitt	[illegible]	[illegible]4
Chrsley	[illegible]	[illegible]3
George	Grn	262
Hannah	Bar	43
James	Bul	187
Joel	Bra	152
John	Mon	348
John	Mon	350
Julius	Clr	145
Lance	Mon	351
Michael	Bul	187
Richd.	Grn	251

Woodard, cont.
Samuel Mon 371
Samuel Mon 372
William Grn 251
Woodburn, James Chr 79
Woodcock, Jno. Nel 5
Wooden, Boal Hnr 356
John Hnr 357
Robert Jef 22
Woodfd, Danl. Jr Hnr 362
Danl. Sr Hnr 362
Woodfield, Andrew She 219
Andw. Hnr 362
Gabriel She 239
Jno. Hnr 362
John She 218
Woodfolk, Thomas Fay 44
Woodford, Thomas Hnd 335
Woodfork, Joseph She 216
Richard Jes 47
Woodland, Henry Mon 373
John Mon 361
Woodly, Francis Cal 16
Woodring, John Nel 18
Woodrow, Alexr. Jef 21
Mary Mas 303
Woodruff, Aaron Fay 12
Aron Cal 9
David Fay 15
Jas. Way 371
Noadiah Fra 176
Woodruffe, David Mad 234
Mary Mad 235
Woodrum, Stepn. Adr 12
Woods, Abner Mer 339
W Adam Fay 39
Adam Mad 236
Adam, Jun Mad 236
Alexd. Clr 144
Amon Jes 43
Anderson Mad 239
Andrew Fay 53
Andrew Grp 274
Andrew Mer 340
Andrew War 264
Archabald Way 368
Archibald Mad 241
Archibald Mer 341
David Bou 115
David Chr 91
David Mer 338
Edward Jes 45
Edward B. Woo 380
Elijah Jes 45
G. Jas. Gar 230
Geo. Cum 173
Henry Chr 58
Henry Mon 361
Isham Grn 253
Isham F. Chr 101
James Bre 156
James Fay 44
James Fle 72
Jas. Gar 230
Jas. Gar 233
Jeremiah Clr 145
Jesse Mon 358
Jessy Chr 101
John Bou 115
John Gar 233
John Mad 241
John Mer 339
John Mon 358
John Nel 18
Jonathan Jes 45
Joseph Fay 15
Joseph Fra 174
Woods, cont.
Joseph Jes 44
Joseph Liv 145
Joseph Mer 340
Lydia Wsh 337
Margaret Fay 12
Mathew Hrs 310
Michael Gar 233
Michael Log 190
Nelly Nel 17
Patrick Mad 236
Richard Gal 196
Robert Liv 145
Searight Sco 180
Saml. Bra 145
Saml. Clr 160
Saml. Way 351
Samuel Fay 53
Samuel Log 190
Samuel Mer 340
Thomas Chr 101
Thomas Jes 45
Timothy Jef 25
William But 197
William But 197
William Fra 178
William Hrs 305
William Jef 25
William Liv 152
William Mad 236
William(red head) Mad 238
William, Mjr Mad 241
Woodside, David Liv 160
Robert Liv 158
Samuel Liv 158
William Fra 175
Woodsides, John She 200
Woodsmall, Shlt. Nel 16
William She 204
Woodson, Henry Knx 87
Jack Fra 178
Saml. Bar 40
Samuel Hop 381
Samuel H. Jes 46
Tarltin Mad 234
Thomas Bar 33
Tucker Jes 47
Wade N. Knx 63
William Pul 128
William Woo 379
Woodsum, Willm. Lin 141
Woodward, Benedict Wsh 339
Henry Liv 154
James Log 175
John Ohi 75
John She 242
John Wsh 337
Peter Hnd 344
Peter Mul 387
Richd. Nel 15
Rosaner Grn 266
William Hnd 342
Woody, Washington Clr 145
Woodyard, Henry Pen 113
Jesse Pen 113
William Pen 113
Woogen, Lewis Bou 133
Nancy Bou 133
Woolbanks, John War 268
Woolcutt, Barnas. Adr 16
Sarah Woo 400
Wooldridge, Edmund Bou 115
Elisha Woo 384
James Adr 16
John Adr 16
John B. Fra 178
John W. Fra 178
Wooldridge, cont.
Josiah Woo 384
Richd. Adr 16
Saml. Adr 15
Thos. Hnr 359B
Wm. Adr 15
Wooldrige, Richard Grn 257
Wm. Bou 115
Woolen, Leonard Nic 64
Wooley, Jeremiah Wsh 338
Woolf, Fealding Chr 87
George Bou 133
Henry Chr 88
Woolfold, Elijah Sco 192
Woolfolk, Augustine Gal 196
Edmond Jef 25
Joseph Hrd 304
Richard Jef 25
Robert Jef 25
Wm. Jef 26
Woolford, Abram Nel 5
John Adr 15
Woolfork, Sowyel Woo 384
William Hnr 354
Woolard, Wm. Grn 254
Woollary, Jacob Hrs 319
John Hrs 319
Joseph Hrs 316
Michael Hrs 312
Woollen, Thomas Fay 24
Woolley, Thomas Wsh 337
Woollum, John Jur Sco 180
John, Senr Sco 179
Zachh. Sco 178
Woolms, Wm. Nic 63
Woolry, Francis Mad 238
Henry Mad 238
Jacob Mad 238
John Mad 238
Lawrence Mad 238
Michael Mad 237
Peter Mad 238
Wools, Daniel Mon 366
Elizabeth Mon 367
Philip Mon 362
Woolsey, Wm. H. War 249
Woolsy, Zephaniah Cum 183
Woolten, Jrriston? Fay 24
Woolwine, Geo. Gar 230
Wooly, Easter Hnr 351
John Chr 91
Levy Bar 38
Woosey, George War 249
Woosley, Thomas Clr 145
Wooten, Charles Grp 277
John Nel 17
Elijah Mul 400
Fredirick Cly 157
Wooton, Moses Cum 181
Nathan War 249
P. Silas Flo 104
Sarah Cly 157
Stephen Hop 373
Woottin, William Ohi 69
Wootton, James Bre 167
Joseph Bar 47
Word, Jonathan Mer 339
Wordlaw, James C. Hnd 327
Worford, Benjamin Pen 109
Work, John Pul 124
Saml. War 251
Worker, Wm. Way 356
Workman, Benjn. Adr 15
George Mon 382
John Adr 8
Saml. Grn 261
Workmon, Joseph She 201

Works, Andrew Sco 179
Joseph, Senr Sco 178
Joseph, Jur Sco 178
Worl, Samuel Hrs 314
Worland, Barnaby Sco 185
Charles Wsh 337
Henry Wsh 337
James Wsh 340
John R. Wsh 337
Ruth Wsh 340
Thomas Sco 184
World, Atte Hrs 305
Worldly, Daniel Mas 294
Worley, Caleb Fay 24
Danl. Nel 6
David Fay 39
Frail Bre 163
George Way 366
Wiley Knx 69
William Adr 19
Worlin, Jonathen Way 362
Wormack, Abra[illegible] War 246
M[illegible]hew War 273
Wilm. War 273
Wormesley, Uriah Mon 357
Wormin, Joseph Adr 16
Wormis, John Mer 340
Wormsley, Cumfort Mon 357
Worner, Martin Cam 28
Wornoch, James Grp 269
Wornock, James Grp 269
Samuel, Grp 269
William Grp 269
Worrel, Rebecca Gar 230
Thomas Jef 26
Worren, William Bou 133
Worrin, Edgeman Chr 78
Worsell, Wm. Boo 64
Worsley, Joseph Gra 238
Worson, Alexander She 223
Robert She 226
Worsted, Jams. Bra 144
Robt. Bra 145
Worters, James Pen 107
Wortham, Jos. Hrd 287
Worthington, Andrew Mul 393
Benjamin Cal 15
Edward Mer 339
Edwd. Hnr 368
I. Thomas Mad 292
Thomas Mul 391
William Mer 397
Wortman, Richard Pen 110
Richard, Jr Pen 110
Worton, John Boo 64
Wotson, David Bar 47
Joseph Mer 339
Woyatt, John Hrs 315
Wrabford, Jacob Way 353
Wray, Daniel Gar 233
Danl. Bar 27
John Bar 45
John, Jnr Gar 231
John, Snr Gar 231
Jos. Gar 231
Mosess Lin 139
Saml. Gar 233
Willm. [illegible]
Wm. [illegible]
Zach. [illegible]
Wren, Isaac Ba[illegible]
Tabitha Gar 230
Willm. Sco 183
Wrenn, James Mon 374
Wright, Adam War 275
Alexdr. Bou 116

Wright, cont.
Alexr. Gar 199
Ariey Cas 38
Asa She 222
Ben Hrd 295
Ben Nel 42
Betsy Clr 145
Bledsoe Fay 26
Charles War 272
Christo. Bar 29
David Hnd 345
Durlin Mad 238
Edwd. Sco 177
Elijah Bul 186
Esau Cum 171
Evan Way 366
Francis Adr 13
Geo. Gar 230
George Hop 381
George War 256
George Wsh 338
Gideon Mad 241
Hugh Bou 115
Isaac Adr 15
Isaac Way 373
Isaiah Hrd 282
Jacob Bar 35
James Bou 133
James Gal 195
James Hnd 329
James Knx 90
James Lin 139
James Mas 300
James Ohi 91
James Sco 174
James Woo 379
Jamis Fle 76
Jane Bou 133
Jarrot War 268
Jeane Fle 82
Jesse Hnr 356
Jesse, Sr Gal 195
Jessee Way 355
Jno. Hrd 285
John Bar 38
John Bar 44
John Bou 133
John Clr 145
John Cum 183
John Cum 184
John Est 1
John Gal 196
John Mul 391
John Pul 124
John She 198
John She 200
John She 220
John She 221
John War 268
John War 279
John Way 368
John Wsh 332
John Wsh 338
John W. Gal 195
Jonathan Lin 139
Joseph Bar 47
Joseph Bre 165
Joseph Lin 139
Joseph Nel 6
Joseph Pul 127
Joseph War 268
Josiah Mas 295
Josiah War 252
Larken Log 186
Levin War 272
Lewis Cum 184
Linsey Lin 141

Wright, cont.
Linsy Lin 139
Mary Wsh 338
Mathew Mas 296
Merideth Clr 145
Morgan Wsh 337
Morris Lin 139
Moses Hrd 296
Nancy Wsh 332
Nathan Gar 230
Nelson Lin 139
N[illegible]s. Way 371
O[illegible]iah She 235
Pate Cas 38
Philbert Cum 182
Rachel Gar 233
Reason Hnr 355
Reason Lew 97
Richard Grn 261
Richard Knx 90
Richard Nel 19
R[illegible] A[illegible] 12
R[illegible] [illegible] 115
R[illegible] Gar 233
Rosana Knx 72
Sally Hnr 360
Saml. Grn 245
Saml. Hnr 356
Saml. Lin 139
Samuel Bou 133
Samuel Pen 113
Samuel She 198
Sarah Bou 133
Sham Pen 115
Stephen Log 186
Stephen Mul 391
Tabitha Hrd 289
Tho. Bar 35
Thomas Clr 145
Thomas Clr 145
Thomas She 216
Thomas Wsh 332
Thomas W. Clr 145
Threlkeld Fra 174
Vincent Hrd 285
William Clr 145
William Clr 145
William Clr 145
William Mad 236
William Nel 19
William Ohi 100
William Wsh 337
William Wsh 338
William Wsh 338
Wilm. War 248
Wm. War 256
Wyant, Jacob Chr 115
Jacob Gal 195
Wyarte, Wm. War 257
Wyat, Jas. Hrd 289
Wyatt, Charles Hop 374
Conquer Cum 176
Emanuel Bou 133
George Hop 374
Henry Bou 114
John Bou 133
John Cal 18
John Clr 145
John Fay 12
John Lin 139
Jonathan Liv 158
Jordan Mad 242
Mark Mad 239
Richard Bou 133
Thomas T. Bou 133
Wm. Cum 178
Zadock Liv 152

Wyatte, Rebeca Lin 139
Wybel, Adam Nel 14
Wycoff, Henry Pen 113
James Pen 113
John Bou 114
Wydick, Jacob Log 174
John Log 174
Wykoff, Ephraim Bou 114
John Bou 114
Samuel Bou 114
Wylie, John Liv 149
John Liv 151
Joseph Liv 154
Wymon, Adam Hnr 359A
Wymore, Frederick Gal 196
George Jef 25
James Fra 176
John Fra 176
Saml. Gal 196

-- Y --

Yaddy, Barnett Est 8
Yager, Ananias Wsh 341
Cornelius Wsh 341
Eleanor Wsh 341
Elija Cam 28
Yagle, Nicholas Woo 386
Yake, Elias Hrs 307
Yaky, Henry Bar 41
Yance, Nicholas Mon 350
Yancy, Burket G. Woo 381
Joel Bar 41
John Bar 36
Ludwell Mas 298
Robert Way 355
Robert Woo 389
Robert Mad 243
Yandel, Andrew Chr 99
Yandle, Henry Way 365
John Chr 64
Yanky, Jacob Mer 340
Yantis, Amos Gar 199
John Gar 234
Yarber, Thomas Mon 361
Wm. Hnr 367
Yarbro, John Mon 371
Yarbrough, James Mon 367
Jeremiah Log 187
Yarbours, ..nally Fle 76
Yarce, Laurance Mul 399
Yarnel, David Hrs 309
Isaac Hrs 311
John Q. Hrs 313
Samuel Hrs 322
Yarnell, Isac Fay 43
Yater, Coonrod Bou 117
Yates, Andrew Nic 65
Benjamin She 242
Enoch Wsh 341
Francis Adr 17
George Adr 17
Henry Gal 197
James Bul 187
Joel Adr 17
John Gra 241
John Bar 26
John Mad 243
John Fay 51
John Wsh 340
John, Senr Bar 28
Joshua Mad 243
Joshua, Junr Mon 372
Joshua, Senr Mon 371
Yates, cont.
Mary Chr 55
Mary Wsh 341
Robert E. Wsh 341
Robt. Bar 29
Saml. Bar 25
Samuel Mon 371
Stephen Wsh 341
Thomas Wsh 341
William Nic 65
William Mer 340
William Mas 298
William Nel 14
William Mad 243
Wm. Mon 371
Zachariah Wsh 341
Yaunt, William She 198
Yeager, Absolam Nel 13
Benjamin Hnd 331
Elijah Fra 180
Elisha Fra 179
Frederick Lin 143
Jacob Fay 27
Jesse Jef 25
Joseph Lin 143
Joseph Knx 83
Josh. H. Nel 13
Josiah Mer 340
Lewiss Lin 143
Lucy Fra 180
Philip Mer 343
Saml. Gar 235
Samuel Fra 180
Yeaky, Frederick Gar 234
Yeanewine, Jacob Jef 23
John Jef 22
Leonard Jef 22
Peter Jef 23
Yearby, Witliam Log 173
Yearly, John Gra 238
William Chr 88
Yeary, Benedick Rck 159
Yeater, Henry Gar 234
Joseph Mon 355
Yeates, Enoch Mon 371
Yeatman, John Fra 180
Yeats, Isaac Jef 22
Joseph Fle 85
Yeazel, Jacob Fle 71
Yeirer?, Jacob Nel 5
Yeizer, Inglehart Fay 12
Yelton, Charles Pen 107
John Pen 107
William Pen 108
Chas. Bou 117
Yewell, James Jef 22
Jeremiah Jef 22
Martin Jef 22
Yizer, Philip Mer 343
Yocom, Francis Mon 356
George Mon 373
Jacob Mon 356
John Mon 357
John, Junr Mon 356
Jonathan Mon 356
Matthew Wsh 341
Matthias Bul 187
Solomon Mon 373
Wm. Mon 370
Wm. Mon 362
Yocum see Gocum
Yocum, George Way 368
George Way 354
Jacob Nel 5
John Mer 340
Matthias Mer 341
Yoder, Jacob She 204
Yokem, John Hnd 339
Yong, Henry Bra 143
Wm. Bra 150
Yongman, Isaiah Bra 151
York, Charles Mon 379
Charles Bra 147
Elijah Bre 164
Ezekiel Mon 358
James Log 166
Jeremiah Fay 27
Jeromah Cly 152
Jerry Hrd 292
John Fay 24
Joseph Way 373
Joshua Cam 24
Joshua Mas 298
Rachel Bra 150
Youcam, Hennery Cas 39
Youcum, Hennery - sin Cas 43
John Cas 42
Young, Aaron H. Fle 65
Abner Jes 42
Alexander Flo 106
Alexr. Nic 65
Alexr. Fle 79
Ambrose Fay 27
Andrew Mon 370
Andrew Wsh 342
Andrew Jef 22
Andrew Jef 22
Barney Gar 199
Benjamin Cal 4
Brice Bra 146
Bryant Nel 13
Cathrine Mad 243
Charity Chr 68
Chas. Cas 38
Christian Jef 22
Christopher But 198
Daniel Mon 351
Daniel War 257
Daniel Cal 13
David War 264
David Bou 117
Drurey War 247
Edward Bar 40
Edward Clr 146
Edwd. Way 362
Elijah She 203
Elisabeth Flo 105
Emanuel Jef 26
Ephraim Mon 360
Garrard Bar 50
George Wsh 341
George Mer 343
George War 277
George Chr 72
Gipson War 277
Henry Jef 25
Henry Chr 103
Henry Chr 93
Henry Chr 93
Hosea Gal 196
Hyram Bou 117
Israel Grn 249
Jacob She 224
Jacob Nel 14
Jacob Nic 65
James Cum 173
James Cum 166
James War 245
James She 206
James Nel 13
James Bar 25
James L. She 225
James But 198

Young, cont.
James Clr 146
James Clr 146
James Mon 352
James Jes 43
James Liv 158
James Flo 106
James Jes 42
James Fle 85
James, Senr Mon 365
Jane Cal 14
Jas. Hrd 299
Joel Jes 43
John Chr 81
John Woo 385
John D. Fay 27
John Fay 27
John Fay 24
John Cu[illegible]
John Ws[illegible]
John Wsh 341
John War 247
John War 245
John War 277
John Nel 13
John She 198
John Cal 3
John Clr 146
John Bra 147
John Chr 92
John Log 182
John Grp 269
John Jef 31
John Jef 23
John Liv 147
John Flo 106
John Gra 240
John Knx 90
John Knx 84
John Lin 143
John Fra 179
John Gar 234
John, Jr Cum 180
John, Senr Cum 173
Jonathan Cum 166
Jos. Sr Hnr 365
Joseph Ohi 98
Joseph Mon 348
Joseph, Jr Hnr 364
Joseph, Sr Hnr 364
Judith Mas 298
Lawrence Fra 179
Leah Lin 143
Leonard Fay 46
Leven Fay 12
Lewis Woo 395
Lewis Jes 43
Martin Wsh 341
Margaret Mad 243
Mary Fay 12
Matthew War 245
Matthew War 245
Micajah She 225
Michael Wsh 342
Minor Jes 43
Nathan Hnd 347
Nathan Bou 117
Nathan War 245
Nimrod Fra 180
Original Mon 351
Original Clr 146
Peter Nel 13
Philip Bar 41
Rachel Hrd 303
Ralph But 198
Reubien Jes 43
Richard Fay 27

Young, cont.
Richard Jes 43
Richard, Jr Woo 392
Richard, Senr Woo 375
Richd. M. Woo 399
Robert Cal 12
Robert Clr 146
Robert Cum 166
Robert Flo 106
Robert Grn 249
Robert Liv 149
Robt. Bou 117
Robt. Jr Hnr 364
Ruben Bar 29
Saml. Cum 170
Saml. Cum 181
Saml. Sco 184
Saml. Way 362
Samuel Hnr 366
Samuel(freeman) Jes 43
Sarah Fra 180
Sinnet Mon 351
Sinnett, Senr Mon 361
Ste. Gar 199
Susanna Bou 133
Tho. Gar 234
Thomas Fle 85
Thomas Jef 22
Thomas Mas 298
William Adr 17
William Chr 91
William Chr 91
William Clr 146
William Fay 27
William Gra 243
William Hrd 302
William Hnr 358
William Jes 42
William Liv 153
William Mul 394
William Mul 399
William Nel 14
William War 245
William Woo 385
William Woo 390
William F. Wsh 341
Willis Bou 69
Wm. Cal 19
Wm. Gar 234
Wm. Jef 23
Wm. Mon 365
Younger, Charles Log 195
Henry Bul 187
Isaac Bul 187
John Fra 180
Joshua Mon 383
Kennard Bul 187
Peter Boo 64
Susannah Ohi 88
William Log 173
Younglove, Samuel Chr 69
Youngman, Jacob Cam 25
Jacob Cam 32
Jesse Mas 298
Youngs, Cable Chr 115
David Chr 115
John Chr 115
Youtsey, Adam Cam 27
John Cam 31
Peter Cam 24
Yowell, James H. She 212
John Mer 340
Thos. Boo 64
William Wsh 342
William Wsh 342
Yunt, George She 221
Jacob She 232

Yunt, cont.
John She 232
John She 232
Jonathan She 240
Nicholas She 232
Nicholas She 232

-- X --

-- Z --

Zachariah, Frederick Mul 399
Zachary, John Pul 124
Nat. Mer 341
William Pul 124
Zarba, Dorathy But 198
Zaringer, Benja. Jef 25
John Jef 23
Philip Jef 23
Philip Jef 25
Jacob Jef 25
Zarman, Anthony Ohi 88
Zarns, Phillip Grp 277
Zedford, Wm. Cum 184
Zelhart, Philip Jef 23
Zicker, Isaac Adr 17
Zimmerman, Frederick Boo 64
Fredk. Sco 189
John Mul 385
Peter Cum 183
William Jes 42
Mathias Mul 400
Zimners, John Mul 401
Zook, Peter Fra 180
Polly Fra 180
Zorens, Wm. Fle 84
Zumwalt, George Hrs 312
Phillip Hrs 312

www.ingramcontent.com/pod-product-compliance
Lightning Source LLC
Chambersburg PA
CBHW071856270326
41929CB00013B/2249
* 9 7 8 0 8 0 6 3 0 8 9 6 8 *